Logic® Pro 9 Power!: The Comprehensive Guide

Kevin Anker and Orren Merton

Course Technology PTR

A part of Cengage Learning

COURSE TECHNOLOGY
CENGAGE Learning™

Australia • Brazil • Japan • Korea • Mexico • Singapore • Spain • United Kingdom • United States

COURSE TECHNOLOGY
CENGAGE Learning™

Logic® Pro 9 Power!:
The Comprehensive Guide
Kevin Anker and Orren Merton

Publisher and General Manager,
Course Technology PTR:
Stacy L. Hiquet

Associate Director of Marketing:
Sarah Panella

Manager of Editorial Services:
Heather Talbot

Marketing Manager: Mark Hughes

Acquisitions Editor: Orren Merton

Project Editor/Copy Editor:
Cathleen Small

Technical Reviewer: Jay Asher

Interior Layout Tech: MPS Limited,
A Macmillan Company

Cover Designer: Mike Tanamachi

Indexer: Sharon Hilgenberg

Proofreader: Sue Boshers

For product information and technology assistance, contact us at
Cengage Learning Customer & Sales Support, 1-800-354-9706

For permission to use material from this text or product, submit all requests
online at **cengage.com/permissions**

Further permissions questions can be emailed to
permissionrequest@cengage.com

Logic is a registered trademark of Apple Inc., registered in the U.S. and other countries. All other trademarks are the property of their respective owners.

All images © Cengage Learning unless otherwise noted.

Library of Congress Control Number: 2009942406

ISBN-13: 978-1-4354-5612-9
ISBN-10: 1-4354-5612-2

Course Technology, a part of Cengage Learning
20 Channel Center Street
Boston, MA 02210
USA

Cengage Learning is a leading provider of customized learning solutions with office locations around the globe, including Singapore, the United Kingdom, Australia, Mexico, Brazil, and Japan. Locate your local office at: **international.cengage.com/region**

Cengage Learning products are represented in Canada by Nelson Education, Ltd.

For your lifelong learning solutions, visit **courseptr.com**

Visit our corporate website at **cengage.com**

Printed in the United States of America
1 2 3 4 5 6 7 12 11 10

Orren Merton wishes to dedicate this book to composers, musicians, and musical hobbyists everywhere who are using Logic to express their creativity.

Kevin Anker dedicates this book to the growing Logic community, those who are just getting their feet wet, and those who have been at it for the last 20+ years. I also dedicate this book to Julli, Taylor, Mom, Dad, my late grandparents, and the rest of my family who have supported me from day one.

Acknowledgments

Orren Merton:

Logic Pro 9 is arguably the best and most complete version of Logic ever, which meant we had our work cut out for us! Thank God for co-writer Kevin Anker. He really took this project by the horns, and this revision would not be half of the book that it is without Kevin's writing and organizing skills!

As ever, I couldn't do anything without the unwavering support of my wife, Michelle, my mother, and in the recent past, my late father, grandfather, and grandmother.

I would also like to thank Dr. Gerhard Lengeling, Manfred Knauff, Marion Freudenthaler, Thorsten Adam, Jan Hennerk-Helms, and everyone at Apple GmbH, both for their part in creating and developing software that assists so many of us to realize our musical creativity and for their part in including me in the processes! Further, I would like to thank the entire Logic FirstClass Community (you know who you are!) for their insight and assistance on my own journey into this program. I want to give a special shout out to Jay Asher, who not only serves as a friend and a sounding board, but who, as technical editor for this book, kept both Kevin and me on track!

Finally, the Course Technology PTR team, of which I am proud to call myself a member, has been exceptional, supporting me in every way I could have hoped all the way through this process. I would especially like to tip my hat to Mark Garvey for always giving me enough rope to hang myself but making sure I never do, and to Cathleen Small, our project and copy editor who keeps the trains (and the text) running!

Kevin Anker:

The day I got the email from Orren telling me that Logic Pro 9 had been released, I was out of the country, out of the loop, and (marginally) out of my mind. Long story that involves a lot of really bad meals interspersed with a few of the finest meals I've had the pleasure of enjoying, but rest assured the news of Logic Pro 9 snapped me back to reality as we began to discuss the new features and our plans for the revision. You can't work on a project that covers an application as deep as Logic without expert assistance, and as far as Logic goes, Orren is truly an expert. It seems that over the last two revisions of this book, I've learned new ideas about and new approaches to Logic from Orren with each chapter. He's as much my teacher as he is my co-writer in that regard, and I'm truly grateful for all the knowledge he's shared.

To spend your days writing books and your nights working gigs, you need a very special and incredibly patient support system. I can't thank my wife, Julli, and daughter, Taylor, enough for all the love and patience they offer me. You guys rock. My parents have always been in my corner, and I simply can't thank them enough. My sister and my in-laws are the greatest, and who can't love a mother-in-law who's okay with her daughter marrying a musician? I am blessed to have such a wonderful family.

I have also been fortunate to have the guidance, friendship, and support of a few experts in Logic and other related applications. My brother, Sean Anker, lent his experience and expertise to my understanding of video with this project, and to my understanding of computers in general since we first started programming in BASIC on an Apple II+ more than 30 years ago. He is the geek I always aspired to be. Eddie Al-Shakarchi has not only helped me check various quirks in Logic on a regular basis, but has also helped me to blow off a lot of steam via Instant Messenger from day one—I hope to return the favor as he finishes his Ph.D.

I also have to acknowledge the music community that has been my extended family for more years that I can recall, particularly Marc Schonbrun, Jeff Jones, Harvey Cook, Lester Johnson, Glenn Hopkins, Tad Robinson, Steve Gomes, David Earl and the entire Severn Records crew, Benjie Porecki (that espresso machine got me through the last few chapters!), Robb Stupka, Earmon Hubbard, Adam Jay Southerland, my late mentors Tony Jessup and Claude Sifferlen, and countless others who have worked with me, taught me, mentored me, and have accepted me into the brotherhood.

Finally, I have to thank my editors. Cathleen Small, who, through two and a half books, has proven herself to keep stranger hours than this professional musician does. That's a true testament to your dedication, and I thank you for all your help making this project better! Jay Asher, thanks so much for your insights. This was a particularly strange revision since Logic was updated midway through the revision, and you caught a lot of important changes and made the book much better as a result.

About the Authors

Orren Merton, co-author of *Logic Pro 8 Power!* and *Logic 7 Ignite!,* and author of *Logic 6 Power!, GarageBand Ignite!,* and *Guitar Rig 2 Power!* has been a computer musician since his days at U.C. Berkeley in 1988. He has been consulting and writing in the professional audio field for more than 10 years. He has done technical writing and editing for many software and hardware pro music–related companies, such as PSPaudioware, Redmatica, THD Electronics, Emagic, and Apple. He writes for numerous pro audio magazines, such as *Electronic Musician, Gearwire, Virtual Instruments,* and *MIX.*

Orren has a master's degree in English from California State University, Long Beach. When he isn't working on his own musical projects, such as Ember After, he helps moderate online Logic users forums, such as the Logic User Group, an online community of more than 23,000 Logic users, as well as Mac OS X Audio, along with co-author Kevin Anker. Orren beta tests for a number of audio software companies. He lives in Orange County, California, and can be reached at author@orrenmerton.com.

Kevin Anker, co-author of *Logic Pro 8 Power!* and author of *Using Logic Pro's Synthesizers,* is a longtime professional musician with more than 15 years of experience in computer-based music production. He has performed, composed, sequenced, engineered, and recorded for a variety of individuals and groups both nationally and internationally. Kevin has been a Logic user since 2002 and is currently an administrator and moderator of www.macosxaudio.com, a large and active online community focused on music production on Mac OS X, which Orren also administrates. Kevin can be reached at logic@kevinanker.net.

Contents

Chapter 3
The Logic Project   43

Chapter 4
Global Elements of Logic   87

Chapter 5
Transport Controls and Recording   133

Chapter 6
The Arrange Window   171

Chapter 7
Working with Audio and Apple Loops   273

Chapter 8
Working with MIDI   339

Chapter 9
Working with Software Instruments   417

Chapter 10
Using Automation in Logic   437

Chapter 11
Mixing in Logic   453

Chapter 12
Working with Files and Networks   531

Chapter 13
The Environment   555

Chapter 14
Advanced Tempo Operations   589

Chapter 15
Synchronizing Hardware with Logic Pro   607

Introduction

If you've gotten this far into the book, you've already figured out that this book deals with Apple's Logic Pro 9 digital audio sequencer. This book takes a different angle than most others. In general, the books written about Logic tend to be geared toward beginners and consist of a few hundred pages of incredibly basic information. If not, they are geared toward specific features of Logic, and not the whole application. This book takes on a fairly ambitious task—to be a complete introduction and reference for Logic Pro 9! It's a goal that no other Logic book really attempts, and while we make no claims of objectivity, we think this book achieves it nicely. We don't attempt to write everything about everything, but we make sure we cover those things that you are likely to run into while using Logic to make music, and we explain them simply, thoroughly, and completely. Moreover, we attempt to go into the philosophy behind *why* Logic works the way it works, so hopefully you will not simply learn the mechanics of how to do something, but you'll really understand what you are doing so when you want to explore on your own, you'll be fully prepared—and successful!

Who This Book Is For

Well, the glib answer is "anyone who owns Logic!" To give you a more complete answer, we're sure some of you with older versions of Logic, Windows versions of Logic, different levels of Logic (Logic, Logic Silver, Logic Audio, Logic Gold, or Logic Platinum), and so on are wondering how much use you can get out of a book focused on the Macintosh OS X–only Logic Pro 9. This is covered in more detail in Chapter 1, but we'll quickly say this—Logic Pro 9 is one of the most important updates Logic has seen in a very long time. It offers many new and updated features, particularly with regard to audio and the ability to run Logic Pro as a 64-bit application. Nonetheless, the basics of how Logic works have not fundamentally changed since the earliest days of Notator Logic for the Atari. Features get added, and the look changes a bit, so the older your version, the fewer features your Logic version may have compared to this one, but the basic operating procedures and features in your Logic version should be covered here in a way that will help you. So if you're looking for help with Logic, this book will help you.

As for what level of user this book is aimed at, really, we took pains to include everyone. The book opens with very basic information aimed at novices and beginners, and then the bulk of this book continues with more intermediate reference information and is sprinkled with expert tips and tricks throughout. The final chapters discuss more esoteric, "expert" functions, but hopefully in a way that is accessible to intermediate users. If you are a beginner, don't feel that only the beginning will be appropriate for you; the chapters are written to bring you up to speed in no time! Intermediate and advanced users, don't feel the beginning of the book is wasted on you, although you're welcome to skip it. It's good stuff, with lots of historical and architectural information you may not be familiar with, even if you're already fast and efficient with Logic and are just looking for a good reference book. Our goals were to start simple, get more advanced, and hopefully leave nobody behind. This book really does try to include something for everyone.

How This Book Is Organized

Every book on computer software starts with a number of assumptions and organizes the chapters accordingly. For this book, we are starting with the assumption that the reader has a very basic knowledge of sequencing and recording and little else. The beginning chapters are introductions—introductions to digital audio, MIDI, sequencing, and Logic. From about Chapter 4 onward, the book becomes far less basic. At that point, as we start getting into the meat of Logic Pro 9, the thought is that you have a working knowledge of the basics and general layout discussed in the previous four chapters, that you have set up your template (don't worry, you'll know what that is soon!), and that you want to start composing, recording, and editing music. The general flow of the chapters follows a Logic project: After setting up Logic, you'll need to learn about the Transport and Arrange, then you'll want to record and edit audio and MIDI, mix down your project, and finally save your project and organize your files. The final chapters are about more advanced, esoteric features of Logic that, as you create more complex compositions and build a more involved project studio, will become more important.

As for each chapter, there is no single model that we adhere to regarding the subdivisions of sections. It is the content that determines the organization of each individual chapter. One thing we do cover, however, is that every time a new Logic window or editor is introduced, we discuss each local menu in that window or editor. This gives you the advantage of getting an overview of many of the functions available in a window or editor before we go deeper into using those functions.

One More Note on Logic Pro 9

Logic Pro 9 is an application in a state of flux, but in a great way. From Logic Pro 9, to Logic Pro 9.1, to the most recent release at this moment, Logic Pro 9.1.1, features have been added and refined again and again, with each update improving Logic immensely. As a result, there are features that may be listed in this book as unavailable, particularly when Logic is in 64-bit mode (which you'll learn about in the coming chapters), that have been restored by an ensuing update. Therefore, it is important that as you update Logic, you pay attention to the release notes for each version of Logic Pro 9 to help you keep track of these changes.

1 Introducing Logic Pro 9

Logic has a reputation for being complex. It isn't, really. Logic Pro 9 offers an incredibly deep and powerful recording and production application that you can have up and running quickly. It has a unique and highly customizable set of tools that allow you to configure a workflow that suits your "logic." Its editing and processing tools are second to none, and its suite of effects and software instruments is truly complete. In this chapter, you'll learn what Logic is, a bit about its history, and its basic working premises.

What Is Logic Pro?

If you hear people discussing Logic, you're likely to hear terms such as "professional," "powerful," "flexible," and "steep learning curve" thrown around. So what is Logic Pro, really?

Put simply, Logic Pro is the most flexible, powerful, comprehensive, professional, and elegant application for producing music on a computer. Although you may consider that a rather contentious statement, after reading through this book you will probably at least concede that this claim is not outrageous. A number of other powerful, professional, and worthy music production programs are on the market today. We don't mean to downplay their functionality. Some applications have a feature or two that Logic lacks, or they implement one of the features that Logic also includes in a way that some prefer. Logic does, however, offer the best combination of features, flexibility, and power of all available music production applications. Logic offers you:

- **Audio recording.** Record audio directly into Logic.

- **Audio editing.** Edit audio files using Logic's many editing tools, including sample-accurate editing and time-stretching audio in the Arrange window.

- **MIDI recording.** Record and play back MIDI information.

- **MIDI editing.** Edit MIDI information in any of several MIDI editors.

- **MIDI notation editing.** Edit and print out professional scores and music charts.

- **Media area.** Manage all your multimedia files and access plug-in presets right in the Arrange window.

1

■ **Global tracks.** Easily set up and edit song marker, tempo, key, chord, and video frame information.

■ **Software instruments.** Use software synthesizers and samplers from within Logic.

■ **Arranging.** View all your song elements as graphic regions and arrange them visually.

■ **Mixing.** Mix your audio tracks and your MIDI tracks within the same song using Logic's highly customizable Mixer.

■ **Processing.** Use Logic's professional offline and real-time processors and functions.

■ **Nodes.** Network as many Macintosh computers as you want for unlimited processing power for Logic's effects and instruments.

■ **Control surface support.** Configure any hardware MIDI controller to be a hardware controller of any Logic function.

■ **Environment.** Build an entire virtual studio and processing environment inside Logic.

■ **64-bit processing.** You can run Logic Pro 9 as a 64-bit application, giving you the ability to access massive amounts of RAM if your computer is so equipped.

For these features and more, Logic earned its well-deserved reputation as the most complete professional music production application, and it continues to break new ground. What about that talk of Logic's steep learning curve? As with most applications that are as deep as this one, it helps to know the application's internal workings to more readily understand how to use it. To give you a solid grounding in the fundamental concepts of Logic, we'll start at the very beginning with where Logic came from and see how the functionality of those previous applications relates to the current version of Logic.

A Brief History of Logic

Once upon a time, in the mid-1980s, during what now would be considered the "prehistoric" era of computer music, a small German software company named C-LAB created a Commodore 64 program called Supertrack. Supertrack, like all early sequencers, was designed to allow users to store, edit, and play back the notes and performance information generated on MIDI synthesizers. (See the section "A Brief Overview of MIDI" later in this chapter for an explanation of MIDI.)

By 1987, this basic program evolved into Creator, and finally into Notator. Notator, which ran on the Atari ST, added a musical notation (or musical score) editor to Creator and became an instant power player in the burgeoning field of computer-based MIDI sequencers. Notator offered a clean, simple interface for four powerful MIDI editors: a real-time musical Notation Editor, an Event Editor for displaying MIDI information in a scrolling list, a Matrix Editor for displaying notes graphically, and a Hyper Editor for editing non-note MIDI data (such as pitch bend). With these editors, you could play a song on your synthesizer or program it on your computer from scratch, then rearrange, edit, and manipulate your data as sheet music in the Notation Editor, in a text list, on a graphic "piano roll," or on a bar graph–style display.

As you can see in Figure 1.1, which shows an edit screen from the final version of Notator for the Atari, the program used the very same concepts and offered many of the same tools for manipulating MIDI information that are still used today. Notator's extensive editing options gave musicians powerful tools for creating and arranging music in an easy-to-use package. Notator won rave reviews from power users and hobbyists alike and garnered a huge following among early MIDI musicians. Even 10 years after its final version, Notator still has a very lively following. In fact, there are websites and mailing lists on the Internet for people who still use Notator today.

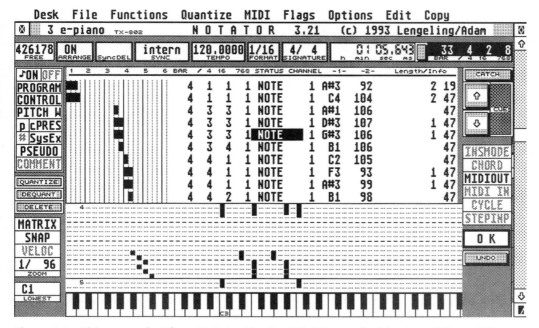

Figure 1.1   This screenshot from Notator Version 3.2.1 shows the Matrix and Event Editors. Users of Notator would feel right at home with the evolved Matrix and Event editors of Logic, which are fundamentally the same a decade later. (Screen image used by permission from the Notator Users Group at www.notator.org.)

By 1993, the principals who developed Notator left to form their own company, Emagic, and built upon their previous efforts by adding a graphical arrangement page and object-oriented editing, among other innovations; this product was named Notator Logic, and later simply Logic. Logic was soon ported to run on the Macintosh computer, which was quickly overtaking the Atari as the music computer of choice for professionals. This early version of Logic introduced the basic architecture and concepts that would form the basis for future iterations of Logic.

By the late 1990s, Logic's developers had ported Logic to run on Windows computers as well as the Macintosh, quietly discontinued the Atari version, and added to the program the ability to record and edit audio in addition to MIDI. To signify this, the developers modified the name of the application to Logic Audio. By the end of the 1990s, there were three versions of the application, each with an expanded feature set. Logic Audio Platinum had the most professional recording options, offering the most hardware options, including unsurpassed support for Digidesign's industry-standard hardware, Pro Tools TDM. Logic Audio Platinum became nearly ubiquitous in the software lists of professional studios worldwide. Logic Audio Gold and Logic Audio Silver offered consumers more affordable versions of Logic with the same depth and power but fewer features. In addition, Emagic developed a separate application, MicroLogic, which was a basic and inexpensive derivative of Logic that offered beginners a way to get their feet wet in music production.

In July 2002, Apple Computer purchased Emagic. The Logic 6 release in February 2003 focused solely on the Macintosh, representing Emagic's return to single-platform development after a decade as a cross-platform application. The names of the three versions of Logic changed again, this time to Logic Platinum, Logic Gold, and Logic Audio. In 2004, Apple Computer streamlined Emagic's Logic line to only Logic Pro and Logic Express, and in late 2004, Apple Computer released Logic Pro 7 and Express 7. September 2007 saw the introduction of Logic Express 8 and the software suite Logic Studio, which included Logic Pro 8. Logic Pro 9 continues to lead the way in professional music production on the Macintosh platform, garnering awards and rave reviews in addition to an honored place in more professional recording studios in the world than any other sequencer package. With the introduction of Logic 9.1 in January 2010, Apple has set the bar even higher, including the ability to run Logic as a full 64-bit processing application if you desire.

As you can see, Emagic and Logic have a long and illustrious history in the computer music field upon which Apple is building. To this day, the Hyper Editor and the Notation, Event, and Piano Roll Editors of even the most recent Logic Pro 9 release would be instantly recognizable to an early Notator user, which speaks volumes about Apple's commitment to supporting its user community.

Will This Book Help You with Your Version of Logic?
The short answer is: Yes!

The long answer is that this book will offer you something no matter which version of Logic you are using. Exactly how much of the material is applicable depends on the specific platform and version number you are using. This book covers the features of the most current, feature-rich version of Logic, Logic Pro 9. This means that this book will cover features that are not found in any other version of Logic on any other platform. If you are using a previous version of Logic, the number of new features explained in this book will be considerable—although many will still be familiar—and the difference in appearance will be considerable as well.

Clearly, if you just purchased Logic 9, this book applies to your version. If you currently do not own Logic at all and you want to learn about it before purchasing it, this book will give you the ins and outs of the most current version of Logic. However, current users of different versions of Logic will find this book eminently useful as well.

The concepts and basic MIDI editing functionality in Logic haven't changed since the program's creation. In other words, users who have held on to Notator Logic 1.5 on their Atari ST could read this book and recognize many of the editors, the nomenclature, the architecture, and so on, even though the developers have seriously updated the look and added many features in the last decade. For users of more recent versions, the differences become even less pronounced. Through Logic 5.5, the features, look and feel, and operation of Logic were nearly identical whether it was running under Windows XP, Mac OS 9, or Mac OS X. Logic 7 was really the first version in nearly half a decade with a significantly redesigned application, and Logic 8 carried that much further, but most operations themselves had not been fundamentally changed. Logic 9 continues the Logic tradition, adding more great features while keeping much of the look and feel of the application intact. As you can see by comparing Figure 1.2a and Figure 1.2b, 2001's Logic Pro 5.5 running under Windows XP and 2009's Logic Pro 9 look different, yet clearly maintain a profound similarity.

In other words, users of previous versions of Logic looking for assistance with basic concepts and operational procedures will find it here. This book will, of course, address the newer features in Logic Pro 9, but users of different versions can easily skip those discussions. In fact, users with earlier or less feature-rich versions of Logic can consider the coverage of the latest features a sneak peak at what the new version has to offer when making the decision about whether to upgrade!

A Brief Overview of MIDI

MIDI (*Musical Instrument Digital Interface*) was formally introduced in August 1983. The MIDI 1.0 protocol was absolutely revolutionary—it allowed MIDI instruments (such as synthesizers, drum machines, and sequencers) to communicate with, control, and be controlled by other MIDI instruments and MIDI controllers. The development of MIDI enabled the rise of electronic music and computer sequencers. MIDI makes possible much of what we use computers for in music production. If you are interested in a complete technical discussion of every aspect of the MIDI protocol, you should read *MIDI Power! Second Edition: The Comprehensive Guide* by Robert Guerin (Thomson Course Technology PTR, 2005), a very thorough and readable exploration of MIDI in depth. Using Logic doesn't require that sort of deep understanding of MIDI, but a basic knowledge of what MIDI is and how it works is invaluable.

The MIDI protocol specified that every MIDI-compliant device that can both send and receive MIDI information must have a MIDI IN port to accept MIDI data, a MIDI OUT port to transmit MIDI data, and optionally a MIDI THRU port for transferring data between other MIDI devices. When you connect the MIDI OUT port of one device to the MIDI IN port of another device, the

Figure 1.2a   Logic Pro 5.5, the final version of Logic developed for Windows XP in 2001.

Figure 1.2b   Logic Pro 9, the most recent version of Logic, running on Mac OS X. You can see that even with the integrated features of the Arrange window, the two versions of Logic still resemble each other.

first device enables you to press a key, turn a dial, engage a control message, and so on, and the second device will receive the data.

In addition to providing hardware specifications that allow devices to send and receive MIDI, the MIDI protocol also defined how to pass data from one device to another. MIDI is a *serial protocol*, meaning that MIDI information is sent one *event* (or MIDI message) at a time. That may sound inefficient, but the speed of MIDI transfer is 31,250 bps (bits per second, where *bit* stands for *b*inary dig*it*), and since each MIDI message uses 10 bits (eight for the information, two for error correction), the MIDI protocol can send 3,906 bytes of data every second (31,250 divided by 8 bits to convert bits to bytes). Since one MIDI note can take up to six bytes, the protocol enables a device to play approximately 500 MIDI notes per second. This might seem like a lot of notes, but as soon as you add a couple five-note chords in a single ten-millisecond span of time, with multiple MIDI control messages, you might very well start seeing some compromised timing. That's why for the most demanding MIDI productions, there are MIDI Time Stamping features on many MIDI interfaces to improve MIDI timing even further.

Even if you have no external MIDI hardware, MIDI is still the protocol that Logic uses for internal playback and automation of virtual instruments, so it's still useful to understand some basics about MIDI.

What MIDI Really Transmits

The most important thing to understand is that MIDI doesn't transmit any sound at all. It only transmits data. In other words, when you record digital audio, you're recording an actual file of digital information that will play back as sound. When you record MIDI data, you'll then need some sort of device—a synthesizer, drum machine, sampler, or software synthesizer—to actually hear that MIDI information. MIDI data can transmit the following:

- Performance events, such as when you play and release notes, and their velocities.

- The pressure with which you press the keys as you play (known as *aftertouch*).

- Information from MIDI controller wheels, knobs, pedal controls, ribbon controllers, pitchbend controllers, and so on that send parameters that affect performance.

- Channel settings. Each MIDI cable can support up to 16 channels, so each device can operate as 16 devices in one. Those devices that can support multiple MIDI channels are called *multitimbral* devices.

- Synchronization information, so that all time-sensitive instruments or functions on various devices can operate from the same master clock and play in sync with each other.

- Program changes and sound bank selections.

- MIDI Time Code (MTC), which allows MIDI devices to lock to devices that use SMPTE (*Society of Motion Picture and Television Engineers*) format time code by translating SMPTE into something that the MIDI device can understand.

- System Exclusive messages, which are unique messages that can alter parameters and control of one specific MIDI device. Most MIDI synthesizers and some multitrack recorders offer unique System Exclusive commands.

MIDI Connections and Signal Flow

As described previously, connecting MIDI devices couldn't be simpler. The most basic type of MIDI connection, in which the MIDI OUT jack of one MIDI device is connected to the MIDI IN jack of another MIDI device, allows the first unit to send MIDI to the second unit, as shown in Figure 1.3.

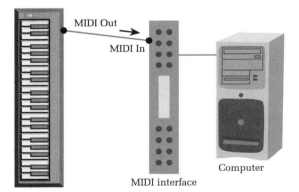

Figure 1.3   A basic MIDI connection between a MIDI OUT jack on a MIDI device and a MIDI IN jack on a MIDI interface, which is then connected to the computer. This type of MIDI connection allows the MIDI device to control MIDI software in the computer.

Note that this type of connection does not allow for two-way communication, only one-way communication. This type of connection is most common when connecting a MIDI controller, which is a MIDI device that does not itself produce sounds (and doesn't *receive* MIDI), but can send MIDI to other devices, such as to a computer MIDI interface or another MIDI device.

An example of another simple but more dynamic MIDI connection is to connect both the MIDI IN and MIDI OUT of one device to the MIDI OUT and MIDI IN of another device, as shown in Figure 1.4.

This enables two-way communication between MIDI devices, so each is capable of both sending and receiving data from the other. This is the most common form of routing between two devices capable of sending and receiving MIDI information, such as two synthesizers or a computer and a synthesizer. When making connections like this, be sure both units have MIDI THRU and/or local control turned off, or else you might end up with a MIDI feedback loop. In a MIDI feedback

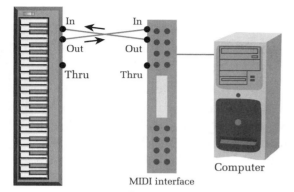

Figure 1.4   A new MIDI connection has been added to the system shown in Figure 1.3.
The MIDI IN on the MIDI device has been connected to the MIDI OUT on the MIDI interface,
allowing the MIDI software on the computer to control the MIDI device.

loop, one unit sends a command to the other, which then sends the command back to the first
unit, and on and on endlessly.

A final example of a basic MIDI connection illustrates how three MIDI devices might be connected together via a MIDI THRU port. The MIDI OUT of the first device is connected to the
MIDI IN of the second device, the MIDI OUT of the second device is connected to the MIDI IN of
the first device, and the MIDI THRU of the second device is connected to the MIDI IN of the third
device (see Figure 1.5).

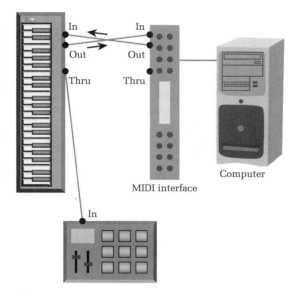

Figure 1.5   A new MIDI connection has been added to the system shown in Figure 1.4.
The MIDI THRU on the original MIDI device has been connected to the MIDI IN on another
MIDI device. This allows the MIDI software on the computer to control the second MIDI device.

In Figure 1.5, complete two-way communication between the first two devices is possible, and the first device (and often the second device) can also send MIDI information to the third device. Such connections are often used when a third MIDI device, such as a drum machine, is not being used to issue any MIDI messages, but only to receive them from the rest of the MIDI setup.

At this point, you should have a good understanding of what MIDI is and the importance of getting MIDI information into Logic. Because Logic can both send and receive MIDI, you will want a *MIDI interface*—a Universal Serial Bus (USB) device that accepts MIDI from MIDI devices and sends it into Logic—that has at least as many MIDI IN and MIDI OUT ports as you have MIDI devices. This will be discussed later in this chapter, in the section entitled "A Brief Primer on Hardware."

A Brief Overview of Digital Audio

These days, recording digital audio is perhaps the most popular use of sequencers such as Logic Pro. In fact, the popular term to describe a computer used as the hub of a music production system is a *Digital Audio Workstation (DAW)*. So what is digital audio? How does it differ from analog audio? Why is it important?

While a complete technical reference on the details of digital audio would result in a book almost as large as this one, it is important to know at least enough about the fundamentals of digital audio to be able to make a good recording. The following subsections should give you just enough of a background to get the most out of your audio recordings.

The Differences between Analog and Digital Sound

We hear sound when our eardrums vibrate. Please read that carefully and realize that it did not say that we hear sound whenever *some object* vibrates. Many objects vibrate outside our ability to hear them. (Think of dog whistles or ultra-low subfrequencies.) Our ears are theoretically capable of registering vibrations (also called *cycles*) that are oscillating between 20 and 20,000 times a second. This is called the *frequency*—pretty logical when you think about it, since the term refers to the frequency of vibrations per second. Theoretically, then, humans can hear frequencies from 20 Hz to 20 kHz. (The measurement hertz, or Hz, is named after Henry Hertz, who in 1888 developed the theory of the relationship between frequency and cycles.) In practice, hardly any adult's hearing reaches that theoretical maximum because people lose the ability to hear certain frequencies (high-pitched ones in particular) as they age, are subjected to loud noises, and so on.

If the frequency of vibration is slow (say 60 vibrations per second, or 60 Hz), we perceive a low note. If the frequency of the vibration is fast (say 6,000 vibrations per second, or 6 kHz), we would perceive a high note. If the vibrations are gentle, barely moving our eardrums, we perceive the sound as soft. The loudness and softness of the sound is called the *amplitude,* because the term refers to the volume, or amplification, of the sound. Thus we can graph sound as you see in Figure 1.6.

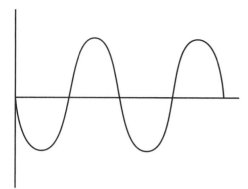

Figure 1.6 A graphical representation of a simple sound wave. This particular kind of even, smooth sound wave is known as a sine wave.

In the graph in Figure 1.6, the frequency is the distance between the oscillations of the waveform, and the amplitude is the height of the waveform. Most sounds we hear in the real world are complex ones that have more than a single frequency in them, as in the graph in Figure 1.7.

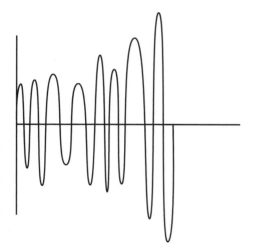

Figure 1.7 A more complex sound wave than the one shown in Figure 1.6.

This example has more than a single tone in it, and not every frequency is being heard at the same volume (amplitude).

Now that you understand a little about sound waves, let's tie it into recording. One way to record sound is to make an exact replica of the original waveform on some other media. For example, you might carve an image of the waveform onto a vinyl surface or imprint the waveform on magnetic tape. In these cases, you have recorded an actual copy of the original sound wave. Now you just need a machine to amplify the sound so it's loud enough to listen to (or to rattle the windows, if that's your style). Because this type of recording results in a continuous waveform, it's called *analog recording*. *Analog* refers to any signal that is represented by a continuous, unbroken waveform.

Because a computer works using mathematical codes instead of actual pictures of objects, to use a computer for recording audio, we need to translate the actual analog signal into math. Luckily, sound can also be represented *digitally*—meaning by use of digits, or numbers. Basically, complex mathematical analysis has proven if we sample a waveform twice in each cycle, or *period*, and record its variation in sound, we can reproduce the waveform. Now, each period is a full cycle, or vibration. This means that if we wanted to reproduce a 60-Hz sound, which is 60 cycles, we'd need to take at least 120 samples. From this, you can see that if you want to be sure to capture the full range of human hearing—20 kHz, or 20,000 cycles—you have to take at least 40,000 samples.

What's Meant by Sampling Frequency and Bit Depth

From the preceding, we understand that we have to represent the sound wave as numbers to store it in the computer, and that by storing two samples per cycle we can represent that cycle. You've probably noticed that every recording interface and program that handles digital audio refers to sample rate and bit depth. Let's explain what these terms mean and how they affect your recording.

As explained previously, it takes two samples per cycle to represent each cycle accurately. It follows that the total number of samples taken of a waveform determines the maximum frequency that will be recorded. This is called the *sampling frequency* or *sampling rate*. For example, the sampling rate of the compact disc is fixed at 44.1 kHz, or 44,100 samples; it's a few thousand samples more than the minimum needed to represent the highest-frequency sound wave that humans can hear.

You've probably noticed that many audio interfaces today boast sampling rates of 96 kHz or even 192 kHz. (kHz is short for kilohertz, or 1,000 Hz.) That means that these devices can represent sounds up to 48 kHz and 96 kHz. The obvious question is, why bother? We can only hear up to a theoretical 20 kHz anyway, right? Of course, it's not quite that simple. Although we may not be able to distinguish sounds accurately above a certain frequency, every sound also contains additional overtones, harmonics, spatial cues, and so on. These features enrich the sound to our ears and help us place it in space and so on. When our sampling rate is too low to represent such features, they are simply discarded and lost forever. We may not consciously notice these "ultrasonic" frequencies when we listen to recordings, but many audiophiles and sound engineers believe that they contribute to a far more realistic listening experience.

That explains sampling rates, but what about bit depth? Remember, the sound wave has two components: the frequency and the amplitude. The mathematical representation of the amplitude at a particular instant in a particular cycle is stored in *bits*. A computer cannot interpolate information in between the amplitudes you have stored—it only knows what the amplitude at a given instant in the cycle is if the amplitude is stored in a bit. The more bits used to store the amplitude per cycle, the more accurate the representation.

Finally, here is a loose analogy, but a good one, to give you a basic understanding of analog versus digital audio, sampling rate, and bit depth. If you make an analog recording, you are left with an actual copy of the audio waveform imprinted onto your media. If you make a digital recording, you are instead taking "snapshots" of the waveform and then attempting to re-create the waveform from those snapshots. Your sampling rate would be the number of snapshots you take every second, and your bit depth would represent the focus and color quality of each snapshot. As you can see, the higher the sampling rate and bit depth, the closer your snapshots will get to the actual sound wave, as follows in Figure 1.8.

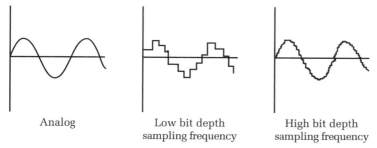

Analog

Low bit depth
sampling frequency

High bit depth
sampling frequency

Figure 1.8 In analog recording, you record an accurate representation of the source, in this case a sine wave. In digital recording, the sample rate and bit depth directly influence the accuracy of the recording. With higher sample rates and bit depths, you can achieve a more accurate digital representation of the source than with lower sample rates and bit depths.

You should also keep in mind that as your bit depths and sampling rates increase, so do the processor, memory, and hard drive requirements. The larger the bit depth and sample rate, the more CPU is required to process it, the more memory the audio requires during processing, and the more space on your hard disk the audio will require.

It is beyond the scope of this book to give comprehensive position papers on the merits of analog versus digital audio, but the important things to remember are that any audio waveform that gets into your computer will be digital audio, and you need to be aware of sampling frequency and bit depth to get the most out of your hardware and out of Logic.

Audio and MIDI in Logic Pro

It's time to relate all of this to what it means for Logic. In its simplest description, Logic can be viewed as a software equivalent of a MIDI and digital audio tape recorder. In other words, if you connect your MIDI devices to your computer, connect your audio devices to your computer, and then activate Record in Logic, you will record your audio and MIDI into Logic. If you then activate Play, you will hear the MIDI and audio you've just recorded. So far, this should be familiar to pretty much anyone who has ever used a tape recorder or VCR.

For Logic to be able to record MIDI and digital audio information, you need a way to capture that information into the computer, and then a way to transfer that information out of the computer when you activate playback. In the case of audio, you capture and transfer this information through your *audio interface*. In the case of MIDI, you handle all of this with your *MIDI interface*.

Unlike a tape recorder, which requires little more setting up than putting in a cassette tape, Logic is famous (and perhaps infamous) for the depth and breadth of setup and configuration options it offers. Logic Pro 9's processes are streamlined so that you can configure your setup on a basic level very quickly, while still allowing the incredible amount of flexibility for which it is famous.

A Brief Primer on Hardware

It is beyond the scope of this book to give you a complete buyer's guide on computer hardware. It is also relatively pointless, since new products are being introduced almost daily, but it is important to touch a little bit on the basic kinds of hardware you'll need to get the most out of Logic.

We'll assume that you already have any musical instruments or MIDI controller devices you will be using. If you already have your computer hardware as well and are ready to set it up, feel free to skip to Chapter 2, "A Quick Tour of Logic Pro."

How Fast Does Your Computer Need to Be?

The simple answer to this question is as fast as possible! The more detailed answer is that it depends on what sort of music production you expect to be doing and what your expectations are.

Apple's stated minimum requirements are for an Intel Macintosh computer. Apple goes on to recommend a minimum of 1 GB of random access memory (RAM); a display with a resolution of 1280 × 800; running the Mac OS X 10.5.7 or later operating system; QuickTime 7.6 or later, which is included in the installation package; 9 GB of disk space, and a DVD drive. If you intend to run a sizable number of effects and software synthesizers, your processor and RAM requirements increase even more. Logic does have a Freeze function and a Bounce in Place function that can help conserve CPU power, but the more processor power and the more RAM you have (we'd recommend at least 2 GB of RAM), the better. If you plan to network computers together as Logic Nodes, those other computers need to be Intel Core computers with Gigabit Ethernet. If you think you'd like to run Logic in 64-bit mode, the minimum system requirements are just a bit higher—Mac OS X v10.6.2 or later and an Intel Core 2 Duo processor(s) are required.

If your computer is old, and you are thinking of pushing the minimum, be warned: Slow computers not only have slower CPUs, but also usually have slower motherboards, hard drives, RAM, and so on. When you ask your computer basically to replace an entire building full of mixing desks, tape machines, effects units, and MIDI synthesizers, you're asking a lot. Although

Logic Pro 9 is a very efficient program, it contains some very powerful, industry-leading tools that can not only inspire you and benefit your productions, but can bring even more recent computers to their knees fairly quickly. Keep that in mind.

Our recommendation is that you get the fastest laptop or desktop Macintosh you can afford and load it with as much RAM as you can. You won't be sorry!

Different Types of Hard Disks

Most storage drives operate on the principle of a set of needles reading and writing data on magnetic platters that spin around incredibly fast. This type of platter hard drive (HDD) has been the industry standard for decades. The differences among the various types of HDDs are mainly in how fast these platters spin and what mechanism they use to connect to the rest of the computer.

Hard disks use two mainstream transfer mechanisms to communicate with the host computer: ATA (*Advanced Technology Attachment*) and SCSI (*Small Computer Systems Interface*). Both formats have different performance subcategories, such as SATA, eSATA, ATA/66 or ATA/100, and SCSI-2 or SCSI-3. SCSI drives have higher top speeds, usually require an additional PCI Express expander or ExpressCard that supports the SCSI protocol, and generally cost more than similar-sized ATA drives. ATA is inexpensive, ubiquitous, and supported internally by every desktop and notebook system designed since 1998. eSATA is an external SATA standard that offers transfer rates that match those of internal SATA drives.

Recording audio files to a hard drive can be a very disk-intensive task, and a faster hard drive can record and play back more simultaneous tracks. Most desktop and external hard drives these days spin at 7,200 RPM, which is fast enough to reliably handle songs with around 64 to 72 audio tracks, which should be more than enough for most people. If you have a 7,200-RPM hard drive and you still need more tracks, you can either record audio to two different hard drives or get a faster drive. These days, hard drives running up to 15,000 RPM are available, although they are expensive and almost always require SCSI.

If you are using a laptop, your internal hard drive could spin at 4,200 RPM, 5,400 RPM, or 7,200 RPM. There are even options available for internal Solid State Drives (SSDs), which have no moving parts and therefore higher potential reads and writes. These drives are similar in nature to the flash storage media used in digital cameras. Many of the more recent MacBook Pros allow easy access to the hard drive, allowing you to easily upgrade the capacity, speed, or type of drive installed. For high-performance mobile use, you should consider using an external hard drive that runs at 7,200 RPM as your audio drive, particularly if you're running a slower internal drive. Several external hard drives are available in USB or FireWire enclosures that offer plug-and-play connectivity to all notebook computers with those ports. If your notebook doesn't have enough USB or FireWire ports and your laptop supports it, you can buy an ExpressCard that will allow you to connect more USB or FireWire devices. You can also find eSATA ExpressCards that will allow you to use eSATA drives with your laptop.

Do You Need a Separate Hard Disk for Audio Files?

In general, the more that a hard drive has to do, the less performance it has left over for audio. In other words, if your hard drive needs to read system files as well as audio files, it needs to divide its attention and not focus on audio file performance. If you have a hard drive devoted to nothing but recording audio files, that hard drive could dedicate 100 percent of its performance to audio-related tasks.

Clearly, having a separate hard drive for audio seems advantageous, but is it absolutely necessary? The answer to this depends on how audio-intensive your projects are. Even a slower hard disk should be able to run both system software and approximately 16–24 tracks of audio. If your needs are modest, you really shouldn't need a separate hard drive for your audio tracks. On the other hand, professional studios that need to record anything from solo singers all the way to full orchestras often have entire banks of hard drives. If you regularly work with songs in excess of 24 tracks or you can easily afford it, you should go ahead and buy a separate hard drive for audio files.

One other consideration is that Logic Pro 9 includes 38 GB of content beyond the 9 GB required for the base installation. If you feel you're likely to use this content, it would be wise to at least consider a separate drive for this.

MIDI Interfaces

The earlier section "A Brief Overview of MIDI" concluded by mentioning the MIDI interface. This device has the same MIDI IN and MIDI OUT ports that your MIDI hardware does and connects to your computer via USB to send that MIDI information from your external units into Logic and vice versa. If you want Logic to be able to communicate with MIDI devices outside the computer, you need a MIDI interface.

So what size interface do you need? That depends completely on how many MIDI devices you have. Do you have only one controller keyboard? Then you just need a simple MIDI interface with one MIDI IN and one MIDI OUT port. If your needs are modest enough, your audio interface may already have all the MIDI ports you need. (See the following section, "Audio Interfaces.") Do you have a full MIDI studio and need 12 MIDI ports? In that case, you need to buy multiple MIDI interfaces of the largest size you can find (usually eight MIDI IN and eight MIDI OUT ports). Also think about whether you plan to expand your MIDI hardware over time; if you do, you might want to get a MIDI interface with more ports than you currently need.

Another thing to consider is whether your MIDI interface needs any professional synchronization features. Some of the more professional interfaces include a lot of video and hardware synchronization options that you might need if you do a lot of sound-to-picture work. Also, many of the larger interfaces include time-stamping functionality, which allows them to stamp the exact time that a MIDI event should occur as part of the MIDI message. Time stamping doesn't have a noticeable effect for small numbers of MIDI devices, but it can make a world of difference with MIDI studios containing large amounts of external hardware.

Finally, keep in mind that many different manufacturers make MIDI interfaces, and these interfaces are all equally compatible with Logic. As long as your interface has a USB connector and drivers for your Mac OS X, it should do the job.

Audio Interfaces

Because there are so many audio interfaces on the market, choosing one might seem daunting. Here are a few tips to help you with your selection.

First, consider how many audio channels you intend to record at one time. Do you see yourself recording a rock band or an entire symphony at once? If so, you will want to investigate those audio interfaces that enable users to daisy chain more than one interface, so you can expand your system as your recording needs grow. Some systems today not only enable users to record 24 or more channels at once, but to connect two or three such boxes for a truly impressive audio recording system. On the other hand, do you see yourself recording only yourself or one stereo instrument at a time? If so, then a single interface with fewer inputs will do.

Next, consider how you would prefer or need your audio interface to connect to your computer. Are you using a laptop? If so, you want an interface that connects to the computer via USB or FireWire, which most Intel Macintosh laptops have. Many MacBook Pro's also allow you to select an ExpressCard format interface. If you have a MacBook Pro, you might also prefer a USB or FireWire interface because those interfaces don't require opening up your machine and installing anything. If you don't mind installing hardware in your MacBook Pro, you can choose an audio interface that is a Peripheral Component Interface Express (PCI Express) card. PCI Express options are usually more expandable and less expensive than USB, FireWire, or ExpressCard interfaces, but are more difficult to install.

You need to consider the sampling frequency and bit depth at which you want to record. Compact discs are standardized at 16 bits, with a sampling frequency of 44.1 kHz. Every audio interface available today can record at least at this level of fidelity. Do you want to be able to record at 24 bits, which is the industry standard for producing music? Do you want to be able to record at higher sampling frequencies, such as the 96 kHz that DVDs can use? Are you going to run Logic in 64-bit mode and does the audio interface have, or does it even require, a 64-bit driver? All these decisions influence what kind of audio interface will fit your needs. Because the higher bit depths and sample rates capture a more accurate "picture" of the sound, as we explained previously, you might want to record and process your audio at higher bit rates than your final format, if you have the computer power to do so.

Finally, you should consider whether you want your audio interface to have additional features. For example, some audio interfaces have MIDI control surfaces and/or MIDI interfaces as part of a package. Does that appeal to you, or would you prefer to fill those areas with other devices?

Now that we've introduced Logic, some of its basic concepts, and the hardware you'll need, it's time to take "A Quick Tour of Logic Pro."

2   A Quick Tour of Logic Pro

Now that you have a basic understanding of what Logic can do, it's time to start exploring. This chapter gives you a broad overview of the application, and the following chapters will delve into the details of the individual areas. At this point, don't worry if you look at the various windows in Logic Pro 9 and are left with all sorts of questions. As you proceed, we promise that it will become clear!

Terminology in Logic

As you begin your examination of Logic, you should already be comfortable with some of the terms that are used in Logic to describe the most common functions and concepts. Of course, every sequencer uses its own terminology, and if you understand this, you'll find it far easier to comprehend the "logic" of the application, both figuratively and literally. Here are the key terms that you'll need to know to work with Logic effectively:

- **Project.** A Logic project contains information about all your editing, MIDI performances, mixing, and recording. A project can also contain audio files, sampler instruments, effects presets, and so on that are used by the song or songs that make up the project. These files are called the project's *assets*. Saving Logic projects with their assets (you'll learn more about that in Chapter 12, "Working with Files and Networks") is a great way to keep every necessary piece of data used in one place.

- **Audio file.** Audio files are files on your computer that contain digital audio information. When you record into Logic, it saves your recording as a digital audio file on your hard drive. When you use Logic to manipulate audio data, that data will always originate from an audio file, regardless of whether it was initially recorded in Logic.

- **Audio region.** An audio region is a graphical representation of a section of audio from an audio file. These graphical representations appear in the Audio Bin, Sample Editor, or Arrange window. An audio region can be as long as the entire audio file in which it is located, or it may be only a few milliseconds long. A single audio file can contain a virtually limitless number of audio regions. When you record or load audio into Logic, it will always contain at least one audio region that is, by default, the length of the entire audio file.

■ **Audio channel.** Every channel strip in the Mixer is assigned to an audio channel, and every audio track in the Arrange window has an audio channel assigned to it. You can have more than one audio track assigned to the same audio channel, but only one at a time can be playing sound.

■ **Apple Loop.** An Apple Loop is a special type of audio file. We will discuss Apple Loops in depth in Chapter 7, "Working with Audio and Apple Loops," but for now, just know that Apple Loops have digital audio information that has been specifically "tagged" so that they will automatically play back at the correct time and in the correct musical key as your Logic project, regardless of the tempo or key in which the original audio was recorded. Apple Loops may also contain MIDI and channel strip information, in addition to audio information.

■ **MIDI region.** Similar to audio regions, a MIDI region is a graphical representation of some MIDI data. Unlike audio regions, however, MIDI regions are not necessarily related to any external information stored in a file on your hard disk. MIDI regions representing sections of MIDI data can be saved to files if you so choose, but they do not need to be stored anywhere other than the Logic project file. If you do save a MIDI file to your hard disk, the MIDI data will still remain in the Logic song as well.

■ **MIDI channel.** This refers to one of the 16 channels that each MIDI port can transmit, or all 16 channels if you have selected the All option. Every MIDI track is assigned to a MIDI channel, except in the case of the All option, in which case the track itself is not assigned to a MIDI channel, but the individual messages are. You can have more than one MIDI track assigned to the same MIDI port and channel.

■ **Track.** Audio and MIDI data are recorded into horizontal lanes in the Arrange window known as *tracks*. The term *tracks* is a holdover from the days of recording onto tape, where each separate strip of a tape recording was known as a *track* (so a stereo cassette would have two tracks, left and right, and an old eight-track tape had—you guessed it—eight tracks).

■ **Event.** An event is a single occurrence of any MIDI message. This can be as simple as a single MIDI message, such as a program change, or it can be a note message, which is actually a compound MIDI message consisting of multiple MIDI messages that are represented as a single MIDI event in Logic.

■ **Object.** The term *object* can broadly apply to nearly anything graphically represented on your display, but in Logic, *object* specifically refers to a virtual studio building block in the Environment.

The Arrange Window

Those coming from pre–Logic 8 versions of Logic will notice that the Arrange window, shown in Figure 2.1, has undergone a significant transformation. Not only is it where you create tracks, record audio and MIDI, slice and splice MIDI and audio regions, and "arrange" them, but you

Figure 2.1 The Arrange window in Logic contains most of the commonly used arrangement and recording functions.

can now access all the various editors, lists, and browsers directly in the Arrange window! If you spent some time working with Logic 8, the Arrange window in Logic 9 looks familiar. For those who are new to Logic, the Arrange window is the first window you see when you launch Logic, and it is the window in which you will do the majority of your work.

At the top of the new Arrange window is the Toolbar, a customizable selection of buttons for many common functions, such as accessing Preferences or importing audio. If you click the Lists or Media button in the Toolbar, a new pane will open on the right side of the Arrange window, giving you access to items such as the Event List, the Audio Bin, and the Library. The Notes button gives you access to notes panes for your entire Logic project or for each individual track. Figure 2.1 shows the Lists area with the Event List displayed.

The left side of the page contains the Inspector, which consists of a Region Parameter box, a Track Parameter box, and the Arrange channel strips. You can show or hide the Inspector by clicking the Inspector button in the Toolbar or by using the key command I. Key commands will be introduced later in this chapter, in "The Key Commands Window" section. To the right of the Inspector is the Track List, which shows the track headers for all tracks in your project and the global tracks. Global tracks are covered in Chapter 4, "Global Elements of Logic." The middle of the window is the Arrange area, which displays horizontal strips for each track and regions of audio or MIDI that are on your tracks. If you have Automation mode on, as in Figure 2.1, you will also see track automation data in a track lane, meaning that track contains some automation data. The bar rule above the Track List displays the measures of the song, and the playhead is the vertical line you see at Measure 64, Beat 1; it shows your exact location.

The Transport bar, located at the bottom of the window, has buttons to activate recording, turn on Cycle mode, and turn the metronome on and off, and it shows you information such as the project tempo, current song position, and loop points. Right above the Transport bar are buttons to open the Mixer and the Sample, Piano Roll, Score, and Hyper Editors. As you can see, there are a lot of tools at your disposal, all in one window. In Chapter 6, "The Arrange Window," you'll explore in depth all the possibilities that the Arrange window offers.

Where's the Song Position Line?   If you're a user of a pre–Logic 8 version of Logic, you're used to calling the vertical line that indicates song position the Song Position Line, or SPL. In Logic 8, the SPL was renamed the *playhead.* The term *playhead* recalls the good old days of tape, in which the tape machine had small magnetic "heads" that glided over the tape—usually one to facilitate recording and another to facilitate playback. The head that was engaged during *play*back was called the *play*head.

The Mixer

The Mixer contains a separate channel strip for every audio and MIDI track in the Arrange window. Normally, it instantly adapts to your current Arrange page, adding, deleting, and re-arranging channel strips based on the state of the Arrange window. As you can see in Figure 2.2, the Mixer resembles a standard mixing desk, with a channel strip for each channel.

You can use the Mixer to mix the volume, panorama, routings, effects, and so on of the audio and MIDI tracks in your song. You can move effects from one slot to another either within or between channel strips in the Mixer. You can choose to view only certain types of channels, all your Arrange channels, or every channel strip in your entire Environment. You can adjust single or multiple channel strips at the same time. Finally, you can print a final stereo or surround audio file of your entire song from the Mixer.

Using the Mixer to mix your song is explained further in Chapter 11, "Mixing in Logic."

The Audio Bin

The Audio Bin is a catalog of all the audio files and audio regions used in a given Logic song. The Audio Bin can be found in the Media area of the Arrange or opened as its own separate window, the Audio Bin window. The Audio Bin might look unassuming compared to some of the others, but don't be fooled—as you can see in Figure 2.3, the Audio Bin is far more than a simple list of audio regions.

Figure 2.2   The Mixer automatically adjusts itself to reflect the audio and MIDI channels currently in your Arrange window.

Using the various tools and menu options in the Audio Bin, you can audition, group, adjust, and loop regions, as well as perform all sorts of file processes and conversions. You can also easily add audio regions to your Arrange window by simply dragging regions from the Audio Bin. The Audio Bin is easily one of the most important areas in Logic when you are using audio in your songs, as you'll see in Chapter 7.

The Sample Editor

When you manipulate audio regions in the Arrange window, you are really only editing Logic's pointers to a given audio file. However, in the Sample Editor, you can operate on the actual audio file itself. The Sample Editor can be opened in the Arrange or in its own separate window. Figure 2.4 shows a stereo audio file in the Sample Editor area of the Arrange window.

To enable you to make the most accurate edits possible, the Sample Editor allows you to view and manipulate your audio with single-sample precision. The Sample Editor is also the location for many of the destructive (in other words, permanent) audio processing options. Chapter 7 will give you more explanation on how to use this editor.

The Event List

As you would imagine, the Event List gives you a detailed list of all the events for the selected window or region. If you are looking at the entire Arrange window, the Event List shows you

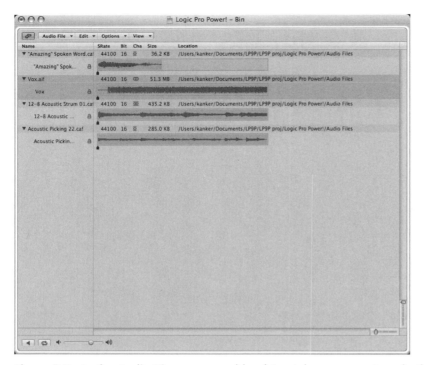

Figure 2.3   In the Audio Bin, you can add, subtract, loop, convert, and otherwise manipulate the audio files and regions in your Logic song.

what region is coming up next; if you're on a MIDI track, the Event List displays a detailed list of all the MIDI events in the track; and so on. Figure 2.5 shows an Event List of a MIDI track in the Arrange window's Lists area. It can also be opened in its own separate window and as a one-line floating window.

The Event List is not simply a textual view of information. It is a very powerful editor, offering you precise access to more parameters than any other editor. The Event List is also an excellent

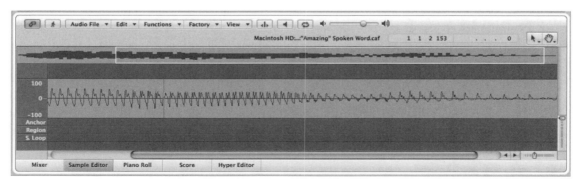

Figure 2.4   The Sample Editor allows you to process and edit an audio file and offers amazingly precise resolution and editing tools.

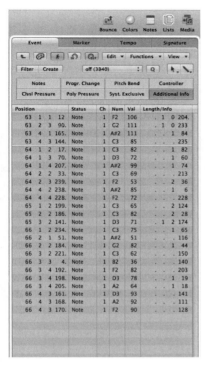

Figure 2.5   The Event List allows users to view and edit data in a text list.

tool to use in tandem with the other editors. For example, you can use an Event List window to give yourself a precise view of your data, while using another editor to operate on your song. You'll learn more about methods of using the Event List in Chapter 8, "Working with MIDI."

The Piano Roll Editor

The Piano Roll Editor is a MIDI note editor that displays MIDI note events as horizontal bars across the screen. The Piano Roll Editor resembles a "piano roll" style of editor (so named because of its similarity to an old-time player piano song roll), with notes scrolling to the right of a graphic keyboard. It can be opened in the Arrange window or in its own separate window, as shown in Figure 2.6.

If you want to program and edit your MIDI notes graphically, the Piano Roll Editor is the place to do it. Not only can you create and manipulate notes and control messages using the Piano Roll Editor, but you can also use its more advanced features, which are detailed in Chapter 8.

The Hyper Editor

The Hyper Editor is one of the least understood editors in Logic. It is a controller editor, a drum editor, and a grid editor all in one. It allows you to save event definitions as *hyper sets*—or *MIDI*

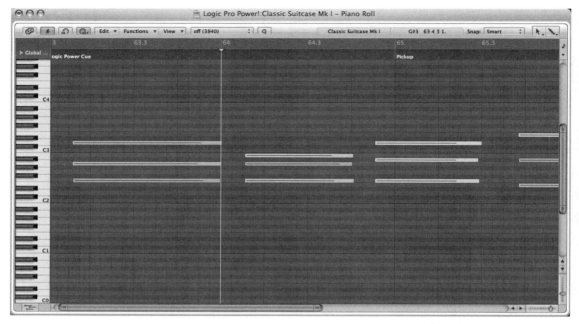

Figure 2.6 The Piano Roll Editor is just one of the powerful MIDI editors in Logic. It allows you to edit MIDI notes and controller values graphically.

view filter templates, if you will—and complements the other Logic editors very well. Figure 2.7 shows a Hyper Editor being used to create and edit MIDI controller data in the Arrange window. It can also be opened in its own separate window.

Don't worry if this definition seems a bit confusing right now. Chapter 8 will describe the many different uses for this powerful and often overlooked MIDI editor. The Hyper Editor might seem unusual at first, but its uniqueness and functionality are among the many features that set Logic apart from the pack.

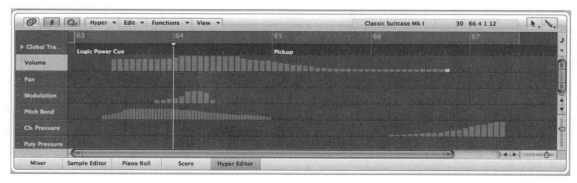

Figure 2.7 The Hyper Editor can be a grid editor, a drum editor, or a controller editor. Here, it's being used to create and edit MIDI controller data.

The Score Editor

If you are comfortable working with musical notation, you will be comfortable with the Score Editor. Logic's Score Editor not only allows you to view, create, and edit MIDI as if you were writing on sheet music instead of a computer, but it allows you to print out professional-quality score charts as well. Figure 2.8 shows a piano part of a song displayed as musical notation in a Score Editor window. You can also open a Score Editor in the Arrange.

The Score Editor offers traditional musicians and composers complete access to the world of sequencing in a familiar format, while being as customizable and powerful as the rest of Logic. The Score Editor of Logic is considered to be one of the best, if not *the* best, in the entire sequencing world, and when you learn about it in detail in Chapter 8, you'll be sure to agree!

The Loop Browser

As discussed earlier in this chapter, Apple Loops are a special kind of audio file. To help distinguish them from the normal audio files in your Audio Bin, Apple Loops get their own special browser, as shown in Figure 2.9.

The Loop Browser allows you to quickly search, audition, and drag loops into your song. Apple Loops that you buy and drag onto the Loop window will automatically be indexed with the rest

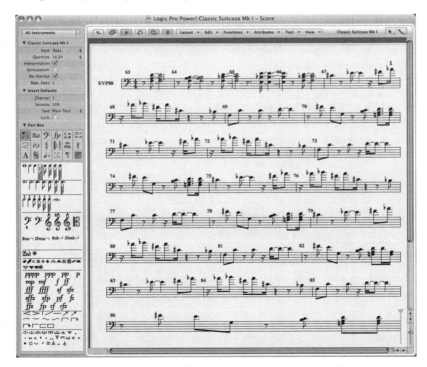

Figure 2.8   The Score Editor allows you to create, view, edit, and print your MIDI tracks in musical notation.

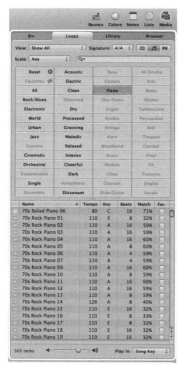

Figure 2.9   The Loop Browser lets you quickly locate and audition Apple Loops, as well as certain other types of loops, such as ACID loops.

of your Apple Loops. You can index Apple Loops that you create however you choose. Other types of loops, such as ACID loops, may be accessible through the Loop Browser but will not be indexed as thoroughly as Apple Loops. The browser is available either as a tab in the Media area or as its own window.

The Browser

The Browser gives you full access to all files on your computer or any connected drives that are usable in Logic. Figure 2.10 shows the contents of a folder in List view.

You can use the Browser to audition audio files and add them directly to the Arrange window or to the Audio Bin for further processing, look for video files, and open Logic projects. We'll go into more depth about the Browser in Chapter 6.

The Library

Sifting through banks of presets across different instruments to find the perfect sound can be difficult at best. The Library tab in the Arrange window, shown in Figure 2.11, makes this problem virtually disappear.

Figure 2.10   The Browser gives you access to all the different files on your drives that Logic can use directly in the Arrange window.

The Library gives you immediate access to presets for all the Logic instruments and effects, channel strip presets, and settings for your Audio Units plug-ins that you save via the plug-in control bar. Additionally, ReWire instruments and External MIDI instruments you have configured either in the Environment or in Audio MIDI Setup (found in your /Applications/Utilities folder) can be accessed in the Library.

A Note on Logic's Use of Mac OS X Directories   You may have already noticed that the Logic Pro file in your Applications directory does not have a folder around it, as some other programs you may own do. This is because Logic Pro follows Apple Inc.'s guidelines for where the support files for applications should go. Logic Pro files are in one of two places.

Factory presets and support files are in the "local" directory (meaning, at the level of your hard drive): /Library/Application Support/Logic.

User presets and support files are in your user directory, with "~" being the UNIX symbol for the Home directory for a given user: ~/Library/Application Support/Logic.

As you see, there's really only a single folder to which you'll be adding information, and that's the user folder above. It's also very convenient to back up just this one folder and know that all your presets, templates, sampler instruments, and so on have been backed up.

The Marker, Tempo, and Signature Lists

There are three other lists that can be found in the Lists area of the Arrange window—the Marker List, the Tempo List, and the Signature List. Each list allows you to create, edit, and delete events for its respective global track. Figure 2.12 shows a Marker List open in the Lists area of the Arrange window. Each of these lists can also be opened in a separate window. These lists will be covered in detail in Chapter 4.

The Environment

The Environment is a window that offers you a library of graphical, onscreen objects that allow you to set up a virtual studio inside Logic, including all your studio objects and hardware routings

Figure 2.11 The Library makes finding the right plug-in preset fast and convenient, giving you instant access to all your Logic presets.

Figure 2.12   A Marker List open in the Lists area of the Arrange window. The Marker, Tempo, and Signature Lists make creating, editing, and deleting events for their respective global tracks very easy.

(see Figure 2.13). The Environment window also allows you to route external hardware with virtual processes and transformers. It's perhaps the most flexible, powerful, and (for some) daunting aspect of Logic. No other sequencer allows you to get under the hood to create unique devices and routings like Logic's Environment, but it will take time for you to feel comfortable using this power.

Notice that the Environment window itself is just an expansive open workspace, and that's exactly what the Environment offers you—an open surface on which to create your ideal studio. You'll learn about the Environment window in depth in Chapter 13, "The Environment." For now, let's just look at one more aspect of the Environment: layers.

Environment Layers

Because the Environment offers nearly infinite routing possibilities, without some sort of organization the Environment window would quickly become an unmanageably large space in which you would find yourself scrolling constantly to get to any structure you have created. To simplify and organize the Environment, Logic introduced the concept of Environment layers. Notice that the left frame of the Environment window in Figure 2.13 includes a box that features a layer

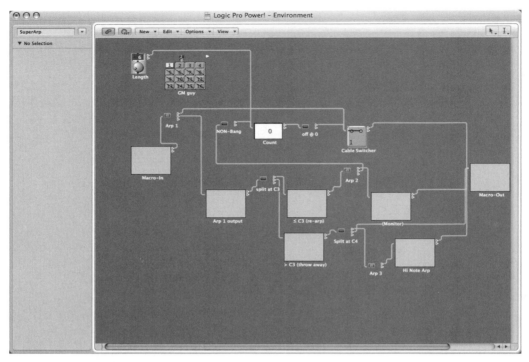

Figure 2.13 The Environment offers you nearly unlimited options for the construction of your own devices and routings inside Logic.

name and a downward arrow—in the case of Figure 2.13, the layer is named SuperArp. That is the Environment Layer pop-up menu, and if you click it, Logic displays a menu that contains all the available layers in that song's Environment, as shown in Figure 2.14.

Layers allow you to organize your Environment into different levels, into which you can put as much or as little as you like, to keep each Environment construction easily accessible. Putting different objects on different layers doesn't affect the way Logic processes the signals, but it does allow you to organize the Environment into more manageable sections.

You'll notice that Logic includes a few Environment layers out of the box. There is a special one worth looking at here: the Environment Mixer layer.

The Environment Mixer Layer

Every Arrange and Mixer channel strip has a corresponding Environment channel strip object. For your convenience, Logic automatically creates an Environment layer, called the *Mixer layer,* that consists of every audio, software instrument, input, output, aux, bus, and master channel strip in your project. By placing all these objects in the Mixer layer of the Environment, you keep the layer's contents separate from all the other layers in the Environment. You can

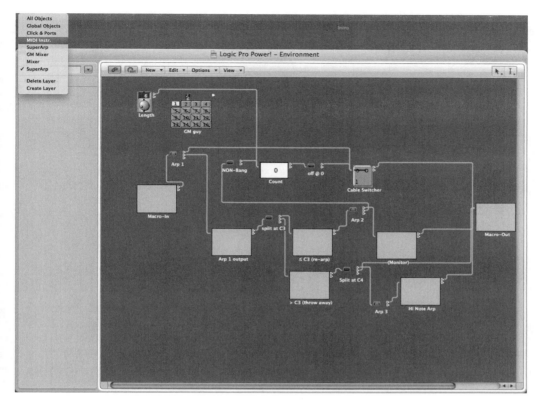

Figure 2.14   This pop-up menu shows all the different layers available in the Environment of this song and enables you to create new layers on the fly.

access this layer from the Layer pop-up menu. Figure 2.15 shows an Environment Mixer for a Logic project.

At first blush, this screen looks a lot like the Mixer shown in Figure 2.2, but the Environment Mixer layer doesn't contain any MIDI channel strips. You'll learn more about both mixers later; for now, you should just know you have a choice.

The Transform Window

The Transform window allows you to alter events according to definable parameters. If that sounds confusing to you, you're not alone—the Transform window is definitely complicated. To give you a quick example of a use for the Transform window, if you wanted to change all the D# notes in a given track to F# without manually editing the notes, you could quickly perform that action in the Transform window, as shown in Figure 2.16.

You can design your own transformations, using amazingly complex data manipulations involving multiple criteria and data mapping, or use the transformations that Apple includes for you with Logic. If all that sounds difficult, don't worry; Chapter 8 explains this feature in detail.

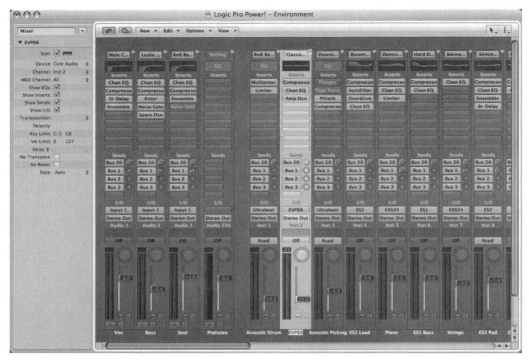

Figure 2.15 The Mixer layer of the Environment contains a complete mixer representing every audio channel and routing that you created for your default song.

The Key Commands Window

Every program allows you to access its features through keyboard shortcuts in addition to selecting commands with the mouse—this is nothing new. However, Logic makes more extensive use of key commands than most applications. In fact, the Key Commands window by itself offers many more options than most applications, as you can see in Figure 2.17.

For most users, accessing functions via key commands is much quicker than using the mouse, so most professional applications offer a vast selection of their functions via key commands. The more flexible applications often allow users to define their own keys to personalize the application to reflect their preferences. Logic takes this a step further—not only can nearly every feature be accessed via a key command, but, in fact, many commands in Logic can *only* be accessed via key command. Also, many key command–only functions do not come with those commands preassigned to keys, so to access such commands, the user first must define them. Setting up your own key commands in Logic is discussed in the following chapter.

It might seem counterintuitive for some commands to only be available via key commands, fueling Logic's reputation for being difficult to learn. In truth, it is for ease of use that some of the advanced, expert features are available only via key commands. Rather than crowd each menu

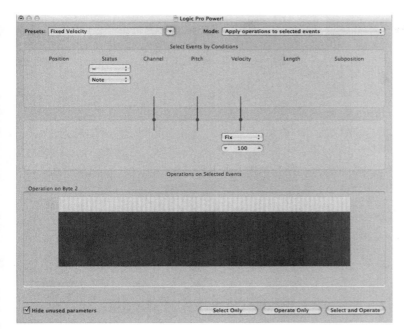

Figure 2.16   The Transform window is powerful enough to make complex global data transformations based on a custom set of criteria. You can also use it to make relatively uncomplicated changes, such as the simple note transposition here.

with commands that most people would never use, Logic makes the least accessed and most obscure functions available for those who need them, but it keeps them out of the way of everyone else.

Right Mouse Button Preferences

If you are using a two-button mouse, you can configure Logic to perform one of four functions when you right-click (or Control-click): You can assign it to a specific tool, to open the Tool menu, to open contextual shortcut menus, or to open combined Tool and contextual menus. Each option has its uses, but it's up to you to decide which one works best for you. It's easy to configure your right-click preference. Simply open the Editing tab in the General Preferences window by selecting Logic Pro > Preferences > General or by selecting General in the Preferences menu in the Toolbar and selecting the Editing tab. Figure 2.18 shows the Editing tab of the General Preferences window.

If you choose Is Assignable to a Tool, you will have three tool options at your immediate disposal at all times. If you select Opens Tool Menu, then every time you click the right mouse button, a menu will open in which you can select the tool you would like to use. If you want to have access to contextual menus with your right mouse button, then select the Opens Shortcut Menu option. If you think that having access to both Tool and contextual menus would work best, you can

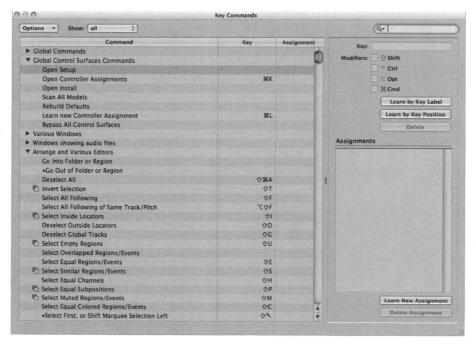

Figure 2.17   Key commands are an integral part of Logic, as you can see by the features of the Key Commands window and the number of commands that are available only as key commands.

assign your right-click preference to Opens Tool and Shortcut Menu, like the one shown in Figure 2.19.

It's important to note that the Tool menu and shortcut menu contents will vary depending on the window, and sometimes even the area of the window, in which you are working.

Screensets

Most sequencers allow you to arrange the various windows and editors onscreen and save these screen formats. As with key commands, however, Logic takes the concept and runs with it in its own uniquely powerful ways. Screensets are not simply an available option in Logic; they are an integral part of how you use the application, as they allow you to create combinations and views of editors that you simply cannot do in the Arrange window alone. Notice that a number appears in the menu bar of Logic, as shown in Figure 2.20. This number (1 in Figure 2.20) indicates the designated number of the screenset that you are currently accessing. You can access up to 99 screensets directly from the numeric keypad, and you can access additional screensets from the Next Screenset and Previous Screenset key commands. As you open, close, and move windows around, Logic automatically remembers them, and the next time you launch your Logic song, it will automatically have the same windows, open in the same location, in each screenset.

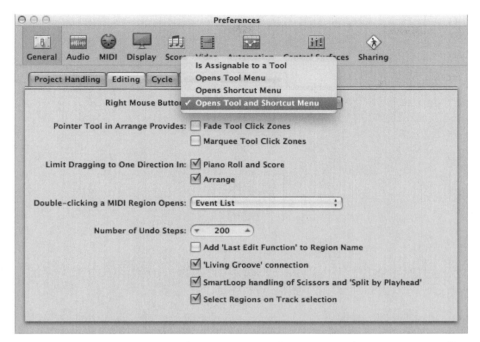

Figure 2.18   The Editing tab of the General Preferences window. You can configure your right-click preference in the Right Mouse Button pop-up menu.

Setting up your screensets helps you create your own ideal workspace and is one of the ways in which Logic is unique—allowing every user to customize Logic to suit himself or herself. In fact, setting up screensets is one of the first things you'll want to do as you customize Logic for yourself, as you will see in the next chapter.

Switching between 32- and 64-Bit Modes

When people talk about "bits" in the context of computer processing, they are referring to how the computer operating system handles addressing. Until recently, the CPUs of most personal computers were 32-bit processors, meaning each program could access 2^{32} addresses. In practical usage, this meant that applications were limited to accessing a maximum of 4 GB of RAM, because 2^{32} is about 4,294,967,295 individual addresses. However, with the introduction of Mac OS X 10.6 (Snow Leopard), Mac OS X is a fully 64-bit operating system, capable of accessing 64 bits' worth of addresses. That is an effectively limitless 2^{64} addresses. (Seriously, this number is huge: 18,446,744,073,709,551,615. That's nearly too big to imagine.) This means that an application that can run in 64-bit mode can access virtually unlimited amounts of memory.

With the introduction of Logic Pro 9.1, Logic can run in Mac OS X 10.6 (Snow Leopard) as either a 32-bit application or a 64-bit application. Which option works best for you is entirely dependent on your workflow, your system, and your needs. First of all, as of this writing, there are a few features that are unavailable when running Logic in 64-bit mode, usually because a particular

Figure 2.19   If you assign your right mouse button preference to Opens Tool and Shortcut Menu, then whenever you right-click, a menu featuring both tools and contextual shortcuts will open.

feature requires a third-party library of code that has not been ported to 64-bit mode itself. These will be pointed out throughout the book as we encounter them. For a complete list of features that currently don't work when Logic runs in 64-bit mode, be sure to read the updated Logic support documents at www.apple.com/logicstudio.

Generally, those features missing when running Logic in 64-bit mode are rather advanced, high-end features, but there are a couple, such as a lack of ReWire/ReCycle support, that may be deal-breakers for many users until these problems are addressed. In addition, most current third-party plug-ins are 32-bit components. In order for Logic running in 64-bit mode to utilize 32-bit plug-ins, Logic launches a separate application, the 32-Bit Audio Unit Bridge, to host 32-bit applications. This is a workaround, and as such, your results may be mixed. Fortunately, most of the time when the 32-Bit Audio Unit Bridge has an issue with a plug-in or becomes unstable for some other reason, it crashes while leaving Logic unscathed. You can easily re-launch the 32-Bit Audio Unit Bridge from the Finder when it crashes.

There are definite benefits to running in 64-bit mode. As we wrote a moment ago, a 64-bit application can access virtually endless amounts of RAM. Of course, current physical limitations dictate the amount of RAM you can install on your system. You may "only" be able to install 8 GB of RAM on your MacBook Pro or 32 GB of RAM in your Mac Pro, but once the OS and any

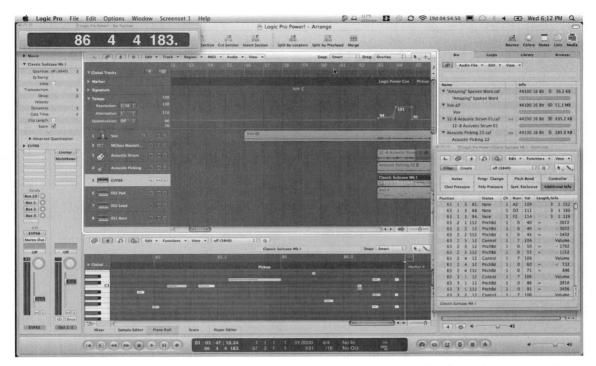

Figure 2.20   Screensets are not an afterthought or a hidden option in Logic. The active screenset is prominently displayed in Logic's menu bar. Here the menu bar shows that Screenset 1 is active.

other processes you may have running on your machine have staked out their little bit of the available RAM, Logic can then have access to whatever RAM remains. Given the extreme size of many current sample libraries and the size of the files that a large 192-MHz/24-bit recording session would need to handle, the ability to maintain large portions of data that would otherwise have to stream from your hard disk in physical RAM greatly improves the performance of your Logic system as a whole. Some users will genuinely be thankful for the performance boost they will see in Logic as a 64-bit application and will be willing to deal with any current limitations for that very reason. Of course, since we know Logic to be a very flexible and customizable application, you don't have to pick either 32-bit mode or 64-bit mode as your permanent, unchangeable version of Logic Pro. As long as your system is capable of running Logic in 64-bit mode—in other words, you have Logic 9.1 installed on a Macintosh computer built in late 2006 or more recently, running Mac OS X 10.6.2 or higher—you can switch between 32-bit and 64-bit modes with just a couple of mouse clicks.

To select which mode Logic will utilize, navigate to the Logic application in the Applications folder in the Finder. Control-click (or right-click) on the Logic application and select Get Info from the menu that opens, as shown in Figure 2.21, or highlight the Logic application in the Finder and press Command+I.

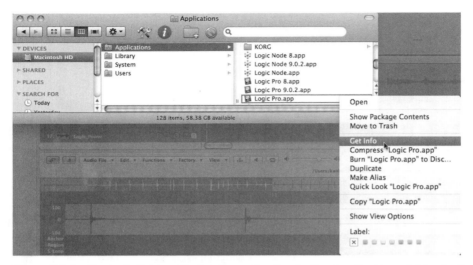

Figure 2.21   Control-click on the Logic application in the Applications folder in the Finder and select Get Info from the menu shown to access the ability to change Logic's default launch mode between 32- and 64-bit modes.

In the Logic Pro.app Info window, you can select the Open in 32-Bit Mode check box to have Logic function as a 32-bit application. If Open in 32-Bit Mode is unchecked, Logic will always open as a 64-bit application. Figure 2.22 shows the Logic Pro.app Info window, with the cursor hovering over the Open in 32-Bit Mode check box.

Remember, once you select which mode Logic will utilize, you're not stuck in that mode. If you want to change back, simply Get Info on the Logic Pro.app in the Applications folder again and switch from one mode to the other. Also note that you can't change the mode Logic is using while Logic is open—you'll have to re-launch Logic for the change to take effect.

Okay, But Seriously—Should I Use 64-Bit or 32-Bit?   Sorry, we're not going to tell you what to do. But here are some good questions to ask yourself:

Can your Macintosh run 64-bit applications? If you have an early 2006 MacBook Pro or iMac, the answer is no. And that settles that.

Does your Mac have enough RAM to take advantage of the extra memory address space available? Obviously, it doesn't matter whether Logic can access more than 4 GB of RAM if your Mac only has 2 GB installed. At that point, you might as well continue running Logic in 32-bit mode.

Are you using sample libraries or plug-ins that can take advantage of the extra RAM? If you're using huge orchestral sample libraries or instruments such as Spectrasonics

Omnisphere that have 50-GB sound libraries and are available in 64-bit mode, that might be a very good reason to run Logic in 64-bit mode.

Does your current Logic project use audio recorded at high sample rates and use Flex often? Flex takes a lot of RAM; higher sample rate audio uses more RAM. These are also very good reasons to run Logic in 64-bit mode.

Does your current Logic project use a lot of 32-bit Audio Unit audio processors? Some plug-ins, such as Waves audio processors, are (at the time of this writing) not compatible with the 32-Bit Audio Unit Bridge. So you might want to stick with running Logic in 32-bit mode.

There is one important thing we'd like to stress: *The audio quality from Logic and its built-in plug-ins will be the same in either 32-bit or 64-bit mode, so sound quality shouldn't affect your choice.* For years now, Logic has used 64-bit *precision* math formulas (which can be run in either 32- or 64-bit operating systems) to get the very best sound quality in its audio path where appropriate, so Logic has always sounded as good as possible. (Many other third-party Audio Units plug-ins use 64-bit precision math as well.) We've run Logic in both modes depending on the project, and you'll get the same professional-sounding results either way. So don't stress the choice, and use what works best for your given system and project.

Now that you have an idea of the possibilities of Logic, it's time to set up your default template. The next chapter, "The Logic Project," will explain how.

Figure 2.22   Use the Open in 32-Bit Mode check box in the Logic Pro.app Info window to define whether Logic will function as a 32- or a 64-bit application.

3 The Logic Project

An important distinction between Logic and other music workstation applications is just how much information is stored in each document file, which is called a *project* in Logic. In most applications, you set up the *application* the way you want to by arranging windows, toolbars, and so on. When you load a document, that document uses the *application* configuration. In Logic, the *project* contains everything about your studio—the setup of all your instruments, editors, windows, screensets, and everything else that is configurable in Logic. In fact, each project in Logic is a self-contained virtual studio. This means that if you create a project in your copy of Logic and then open it in someone else's copy of Logic, you will still find your own familiar virtual studio waiting for you.

When you launch Logic for the first time, it automatically presents you with a selection of different templates in the New dialog. These templates represent Apple's effort to provide an array of ready-made project setups that people will find generally useful. Figure 3.1 shows the New dialog.

Templates are blank songs with a specific configuration from which you might want to start. Apple's templates are stored in the Application Support folder for Logic, which you can find at the following path: /Library/Application Support/Logic/Project Templates. This chapter is going to deal with creating and saving your own custom template, which will help you get right down to the business of creating music every time you open Logic.

You should explore the templates that Apple includes with Logic to get a feel for some of the myriad different ways you can configure Logic—Apple has included templates for uses as varied as electronic music composition, music for picture, surround mastering, and even a TDM configuration for working with a Pro Tools TDM system. To open a template in the New dialog, simply click on its icon. Each time you close a template, you can access the New dialog by selecting File > New or pressing Command+N.

After you have explored some of these templates, open an empty project by selecting File > New or pressing Command+N and clicking on the Empty Project icon. We'll be using this empty project to create your template. When complete, this template will allow you to have Logic immediately open into your personal virtual studio instead of a general default song. Trust us on this: *Creating your template project is one of the most important things you will do in Logic!*

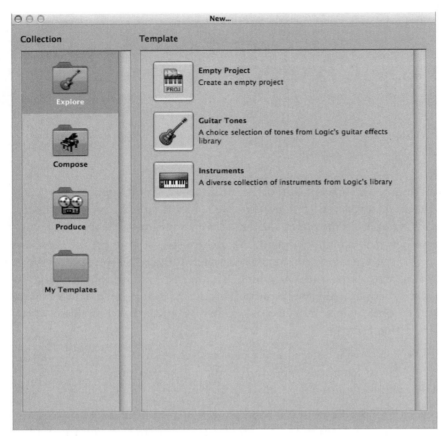

Figure 3.1 The New dialog. When you first launch Logic, or when you use the File > New command, the New dialog opens. You can select a template to use or open an empty project by clicking the desired template's icon.

The actual mechanics involved in creating a template couldn't be simpler: You set up a Logic project, name it, and select File > Save As Template. Exactly how you set up the template, however, takes some serious thought and preparation. Creating your template project is a continuous process—as you learn more about Logic and your working preferences, you can always go back and change your template project accordingly. You can even create a number of different templates designed for different purposes, much like the templates that Apple has included with Logic. To get you started, here are a few points that you need to consider.

Visualizing Your Workspace

The first and most important aspect of creating your template project is to have a general idea of what aspects of the program you'll want to access. Chapter 2 gave you an overview of some of the windows and editors in Logic. Did you already get a sense of which ones you expect to use the most? Do you imagine yourself needing the Arrange window and the Sample Editor window all the time, the Piano Roll Editor a little, and the Score Editor not at all? Do you imagine that your most important windows will be the Score Editor and Event Editor, and then the Arrange and the Mixer? Do you need to access Environment objects creatively for each composition? You don't need to know how to use all the windows and editors yet—that's what the rest of the book is for. For now, consider how you might want to work and which windows you'll want to have readily available.

Next, consider how much screen real estate you have. Do you have dual 30-inch screens so you can spread out everything you'll need at once? Are you making do with a 13-inch laptop screen? Do you like to work with one single window on the screen at one time, or do you like to have each editor in its own separate window? Luckily, Logic's screensets allow you to build your template project to fit any of these configurations; all you need to have is a general idea of where you'd like to start.

Remember, the core idea behind Logic is to be as configurable as possible to allow you the flexibility to create your own ideal workspace. If you have an image of what the makeup of that ideal space will be, then it will be that much easier to create it. The name of the game here is experimentation—if you're not sure you'll have enough room for an editor, open the editor in the Edit area of the Arrange or its own window, resize it as much as possible, move it around, and see how it feels to use it in that size and position. When you're comfortable with Logic, rearranging your template will be as simple as opening the application, placing the window you need in the screenset you desire, perhaps locking the screenset (explained later in this chapter in the section "Setting Up Screensets"), and resaving the project. For now, with just what has already been discussed and a bit of careful planning, you can already set up an almost optimal template project.

Creating Your Template

Not too long ago, creating a new workspace from scratch in Logic meant getting your hands dirty and digging around in menus and the Environment. Having to figure out how to create and configure instrument objects, audio objects, Environment Mixers, and so forth helped add to the impression that Logic was an application with a very steep learning curve. The process is so much simpler these days that getting a template started with a full complement of audio, software instrument, and External MIDI tracks takes little more than a few mouse clicks and keystrokes.

To begin creating your template project, select Empty Project in the Templates dialog (if you do not already have an empty project open). When you create an empty project, you are greeted with an empty Arrange window showing a New Tracks drop-down dialog, as seen in Figure 3.2.

In the New Tracks dialog, you can add and configure audio, software instruments, and External MIDI tracks. Let's begin by adding some Audio tracks to the empty project.

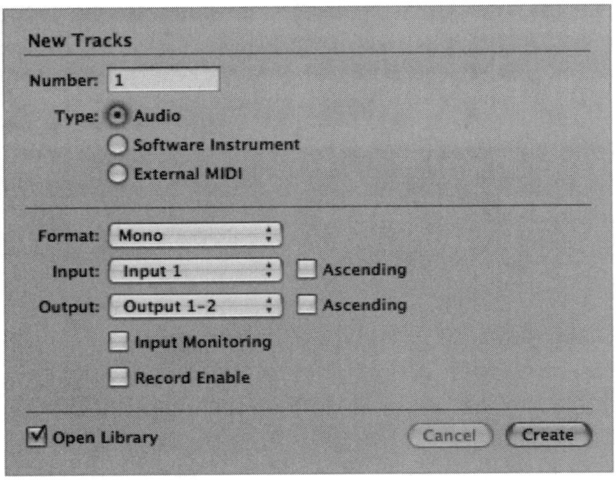

Figure 3.2   The New Tracks dialog.

Adding Audio Tracks

To add Audio tracks to your project, select the Audio radio button in the New Tracks dialog in the Type area. In the Number field, enter the number of Audio tracks you would like to add to your project. Don't worry about getting it right the first time. You can always add more tracks later. You then need to configure your Audio tracks. The New Tracks dialog gives you the following options regarding the configuration of your Audio tracks to allow you to have your new Audio tracks ready to go immediately after creation:

- **Format.** In this pull-down menu, you can choose between mono, stereo, and surround. Whichever format you choose, all of the Audio tracks you are currently creating will have the same format. For example, if you choose to create 16 new Audio tracks and select Stereo as the format, you will create 16 new stereo Audio tracks.

- **Input.** The Input pull-down menu allows you to assign hardware inputs, busses, or no input to your new Audio tracks. With No Input tracks, you can configure the input later if desired. If you choose Surround as the format for your new Audio tracks, Logic will configure your hardware inputs per the assignment in the Input tab of the I/O Assignments tab of the Audio Preferences window, covered in the "Configuring Surround Inputs" section later in this chapter. You also have the option of selecting No Input or a bus for the input of surround Audio tracks. If you are creating more than one new Audio track assigned to hardware inputs or to busses and you select the Ascending check box next to the Input menu, then Logic will automatically assign hardware inputs or busses to your new Audio tracks in ascending order. If you are assigning your new Audio tracks to hardware inputs and are creating more new Audio tracks than you have hardware inputs, once Logic has assigned all your hardware inputs to Audio tracks, Logic will start back at Hardware Input 1 and continue assigning subsequent inputs in ascending order. Therefore, if you create 10 new mono Audio tracks and select the Ascending check box, but you only have eight hardware inputs, Logic will assign Audio Tracks 1–8 to Hardware Inputs 1–8, respectively, and then assign Audio Track 9 to Hardware Input 1 and Audio Track 10 to Hardware Input 2.

■ **Output.** The Output pull-down menu allows you to assign your new Audio tracks to hardware outputs, busses, no output, or surround. If you select No Output, you can configure the output later if desired. If you select Surround as your output format, then Logic will configure your hardware inputs per the assignment in the Output tab of the I/O Assignments tab of the Audio Preferences window. Surround outputs and the Output tab of the I/O Assignments tab of the Audio Preferences window are covered in detail in Chapter 11, "Mixing in Logic." If you are creating more than one new Audio track assigned to hardware outputs or to busses and you select the Ascending check box next the Output menu, Logic will automatically assign hardware outputs or busses to your new Audio tracks in ascending order. If you are assigning your new Audio tracks to hardware outputs and are creating more new Audio tracks than you have hardware outputs, once Logic has assigned all your hardware outputs to Audio tracks, Logic will start back at Hardware Output 1 and continue assigning subsequent outputs in ascending order.

■ **Input Monitoring.** Selecting the Input Monitoring check box activates your new Audio tracks' input monitoring buttons, allowing you to monitor signals passing through your new Audio tracks' channel strips when the Audio tracks are not record enabled.

■ **Record Enable.** Selecting the Record Enable check box activates your new Audio tracks' Record Enable button, allowing you to begin recording to your new Audio tracks almost immediately.

■ **Open Library.** Selecting the Open Library check box opens the Library in the Arrange window when you create your new Audio tracks, allowing you to instantly access channel strip settings for your new audio channel strips.

Once you have configured all the options in the New Tracks dialog, click Create, and the specified number of new Audio tracks will be created. Your new Audio tracks will be visible in the Arrange window, and channel strips for each new Audio track will be added to the Mixer. Channel strips will also be created in the Mixer layer of the Environment for each new Audio track.

What if you created eight mono Audio tracks, but you would like to add eight stereo Audio tracks? You can open the New Tracks dialog by clicking the + symbol at the top of the Track List, by selecting Track > New in the Arrange window, or by pressing Option+Command+N. If you want to add a track that is identical to a track you have selected in the Track List, you can select Track > New with Duplicate Setting or press Command+D. When you use either command, the new tracks will appear directly below the selected track in the Track List, and the new track will be selected.

Configuring the Audio Track Parameter Box

Although all the parameters you need to get started are configured using the New Tracks dialog, there are a couple of other options you may want to change in the Track Parameter box. Each track has its own Track Parameter box, although if a track shares a channel strip with other tracks, then they all share the same Track Parameter box. Figure 3.3 shows an Audio track and its Track Parameter box.

Figure 3.3   An Audio track and its Track Parameter box.

The Audio Track Parameter box options are as follows:

- **Icon.** Use this setting to select the icon you want to represent the Audio track. If you click and hold the mouse on the image, Logic will display a pop-up menu of available icons. If you know that certain Audio tracks will always be assigned to a particular purpose—for example, Audio Track 1 might always be a vocal track, and Audio Track 2 might always be the bass track—then feel free to go ahead and assign an appropriate icon to each track.

- **Core Audio.** This setting specifies the Core Audio driver that your audio hardware is using. In the Arrange window, this setting is grayed out. You won't need to adjust this setting unless you are using a DAE or Direct TDM device. If you are, you can open the Mixer layer of the Environment, select the desired channel strip, and change this parameter in the Environment's Inspector. Core Audio, DAE, and Direct TDM devices are discussed in the section "Configuring Your Audio Device" later in this chapter. The Mixer layer of the Environment is discussed in Chapter 11.

- **MIDI Channel.** In old-style automation in Logic, this parameter determined what channel the automation for the track would need to be on. Since Logic 5, this parameter hasn't been of much use, although it still appears if you are using some of the region-based automation (explored in Chapters 6 and 10), which is steeped in MIDI.

- **Freeze Mode.** The Freeze Mode parameter lets you specify whether the track will include effects in the resulting Freeze file if you freeze the track. The Freeze Mode parameter and Freeze tracks will be covered in Chapter 6.

- **Q-Reference.** Logic Pro 9 lets you easily quantize audio. With the Q-Reference button selected, the Audio track will give its region's transients as quantization reference points. Quantizing audio will be covered in Chapter 6.

- **Flex Mode.** In addition to quantizing audio, Logic Pro 9 lets you treat audio in an elastic manner, changing the timing of an audio file in a nondestructive manner. The Flex Mode parameter helps you define what kind of Flex Time editing process will work on the audio. Flex Time editing and the Flex Mode menu will be covered in Chapter 6.

Adding Software Instrument Tracks

The Software Instrument track represents a simple MIDI device that plays on only one MIDI channel, but which produces audio via software instruments. To add Software Instrument tracks to your project, click the + symbol at the top of the Track List, select Track > New in the Arrange window, or press Option+Command+N. Click the Software Instrument radio button. Figure 3.4 shows the New Tracks dialog with the Software Instrument radio button selected.

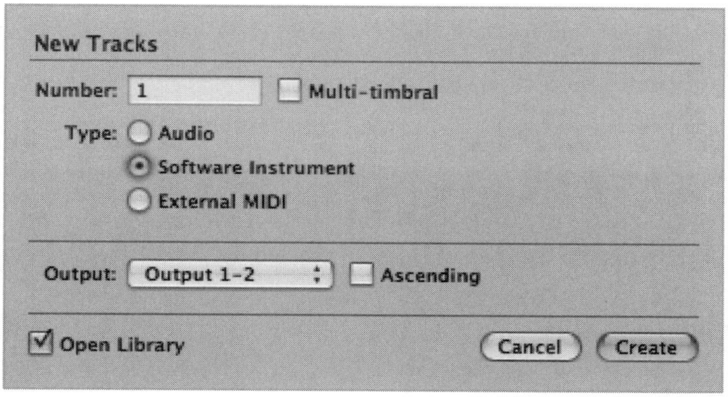

Figure 3.4   The New Tracks dialog configured for creating new Software Instrument tracks.

When you select the Software Instrument radio button, the New Tracks dialog presents you with the following options:

- **Multi-Timbral.** Selecting the Multi-Timbral check box next to the Number field creates your new software instrument as a multitimbral instrument. Creating and using multitimbral software instruments is covered in Chapter 9, "Working with Software Instruments."

- **Output.** The Output menu allows you to assign your new Software Instrument tracks to specific hardware outputs or busses. If you select the Ascending check box, Logic will automatically assign hardware outputs or busses to your new Software Instrument tracks in ascending order.

- **Open Library.** Selecting the Open Library check box opens the Library in the Arrange window when you create your new Software Instrument tracks, allowing you to instantly access channel strip settings for your new Software Instrument channel strips.

After you configure the New Tracks dialog to create your software instruments, click the Create button. The specified number of Software Instrument tracks will be created. Your new Software Instrument tracks will be visible in the Arrange window, and channel strips for each new Software Instrument track will be added to the Mixer. Channel strips will also be created in the Mixer layer of the Environment for each new Software Instrument track.

If you need to create any more Software Instrument tracks, you can use any of the methods described earlier for creating more Audio tracks.

Configuring the Software Instrument Track Parameter Box

Because a Software Instrument track is a hybrid track that incorporates both MIDI sequencing capabilities and audio output, it has a wider range of track parameters than an Audio track does. Figure 3.5 shows a newly created Software Instrument track and its parameter box.

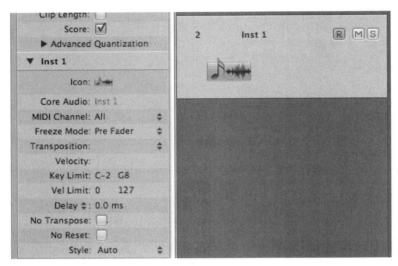

Figure 3.5   A Software Instrument track with its parameter box.

The Software Instrument track parameters are:

- **Instrument name.** If you know what software instrument you are going to assign to a particular Software Instrument track, you can double-click on the default name to the right of the disclosure triangle—Inst 1 in Figure 3.5—and Logic will display a text entry box in which you can type the new track name. For example, if you know you will be adding an EVP88 to Software Instrument Track 1 of your template, you could name Software Instrument Track 1 "EVP88".

- **Icon.** Use this setting to select the icon you want to represent the Software Instrument track. If you know you'll be dedicating a Software Instrument track to a specific software instrument, then feel free to assign an icon to that Software Instrument track. If you click and hold down the mouse button on the small picture next to Icon, a large pop-up menu will appear with small picture options. Find one that represents your software instrument in some way. (For example, if it's EVP88, you can use the EVP image; if it's Ultrabeat, the UB image; and so on.)

- **MIDI Channel.** This parameter assigns the MIDI channel for your Software Instrument track. If you set the Channel parameter to All, then your software instrument will respond to any MIDI input when its track is selected. If you set the Channel parameter to a specific MIDI channel—channel 3, for example—then your software instrument will only respond to MIDI input on MIDI channel 3 when its channel is selected.

- **Freeze Mode.** The Freeze Mode parameter lets you specify whether the track will include effects in the resulting Freeze file if you freeze the track. The Freeze Mode parameter and Freeze tracks will be covered in Chapter 6.

- **Transposition.** If you enter a value here, every time you play this software instrument, Logic will automatically transpose the note it sends the software instrument up or down by the amount you specified. You can either double-click in the space to the right of Transpose to display a text box or drag the mouse up or down to add or subtract up to 96 steps (a full eight octaves!) from the original value in single-step (half-note) increments. If you click on the double-arrows to the right, you can quickly octave shift up to three octaves up or down.

- **Velocity.** If you enter a value here, every time you play this software instrument, Logic will automatically increase or reduce the velocity of the MIDI note it sends to the software instrument by this value. You can click to the right of Velocity to display a text box or drag the mouse up or down to increase or reduce the velocity of the MIDI note by up to 99 steps. (MIDI values are represented from 0 to 127, so this parameter can be used to adjust velocities through nearly the entire velocity range.)

- **Key Limit.** This parameter sets the upper- and lower-note boundaries of the software instrument. You can use this parameter to make certain that you do not send a software instrument a note outside of its range or to reduce artificially the range of the notes you choose to send a software instrument. (So, for example, even though EVB3 is capable of reproducing notes outside the actual range of a Hammond B-3, you might want to limit the notes to a Hammond's real range to ensure a realistic organ sound.) As with the previous two parameters, you can either double-click on the values to display a text box or click and hold on either value to use the mouse to raise or lower the value.

- **Vel Limit.** This parameter sets up the upper and lower velocity boundaries of the instrument. As with the previously discussed parameters, you can double-click on each value to display a text box or click and hold on the value to use the mouse to raise or lower the values.

- **Delay.** The term *delay* has many meanings in a musical (and even in a MIDI-related) context. In this context, it warrants further explanation. Basically, this Delay parameter allows you to send MIDI information to this software instrument either early or late, depending on the setting. This parameter is not a "MIDI echo" that allows you to create doubling or echo effects that are also often called *delay*. This parameter only adjusts the point at which Logic will commence sending data to your software instrument. Clicking on the double-arrows lets you select between delaying in ticks or delaying in milliseconds. You can double-click in the space to the right of Delay or click and hold the mouse to raise or lower the value between –99 and +99 ticks or –500.0 and +500.0 ms, depending on your Delay value setting. (A *tick* is the smallest amount of distance possible on the Arrange window's Time ruler.)

■ **No Transpose.** If you check this box, the software instrument is set to No Transpose. This means that even if you are transposing all MIDI tracks globally or with the Transpose setting in the Region Parameter box (which is discussed in Chapter 6, "The Arrange Window"), the process will not affect this instrument. This check box is especially valuable for percussion tracks, where transposing notes often results in selecting completely different sounds.

■ **No Reset.** If you check this box, this software instrument will not respond to MIDI Reset messages, such as mod wheel and pitchbend resets, even if they are sent to all devices.

■ **Style.** This parameter is set to Auto by default. If you click and hold the up/down arrows to the right of the parameter name, Logic displays a pop-up list of all the available default Score Editor styles. In the Auto style, Logic picks an appropriate style based on the pitch range of the notes on the track. If you do not use the Score Editor, you can ignore this parameter.

Adding External MIDI Tracks

To add External MIDI tracks to your project, click the + symbol at the top of the Track List, select Track > New in the Arrange window, or press Option+Command+N. Click the External MIDI radio button. Figure 3.6 shows the New Tracks dialog with the External MIDI radio button selected.

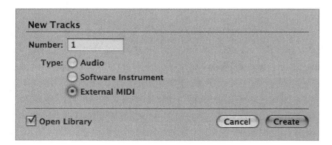

Figure 3.6   The New Tracks dialog configured for creating new External MIDI tracks.

As you can see in Figure 3.6, the only options available when you select the External MIDI radio button in the New Tracks dialog are the Number field and the Open Library check box. How many External MIDI tracks you should add is dependent on how many MIDI OUT ports your MIDI interface has or how many ReWire instruments you want to use. For each MIDI OUT you have, you can access 16 MIDI channels. It is very beneficial to have a dedicated MIDI connection for each of your External MIDI instruments, as this gives you access to all the power Logic offers for utilizing all your External MIDI hardware to the fullest. This is particularly true of multitimbral External MIDI equipment, which can allow you to access up to 16 MIDI channels simultaneously from one MIDI instrument.

When you create a new External MIDI track, Logic creates a General MIDI multi-instrument object (GM Device) in the Environment, which is shown in Figure 3.7. Don't worry that it's a GM Device—you can always reconfigure it for your specific piece of MIDI hardware, as you'll see a little later in this chapter.

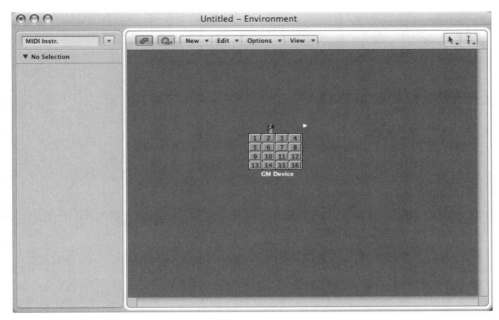

Figure 3.7   A General MIDI multi-instrument object in the Environment. When you create an External MIDI track, a multi-instrument object is automatically created in the Environment.

If you create more than 16 External MIDI tracks in the New Tracks dialog, Logic automatically creates a new multi-instrument object for each new set of 16 tracks in addition to the GM Device. Note that the number of multi-instrument objects that are created is dependent on the number of MIDI OUT ports you have available on your MIDI interface. Therefore, if you have 4 MIDI OUT ports on your MIDI interface, you can create up to 64 External MIDI tracks in the New Tracks dialog and have four multi-instrument objects automatically added to the Environment along with the GM Device, for a total of five multi-instrument objects. You can always add more instrument objects and multi-instrument objects in the Environment later if need be, as you'll discover in Chapter 13, "The Environment."

Setting Up Multi Instruments

A multi instrument, or multitimbral instrument, is an instrument that can play sounds on up to 16 MIDI channels simultaneously. When you first create new External MIDI tracks, you should open an Environment window and configure your multi-instrument objects. Click the downward-pointing triangle button in the upper-left corner of the Environment window to open the Layer menu. Select the MIDI Instr. layer from the Layer menu, and you'll see your multi-instrument object(s) and the Parameter box shown in Figure 3.8.

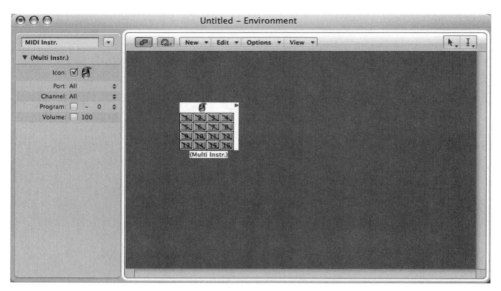

Figure 3.8   A multi-instrument object and its Parameter box.

The functions of the parameters in the multi-instrument Parameter box are as follows:

- **Instrument name.** To give your new multi instrument a name, simply click on the word "(Multi Instr.)" to the right of the disclosure triangle, and Logic will display a text entry box in which you can type the new name.

- **Icon.** The added visual cue of an icon can help you visualize your device, and you might as well take care of this while configuring your multi-instrument object. Selecting an icon was discussed earlier, in the "Configuring the Software Instrument Track Parameter Box" section.

- **Port.** You'll also want to make sure your instrument is set to the correct port. Click the number (or it might be the word All, as in Figure 3.8) next to the Port parameter, and you'll see a list of all your available MIDI ports. Choose the one to which your device is connected. MIDI ports are covered in more detail later in this chapter, in the "Selecting MIDI Ports" subsection.

- **Channel.** If your device is only capable of operating on a single MIDI channel, or if your instrument represents only a single patch on a synth, you want to be sure to select that channel in the Channel parameter. Click the number next to Channel and select the proper

MIDI channel, from 1 to 16. If you want the notes in your MIDI regions to determine the MIDI channel, set the Channel parameter to All.

- **Program.** Check this box and select a program number between 0 and 127 if you want this instrument to always select a specific patch in your MIDI device.

- **Volume.** Check this box and select a MIDI volume level between 0 and 127 if you want this instrument to always set your MIDI device to a specific volume.

After you have set parameters for the multi-instrument object as a whole, it's time to activate its individual subchannels. All 16 boxes in the multi-instrument object have lines through them because every subchannel is turned off by default. You'll want to activate as many subchannels as your instrument supports; for example, if your synth is eight-part multitimbral, you'll activate eight subchannels in the multi instrument by clicking on them. Figure 3.9 shows the multi-instrument object after you have activated some subchannels.

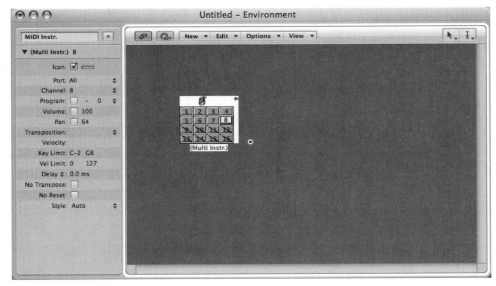

Figure 3.9   A multi-instrument object once eight subchannels have been activated. The Parameter box shown is the unique Parameter box for Subchannel 8.

Notice that each subchannel has its own on/off toggle and associated Parameter box. Each parameter you see in the Parameter box that is identical to those in the software instrument Track Parameter box previously discussed functions identically.

Since each subchannel of a multi instrument is basically a unique single-channel MIDI instrument, you get a set of six "general" parameters for the entire MIDI instrument, but you might want each subchannel to be completely unique. If you already know how you want to set up your subchannels, go ahead and set the Parameter boxes as you activate the channels. Be careful about setting a global port value, however, as it applies to the entire multi instrument.

The Multi Instrument Window

The other window that you can access from a multi-instrument object is called the Multi Instrument window. If you double-click any multi-instrument object, Logic displays the window shown in Figure 3.10. Here you can set up the banks and patch names of your multi instrument.

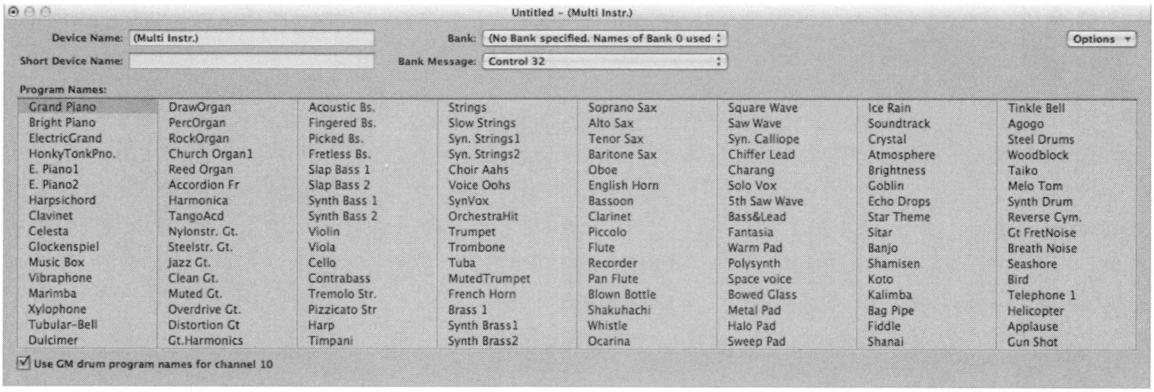

Figure 3.10   A Multi Instrument window of a multi-instrument object.

You can set several parameters in this window:

- **Device Name and Short Device Name.** The device name is simply the name of your multi-instrument object. You should have already named your multi instrument, and that name should already appear in the Device Name box. In the Short Device Name box, you can type in a short abbreviation of the instrument name that will appear in the Arrange window Track List when a multi instrument's program name is also being displayed.

- **Bank menu.** This pull-down menu allows you to select among banks of patches on your MIDI device. Each multi-instrument object allows up to 15 banks, numbered 0–14. If you choose Bank 1–14, Logic asks whether you want to initialize the bank. If you want to enter your own bank names, then press Enter. If you want to use the generic General MIDI names from Bank 0, click Cancel. In general, unless your instrument is specifically a General MIDI device, you'll want to input your own names.

- **Bank Message menu.** This pull-down menu allows you to select among different MIDI messages that will be sent to your MIDI device when you switch banks. Different manufacturers and devices use different messages to switch banks, so you need to consult your MIDI device's documentation to see which selection is appropriate for each device.

- **Program Names.** You'll notice that 128 program names are visible in the Multi Instrument window for each bank. You can enter the specific names for the various programs of your device here. You can do this in a number of ways:

  - Double-click on each program name one by one and manually type the new program name in the text boxes that appear.

- Copy data from the Clipboard by using the Options pull-down menu to the right of the Bank Message menu (see Figure 3.11). You can easily type the program numbers and names into a word processing program and simply use the menu to copy them all to the correct program. You can also copy and paste program names from another multi-instrument object by using either this menu or the Copy and Paste global commands.

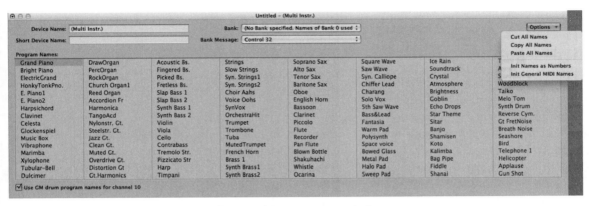

Figure 3.11   The Text Import menu of the Multi Instrument window.

- If you just want program numbers instead of names, select Options > Init Names as Numbers.

- If you wish to use General MIDI program names, select Options > Init General MIDI Names.

- **Use GM Drum Program Names for Channel 10.** In General MIDI devices, Channel 10 is reserved for drums. The General MIDI drum kit also contains a standard set of drum kits. If you check this box, Logic automatically uses the standard drum set names for Subchannel 10.

Once you have configured all your multi-instrument objects, you can easily reassign External MIDI tracks to different MIDI devices and different MIDI channels in those devices using the Library in the Arrange window. Simply open the Library by clicking the Media button in the Toolbar and selecting the Library tab, or by pressing R, and browse the different folders that represent your multi-instrument objects.

Expert Tip: Create Multi-instrument Objects for All Your MIDI Synths   The best part about customizing the program names for your multi-instrument objects is that if you select the multi-instrument object in a track in the Arrange window and your track lane has enough room, it will display the actual track name. Also, if you have the Program button (one of the performance parameters in the instrument Parameter box mentioned but not detailed earlier) checked for that subchannel, you can send your device program changes from the Arrange window by clicking on program names (and scroll through your synth's programs by scrolling through the program names on the Arrange window). Because you have all the names typed in, you can send changes by name rather than by number. For this reason, even for mono synths that are not multitimbral, you should seriously consider using a multi-instrument object for the device and only activating one subchannel. This might seem like overkill, but it conveniently enables you to customize patch names, which is worth the minimal additional effort.

Adding ReWire Tracks

Although adding and configuring ReWire tracks is covered in detail in Chapter 9, if you know you will be using a ReWire slave with Logic, you may want to add some ReWire tracks to your template project.

To add ReWire tracks to your project, you need to create some new, or configure some existing, External MIDI tracks. To configure your External MIDI tracks for ReWire use, open the Library tab of the Media area. Then, select the External MIDI track you wish to configure. In the Library Browser list, double-click the name of the ReWire application you want to use for your selected External MIDI track. This will launch the selected ReWire application. Once the ReWire application has launched, you can access any available ReWire instruments in the Library, as seen in Figure 3.12, and assign a ReWire instrument to your selected External MIDI track.

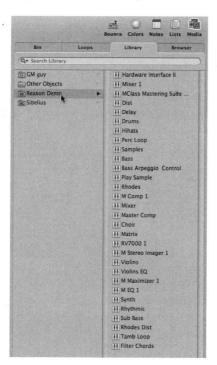

Figure 3.12   You can use the Library tab of the Media area to launch ReWire applications and assign the instruments available in your ReWire applications to External MIDI tracks.

Once you have configured your External MIDI tracks for ReWire transmission, you can play and sequence the instruments in your ReWire applications from Logic. To route the audio from your ReWire applications into Logic, you will need to create and configure auxiliary channel strips. Creating auxiliary channel strips is covered in the next section of this chapter. Configuring auxiliary channel strips for ReWire audio transmission is covered in detail in Chapter 9. Note that ReWire is not currently compatible with Logic in 64-bit mode.

Adding Auxiliary Tracks

Auxiliary channel strips, or aux channel strips, are destinations for busses in Logic. For those unfamiliar with auxes and busses, they are covered in Chapter 11. Briefly, a bus is used to transmit audio from one or more channel strips to another channel strip in Logic. An aux is the most common destination for a bus. One common use of an aux channel strip is to instantiate a reverb effect in the aux channel strip and to send audio from a variety of Audio or Software Instrument tracks through a bus to the aux, allowing them all to utilize the same reverb effect. If you are familiar with auxes and busses, or you think you can see the value of having a few auxes ready to be used in your template, then you may want to add a few to your template.

Creating Auxiliary Channel Strips

To create a new aux, open the Mixer either in the Arrange window by pressing X or clicking the Mixer button at the bottom of the Arrange area, by dragging the Mixer button to create a new Mixer window, or in a Mixer window by selecting Window > Mixer or by pressing Command+2. In the Mixer's local Options menu, select Options > Create New Auxiliary Channel Strips, click the + symbol on the left side of the Mixer window, or use the key command Option+Command+N. This will open the New Auxiliary Channel Strips dialog, shown in Figure 3.13.

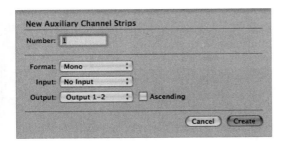

Figure 3.13   The New Auxiliary Channel Strips dialog.

The options in the New Auxiliary Channel Strips dialog are identical in function to the options of the same name in the New Audio Tracks dialog, discussed in the "Adding Audio Tracks" section earlier in this chapter.

The Wrong Mixer Window...   When we say *Mixer,* that's exactly what we mean: the separate window called Mixer, or the Mixer that's integrated in the Arrange window.

We do not mean the Mixer layer of the Environment, which does not have the $+$ button. If you think you opened the Mixer window but you don't see the button, make sure you didn't open the Environment Mixer! For more on this distinction, check out Chapter 11.

Adding Auxiliary Tracks to the Arrange Window

Now that you have created some aux channel strips, you can add auxiliary tracks to the Arrange window. Having auxiliary tracks in the Arrange can be valuable because it allows you to easily automate and edit the automations for a wide variety of aux channel strip parameters and insert effect parameters, as we'll explore in Chapter 10, "Using Automation in Logic."

In the Arrange window, create a new track for each aux you would like to have in the Arrange. It doesn't matter what type of tracks you create, because you will be reassigning them. To reassign a track to an aux, Control-click (or right-click) on the selected track header. This will open the pop-up menu shown in Figure 3.14.

Figure 3.14 Control-clicking (or right-clicking) on a track header opens this pop-up menu.

Select Reassign Track in the pop-up menu and navigate the path Reassign Track > Mixer > Aux, as shown in Figure 3.15.

Finally, select the aux channel strip you want to assign to the current track in the Aux submenu.

Setting Up Your Arrange Window

We've spent quite a few pages discussing basic setup of your template project, but no less important is setting up the Arrange window. For example, Figure 3.16 contains the Arrange window generated by the Instruments template from the Explore folder in the New dialog.

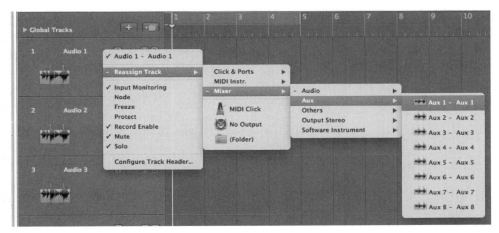

Figure 3.15   To reassign a track to an auxiliary track, navigate to the Reassign Track > Mixer > Aux submenu and select the aux you wish to assign to the track.

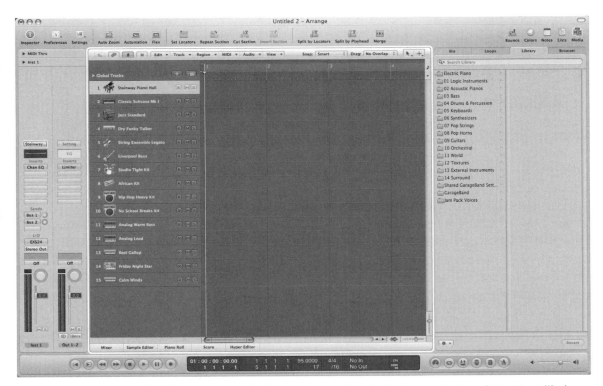

Figure 3.16   An example of an Arrange window generated by the Instruments template. Most likely, you will prefer a different configuration for your own personalized template.

Does this look like your ideal workspace? Or do you imagine yourself using a different combination of tracks? Perhaps with different instrument names? Do you want your track lanes to have more room? The Arrange windows in the provided templates are designed to offer users a sampling of available track types and configurations, in the hopes that some of what they need might be included in a particular template. For your template, you want your Arrange window to represent *your* personal working needs.

Expert Tip: Use Key Commands!   As you can already see, using key commands in Logic is a major timesaver. Creating tracks isn't fun, creative work—it's an administrative task that most people just want to finish as soon as they can. If you are creating 50 or more tracks of different types, that means you have to navigate to the menu option, then re-navigate to the menu option, then re-navigate to the menu option...if you're using menu commands. (Are you getting the idea?) However, if you use the key command, creating each new track is as rapid as tap, tap, tap. We'll continue to show you the menu options as well as the default key commands throughout this book, but you should commit some time to learning to use Logic via the key commands. Now is an excellent time to start!

Setting Up Tracks

Although many of the steps involved in creating your tracks are simplified and streamlined in Logic these days, there are still a few more things you may want to set up to finish configuring your template.

Naming Tracks

Now that you've created as many tracks as you think you'll need, you might want to think about giving them slightly more descriptive names than simply Audio 1, Audio 2, and so on. Of course, you probably don't know what your final track names will be, but perhaps you expect you will need 12 separate Audio tracks for your drums, for example. If so, you might name Audio 24–36 (or whichever tracks you choose) as Drums 1–12 instead of Audio 24–36. Did you only need eight MIDI tracks that you divide between two separate MIDI synths, such as a Roland and a Korg synth? Why not name the MIDI tracks Korg 1 to Korg 4 and Roland 1 to Roland 4 to be more descriptive? Remember, customizing your Arrange window to be your personal workspace is the name of the game!

The easiest way to name tracks is to double-click the instrument name in the Track Parameter box in the Inspector or to double-click the name in the track header. As soon as you do, a text box will appear with the current name of the track highlighted, as shown in Figure 3.17. Type any name you want, then press Return or click anywhere outside of the text box.

You can also use a menu command to name tracks: Track > Create Track Name. As you'll see in the "Defining Key Commands" section later in this chapter, you can define a key command for this function. If you change track names using the menu command, you are actually naming the

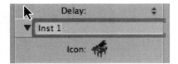

Figure 3.17   To rename a track in your Track List, double-click the track name next to the triangle in that track's Parameter box as shown, or double-click the track name in the track header. When the text box appears, type the new name.

track itself. By default, this distinction makes no difference; however, if you decide to display the second name of your tracks by selecting the check box in the Names section of the Track Configuration dialog, you can configure Logic to display not only the track name or the name created with the Create Track Name command, but a variety of different name types for either the first or second track name. To open the Track Configuration dialog, select View > Configure Track Header or Control-click on the track header and select Configure Track Header from the pop-up menu. Figure 3.18 shows the Names section of the Track Configuration dialog.

Figure 3.18   The Names section of the Track Configuration dialog. Selecting the check box displays the second names of your tracks.

Both pop-up menus in the Names section of the Track Configuration dialog offer the same options:

- **Auto Name.** This option names your tracks based on the following criteria, in order: user-entered names, channel strip settings or software instrument names, and in the absence of one of the previous options, the parent channel strip's name.

- **Track Name.** This option displays track names that you enter by double-clicking on the track names in the track header.

- **Channel Strip Setting Name.** This option displays the channel strip setting name for the parent channel strip of each track.

- **Software Instrument Setting Name.** This option displays the software instrument setting name for each Software Instrument track.

- **Channel Strip Name.** This option displays the channel strip name of each track's parent channel strip in the Mixer.

- **Channel Strip Type and Number.** This option displays the type and number of each track's parent channel strip. For example, if a track's parent channel strip is the third auxiliary channel strip, the track's name will be Aux 3.

The first menu is always active and is set to Auto Name by default. Selecting the Allow Two Lines check box enables a second track name line in the track header. The second line is only visible with Auto Name or Channel Strip Type and Number selected and without the second menu active. It allows you to name a track, but also see its actual track number. The second menu is only active when you select the check box to the left of the second menu. When you enable the second name, the track header expands, and a movable dividing line appears. The second name is displayed to the right of this dividing line.

Thus, you could have a track named Nord Electro on a track named Wurlitzer, for example, or a track named Ambient Guitar on a track named Audio 6. Figure 3.19 shows a track with this view enabled.

Figure 3.19   If you have chosen to display second names in the track header, you'll see the two names you have designated in the pop-up menus found in the Names section of the Track Configuration dialog.

The primary disadvantage to displaying both the instrument name and the track name is screen clutter. The second line option can help mitigate this, although this option is slightly less flexible. That said, you might find it advantageous to display second names, particularly on a larger monitor. For example, you could be using a software instrument, and you could configure the first name to display the channel strip name (which you could name EXS24, for example) and set the second name to display the software instrument setting name, telling you which preset you are using in that EXS24 instance.

A Rose by Any Other Name . . .   For ages, Logic has had fairly unintuitive track and channel strip naming practices. Naming a track didn't name its channel strip, naming a channel strip didn't name its track—it could be a confusing mess getting your Arrange window and your Mixer names unified. Logic Pro 9 has finally straightened this out—naming a track names its channel strip and vice versa. You can now easily name your tracks in the Arrange window using the track header, the Track Parameter box, or the selected track's Arrange channel strip; in the Mixer; or in the Environment Mixer layer. The name of a track is now unified across the entire application!

Coloring Tracks

As a final method of customizing your template tracks, you might want to think about coloring them. Certainly it won't affect your music or creativity in any way if you do or do not use a unique color for each track, but it does help to keep tracks separate and to visually group tracks that you want to keep together, such as tracks for the same MIDI instrument or for similar types of audio recordings. (For example, you might color all your drum tracks the same color.)

First, to see the colors you are choosing before each track lane has any regions on it, make sure Track Color Bars is selected in the Configure Track Header menu. You can access the Configure Track Header menu, which will be covered in full detail in Chapter 6, by Control-clicking in any track's track header. With Track Color Bars selected, you will then be presented with a small line at the right of each track name that shows you the color for that track. To change the color, display the Color palette by selecting View > Colors or (better yet) by pressing the key command Option+C. Logic then presents its Color palette, as shown in Figure 3.20. When you click on any of the palette's colors, you will see the line of color change to the selected color.

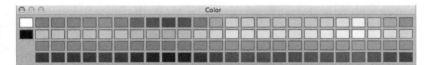

Figure 3.20   Logic's Color palette. Click on a color to choose it for the selected track in the Arrange window.

If you want a color that is not represented in Logic's Color palette, you can double-click any color to bring up the standard Mac OS X Pro Application color wheel. You can then adjust that color to taste and apply it to your track. Changing a color this way will also change the color of any region, object, and/or track already using that color.

Configuring the Initial Zoom and Automation Settings

You may want all of your track lanes to be wider or thinner than the default "skinny" tracks that Logic creates in the Arrange window. Basically, the skinnier the track lane, the more tracks will fit in the Track List, but the less detail you will see for each track. You may also want the horizontal zoom in the Arrange to be more zoomed in (for more precise detail) or more zoomed out (for an overview of an entire song). Many Logic users choose to set up an initial screenset with an Arrange window with wider track lanes and a tight horizontal zoom to focus on a specific group of tracks, and then another screenset with an Arrange window with very skinny track lanes horizontally zoomed out for viewing the whole song at once.

To accomplish this, you can use the zoom sliders at the bottom right of the Arrange area. These sliders are shown in Figure 3.21. The vertical slider controls vertical zoom. Dragging the slider down increases the track lane height, and dragging the slider up decreases the track lane height. The horizontal slider controls horizontal zoom. Dragging the slider left decreases how much horizontal space is shown between each bar/SMPTE location, and dragging the slider right increases how much horizontal space is shown between each bar/SMPTE location. You can also use the zoom key command, which is Control+Arrow. Press the appropriate arrow key, depending on whether you are increasing (up) or decreasing (down) the vertical zoom or increasing (right) or decreasing (left) the horizontal zoom.

Figure 3.21 The vertical and horizontal zoom sliders allow you to adjust vertical and horizontal zoom for the entire Arrange window track lane area.

The horizontal zoom setting can also be changed with the playhead. If you click and hold on the triangle at the top of the playhead, the cursor changes to a resize cursor, as shown in Figure 3.22. Simply drag your mouse vertically, and you can change the horizontal zoom of the Arrange.

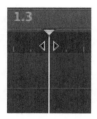

Figure 3.22 If you click and hold on the triangle at the top of the playhead, the cursor changes into a resize cursor, allowing you to change the horizontal zoom of the Arrange window by dragging your mouse vertically.

Logic also gives you a number of ways to vertically resize individual tracks without resizing the other tracks on the Arrange window. First of all, if you move the mouse to the bottom-left edge of a track, the cursor will turn into a finger, as shown in Figure 3.23. When the cursor is a finger, you can click and drag the mouse vertically to increase or decrease the height of that individual track. You can also select a track and use the key commands for Individual Track Zoom In (Control+ Option+Command+Up) and Individual Track Zoom Out (Control+Option+Command+ Down). Finally, you can activate the Auto Track Zoom feature in the View menu. Auto Track Zoom will increase the size of whichever track in the Arrange you have currently selected, leaving all unselected tracks at their normal height.

Figure 3.23 If you move the cursor to the bottom-left side of an Arrange track, the cursor will turn into a finger, indicating that you can adjust the height of the track by dragging up or down with your mouse.

Another function that increases the height of all your tracks is automation. We'll discuss automation a bit more in the next chapter and in depth in Chapter 10. For now, you just need to know that Logic has a very powerful automation system that allows you to set up mixing moves that will happen automatically, without you having to control them every time you play the song. When you turn on automation, all your track lanes will zoom out so that each track has enough room to display the automation information. If automation seems like something you'll definitely be using, you can turn automation on by selecting View > Track Automation or by pressing A. You will see every track instantly widen.

Setting Up Screensets

We've already discussed screensets, which are one of Logic's indispensible customization tools. Using screensets, you can set up each view in Logic to have its own unique set of editors and windows, and you can switch between the views conveniently by using the numeric keys. Press a numeric key or two to get a quick glimpse at what screensets can do for you. It's kind of like having multiple workflows or templates within your projects. Setting them up couldn't be simpler: You simply press a number key to go to a screenset, organize the various windows and editors as you like, and when you save your template project, all your screensets are automatically saved as well. No muss, no fuss! There are only a couple of special options for creating screensets that you might want to consider using, and they are discussed in this section.

First, if you open the Screenset menu, you'll notice a list of any current screensets and, below that, a menu of screenset options, as shown in Figure 3.24.

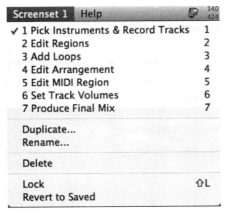

Figure 3.24   The Screenset menu displays a list of your screensets plus screenset options.

If you know that, even if you open and close windows while using Logic, you'll want the windows of a particular screenset to never change from Logic session to Logic session, you can choose to lock the screenset using the Lock menu command (or pressing Shift+L). If you want to create a new screenset using the current screenset as a base, you can select Duplicate. This opens the Duplicate Screenset dialog, where you can assign the duplicate screenset to the number of your choice, and you can name the screenset. Selecting the Rename option opens the Rename Screenset dialog, where you can rename your screenset. You can use the Delete command to delete the current screenset. Be advised that there is no warning dialog when using this command. The Revert to Saved command simply returns the current screenset to its original state, just like you used the key command for selecting that particular screenset.

Setting up your screensets in your template is really this easy! Trust us: Using screensets is one of the best ways to configure Logic to reflect how you want to work.

Defining Key Commands

Don't worry; you're not going to give every command in Logic a key command at this point, but as you work on your template, you should begin to get a feel for which commands you might like to access from the keyboard instead of the menus, so you can begin defining your own key commands. Logic makes this process simple with its extremely powerful and intuitive Key Commands window.

First, you need to access the Key Commands window by selecting Logic Pro > Preferences > Key Commands, selecting Key Commands from the Preferences menu in the Arrange Toolbar, or simply pressing Option+K. Figure 3.25 shows Logic's Key Commands window.

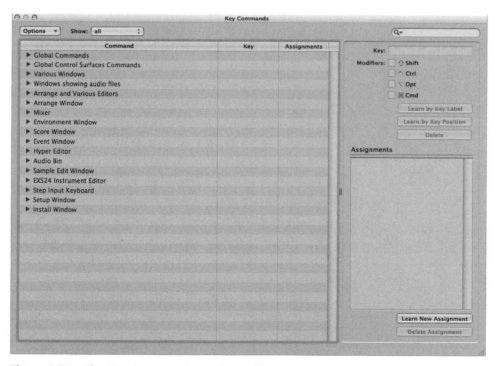

Figure 3.25   The Key Commands window offers many different methods to search for and assign key commands.

You will notice that the key commands are grouped into commands relating to specific windows and editors in the Command List. You can click open any of the disclosure triangles from any or all of the groups to see what key commands are available for that window or editor.

The easiest way to define a key command is simply to search for it, then have Logic learn the key you wish to be the key command. For example, suppose you want to assign a key command to the Duplicate Screenset command. Type the word **screenset** into the Search field of the Key Commands window, as shown in Figure 3.26. Logic will display a list of all key commands with the word *screenset* in their name. Select the Duplicate Screenset command from the list.

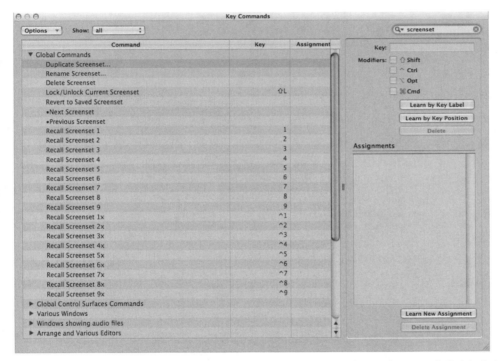

Figure 3.26   To search for key commands, type a search word into the Search field of the Key Commands window.

First, you need to select the command for which you wish to assign a key command. From here, assigning keys (and more) to a command couldn't be easier. There are three ways to assign keys to a command, depending on your preference.

■   **Learn by Key Label.** This learns key sequences based on the label of the key you press. In other words, if you press a key labeled 3, then 3 will be assigned to that command. In this example, press the Learn by Key Label button, then press Control+Shift+2. You will see the Key Assignment window and boxes reflect your choice, as you see in Figure 3.27. You can now press Control+Shift+2 (the 2 on either the keyboard or the numeric keypad) to duplicate a screenset. Your new key command is listed in the Key column of the Command List.

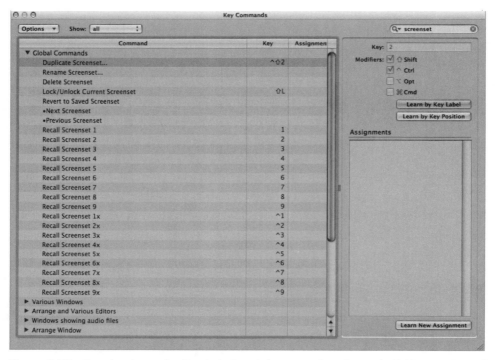

Figure 3.27   Pressing Learn by Key Label and then pressing Control+Shift+2 assigns the key sequence Control+Shift+2 to the Duplicate Screenset command.

- **Learn by Key Position.** This key command option allows you to assign a key command not based on the label on the key, but based on the position of the key on the keyboard. The advantage of this is that you can assign different key commands to the number 2 above the keyboard and the number 2 in the numeric keypad. It also means that if you switch between different languages, your key assignments will remain the same. Using the same example, if you press the Learn by Key Position button and Control+Shift+2, the Key Assignment window will reflect the location code (or scan code) of the key pressed (in this case, the number 2 above the keyboard, not the numeric keypad), and only those exact keys will be assigned to the command, as Figure 3.28 illustrates. Your new key command is listed in the Key column of the Command List.

- **Learn New Assignment.** If you want to assign a command to a control surface, press this button, then move or press the control on the control surface you wish to assign to this command. The Assignments window will reflect what you pressed, as in Figure 3.29.

That's it! You've just activated a new key command! As you become more familiar with Logic, you will use these methods not only to activate key commands that do not have defaults, but also

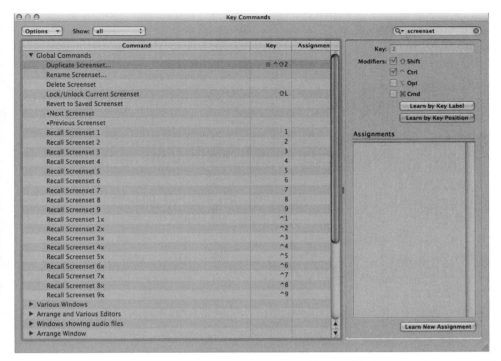

Figure 3.28   Using Learn by Key Position memorizes the specific keys you have pressed and assigns that sequence to your key command—in this case, Control+Shift+2 (above the keyboard, not on the numeric keypad).

to assign different key commands than the Logic default key sequences to better suit your own working methods.

Keyboard Covers and Cheat Sheets   If you are unfamiliar with Logic's key commands and want to get in the habit of using them, a great way to learn key commands is to make yourself a cheatsheet of your most used key commands and leave it right next to your keyboard. This can be an index card, a sheet of paper, or any other material that works for you.

Also, there are companies such as KB Covers (www.kbcovers.com) that sell silicon overlays for Mac keyboards that are printed with the default key commands for many different applications. Both authors of this book, in fact, have been consulted by KB Covers for the Logic covers, and we feel that they do a fine job of including the basic commands. Use cheatsheets or keyboard covers to help familiarize you with key commands until they become second nature to you!

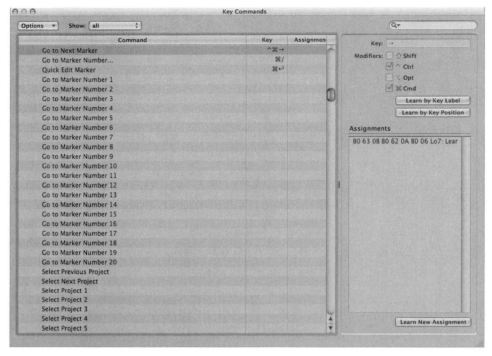

Figure 3.29   You can assign key commands to control surfaces as well as keyboards and MIDI devices by using the Learn New Assignment button.

Setting Up Your Hardware

There are many options today for hardware that can interface with a DAW, and having Logic configured to work with your hardware is essential to ensuring the kind of ease of use that keeps inspiration flowing when it hits. Before you finalize your initial setup of Logic, we need to look at configuring your audio interface, your MIDI gear, and any control surfaces you may be using.

Interfaces and Drivers

Sometimes, simply plugging your audio interface into your computer is enough to enable your computer to recognize the interface so that you can start using it. Other times, the audio interface comes with *drivers*—files that explain to your computer how to communicate with your interface. For example, with Mac OS X, audio and MIDI interfaces that use the support for standard USB or FireWire Class Compliant drivers that are built into Core Audio (explained in the next section) and Core MIDI do not require additional drivers, whereas all other audio and MIDI devices require installation of manufacturer-supplied drivers. If your hardware requires manufacturer-supplied drivers, you may need to make sure they work with Logic in 64-bit mode before you try working in 64-bit mode.

In general, most of the configuration of audio and MIDI devices is done inside Logic, so the driver installation is usually a very straightforward process of inserting the CD that came with your hardware or perhaps downloading drivers from the Internet, and then launching an installation application. Most device driver installations require you to restart your computer at the end of the process, as most operating systems scan for new drivers only when the system starts up.

Configuring Your Audio Device

To get the most out of your system, you will want to tell Logic exactly how you want to use your hardware. You can configure how Logic will interact with your audio interface in the Devices tab of the Audio Preferences window, which you can access at Logic Pro > Preferences > Audio, by selecting Audio in the Preferences menu in the Toolbar, or by pressing Option+= and then clicking on the Devices tab. The Devices tab of the Audio Preferences window is shown in Figure 3.30.

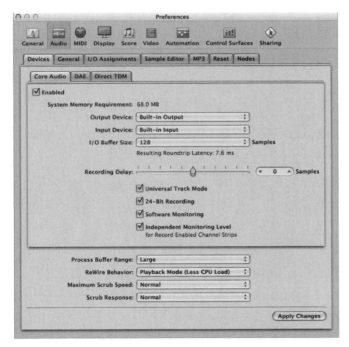

Figure 3.30   The Devices tab of the Audio Preferences window. Here you can configure how you want Logic to use your audio device.

The first thing you'll notice is a tab for each of the audio engines that Logic can use. In Figure 3.30, the Core Audio driver is selected, but you can also choose to use any of the other available drivers if you have compatible hardware. Unlike many other audio applications, Logic allows you to use multiple audio engines simultaneously. Here is a quick explanation of each audio engine in the Devices tab:

- **Core Audio.** This is the built-in audio engine of the Mac OS X operating system. Almost every new audio device comes with Core Audio drivers, and this is the audio engine that you will most likely keep checked. In fact, since the built-in audio jack of your Macintosh uses Core Audio (as you can see in Figure 3.30), even if you have one of the other audio engines checked, you can still run Core Audio alongside it. Core Audio is a *native* audio engine, which means that when you use Core Audio, all of your Audio tracks, effects, and so on will run from the central processing unit (CPU) of your computer, instead of running on external hardware. Core Audio gives you full access to all of Logic's effects and synthesizers and to all third-party native Audio Unit (AU) plug-ins.

- **DAE.** This is the Digidesign Audio Engine. Select this engine if you wish to use the DSP (*Digital Signal Processing*) engine of Digidesign HD hardware. You will not have access to native audio and effects (such as VST [*Virtual Studio Technology*] or AU) unless you are also running a native audio engine in addition to DAE. With ProTools 8.0.3 and all subsequent future releases, Avid will no longer support Logic as a DAE front end for an HD/TDM system.

- **Direct TDM.** If you want to use Avid Pro Tools|HD audio hardware with the native plug-ins instead of the HD DSP, Direct TDM allows you to do so.

When you click the tab for the Core Audio engine, you see a number of options. Some are self-explanatory; others are less so. We'll briefly go over all of the options here. Because the Process Buffer Range and Software Monitoring options are more complex and require detailed explanation, each will get its own section later in this chapter and in Chapter 5.

- **Output Device.** Use this menu to select the audio device to which Logic will output audio.

- **Input Device.** Use this menu to select the audio device from which Logic will receive audio.

- **I/O Buffer Size.** This is explained in detail in the "I/O Buffer Size" section later in this chapter.

- **Recording Delay.** If your audio interface properly discloses how long it takes for audio to travel from its inputs into the computer, Logic can compensate for this delay to make sure that everything you record appears on Logic's Arrange page exactly at the instant you recorded it. However, some devices do not report their delay, so Logic would have no way of knowing exactly how to compensate for this "record offset" caused by your hardware. The Recording Delay parameter allows you to manually adjust Logic's recording offset compensation, so that you can even compensate for devices that do not report their delay. If this sounds complicated, and/or if your tracks don't sound like they are out of time, you don't need to worry about this parameter. For most modern interfaces, you won't need to adjust this.

- **Universal Track Mode.** When this is turned on, all stereo tracks take up a single Mixer channel. Without Universal Track Mode selected, a stereo track takes up two Mixer channels (one for the right channel and one for the left channel). With Universal Track Mode off, you have some extra routing options (such as routing one side of a stereo track to a different destination than the other side), but you will not be able to save a stereo track into a single file. Most users will want to keep Universal Track Mode active just for the simpler option of having a single Mixer strip for stereo objects and saving them as a single file.

Universal Track Mode and the DAE Audio Engine   The DAE engine cannot use Universal Track Mode, so this option does not appear at all in the DAE parameters.

- **24-Bit Recording.** If you want to record into 24-bit audio files, keep this option checked. Using 24-bit files takes up more processing power and hard disk space, so some users prefer to record at 16-bit to conserve their CPU and hard disk. In addition, some older or inexpensive audio interfaces do not have 24-bit recording capability. These days, almost every device is capable of 24-bit recording. As Chapter 1's sections about digital audio explained, it is advantageous to use the highest bit rate you can, so you should keep this option selected if your system is capable.

- **Software Monitoring.** This button selects or deselects software monitoring. Software monitoring is explained in detail in Chapter 5, "Transport Controls and Recording."

- **Independent Monitoring Level for Record Enabled Channel Strips.** Engaging this option allows you to set a separate record monitoring level for a record-enabled track. You can record enable a track, then set the level fader for that track to the level you wish to monitor at while recording. When you disengage the Record button for that track, the level fader will return to its previous setting. *This does not affect the input level of your source!* Therefore, you must still take care to set your input levels properly on your audio interface to avoid overloading your converters.

- **Process Buffer Range.** Process buffer range is explained in detail in the "Process Buffer Range" section later in this chapter.

- **ReWire Behavior.** ReWire is a technology developed by Propellerhead Software (the Swedish audio software company famous for ReCycle, ReBirth, and Reason) to allow separate standalone audio applications to inter-operate. Setting up Logic as a ReWire host is addressed in detail in the "Using ReWire 2 Instruments" section of Chapter 9. This Preference determines whether Logic utilizes ReWire in Playback mode, which takes up less CPU processing, or in Live mode, which allows you to send MIDI from Logic to your ReWire applications with lower latency, at the expense of a high CPU load.

- **Maximum Scrub Speed.** *Scrubbing* refers to moving the playhead over an audio file with the mouse while Logic is paused to play it back, as opposed to simply pressing Play. You can also scrub if you click and drag on a region with the Scissors tool. This option is particularly useful if you are doing some very fine editing and are listening for a very specific point in the song. The Maximum Scrub Speed option determines the maximum possible playback speed when you scrub: Normal or Double Speed. When you select Normal, even if you scrub your mouse as quickly as you can across a section of audio, you'll never hear it faster than real time. If you select Double, you will hear the section play back at double the normal speed. You might want to change the scrub speed if you want to be able to quickly scrub through your song.

- **Scrub Response.** This Preference determines how quickly the Scrub function will react to changes in your mouse speed. Your options are Slow, Normal, Fast, and Faster. The faster the response, the more the playback reflects your actual speeding up and slowing down, but the more jerky the sound will be unless you keep your speed extremely steady.

Adjusting the Audio Hardware Buffers

One of the most important reasons for opening the Devices tab of the Audio Preferences window is to adjust the various input and output buffers. Adjusting buffers is how you fine-tune Logic's performance to get the most out of your system. To do this properly, it is important to know what each of the buffers does, so you can tailor the settings to meet your requirements exactly.

The fundamental concept is that it takes a set amount of time for the CPU to do a given amount of work. Because timing is so integral to making music, having control over the exact amount of time it takes the CPU to complete a given task is crucial. Logic allows users to have independent control over two separate but related audio buffers—the input/output (I/O) buffer and the process buffer—and gives you the option of engaging an I/O safety buffer.

I/O Buffer Size.   When you record audio into Logic, it naturally takes a certain amount of time before you hear it played back through the audio interface's outputs. First, the audio has to travel from your audio interface into the audio driver of your audio interface. The driver then passes the signal information to Logic. After Logic records the audio onto your hard drive, Logic then returns the audio to your audio driver for output, and finally the driver sends the audio to your interface. This is shown in Figure 3.31.

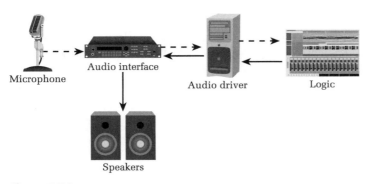

Figure 3.31

As this diagram shows, the audio driver is in charge of regulating the input and output of audio to and from the application. To do this effectively and in perfect synchronization, the audio driver passes to Logic a chunk of audio that consists of a variable number of samples, and Logic then sends to the driver chunks of audio with that same number of samples. The amount of time that elapses in this process is called *latency*.

If the number of samples in each chunk of audio is very small, the latency will be very low. The drawback is that the audio driver has to work very quickly to keep those small chunks of audio moving. This requires more CPU power and, if the audio drivers are not well written, can cause audible crackles and pops as the audio driver struggles to keep up with the demands placed on it. If the number of samples in each chunk is very large, the driver does not need to work nearly as hard, resulting in a far lower CPU drain and better performance from audio drivers. However, large buffers result in a higher latency.

Figure 3.32 shows the I/O Buffer Size pop-up menu.

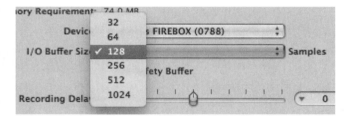

Figure 3.32   You can select any of these different buffer sizes in the I/O Buffer Size pop-up menu.

There are a number of situations in which you need your latency to be as low as possible:

- To get the most out of software monitoring (see the "Recording, Software Monitoring, and Latency" section in Chapter 5)

- To play virtual instruments in real time

- To use external hardware alongside playback from Logic

In these cases you should set your buffer as low as your system can handle without glitches (audible pops and crackles during playback), which usually ranges between 64 and 256 samples. Otherwise, you can set your buffer to a high setting, because higher settings usually offer the best CPU performance—try 512 and 1,024 samples. As a rule, you should start with as low a setting as you can, and if you notice audio glitches or sluggish computer performance due to the CPU strain, slowly raise the I/O buffer until you reach the lowest comfortable setting. After you change the buffer size, you must then click on Apply Changes. Logic Pro will then reload any software instrument's data that exists in the project, which can take a little while in a full project.

Process Buffer Range.   As described in the explanation of the audio engines, when you use a native audio engine, your computer's CPU handles all the audio processing. Just as the audio drivers handle audio in chunks to increase efficiency, the CPU also handles audio processing in chunks. The size of these chunks is set with the Process Buffer Range pull-down menu. The process buffer size may be small, medium, or large. The smaller the buffer, the faster audio is processed, but the more CPU is required, leaving less total CPU power available for other processing. The larger the buffer, the slower the CPU processes audio, which leaves more power available for everything else (such as playing tracks, doing screen redraws, and so on).

If your process buffer is too small for your system, your system will quickly run out of power, presenting you with cryptic messages informing you "Error: Core Audio too slow," and the like. Regardless of the exact text, the reason is the same: Logic can't keep up with everything you're asking it to do. If your buffer is too large, you may find that some operations that rely on fast response—such as external storage devices, recording, or real-time processing—will become out of sync because each chunk is too large to keep up with the rest of the song. You have to adjust this setting to find the ideal buffer size for your particular system, but in general you should keep the process buffer as small as possible. Most modern computers should be able to handle a process buffer of Small or Medium without a problem. As with the I/O buffer, start with a setting of Small, and then increase it as necessary to find the ideal setting.

Setting Up Your MIDI Hardware

Because most MIDI devices don't have many configurable options, setting them up is far more straightforward than with audio devices. When connecting your MIDI hardware to your MIDI interface, however, you need to be conscious of MIDI ports.

Selecting MIDI Ports

The most basic MIDI interfaces have a single MIDI IN and a single MIDI OUT jack. However, most MIDI interfaces will have multiple jacks (usually two to eight of each). Each pair of IN and OUT jacks is referred to as a *MIDI port*. You'll need to keep track of which device you have plugged into which port because although Logic can detect that something is connected to any MIDI port, it's up to you to tell Logic what that device is and what it can do. This becomes especially important when you add devices or change the port to which they are connected. You can run into problems such as devices not being detected or, if you select the wrong MIDI port, MIDI data being sent to the wrong devices.

Every External MIDI track in Logic has a Parameter box; the second parameter (right under the Icon check box) is the Port setting. Figure 3.33 shows an External MIDI track in the Arrange with its port set to Port 2.

If you change the MIDI ports to which your MIDI devices are connected, make sure that the Port settings of your External MIDI tracks are still accurate. While audio settings are global for all Logic songs, MIDI settings are project-specific and may need to be updated. Ideally, you want to keep your MIDI equipment configured the same way all the time to increase the effectiveness of

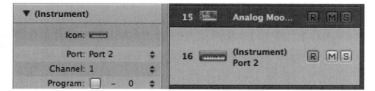

Figure 3.33   By looking at the Port setting in the Parameter box of this MIDI object, you can quickly determine that the device is connected to Port 2 of the MIDI interface.

your template. If you remove devices that are being sent MIDI data from Logic, or perhaps you get a new piece of MIDI equipment, be sure to set the MIDI port on those External MIDI tracks to the new device to which you'd like the signals sent. Keeping Logic and your template properly up to date with what MIDI device is connected to which MIDI port is an essential part of setting up and maintaining your system.

Logic Pro and Surround

Surround material is pervasive in modern music and video, from 5.1 DVD-Audio releases to 7.1 SDDS movie releases. Logic Pro offers full surround support, including recording, bouncing, mixing, and processing in a wide variety of surround formats. Although topics such as surround mixing and bouncing will be covered in Chapter 11, knowing what the supported surround formats are and how you can configure your audio interface for surround input is necessary if you are considering using surround in Logic.

Supported Surround Formats

Logic offers the following surround format options:

- **Quadraphonic.** Quadraphonic, or Quad, is a fairly old format whose height of popularity was in the 1970s. The format uses four channels: one right, one left, one right rear, and one left rear.

- **LCRS (Pro Logic).** LCRS is the original Dolby Pro Logic Surround format, which is another four-channel format consisting of left, center, right, and surround (rear) channels.

- **5.1 (ITU 775).** This is the surround format most commonly in use today. This is the format that 5.1 DVD-Audio uses, and it is typical in home theater systems. This format uses a total of six channels: left, center, right, left rear, right rear, and the LFE (*Low Frequency Effect*) channel.

- **6.1 (ES/EX).** This setting is used for the DTS ES or Dolby Digital EX format. This is a seven-channel format utilizing left, center, right, left rear, surround, right rear, and LFE channels.

- **7.1 (3/4.1).** This is a common cinema format similar to 5.1, but adding two more surround channels, a left side channel, and a right side channel.

■ **7.1 (SDDS).** SDDS is a Sony format used in movie theaters. It consists of eight channels: left, left center, center, right center, right, left rear, right rear, and LFE.

Setting the Project Surround Format

To set the surround format for your project, you need to open the Audio tab of the Project Settings window by choosing File > Project Settings > Audio, selecting Audio from the Settings menu in the Toolbar, or pressing Option+P. Figure 3.34 shows the Audio tab of the Project Settings window.

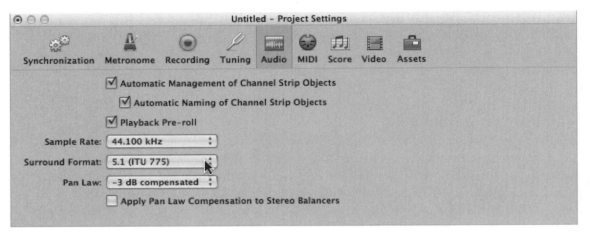

Figure 3.34   The Audio tab of the Project Settings window. You can assign a surround format to your project with the Surround Format pop-up menu.

To assign a surround format to your project, simply select your desired format in the Surround Format pop-up menu.

Configuring Surround Inputs

To set the surround input format, open the Input tab of the I/O Assignments tab of the Audio Preferences window (see Figure 3.35).

Use the Show As pop-up menu to set the desired surround format. Selecting a surround format automatically configures the various pop-up menus in the Input Assignment section to the default input settings for the chosen format. In Figure 3.35, the surround format is 5.1 (ITU 775), and the Input Assignment menus reflect the default settings. You can reassign any channel to any available input.

Setting Up Your Control Surface

If you have a software controller, you are in for a special treat. A control surface can actually be any MIDI device capable of sending and receiving MIDI in order to control functions within Logic. The most common control surfaces, however, resemble hardware mixers, except instead

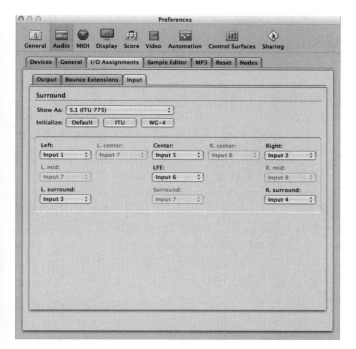

Figure 3.35   The Input tab of the I/O Assignments tab of the Audio Preferences window.
You can configure your audio interface for surround input in this tab.

of controlling audio, they control your Logic software. A full explanation of how to use your control surface is beyond the scope of this book; this section will just focus on how to set up your control surface to work with Logic.

Setting Up a Supported Control Surface

Logic already has complete built-in support for a number of popular control surfaces. As of this writing, Logic Pro 9 ships with built-in support for the following devices:

- **CM Labs.** Motor Mix.

- **Euphonix.** MC Pro, System 5-MC, MC Control, MC Mix, MC Transport. EuCon devices such as these are not currently supported when Logic is in 64-bit mode.

- **Frontier Design.** TranzPort, AlphaTrack.

- **JL Cooper.** CS-32 MiniDesk, FaderMaster 4/100, MCS3.

- **Korg.** microKONTROL, KONTROL49.

- **M-Audio.** iControl, Project I/O.

- **Mackie Designs.** Baby HUI, HUI, Logic Control (Mackie Control), Logic Control XT (Mackie Control XT), Mackie Control C4.

- **Radikal Technologies.** SAC-2k.

- **Roland.** SI-24.

- **Tascam.** FW-1884, US-224, US-428, US-2400.

- **Yamaha.** 01V96, 02R96, DM1000, DM2000.

Apple is always adding support for new control surfaces, so if you have a control surface that is not listed above, keep checking with Apple to see whether support for it has been added.

Depending on your control surface, you may need a MIDI interface to connect it. (See your owner's manual for your control surface for instructions on proper hookup.) Logic will automatically detect most control surfaces. When Logic first opens, you will be presented with the Control Surface Setup window, as shown in Figure 3.36. This indicates that Logic was able to sense immediately that you had a control surface plugged in, and that all is well.

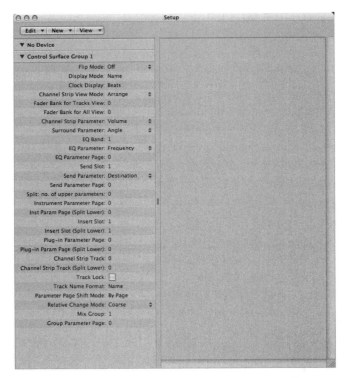

Figure 3.36   The Control Surface Setup window. If Logic automatically opened to this window, you're home free. Otherwise, you may need to connect to your control surface manually.

If this window does not detect your control surface immediately, don't worry, as all is not lost. In the Setup window, select New > Scan All Models, and Logic will rescan your MIDI interface to find any connected control surfaces. If your control surface does not support automatic scanning, then you need to add it manually by selecting New > Install in the Setup window, choosing your control surface from the list, and clicking Add. If your control surface is found but does not seem to be responding, then from the global Logic Pro menu, select Logic Pro > Preferences > Control Surfaces > Rebuild Defaults. That should do the trick. If this works, it means that Logic always knew where your control surface was among your devices, but it was simply not connecting. If that doesn't work, you'll need to start looking for loose cables and hardware connections, then try again. If nothing works, don't be afraid to call tech support and ask them to walk you through the connection process.

Once Logic senses your control surface, you're ready to go. Close the window and bask in the joy of your control surface!

Setting Up Any MIDI Device as a Control Surface

As mentioned earlier, if your control surface is not supported, you can still configure Logic to use it to control the application. If you want to use an unsupported control surface, you will need to set up what each knob, fader, and button on your controller does. The basic procedure is to first click on an onscreen control or menu option. After you have done this, immediately select Logic Pro > Preferences > Control Surfaces > Learn Assignment For. You will immediately notice the word following "for" will be the control or command that you just selected. Figure 3.37 illustrates how this should work.

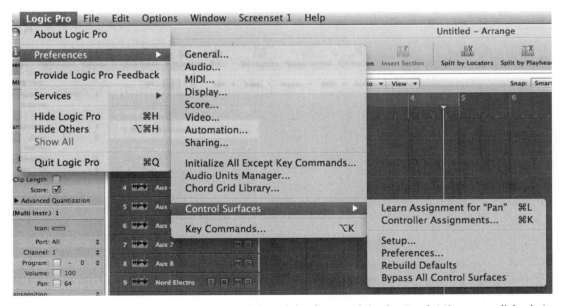

Figure 3.37   In this example, the volume slider of the first track in the Track Mixer was clicked. As you can see, the Learn Assignment parameter now says Learn Assignment for "Pan," reflecting that any controller assignment you make will be mapped to the panorama of that track.

After you select the Learn Assignment command or press Command+L, you will be presented with the Controller Assignments window shown Figure 3.38. At this point, simply press the Learn Mode button and twist, press, slide, or otherwise manipulate a control on your MIDI controller, and it will be automatically assigned to the chosen control or command in Logic. You can use this to assign each button, knob, and fader on your MIDI controller to control a function in Logic.

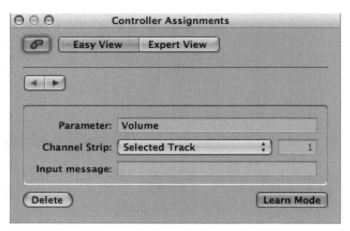

Figure 3.38 Once you have activated Learn Assignment, you will be presented with the Controller Assignments window. Press Learn Mode and move a control on your MIDI device, and it will be assigned to that control or command.

As you can see, this is an amazingly powerful feature in Logic, allowing virtually every aspect of the application to be remotely controlled! As you can also see, going into every detail of this extremely powerful feature would take a whole chapter by itself, and it's beyond the scope of this book. This description should be enough to get you started with a basic setup, and when you want to get into more complex and esoteric assignments, the Logic Pro 8 Control Surfaces Support manual offers a complete description of the Controller Assignments feature.

Saving Your Template

When you are ready to save your template project, you'll want to select File > Save As Template. You will be presented with the Save As dialog box, already opened to the Project Templates folder in the user directory. Click Save, and your template is ready for you to use as a starting point any time you need it!

Expert Tip: Protecting Your Template Being that your template is so important and painstakingly constructed, you most likely will want to save it from being accidentally modified. Luckily, the Mac OS offers two easy methods to protect a file. For either, you'll need to select your template in the Mac OS Finder and choose File > Get Info (or press

Command+I). When the Get Info box appears, you'll notice two check boxes. If you check the Stationary Pad box, Logic will open a copy of your template and name it Untitled instead of your actual template file; this way, accidentally hitting Return creates a new file and doesn't overwrite your previous template. You may also want to check the second box in the Get Info window, labeled Locked. With this checked, you simply cannot make any changes to the template file without unlocking the file in the Finder first. Either method will protect your template from any accidental changes.

A Note on Logic's Use of Mac OS X Directories   You may have already noticed that the Logic Pro 9 file in your Applications directory does not have a folder around it, as some other programs you may own do. This is because Logic Pro follows Apple's guidelines for where the support files for applications should go. Logic Pro files are in one of two places:

Factory presets and support files are in the local directory (meaning, at the level of your hard drive):

/Library/Application Support/Logic

User presets and support files are in your user directory, with "~" being the UNIX symbol for the Home directory for a given user:

~/Library/Application Support/Logic

So as you see, there's really only a single folder you'll be adding information to, and that's the user folder. It's also very convenient to back up just this one folder and know that all your presets, templates, sampler instruments, and so on have been backed up.

You should now understand the basics of what Logic is and what Logic can do, and you should also have completed the basic configuration of your template project. From this point forward, the focus shifts from explaining to exploring, and as such, you will encounter many details very quickly. Don't feel intimidated if you need to slow down or reread a section a few times before you are comfortable with the information. Logic is a very deep program, and it takes time to absorb. In the next chapter, you will start exploring some of the global functions, options, menus, and tracks Logic has to offer.

4 Global Elements of Logic

M ost of Logic's commands and options only make sense within the specific window where the command or feature is used. For example, having a function to select notes wouldn't make sense in the Mixer, and having a way to adjust the stereo field of an audio track doesn't matter in the Score Editor. That's why most commands and tools in Logic reside in *local* menus—menus specific to the window you are using. This allows Logic to put many more commands at your fingertips than if it were limited to the few menus in the OS X menu bar.

There are some functions that apply to more than one window, affect the entire song, or affect the whole application. These elements of Logic can be considered *global*. Before covering the more specific elements of Logic Pro 9, we'll use this chapter to give you one more broad view of the kinds of options and features available to you in Logic.

What Do You Know? Believe it or not, trying to decide where to put this chapter in the book was actually one of our tougher decisions. For intermediate and advanced music software users, it's not a problem—you're familiar with the concepts of global menus, local menus, using tools from a Tool menu, and so on. Intermediate and advanced Logic users may already understand what most of the features, functions, and concepts are all about. For a beginner, on the other hand, reading about these menus and later learning how to create and manipulate data in global tracks might seem overwhelming.

In the end, we decided that because the global menus and global tracks play a part in almost every section after this one, we really had no choice but to cover them here. If you feel that you need more details about some of these features, we list the sections that cover the issues more in depth so you can find answers to any questions you might be left with. Hopefully, for those of you who are a bit perplexed, after you've read a little further, you can come back to this chapter and everything will be clearer.

The Global Menus

You've already looked at and used commands from both global and local menus. The following chapters will explore all of the local menus throughout the various editors, windows, and tabs in Logic in depth. Detailed information on many functions of the global menus will be offered later on in the appropriate chapters, but this chapter offers a brief description of each global menu and its contents. When menu commands have default key commands, these will also be listed with the menu command.

The Logic Pro Menu

The Logic Pro menu, shown in Figure 4.1, contains commands and options that affect the entire application.

Figure 4.1   The Logic Pro menu.

It contains the following commands and submenus:

- **About Logic Pro.** Obsessed with trying to figure out whose name is on the platinum album on the Logic Pro 9 splash screen? You can get another look at the splash screen by selecting this command. To close the splash screen, simply click anywhere inside it.

- **Preferences.** The Preferences submenu, detailed in the following section, offers shortcuts to the main tabs in the Preferences window. The Preferences themselves are described in the following chapters, where appropriate.

- **Provide Logic Pro Feedback.** Selecting this command will open your Internet browser and take you to a page on the Apple website where you can submit feedback to Apple about Logic Pro. We can't stress how important it is for you to use this feature to submit new ideas and report any bugs you may encounter.

  There are bugs in nearly every program that won't crash the program but may affect your workflow. Since they don't show up in crash logs, the only way a developer can fix these bugs is from user feedback, detailing what the bug is and how to reproduce it. Believe us when we say that developers appreciate this kind of user feedback. No one tries to write bugs into their software, and Apple does listen to your feedback, be it about wish-list features or any bugs. Many of the new features you will learn about in this book are a direct result of user feedback.

- **Services.** This is a standard Mac OS X submenu included by the system in every Mac OS X application. This submenu is of no use in Logic.

- **Hide Logic Pro.** This command will remove all the Logic Pro windows from your screen until you select the application in the Finder or the Dock. The key command for this is Command+H.

- **Hide Others.** You can hide every application except Logic Pro with this command. The key command for this is Option+Command+H.

- **Show All.** You can reveal all applications, including those that are hidden, with this command.

- **Quit Logic Pro.** Use this command to quit Logic Pro. The key command for this is Command+Q.

The Preferences Submenu

The Preferences submenu, shown in Figure 4.2, gives you access to the individual tabs of the Preferences window and other global Preference-related elements of Logic Pro. Preferences govern the application as a whole, and therefore apply to any project open within the application.

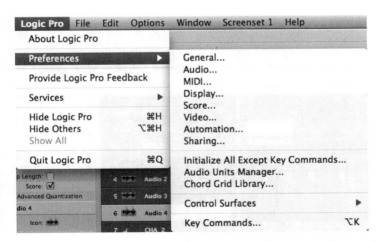

Figure 4.2   The Preferences submenu. Selecting any of these options will open the Preferences window to that particular Preferences tab.

The commands in the Preferences submenu are:

- **General, Audio, MIDI, Display, Score, Video, Automation, and Sharing.** Each of these will open the Preferences window to the specific Preferences tab you have selected. Each

Preferences tab has a number of sub-tabs to which you'll have to navigate from there. The different Preferences tabs will be explained in the chapter appropriate for each particular set of Preferences.

- **Initialize All Except Key Commands.** You can reset every Preference except your key commands by selecting this command.

- **Audio Units Manager.** You can launch the Audio Units Manager with this command. The Audio Units Manager allows you to turn on and off individual Audio Unit plug-ins within Logic. Chapter 11, "Mixing in Logic," details the functions of the Audio Units Manager.

- **Chord Grid Library.** Selecting Chord Grid Library opens the Chord Grid Library, where you will find a library of more than 4,000 different guitar chords displayed in tablature for use in the Score Editor. You can also use the Chord Grid Library to create your own guitar chord tablature for use in the Score Editor. The Chord Grid Library will be covered in detail in Chapter 8, "Working with MIDI."

- **Control Surfaces.** This submenu, explained in the following section, contains options for configuring and using MIDI control surfaces with Logic.

- **Key Commands.** This command opens the Key Commands window. Using the Key Commands window was described in Chapter 3. The key command for this is Option+K.

The Control Surfaces Submenu. The Control Surfaces submenu, shown in Figure 4.3, offers commands relating to the use and configuration of MIDI devices to be used as control surfaces for Logic.

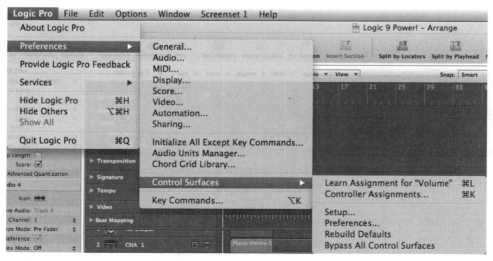

Figure 4.3 The Control Surfaces submenu of the Preferences submenu.

The commands in this submenu include the following:

- **Learn Assignment.** This command launches the Controller Assignments window for the selected option or command. This was discussed in Chapter 3. The key command for this is Command+L.

- **Controller Assignments.** You can launch the Controller Assignments window without previously selecting an option or command directly here. The Controller Assignments window was discussed in Chapter 3. The key command for this is Command+K.

- **Setup.** This launches the Control Surface Setup window. This window was discussed in Chapter 3.

- **Preferences.** You can set a number of Preferences for control surfaces here.

- **Rebuild Defaults.** This will reset the Preferences for your control surface.

- **Bypass All Control Surfaces.** When selected, this option disables your control surface.

The File Menu

Not surprisingly, the File menu, as shown in Figure 4.4, contains options and commands that involve files. Most commands here will get files either into or out of Logic. If not otherwise noted, most of these commands will be explored in more detail in Chapter 12, "Working with Files and Networks."

Figure 4.4   The File menu.

The following list describes the entries in the File menu:

- **New.** This command opens the Templates window, which was covered in Chapter 3. The key command for this is Command+N.

- **Open.** The Open command opens a song or project created by Logic (any version or platform of Logic from Logic 5 to Logic 9). It can also open all the file types Logic supports—GarageBand, Notator SL, MIDI, OMF, AAF, OpenTL, and XML (Final Cut Pro). The key command for this is Command+O.

- **Open Recent.** The Open Recent submenu contains a list of your recently opened projects. If the list gets too long, you can use the Clear Menu option in the Open Recent submenu to clear the Open Recent list.

- **Close.** This command will close the uppermost open window. If only one window is open, it will prompt a Save dialog, allowing you to close the current project. It will not close a floating window, but you can use it to close a plug-in window if the plug-in window has been selected. The key command for this is Command+W.

- **Close Project.** This command closes the current project. The key command for this is Option+Command+W.

- **Save.** This will save the current project. The key command for this is Command+S.

- **Save As.** This command brings up a Save dialog box for you to name and save your project. The key command for this is Shift+Command+S.

- **Save a Copy As.** This command brings up a Save dialog box for you to save a copy of your project.

- **Save as Template.** This command saves the current project as a template.

- **Revert to Saved.** If you aren't happy with the current state of your project, Revert to Saved will reload the last saved version of your project. Obviously, this only works if you'd previously saved your project!

- **Project.** The Project submenu, described below, offers you a few options for managing Logic projects:

    - **Clean Up.** You can use this command to find and display unused project files, allowing you to selectively delete them.

    - **Consolidate.** You can take a Logic song that does not have its dependent files in the proper project folder structure and consolidate it into the correct structure with this command.

    - **Rename.** This allows you to rename a project.

- **Project Settings.** The Project Settings submenu, described in the following section, allows you to open the Project Settings window to a specific settings tab. Project settings are specific to the particular project in which you are working. If you have a preferred, standard set of project settings, save them as a part of your template. You can then alter them on a per-project basis as needed.

- **Page Setup.** This command opens the Page Setup window of your printer driver.

- **Print.** This prints the contents of the selected window. This is useful if you want to print musical notation from the Score Editor, for example. The key command for this is Command+P.

- **Open Movie.** The Open Movie command opens a file browser in which you can search for a movie to open and score in your Logic project. While the Video track is discussed briefly at the end of this chapter, you'll find much more information on using video in Logic in Chapter 16, "Working with Video."

- **Remove Movie.** The Remove Movie command removes an opened movie from your Logic project.

- **Import Audio from Movie.** The Import Audio from Movie command lets you import the Audio track from a movie file that has been opened in your Logic project.

- **Export Audio to Movie.** The Export Audio to Movie command allows you to export the audio from the area in your Logic project that is concurrent to the opened movie file to the movie, replacing the original audio.

- **Import.** The Import command brings up the Open File window. It allows you to import any of the file types mentioned earlier that Logic supports, except Notator SL. The key command for this is Command+I.

- **Import Audio File.** Using this command allows you to find, audition, and import all Logic-supported audio file types—WAV, Broadcast Wave, AIFF, SDII, CAF, MP3, AAC, Apple Lossless, Apple Loops, and ReCycle—to the Audio Bin. The key command for this is Shift+Command+I.

- **Export.** In the Export submenu, you can export your Logic project into any of the afore-mentioned formats that Logic supports except GarageBand and Notator SL. You can also export a single region, track, or all of your tracks into individual files. The various Export options are discussed in Chapter 7, "Working with Audio and Apple Loops," and Chapter 12, "Working with Files and Networks."

- **Bounce.** This command allows you to create a stereo mixdown of all the tracks in your song. The Bounce command is discussed in Chapter 11. The File menu Bounce command can only bounce the audio routed to Output 1–2.

The Project Settings Submenu

When you set Logic's Preferences, those settings apply to the entire application, regardless of the project. The Project Settings submenu is shown in Figure 4.5.

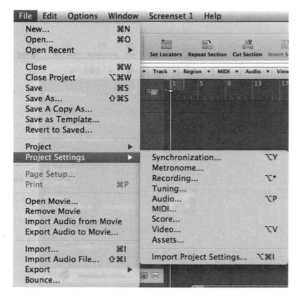

Figure 4.5   The Project Settings submenu.

The Project Settings submenu contains the following items:

- **Synchronization.** You can open the Project Settings Synchronization tab here. These settings are described in Chapter 15, "Synchronizing Hardware with Logic Pro." The key command for this is Option+Y.

- **Metronome.** You can open the Project Settings Metronome tab here. These settings are described in Chapter 5, "Transport Controls and Recording."

- **Recording.** You can open the Project Settings Recording tab here. These settings are described in Chapter 5. The key command for this is Option+*.

- **Tuning.** You can open the Project Settings Tuning tab here.

- **Audio.** You can open the Project Settings Audio tab here. These settings are described in Chapter 6, "The Arrange Window." The key command for this is Option+P.

- **MIDI.** You can open the Project Settings MIDI tab here. These settings are described in Chapter 6.

- **Score.** You can open the Project Settings Score tab here. These settings are described in Chapter 8.

- **Video.** You can open the Project Settings Video tab here. These settings are described in Chapter 16. The key command for this is Option+V.

- **Assets.** You can open the Project Settings Assets tab here. These settings are described in Chapter 12.

- **Import Project Settings.** This command allows you to import the project settings of another Logic project. Selecting this command brings up a File dialog for you to choose the project from which you want to import settings. You may choose to import any or all of the following: Screensets, Transform Sets, Hyper Edit Sets, Score Instrument Sets, Score Styles, and/or Score Settings. The key command for this is Option+Command+I.

The Edit Menu

The Edit menu, shown in Figure 4.6, includes a standard set of global editing, moving, selection, and undo commands.

Figure 4.6 The Edit menu.

The commands in the Edit menu are explained below:

- **Undo.** If you are not happy with your most recent action, Undo will revert Logic to the condition before that action. Not all actions can be undone. If you try to undo an action that cannot be undone, the command will be grayed out and will read "Can't Undo." The key command for this is Command+Z.

- **Redo.** If you have undone an action and you want to bring it back, you can use the Redo command. Not all actions can be redone. If you try to redo an action that cannot be redone, the command will be grayed out and will read "Can't Redo." The key command for this is Shift+Command+Z.

- **Undo History.** Logic has multiple levels of undo. This means that each action gets stored in the Undo History window, and you can decide at any time to go back and undo as many actions as you'd like. The Undo History window is explored in more detail in Chapter 6. The key command for this is Option+Z.

- **Delete Undo History.** Use this command to empty the Undo History window and start over with a brand-new list of actions, starting from the action after selecting Delete Undo History.

- **Cut.** This command removes the selected data from its current location and adds it to the Clipboard. The key command for this is Command+X.

- **Copy.** This command adds the currently selected data to the Clipboard without removing it from its current location. The key command for this is Command+C.

- **Paste.** This command adds the data in the Clipboard to the current pointer location. Note that this only works for compatible data. For example, if an audio file is in the Clipboard, you can't paste it into the Score Editor, only into the Audio window, Sample Editor, or Arrange window, as these windows can contain audio data. The key command for this is Command+V.

- **Delete.** This command will delete the selected data without adding it to the Clipboard.

- **Select All.** This command will select all of the data in the current window. The key command for this is Command+A.

Note that there may be more commands available in the main Edit menu, but that they are dependent on the currently selected window.

The Options Menu

The Options menu, as shown in Figure 4.7, is a catchall menu for commands and options that impact the project as a whole, more than one window, global tracks, and so on. Most of these submenus are described later in the book, where appropriate.

Figure 4.7   The Options menu.

The following list describes the entries in the Options menu:

- **Audio.** This submenu, which offers you a variety of audio-related tools, is detailed in the following section.

- **Marker.** This submenu includes options relating to song markers. Markers, including the options in this submenu, are explained in "The Marker Track" section later in this chapter.

- **Tempo.** This submenu includes options relating to Logic's display and control of tempo. The options in this submenu are explored in Chapter 15.

- **Open Signature List.** This command launches the Signature List. This editor is used for entering new time signature and key change information. This window is explored in "The Signature Track" section later in this chapter.

- **Step Input Keyboard.** This command opens a Step Input Keyboard window that can be used to input MIDI note information into the Event List and Score and Piano Roll Editors.

- **Event Float.** If you want a one-entry Event List in a floating window to always show you the currently selected data, you can launch one with this command. The key command for this is Option+E.

- **Region Inspector Float.** Selecting this command opens a floating Region Playback Parameter box, which will display the playback parameters for the selected region. The floating Region Playback Parameter box is an exact duplicate of the Region Playback Parameter box in the Inspector, which is covered in Chapter 6.

- **Project Information.** You can open the Project Information window, shown in Figure 4.8, using this command. It gives you a concise list of all the elements of your song and how much memory they require.

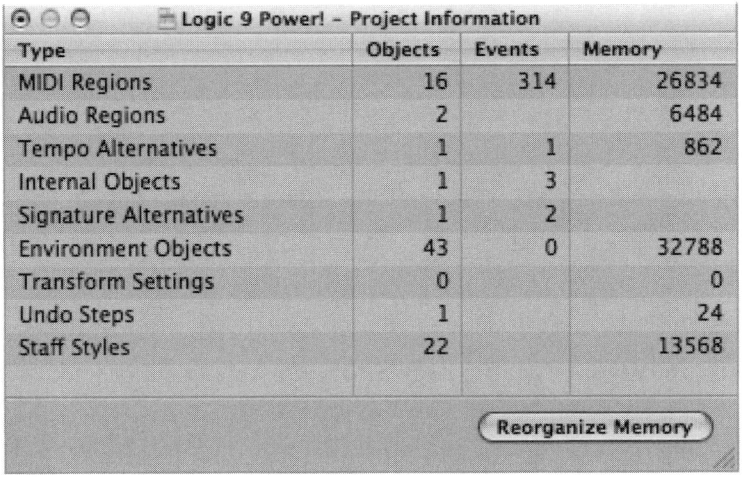

Type	Objects	Events	Memory
MIDI Regions	16	314	26834
Audio Regions	2		6484
Tempo Alternatives	1	1	862
Internal Objects	1	3	
Signature Alternatives	1	2	
Environment Objects	43	0	32788
Transform Settings	0		0
Undo Steps	1		24
Staff Styles	22		13568

Reorganize Memory

Figure 4.8   The Project Information window.

■ **Send to MIDI.** This submenu contains a few options for resetting hardware MIDI devices, sending them global volume increases, and so on. If you're having problems with your MIDI hardware, these options might come in handy.

The Audio Submenu

The Audio submenu, shown in Figure 4.9, contains a small but diverse collection of tools for handling various audio-related processes in Logic.

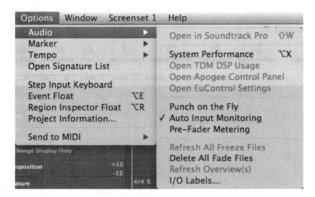

Figure 4.9   The Audio submenu.

■ **Open in Soundtrack Pro.** This command opens the selected audio region in Soundtrack Pro. The key command for this is Shift+W.

■ **System Performance.** This command opens the System Performance window, which contains meters that show the performance of the CPU, hard drives, and any Nodes you may be running. The System Performance window is covered in Chapter 5. The key command for this is Option+X.

■ **Open TDM DSP Usage.** If you're using a Pro Tools|HD system with Logic, you can use this command to open a TDM DSP Usage window, which reports the current DSP load of your project.

■ **Open Apogee Control Panel.** This control panel displays the parameter set for connected, supported Apogee hardware.

■ **Open EuControl Settings.** This control panel displays the parameter set for connected devices that support the Euphonix EuCon protocol.

■ **Punch on the Fly.** If you want to be able to immediately drop into Record mode when needed, you can check this command. This is described in detail in the next chapter.

■ **Auto Input Monitoring.** If you want to monitor what is coming through your hardware inputs into Logic, you can check this command. This is described in detail in the next chapter.

- **Pre-Fader Metering.** This sets up the channel strip meters to show the level of your audio *before* it is processed by the channel strip. Without this checked, the channel strip meters will show the level of your audio *after* it has been processed by any effects and adjustments made on the channel strip.

- **Refresh All Freeze Files.** If you have used Freeze on any Arrange tracks, then turned off Freeze to edit those tracks and turned it on again, this command will re-freeze those tracks. The Freeze Tracks function is described in detail in Chapter 6.

- **Delete All Fade Files.** This command deletes all fade files from the Fade Files folder in your Project folder.

- **Refresh Overview(s).** This command allows you to refresh the overview of an audio file or audio files you have replaced or edited in an external audio editor.

- **I/O Labels.** This command opens the I/O Labels window, which allows you to rename your Input, Output, and Send channel strips. The I/O Labels window is covered in Chapter 11.

The Window Menu

The Window menu, as shown in Figure 4.10, contains commands related to opening and manipulating windows.

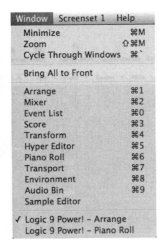

Figure 4.10   The Window menu.

The Window menu contains the following commands:

- **Minimize.** This command minimizes the currently selected window to the Dock. The key command for this is Command+M

- **Zoom.** You can instantly resize a window to fill the entire screen using this command. The key command for this is Shift+Command+M.

- **Cycle Through Windows.** You can switch from the current window to the next unselected window using this command. The key command for this is Command+'.

- **Bring All to Front.** Selecting this command brings all Logic windows to the front of any other open windows.

- **Arrange.** This command will launch an Arrange window. The Arrange window is discussed in Chapter 6. The key command for this is Command+1.

- **Mixer.** This command will launch a Mixer window. The Mixer is discussed in Chapter 11. The key command for this is Command+2.

- **Event List.** This command will launch an Event List window. The Event List is discussed in Chapter 8. The key command for this is Command+0.

- **Score.** This command will launch a Score Editor. The Score Editor is discussed in Chapter 8. The key command for this is Command+3.

- **Transform.** This command will launch a Transform window. The Transform window is discussed in Chapter 8. The key command for this is Command+4.

- **Hyper Editor.** This command will launch a Hyper Editor. The Hyper Editor is discussed in Chapter 8. The key command for this is Command+5.

- **Piano Roll.** This command will launch a Piano Roll Editor. The Piano Roll Editor is discussed in Chapter 8. The key command for this is Command+6.

- **Transport.** This command will launch a Transport window. The Transport window is discussed in Chapter 5. The key command for this is Command+7.

- **Environment.** This command will launch an Environment window. The Environment window has been discussed previously, but will be discussed in depth in Chapter 13, "The Environment." The key command for this is Command+8.

- **Audio Bin.** This command opens the Audio Bin. The Audio Bin is explored in Chapter 7. The key command for this is Command+9.

- **Sample Editor.** This command opens the Sample Editor window. The Sample Editor is explored in Chapter 7.

- **List of Open Windows.** At the bottom of the Window menu is a list of all the windows currently open in Logic. In Figure 4.10, for example, the open windows are an Arrange window and a Piano Roll window from the Logic 9 Power! project.

Screenset Menu

This menu includes commands relating to screensets. This menu was explored in Chapter 3.

Help Menu

The Help menu is the standard Mac OS X Help menu with some great added features. In addition to the Help menu's Search dialog, the Help menu gives you direct access to all your Logic Pro manuals in PDF format. The Help menu also contains a number of helpful Logic web links.

Global Tracks

Global tracks are unique tracks that contain information that pertains to the entire Logic project, such as the project's tempo, key signature, time signature, song markers, thumbnails of video for which you are composing audio, and so on. Global tracks can be displayed in the Arrange window and in the Piano Roll, Score, and Hyper Editors. There are seven types of global tracks:

- **Marker track.** This track contains song markers, or position holders you can use to label and separate sections of your project.

- **Signature track.** This track contains all your time signatures and key signatures for your project.

- **Chord track.** This track contains chord symbols and acts as a chord chart for your entire project.

- **Transposition track.** This track shows any global transposition events—in other words, any chord changes or note transpositions that would result in all MIDI regions and Apple Loops being transposed from their original pitch.

- **Tempo track.** This track contains the tempo and tempo changes for your project.

- **Beat Mapping track.** This powerful addition to Logic allows you to use any audio or MIDI region with strong rhythmic accents to create a "beat map" that Logic will use to adjust the musical timeline.

- **Video track.** This track contains thumbnail frames of QuickTime video in sync with Logic.

Figure 4.11 shows all the global tracks expanded in an Arrange window.

As you can see in Figure 4.11, global tracks can eat up your screen real estate quickly! Don't worry—you don't need to view them all at the same time. The local View menu of any window that can show global tracks includes the Configure Global Tracks command. You can also right-click any global track header and select this command from the shortcut menu, or use the key command Option+G. This will bring up a sliding window allowing you to choose to show only those global tracks that you want to see (see Figure 4.12). There are also key commands to toggle each global track on or off. Using this Global Tracks Configuration window, you can, for example, choose to view only the Marker and Video tracks, or you might choose to show the Tempo track in the Arrange window but not in the Score Editor.

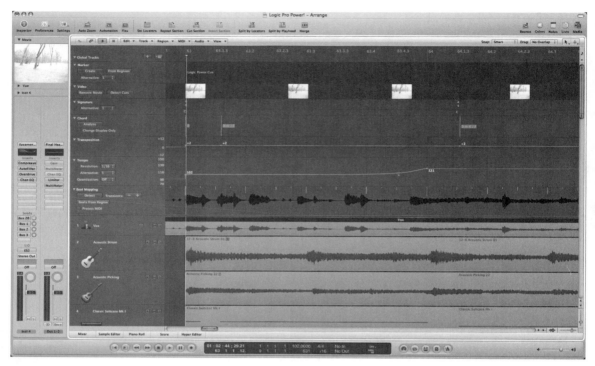

Figure 4.11   An Arrange window with all seven global tracks displayed and expanded.

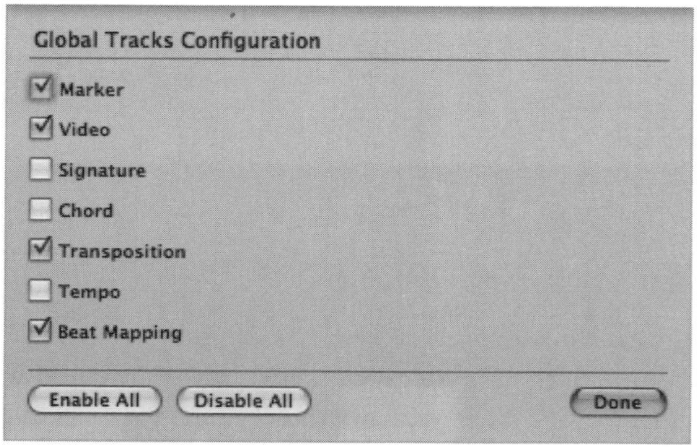

Global Tracks Configuration

☑ Marker

☑ Video

☐ Signature

☐ Chord

☑ Transposition

☐ Tempo

☑ Beat Mapping

(Enable All)   (Disable All)   (Done)

Figure 4.12   The Global Tracks Configuration sliding window lets you check which global tracks you would like to show.

Each global track also has a disclosure triangle at its left edge, which you can use to expand or collapse the global track. If you want to rearrange your displayed global tracks, you can do this by grabbing a global track in the Track List and dragging it to its new location. Finally, when you move the cursor to the border of a global track, it turns into a resize cursor, and you can drag that track to resize it. Figure 4.13 gives an example of these global track features.

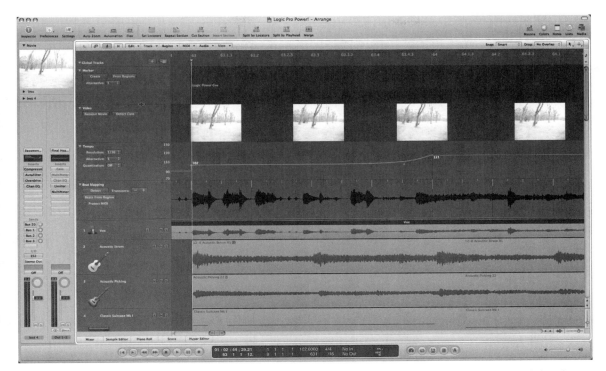

Figure 4.13   In this figure, only four of the seven global tracks are showing. The Marker track has been resized to be larger via the resize cursor (shown). The Video and Beat Mapping tracks have been collapsed via their disclosure triangles. Finally, the Tempo track is expanded and normal size.

Common Features of Global Tracks

The Video and Beat Mapping tracks are quite unique in their functions and features, but the other five global tracks share a number of common features. The data on these global tracks consists of *global events*. These global events are different types of data depending on the specific global track, but they can be created, moved, copied, and deleted similarly. The next sections will explain how.

Creating a Global Event

To create a global event on a global track, simply click with the Pencil tool at the desired position in the track. As the mouse button is down, a help tag with the exact position (and value, if applicable to that global track) will be displayed below the cursor. Figure 4.14 illustrates creating a global event in the Tempo track.

If you have not changed the default tool to the Pencil tool, you can access the Pencil tool with the Command key by assigning the secondary Tool menu to the Pencil tool.

You can also access the Tool menu by pressing the ESC key. If you have set your Right Mouse Button Preference in the Logic Pro > Preferences > Global > Editing tab to Opens Tool Menu, you can use your right mouse button to open the Toolbox and select the Pencil tool.

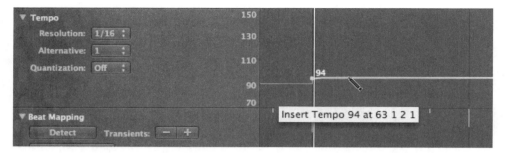

Figure 4.14 Inserting global events in the Tempo track. Just click in the track with the Pencil tool to create the event. The help tag below your Pencil tool will give you the exact information and position regarding your action.

If the concept of tools and Tool menus isn't familiar to you, you might want to skip to Chapter 6, where, in the context of the Arrange page tools, we explain the Tool menu and the Pencil tool in detail.

Selecting and Moving Global Events

You can select global events using the common selection methods you are familiar with from other applications. Click on an event with the mouse pointer to select it. To select multiple global events, Shift-click on the events you want to select. If you want to make a "rubber band" (sometimes called *lasso*) selection, you can drag the cursor over a group of events while holding down the Control key. If you click the track header of the global track in the Track List, you will select all the events on that track.

Once selected, global events can be moved and/or changed simply by dragging them. As the mouse button is down, a help tag with the exact position (and value, if applicable to that global track) of your global event will be displayed below the cursor. Figure 4.15 shows a global event on the Tempo track being moved.

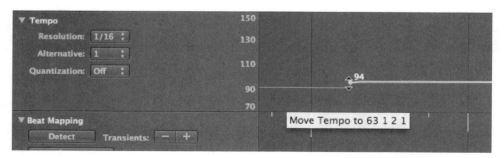

Figure 4.15 In this figure, a global event on the Tempo track has been selected and is being moved to the left.

Copying and Deleting Global Events

You can copy and delete global events using the standard Macintosh methods for copying and deleting information.

To copy data using the mouse, you can Option-drag any selected data. You can also use the Edit menu and keyboard commands for Cut and Paste or Copy and Paste.

To delete data using the mouse, you can click on the data with the Eraser tool from that window's Tool menu. You can also use the Delete or Backspace key on your keyboard. Finally, you can use the Edit menu command for Delete.

The Marker Track

The Marker track displays project markers. Markers are very useful position-holders for locations or sections of your project. They can appear as short placeholders with a line or two of text in the Marker track or as much longer messages in their own Marker Text window. The background and text of the markers can be colored if you wish. Figure 4.16 shows the Piano Roll Editor with the Marker track displayed.

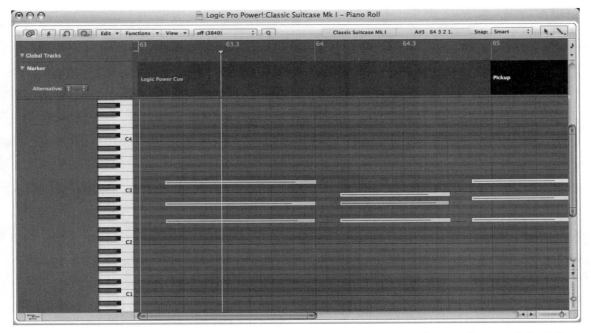

Figure 4.16   This Piano Roll Editor has a Marker track displaying song markers at the top of the Editor.

If you do not have the Marker track displayed, the markers themselves will still appear as they do in Figure 4.17 at the bottom of the Bar ruler.

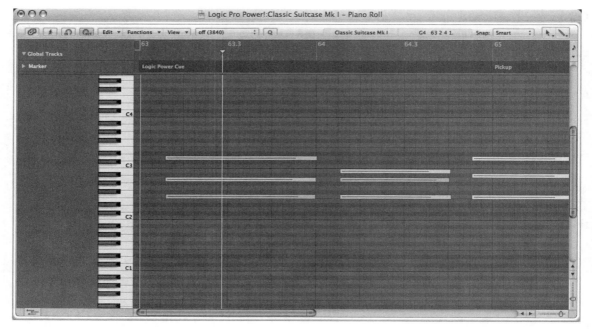

Figure 4.17   In this Piano Roll window, the Marker track is not displayed, but the markers themselves are still visible on the Bar ruler.

Markers are an invaluable aid in arranging your song and are very easy to create and use, as you will soon see. They are even embedded in any audio files you bounce or export from Logic, allowing you to use them across multiple projects.

The Marker List

In addition to being visible in the global track or on the Bar ruler, Logic stores the locations of all of a song's markers in a specialized Event List called the Marker List, available either in the Lists area of the Arrange window or as its own window. The Marker List displays all the markers currently created in your project. It allows you to edit the positions of markers, create markers, and perform some additional functions as well. You can bring up the Marker List window by selecting Options > Marker > Open Marker List. You can display the Marker List in the Arrange window by clicking on the Marker tab in the Lists area or by using the key command Option+M to toggle the display of the Marker List in the Arrange. Figure 4.18 shows a Marker List window.

The Marker List serves as a single location in which to quickly view all your markers. If you like to navigate or edit markers from a list, the Marker List serves that purpose, too. If you make regular use of markers, a Marker List window can be an invaluable addition to your screensets.

The Marker List incorporates some unique buttons and menus, which we will now explore.

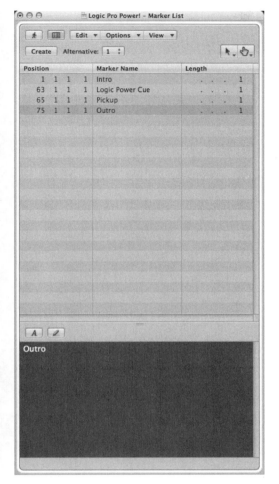

Figure 4.18 In the Marker List, you can add markers, edit their position and length, and more.

The Edit Menu.   The Marker List Edit menu, shown in Figure 4.19, features many of the same functions as the global Edit menu. Refer back to that section for information on these functions.

The Options Menu.   The Options menu contains commands for creating and altering markers. Figure 4.20 shows the Marker List Options menu.

The Marker List Options menu commands are:

■ **Create.** The Create command creates a new marker at the bar nearest to the current playhead position. The key command for this is Command+'.

■ **Create Without Rounding.** The Create Without Rounding command creates a new marker at the current playhead position. The key command for this is Shift+Command+'.

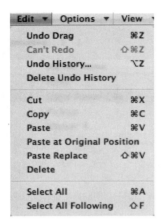

Figure 4.19 The Marker List Edit menu.

Figure 4.20 The Marker List Options menu.

- **Marker Alternatives.** Selecting Marker Alternatives opens the Marker Alternatives submenu, allowing you to select an alternative set of markers for your project. Marker Alternatives are covered in more detail in the "Marker Alternatives" section later in this chapter.

- **Unlock SMPTE Position.** If you have a marker locked to a SMTPE position, you can unlock it using this command. This is particularly applicable to video markers, which will be covered in more detail in "The Video Track" section later in this chapter and in Chapter 16. The key command for this is Command+Page Up.

- **Lock SMPTE Position.** This command locks your marker to its current SMPTE position. The key command for this is Command+Page Down.

- **Convert to Scene Marker.** This command converts a standard marker into a movie scene marker.

- **Convert to Standard Marker.** This command converts a movie scene marker into a standard marker.

The View Menu.   The View menu contains a couple options to change the display of information in the Marker List. Figure 4.21 shows the Marker List View menu.

Figure 4.21   The Marker List View menu.

The Marker List View menu options are:

- **Event Position and Length in SMPTE Units.** This command changes the display of the Position and Length columns in the Marker List from displaying information in bars to SMPTE. This is very useful when working with movie scene markers. The key command for this is Control+Option+R.

- **Length as Absolute Position.** This command changes the display of the Length column from displaying the relative length of the marker to the actual bar position of the length of the marker. The key command for this is Control+A.

The Marker List Buttons.   The Marker List has three buttons on the upper-left side of the Lists area and a Tool menu on the upper-right side. Brief explanations of their functions follow:

- **Catch.** When lit, this button ensures the Marker List follows along the playhead.

- **Open Book.** This button opens the Marker Text area at the bottom of the Marker List. The Marker Text area will be covered in the subsection "The Marker Text Area" later in this chapter.

- **Create.** Clicking this button creates a new marker at the beginning of the nearest bar.

The Market List Tool Menu.   The Marker List Tool menu can be accessed by clicking on the Pointer button in the upper-right corner of the Marker List. Figure 4.22 shows the Marker List Tool menu.

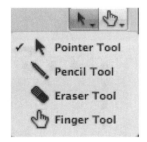

Figure 4.22   The Marker List Tool menu.

The Marker List tools are:

- **Pointer.** This is a normal selection tool. If you double-click on the position or length parameters of a marker, a text entry box will open, allowing you to enter new values manually. You can also click on a parameter to use the mouse as a slider for adjusting values. Double-clicking on the name of a marker opens the Marker Text area at the bottom of the Marker List, open to the selected marker.

- **Pencil.** If you double-click on a marker, this tool creates a marker identical to the selected marker. You can then edit the marker to suit your taste.

- **Eraser.** When you click on a marker with this tool, it erases (deletes) the marker.

- **Finger.** This tool not only selects a marker when you click on it, but it moves the playhead to the beginning of that marker and sets the locators to the marker boundaries. If you hold down the mouse button, Logic begins playing your song from the beginning of this marker as long as you hold down the button.

The Options > Marker Submenu
In addition to the commands available in the Marker List, there are also commands pertaining to the creation and use of markers available in the global Options menu, as shown in Figure 4.23.

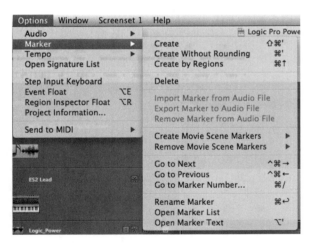

Figure 4.23   The Options > Marker submenu.

The Marker submenu commands are:

- **Create.** The Create command creates a new marker at the bar nearest to the current playhead position. The key command for this is Shift+Command+'.

- **Create Without Rounding.** The Create Without Rounding command creates a new marker at the current playhead position. The key command for this is Command+'.

- **Create by Regions.** The Create by Regions command creates new markers at the position of each selected region. The markers also span the length of each selected region and take on the name of their respective parent region. The key command for this is Command+Up Arrow.

- **Delete.** The Delete command deletes the marker at the current playhead position.

- **Import Marker from Audio File.** When you record or bounce an audio file in Logic, the marker information that falls within the borders of that audio file is included in the bounced file. The Import Marker from Audio File command lets you import this information into your Logic project, a handy feature if you want to share markers across multiple projects. You'll learn more about bouncing audio in Chapter 11.

- **Export Marker to Audio File.** The Export Marker to Audio File command allows you to export marker information directly into an audio region.

- **Remove Marker from Audio File.** The Remove Marker from Audio File command removes the maker information from an audio file, which is helpful if you are sharing audio across projects and want to remove any marker information from the audio on a per-project basis.

- **Create Movie Scene Markers.** The Create Movie Scene Markers submenu offers a variety of options for creating movie scene markers. It's covered in Chapter 16.

- **Remove Movie Scene Markers.** The Remove Movie Scene Markers submenu offers a variety of options for removing movie scene markers. It's also covered in Chapter 16.

- **Go to Next.** The Go to Next command lets you navigate your project via markers. Selecting Go to Next moves the playhead to the next marker. The "Go to" marker key commands are particularly good ones to learn. The key command for Go to Next is Control+Command+Right Arrow.

- **Go to Previous.** The Go to Previous command moves the playhead to the previous marker. The key command for this is Control+Command+Left Arrow.

- **Go to Marker Number.** The Go to Marker Number command opens the Go to Marker dialog. Figure 4.24 shows the Go to Marker dialog.

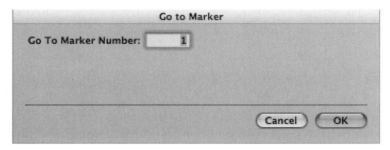

Figure 4.24 The Go to Marker dialog lets you move the playhead to the marker number you enter in the Go to Marker Number field.

Simply type a marker number in the Go to Marker Number field, press OK, and the playhead will move to that marker. The key command for this is Command+/.

- **Rename Marker.** The Rename Marker command lets you rename the selected marker. When you use this command, a text window will open above the marker in the Marker Track lane, where you can input a new name and then press Return. The key command for this is Command+Return.

- **Open Marker List.** The Open Marker List command opens a Marker List window.

- **Open Marker Text.** The Open Marker Text command opens a Marker Text window. The Marker Text window will be discussed in "The Marker Text Area" later in this chapter. The key command for this is Option+'.

Creating, Copying, Resizing, Moving, and Deleting Markers

As discussed earlier, markers are global events and can be created, copied, moved, resized, and deleted the same way as any global event on a global track. The Marker List gives you the ability to accomplish the same things in a text-based editor using standard Edit menu commands, mouse input, and keyboard input. The Marker submenu of the Options menu offers a number of other ways to work with markers. In addition to the methods discussed earlier, Logic offers a few additional ways to work with markers in your project.

- You can use the Create Marker, Rename Marker, and Delete Marker commands by invoking the Control-click shortcut menu when mousing over the Marker lane.

- You can drag one or more regions from the Arrange window into the Marker track. A marker will be created with the same length and position as the dragged region(s).

- If you click the From Regions button in the Marker track, Logic will automatically create a new marker for each selected region. The markers will have the same position, length, and name as the selected regions.

- Markers that you create using regions may be rounded to the closest bar line. If you want your marker to be at the exact position the regions are, even if they are not on a bar line, you can choose the Create Without Rounding command at Options > Marker > Create Without Rounding. The key command for this is Command+'.

- If the marker global track is not displayed, you can click any point in the bottom third of the Bar ruler while holding down the Option+Command keys, and Logic will create a marker where you clicked. A text field will open, allowing you to name your marker.

- You can create a marker that corresponds to a cycle area if Cycle mode is on (see Chapter 5) by dragging the cycle area down into the Marker track or down into the bottom third of the Bar ruler.

If you attempt to create a marker where one already exists within a quarter note in either direction, Logic will not create the new marker. If you want to assign a marker to an absolute time position regardless of the song's tempo (this is very useful for film scoring and audio post-production for video), create a marker (or select a previously created marker) and use the Lock SMPTE Position command from the Arrange window's local Region menu. The key command for this is Command+Page Down.

If you decide that you no longer need a marker, deleting it is very simple. You can simply select the marker in the Marker track and press Delete, or you can delete it from the Bar ruler and the Marker List. In the Bar ruler, Command-drag the marker below the Bar ruler, and the marker will vanish. You can also use the Eraser tool or the Delete key in the Marker List window. Lastly, you can choose Options > Marker > Delete.

Adding or Changing Marker Color

You can easily add or change the color of a marker on the Marker track. First, open the Color palette from the local View menu of the selected window (View > Colors) or press Option+C. Select one or more markers and click the color in the palette you wish to add to the marker(s). The markers will then have the selected color.

The Marker Text Area

The Marker Text area, shown in Figure 4.25, is where you customize the look and the text of the marker you have created.

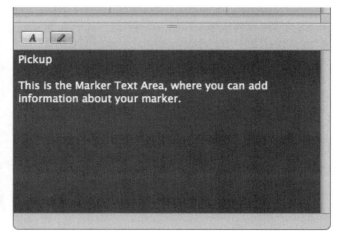

Figure 4.25   The Marker Text area contains all your options for customizing markers.

As you can see in Figure 4.25, there are two buttons above the text-entry area. These buttons have the following functions:

- **A.** This button opens a Font window containing options for selecting a font, resizing the font, and choosing the font style and color.

■ **Pencil tool.** When the Pencil tool is engaged, you can enter text in the Marker Text window. This tool defeats all Logic local key commands, allowing you full access to all the available letters, numbers, and symbols in OS X. Some global key commands, such as copy and paste, are still functional.

If you have text in the Clipboard, you can paste it into a marker, or you can copy the text here into the Clipboard to paste it elsewhere.

Keep in mind that in the Arrange window, the Marker space in the Bar ruler is too small to display anything besides the name and color of your marker. You can resize an expanded Marker track to display all the text if desired. You'll need to keep the Marker Text window open in your screenset to view customized marker text—the Marker track itself uses only its default font.

Marker Background Color with More Than One Text Paragraph   If you create more than one paragraph of text in the Marker Text area by pressing the Return key and then change the background color, in the Marker Text window, the new background color will fill the entire text window. In the Marker track, however, it will not. A line will divide the first-paragraph and second-paragraph text through the marker, and your color will only appear in the top half. There is currently no way to add color to the bottom half of a marker on a Marker track.

Expert Tip: When Marker Text Is Important, Open the Text Window   Clearly, the markers in the global track or the Bar ruler are not designed for large amounts of text. They are perfect for a quick title and maybe a note or a lyric or two, but not much more than that. If you want your markers to contain extensive notes and information for collaborators, future reference, and so on, you would be better off to keep the Marker Text window open permanently. A great way to do this is by selecting Options > Marker > Open Marker Text. This creates the Marker window as a "floating" window, meaning it will not get lost behind other windows and will always be visible. One thing to keep in mind, however, is that with the addition of the Notes feature of Logic 9, there is far less need to use markers for extensive notes. You can read about the Notes feature in Chapter 6.

Using Markers

We've already discussed using markers as a visual cue to organize your song or to create extensive text boxes filled with notes, lyrics, and such that will automatically follow your song. You can also use markers to move the playhead and set a cycle area.

If you click on a marker in the Marker track using the Option key, the playhead moves to the start of the marker. If your global tracks are not showing, you can click on a marker in the Bar ruler while holding the Command key to do the same thing. If you Command-drag a marker up to the top of the Bar ruler, it will set the locators and turn on Cycle mode for the length of that marker.

Marker Alternatives

The Marker Alternative feature allows you to switch between nine completely unique Marker List variations for each project. The Marker Alternative pull-down menu in the Marker track, shown in Figure 4.26, gives you instant access to all nine Marker List variations.

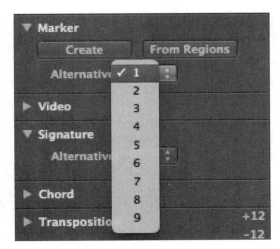

Figure 4.26   The Marker Alternative menu in the Marker track. You can save and access entire sets of alternative markers in this menu.

Simply select a marker alternative and create markers for it using any method described previously. You can hold the Option key while selecting the Marker Alternative menu to copy all the marker events from one marker alternative to another. The Marker Alternatives submenu of the local Marker List Options menu and the Alternative pull-down menu in the Marker List also let you switch among alternative sets of markers.

Importing Markers from Other Projects

One very cool feature in Logic is the ability to import settings from one project directly into another. While templates do a great job of giving you a customized blank slate from which to start, sometimes you'll find that you'd really like to import things like aux routings, entire mixer configurations, and global tracks. In addition to being able to import markers from an audio file, you can import the Marker track from one project into another in the Browser. This will be covered in detail in Chapter 12.

The Signature Track

The Signature track shows any time and key signatures associated with the song. If you haven't set any, Logic will default to a time signature of 4/4 and a key of C. If you import a GarageBand song, your initial key and time signature settings from GarageBand will be carried over. If you are not familiar with music notation or otherwise do not generally use time and key signatures in your music, you most likely will not use this global track very often. Figure 4.27 shows a Signature track open in a Score Editor window.

Figure 4.27 This figure shows the Signature track with some time and key signature changes displayed in a Score Editor.

In general, the Signature track information is more for display purposes than anything else. Any key signature changes after the initial key signature affect the display of MIDI notes in the Score Editor but don't have any effect on playback. Similarly, even time signature changes don't affect the playback, only the display of measures in the Score Editor and the Bar ruler and the emphasis of the metronome.

The Signature track does interact in some ways with the Chord track. Apple Loops and transposable MIDI regions will be transposed based on the root note of chords in the Chord track. These root notes determine whether there will be any transposition relative to the current key signature shown in the Signature track. If no chords are available in the Chord track, the global playback key for Apple Loops and MIDI regions is determined by the very first key signature.

Creating Time and Key Signature Global Events

You can create time and key signatures by creating global events in the Signature track as described in the "Creating a Global Event" section earlier in this chapter. If you click with the Pencil tool in the top half of the Signature track, you will be shown the dialog box in Figure 4.28 to add a time signature event. If you click the Pencil tool in the bottom half of the Signature track, you will be shown the dialog box in Figure 4.29 to add a key signature event.

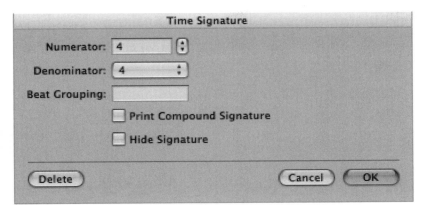

Figure 4.28   When you use the Pencil tool to create a time signature event, this dialog box lets you enter the time signature information. When you click OK, the time signature will be added to the Signature track.

Figure 4.29   When you use the Pencil tool to create a key signature event, this dialog box lets you enter the key signature information. When you click OK, the key signature will be added to the Signature track.

If you collapse the Signature track height, you will only be able to create a time signature event. Only when the Signature track is expanded will both lines for time and key signatures be visible.

Time and key signatures can also be added in the Score Editor. This will be discussed in Chapter 8.

Copying, Resizing, Moving, and Deleting Signatures

Events on the Signature track can be selected, moved, deleted, and copied in the same way as other global events. If you want to edit an existing signature, double-click a signature, and the corresponding dialog box shown in Figures 4.28 and 4.29 will open. If you Shift-double-click anywhere in the Signature track, you will open the Signature List in the Lists area of the Arrange window, as shown in Figure 4.30. Time and key signatures are shown in a list style editor, much like the Marker List. Any other score symbols, such as repeat signs, double bar lines, and so on, will also be shown in this list. You can also open the Signature List in its own floating window by going to Options > Open Signature List.

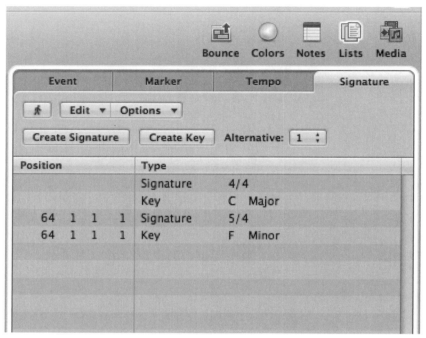

Figure 4.30   The Signature List shows all your time signatures and key changes in a list format.

The Edit menu in the Signature List is a typical Edit menu, full of familiar commands. The Options menu in the Signature List gives you access to signature alternatives, which are also available directly in the Alternative drop-down menus in the Signature List and in the Signature track header. You can use the Create Signature and Create Key buttons to create new signature and key events, respectively.

Cutting Measures in the Signature Track

If you want to cut measures in the Signature track—for example, if you want to divide one 5/4 measure into a 3/4 measure and a 2/4 measure—you can select the Scissors tool from the Toolbox of the selected window and click at the desired location. If you make a cut in the middle of a bar in which there are no time signature changes, you will create two shorter measures with the original time. You can also merge two measures into one longer measure by using the Glue tool in the Signature track.

Signature Alternatives

The Signature track can utilize nine different signature alternatives. See the "Marker Alternatives" section earlier in this chapter for details on using global track alternatives.

Importing Signature Tracks from Other Projects

Like Marker tracks, Signature tracks can also be imported from one project directly into another in the Browser. This will be covered in Chapter 12.

The Chord Track

The Chord track contains letters symbolizing the chords in your song. The main uses of this track are for a visual display of the chord structure of your song and for determining the global transposition of MIDI regions and Apple Loops throughout your song. Figure 4.31 shows a Chord track displayed in an Arrange window.

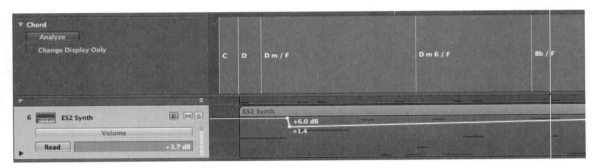

Figure 4.31   The Chord track displayed in this Arrange window reflects the current chord that will affect global transposition at each point of the song.

Creating Chord Track Global Events

There are a number of ways to create global events on the Chord track:

- As explained in the first section on creating global events, you can click the Pencil tool at the desired position in the Chord track. This will open the dialog box shown in Figure 4.32 for you to define your chord event.

- You can select one or more MIDI regions (preferably containing complete chords) and click the Analyze button in the Chord track list. Logic analyzes the MIDI region and adds the resulting chords to the Chord track.

- You can select one or more MIDI regions and drag them onto the Chord track. This has the same effect as selecting MIDI regions and clicking the Analyze button.

- When you create or alter a transposition event (see "The Transposition Track" section later in this chapter), the root note of any affected chords on the Chord track will be shifted accordingly.

Global Transpositions Generated by the Chord Track

Any chord in the Chord track has the potential to affect global transposition, meaning it can affect the playback key of Apple Loops and MIDI regions. You can keep the MIDI regions on an

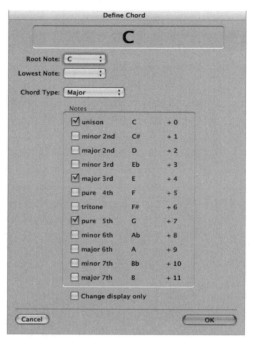

Figure 4.32   The Define Chord dialog box opens when you use the Pencil tool to create a chord event.

Arrange track from being transposed by clicking the No Transpose check box in its Region Parameter box. (Region Parameter boxes will be discussed in Chapter 6.) Logic derives the transposition interval from the gap between the chord root and the first key signature root in the Signature track. If a chord is created, this will also be reflected in the Transposition track.

Although Logic's chord analysis algorithm usually delivers accurate results, you still might find incorrect or missing chords in the Chord track occasionally. In these circumstances, you'll want to check the Chord track's Change Display Only button, which you can see in Figure 4.32. With this mode active, you can adjust the chords manually, and the transposition events in the Transposition track will adapt accordingly. Changes you make to chords while Change Display Only mode is active don't affect playback of the corresponding MIDI regions; your changes only adapt the chords displayed in the Chord track to the chords played in the MIDI region.

You cannot use Change Display Only mode to adjust the chords of a song to the chords in an audio-only Apple Loop. In general, this doesn't matter, since chord events are generally derived from MIDI regions. However, some Apple Loops do contain chord progressions. This means that your Apple Loop might end up getting transposed, even if you don't want it to. To get around this, you can cut an Apple Loop whenever chord changes happen and match the chords displayed in the Chord track with the chord progression in the cut Apple Loop. You can also use global transposition events in the Transposition track to make sure the Apple Loop matches its original parts. If you do not use the Chord track, this is obviously not an issue.

Moving, Copying, Resizing, Editing, and Deleting Chord Events

Chord events on the Chord track can be moved, copied, resized, and deleted as described in the first section on global tracks. If you want to edit a chord event, simply double-click it, and the Define Chord window from Figure 4.32 will open, and you can change the event as you wish.

The Transposition Track

The Transposition track shows global transposition events that affect the transposition of Apple Loops and MIDI regions. In MIDI regions, the MIDI events themselves are changed, but non-destructively, meaning that the original data itself is not deleted—so if you remove the transposition, the original data will return. Apple Loops will be pitch-shifted based on the transposition events on the Transposition track. Regular audio regions and Apple Loops with no key information will not be transposed. Figure 4.33 shows an Arrange window displaying the Transposition track.

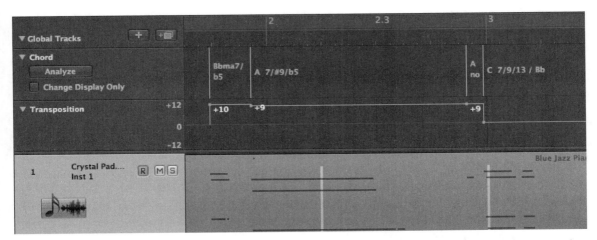

Figure 4.33 The Transposition track in an Arrange window. Notice the close relationship between the Chord track and the Transposition track.

The transposition events relate closely to the progression of the chord root notes in the Chord track. If you change a chord root in the Chord track, it will be reflected in the Transposition track, and vice versa. Creating or editing a transposition event will generate or alter the corresponding chord in the Chord track. All Apple Loops and MIDI regions will be pitch-shifted accordingly. If you do not want a MIDI region to transpose, click the No Transpose check box in its Region Parameter box. The current key signature in the Signature track determines the "zero position" of the Transposition track. If the key signature changes during a song, the zero position of the Transposition track also changes. The Transposition track always shows the difference between the Chord track and the Signature track at the position of the appropriate chord.

Editing Events in the Transposition Track

Transposition events on the Transposition track take the form of Nodes (round dots). These transposition events are connected with vertical and horizontal lines. The transposition event determines the global transposition value until the song position reaches the next transposition event (Node) during playback.

You can create, copy, move, and delete transposition events as described in the "Common Features of Global Tracks" section earlier in this chapter. Transposition events are limited to being moved horizontally (along the timeline) or vertically (by the transposition value), not diagonally. The help tag will appear below the cursor when the mouse button is pressed, with the exact transposition value and bar position of the current transposition event.

Pressing Control+Option+Command while clicking in the Transposition track opens a text window, as shown in Figure 4.34. You can directly enter a transposition value in the box, and, after pressing Return, you will create a transposition event of the typed value at the clicked position.

Figure 4.34   If you Control+Option+Command-click on the Transposition track, a text window will appear. When you type a value and press Return, a transposition event will be created at that location.

The scale range for the display of transposition events is +/−12 semitones.

The Tempo Track

Tempo, meaning speed and timing, is one of the most important elements in music. Tempo management can be as simple as agreeing on the timing of a song and asking all the musicians to play in time, or it can be as complicated as keeping track of multiple tempo changes throughout a musical movement—or even continuous tempo changes. With digital audio sequencers being the nerve center for both electronic and acoustic programmed and performed tracks, it becomes vital that the sequencer can keep everything synchronized and that it gives the user the tools to fully implement whatever tempo requirements he has. The Tempo track gives you a visual track for displaying, setting, and editing tempo events for your song. Figure 4.35 shows the Tempo track in an Arrange window.

Like the Transposition track, the Tempo track is made up of Nodes along a line. These Nodes are tempo events, and the line is the current tempo.

Inserting, Deleting, Moving, and Copying Tempo Changes

You can insert tempo changes like any other global event—clicking in the Tempo track with a Pencil tool to create a tempo change at the current position. Pressing Control+Option+Command

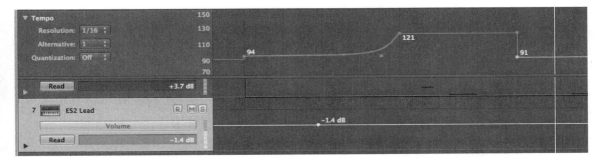

Figure 4.35 The Tempo track offers both a visual display and a convenient editing track for tempo changes in your song.

while clicking in the Tempo track opens a text window, as shown in Figure 4.36. You can directly enter a transposition value in the box, and after pressing Return, you will create a tempo change of the typed value at the clicked position.

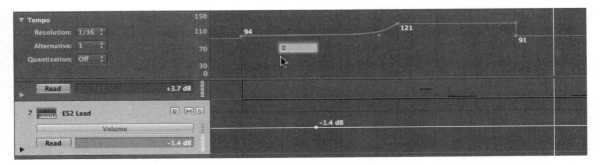

Figure 4.36 If you Control+Option+Command-click on the Tempo track, a text window will appear. When you type a value and press Return, a tempo change will be created at that location.

You can also record tempo changes in real time, as explained in Chapter 14, "Advanced Tempo Operations," and they will be reflected in the Tempo track.

Moving, copying, and deleting tempo changes is handled exactly the way other global events are handled. If you want to create a continuous transition between two tempi, select the Node at the tip of the right angle formed by the first and second Nodes and drag it inside the angle. A curve or diagonal line will form. The pull-down Tempo Resolution menu, visible in the Tempo track header in Figure 4.35, defines how minimum division size for tempo changes along the project timeline. Shorter divisions mean more tempo changes; longer divisions mean fewer tempo changes. You can define this differently for each Node.

The range for the display of tempo events adjusts automatically: Dragging a tempo event beyond the current upper and lower boundaries of the Tempo track results in an automatic adjustment of the range. You can manually define the maximum and minimum of the tempo scale by grabbing the maximum and minimum values and dragging them vertically or by double-clicking on them and typing the desired value into the text window that appears. These user-defined values are displayed in yellow. To reset to the automatic adjustment mode, repeat the procedure and leave the text window blank.

Tempo Alternatives

The Tempo Alternatives feature works similarly to the Marker Alternatives function discussed earlier in this chapter.

Importing Tempo Tracks from Other Projects

Like the Marker and Signature tracks, Tempo tracks can also be imported in the Browser.

Accessing Logic Pro's Advanced Tempo Functions from the Tempo Track

Logic Pro 9 offers a number of more advanced tempo features, a few of which can be accessed directly from the Tempo track. These will be discussed in Chapter 14.

You can press Shift while double-clicking in the Tempo track to open the Tempo List, a list view of your project's tempo changes. The Tempo List opens in the Lists area of the Arrange window.

The Tempo track has a close relationship with the Beat Mapping track, described in a moment. After you use the Beat Mapping function in the Beat Mapping track, do not make any more changes in the Tempo track!

The Beat Mapping Track

The Beat Mapping track is perhaps one of the most unique and powerful global tracks in Logic. It does exactly what the name implies—it maps Logic's tempo to a beat. In other words, suppose you recorded a fantastic audio or MIDI performance of an instrument, but the timing was a bit off the metronome click. Or maybe you recorded a live band without any metronome at all. The Beat Mapping track analyzes the performance and then creates a musically meaningful tempo map so that the bars and measures will fall in useful places. The performance is in no way moved or altered; it is only the tempo map and Bar ruler of Logic that are adjusted to fit the performance. Beat Mapping allows you to then use a metronome that will follow the tempo of your recorded performance; you can quantize other regions to the performance, loops will play in tune, and so on. Figure 4.37 shows the Beat Mapping track.

Beat Mapping Is Not Flex Time   For new Logic users, a common mistake is to think that beat mapping is the same thing as Logic 9's new audio tempo manipulation features, collectively called *Flex Time.* In fact, beat mapping and Flex Time are the exact opposite. Beat mapping conforms Logic's tempo map to the existing tempo of your performance. Flex Time conforms your performance to Logic's tempo map. You'll learn more about Flex Time and when you'll want to use it in Chapter 6.

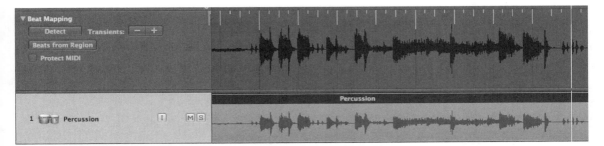

Figure 4.37   The Beat Mapping track shown in the Arrange window.

Beat Mapping Process

The beat mapping process basically consists of two steps. First, you graphically link musical events (MIDI notes or audio transients, which correspond to the initial accent of rhythmically important notes) to the desired bar positions in the Beat Mapping track. Then, you tell the Beat Mapping track which measures to line up with which beat position lines. Logic will automatically insert tempo changes, causing the musical bars to correspond to the positions of the beat position lines.

As you can imagine, manually adding each and every beat position line for a song that is hundreds of bars long would require massive amounts of work! Luckily, Logic offers a number of automatic beat-mapping functions to make this process as fast and intuitive as possible.

Beat Mapping from MIDI Regions.   Beat mapping from MIDI regions is simple. First, you need to select a MIDI region for Logic to beat map. As soon as you select a MIDI region, horizontal beat position lines for each MIDI note, similar to those found in the Piano Roll, will appear at the bottom of the Beat Mapping track, as shown in Figure 4.38.

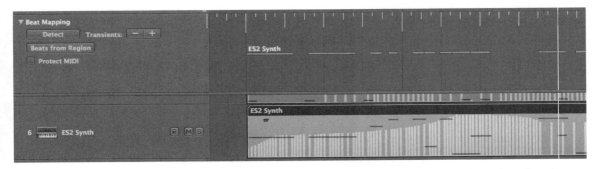

Figure 4.38   As you can see from the figure, the MIDI region ES2 Synth has been selected, and each note in the region has a corresponding horizontal line in the Beat Mapping track.

Now you need to tell Logic exactly which position on the Bar ruler you want to correspond to each note. At the first position you want to assign to a MIDI note, click and hold the mouse button. A yellow vertical line will appear in that location, as shown in Figure 4.39. The help tag will reflect your action and the pointer's exact location.

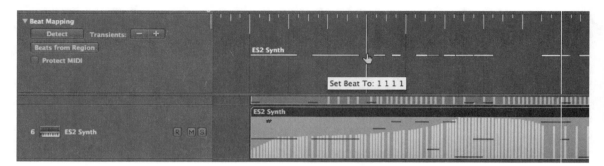

Figure 4.39   Click and hold the mouse at the first position on the Bar ruler where you want to assign a MIDI note.

Now drag the vertical yellow line toward the beat position line to which you want to assign the selected bar position. A darker yellow line will extend from the selected bar position location to the beat position line you have selected, as you see in Figure 4.40. The help tag will reflect your action and the pointer's exact location.

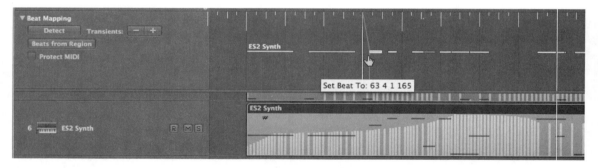

Figure 4.40   Drag the vertical yellow line to the beat position line you want to assign to your selected bar position. A line will extend from the original vertical yellow line to the beat position line.

When you release the mouse button, Logic inserts a tempo change in order to shift the Bar ruler so that the position you chose is linked to the note you chose, as shown in Figure 4.41.

That's the whole procedure! Simply repeat the aforementioned steps for any additional Bar ruler positions you want to map to MIDI notes. If you want to connect a bar position line to a position in which there is no beat position line, you can do this by dragging the yellow vertical line while pressing the Control key.

If you are not happy with a mapped beat, you can erase any beat allocation by double-clicking on it, clicking on it with the Eraser tool from the selected window's Tool menu, or selecting it and

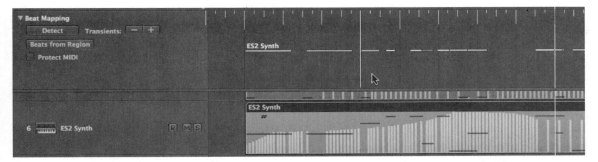

Figure 4.41   When you release the mouse button, a tempo change will be created to shift the Bar ruler to match the beat position. Notice between Figures 4.40 and 4.41, the entire Bar ruler has moved over. No musical events have been affected at all, however—only the tempo map.

pressing Delete. You can erase all your beat mapping by clicking in the Track List of the Beat Mapping track (except, obviously, the buttons or menus) and pressing Delete.

Expert Tip: Beat Map MIDI Regions in MIDI Editors   This example illustrated beat mapping a MIDI region on the Arrange window, but keep in mind that the global tracks all appear in the Piano Roll, Score, and Hyper Editors. You might find it more convenient to beat map MIDI regions in one of these MIDI editors, where you have a much better view of the actual MIDI notes.

Beat Mapping from Audio Regions.   Beat mapping from audio regions follows the same procedure as beat mapping from MIDI regions—you click on a Bar ruler position to create the vertical yellow line, drag it to the vertical beat position line to which you wish to allocate that bar position, then release the mouse. Repeat this procedure until you have the completed beat map. There is one very significant difference, however, between beat mapping a MIDI region and an audio region: Whereas the notes of the selected MIDI region(s) will automatically generate beat position lines in the Beat Mapping track, audio regions must be *analyzed* first. This means that Logic must search the audio region for transients, or the initial attack of strong notes. (In the waveform, these transients look like spikes in the signal.) Generally, the more rhythmic the instrument (drums, percussion, and so on), the more distinct and accurate Logic's analysis of the transients will be.

To do this, simply select an audio region (or regions) and click the Detect button in the track header of the Beat Mapping track. Logic will analyze the region(s) for transients and generate corresponding beat position markers in the Beat Mapping track. You can also drag an audio region (or regions) directly onto the Beat Mapping track to begin the analyzing process.

The Transients buttons in the track header of the Beat Mapping track (see Figure 4.37) allow you to change the sensitivity to transients of the beat mapping algorithm. You can click on these buttons to increase or decrease the sensitivity of the detection algorithm to transients. Generally, the most useful results will happen within a couple of clicks up or down from the default analysis. High Transients settings work well for regions with less distinct accents, but they will detect too many peaks as transients in other files. If even a Transients setting somewhere in the middle of the range detects extraneous transients that are not musically useful, you can try a lower Transients setting. After you press Detect, you can click through the entire Transients range to find a setting that works for your selected region.

Beats from Regions.   Using this option, you create a metronome region that you use to guide the Beat Mapping track as to where to generate beat position lines. For veteran Logic users, this is almost identical to using a guide region in the Reclock function. The advantage to using Beats from Regions is that the metronome region you create will often be easier for the Beat Mapping track to detect beats from, resulting in more accurate beats. For example, you might want to beat map your song to an acoustic guitar part, but the accents may be too soft to accurately analyze. In that case, creating a metronome region with the same timing as the acoustic guitar track and using Beats from Regions will result in the beat map you want.

To use this option, first create a MIDI track with an appropriately distinct rhythm, tapping out the exact beat to which you want Logic to beat map. If your metronome region isn't exactly right, you can use the MIDI editors to shift notes or keep trying until you get it right. When you are completely satisfied with the metronome region, click the Beats from Region button. You will be presented with the Set Beats by Guide Region(s) window shown in Figure 4.42.

Figure 4.42   Choose the note division of your metronome region in the Set Beats by Guide Region(s) window.

Select the note division you want for your metronome region and click OK. The Bar ruler of your song will be beat mapped to the metronome region, as shown in Figure 4.43.

Beat Mapping to Scene Markers.   This feature of the Beat Mapping track is especially useful for those scoring to picture. If you are using a Video track with a loaded QuickTime movie and you have used the Detect Cuts function on the movie (see "The Video Track" section later in this

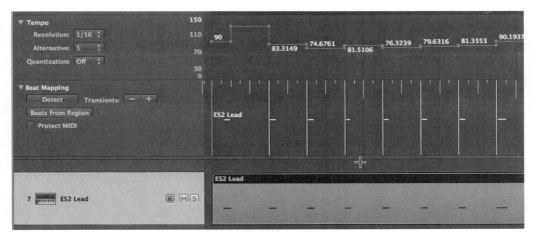

Figure 4.43   After the Beats from Regions process, your Bar ruler will be mapped to the beats of your metronome region.

chapter), the detected scene cuts will create markers, which can be used to generate beat position lines in the Beat Mapping track. If you want to define cut positions as the first downbeat of a bar, simply allocate the bar position to the beat position line as described in the "Beat Mapping from MIDI Regions" section earlier in this chapter.

Beat Mapping to Markers.   You can even beat map to the markers in the Marker track, if that track is visible. Simply select one or more markers, and the beginning of the marker(s) will appear as beat position lines in the Beat Mapping track. This works with standard markers and with scene markers.

Protecting MIDI Event Positions.   When you beat map an audio region, all MIDI events also move to reflect the new tempo map. However, this is not always a desirable result. For example, suppose you have a MIDI drum pattern that needs to line up correctly with a piano audio region you are beat mapping. To maintain the absolute position of all your MIDI events relative to the Bar ruler, you can select the Protect MIDI check box in the Beat Mapping track header (see Figure 4.37).

The Video Track

The Video track, unlike the other global tracks, does not contain any global events. Instead, it contains thumbnail images of single frames of a QuickTime movie loaded with your song. This track is especially for users who are doing sound for picture. Figure 4.44 shows an Arrange window with a Video track displayed.

Figure 4.44 The Video track shows thumbnails of a QuickTime movie.

You can open a QuickTime movie by clicking the Open Movie button in the Track List of the Video track or by clicking in the Video track with the Pencil tool of the window you are in to insert a movie into the Video track at the current mouse position.

You can also use the Browser in the Media area of the Arrange window to search for and open the video file on any connected volume. There are three ways to open a movie from the Browser: drag the movie file directly into the Video track at the desired position, double-click on it, or select the file and click the Open button. All of these actions cause the Drop Movie dialog, shown in Figure 4.45, to open.

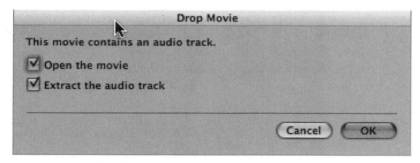

Figure 4.45 The Drop Movie dialog.

In this dialog, you can choose to open the movie, extract its audio, or both.

The number of thumbnails you see depends on the current zoom level. The frames are always left aligned, with the exception of the final movie frame, which is right aligned. In other words, the left border of every frame except the final frame represents the correct song position for that frame. The final frame is right aligned to ensure that regardless of your zoom level, at least the first and last frames of a movie will be visible. No editing operations are possible on Video thumbnail tracks.

Because the Video track doesn't contain any global events, you can't do any editing. You can, however, use the Detect Cuts feature, which searches for scene cuts in the movie. To do this, click the Detect Cuts button in the Video track's Track List. Doing this creates movie scene markers, which are special markers locked to a specific SMPTE time and which can be deleted if the movie is removed from the song. Finally, as described in "The Beat Mapping Track" subsection, you can use the detected cut scenes from a Video track to generate beat position lines in the Beat Mapping track.

Now that you are familiar with some of the global options that you will be able to access from several areas of Logic Pro 9, it's time to start exploring the individual program areas, starting with the Transport in the next chapter.

5 Transport Controls and Recording

The Transport contains perhaps the most fundamental functions in Logic—the controls for recording, playback, and project position. The Transport is modeled after the "transport" section of a tape machine, so named because pressing the buttons physically moves (transports) the magnetic tape. Of course, there's no tape in your computer, but because the metaphor of the tape machine transport for these controls is quite intuitive, it has found its way into Logic (and, in fact, almost all modern software-based audio applications). Figure 5.1 shows the default Logic Pro Transport.

Figure 5.1 In the Transport, you can control recording, playback, and related functions. The Transport also offers project position display and other data viewing options.

Notice that the Transport in Logic offers many more options than a standard tape machine. This is because Logic offers far more functionality than simply recording and playback. Logic Pro 9 adds more functionality to the Stop and Play buttons in the form of shortcut menu options. All of the functions accessible on the Transport are directly related to playback or recording, as you'll explore in the next sections.

The Transport Buttons

The most immediately noticeable features of the Transport are the Transport buttons themselves. These are the buttons that directly correspond to those buttons on a tape machine that "transport" the tape. When you record on a computer, no actual tape is physically moved, so Logic uses a playhead—a vertical line in the Arrange window from the Bar ruler to the bottom of the Arrange window—to indicate the current playback location in the song. Figure 5.2 shows the default Transport buttons.

Figure 5.2 The Transport buttons.

133

If you have help tags enabled, holding the mouse over these buttons will reveal the names of the buttons. Although the functions of these buttons are self-evident if you've previously used a tape recorder, here is specific information about how these buttons function in Logic, starting from left to right in the Transport shown in Figure 5.2.

- **Go to Beginning.** This button moves the playhead back to the first bar of the project. The key command for this is Return.

- **Play from Selection.** This button moves the playhead to the beginning of the selected region or event and starts playback. The key command for this is Shift+Enter.

- **Rewind.** Pressing this button moves the playhead backward. If you click and hold this button, the playhead moves backward faster. The key command for this is Shift+, (comma). If you *short-click* the button (that is, click the button very quickly), the playhead jumps back one bar. The key command for this is , (comma). It might be easier to remember that these rewind commands use the < (less than) key rather than the comma, as the < resembles the left-facing arrows of a Rewind button on a tape, CD, or DVD player's transport controls. If you click and hold the button and drag your mouse to the left or right, you can shuttle the playhead backward *or* forward. If you Command-click on the Rewind button, you will move the playhead to the previous marker. The key command for this is Control+Command+Left Arrow.

- **Fast Forward.** This button moves the playhead forward. If you click and hold this button, the playhead moves forward faster. The key command for this is Shift+. (period). If you short-click the button, the playhead jumps forward one bar. The key command for this is . (period). It might be easier to remember that these fast forward commands use the > (greater than) key rather than the period, as the > resembles the right-facing arrows of a Fast Forward button on a tape, CD, or DVD player's transport controls. If you click and hold the button and drag your mouse to the left or right, you can shuttle the playhead forward *or* backward. If you Command-click on the Fast-Forward button, you will move the playhead to the next marker.

- **Stop.** By default, pressing Stop halts playback or recording. If Logic is not currently playing or recording when you press Stop, the playhead will return to the first bar of the project or cycle. The key command for this is 0. The Stop button has a shortcut menu that can be revealed by clicking and holding or Control-clicking on the Stop button. The Stop shortcut menu will be covered in "The Stop Button Shortcut Menu" section later in this chapter. You can also toggle playback with the spacebar.

- **Play.** By default, pressing this button begins playback at the current playhead or from the left locator. If you are in Cycle mode, playback begins at the start of the cycle. The key command for this is Enter. The Play button has a shortcut menu that can be revealed by clicking and holding or Control-clicking on the Stop button. The Play shortcut menu will be covered in "The Play Button Shortcut Menu" later in this chapter. You can also toggle playback with the spacebar.

■ **Pause.** Pressing this button momentarily stops playback or recording. Pressing it again, or pressing Play, continues playback or recording. The key command for Pause is the decimal point on your keyboard's number pad.

■ **Record.** When you press this button, it turns red, along with the Bar ruler, and Logic begins recording. The key command for this is *. If you have designated a count-in or a pre-roll, covered later in this chapter, Logic will play the count-in or pre-roll before engaging record. Any data sent by connected MIDI controllers is recorded on the selected MIDI track in the Arrange window. Any audio sent into one or more channels of your audio interface is recorded as audio on record-enabled Audio tracks with one of those channels selected as an input. Logic creates a region in the Arrange window for each track you record. The region will span the actual length of the time you recorded, from the end of the pre-roll (if applicable) to the moment Stop was pressed. If you click and hold down the Record button, you can access the Recording Settings window, which is explained in "The Recording Settings Window" section later in this chapter.

Expert Tip: Transport Key Commands   Remember, Logic is designed to allow users to really fly by using key commands everywhere possible. This means that not only are there key commands for all the Transport buttons, but there are key commands relating to Transport functions that offer even more functionality. For example, simply pressing Play will start playback at the current playhead position or at the beginning of a cycle, but there are also key commands for Play from Beginning to begin playback from the start of the song, Play from Previous Bar to begin playback one bar behind the current playhead position, Play from Selection to begin playback from the start of a selected region, and so on. You can use a key command to Stop and Go to Left Locator or to Stop and Go to Last Play Position, and there are key commands to increase or decrease Forward and Rewind speed. Assigning and using these and other Transport-related key commands will vastly speed up your workflow. Give them a try!

Mode Buttons

The mode buttons, which are located under the Transport buttons, toggle Logic's Playback and/or Record mode. Figure 5.3 shows the default mode buttons.

Figure 5.3   The Low Latency, Cycle, Autopunch, and Replace mode buttons.

If you have help tags enabled, holding the mouse over these buttons will reveal their functions. From left to right, here is a description of these buttons:

- **Low Latency.** This button engages Low Latency mode, which lets you limit how much plug-in delay you will incur when you record. If you are monitoring through Logic while recording with latency-inducing plug-ins running, you will need to click Low Latency mode on when you are recording and off when you are finished. Please see the subsection on Low Latency mode in the "Recording, Software Monitoring, and Latency" section later in this chapter.

- **Cycle.** This button toggles Cycle mode on or off. Basically, in Cycle mode, playback and recording repeat within a given range defined by the left and right locator positions. You can numerically input the boundaries of the cycle in the Locator display (see the "Locators" section later in this chapter), or you can graphically set the cycle boundaries in the Arrange window. The Cycle button has a shortcut menu that can be revealed by clicking and holding or Control-clicking on the Cycle button. Cycle mode and the Cycle button shortcut menu are explained in more detail in Chapter 6, "The Arrange Window."

- **Autopunch.** This button toggles Autopunch mode on or off. Autopunch mode, formerly known as *Drop mode,* automatically sends Logic into Record mode and Exit Record mode at predefined positions. You can set the locators by typing in numeric values for them in the Locator display or set them graphically in the Arrange window by dragging the red bar in the middle of the Bar ruler. You can also add special punch locators to the Transport if you choose to customize your Transport, which is covered in the "Customizing the Transport" section later in this chapter. Note that if you have both Cycle and Autopunch mode on, Logic will have two Locator displays and two white bars in the Bar ruler to represent the locator positions for each mode.

- **Replace.** This button toggles Replace mode for audio recording on and off. In Replace mode, any data you record onto a track will supersede previously recorded data on that track. In other words, if you record a region on a track, turn on Replace mode, and then record over that original region, the old data will be gone, and the new data will be all that is left on that track. If Replace mode is off, recording over a region on a track leaves the original region intact—the old region is still present but will not play back until you move it to an empty track. If you are using Replace mode and Cycle mode simultaneously, an existing region is only deleted on the first pass. As you continue to cycle, each subsequent pass is retained.

There are two more mode buttons: Solo and Metronome. Both of these buttons require the additional explanation provided in the following subsections.

The Solo Button

Next to the default mode buttons is the Solo mode button, which appears like an S in a box, as shown in Figure 5.4. When Solo mode is active, you may play back your song while only listening to those selected regions you wish to hear.

Figure 5.4   The Solo button. Click it once to turn Solo on. Click again to turn Solo off.

In Logic Pro, you have two ways to solo tracks or regions in the Arrange; you can select one or more regions and click the Solo button, or you can click the Solo button on a track to solo the entire track. You can also press the key command S to toggle solo on and off. If you press Shift while the Transport Solo button is engaged, you can solo the regions on multiple Arrange tracks by clicking in their track headers.

If Solo mode is active and all selected regions are being soloed, what if you want to select a region for editing or moving but you don't want it to be soloed? Logic facilitates this by offering a Solo Lock feature. If you Option-click the Solo button, you will activate Solo Lock, which locks the Solo function to those regions already selected. You can also access the Solo Lock function by clicking and holding or Control-clicking the Solo button and selecting Solo Lock from the shortcut menu that opens. Figure 5.5 shows the Solo button shortcut menu.

Figure 5.5   The Solo button shortcut menu, which contains the Solo Lock function. You can access this menu by clicking and holding or Control-clicking on the Solo button.

With Solo Lock active, you can go ahead and manipulate any other region without changing the solo selection. If you want to return to selecting only the soloed regions, you can assign a key command for Reselect Solo-Locked Objects.

When Solo is activated, the button and the Bar ruler glow yellow. When Solo Lock is activated, the button icon changes to a small padlock image with an S in it, as you can see in Figure 5.5.

The Solo function is one that spans multiple windows and has some deeper functionality, which will be explored in Chapter 6, "The Arrange Window," and Chapter 11, "Mixing in Logic."

The Metronome Button

The Metronome button, shown in Figure 5.6, turns the Metronome on and off in Logic. You can also press the key command C to toggle the Metronome on and off. The Metronome emits a constant click at the current song tempo.

Figure 5.6   The Metronome button. This turns the Metronome on and off and gives you access to the Metronome Settings dialog box.

If you hold the mouse button down over the Metronome button, Logic displays a pull-down menu that lets you open the Metronome Settings window.

Metronome Settings

The Metronome Settings window, shown in Figure 5.7, consolidates all the various settings that affect the Metronome. The MIDI settings can also be accessed from the Metronome object's Parameter box in the Environment. The Recording Settings window, covered later in this chapter, offers control of the Metronome on count-in or record pre-roll. You can also access the Metronome Settings window by clicking and holding the Metronome button and selecting Metronome Settings from the pop-up menu (shown in Figure 5.8), selecting File > Project Settings > Metronome, or selecting Metronome in the Settings menu in the Toolbar.

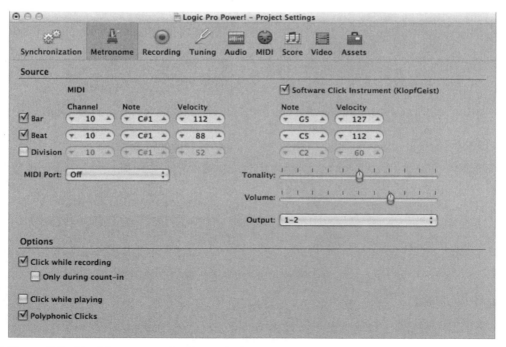

Figure 5.7   The Metronome Settings window.

Figure 5.8   Clicking and holding the Metronome button opens this pop-up menu.

All the parameters in the top left of the Metronome Settings window allow you to configure an external MIDI synthesizer to be your Metronome. You can set the MIDI port of a hardware synth; determine whether you want different MIDI notes to be played on the bar, beat, or division; and set the channel, note, and velocity of each Metronome note.

Most often, however, you will probably want to use Logic's internal click as a Metronome. It's not only more convenient, but because an internal Logic software instrument generates the click, the timing is always sample-accurate, which means that the beat will always occur precisely when the master digital clock tells it to occur, not early or late. To use the internal software instrument for your Metronome, check the box named Software Click Instrument (KlopfGeist) at the top right. KlopfGeist is the name of the Metronome software instrument in Logic. *KlopfGeist* translates literally to "knocking ghost"—so when you use it, you can honestly say there is a ghost in the machine!

As with the MIDI Metronome object, you can have different notes for different time divisions, and you can set the note and velocity. You also have a control for Tonality, which allows you to tone-shape the sound from KlopfGeist to a limited degree, and Volume, which sets the volume of the software instrument. Finally, you can select the output from which KlopfGeist will sound.

If you are using your computer's built-in sound, the Metronome Plays through Built-In Speakers check box enables you to choose whether to have your computer's built-in speaker emit a Metronome click. In general, if you use KlopfGeist, you do not need to select this option as well. In fact, if you check this box and then you check the KlopfGeist check box, Logic unchecks Metronome Plays through Built-In Speakers for you, under the assumption that you won't need both clicks.

Below these settings are check boxes that determine when you will hear the Metronome. If you select Click While Recording, you'll hear the click when you are recording. Selecting Click While Playing ensures that you'll hear the click when you're recording. These two options can also be selected in the Metronome button pop-up menu, as shown in Figure 5.8. If you select Only During Count-In, the click will play only during the count-in, or the measures before the recording begins.

You can set your click to be monophonic (one voice) or polyphonic (more than one voice) by checking or unchecking the Polyphonic Clicks check box. If you are using KlopfGeist, this setting will have no effect.

The Positions Display

To the right of the Transport buttons is the Positions display, shown in Figure 5.9.

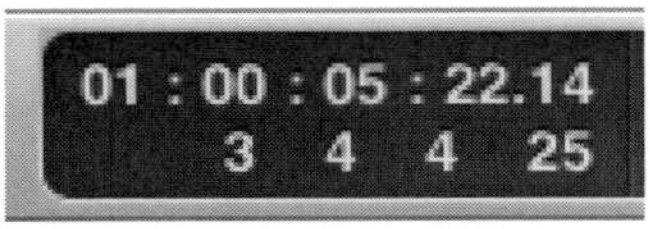

01 : 00 : 05 : 22.14
3   4   4   25

Figure 5.9   The Positions display, located to the immediate right of the Transport buttons.

The Positions display shows you a numeric representation of where the playhead currently is in your song. The top number is shown in SMPTE time format (hours: minutes: seconds: frames/subframes), and the bottom number is in bar position format (bar—beat—division—tick). SMPTE (*Society of Motion Picture and Television Engineers*) is the standard format used for synchronizing sound to pictures. The bar position format is so named because it follows the musical notation structure of bars and beats. This is the same format shown in the Arrange window on the Bar ruler, unless you choose to show SMPTE time format in the Bar ruler. SMPTE sync and the Bar ruler display modes are covered in detail in Chapter 15, "Synchronizing Hardware with Logic Pro."

Positions Display Format Preferences

You have some options in how you display the two formats. If you select Logic Pro > Preferences > Display, in the General tab are two pull-down menus that enable you to customize the display of the two formats. You can adjust the display of SMPTE time via the Display SMPTE pull-down menu shown in Figure 5.10.

Figure 5.10   The Display SMPTE pull-down menu in the Display Preferences General tab alters the way the SMPTE format appears in the Positions display.

These options change the way that SMPTE appears in the Positions display. You also can choose zeros to be displayed as spaces by checking the Zeros as Spaces box. Change the default SMPTE display only if you need a different format in order to synchronize your Logic song to a picture in that format.

If you pull down the Clock Format menu, Logic displays the various clock formats shown in Figure 5.11.

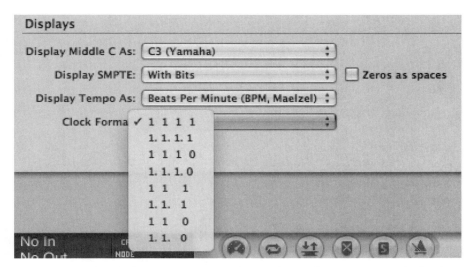

Figure 5.11   The Clock Format menu in the Display Preferences General tab. These parameters allow you to change the look of the clock in the Positions display to a different view.

These options allow the clock to take on a slightly different look. It's worth browsing through the different options here so you can find out which one you prefer working with. If you have a smaller screen, you might prefer the smaller numbers to save screen space, whereas if your screen is larger, you might prefer the larger numbers.

Using the Positions Display to Move the Playhead

The Positions display has another function in addition to offering a numeric visual reference to the location of the playhead. If you double-click one of the numbers, the display presents a text box, as shown in Figure 5.12. Enter the desired numeric location here, and when you press Return, the value of both numeric displays will change, and the playhead will jump to the specified location.

Figure 5.12   If you double-click on one of the numeric displays, the Positions display presents a text box in which you can enter a new playhead location.

You can also click and drag vertically on any component of either the SMPTE display or the clock display to move the playhead in those units. In other words, if you click and drag on the division area in the clock display, you can move the playhead backward and forward in divisions.

Locators

Directly to the right of the Positions display is a display window for the locators. Figure 5.13 shows the Locators display.

Figure 5.13   The locators are displayed numerically to the right of the Positions display.

The locators define the start and end for Cycle mode. As with the Positions display, if you double-click the numeric values, a text box appears in which you can enter the position of each locator. Also, as in the Positions display, clicking and dragging vertically on any component of either the start or end locator allows you to alter the position of that locator.

The Tempo/Project End Display

To the right of the Positions display is the Tempo/Project End display box, shown in Figure 5.14.

Figure 5.14   The Tempo/Project End display box.

The tempo value displays the tempo of the current song in either beats per minute (BPM), frames per second, or quarter notes per minute. You can choose how tempo will be displayed in the Display Tempo As pull-down menu in the General tab of Logic Pro > Preferences > Display, as shown in Figure 5.15.

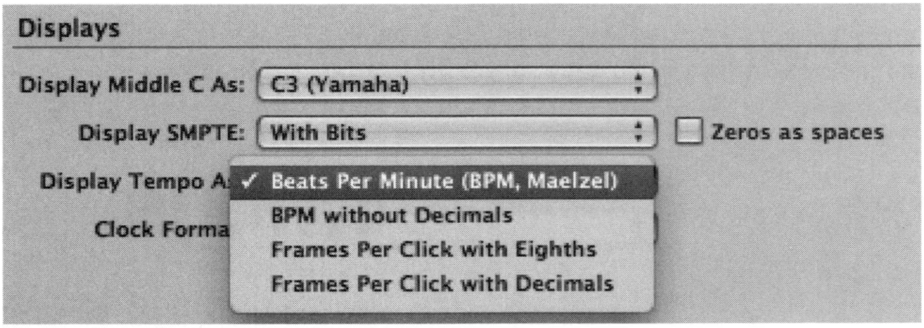

Displays

Display Middle C As: C3 (Yamaha)

Display SMPTE: With Bits   Zeros as spaces

Display Tempo A ✓ Beats Per Minute (BPM, Maelzel)
                   BPM without Decimals
Clock Forma   Frames Per Click with Eighths
                 Frames Per Click with Decimals

Figure 5.15   The Display Tempo As pull-down menu in Logic Pro > Preferences > Display (General tab).

Logic offers a BPM range of 5–990 BPM, with four-decimal-place precision, which should be enough tempo range for most users! You can change the tempo of the project inside the Transport in two ways—first, by double-clicking the tempo value to bring up a text box, then entering the new value; and second, by clicking on the tempo number and dragging the mouse up or down. Logic allows for more complicated tempo programming and changes using either the Tempo track in the global tracks discussed in Chapter 4 or the other tempo functions explored in Chapter 14, "Advanced Tempo Operations."

The Project End box below the Tempo display shows you the final bar in the song. When the playhead reaches this measure, Logic stops playback. You can double-click in this box to display a text box in which you can change the value or click and drag on the Project End box. The maximum project length in Logic is around 12 hours; exactly how many bars this will add up to depends on the time signature and tempo of your project.

The Signature/Division Display

To the right of the Tempo/Project End display is the Signature/Division display, as shown in Figure 5.16.

Figure 5.16   The Signature/Division display.

The Signature value represents the time signature at the currently selected measure in the project. You can add as many time signature changes as you like to your project using the Signature track as described in Chapter 4, or the Score Editor, which will be explained in Chapter 8, "Working with MIDI." If you want to remove a time signature change, simply change the time signature back to its original value.

The Division value lets you determine what note value will get the third position in the bar—beat—division—tick display. This also will affect the resolution of the Bar ruler in the Arrange window. You can also assign key commands to allow you to raise and lower this division value quickly.

The MIDI Activity Display

To the right of the Time Signature/Division display is the MIDI Activity display, shown in Figure 5.17.

Figure 5.17   The MIDI Activity display.

The MIDI Activity display gives you visual feedback as to whether Logic is sending or receiving MIDI events. If the MIDI events being sent are a chord, Logic's Auto Chord Recognition feature will show you the proper name for the chord, rather than showing you all of the individual notes. If your MIDI devices get stuck notes (in other words, they can't stop playing) or are otherwise unresponsive, you can click in the MIDI monitor to send a MIDI Reset command to them. If that doesn't work, you can double-click to send a MIDI Panic Off—basically, this will send individual note-off commands for every note on every channel.

The Load Meters

The load meters, shown in Figure 5.18, display the CPU and hard disk loads of your project in real time, as well as any Nodes you may be running.

Figure 5.18 The load meters display the CPU and hard disk loads of your project.

If you double-click on the load meters or press Option+X, you can open the System Performance window, which displays your project's loads in greater graphic detail in its own floating window. Figure 5.19 shows the System Performance window.

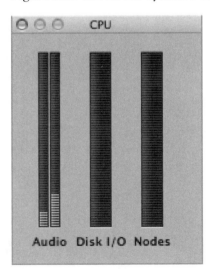

Figure 5.19 Double-clicking the load meters opens the System Performance window.

For some reason, while Logic saves the position of every window and every song setting with each project, it doesn't want to save the position of the System Performance window. So if you like to display it, you'll need to re-launch it every time you open your project.

The Transport Display Menu

If you Control-click in the Display area of the Transport, you can access the Transport Display menu, shown in Figure 5.20.

Figure 5.20   Control-clicking in the Display area opens the Transport Display menu.

Here is a brief explanation of the menu options:

■ **Big Bar Display.** Selecting this will change the Display area of the Transport into a large display of the current bar—beat—division—tick position. Figure 5.21 shows this display.

Figure 5.21   The Big Bar Display option of the Transport.

■ **Big SMPTE Display.** Selecting this option changes the Display area of the Transport into a large display of the current SMTPE position. Figure 5.22 shows this display.

Figure 5.22   The Big SMPTE Display option of the Transport.

■ **Open Giant Bar Display.** Selecting this option opens a separate, resizable window with a very large display of the current bar—beat—division—tick position. Figure 5.23 shows this display.

Figure 5.23   The Giant Bar Display option in the Transport Display menu opens a separate giant Bar display window.

- **Open Giant SMPTE Display.** Selecting this option opens a separate, resizable window with a very large display of the current SMTPE position. Figure 5.24 shows this display.

Figure 5.24   The Giant SMPTE Display option in the Transport Display menu opens a separate giant SMPTE display window.

- **Use SMPTE View Offset.** This option allows you to display a different SMPTE time for the start of your song than the true SMPTE start time that an external device is sending to Logic. For this to work, you need to check the Enable SMPTE View Offset option in the General tab of the Synchronization Settings window, accessible by selecting File > Project Settings > Synchronization, by selecting Synchronization from the Settings menu in the Toolbar, or by pressing Option+Y. You can then choose Use SMPTE View Offset. Synchronizing to external SMPTE is explained further in Chapter 15.

- **Display Locators as Time.** This option lets you view the Locators display as SMTPE, which you can see in Figure 5.25.

Figure 5.25   Selecting Display Locators as Time lets you view the Locators display as SMPTE.

The Master Level Slider

To the far right of the Transport is the Master Level slider. The Master Level slider, shown in Figure 5.26, is directly linked to the master channel strip in the Mixer, controlling the level of your entire Logic project.

Figure 5.26   The Master Level slider in the Transport.

Clicking the speaker icon to the left of the Master Level slider allows you to quickly lower the output level of Logic to a specified level, called the *dim level*. To change the dim level, open the General tab of the Audio Preferences window. There you can adjust the dim level by moving the Dim Level slider, by double-clicking in the Dim Level text box, by clicking the up and down arrows in the Dim Level text box, or by clicking and dragging in the Dim Level text box. The Dim Level Preference settings are shown in Figure 5.27.

Figure 5.27   The Dim Level settings in the General tab of the Audio Preferences window.

If you have changed the Master Level slider setting, you can quickly return it to 0.0 dB by clicking the speaker icon to the right of the slider.

Customizing the Transport

If you Control-click in an empty area of the Transport, the Customize Transport Bar menu shown in Figure 5.28 will open. The Customize Transport Bar option is also available in any of the other shortcut menus available in the Transport.

Figure 5.28   Control-clicking in the Transport opens the Customize Transport Bar menu.

Selecting Customize Transport Bar causes Logic to open the Customize Transport dialog, as seen in Figure 5.29. This dialog allows you to customize the display of the Transport. There are three columns in the Customize Transport dialog, which are directly related to the three different areas of the Transport. The Transport column allows you to customize what Transport buttons will be displayed. The Display column options affect the Display area. Finally, the Modes and Functions column gives you access to a variety of Mode area buttons.

Although there are many unique and valuable functions that you can add to the Transport via this dialog, covering all of them here would be impossible. Rest assured, most of these functions are covered throughout this book, and anything we don't cover can be found in the manual. That said, there is one very important mode button and one very important display mode, and one function that adds both a button and a display option accessible in the Customize Transport dialog that we will cover now.

The Sync Button

Selecting Sync from the Modes and Functions column of the Customize Transport dialog adds a Sync button, shown in Figure 5.30, to the Transport. Turning on Sync mode allows you to slave the sequencer in Logic Pro to external hardware, such as tape machines, external hard disk recorders, hardware sequencers, and any other device that is capable of sending compatible time code, as well as internal software applications that receive MIDI Clock via Core MIDI. If Logic is the slave, that means Logic is taking its tempo cues from the external hardware. If you don't have any external hardware that generates its own tempo, or if all your external devices are slaves and Logic is the master, you will not need to use Sync mode in Logic.

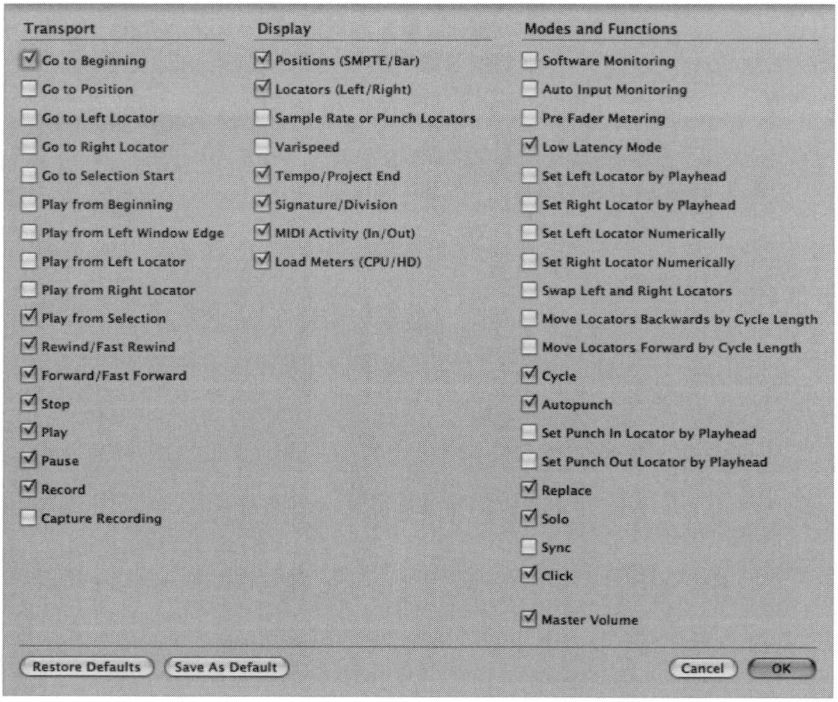

Transport	Display	Modes and Functions
☑ Go to Beginning	☑ Positions (SMPTE/Bar)	☐ Software Monitoring
☐ Go to Position	☑ Locators (Left/Right)	☐ Auto Input Monitoring
☐ Go to Left Locator	☐ Sample Rate or Punch Locators	☐ Pre Fader Metering
☐ Go to Right Locator	☐ Varispeed	☑ Low Latency Mode
☐ Go to Selection Start	☑ Tempo/Project End	☐ Set Left Locator by Playhead
☐ Play from Beginning	☑ Signature/Division	☐ Set Right Locator by Playhead
☐ Play from Left Window Edge	☑ MIDI Activity (In/Out)	☐ Set Left Locator Numerically
☐ Play from Left Locator	☑ Load Meters (CPU/HD)	☐ Set Right Locator Numerically
☐ Play from Right Locator		☐ Swap Left and Right Locators
☑ Play from Selection		☐ Move Locators Backwards by Cycle Length
☑ Rewind/Fast Rewind		☐ Move Locators Forward by Cycle Length
☑ Forward/Fast Forward		☑ Cycle
☑ Stop		☑ Autopunch
☑ Play		☐ Set Punch In Locator by Playhead
☑ Pause		☐ Set Punch Out Locator by Playhead
☑ Record		☑ Replace
☐ Capture Recording		☑ Solo
		☐ Sync
		☑ Click
		☑ Master Volume

(Restore Defaults) (Save As Default)   (Cancel) (OK)

Figure 5.29   The Customize Transport dialog allows you to create highly customized Transports, giving you access to a wide range of Transport buttons, Display area fields, and mode buttons.

Figure 5.30   The Sync button. Turn on Sync mode to slave Logic Pro to an external tempo.

If you click the Sync button, you will toggle the Sync mode. If you hold down the button, you access a menu of synchronization options. These options allow you to select the type of sync that Logic will send, give you access to tempo editors, and so on. Chapter 15 explains synchronization and Logic Pro's sync options in more detail.

The Sample Rate or Punch Locators

If you select the Sample Rate or Punch Locators option in the Customize menu, the Sample Rate or Punch Locators display is added to the Display area, as shown in Figure 5.31.

Figure 5.31   The Sample Rate or Punch Locators display.

If you do not have Autopunch mode engaged, then the Sample Rate or Punch Locators display shows the project sample rate. When you engage Autopunch mode, the display changes to show the punch locator positions, as in Figure 5.31.

The Varispeed Display and Button

Selecting the Varispeed option in the Customize Transport dialog adds the Varispeed display and Varispeed button to the Transport. Figure 5.32 shows a Transport customized to show the Varispeed display and the Varispeed button next to each other.

Figure 5.32   The Varispeed display and button.

Varispeed is a very powerful addition to Logic Pro 9, giving you the ability to speed up or slow down your entire project nondestructively and instantaneously. For example, you can use Varispeed to slow down the project a little bit to practice a part or speed it up to see how it feels at a faster tempo. Varispeed and the Varispeed display and button will be covered in the "Using Varispeed" section later in this chapter.

Hiding the Transport

Although the Transport is a very handy tool full of many important functions, there are times when you may want to hide the Transport. Perhaps you have all your necessary Transport key commands assigned and memorized, or you have a control surface that has all the necessary Transport controls configured. Maybe you're in the middle of a large project and you find you need the extra bit of screen real estate in the Arrange window that hiding the Transport would offer. Hiding the Transport is simple—you can drag the Arrange window down over the Transport with the Resize pointer shown in Figure 5.33; in the Arrange window's local View menu, you can select View > Transport; or you can assign the Toggle Transport key command.

Figure 5.33   You can hide the Transport in the Arrange window with the Resize pointer.

To show the Transport again, simply use the Resize pointer at the bottom of the Arrange window, access the View > Transport command from the Arrange window's local View menu, or use the Toggle Transport key command.

Opening the Transport Window

Having the Transport display directly in the Arrange window is convenient as long as you are working in the Arrange. However, there may be times when you are working in a screenset that doesn't include the Arrange window, or you may want to have multiple Transports open displaying different things, such as a conventional Transport, a Big Bar display, and a Giant SMPTE display. You can open separately movable, resizable, and configurable Transport windows by selecting Window > Transport from the global Window menu or by pressing Command+7.

Expert Tip: Opening More Than One Transport When Using Giant Displays   If you select the Giant SMTPE Display or the Giant Bar Display option, you will lose all the other functions of the Transport. But never fear: Logic allows you to open as many of each kind of window as you like, so you can also open up multiple Transports if you want. This way, you can open one Transport and configure it as a Giant Bar display, for example, and then open a second, fully featured Transport.

Resizing the Transport Window

To resize a Transport window, click and hold the mouse on the lower-right corner and drag the Transport to the desired size, as shown in Figure 5.34. Note that the Transport window can only be resized horizontally.

Figure 5.34   To resize the Transport window, simply drag the lower-right corner with your mouse.

Recording

For our purposes, the most basic definition of recording is capturing performances with Logic. Logic Pro offers a large number of recording modes and options. First of all, to record in Logic, you need to select a MIDI track or record-enable one or more Audio and/or Software Instrument tracks. (This is explained further in the next chapter.) If you are recording a single Audio track, the selected Audio track will automatically record-enable when you press Record. To activate the normal Record mode, simply click the Record button. After the count-in that is set in the Metronome Settings window, Logic begins capturing data. MIDI information and arrangement data (such as live recorded automation, tempo changes, and so on) are stored in the Logic project itself, while audio is saved onto your hard drive. All of this immediately shows up in the Arrange window of Logic. Figure 5.35 shows a recording in progress.

Figure 5.35   Logic Pro 9 recording away!

In the good (but featureless) old days, there was only one record option: Press the Record button, and the tape started rolling, ready to print your performance. However, we are in the software age, and Logic Pro offers myriad recording and monitoring options. If you hold down the Record button or Control-click it, Logic displays the pop-up menu shown in Figure 5.36.

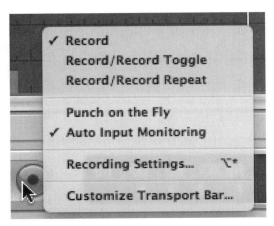

Figure 5.36   You access this pull-down menu by clicking and holding down on the Record button in the Transport.

Here is an explanation of the menu options:

- **Record.** This starts the normal Record mode. Selecting this is the same as simply clicking the Record button without accessing the Record pull-down menu.

- **Record/Record Toggle.** Record Toggle switches between Record and Playback modes. Accessing this command using the mouse during recording is very awkward; if you find yourself wanting to use this command, do yourself a favor and assign and use a key command for the action instead.

- **Record/Record Repeat.** This option starts recording at the previous drop or record-start point.

- **Punch on the Fly.** If you are recording audio, normally you set up a track and start recording from the beginning of the song, or you set recording to begin at predetermined drop locators. If you turn on Punch on the Fly, you can be in Play mode and simply switch into Record mode immediately. This is punching "on the fly" because you did not previously configure Logic to record at the specific location you chose. You should record on the fly sparingly because it's pretty taxing on your computer's resources to punch in completely cleanly without clicks or gaps. Instead, you should use the drop locators to set locator points in advance so that Logic can allocate and conserve the resources ahead of time. Also, keep in mind that even though you are punching in on the fly, you'll still need to have an Audio track record-enabled in order to record your punch-in.

Why Call It Punch-In?   The term *punch-in* comes from the fact that when recording to tape, in order to start recording on the fly, engineers would "punch in" (not literally) the recording head while the playback head was operating. With digital recording, there are no tape heads to punch, but Logic still has to switch instantly from Playback to Record mode, which in itself is quite a task.

Power User Tip   To do true "tape-recorder style" punch in/punch out without stopping and starting the sequencer, use the tandem of Punch on the Fly and Record/Record Toggle.

- **Auto Input Monitoring.** This allows you to monitor in Logic what is coming in through the hardware inputs when Logic is stopped and in Record mode. When in Playback mode, Logic plays any prerecorded audio regions on the Audio track that are record-enabled. You'll almost always leave this option on unless your audio hardware has a special monitoring mode or you want to free additional resources in the host computer. As we discussed in Chapter 2, keep in mind that whenever you are monitoring audio through software, there is some latency.

- **Recording Settings.** This brings up the Recording Options dialog box. You can also access this dialog box by pressing the key command Option+*, by selecting File > Project Settings > Recording, or by selecting Recording in the Settings menu in the Toolbar. The Recording Settings window is explored further in the next section.

The Recording Settings Window

The Recording Settings window, shown in Figure 5.37, presents a number of options to customize how you record with Logic.

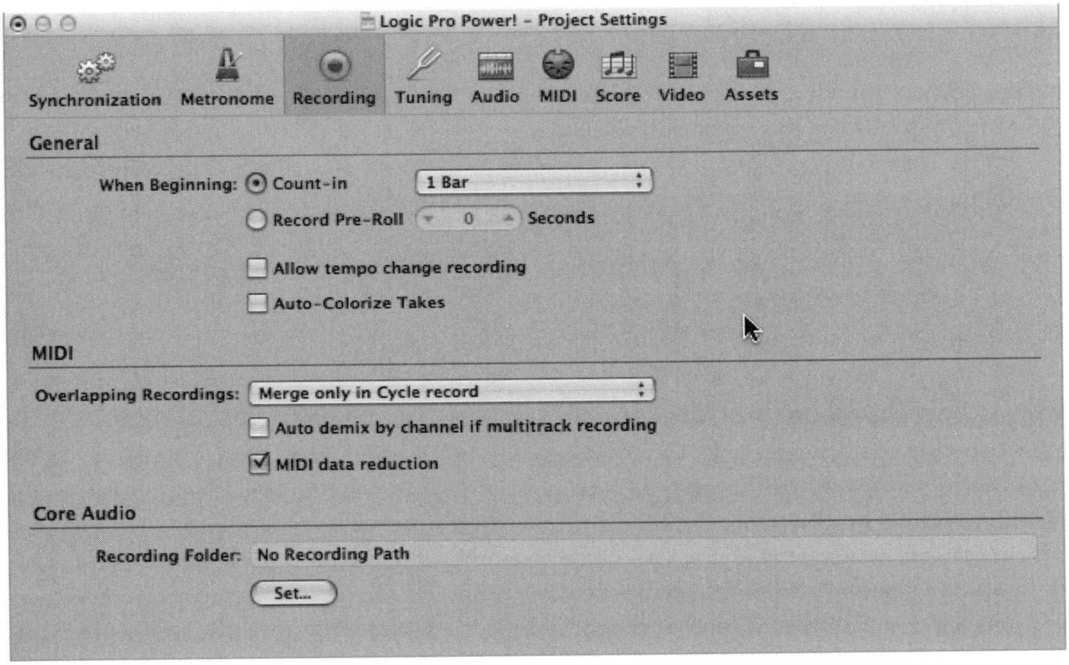

Figure 5.37   The Recording Settings window.

Some of these parameters are explained elsewhere in the book, and some parameters appear in other windows as well. Following are brief descriptions of some of these parameters:

- **Count-In/Record Pre-Roll.** Use these radio buttons to determine how many bars or seconds Logic will rewind the playhead when you start recording.

- **Allow Tempo Change Recording.** This option allows you to record tempo changes.

- **Create Take Folders, Merge with Selected Regions, and Merge Only in Cycle Record, Create Tracks in Cycle Record, Create Tracks and Mute in Cycle Record.** These settings all relate to MIDI recording only. Create Take Folders is covered later in this chapter. The rest of these options all control how Logic records when in Cycle mode. These parameters are defined in the "Cycle Mode" section of Chapter 6.

- **Auto Demix by Channel If Multitrack Recording.** If this option is selected and you are recording on more than one MIDI channel at a time, Logic will automatically create a new

MIDI track for each MIDI channel that is recorded. Each MIDI track that is created will contain a single MIDI region with all of the information recorded from that channel.

- **MIDI Data Reduction.** If this is checked, Logic filters MIDI information according to your specification. You can select which MIDI messages you want Logic to filter out by selecting Files > Project Settings > MIDI Options and configuring the MIDI Options dialog box's settings.

- **Recording Folder.** Clicking the Set button brings up a dialog box in which you choose the directory into which you will save the audio files for your project. The audio record path is saved with each project, so you don't have to define it more than once per project unless you want to change it. If you have not set an audio record path when you attempt to record your first Audio track in a project, it will bring up the Set Audio Record Path dialog box automatically. Keep in mind that you should not set an audio record path in your template; otherwise, Logic will automatically use that folder for all the audio you record for any subsequent projects.

Recording Using Key Commands

While Logic's menus offer a large selection of recording modes and parameters, if you want to record quickly, you should assign key commands to all of the modes, functions, and options that you access regularly. In addition, some powerful recording functions are available only via key commands; for example, Record Off for All—a key command that turns off the record status of all record-enabled tracks—is available only via key command. As you are starting to see, the more key commands you assign and use while recording, the faster and more efficiently you will be using Logic.

Method Tip: How to Record in Logic   Don't let all these recording options confuse you into thinking that basic recording of audio or MIDI in Logic is difficult. It's not. The basic procedure couldn't be easier:

- **To record audio.** Select one or more Audio tracks in the Arrange window. Record-enable the Audio tracks and start recording (via Transport button, key command, control surface, and so on). In order to arm more than one Audio track at a time, each track must be assigned to a different input.

- **To record MIDI.** Select a MIDI track and start recording.

- **To record MIDI and audio at the same time.** Record-enable one or more Audio tracks and then record-enable an External MIDI or Software Instrument track. With all your Audio tracks record-enabled and your MIDI track selected, start recording.

We'll discuss more about record-enabling Audio tracks in the next chapter.

Recording, Software Monitoring, and Latency

Whenever you are recording audio into a computer, you will have to deal with latency. Why? Physics, I'm afraid, and as Scotty told Captain Kirk so many times, "I cannot change the laws of physics!"

Here is the simplest explanation that we can give. When recording audio onto a tape machine, the instant the Record button is pressed, the record head engages the tape, and any material streaming through the record head is printed onto the tape. There is no delay inside that tape head; the audio material instantly streams through the record head.

When you record audio into a computer, first that audio is converted into a digital signal inside your audio interface. This process requires the interface to process a number of *samples* before it can stream the digital audio. (See "The Differences between Analog and Digital Sound" in Chapter 1 for the full explanation of digital audio, samples, and so on.) Then the digital audio streams into your Macintosh. It then needs to go through Mac OS X's system to get into Logic Pro. Core Audio, the Mac OS X audio system, also needs to hang onto a few samples' worth of information before it can pass it onto Logic. After that, in order to most efficiently process the streaming audio, Logic buffers the audio and processes it in chunks. How much time this takes depends on the size of the buffer. All these samples of delay are called the *recording latency*, or the time lag between when a sound enters your audio interface and when it ends up on the Arrange of Logic. The exact amount of time will depend on the total number of samples, divided by the sample rate at which you are recording.

The recording latency, however, is only half the story. If you want to hear what you are recording—in other words, to *monitor* your recording—you will have to deal with monitoring latency as well. There are basically two types of monitoring. The first, *hardware monitoring*, means that you monitor what you are recording *before* the signal passes through Logic. The second, *software monitoring*, means that you are monitoring your signal *after* it is recorded into Logic.

How Recording Latency Can Cause Recording Offset

Imagine this scenario: You are using a 4/4 drum loop in which every beat is exactly on the bar. You start recording. The first beat hits at 1.1.1.0. You play the part you wish to record exactly on time. However, your recording latency is 441 samples. If Logic were to place the digital audio at the exact point in the Arrange that it appeared in Logic, there would be a *recording offset*, or a difference between when the source audio was recorded and when the digital audio was placed on the Arrange, of 441 samples.

Thankfully, Logic is extremely smart regarding recording offset. All audio interfaces report how many samples they take to do their processing to Core Audio. Core Audio then adds to that number how many samples it uses to process the audio and passes that information to Logic. Logic takes that number from Core Audio, adds the setting of its own audio buffer to it, and then places that digital audio on the Arrange at the correct spot. So using our earlier example, Logic would figure out that there was a recording latency of 441 samples and place the audio back-wards at 1.1.1.0 on the Arrange, thus eliminating the record offset. Your performance is exactly in time with the drum loop!

However, not all audio drivers report the correct recording offset to Core Audio. In this situation, Logic does the only thing it can—it places the audio where it *thinks* it should, based on the inaccurate numbers it has to work with. If you play back what you just recorded and it sounds consistently off, as if your recording is consistently early or late, this may very well be the reason.

If you do discover that there is a recording offset, the first thing to do is to fire off an email to the manufacturer of your audio interface informing them of the problem. If you are an advanced user and have used the Logic Pro Sample Editor to count exactly how many samples of record offset there are, be sure to send that information as well. Hopefully, this will help the manufacturer write a new Core Audio driver that reports the correct sample delay.

Fortunately, you're not simply left at the mercy of the manufacturer. In Preferences > Audio > Devices > Core Audio, Logic offers a Recording Delay slider (see Figure 5.38). You can use this to manually adjust Logic's record offset correction amount. So if, for example, you have de-termined that all your audio is being placed 140 samples early, you can use this slider to delay the placement of the audio by 140 samples. If you determine that the audio is being placed 140 samples late, you can use this slider to subtract 140 samples. If you're not sure, just experiment with different amounts until you get as close to zero as you can.

Figure 5.38   The Recording Delay parameter in Preferences > Audio > Devices > Core Audio lets you manually adjust for record offset.

Hardware Monitoring versus Software Monitoring

As we stated in the introduction, you also have to deal with latency when listening to what you are recording. However, in this case one of the ways we can deal with it is to virtually eliminate it by using *hardware monitoring*. As stated earlier, this means that we are directly listening to the source we are recording in hardware, before it hits the Logic Pro software.

This can be done in a couple of ways. Most audio interfaces offer *direct monitoring* or *direct hardware monitoring*. This means that the interface sends the source audio signal both into your Macintosh and out of one of its hardware outputs. The audio that is fed directly from the audio input to the audio output incurs virtually no delay at all. We say "virtually" because there may still be a small delay from digital-to-audio and audio-to-digital conversion, but this will be neg-ligible. If your audio interface allows direct monitoring, there will be either a physical switch or button on your interface, or a software mixer included with your interface, to set this up. Read the manual for your audio interface for more information.

However, you might not have an interface capable of hardware monitoring. In this situation, you have two choices: Either buy an external mixer and send one signal from the mixer to your audio interface and another to your speakers/headphones, or use software monitoring. There are other reasons to use software monitoring, too. If you want to monitor through Logic's effects—for example, if you want to record your guitar using Amp Designer and Pedalboard as your guitar amp and effects—you have no choice but to use software monitoring. Also, when you monitor through hardware, you can't be sure exactly what the signal sounded like as Logic recorded it—perhaps your mic preamp levels were too high, and so on—but when you monitor through software, you are monitoring exactly what is going through Logic, so you can stop the recording immediately to fix any problems. Software monitoring can be engaged via the Software Monitoring check box in Preferences > Audio > Devices > Core Audio, shown in Figure 5.39; via key command; or via the Software Monitoring button on the Transport, if you have customized your Transport to include the Software Monitoring button.

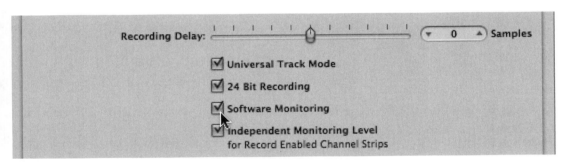

Figure 5.39   The Software Monitoring check box.

The major drawback to software monitoring is that all of the delay you incurred earlier, in the recording latency section, you incur again—the signal goes back through Logic's buffer, through Mac OS X, into your audio interface's converters, and so on. That means if you use software monitoring, your monitoring latency is double your record latency. Also, if you are using plug-ins that cause latency, software monitoring really messes with Logic's ability to compensate for record offset. Thankfully, this shortcoming of software monitoring can be addressed using Low Latency mode, explained in a moment, but in general, the drawbacks of software monitoring are severe enough that we *highly* recommend that when you record, you use hardware monitoring whenever possible.

Low Latency Mode
As explained earlier, Logic can correct for recording offset created by your audio interface, Core Audio, and Logic's own buffer. However, when you record through plug-ins that cause delay (plug-in delay is discussed in Chapter 11), that delay happens after Logic has internally

compensated for record offset. In other words, your recording will be placed on the Arrange late and won't sync up with the rest of your audio.

However, when Low Latency mode is engaged, Logic creates an alternate signal path that completely ignores plug-ins that cause more than a user-defined amount of delay. In other words, if you manually set the delay limit for 5 milliseconds, if there are plug-ins that cause more than 5 ms of delay in the signal path, turning on Low Latency mode will create an alternate signal path without those plug-ins.

This guarantees that the total plug-in delay of the entire signal flow of the selected channel, including any aux channel strips or output channel strips, stays under this user-defined maximum value. To set the maximum plug-in delay for Low Latency mode, open the General tab of the Audio Preferences window and adjust the Limit value in the Plug-In Delay area of the General tab. In addition to using the Low Latency Mode button, you can engage Low Latency mode by clicking the Low Latency Mode check box in the General tab of the Audio Preferences window, as shown in Figure 5.40.

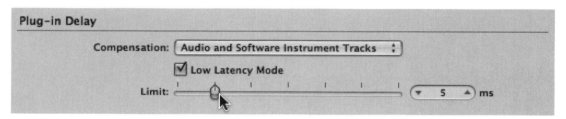

Figure 5.40 Set the maximum plug-in delay limit for Low Latency mode in the General tab of the Audio Preferences window.

With Low Latency mode engaged, your recording will be placed far closer to its "correct" position when recording through delay-causing effects. We say "closer" because depending on your latency threshold, there may still be some amount of offset, but not enough for you to notice.

You should be aware that engaging Low Latency mode will most likely change the sound of your track, perhaps drastically, since you are bypassing plug-ins that would otherwise be affecting the sound of your track. For this reason, you should *only* engage Low Latency mode very briefly, to specifically record tracks through delay-causing plug-ins when you have software monitoring turned on. If you are not using software monitoring, you will not need Low Latency mode. If you are not recording through effects that cause delay, you will not need Low Latency mode.

Software Monitoring and I/O Buffer Size
As explained earlier, when you record through software monitoring, your monitoring latency is double your recording latency. If this latency is too high, it will actively hinder your performers, because there will be a noticeable and jarring delay between the time an instrument is played or a lyric is sung and when that performance is heard back. Clearly you want your total monitoring latency to be as low as possible, to inhibit your performers as little as possible.

The main parameter you have to reduce latency is the I/O Buffer Size pop-up menu, found in Preferences > Audio > Devices > Core Audio and shown in Figure 5.41. The lower the buffer size you select, the fewer samples are processed at a time, and the less latency you will experience.

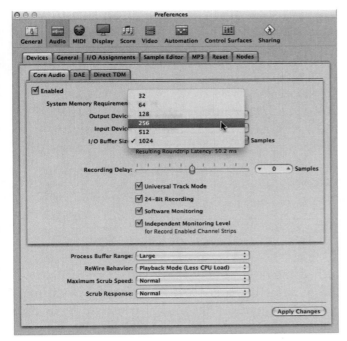

Figure 5.41   The I/O Buffer Size pop-up menu lets you choose the size of the audio buffer Logic uses when streaming digital audio into and out of Logic.

The temptation is to use the smallest audio buffer available, which is 32 samples. Unfortunately, not all audio interfaces can operate efficiently when the number of samples is too small, which can result in crackles and pops in your recorded audio. Also, the smaller the buffer, the more CPU power is required to stream audio into and out of your Mac. Depending on how much processing power your computer has and how much processing power your Logic project is using, setting your I/O buffer size too low can result in crackles and pops in your recorded audio, or overload errors, which will stop recording.

To help you determine what sort of monitoring mode to use and help determine what buffer size to use, Logic reports the total I/O latency in milliseconds beneath the I/O Buffer Size menu, as you can see in Figure 5.41. You can click on the Resulting Roundtrip Latency area, and it will change to display the Resulting Output latency, letting you know what your output latency is for the current buffer setting. While these things won't tell you exactly how to use your system, they can be beneficial aids in balancing what latency you incur at different buffer settings with your monitoring needs.

Logic Pro, Latency, and TDM Hardware   *Logic Pro 9 Power!* focuses on using Logic with Core Audio devices, but as we've mentioned before, you can also use Logic with Avid's Pro Tools|HD systems using the DAE driver in Logic. One of the main advantages Avid's Pro Tools|HD systems have is their ultra-low latency. In an HD system, the audio never goes through the computer—the audio is handled completely on the DSP cards installed inside your Macintosh. By cutting the computer out of the latency path, HD hardware latency is extremely small.

For example, native systems can rarely achieve practical, real-world monitoring latencies under about 6 ms, and that takes an exceptional amount of processing power. Logic systems running under the DAE audio engines routinely have latencies under 2 ms, and that is achieved without worries about I/O buffer size and with no loss whatsoever in processing power. Pro Tools|HD systems are incredibly expensive, but for those to whom low-latency recording is mandatory, using Logic with HD hardware is the answer. Unfortunately, these DAE systems are no longer supported as of Pro Tools|HD 8.0.3, although you can still use Pro Tools|HD hardware as a front end for Logic via Core Audio.

Recording Takes

In the world of multitrack recording, it's fairly common to record a particular section of a song repeatedly. Perhaps you are looking for a few different vocal recordings to work with on a chorus, or you would like to have a number of different piano solo options from which you can choose. You may even want to use multiple performances of the same section of the song to compile a single performance from the best bits of the different recordings. Recording multiple performances of the same material is known as recording *Takes*. With Logic's Takes recording, recording and managing audio and MIDI Takes has been simplified and streamlined to an amazing degree.

Recording Audio Takes

Recording audio Takes in Logic Pro 9 requires no special configuration—the ability to easily record, edit, and manage Takes is the default behavior in Logic. Why even cover recording audio Takes, then? Because how Logic handles audio Takes, and the things you can do with your audio Takes, such as Quick Swipe Comping (covered in Chapter 6), are likely to become integral parts of your workflow.

To record audio Takes, you need to either engage Cycle mode and record more than one pass in the cycle or record over at least 50 percent of an existing audio region. Logic automatically creates a Take folder for that region. An audio Take folder is a single audio file containing all your passes over a particular region. In the Arrange window, a Take folder resembles a typical audio region with three very important differences: There is a disclosure triangle in the upper-left corner of the Arrange region, there is an arrow in the upper-right corner that gives you access to the Take

Folder menu, and next to the Take Folder menu is the Quick Swipe Comping button. Figure 5.42 shows a Take folder in the Arrange window.

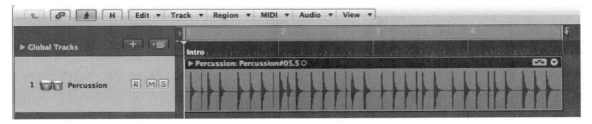

Figure 5.42   An audio Take folder in the Arrange window.

Opening an Audio Take Folder

Clicking the disclosure triangle in the upper-left corner of a Take folder opens the Take folder. You can also open a Take folder by double-clicking it or by using the key command Option+F. Figure 5.43 shows an open Take folder.

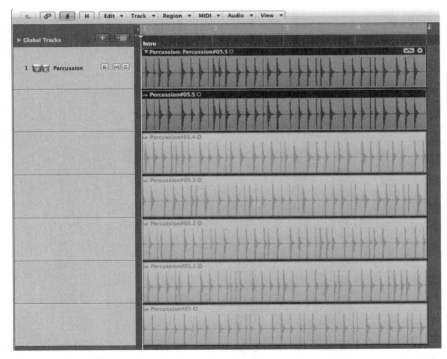

Figure 5.43   Clicking the disclosure triangle in the upper-left corner of a Take folder opens the Take folder.

You can select different Takes for playback in an open Take folder by clicking on the desired Take. Be aware that the top level still represents the actual Take folder, and the individual Takes are displayed below the Take folder. The last Take is displayed just below the Take folder, the first at the bottom. You can also select the desired Take from either an open or a closed Take folder by using the Take Folder menu or by Control-clicking on a Take folder. You can reorder Takes by dragging a Take onto the Take folder. That Take will now be the first Take in the Take folder.

The Take Folder Menu

Clicking on the triangle in the upper-right corner of a Take folder opens the Take Folder menu, as shown in Figure 5.44.

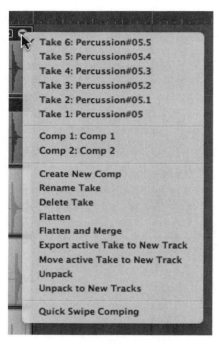

Figure 5.44   The Take Folder menu.

The functions of the commands in the Take Folder menu are as follows:

- **Takes and Comps list.** At the top of the Take Folder menu is a list of the Takes and Composite Takes, called *Comps*, in the selected Take folder. To switch Takes or Comps, simply select a different Take or Comp from the list.

- **Create New Comp.** This command saves a Comp you have created in a Take folder and adds it to the Takes and Comps list. If you have created a Comp, and the Comp is selected in the Takes and Comps list, this command becomes the Duplicate Comp command, which saves the current Comp and creates a duplicate of the Comp. Logic's new comping features will be covered in Chapter 6.

- **Rename Take/Comp.** This command opens the Rename Take or Rename Comp dialog, depending on whether you have a Take or a Comp selected. You can rename the selected Take or Comp in this window. Figure 5.45 shows the Rename Take dialog.

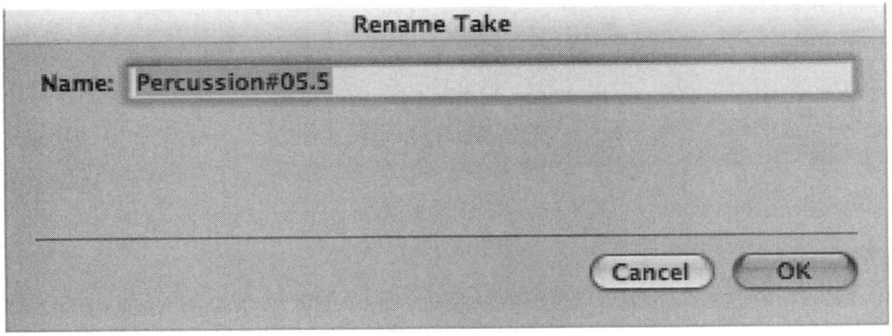

Figure 5.45   The Rename Take dialog. You can rename a selected Take in this window.

- **Delete Take/Comp.** This command deletes the selected Take or Comp.

- **Delete All Other Comps.** This command is only displayed if you have more than one Comp, and you have one Comp selected. The Delete All Other Comps command deletes all but the selected Comp.

- **Flatten.** The Flatten command replaces the Take folder with regions created from the Comp selections you have made to your Takes. The new regions are independent of each other and therefore can be moved, copied, pasted, and edited individually.

- **Flatten and Merge.** The Flatten and Merge command creates a single new audio region from the Comps you have made in your Take folder. The new region is the same length as its parent Take folder.

- **Export Active Take/Comp to New Track.** The Export Active Take to New Track command exports either the selected Take or the current Comp to a new Audio track utilizing the same channel strip as the parent track. Since the Take/Comp has been exported, the Take/Comp also remains in the Take folder.

- **Move Active Take/Comp to New Track.** The Move Active Take to New Track command moves either the selected Take or the current Comp to a new Audio track utilizing the same channel strip as the parent track. Since the Take/Comp has been moved, the Take/Comp no longer exists in the Take folder.

- **Unpack.** The Unpack command creates new tracks for each Take and each Comp in the selected Take folder utilizing the same channel strip as the parent track. The key command for this is Control+Command+U.

- **Unpack to New Tracks.** The Unpack to New Tracks command creates new tracks for each Take and Comp in the selected Take folder utilizing new channel strips for each new track, but with the settings of the parent track's channel strip. The key command for this is Control+Shift+Command+U.

■ **Quick Swipe Comping.** The Quick Swipe Comping option lets you toggle Quick Swipe Comping mode. When Quick Swipe Comping is engaged, you can create and edit Comps. When Quick Swipe Comping is disengaged, you can't create or edit Comps, but you can access Logic's full complement of editing features, including the new Flex Audio features. You can also toggle Quick Swipe Comping mode by clicking the Quick Swipe Comping button or by using the key command Option+Q.

Audio Take Folder Behaviors

Because recording Takes and creating Take folders involves recording over existing regions, there are some behaviors that are unique to recording Takes and to Take folders. The behaviors are designed to be helpful, but because there is a wide variety of ways you can employ Take recording, there are some specific guidelines you need to be aware of to understand recording Takes and utilizing Take folders.

If you are working on a project alone or you are having a musician perform the same section over a few times, then using cycle recording to record a section repeatedly has obvious benefits. As mentioned earlier, cycle recording an audio track automatically creates a Take folder after the second pass. What happens when you stop cycle recording? That depends on where you stop in the cycle. If you stop recording in the first bar of a cycle, Logic will automatically discard the "extra" bit that went into the next cycle and will truncate the recording to the end of the previous cycle. If you stop recording after the first bar of a new cycle, Logic will automatically add the small section of the new cycle with the previous cycle. This can be handy if you don't like what you played at the start of a cycle, and you decide you can fix it by playing into the next cycle.

If you have already created a Take folder on a track and you record over the Take folder, then the new region is automatically added to the Take folder. If your new region starts before or ends after the Take folder, then the Take folder is lengthened to match the length of the new audio region. If the new region begins and ends inside the boundaries of the Take folder, a new Comp is made of the new recording and the previous Take or Comp.

If you record over multiple Take folders in a single track lane, then the new audio file is split into separate Takes at the beginning of each Take folder, and the resulting Takes are added to those Take folders. If there were any gaps between the Take folders previously, the Take folders are lengthened to match their new Takes.

You can also add existing audio regions to a Take folder by simply dragging them to the Take folder and dropping them at the desired position. If the new region is the same length as the Take folder, then it is added as a Take. If the new region is longer than the Take folder, the Take folder is lengthened to match the length of the new region, and if the new region is shorter than the Take folder, a new Comp is created from the new region and the existing Take or Comp.

It is also possible to multitrack Takes. For example, suppose you need the bass player and the guitarist to record a few new Takes on the second verse of a song. You can record their Takes at the same time, and the new regions will be added to Take folders on their respective tracks, allowing you to create edits later.

Finally, you cannot record Takes with Replace mode engaged, because Replace mode discards any previously recorded audio.

Can I Disengage Audio Takes Recording?   Takes offer extremely powerful and intuitive organization and editing tools. Moreover, Logic 9 has improved Takes recording even further, allowing full editing capabilities. We love Logic's Takes feature and highly recommend that you learn to integrate it into your workflow.

However, for those who started using Logic before the Takes feature, you may be set on older ways of working. There is no preference to turn off audio Takes recording. However, once you have recorded audio, you can use the key command or Takes Folder command to unpack your Takes folder to new Audio tracks. If you are determined to never get used to Take folders, you can unpack every Take folder via key command as soon as it's created, even on the fly.

There have been complaints that the Takes feature can't be turned off, but frankly, these complaints are unfounded—this requires a grand total of one extra key press after recording. And again, we highly recommend everyone give Takes recording a chance—we believe it's worth the effort.

Recording MIDI Takes

Although there are similarities between audio Take recording and MIDI Take recording, there are some aspects of MIDI Take recording that are different. First of all, because the default behavior in Logic is to add any new events to an existing MIDI region when recording, you actually have to tell Logic that you want to record MIDI Takes. To do this, simply open the Recording Settings window by selecting File > Project Settings > Recording, select Recording in the Settings menu of the Toolbar, or press Option+*. In the Overlapping Recordings menu, select Create Take Folders. Figure 5.46 shows the Overlapping Recordings menu.

With Create Take Folders selected, recording in Cycle mode or recording over a MIDI region creates a MIDI Take folder. Figure 5.47 shows a MIDI Take folder.

Like audio Take folders, MIDI Take folders also have a disclosure triangle in the upper-left corner for opening the Take folder and a triangle in the upper-right corner for opening the Take Folder menu. Figure 5.48 shows the Take Folder menu.

As you can see, the functions in the Take Folder menu of a MIDI Take folder are identical to some of the functions in the Take Folder menu of an audio Take folder. You can reference the audio Take

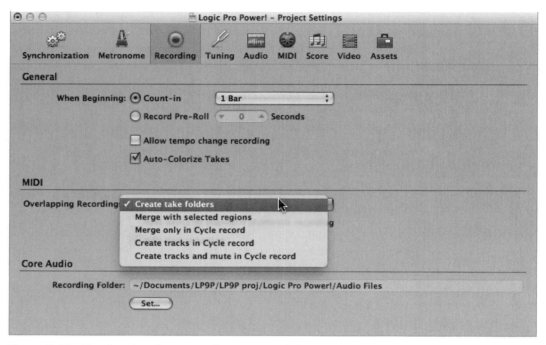

Figure 5.46 The Overlapping Recordings menu of the Recording Settings window. Selecting Create Take Folders allows you to record MIDI Takes.

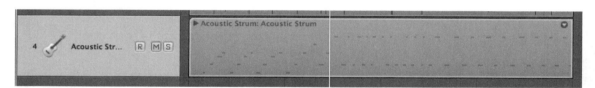

Figure 5.47 A MIDI Take folder.

folder menu section for an explanation of these commands; however there is one big difference worth noting. The Flatten command replaces the Take folder with the currently selected Take.

MIDI Take Folder Behaviors

Recording over an existing MIDI Take folder adds the new MIDI region to the MIDI Take folder. If you record over multiple MIDI regions, the existing regions will be merged and will show as the first Take, and the new region will show as the newest Take. If you are recording to multiple MIDI tracks, the regions will be merged into Take folders per track. Recording over existing MIDI Take folders will merge the existing folders into first Takes per track, and the new region will show as the newest Take.

MIDI Take folders do not share the comping functionality of audio Take folders. However, you can open individual Takes in Logic's powerful MIDI editors and use the editors to create your

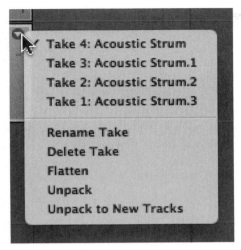

Figure 5.48   The Take Folder menu for a MIDI Take folder.

own MIDI Comps by selecting and deleting sections from different MIDI Takes to create the perfect performance! Logic's MIDI editors will be covered in detail in Chapter 8.

Auto-Colorizing Takes

By default, all Takes assume the color of the parent region. You can also colorize individual Takes using the Colors menu by selecting View > Colors (or clicking Option+C), selecting a color, and clicking on a Take. Logic also will automatically make each Take a different color when you select the Auto-Colorize Takes option in the General area of the Recording Settings window, shown in Figure 5.49.

Figure 5.49   When you select Auto-Colorize Takes, Logic automatically assigns a different color to each Take.

This is particularly helpful for keeping track of which Comp comes from which Take.

The Play Button Shortcut Menu

If you click and hold or Control-click on the Play button, the Play button shortcut menu opens, giving you a variety of options for what happens when you press Play. Figure 5.50 shows the Play button shortcut menu.

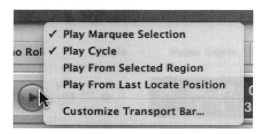

Figure 5.50   The Play button shortcut menu lets you control the behavior of the Play command.

The Play button shortcut menu options are:

- **Play Marquee Selection.** If you select Play Marquee Selection, playback will start from the beginning of your Marquee selection, and end at the end of your Marquee selection. Marquee selections and the Marquee tool will be covered in Chapter 6.

- **Play Cycle.** If you select Play Cycle, playback will start from the beginning of the cycle area when Cycle mode is engaged, and playback will continue to cycle until it is manually stopped.

- **Play from Selected Region.** If Playback from Selected Region is selected, playback will begin at the beginning of the selected region.

- **Play from Last Locate Position.** If Play from Last Locate Position is selected, playback will begin at the last point Play was engaged.

These are only some of the Play options available to you in Logic. There are more Play options available in the Key Commands window. You should check them out and maybe even assign a few you find useful to key commands.

The Stop Button Shortcut Menu

The Stop button has its own shortcut menu, accessible by clicking and holding or Control-clicking the Stop button. Figure 5.51 shows the Stop button shortcut menu.

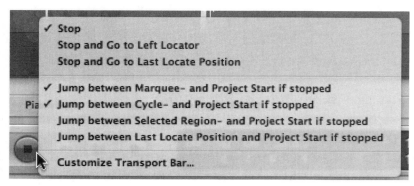

Figure 5.51   The Stop button shortcut menu gives you options to control the Stop command's actions.

The Stop button shortcut menu has the following options:

- **Stop.** With Stop selected, playback stops at the current playhead position when you press Stop.

- **Stop and Go to Left Locator.** If you select Stop and Go to Left Locator, the playhead moves to the left locator when you press Stop.

- **Stop and Go to Last Locate Position.** If you select Stop and Go to Last Locate Position, the playhead returns to the last locate position. For example, if you were playing a Marquee selection and pressed Stop with this Stop mode engaged, the playhead would return to the beginning of the Marquee selection.

- **Jump between Marquee- and Project Start If Stopped.** With Jump between Marquee- and Project Start If Stopped selected, you can toggle the playhead position between the project start and the start of your Marquee selection by pressing Stop.

- **Jump between Cycle- and Project Start If Stopped.** With Jump between Cycle- and Project Start If Stopped selected, you can toggle the playhead position between the project start and the start of your cycle area by pressing Stop.

- **Jump between Selected Region- and Project Start If Stopped.** With Jump between Selected Region- and Project Start If Stopped selected, you can toggle the playhead position between the project start and the start of your selected region by pressing Stop.

- **Jump between Locate Position and Project Start If Stopped.** With Jump between Locate Position and Project Start If Stopped selected, you can toggle the playhead position between the project start and the last locate position by pressing Stop.

Using Varispeed

As we mentioned earlier, Varispeed lets you alter the speed of your entire project instantly and nondestructively. Varispeed allows you to slow down a project by up to half, or speed it up to a maximum of double speed. To use Varispeed, customize your Transport to include the Varispeed controls. To turn Varispeed on, simply click the Varispeed button. You can then adjust your project speed by clicking and dragging the Varispeed value in the Varispeed display or by double-clicking the Varispeed value and entering a value manually. If you click on the top half of the Varispeed display, where the Varispeed mode is displayed, a menu opens, giving you a variety of Varispeed options. Figure 5.52 shows the Varispeed menu.

The Varispeed menu options are:

- **Speed Only.** If you select Speed Only, changing the Varispeed value only affects the speed of playback, not the pitch. This mode is best for checking how the project sounds and feels at different tempos and for practicing or recording difficult sections of a project.

- **Varispeed (Speed and Pitch).** With Varispeed (Speed and Pitch) enabled, Varispeed functions like an analog tape machine or a record player would, where speeding up or slowing down

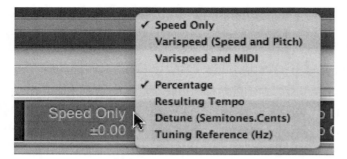

Figure 5.52   The Varispeed menu.

the playback also affects pitch. This mode is particularly good for working with vocal performances, slowing the speed and lowering the pitch a little to help a singer in more difficult sections. As the speed can be decreased up to half and increased up to double the original speed, slowing the speed down by half lowers the pitch an octave, and speeding it up to double raises the pitch an octave. Obviously, the further one gets from the actual pitch, the less desirable the results may be.

- **Varispeed and MIDI.** The Varispeed and MIDI mode transposes any MIDI tracks (other than drum tracks) to match the pitch change your audio incurs using Varispeed. If you are using MIDI tracks and trying to alter the speed and the pitch of the project, this is the mode to use.

- **Percentage.** Percentage displays the Varispeed value as a percentage of the original tempo.

- **Resulting Tempo.** Resulting Tempo displays the Varispeed value as the tempo that will result from the current Varispeed setting. This view mode is good for trying out new tempos.

- **Detune (Semitones.Cents).** Detune (Semitones.Cents) displays the Varispeed value as the amount of detuning incurred in semitones and cents.

- **Tuning Reference (Hz).** Tuning Reference (Hz) displays the Varispeed value as the actual tuning of the project compared to 440.0 Hz. This mode is great for working with instruments tuned to a different standard than A440 and having them fit in projects recorded with A440 as the standard tuning note.

Now that we have a good sense of how to use the Transport, how to use some of Logic's playback features, and how to record Takes, it's time to dig into the next chapter on the Arrange window, including more detail on comping.

6   The Arrange Window

The Arrange window is the central window in Logic. As we mentioned in Chapter 2, the Arrange window has seen some significant changes since Logic Pro 7. The Arrange window gives you integrated access to all the editors, browsers, and lists that were previously only available in separate windows. Here you create and manipulate all the various tracks of your project, along with those tracks' adjustable parameters. You can record data onto tracks in the Arrange page, and that data is graphically represented in track lanes as one or more regions. These regions can then be arranged (meaning manipulated into new organizations that do not necessarily reflect the original data organization), processed, and automated. You can use the Arrange to give you an overview of an entire project or a sample-accurate close-up of a few tracks. You can play your Logic project from beginning to end or set up project locators at any two points and just focus on your project from there. Figure 6.1 gives you a look at an Arrange window showing a selection of Audio and MIDI tracks along with their regions, some automation, a global track (an expanded Marker track), and the Bin and the Piano Roll Editor open.

You will find that you spend much of your time using Logic in the Arrange, so you'll need a solid understanding of what functions and features are available to you in here.

An Overview of the Arrange Window

While every different area in the Arrange window is covered in depth throughout this book, we will still touch on each area briefly before going into detail on the more "traditional" functions in the Arrange. With the exception of the Track List and the Arrange area, all other areas in the Arrange window can be hidden if desired. The Arrange window interface consists of the following different areas:

- **Arrange area.** The Arrange area is the central area of the Arrange window, where you find the Track List, global tracks, local menus, and track lanes. This is the area where you perform the bulk of your editing and arranging tasks. Figure 6.2 shows the Arrange area.

- **Toolbar.** The Toolbar is a customizable area that sits across the top of the Arrange window. In it, you can place mouse shortcuts for different commands and windows, and for the Lists and Media areas. The Toolbar will be covered in the section "Configuring the Toolbar" later in this chapter.

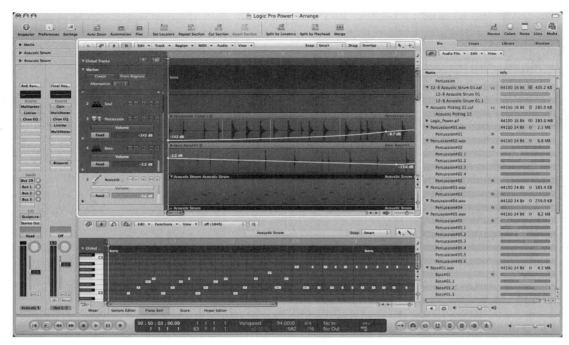

Figure 6.1   The Arrange window in Logic Pro 9. You will spend much of your time using Logic in this window, so getting comfortable with it will make your Logic experience a productive one.

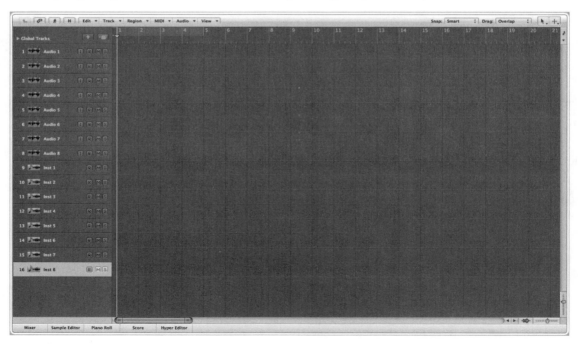

Figure 6.2   The Arrange area is where you will perform most editing and arranging tasks.

■ **Inspector.** The Inspector is found on the left side of the Arrange window. It consists, from top to bottom, of the Region Parameter box, the Track Parameter box, and the Arrange channel strips. You can toggle the Inspector by selecting View > Inspector, by clicking the Inspector icon in the Toolbar, or by pressing the key command I. Each component of the Inspector gives you some added control over individual tracks or regions in the Arrange. The different components of the Inspector are covered in detail in the "Track Parameters" and "The Arrange Channel Strips" subsections later in this chapter. Figure 6.3 shows the Arrange window Inspector.

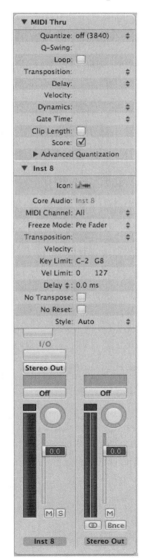

Figure 6.3   The Inspector contains the Region Parameter box, the Track Parameter box, and the Arrange channel strips.

■ **Notes area.** The Notes area is found on the right side of the Arrange window. The Notes area lets you create notes for individual tracks or for your project as a whole, making it very easy to create specific reminders for yourself or for your collaborators. Figure 6.4 shows the Notes area.

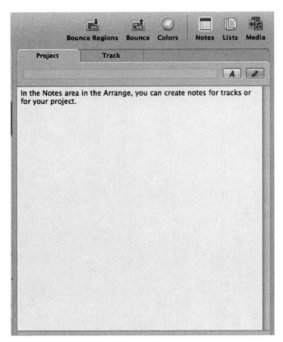

Figure 6.4   The Notes area of the Arrange window. You can create notes for individual tracks or for the project as a whole in this area.

■ **Lists area.** The Lists area occupies the same space as the Notes area. The Lists area is used for editing different types of data in a text-based interface. It contains tabs for the Event, Marker, Tempo, and Signature Lists, as seen in Figure 6.5.

■ **Media area.** The Media area occupies the same space as the Notes and Lists areas. Selecting a component of any of these areas while a component of the other area is showing automatically hides the first. For example, if you are working in the Event List in the Lists area and you open the Loops tab of the Media area, the Event List is hidden and the Loop Browser is shown. The Media area is a repository of browsers for different media files, such as audio files, video files, and effect presets. The Media area contains tabs for the Audio Bin, the Loop Browser, the Library, and the Browser, as seen in Figure 6.6.

■ **Transport.** At the bottom of the Arrange window is the Transport, which contains a variety of buttons and displays related to recording and playback. The Transport was covered in depth in Chapter 5.

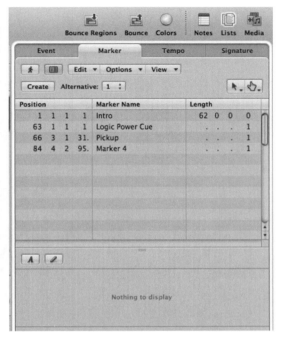

Figure 6.5   The Lists area of the Arrange window. Here you can access the Event, Marker, Tempo, and Signature Lists directly in the Arrange window.

■ **Editor area.** At the bottom of the Arrange area, right above the Transport, is the Editor area. The Editor area contains tabs for the Mixer, Sample Editor, Piano Roll, Score, and Hyper Editor. Figure 6.7 shows the Editor area.

Local Menus

Every editor and window in Logic has its own local menus. These menus conveniently contain commands users need within that window and editor. Keep in mind that some commands that can be used in a given window will not be in local menus because they are already located in the global application menus or because the given function is only available using key commands.

The following subsections describe the local menus in the Arrange window of Logic and the commands that they contain.

The Edit Menu

The Edit menu, shown in Figure 6.8, is the first local menu in the Logic Arrange page. An explanation of its commands follows. Whenever a key command is defined by default, we have listed it at the end of the definition. Remember that even for menu commands that do not have default key commands assigned, you can assign one yourself in the Key Commands window.

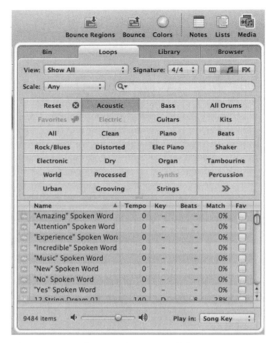

Figure 6.6   The Media area of the Arrange window. Here you can access the Audio Bin, the Loop Browser, the Library, and the Browser.

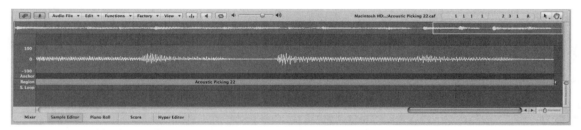

Figure 6.7   The Editor area of the Arrange window gives you access to the Mixer, Sample Editor, Piano Roll, Score, and Hyper Editor via the buttons in the bottom-left corner of the Editor area. In this figure, the Sample Editor is open in the Editor area.

Following are descriptions of each command in the Edit menu:

- **Undo.** This command will undo the last action in Logic. Be careful about relying on Undo, however, since not every action can be undone. If an action cannot be undone, this command is grayed out and changes to Can't Undo. The key command is Command+Z.

- **Redo.** This will redo the option previously undone. Be careful about relying on Redo, however, since you cannot redo every option that you can undo. If an action cannot be redone, this command is grayed out and changes to Can't Redo. The key command is Shift+Command+Z.

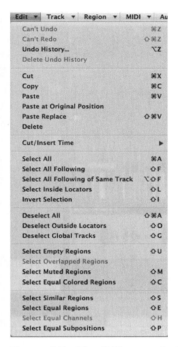

Edit ▾	Track ▾	Region ▾	MIDI ▾	Au
Can't Undo			⌘Z	
Can't Redo			⇧⌘Z	
Undo History...			⌥Z	
Delete Undo History				
Cut			⌘X	
Copy			⌘C	
Paste			⌘V	
Paste at Original Position				
Paste Replace			⇧⌘V	
Delete				
Cut/Insert Time			▶	
Select All			⌘A	
Select All Following			⇧F	
Select All Following of Same Track			⌥⇧F	
Select Inside Locators			⇧L	
Invert Selection			⇧I	
Deselect All			⇧⌘A	
Deselect Outside Locators			⇧O	
Deselect Global Tracks			⇧G	
Select Empty Regions			⇧U	
Select Overlapped Regions				
Select Muted Regions			⇧M	
Select Equal Colored Regions			⇧C	
Select Similar Regions			⇧S	
Select Equal Regions			⇧E	
Select Equal Channels			⇧H	
Select Equal Subpositions			⇧P	

Figure 6.8   The Edit menu in the Arrange.

- **Undo History.** Logic has more than a single level of undo. Logic offers multiple undo, meaning that Logic will maintain a list of undoable actions, and you can choose to undo any or all of them at any point. And this does mean at *any* point—your undo list is saved with your project, so the list of all your undoable actions is always available (unless you choose to delete it; see the description of Delete Undo History). You determine how many levels deep your Undo History will be via a preference found in the Editing tab of the General Preferences, which you can access by selecting Logic Pro > Preferences > General or by selecting General in the Preferences menu in the Toolbar. The default is 30 steps, but you can choose any number up to 200 steps.

When you select this command, you are presented with the Undo History window shown in Figure 6.9.

The obvious features of the Undo History window are a list of your previous actions in Logic and two buttons in the bottom-left corner: a button labeled Undo and a button labeled Redo. Notice that as you click on an option inside the window, that option is highlighted. You can change what step you have highlighted by either clicking on another step or using the up and down arrows. The actions above the selection appear as normal, and those below the selection are grayed out. This means that if you were to click the Undo button, all of the options below the line would be undone. If you want to redo those actions, clicking the Redo button will redo them. Clicking Undo or Redo will move the highlighted area up or down a step accordingly. Keep in mind that you can redo what you have just undone only if you have not

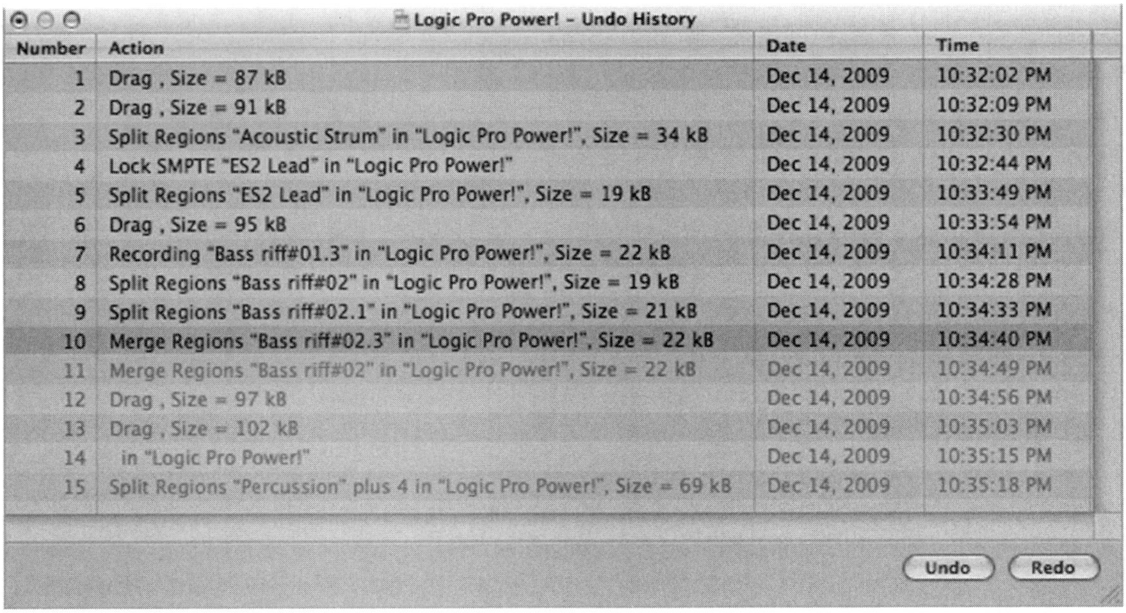

Number	Action	Date	Time
1	Drag , Size = 87 kB	Dec 14, 2009	10:32:02 PM
2	Drag , Size = 91 kB	Dec 14, 2009	10:32:09 PM
3	Split Regions "Acoustic Strum" in "Logic Pro Power!", Size = 34 kB	Dec 14, 2009	10:32:30 PM
4	Lock SMPTE "ES2 Lead" in "Logic Pro Power!"	Dec 14, 2009	10:32:44 PM
5	Split Regions "ES2 Lead" in "Logic Pro Power!", Size = 19 kB	Dec 14, 2009	10:33:49 PM
6	Drag , Size = 95 kB	Dec 14, 2009	10:33:54 PM
7	Recording "Bass riff#01.3" in "Logic Pro Power!", Size = 22 kB	Dec 14, 2009	10:34:11 PM
8	Split Regions "Bass riff#02" in "Logic Pro Power!", Size = 19 kB	Dec 14, 2009	10:34:28 PM
9	Split Regions "Bass riff#02.1" in "Logic Pro Power!", Size = 21 kB	Dec 14, 2009	10:34:33 PM
10	Merge Regions "Bass riff#02.3" in "Logic Pro Power!", Size = 22 kB	Dec 14, 2009	10:34:40 PM
11	Merge Regions "Bass riff#02" in "Logic Pro Power!", Size = 22 kB	Dec 14, 2009	10:34:49 PM
12	Drag , Size = 97 kB	Dec 14, 2009	10:34:56 PM
13	Drag , Size = 102 kB	Dec 14, 2009	10:35:03 PM
14	in "Logic Pro Power!"	Dec 14, 2009	10:35:15 PM
15	Split Regions "Percussion" plus 4 in "Logic Pro Power!", Size = 69 kB	Dec 14, 2009	10:35:18 PM

Figure 6.9   The Undo History window. In this example, you can undo action 10 and below by clicking the Undo button. If you undo these actions, you can redo them by clicking the Redo button.

already gone ahead and performed other actions. If you have, these new actions start where your Undo action left off, and you'll no longer have Redo as an option. As with the single Undo and Redo commands, not every action will appear in your Undo History, as not every action can be undone or redone. The key command is Option+Z.

■ **Delete Undo History.** This option completely empties the Undo History window for the project. After this, no previous actions will be undoable. The Undo History window immediately starts recording all undoable actions after the Delete Undo History command, and those subsequent actions remain undoable until the next time you select Delete Undo History.

■ **Cut.** The Cut command removes the contents of any selection you make in a text box or track lane of the Arrange and places it onto the Clipboard. You can then use the Paste command to replace the Cut selection. The key command for the Cut function is Command+X.

■ **Copy.** The Copy command copies the contents of any selection you make in a text box or track lane of the Arrange and places it onto the Clipboard. The original data is not removed. You can then use the Paste command to insert a copy of the data on the Clipboard. The key command for the Copy function is Command+C.

■ **Paste.** Paste inserts the data from the Clipboard at the current playhead location. Keep in mind that if you have text on the Clipboard, you have to paste it into a text window, and if you have a region from a track lane on the Clipboard, you cannot paste that into a text box. The key command is Command+V.

- **Paste at Original Position.** If you select Paste at Original Position, the regions on the Clipboard will be pasted to the exact position they were cut or copied from, instead of being inserted at the current project location.

- **Paste Replace.** Instead of inserting the regions from the Clipboard at a given location, Paste Replace overwrites any regions that occur at the same point in the timeline with regions from the Clipboard. The key command is Shift+Command+V.

- **Delete.** Delete erases any currently selected regions. The key command is, obviously, Delete.

- **Cut/Insert Time.** The Cut/Insert Time submenu is covered later in this chapter, in "The Cut/Insert Time Submenu" section.

- **Select All.** This command selects all regions on every Arrange track lane. The key command is Command+A.

- **Select All Following.** If you select a region on the Arrange, this command selects all other regions on every Arrange track lane beyond the selected region. This command does not select any region whose starting point comes before your originally selected region, even if the end of the region extends to (or past) the selected region. The key command is Shift+F.

- **Select All Following of Same Track.** If you select a region on the Arrange, this command selects all other regions beyond the selected region on the same Arrange track lane. This command does not select any region whose starting point comes before your originally selected region, even if the end of those regions extends to (or past) the selected region. The key command is Option+Shift+F.

- **Select Inside Locators.** This command selects all regions that are between the left and right locators. The key command is Shift+L.

- **Invert Selection.** This powerful command toggles the selection status of regions on the Arrange. In other words, if you currently have four regions selected, this command deselects those four regions and selects every other region on the Arrange. The key command is Shift+I.

- **Deselect All.** Any selected regions will be deselected with this command. The key command is Shift+Command+A.

- **Deselect Outside Locators.** When you select this command, any regions you've previously selected outside the left and right locators will be deselected. Regions between the two locators will be unaffected. The key command is Shift+O.

- **Deselect Global Tracks.** This command will deselect any global tracks and/or global events on global tracks that have been selected. The key command is Shift+G.

- **Select Empty Regions.** If you have regions that do not contain any data, this command selects them. Because empty regions don't often serve much purpose, this command is often used in tandem with Delete (or the Delete key) to remove unnecessary regions from the Arrange window. The key command is Shift+U.

- **Select Overlapped Regions.** This command selects every region that is overlapping (or overlapped by) another region.

- **Select Muted Regions.** You can use this command to select all the regions that you have previously muted in the Arrange. The key command is Shift+M.

- **Select Equal Colored Regions.** If you are using color to organize your tracks in the Arrange window, this command will select all the regions that have the same color. The key command is Shift+C.

- **Select Similar Regions.** If you select a region, this command selects regions that process the same type of MIDI data as the one you have selected. The key command is Shift+S.

- **Select Equal Regions.** If you select a region, this command selects regions identical to the region you have selected. (For example, if you have copied and pasted a region a number of times, this will select each of the copied regions.) The key command is Shift+E.

- **Select Equal Channels.** This command selects all regions that are of the same type (audio or MIDI) or on the same MIDI channel as a region you have selected. The key command is Shift+H.

- **Select Equal Subpositions.** To use this command, first select a region that is at the desired relative position in a bar of your project—for example, on the first downbeat. After that, if you choose Select Equal Subpositions, all regions at that relative position—in this example, at the first downbeat of a bar—will be selected. The key command is Shift+P.

The Track Menu

The Track menu is the local menu on the Arrange that contains many of the commands regarding the creation, deletion, and sorting of tracks. Figure 6.10 shows the Track menu of the Arrange window.

Explanations of the Track menu commands follow:

- **Track Automation.** The Track Automation submenu offers a number of options for working with track automation and is covered in depth in Chapter 10, "Using Automation in Logic."

- **New.** This command opens the New Tracks dialog, where you can create new Audio, Software Instrument, and External MIDI tracks. The New Tracks dialog was covered in detail in Chapter 3. The key command is Option+Command+N.

- **New with Duplicate Setting.** This command creates a track directly below the currently selected track. The track created is a duplicate of the selected track, including input and output assignments, the channel strip format, and any channel strip settings used. New tracks will be numbered sequentially starting from the last track of that type created. In other words,

Figure 6.10 The Track menu of the Arrange window.

if you created 24 Audio tracks, but you decide to duplicate Track 17, your new duplicate tracks will begin with number 25. You can also use the New with Duplicate Setting button at the top of the Track List, next to the New Tracks button. The key command is Command+D.

- **New with Next MIDI Channel.** This command creates a new Software Instrument or External MIDI track directly below the currently selected Software Instrument or External MIDI track and sets the MIDI channel to the next MIDI channel, in ascending order. If the selected track's MIDI channel is set to All, the new track will be set to MIDI channel 1. If the selected track's MIDI channel is set to 16, the new track will be set to MIDI channel 1. The key command for this is Option+Command+M.

- **New with Next Channel Strip/Instrument.** This command creates a track directly below the selected track. The created track follows the selected Environment object in sequence, even if the Track List already contains a track that follows the selected instrument sequentially. In other words, if you select Audio 5, using this command creates Audio 6, even if the next track already on the Track List is Audio 6. The key command is Option+Command+X.

- **New with Same Channel Strip/Instrument.** This command creates a track below the selected track that is literally identical to the selected track in every way. The key command is Option+Command+Return.

- **New for Overlapped Regions.** If you select a number of regions on a track lane that overlap, this command creates one new track for each region.

■ **New for Selected Regions.** Similar to the New for Overlapped Regions command, this command creates a new track for each region you have selected. This command does not require regions to be overlapping.

■ **Drum Replacement/Doubling.** The Drum Replacement/Doubling command lets you easily replace or double a drum track with sampled drum sounds. The Drum Replacement/Doubling command will be covered in the "Replacing and Doubling Drum Tracks" section later in this chapter.

■ **Bounce Track in Place.** The Bounce Track in Place command lets you bounce an Audio or Software Instrument track, including all effects and automation, and have the resulting bounce automatically replace the original track data. The Bounce Track in Place command will be covered in the "Bouncing Tracks in Place" section later in this chapter.

■ **Bounce-Replace All Tracks.** The Bounce-Replace All Tracks command performs a bounce in place for all Audio and Software Instrument tracks, including all effects and automation. This command will be covered in the "Bouncing All Tracks in Place" section later in this chapter.

■ **Delete.** This command deletes a track from the Track List.

■ **Delete Unused.** This command deletes any track from the Track List that does not have any regions in its track lane.

■ **Create Track Name.** This command presents you with a text box to enter a name for the selected track in the track header.

■ **Delete Track Name.** This command erases the name of the selected track.

■ **Sort Tracks By.** This option opens a hierarchal menu of track sorting options, as shown in Figure 6.11.

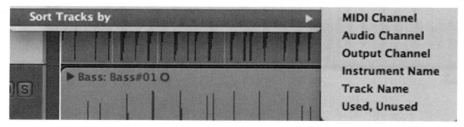

Figure 6.11   The Sort Tracks By submenu of the Track menu.

The Sort Tracks By options are:

■ **MIDI Channel.** If you choose this option, Logic sorts all the tracks in your Track List in order of their MIDI channel. Even audio channels will be sorted in order of the MIDI channel in their Parameter box.

- **Audio Channel.** This option sorts Audio tracks by their audio channel. MIDI channels, which don't have an audio channel, will be sorted to the top of your Track List.

- **Output Channel.** This option sorts Audio tracks by their output channel. Tracks assigned to the same output will be sorted alphabetically. MIDI channels, which don't have an audio channel, will be sorted to the top of your Track List.

- **Instrument Name.** This option sorts tracks alphabetically by instrument name. This option only works if you have selected View > Instrument Name.

- **Track Name.** This option sorts tracks alphabetically by track name. This option only works if you have selected View > Track Name.

- **Used, Unused.** This option sorts tracks into groups that are used and that are not used.

The Region Menu

The Region local menu contains commands and subfolders of commands that act on regions in the Arrange window. Figure 6.12 shows the Region local menu.

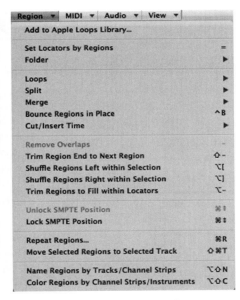

Figure 6.12 The Region local menu.

As you can see, this local menu contains a fair number of submenus filled with commands. Following are descriptions of the Region menu commands, as well as its submenus and commands.

- **Add to Apple Loops Library.** This command allows you to add a selected region to the Apple Loops library as an Apple Loop. The Add to Apple Loops Library command is covered in detail in Chapter 7, "Working with Audio and Apple Loops."

■ **Set Locators by Regions.** This command moves the left locator to the leftmost boundary of the leftmost region you have selected and the right locator to the rightmost boundary of the rightmost region you have selected. The key command is =.

■ **Folder submenu.** See the following "Folder Submenu" subsection.

■ **Loops submenu.** See the following "Loops Submenu" subsection.

■ **Split submenu.** See the following "Split Submenu" subsection.

■ **Merge submenu.** See the following "Merge Submenu" subsection.

■ **Bounce Regions in Place.** The Bounce Regions in Place command bounces the selected regions, including all effects and automation, and automatically replaces them with the resulting bounce files. Bouncing regions in place will be covered in the "Bouncing Regions in Place" section later in this chapter.

■ **Cut/Insert Time submenu.** See the following "Cut/Insert Time Submenu" subsection.

■ **Remove Overlaps.** If you have overlapping regions on your track, this command shortens the length of the earlier region to stop at the beginning of the later region. The key command is - (hyphen).

■ **Trim Region End to Next Region.** This command extends all selected regions so that they end at exactly the beginning of the subsequent region on the track. For audio regions, this only works if the audio file is long enough for the region to extend to the beginning of the subsequent region. The key command is Shift+-.

■ **Shuffle Regions Left within Selection.** This command does not alter the length of the selected regions, but Logic will move all subsequent regions so that they begin precisely at the end of the previous region. The key command is Option+[.

■ **Shuffle Regions Right within Selection.** This command does not alter the length of the selected regions either, but Logic will move all regions right so that they begin precisely at the beginning of the next region. The key command is Option+].

■ **Trim Regions to Fill within Locators.** This command elongates all regions between the locators on the same track so there are no gaps between them. The key command is Option+ . When applied to regions on separate tracks, the regions will simply be extended to the locators.

■ **Unlock SMPTE Position.** This command unlocks the selected regions from their SMPTE position. At this point, these regions are tied to their bar position, like every other region. The key command is Command+Page Up.

■ **Lock SMPTE Position.** This command locks any selected region to its SMPTE position, so that any changes in bar length, tempo, meter, and so on will not affect those regions' time positions, even as their bar location changes. The key command is Command+Page Down.

- **Repeat Regions.** This command repeats the selected region. It presents a small dialog box for you to select the number of repetitions, if you want real or alias copies, and if you want to quantize the copies (in other words, force the repeats to end on an exact bar line, even if the original does not). The key command is Command+R.

- **Move Selected Regions to Selected Track.** If you have a track selected in the Track List and then you select one or more regions on different track lanes, this command moves all the regions you have selected to the selected track. The key command is Shift+Command+T.

- **Name Regions by Tracks/Channel Strips.** When you select a track and then use this command, all of the regions on that track will be given the name of the track. The key command is Option+Shift+N.

- **Colors Regions by Channel Strips/Instruments.** When you select a track and then use this command, all of the regions on that track will be given the same color as the track. The key command is Option+Shift+C.

Folder Submenu

Logic Pro uses two different kinds of folders. Folder tracks are tracks that are containers for the data of one or more other tracks. This allows you to organize tracks into their own little Arrange window groups and move and edit the entire group as a single track. With Folder tracks, for example, you could keep your "main" Arrange window organized by creating Folder tracks for all your drum loops, synth lines, backup vocals, and so on. We will explain Folder tracks in more depth later in this chapter.

Folders are also used for recording *Takes*. Takes are multiple recordings of the same section of a project on the same track. Take recording and Take folders were covered in Chapter 5. The Folder submenu, shown in Figure 6.13, contains commands that operate on Folder tracks and Take folders.

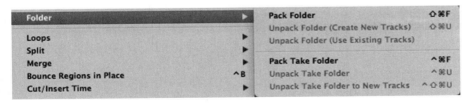

Figure 6.13 The Folder submenu of the Region local menu.

The commands in the Folder submenu are as follows:

- **Pack Folder.** This command combines all the selected tracks into a single Folder track. The key command is Shift+Command+F.

- **Unpack Folder (Create New Tracks).** When you select a Folder track, this command removes each track from the folder and creates a new track in your Track List for each track in the folder. The key command is Shift+Command+U.

- **Unpack Folder (Use Existing Tracks).** This command also removes each track from the selected folder. If you do not have any existing tracks on your Arrange that match the Folder track, it creates new tracks. If empty tracks already exist that match the name of the Folder track, it places the contents of each track on the matching empty track.

- **Pack Take Folder.** The Pack Take Folder command places all selected regions in a new Take folder. Take folders were covered in more detail in Chapter 5. The key command for this is Control+Command+F.

- **Unpack Take Folder.** This command unpacks a Take folder to new tracks, all using the same channel strip. The key command for this is Control+Command+U.

- **Unpack Take Folder to New Tracks.** This command unpacks a Take folder to new tracks, all with their own channel strips but with the original track's channel strip setting. The key command for this is Control+Shift+Command+U.

The Loops Submenu

These commands relate to functions you can access inside a region's Parameter box, such as looping. Figure 6.14 shows the Loops submenu of the Region menu.

Figure 6.14   The Loops submenu of the Region local menu.

There are only two commands in the Loops submenu:

- **Convert to Real Copies.** This command turns any loops of the selected region into an actual copy of the selected region. The key command is Control+L.

- **Convert to Aliases.** This command turns any loops of the selected region into aliases of the selected region.

The Split Submenu

This submenu includes two commands that divide regions in different ways. Figure 6.15 shows the Split submenu.

Figure 6.15   The Split submenu of the Region local menu.

An explanation of the two commands in the Split submenu follows.

- **Split Regions by Locators.** This command creates a split in any selected regions at the current locator positions. The key command is Command+\.

- **Split Regions by Playhead.** This command splits any selected regions at the current playhead position. The key command is \.

The Merge Submenu

This submenu offers a couple of options for merging regions, as shown in Figure 6.16.

Figure 6.16   The Merge submenu of the Region local menu.

The submenu's two options are as follows:

- **Regions.** This command merges the data from any selected regions into a single region. The new object will be given the same name and will be on the same track as the track of the first selected object. If you have MIDI regions on different tracks, the merged data will retain its position in time but not its MIDI channel; the MIDI channel of the newly created MIDI region will be the MIDI channel that the instrument on the selected track is using. If you use this command on noncontiguous audio regions, Logic will create a new audio file containing the merged regions, just as if you had used the Glue tool (described in "The Arrange Tool Menu" section later in this chapter). The key command is Control+=.

- **Regions per Tracks.** This is the same as the preceding option, except that if the selected objects are on different tracks, rather than a single region being created on the track of the first region, Logic will create regions on each track on which there are selected regions. This means that merged MIDI regions will retain the MIDI channel of the events in the original regions because they are not changing MIDI instruments. New audio files will be created for merged audio regions on their respective tracks. The key command is Control+Shift+=.

The Cut/Insert Time Submenu

This submenu, also found in the local Edit menu, includes a few commands that add or remove time from the project. Figure 6.17 shows the Cut/Insert Time submenu.

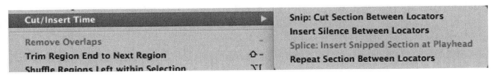

Figure 6.17   The Cut/Insert Time submenu of the Region local menu.

An explanation of the options in the Cut/Insert Time submenu follows:

- **Snip: Cut Section Between Locators.** This command removes an amount of time determined by the project locators. Regions after the right locator move to the left locator, and all information between the locators is removed from the project to the Clipboard.

- **Insert Silence Between Locators.** This command creates a gap of empty space between the two locators. Any regions between the locators move to the right of the right locator.

- **Splice: Insert Snipped Section at Playhead.** This command inserts all the information cut by the Snip command back into the project at the current playhead position. All regions to the right of the inserted objects are pushed back so they begin at the end of the inserted regions.

- **Repeat Section Between Locators.** This command takes all selected regions inside the locators and any sections of any selected regions inside the locators and copies them to the right of the right locator.

The MIDI Menu

The MIDI local menu consists of commands and submenus of commands relating to MIDI regions. The MIDI local menu is shown in Figure 6.18.

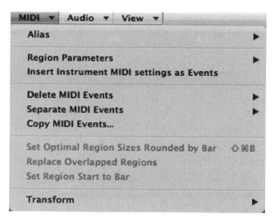

Figure 6.18 The MIDI local menu of the Arrange window.

The commands and submenus of the MIDI menu are described below:

- **Alias submenu.** See the upcoming "The Alias Submenu" subsection.

- **Region Parameters submenu.** See the upcoming "The Region Parameters Submenu" subsection.

- **Insert Instrument MIDI Settings as Events.** When you select a MIDI track, choosing the Insert Instrument MIDI Settings as Events command creates MIDI events for program, volume, and pan if they are checked in the Object Parameter box and places those events in the track.

- **Delete MIDI Events submenu.** See the upcoming "The Delete MIDI Events Submenu" subsection.

- **Separate MIDI Events submenu.** See the upcoming "The Separate MIDI Events Submenu" section.

- **Copy MIDI Events.** This command opens the dialog box shown in Figure 6.19. From this box, you can select exactly where your data to copy is, if you want to copy it to the Clipboard or to another location on the Arrange, what type of copy mode (merge, replace, and so on) you wish for your MIDI data, and how many copies you want to make. This command is a very powerful way to move large amounts of MIDI data around your project. If you work with MIDI a lot, assigning this command to a key command is a must.

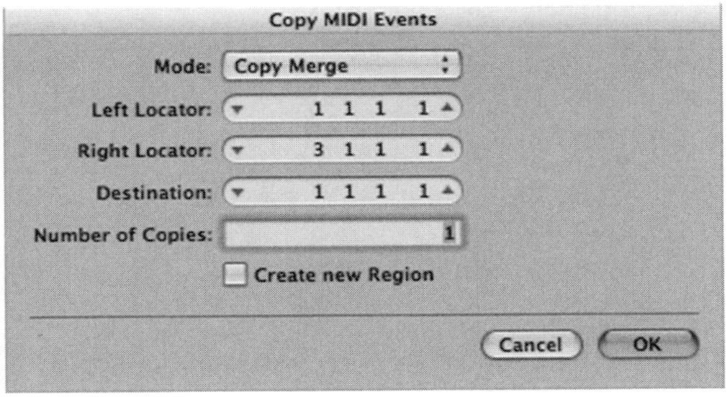

Figure 6.19   The Copy MIDI Events dialog box. Use this to copy or move large amounts of MIDI data around your project.

- **Set Optimal Region Sizes Rounded by Bar.** This command reduces or increases the length of a MIDI region to be just large enough to contain the MIDI events within it, rounded to the nearest bar. Most regions tend not to be too much larger than the amount of data inside them to begin with, so you are unlikely to need this command. Its main uses include if you record a MIDI part and don't stop recording quickly, leaving you with a large empty space in the MIDI region without notes, or if you are editing a MIDI region in a MIDI editor and you delete notes at the beginning or end of the region. The key command is Shift+Command+B.

- **Replace Overlapped Regions.** This command moves selected overlapping regions so that they no longer overlap. It does so by deleting the regions that the selected region overlaps, lengthening the selected region to fill the space previously occupied by the deleted region, and adding the MIDI data from the deleted region to the lengthened region.

- **Set Region Start to Bar.** This command rounds your MIDI regions to start at the nearest bar.

- **Transform submenu.** The Transform submenu offers shortcuts to the functions in the Transform window. Selecting one of the options in the Transform submenu opens the

Transform window, with the selected Transform process ready to be used. The Transform window will be covered in Chapter 8, "Working with MIDI."

The Alias Submenu

Aliases are regions that do not themselves contain data, but that are pointers to other regions that contain data. This submenu offers a selection of commands relating to the creation and selection of aliases. Figure 6.20 shows this submenu.

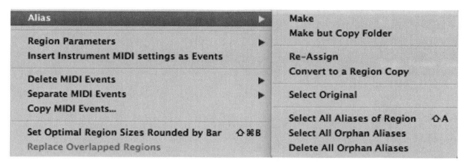

Figure 6.20   The Alias submenu of the MIDI menu.

An explanation of the commands in the Alias submenu follows:

- **Make.** This command makes an alias of the selected region.

- **Make but Copy Folder.** If you select a Folder track and then choose this command, Logic creates a copy of the Folder track that contains aliases of all the regions in the original folder. This command has no effect if no folder is selected.

- **Re-Assign.** By selecting an alias and the desired region you wish to reassign that alias, this command reassigns the selected alias to point to the selected region instead of the initial region to which the alias pointed.

- **Convert to a Region Copy.** This command turns an alias into a real copy of the original region, meaning it will now contain data identical to that of the original region, and not simply a pointer to the original region. The benefit of this command is that you can then edit events in the new region or the region as a whole.

- **Select Original.** If you select an alias and then choose this command, the original region to which the alias is pointing is selected as well.

- **Select All Aliases of Region.** If you select a region and choose this command, all the aliases of the original region are selected as well. The key command is Shift+A.

- **Select All Orphan Aliases.** If you have unassigned aliases in your Arrange because you deleted the original region to which they pointed, this command selects those aliases.

- **Delete All Orphan Aliases.** This command deletes all aliases that point to deleted regions.

The Region Parameters Submenu

This submenu contains a number of commands that relate to the parameters specific to MIDI regions. Figure 6.21 shows the Region Parameters submenu.

Figure 6.21   The Region Parameters submenu of the MIDI menu.

The following are descriptions of the Region Parameters submenu's options:

■ **Normalize Region Parameters.** This command permanently adjusts the values in the Parameter box of a MIDI region. The key command is Control+N.

■ **Normalize without Channel.** This command normalizes the parameters of a MIDI region without normalizing the MIDI channel value.

■ **Normalize without Channel and Delay.** This command normalizes the parameters of a MIDI region without normalizing the MIDI channel or the MIDI delay.

■ **Apply Quantization Settings Destructively.** This command permanently applies the playback quantize value assigned to the MIDI region in its Parameter box. The key command is Control+Q.

The Delete MIDI Events Submenu

This submenu contains different options for deleting MIDI events in a track. Figure 6.22 shows the Delete MIDI Events submenu.

Figure 6.22   The Delete MIDI Events submenu of the MIDI menu.

Explanations of the commands in the Delete MIDI Events submenu follow:

■ **Duplicates.** This command erases all duplicate MIDI events (meaning, similar events at the same time position in your project) in selected regions. The key command for this is D.

- **Inside Locators.** This command erases all MIDI events in selected regions inside the left and right locators.

- **Outside Locators.** This command erases all MIDI events outside of the left and right locators in selected regions.

- **Outside Region Borders.** Use this command to erase all of the MIDI events outside the borders of a selected region.

- **Unselected Within Selection.** This command erases all the unselected MIDI information inside an area you have selected.

The Separate MIDI Events Submenu

The Separate MIDI Events submenu, shown in Figure 6.23, contains two commands for separating MIDI events. For those coming from an earlier version of Logic, this menu contains the Demix commands from the old Region > Split/Demix submenu.

Figure 6.23   The Separate MIDI Events submenu.

The Separate MIDI Events submenu commands are:

- **By Event Channel.** If you have a MIDI region selected, this command creates a new track for each MIDI channel used by events in the parent region. Each new track will contain the events from the original region that were on that MIDI channel. This command is useful for recording many different MIDI parts on different MIDI channels at once and then moving each part to its own track afterward. Remember that if you select a track header, all the regions on that track are selected, allowing you to demix an entire track with one command.

- **By Note Pitch.** If you have a MIDI region selected, this command creates a new track for every MIDI note in the parent region. This command is especially useful for recording a MIDI drum performance, in which each note is a separate drum, and then placing each drum note on its own separate track afterward.

The Audio Menu

The Audio local menu of the Arrange contains commands that only affect audio regions. Figure 6.24 shows the Audio menu. The next chapter, "Working with Audio and Apple Loops," explains the use of these functions in more depth.

Following are descriptions of the options in the Audio menu:

- **Move Region to Original Record Position.** This command returns all selected audio regions to the positions at which you initially recorded them. This works only for audio regions

Figure 6.24   The Audio menu of the Arrange window.

consisting of audio recorded in Logic or Sound Designer II and Broadcast WAV files that have embedded start information; because a region that you imported from a disk of audio samples would have no "original record position," this command would not have any effect. The key command is Option+Shift+Command+R.

- **Convert Regions to New Regions.** This command makes independent audio regions in the Audio Bin for regions previously considered sub-regions of a "parent" audio region (meaning, audio regions carved from what was one initial audio region). The key command is Option+Command+R.

- **Convert Regions to New Audio Files.** This command can save all the audio regions you select as separate audio files on your hard disk. This command is incredibly useful if you want to export specific regions to other audio applications. You may also need to use this command if you want to make an Apple Loop of a specific region that is a part of a longer audio file. The key command is Option+Command+F.

- **Convert Regions to New Sampler Track.** This command lets you convert the selected region(s) to zones in an EXS24 instrument. The new EXS instrument will be loaded on a new Software Instrument track, which will contain a region with notes automatically placed to play back the converted regions at their original positions. This command will be covered in more detail in "Converting Regions to Sampler Tracks" later in this chapter. The key command is Control+E.

- **Strip Silence.** When you select an audio region, you can choose Strip Silence to scan the audio region for points in which the audio material is below a threshold you define, and then create a number of new audio regions out of those regions above the threshold. This command is extremely useful for removing any pauses in a recording. This command is covered in more detail in Chapter 7. The key command is Control+X.

■ **Detect Tempo.** The Detect Tempo command opens the Detect Tempo of Audio Regions dialog, which is covered in detail in Chapter 14, "Advanced Tempo Operations."

■ **Time Stretch Region to Locators.** When you select an audio region and choose this command, Logic will time stretch or compress your audio to the length of the locators. Note that no audio region can be stretched more than 400 percent or compressed to less than 25 percent of its original length. The key command is Option+Command+L.

■ **Time Stretch Region to Nearest Bar.** This command results in Logic using time stretching or compressing to adjust the length of a selected audio region to the nearest bar. Note that no audio region can be stretched more than 400 percent or compressed to less than 25 percent of its original length. The key command is Option+Command+B.

■ **Time Stretching Algorithm.** When Logic time stretches or compresses an audio region, it uses unique and high-quality algorithms created for its Time Machine in the Sample Editor, which is explored in the next chapter. The Time Stretching Algorithm submenu is explained in the following subsection.

■ **Show Selected Audio File(s) in Finder.** This command will bring up a Finder window showing you the actual file on your hard drive referenced by the selected audio region(s). The key command is Shift+Command+R.

■ **Copy as ReCycle Loop.** If you want to copy audio in your Arrange for use in Propellerhead's ReCycle, you can select the audio files and copy them to the Clipboard using this command. As of this writing, this command does not exist in the 64-bit version of Logic.

■ **Paste ReCycle Loop.** If you have copied a REX or REX2 loop into the Clipboard, you can paste it at the current playhead position using this command. As of this writing, this command does not exist in the 64-bit version of Logic.

■ **Snap Edits to Zero Crossings.** This command sets a preference to search selected audio regions for points at which the amplitude of the audio wave crosses the zero line. Any subsequent attempts to edit the length of an audio region will be restricted to zero crossings. This is useful in matching up audio edits.

The Time Stretching Algorithm Submenu

You can choose from several Time Stretching algorithms, each of which is optimized differently. Figure 6.25 shows the hierarchal menus of the Time Stretching Algorithm.

You can select from the following algorithms:

■ **Legacy Algorithms submenu.** These algorithms come from earlier versions of Logic. The Legacy algorithms are:

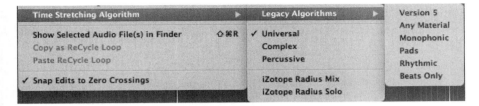

Figure 6.25   The Time Stretching Algorithm submenu of the Audio menu.

- **Version 5.** This is the Time Stretching algorithm from Logic 5.

- **Any Material.** This algorithm has been designed to give high-quality results when stretching and compressing audio regions containing any variety of material.

- **Monophonic.** This algorithm is optimized for material that uses only a single voice (such as a single singer, wind instrument, mono synthesizer, and so on).

- **Pads.** This algorithm is optimized for polyphonic material, such as pads, choirs, and so on.

- **Rhythmic.** This algorithm is optimized for instruments with dramatic rhythmic peaks, such as percussion, steel drums, pulsing rhythmic synths, and so on.

- **Beats Only.** This algorithm is designed for non-pitched material with strong rhythmic peaks, such as drums. You can use this algorithm to adjust the spaces between peaks, which produces excellent results on drums and such. However, the algorithm is often ineffective or unusable on melodic audio parts.

- **Universal.** This algorithm is designed to supplant the Any Material algorithm. Most of your time stretching and compressing needs can be addressed with this setting.

- **Complex.** This algorithm is designed for time stretching or compressing particularly dense and complex material.

- **Percussive.** This algorithm is designed to maintain the rhythmic integrity of your more percussive audio material when time stretching or compressing. Don't let the name fool you—this algorithm works beautifully on percussive material played on harmony instruments as well as drums and other percussion instruments.

One of the advantages in the way Logic implements its Time Machine is that third parties can release their own extremely high-quality Time Stretching algorithms that you can use within Logic. For example, notice that at the bottom of the Time Stretching Algorithm submenu in Figure 6.25, there are options for using two iZotope Radius algorithms in addition to the Logic algorithms. If you have any third-party algorithms installed, such as the iZotope Radius for Logic AU or Serato Pitch 'n Time LE AU installed, you will see their available algorithms in this menu, and you can use these algorithms seamlessly in the Time Machine. They will also be available to you in the Time and Pitch Machine in the Sample Editor.

At this time, there are other high-quality algorithms being developed by other companies as well, so be sure and do some research as to the current state of the art if you are looking for some professional Time Stretching algorithms. Finally, as of this writing all of the third-party algorithms are currently available only as 32-bit Audio Units. If you are using the 64-bit version of Logic 9.1, that means these time and pitch algorithms will not be available. Be sure to keep checking for upgrades of these plug-ins that offer 64-bit compatibility.

The View Menu

The View menu is loaded with options you can use to specify what you will see as part of your Arrange page. Most of these options simply allow you to check or uncheck various items to determine whether they will appear on your Arrange window. Figure 6.26 shows all the various items that you can choose to view or not to view on your Arrange page.

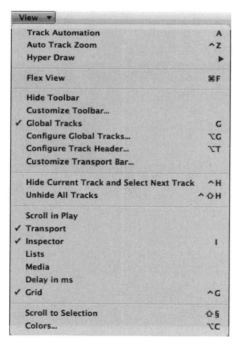

Figure 6.26　Use the View menu of the Arrange window to select which items you will view in your Arrange.

Because these items are simply checked on or off and are described individually later in this chapter or are covered in detail in other chapters, this menu doesn't call for a definition of options here. The main thing to remember about the View menu is that when you need to toggle the view of any feature of the Arrange, you use this local menu.

The Arrange Tool Menu

The Arrange window Tool menu contains a collection of tools for use in the Arrange. These tools each have a different function when graphically manipulating and editing regions. In addition to the Tool menu in the local menu bar, you can press the ESC key to create a floating Tool menu at the current cursor position, or you can right-click with your mouse if you have set right-click to open the Tool menu in the editing tab of Logic Pro > Preferences > General. Figure 6.27 shows the Tool menu.

Figure 6.27   The Tool menu in the Arrange window.
Each window and editor contains its own set of tools.

Brief descriptions of each tool follow, from top to bottom:

- **Pointer.** This tool looks like an arrow pointing upward and left. The pointer should be familiar from most other computer applications and is the default tool in Logic. You can use it to select regions by clicking on one or more regions or click-dragging over a group of regions to create a "rubber band" or "lasso" that will select them all.

- **Pencil.** The icon for this tool resembles—surprise, surprise—a pencil. It is used to add or alter the length of regions.

- **Eraser.** This tool looks like an eraser. It is used to remove ("erase") any regions you have selected from the Arrange.

- **Text.** This tool looks like a text-entry bar. It is used to name regions.

- **Scissors.** The Scissors tool conveniently looks like a pair of scissors. It is used to split regions. You hold the Option key down while splitting regions to divide the entire region into multiple equally spaced regions the same length as your initial split.

- **Glue.** This tool looks like a tube of glue. It is used to join selected regions into one single region, which is given the name and track position of the initial region. When the Glue tool is used to glue audio regions that were not originally next to each other, Logic will need to create a new audio file.

- **Solo.** The Solo tool is represented by the letter S in a box. This tool solos any selected regions.

- **Mute.** The Mute tool is represented by the letter M in a box. This tool mutes any selected regions.

- **Zoom.** This tool resembles a magnifying glass. When you use this tool to select an area containing regions, Logic zooms in on that area.

- **Crossfade.** This tool looks like a less-than symbol ($<$) in a box. This tool, when dragged over two adjacent audio regions, creates a crossfade between them. See the next chapter for an explanation of crossfades.

- **Automation Select.** The Automation Select tool resembles a bent arrow pointing upward and left, with a solid arrowhead. The Automation Select tool can select automation data in the automation lane. Chapter 10 discusses automation and the Automation Select tool in depth.

- **Automation Curve.** The Automation Curve tool resembles a bent arrow pointing upward and left, with an open arrowhead. The Automation Curve tool can create curves between two automation Nodes. Chapter 11, "Mixing in Logic," discusses automation in depth.

- **Marquee.** This tool looks like a crosshair. The Marquee tool is a unique and powerful tool. Briefly, the Marquee tool is not limited to selecting entire regions, but can make selections within regions for subsequent editing. (The name *marquee* was adopted from graphics applications, in which some selection boxes featured moving, broken selection lines often resembling an old theater marquee with rotating lights.)

- **Flex.** The Flex tool allows you to perform some Flex Time edits when Logic is not in Flex view. The Flex tool will be covered in the "Using the Flex Tool" section later in this chapter.

Expert Tip: Use Key Commands to Bring Up Tools   Logic offers key commands to accomplish the function of many of these tools and offers key commands that enable you to select tools without having to use the Tool menu. If you want to get as fast with Logic as you can, be sure to assign and use those key commands!

Track Classes

By now you realize that all tracks are not created equal. Logic provides several different track classes. Each track contains different sorts of data and has a different purpose. Let's briefly go over them:

- **External MIDI tracks.** An External MIDI track is assigned to an External MIDI instrument or a MIDI channel of a multitimbral MIDI instrument and contains MIDI data. You can only record and play back MIDI information from an External MIDI track.

- **Audio tracks.** An Audio track is a track assigned to an audio channel. It may contain, record, and play back audio information. An Audio track doesn't have to contain audio data, however; you can create Audio tracks to represent audio, bus, auxiliary, output, input, and other tracks that do not actually contain information but are assigned to an audio channel. Reasons for creating these sorts of tracks are to access their channel strips from the Arrange window, to include the multiple outputs of a software synthesizer with its Software Instrument track, to automate them using track automation, and so on.

- **Software Instrument tracks.** These are also Audio tracks, but a special kind of Audio track. A software instrument outputs audio produced by the instrument through Logic's audio engine. So a Software Instrument track uses an audio channel and has a channel strip similar to the channel strips of the other audio channel strips. However, since Software Instrument tracks contain instruments, the track itself contains only MIDI data that triggers the instrument. As such, the parameters and channel strip of a Software Instrument track look like an Audio track, but the regions on a Software Instrument track look like those of a MIDI track.

- **Folder tracks.** As explained previously, Folder tracks are containers for other classes of tracks. Tracks packed in folders can be arranged and edited as a single track. An advantage of this capability is that if you have a group of tracks that you want to keep together—for example, a full choir—you can put them all in a folder, and then when you move, split, or otherwise change that Folder track, all of your choir tracks will be moved and edited together, so that you need not operate on each individual track. Folders are also great organizational tracks, in that packing tracks into folders can help keep your main Arrange window from becoming cluttered. There are commands in the Region > Folder submenu to both pack folders (load a folder with tracks) and unpack folders (unload all of the tracks in a folder onto the Arrange). See the "Folder Submenu" subsection earlier in this chapter for a description of those commands.

Method Tip: Uses for Folder Tracks   Len Sasso, author of *Emagic Logic Tips and Tricks* (Course Technology PTR, 2003), offers a few expert uses for Folder tracks:

"Create a screenset with two Arrange windows, one primary, and one secondary. Click your secondary Arrange window's Link button until it is yellow, indicating

Contents-Link mode. Any folder you select in the primary Arrange window will now have its contents shown automatically in the secondary Arrange window."

Sasso also explains how to unpack only part of a folder:

"When you want to unpack only some of the regions in a folder, select the regions you don't want unpacked and pack them into a sub-folder of their own. Then unpack the original folder and you will have the desired regions unpacked and the rest in their own folder. That's easier than trying to find and re-pack the desired regions in the full Arrange window."

- **Metronome track.** This is the track reserved for the Metronome in Logic, named *click* by default. You can use this track to adjust the parameters of your click to best assist your live performance. You will only want a single Metronome track per project. Keep in mind that you don't actually need to have a Metronome track in your Arrange to use the Metronome.

- **No Output track.** This special track, as its name implies, does not output any MIDI data to MIDI devices or audio data to audio outputs. The No Output Track option is mostly used for storing synth SysEx data you don't want to send, or as a temporary assignment for tracks you want to turn off momentarily.

You can change the class of a track and/or instrument of a track by Control-clicking (or right-clicking) the mouse over a track in the Track List. Place the cursor over the Reassign Track option, and a hierarchal menu will appear, containing all of the previously discussed track classes, and all of your instrument and audio options divided into submenus based on the Environment layer in which they appear. Generally, you will use the Mixer submenu in the Reassign Track menu to change the class of a track. Figure 6.28 shows this hierarchal menu of track classes.

Figure 6.28 When you Control-click (or right-click) on a track header, a hierarchal menu will appear of all available track classes and instruments on the various Environment layers.

To change the track, simply select a new track class or instrument.

Expert Tip: Folders on Nonfolder Tracks   There is an exception to the preceding rule, as aforementioned author Sasso points out:

"Normally folders are placed on special Folder Tracks, which are not assigned to particular channel strip, unlike other tracks. That's what Logic does automatically when you create a folder, but you can reassign the track to its own channel strip using the Reassign Track menu, and you can also move the folder to another track. When a folder is on a normal track, all of its output is routed to the channel strip assigned to that track. That holds for the 'No Output' track as well."

Configuring the Toolbar

The Toolbar is a handy repository of buttons for opening different windows and Arrange areas, accessing Preferences and settings, and even executing commands. In keeping with the overall customizable nature of Logic, you can configure the Toolbar to contain the buttons you find most useful, or you can hide the Toolbar entirely. Figure 6.29 shows the default Toolbar configuration.

Figure 6.29   The default Toolbar configuration. The Toolbar can be configured to display buttons for different functions and commands or can be hidden from view.

To hide the Toolbar, click the oval button in the upper-right corner of the Arrange window. To configure the Toolbar, Control-click (or right-click) anywhere in the Toolbar. This opens the contextual menu shown in Figure 6.30.

Figure 6.30   Control-clicking in the Toolbar opens this contextual menu.

With the options in this menu, you can choose to display the items in your Toolbar as icons and text, icons only, and text only. There is also an option to remove an item, and if you Control-click or right-click directly on a button, there is also an option to keep the item visible. At the bottom of this menu is an option called Customize Toolbar. Selecting this option opens the Customize Toolbar dialog, shown in Figure 6.31.

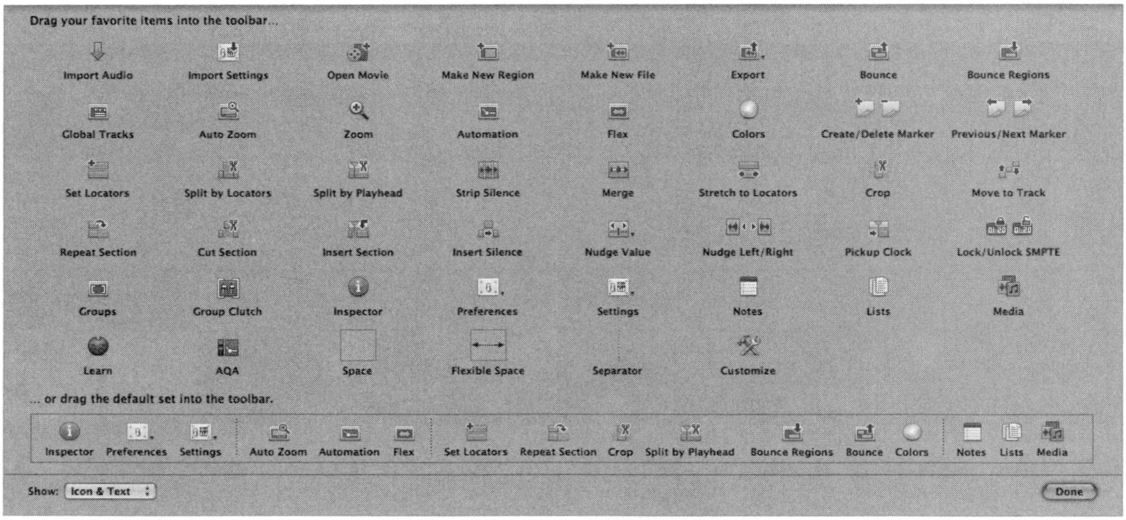

Figure 6.31   The Customize Toolbar dialog. You can add buttons controlling a wide variety of functions to your Toolbar with this dialog.

To add an item to your Toolbar, click and hold on the icon in the Customize Toolbar dialog, drag it to the place in your Toolbar you wish to put it, and release the mouse button. You can also rearrange items in your Toolbar by click-holding the item you wish to move, moving it to the location you wish, and releasing the mouse button. It is also possible to remove items from the Toolbar when the Customize Toolbar dialog is open by click-holding an item, dragging it out of the Toolbar, and releasing it.

You can use the pop-up menu in the lower-left corner of the Configure Toolbar dialog to change the icon and text display mode of the Toolbar. When you are finished customizing your Toolbar, simply click the Done button in the lower-right corner of the dialog or press Return.

Adding Tracks to the Arrange Window Track List

We already discussed how to add tracks to the Arrange window Track List in Chapter 3, and from the menu descriptions in this chapter, you have already seen the various commands relating to creating tracks in the Track local menu. You can also use the Append Track to Track List command. If you want to append a new track to the very bottom of your Track List, you can do so by double-clicking in the empty space below the final track in your Track List. This creates a new track that is identical to whichever track you have selected in the Track List. You can also define a key command for this function in the Key Commands window.

Track Parameters

We've already seen and discussed the different Track Parameter boxes in Chapter 3, but it bears repeating that every single track has two Parameter boxes in the Inspector. Figure 6.32 shows both Parameter boxes.

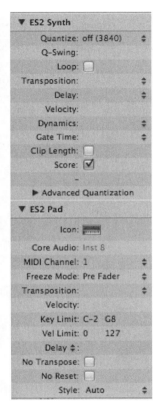

Figure 6.32 The Region Parameter box and the Track Parameter box of a Software Instrument track. The Track Parameter box should be familiar from Chapter 3. The Region Parameter box contains playback parameters for MIDI regions.

The upper box in the Inspector is the Region Parameter box. It acts as the MIDI THRU Parameter box if no region is selected, but if any regions are selected, it acts on the region playback parameters for the selected regions. The second box is the familiar Track Parameter box. Chapter 3 explained the track parameters, and the next section describes the region parameters.

Region Playback Parameters

Figure 6.33 shows the region playback parameters that you will find for a MIDI or Software Instrument track. They are called *playback parameters* because these settings do not affect recording, and they are not written to the region itself, but only affect the way Logic plays back the track, unless you apply the Normalize Region Parameters command.

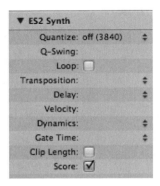

Figure 6.33   The Region Playback Parameters box of an External MIDI or Software Instrument track.

Descriptions of the parameters follow:

- **Quantize.** This is the quantize setting. To *quantize* MIDI data means to lock its playback to a beat count, so that regardless of the timing of the data, it will be played back with the exact timing selected in the Quantize parameter. If you click to the right of the parameter, a pull-down menu will appear that offers you myriad beat and note options from which to choose. Quantizing is explored in more depth in Chapter 8.

- **Q-Swing.** This controls how tightly the quantization feature locks every second beat to its quantization grid to give the MIDI part a more "pushed" or "laid-back" feel. You can adjust this parameter from 1 percent to 99 percent, with values under 50 percent resulting in an early beat, and values over 50 percent resulting in a delayed beat.

- **Loop.** Clicking in the box to the right of this parameter turns on "old-style" looping for that track or region. When activating old-style looping, the looped region will continually repeat for the length of the project or until another region on the same track interrupts the looping. When old-style looping is activated for a region, a number of grayed regions representing the repeats of the looped region extend until the end of the project or until looping is interrupted by another region. You can also engage looping by pressing L. Looping will be explained in more detail later in the chapter, in the "Looping Regions in the Arrange" section.

- **Transposition.** This parameter allows you to transpose the pitch of playback higher or lower by up to 96 semitones.

- **Delay.** This parameter offsets when a region plays back. The range of this parameter is –999 to 9999 ticks; a tick is the smallest time resolution in the sequencer, 1/3840th of a quarter note. You can turn on Delay in Milliseconds by choosing View > Delay in Ms, which displays this range in milliseconds instead of ticks. This parameter is useful if you are trying to align audio and MIDI data, and your MIDI seems to play back a tiny bit ahead of or behind the audio.

- **Velocity.** You can also offset the velocity of a MIDI track or region up or down. The range of velocity is the standard MIDI parameter range of 0–127, and you can add or subtract up to 96 to or from that value, up to the maximum value of 127.

- **Dynamics.** Adjusting the Dynamics parameter affects the velocity, except that instead of offsetting the maximum value, Dynamics offsets the distance between the loudest and softest velocities in the region. This can compress or expand the difference in volume between the notes, affecting the perceived volume. If you select this parameter, a pull-down menu will open that offers adjustment steps from 25 percent to 400 percent, with values below 100 percent increasing the dynamics and values above 100 percent reducing the dynamics. The Fixed option plays back all the notes at the same velocity.

- **Gate Time.** Gating literally opens or closes playback of the note that is being played, reducing or expanding its length. This scales the note duration, forcing playback to be staccato (shorter) or legato (longer). This parameter offers a pull-down menu of adjustment steps from 25 percent to 400 percent, with values below 100 percent reducing note duration and values above 100 percent increasing note duration. The Fixed option will create an abrupt staccato effect, while Legato will remove all space between all notes in the selected region.

- **Clip Length.** When the end of a MIDI region is reached, this parameter determines whether any notes that sustain past the end of the region will be played back to their completion or cut off. If the parameter is checked, any sustaining notes are stopped. If the check box is unchecked, the notes continue playing normally.

- **Score.** This parameter determines whether the MIDI region is available in the Score Editor. Check this box to make the region available in the Score Editor. This parameter is of use when a MIDI region contains only nonmusical MIDI information, such as controller messages, and you don't need to display the region in the Score Editor.

Advanced Quantization Parameters

If you click the disclosure triangle at the bottom of the Region Parameter box, the Region Parameter box will expand to display the Advanced Quantization Parameters, which offer more options than the standard Region Playback Parameters box. The Advanced Quantization Parameters box is shown in Figure 6.34.

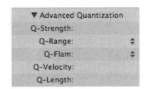

Figure 6.34 The Advanced Quantization Parameters for the track in Figure 6.33.

As you may have guessed from the name "Advanced Quantization Parameters," most of these parameters offer finer control over the Quantize function. Again, Chapter 8 explains quantizing in more detail.

The Advanced Quantization Parameters are as follows:

■ **Q-Strength.** This parameter determines how close to move each note to the nearest quantization grid position. You can adjust the value from 0 percent to 100 percent, with 0 percent resulting in no movement of the note at all, and 100 percent moving the note completely to the grid.

■ **Q-Range.** If you set this parameter, notes that are farther away than the number of ticks you set are not quantized. The range can be from –3,840 to 3,840 ticks. There are some exceptions to this, however. A negative setting means that only those notes farther away are quantized; this is useful to quantize only those notes farther away from the grid than you would like. Also, a value of 0 basically turns off the Q-Range function, in which case all notes are quantized.

■ **Q-Flam.** This parameter spreads out notes that fall on the same point; in other words, it rolls the chords. A positive value creates an upward roll; a negative value creates a downward roll. You can set the range from –3,840 to 3,840 ticks.

■ **Q-Velocity.** This parameter sets how much the velocity values of a template MIDI region will affect the velocity of the notes. You can adjust this parameter from –99 percent to 127 percent, with negative numbers and numbers over 100 percent creating the greatest velocity deviation from the template MIDI region, 0 percent leaving the notes unaffected by the note velocities of the template MIDI region, and 100 percent meaning the notes adopt the note velocities of the template MIDI region completely.

■ **Q-Length.** This parameter determines how the note lengths of a template MIDI region affect the note length of your MIDI region in the Arrange. You can adjust this parameter from –99 percent to 127 percent, with negative numbers and numbers over 100 percent creating the greatest note length deviation from the template MIDI region, 0 percent leaving the notes unaffected by the note lengths of the template MIDI region, and 100 percent meaning the notes adopt the note lengths of the template MIDI region completely.

The Audio Region Parameter Box

If you select an audio region, a different Region Parameter box will appear that contains parameters specific to audio regions. Figure 6.35 shows the Audio Region Parameter box.

The parameters are as follows:

■ **Loop.** This setting is the same as that described for the region playback parameters.

■ **Delay.** This setting is the same as that described for the region playback parameters.

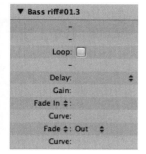

Figure 6.35   The Parameter box of an audio region.

■ **Gain.** The Gain parameter lets you adjust the volume of the selected audio region, + or −30 dB.

■ **Fade In.** You can adjust this parameter to determine the length in milliseconds of a fade-in at the beginning of an audio region.

■ **Speed Up.** If you click on the Fade In parameter name, a menu will open in which you can select between the Fade In parameter and the Speed Up parameter. The Speed Up parameter combines a fade-in with an effect that sounds like tape speeding up to its proper playback speed, per the length in milliseconds you define, at the beginning of an audio region.

■ **Curve.** This setting determines the strength and shape of the curve of the fade-in or speed up, if any.

■ **Fade Out.** This parameter determines which kind of fade there will be at the end of your audio region. The options are Out (for fade-out), X (for crossfade), EqP (for equal-power crossfade), or X S (for equal-strength crossfade).

■ **Slow Down.** If you click on the Fade Out parameter name, a menu will open in which you can select between the Fade Out parameter and the Slow Down parameter. The Slow Down parameter combines a fade-out with an effect that sounds like tape down from its proper playback speed, per the length in milliseconds you define, at the end of an audio region. The Slow Down setting only works with the Out setting.

■ **Curve.** This setting determines the strength and shape of the curve of the final fade or slow down, if any.

A Word about Fades   Don't worry if you are completely unfamiliar with the concept of audio fades right now; you'll learn more about this in Chapter 7.

The Arrange Channel Strips

To make mixing and accessing mixing parameters more convenient, Logic displays the channel strip for the selected track below the Parameter boxes in the Inspector, along with a second channel strip. The second channel strip is the "signal flow" channel strip. It can display any channel strip to which your primary channel strip is routed. In other words, you can have the second channel strip display the primary channel strip's Output channel strip by simply clicking on the Output field of the primary channel strip, or to an Aux channel strip by clicking on the Bus field on the primary channel strip for the desired Aux. You need to have the Inspector turned on in the View menu (View > Inspector) in order to see the Arrange channel strip. Figure 6.36 shows the Arrange channel strips of an Audio track.

The Arrange channel strips take up a lot of vertical space, so depending on how large your Arrange window is and how many items you are viewing, the channel strips may not fit in the window and may appear cut off at the top of its frame. To fit both channel strips in the window, you might need to close either or both of the Parameter boxes by clicking on their disclosure triangles in the top-left of each box. A monitor with more vertical resolution would allow you to display all the items in the Inspector.

Configuring the Track Header

At the left side of each track lane is the track header, which contains a variety of track information and controls. As with so many other aspects of Logic, the track header is customizable. Perhaps you are using multiple control surfaces and need a quick visual reference for which tracks are tied to which control surface, or maybe you need to enable certain tracks for Node processing. While some of the most fundamental tools are displayed in the track header by default, configuring the track header allows you to put tools you need at your fingertips. Figure 6.37 shows an Audio track with the default track header.

To configure your track headers, select View > Configure Track Header or Control-click (or right-click) on a track header and select Configure Track Header. This will open the Track Header Configuration dialog, as seen in Figure 6.38.

Many of these options will be explained in detail elsewhere in the book. For now, here is a quick description of the functions that each option represents:

■ **Control Surface Bars.** Selecting this option displays the track control bars that show the tracks that are controlled by any connected control surfaces.

■ **Track Numbers/Level Meters.** Selecting this option displays the track number for each track. During playback and recording, the track number is replaced by a small level meter, giving you a quick reference for the velocity of Software Instrument and External MIDI tracks and the level of Audio tracks.

Figure 6.36   The Arrange channel strips of an Audio track. This Software Instrument track is routed through a number of busses, but the Aux channel strip for Bus 1 is displayed to the right. You can select any output on the primary channel strip, and it will display in the second channel strip. As you can see, you'll need to close the Region or Track Parameter box to fit the entire strip on the page on many monitors.

■ **Track Icons.** If you select this option, track icons will be displayed in the track header. There is a sub-option, Allow Large Icons, which, when enabled, allows for larger icon sizes in the headers of track lanes that have been expanded. Track icons are covered in greater detail in the next section.

Figure 6.37   An Audio track with the default track header configuration.

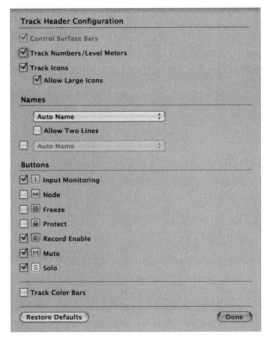

Figure 6.38   The Track Header Configuration dialog.
You can customize your track headers in this dialog.

- **Names.** This section provides a number of options for naming your tracks. There are two pop-up menus, each containing the same list of options regarding the nature of the name(s) displayed for your tracks. The second menu becomes available if the Allow Two Lines check box is selected. The Names section of the Track Header Configuration dialog was covered in Chapter 3.

- **Input Monitoring.** Selecting the Input Monitoring button allows you to monitor audio signals through Logic when a track is not record enabled. When selected, the Input Monitoring button glows orange. The Input Monitoring button is displayed in the track header of Audio tracks by default.

- **Node.** Nodes are a powerful and elegant feature of Logic Pro that allow you to distribute the processing of Logic's built-in plug-ins and synthesizers to other Node computers. If you engage this button, the compatible plug-ins and synthesizers on an Audio or Software Instrument track will be processed on your Logic Node computers. When engaged, the Node button glows green. The Node feature is explained in detail in Chapter 11.

- **Freeze.** The button with a snowflake icon is the Freeze switch (Audio tracks and Software Instrument tracks only). Clicking this button freezes Audio tracks or Software Instrument tracks. (See the "Freezing Tracks" section later in this chapter.) The button glows green when the Freeze switch is active for that track. If you click the button again, the track will unfreeze.

- **Protect.** This is the Track Protect switch. When clicked, this button locks the regions on the track in time and disallows recording on that track. (The R button vanishes.) When selected, the button glows green, and the icon changes to an image of a closed lock. When you click the button again, the track is no longer protected, and the icon returns to the image of an open lock.

- **Record Enable.** This button allows the track to receive audio as soon as you begin recording. When you click the button, the track is record enabled, and the button glows red. Clicking again disables record enable.

- **Mute.** This button mutes (silences) the track. When you click this button, the track is muted, the regions' colors become grayer, and the button glows turquoise. Clicking again unmutes the track.

How the Mute and Solo buttons on an Arrange track interact with the Mute and Solo buttons on that track's parent channel strip can be controlled via the Track Mute/Solo Preference found in the General tab of the Audio Preferences window. You can access the General tab of the Audio Preferences window by selecting Logic Pro > Preferences > Audio > General, by clicking on the Preferences menu in the Toolbar and selecting Audio, or by pressing Option+=. The Track Mute/Solo pop-up menu offers two options, as seen in Figure 6.39—CPU-Saving (Slow Response) and Fast (Remote Channel Strips).

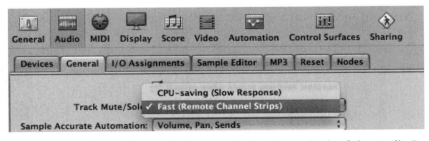

Figure 6.39   The Track Mute/Solo menu in the General tab of the Audio Preferences window. This Preference controls the interaction of a track's Mute button and the Mute button of its parent channel strip.

The Fast (Remote Channel Strips) setting allows you to link the action of the Mute and Solo buttons on a channel strip and all of its dependent tracks. In other words, engaging the Mute button of an Arrange track engages the Mute button on its parent channel strip *and* the Mute buttons on any tracks dependent on that channel strip.

The CPU-Saving (Slow Response) setting makes all Mute and Solo buttons on any tracks that share a parent channel strip independent from each other and from the parent channel strip. That means you can mute or solo tracks that share a channel strip individually. It is also CPU-saving because the track is unloaded from memory, since Logic assumes that you will not need to play this track along with the rest of your project. That's why this is the "slow response" option; if you click the Mute or Solo button on a track with this option selected, the track will load or unload completely from memory, which will take a noticeable amount of time. Remember that muting a channel strip mutes its output, regardless of the setting of any of its dependent tracks.

■ **Solo.** This button will solo all the regions on the selected track and enable Solo mode in the Transport. When you engage the Solo button, only other tracks with their Solo buttons engaged, or regions that have been soloed, will play back, and the Solo button will glow yellow. With Solo engaged, the Bar ruler will become yellow, and a yellow outline will surround all the regions in the soloed track.

■ **Track Color Bars.** If you select this option, then a thin strip of color will be visible on the right edge of the track header. The color for each track is determined by the color assigned to its parent channel strip.

You can also enable and disable different options through the contextual menu available in the track header. Figure 6.40 shows the track header contextual menu.

Figure 6.40   The track header contextual menu lets you enable and disable different track header options quickly and easily.

Unless you have a particularly large display, you will probably want to be fairly selective with the options you enable for your track headers. Figure 6.41 shows a track lane with every possible track header configuration option activated.

Figure 6.41   A track header with all options visible. As you can see, this takes up quite a lot of screen space.

Method Tip: Quickly Toggling Multiple Buttons   If you want to toggle on or off multiple buttons of the same type, navigating to each track one by one to click its relevant track button will become quite time-consuming. Luckily, you can click-hold the mouse over a button and then mouse up or down over the other similar track buttons to activate or deactivate multiple buttons at the same time. For example, suppose you want to mute 10 tracks. Rather than selecting each track individually and clicking each individual Mute button, you could click-hold the first Mute button, then slide your mouse over the other nine Mute buttons to mute the rest of the tracks.

You can only use this feature on the same type of button—in other words, you can't click-hold on the Mute button of one track and then slide over the Solo button of another. Nonetheless, you'll find this feature to be a massive timesaver!

Track Icons

Every track may have an icon associated with it if you have Instrument Icons and Instrument Icons (Large) turned on in the Track Configuration menu. This track icon represents the channel strip and/or Environment object to which that track is linked. Logic features excellent, high-resolution icons, as you can see in Figure 6.42. These icons are scalable from 128×128 pixels downward.

To assign an icon to a track, simply click and hold on the icon in the Track Parameter box in the Inspector, and a window will open in which you can select the icon for your track.

You are not limited to the icons that ship with Logic Pro 9. You can also create your own unique icons for use within Logic. The icons you create must be 128×128 pixels in size, have an alpha channel for transparency, and be saved in the Portable Network Graphics format with the file extension .png. Filenames for Logic icons must begin with a three-digit number so Logic knows where in its icon list to place the new icon. Be aware that if you choose a number less than 325,

Figure 6.42   Here you can see both the mini-icon in the Audio Track Parameter box and the large icon in a fully zoomed-out track lane.

your icon might replace a Logic icon that is named with the same three-digit number; however, many numbers aren't used, and you may want to replace an older Logic icon, so you have that option.

For Logic Pro 9 to use your homespun icons, you need to place them in an Icons folder in the following directory: ~/Library/Application Support/Logic/Images/Icons. If folders named Images or Icons do not yet exist inside your Applications Support/Logic folder, you will need to create them yourself. After placing your properly formatted icons in this folder, they will appear in the pull-down menu of icons alongside all of Logic's other icons.

Hide Tracks

Suppose you have tracks in the Track List that have project-related MIDI data, such as SysEx data, that you do not need to see on the Arrange. Or perhaps you created a number of tracks for audio channel strips that you wanted to appear in the Mixer, but which you do not need to display in the Track List. Maybe you just want to focus on a particular set of tracks, and you wish to group the other tracks for quick hiding and unhiding. For those situations where you have tracks in the Track List that you do not need or want to have visible, Logic offers the Hide Track feature.

There is a global Hide View button at the top of the Arrange. It appears to the right of the Catch button and looks like a large H, as you can see in Figure 6.43.

Figure 6.43   The global Hide View button. It is currently green, indicating you can click on the Hide button on individual tracks to hide them.

When you click on the Hide View button, it glows green, and Hide buttons in the individual track headers become available. You can now activate the individual Hide buttons on the desired tracks, which will also glow green when activated. When you deactivate the global Hide View button, all those Arrange tracks with Hide activated will no longer be visible, and the Hide View button will glow orange to let you know that the Track List includes hidden tracks. The Hide button will also disappear from the remaining track headers. When you want to see the hidden tracks again, or to have access to Hide buttons for your remaining tracks, simply re-activate the Hide View button.

Several key commands relate to the Hide Track feature. Even when the global Hide View button is deactivated, you can still hide an individual track by using the key command for Hide Current Arrange Track and Select Next Track, Control+H, or by selecting View > Hide Current Track and Select Next Track. You can toggle the state of the Hide View button using the key command H to Toggle Hide View. Finally, there is a key command to Unhide All Tracks that resets the Hide buttons of each track, making them all visible, Shift+Control+H.

Keep in mind that hiding a track does not affect its playback in any way. Also, you can link the Hide functions of all the tracks belonging to a group if you select Hide in the Group Property Settings. We will discuss groups a little bit later in this chapter and in greater detail in Chapter 11.

Hide Tracks and Snip/Insert Time   Let's say you wanted to add or remove some measures from your entire project. Any easy way to do this would be to select all of your tracks on the Arrange and then use the Snip/Insert Time commands from the local Region menu. Unfortunately, this way of adding or removing time skips over any hidden tracks. So be sure that if you have hidden tracks, you have clicked the Hide button so it is green when you use either of these commands.

Freezing Tracks

Freeze is one of the most powerful features in Logic. Now, most applications have some form of freeze function, but Logic was the first major sequencer to add Freeze. Freeze can extend the power of your computer if you find your CPU beginning to strain under the processing load of your project. You can also freeze your Software Instrument tracks on one computer, take your Logic project to a computer without those software instruments installed, and then play the project, including the missing instruments. If you use audio or software instruments, you may find yourself wanting to use Logic's Freeze function.

What Is Freeze?

When you start using audio effects and software instruments, particularly at high sample rates and bit depths, you'll quickly realize that real-time effects and synth processing can take up a large amount of CPU power. Each effect and synth takes up a different amount of CPU power, of course, but the more you use, the higher the load on your CPU. What happens when you reach the limit of your Mac's CPU capability? You get a System Overload error message, your project stops playing, and you need to turn off some of the synths or effects you have turned on.

This is where Freeze comes in. With a simple click of the Freeze button, Logic will make a temporary 32-bit floating-point audio file of your Audio or Software Instrument track, including all effects and effects automation, and then link that track to the temporary audio file, bypassing all the effects (and the software instrument, if the track is a Software Instrument track). This means that instead of your CPU having the heavy load of real-time synths and effects, it only has the lighter duty of playing back the referenced audio file. All of the processing power required by the synth and the effects utilized by that track are now released.

You may want to use Freeze if you want to use effects and/or softsynths after you've run out of CPU power. Another very handy way to use Freeze is if you are trying to play back a Logic project created on a computer with greater power (or that used a number of Logic Node computers for extra processing muscle), you can use Freeze until the CPU load is reduced to the point that the project will play back. Keep in mind that if your project's real-time processing demands are not causing any processing problems, you do not need to freeze any tracks.

How to Freeze Tracks

Freezing tracks is an incredibly easy procedure. First, make sure that the Freeze button, which looks like a snowflake, is visible on your track. If it isn't, you can turn it on either by selecting View > Configure Track Header or by Control-clicking (or right-clicking) on the track header and selecting Configure Track Header, and then checking the Freeze check box.

Once the button is visible, simply click on it. The button will glow green, as shown in Figure 6.44. Repeat this procedure for all the tracks in your project that you want to freeze. If you want to freeze many tracks at once, you can use the Method Tip "Quickly Toggling Multiple Buttons" to engage multiple Freeze buttons. The next time you issue the Refresh Freeze Files command (via key command or found in the global menu at Options > Audio > Refresh All Freeze Files) or the Play command (via the Transport, a key command, or a software controller), instead of beginning playback of your project, Logic will freeze all of the tracks that you have selected. That's it!

Figure 6.44 An Audio track with Freeze Track turned on. This button tells you that the plug-ins on this track will not be played back in real time, but instead the track is playing an audio file that is an exact duplicate of the track.

Logic 9 adds a new parameter to the Track Parameter Inspector box: Freeze mode. There are two modes:

- **Source Only.** This freezes the software instrument or source audio file (including Flex adjustments), but not any of the plug-ins on the track. This is very useful if you have a very CPU-heavy software instrument and want to freeze the instrument, but you want to keep the plug-ins "live" so you can adjust them. Source Only also can be used if you have an Audio track that is very heavily Flexed, as Flex takes up CPU resources when used in real time. In this mode, the Freeze button will turn blue.

- **Pre Fader.** This is the traditional Logic Freeze mode. The source audio or software instrument and all plug-ins (in other words, everything before the fader) will be frozen. This saves the most CPU and turns the Freeze button green.

When you freeze a track, you can no longer edit the track or adjust the automation of your effect or software instrument parameters, since the track is no longer playing back the regions in the track lane in real time, but linking to the recorded file. If you selected Source Only mode for freezing, you can still adjust and add/remove plug-ins, but in Pre Fader mode you cannot. If you attempt to edit any of these parameters, Logic will display the error message, "Current track or object is frozen. Do you wish to unfreeze it?" As this message informs you, if you want to make further changes or edits to the regions, effects, or effects automation, just click the Unfreeze button in the message or click the Freeze button again to unfreeze the track. When you are finished editing your track, simply reactivate the Freeze button, and then the next time you activate Play, the track will refreeze with your changes. If you create an edit after unfreezing a track, the Undo command will undo the edit but will not return your track to a Freeze track, so be sure to Freeze your track again even if your edits are undone.

Not every function of the track is frozen, however; you can still adjust the effect send level and destination, the pan and surround parameters, and the volume, and toggle the channel strip's mute and solo (as well as automation for these features).

The Freeze process always attempts to freeze for the full length of the project; however, if your track contains only audio (or MIDI data for a software instrument) for a portion of the project, you may want to stop the Freeze procedure manually. Even though the Freeze Tracks procedure happens faster than real time, Logic does allow you to stop it. When tracks are freezing, Logic displays a dialog box with a progress bar showing you how much is left to freeze, and you will see the playhead speed through the project, showing you visually how much of your project has been frozen. You can interrupt the Freeze Tracks procedure by pressing Command+. (period key) when Logic passes the point at which you want to freeze. The partially frozen track will now play back the Freeze file to the end of the file, and then the track will fall silent.

Keep in mind that since Freeze operates by printing files faster than real time, in order for Freeze to work, the audio engine and processors you are using must be capable of working faster than real time. All native plug-ins and most DSP accelerator cards have no problem with this, but if you are using a Digidesign HD system, the DAE audio engine, which can only run in real time, cannot freeze tracks. Also, if you are using the I/O plug-in to access external hardware in real time, you cannot use Freeze.

Cycle Mode

We touched on Cycle mode in Chapter 5, but now we'll go into it in detail. As you recall, Cycle mode allows you to loop a predefined section of your project continually. You might want to do this to listen critically to a specific section of your project, to practice performing a specific part of your project, to edit events only in a given section, and so on.

You can turn on Cycle mode in a number of ways:

- Click the Cycle button on the Transport.

- Press the Cycle key command.

- Click the top of the Bar ruler.

- Define the cycle region.

When Logic is in Cycle mode, the playhead plays back the project only within the cycle region. When the playhead reaches the end of the cycle, it immediately returns to the beginning of the cycle, interrupting playback of whatever sounds are at the end of the cycle.

Combining Cycle Mode and Recording

One of the most powerful combinations of features in Logic is to use Cycle mode with recording. This can greatly facilitate creativity and frees you to improvise parts over a section of your project without worrying about creation and organization of tracks and so on. It can also be beneficial when recording Takes, as we saw in Chapter 5. The Recording tab of the Project Settings window offers a number of Preferences as to how cycle recording will operate within a given project. You can access these parameters by selecting File > Project Settings > Recording, click-holding the Record button in the Transport and selecting Recording Options, selecting Recording from the Settings menu in the Toolbar, or pressing the key command Option+*.

You already saw the Recording tab of the Project Settings window in Figure 5.37 of Chapter 5. Please refer back to Chapter 5 if you would like more information on the Recording tab as a whole—here are short explanations of each parameter that relates to Cycle mode MIDI recording (and MIDI recording only):

- **Create Take Folders.** This option tells Logic to create a Take folder automatically when a second cycle has passed the first bar of the cycle region. Take folders and Take recording were covered in detail in Chapter 5.

- **Merge with Selected Regions.** This parameter merges the data from each recording pass into a single region on the track to which you are recording. If you do not select this option, Logic will create a new region for each recording pass.

- **Merge Only in Cycle Record.** This setting allows you to record the first pass as a unique region. Then Logic merges all subsequent recording passes into another region. If you do not check this box, Logic will create a new region for each recording pass.

- **Create Tracks in Cycle Record.** This option not only creates a new region for each recording pass, but creates a new track as well. The newly created tracks appear sequentially beneath the original track to which you began recording. Obviously, this function deactivates the merge options.

- **Create Tracks and Mute in Cycle Record.** If you select this option, each pass will be muted as soon as it is finished recording, so you will not have to listen to it when recording subsequent passes. This setting is independent of your setting regarding Logic creating new tracks or merging tracks for each pass; regardless of whether your data is being recorded to one region or separate regions, you will hear only the current recording pass.

Defining the Cycle Region

There are a number of different ways to set the cycle region in Logic. The most straightforward method is to click in the top third of the Bar ruler and then drag your mouse to the point at which you want the cycle to end. As you drag the mouse, a green bar will travel behind your mouse to the point at which you stop. This green bar represents the cycle region. Figure 6.45 shows a defined cycle region.

Figure 6.45   The green bar between Measure 2 and Measure 6 represents the defined cycle region.

You can grab one of the edges of the cycle region to redefine it—even during playback! You can also click in the middle of the cycle region to move it over. If you want to reset one of the cycle region boundaries to a specific point near that boundary, you can click on that point while holding down the Shift key. You can also drag a marker from the Marker track (or Bar ruler) into the upper portion of the Bar ruler to set the cycle region.

In addition to setting the cycle region graphically, you can set it by directly inputting the measure numbers into the position display of the Transport. You might also define several key commands to set the cycle region. If you do a key command search for *locators*, you will find a host of key commands that can set the cycle regions by objects, markers, and so on. Very few of these key commands are defined by default—it's up to you to decide which ones you want to use and then to define them.

Using Skip Cycle

Skip Cycle is a variation of Cycle mode. Skip Cycle mode allows you to define a region that will be skipped over rather than used during playback. You can create a Skip Cycle region by dragging from the right to the left boundary of the region you want to skip, by dragging the left locator of a cycle region to the right of the right locator, or by using the Swap Left and Right Locators key command, J. A Skip Cycle region is defined by a striped green bar at the top of the Bar ruler, as shown in Figure 6.46.

Figure 6.46   Here a Skip Cycle region is defined between Measures 2 and 6.

When a Skip Cycle region is defined, Logic simply ignores that section of the project during playback or editing. The playhead jumps from the beginning of the Skip Cycle region instantly to the end and continues as if the section did not exist. When Skip Cycle mode is turned off, the region plays back as normal.

Looping Regions in the Arrange

We've already touched on the Loop parameter in the Region Parameter box, and you've seen some of the commands related to looping in the Arrange local menus. If you loop a region, Logic repeats that region again as soon as it ends. You will be able to see this visually on the track lane as well; grayed boxes with the identical length of your original region will emanate from the end of your original region. This is illustrated in Figure 6.47.

Figure 6.47   The grayed boxes attached to the Take folder region offer visual feedback on the track lane that the region is looped.

Looping Regions with the Loop Tool

The traditional method, or "old style," of looping in Logic consists of clicking the check box of the Loop parameter in the Region Parameter box. You can also use the key command Toggle Loop (default key command: L) to turn the Loop parameter on and off for a selected region. Once looping is engaged, grayed boxes representing *loops*—repeats of your region—will extend from the selected region until they reach either the end of the project or another region in the same track lane. If you don't want the loop to extend to the end of the project, the old-style method of controlling how many measures a region will loop is to use the Pencil tool to create an empty region at some point in the track after a region that you want to loop; when you turn on looping for the original region, it loops until it reaches that empty region, and then the looping ends. As you move that empty region around, you can extend or reduce the number of loops for that original region. You will also notice that as you extend or reduce the length of your project, those loops that extend to the end of your project will be extended or reduced along with the project length. You could also cut loops using the Marquee tool (which is covered in the "Splitting and Resizing Regions Using the Marquee Tool" section later in this chapter).

You can also loop regions directly in the Arrange area, which for distinction's sake we will call "new-style" looping. Users of GarageBand or other ACID-loop-style applications will be familiar with this method of looping. For users unfamiliar with this kind of looping, you are in for a treat, because it couldn't be easier. Here's how it works.

First, move the cursor to the upper-right edge of a region. The pointer becomes the Loop tool, as shown in Figure 6.48.

Figure 6.48 When you move the Pointer tool to the upper-right edge of a region, it becomes the Loop tool.

Then click-drag the loop out as many measures as you wish, as you can see in Figure 6.49. The cursor info tag will indicate which region you are looping, where you are in your project, and how many times the region has been repeated. Note that the resolution to which you can drag a loop is determined by the Snap value, which is covered in "The Snap and Drag Menus" section later in this chapter.

Figure 6.49 To loop your region, simply click-drag the region as far to the right as you would like your region to loop.

That's it! Looping in Logic couldn't be simpler! If you want a loop to continue for an entire project or for so many measures that manually dragging the loop would be tedious, that's where the old style of looping comes in.

You can also use the Loop tool to edit any loop—old-style loops, new-style loops, and Apple Loops. If you simply move the pointer to the upper-third of a loop, it will turn into the Loop tool, as shown in Figure 6.50.

Figure 6.50 Moving the cursor to the upper-third of any loop will turn the pointer into the Loop tool, and you can then split and drag the loop.

You can then click on the loop to stop looping at that point. You can also drag the new end point exactly as you would a new-style loop. You can cut loops with the Loop tool regardless of whether they were looped using old- or new-style looping.

If you wish to operate on a loop that resides on a track in which the automation lane is showing, you will have to Option-click and Option-drag the loop. The reason is that when the automation lane is in view, there is a very small area that must be shared by both looping and resizing functions. You will read more about resizing and track automation later in this chapter.

Note on Old- versus New-Style Looping   One more time, just to be clear: There is no actual distinction made by the application between either looping method. We simply call the previous methods old-style and the recently introduced methods new-style for the sake of upgraders who are familiar with traditional looping in Logic but unfamiliar with the updates to looping since Logic Pro 7.

Clicking on a loop selects the looped region and all its loops. Click-holding on a loop turns the cursor into a Hand tool, allowing you to grab and move the looped region. Click-holding on a loop's track turns the cursor to a rubber band, like normal. The Marquee tool is capable of making rubber-band selections of portions of a loop.

The Convert to Real Copies command, key command Control+L, changes all the loops from a selected region into new, independent regions that are identical to the original region. The Convert to Aliases command will change all the loops from a selected region into new, independent regions that contain no data but point to the original region.

Expert Tip: Folders and Looping   Len Sasso, author of *Emagic Logic Tips and Tricks*, offered some tips on using Folder tracks earlier in the chapter. He also has some tips specifically regarding using Folder tracks for looping. "When you want to create a composite loop incorporating several regions," he explains, "pack the regions into a folder and loop the folder." In fact, if you use Propellerhead's ReCycle (REX) files, you will see that they use this same concept—REX files in Logic are folders packed with individual audio slices.

Creating Regions

At first, your tracks will not have regions on their track lanes. There are basically three ways for you to create regions on the Arrange:

- You can record audio or MIDI onto your various tracks. (Refer to Chapter 5 for more information on recording.) Logic will create audio regions and MIDI regions consisting of what you record.

- You can use the Pencil tool to create regions. If you click the Pencil tool in a MIDI track lane, an empty region one bar long will be created. If you Shift-click the Pencil tool in an Audio track, you will be presented with the Add File dialog for you to choose an audio file to add to the Arrange at the current cursor location. The created audio region will be the length of the audio file you select.

- Finally, you can create regions on the Arrange by adding audio or MIDI files to your Arrange by dragging them onto the Arrange window. You can drag MIDI files from the Finder directly into Logic or from the Library (discussed in Chapter 12, "Working with Files and Networks"), and you can drag audio files from the Finder, the Audio Bin (discussed in Chapter 7), or the Library. You can also use the Add to Arrange command in the Audio Bin.

Editing in the Arrange Window

After you create your Track List and you've got some regions on the Arrange, you most likely will want to edit and rearrange them. As you would imagine, the Arrange window is ideal for re-arranging regions. Every region displayed in the track lanes of the Arrange is ready and waiting for you to manipulate using Logic Pro's powerful tools and features.

Making Selections

The first step in editing your project is to select one or more regions, or portions of regions, that you want to edit further. Selected regions will have darker outlines and black title bars. Figure 6.51 shows a number of selected regions on the Arrange.

Logic offers a number of methods for selecting regions.

Selecting Regions Using Commands

You can use many different commands to select regions, such as the Select commands. These commands were previously listed in the local Edit menu earlier in this chapter. If you do a search

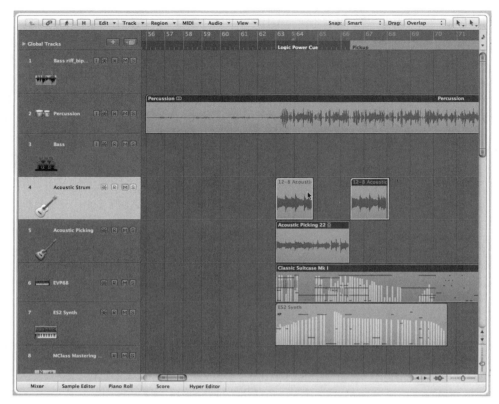

Figure 6.51   An Arrange with several regions selected. The dark color and title bar indicate which regions are selected.

in the Key Commands window, you will also find many selection commands, some of which are unassigned.

The two most common key commands for selecting regions are the Select Next Region and Select Previous Region commands. These keys move you to the following or previous region, using the right or left arrow, respectively. These commands select one region at a time. If you want to use the arrow keys to select more than one region, hold down the Shift key while navigating to the various regions with the arrow keys.

If you have the Select Regions on Track Selection check box selected in the Editing tab of the General Preferences window and you have selected a track using the Select Previous Track or Select Next Track key command, you select every region on that track. If you have not checked the Select Regions on Track Selection Preference, then none of the regions on a track will be selected when you select the track.

Finally, you can choose the Edit > Toggle Selection command (or key command Shift+I) to reverse the selection status of the regions you have selected, so everything you select will become unselected, and instead all the rest of the regions in your project will be selected.

Selecting Regions Using the Pointer Tool

Clicking on any region in the Arrange window with the Pointer tool will select that region. Remember that if you have Track Automation view enabled, you will need to click on the top solid bar of any region you wish to select, or you will inadvertently edit your automation.

Perhaps the most popular method of selecting regions is by using the Pointer tool to rubber band a group of regions. To do this, simply click the Pointer tool on an empty spot on the Arrange near the objects you want to select and then drag a selection square over all the regions you want to select.

If you have selected Select Regions on Track Selection on the Editing tab of the General Preferences window, you can also click on a track header to select every region in that track.

Making Selections with the Marquee Tool

The Marquee tool is unique in that instead of selecting a number of entire regions, it can select a *portion* of regions, as shown in Figure 6.52.

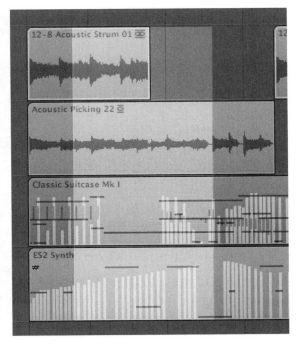

Figure 6.52   A marquee selection spanning a number of regions and tracks. The area in which the colors of the tracks are inverted is the marquee selection.

To use the Marquee tool, select the tool and then drag it over a portion of one or more regions. When you release the mouse button, the colors inside your selection area will be lightened; this is the selected area. You can hold Control+Shift when selecting a marquee area to snap to either ticks or samples depending on your zoom level. Pressing Control while selecting a marquee area will snap to the current Division setting. By holding down Shift, you can adjust the borders of the current marquee selection from either the left or the right side (not up or down).

You also have the option to display the marquee stripe, which sits above the Bar ruler and displays a white-striped bar over the area selected with the Marquee tool. To enable the marquee stripe, click on the down arrow at the end of the Bar ruler, which opens the menu shown in Figure 6.53, and select Marquee Stripe.

Figure 6.53 To enable the marquee stripe, click the down arrow at the end of the Bar ruler and select Marquee Stripe.

Figure 6.54 shows the marquee stripe and an area of a region selected with the Marquee tool.

Figure 6.54 The marquee stripe displays a white-striped bar over the area selected with the Marquee tool.

You can use the marquee stripe for a quick visual reference for the length of a selection you have made with the Marquee tool or for precise manipulation of the edges of the marquee selection. To adjust the borders of a marquee area with the marquee stripe, drag the cursor to the edge you wish to alter. The cursor will become the Resize tool. The resolution you can achieve with the Resize tool is dependent on the Snap setting, which is covered in "The Snap and Drag Menus" section later in this chapter. You can also move the marquee area by moving the marquee stripe. Just place the cursor over the marquee stripe, and the cursor will change to a Hand tool. You can then click-drag the marquee stripe.

Almost every editing function that is available when you select entire regions is available when you select portions of regions with the Marquee tool.

Adjusting the Marquee Borders by Transient

One of the extremely powerful features of the Marquee tool is that it can help you arrange and edit regions by transient. As we already discussed when talking about the Beat Mapping track in Chapter 4, transients are musically relevant peaks in audio material. You may want your marquee selection to fall not on the measure line, but on the beat, or the upstroke of an acoustic guitar strum, or the accented stroke of a violin bow, and so on.

Previously, if you wanted to do this, you had no choice but to try to visually find the transients by looking at the zoomed-in audio region and painstakingly set the marquee start and end to those transients. If you then realized that you set your marquee too long, and you wanted your selection to be one transient shorter, or your marquee selection needed to be a couple transients longer, you had to grab the start or end of the marquee and try to visually reset it again. As you can imagine, this took a long time and wasn't always accurate. Fortunately, Logic Pro includes these four key commands:

- **Set Marquee End to Previous Transient.** This sets the end of the current marquee selection to the transient before the current marquee end. The key command is Left Arrow.

- **Set Marquee End to Next Transient.** This sets the end of the current marquee selection to the transient after the current marquee end. The key command is Right Arrow.

- **Set Marquee Start to Previous Transient.** This sets the start of the current marquee selection to the transient before the current marquee start. The key command is Shift+Left Arrow.

- **Set Marquee Start to Next Transient.** This sets the start of the current marquee selection to the transient after the current marquee start. The key command is Shift+Right Arrow.

These commands allow you quickly to shift the start and end points of the marquee selection to the transients you wish. Combined with the editing commands, these make the marquee an even more precise editing tool.

The Arrange Grid

Most of what you'll be doing in the Arrange window will be editing and moving regions. For many users, the playhead and the Bar ruler offer enough of a guide. If you want more obvious guidelines, you're in luck. If you select View > Grid (or press Control+G), you will activate the Arrange grid. This tool puts guidelines at every bar of your project; the resolution of the grid depends on your current zoom level and the numerator of the time signature of your project. Figure 6.55 shows an Arrange with the grid turned on.

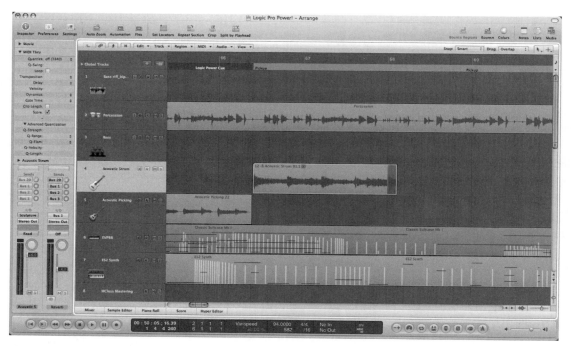

Figure 6.55 This Arrange window has the Arrange grid activated. Due to the zoom level and the 4/4 time signature, you can see a grid line every quarter note.

The grid is a purely visual tool; it does not affect region movement or editing at all, but it can assist you in moving regions and perfoming edits on specific grid positions. If the grid makes working in the Arrange easier for you, turn it on whenever you need it.

Zooming in the Arrange

As you begin moving and editing regions, you'll find that sometimes you'll want an overview of a portion of the project, and other times you'll want to focus in on a very small area. To do this, you'll want to zoom in and out.

In Chapter 3, we discussed using the zoom sliders in the bottom-right of the Arrange window to adjust the size of the track lanes. Using the horizontal zoom increases or decreases the number of bars that are visible onscreen at a time. When your project is fully zoomed out, you can easily fit the entire length of the project on your monitor at once for arranging regions, and if you zoom in all the way, you'll be able to view each individual sample of your audio to enable very precise editing. Figure 6.56 shows a project zoomed out and zoomed in completely.

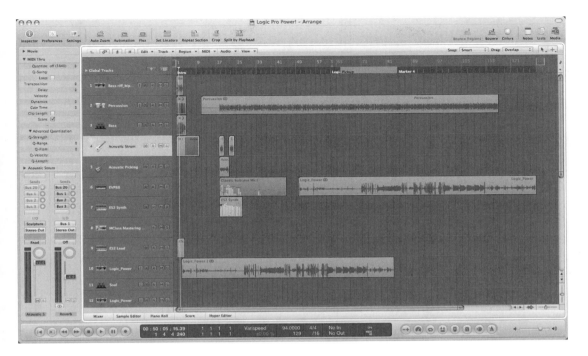

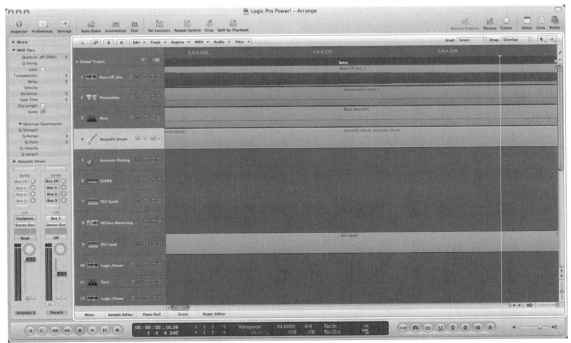

Figure 6.56 Using the zoom in Logic: (a) a project with the Arrange window zoomed out far enough to show the entire project; (b) the same project, but with maximum zoom, so you can see each sample of audio.

By now, it should be no surprise that Logic offers a full complement of key commands to facilitate zooming in addition to the zoom sliders. By default, pressing Control+Option+Arrow zooms in and out, horizontally or vertically, depending on the arrow key. There are also key commands to zoom in and out for individual tracks, to change instantly to user-definable zoom settings, to zoom to fit selection, and more. Be sure to do a search for *zoom* in the Key Commands window; you'll find a lot of fantastic timesaving key commands just waiting to be assigned.

Finally, you can select Auto Track Zoom either via key command or by selecting View > Auto Track Zoom. This command automatically increases the vertical zoom of the selected track for as long as that track is selected. This command is useful if you want to keep your tracks vertically short in order to fit more tracks on the screen, but you want the specific track you are working on to be larger for more precise moves and edits.

Splitting and Resizing Regions

Two operations that go hand in hand with zooming are splitting and resizing regions. You can zoom out or in to get the optimal view of a section of project and then edit that section to suit your taste. This is one of the most important uses for sequencers, and Logic's Arrange window offers users powerful and intuitive tools and commands for this purpose. This section describes some of the most popular commands, functions, and tips for splitting and resizing regions.

Splitting Regions

Logic offers a number of different functions and methods to split one region into two or more regions. Perhaps the most graphically intuitive way to split a region into two parts is to select the Scissors tool from the Tool menu and then click on a portion of a region. Logic then splits that region into two regions at the point at which you clicked. Figure 6.57 shows a region that is being split into two regions using the Scissors tool.

Figure 6.57   Splitting a region with the Scissors tool: (a) the Scissors tool over a region in the Arrange; (b) the resulting two regions after clicking with the Scissors tool.

If you try to split a MIDI region that has a note that overlaps the split by more than 1/16 note, Logic will display a dialog box asking whether you want to keep, shorten, or split those notes. Keep, the default option, leaves the note lengths unaltered, and you will simply have notes in the first region that play past the end of the region. If Clip Length in the track's Extended Region Parameters box is checked, however, the note will still be cut off. If you select Shorten, the over-lapping notes are truncated at the end of the first region. Finally, selecting Split creates two notes to represent the original overlapping note: one note in the first region that is truncated at the end of the first region, and a new note at the beginning of the second region that consists of the remainder of the original note. Click the option you prefer in the dialog box.

Logic also enables you to split a region into multiple regions using the Scissors tool. If you hold down the Option key while splitting your region, the Scissors tool will appear with a + sign above the teeth of the scissors, and it will split the region into multiple regions of equal size. Figure 6.58 illustrates this.

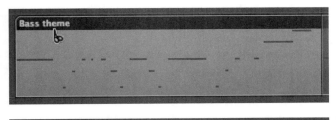

Figure 6.58   Using the Scissors tool to split a region into multiple regions: (a) the Scissors tool about a 1/4 note into a MIDI region; (b) the results of clicking with the Scissors tool and while pressing the Option key.

You can also use a number of commands to split regions. As explained previously, the Region > Split submenu offers the commands Split Region by Locators and Split Region by Playhead. These commands split a selected region by using the locators in the Bar ruler or by using the playhead, respectively. You can also use the key commands for these commands, as well as the key command for Split Region by Rounded Playhead Position, which splits the region at the bar line nearest to the playhead.

Splitting Regions That Are Looped: SmartLoop   In the Editing tab of the General Preferences window, there is a check box for SmartLoop Handling of Scissors and 'Split by Playhead.' If you have this check box selected and you split a region that has been looped, the loop immediately following the split region will be turned into a copy of the original region, and the original region will be split. This is a special feature in Logic called *SmartLoop*. Logic does not assume that just because you want to split a looped region you necessarily intend to split every single loop that comes after it. By creating a copy, Logic automatically keeps the loop identical to how it was before you split the looped region, giving you a "new" original for the following loops. This procedure of creating a copy, looping the copy, and then splitting the original used to take a number of steps and a fair amount of time. Now, Logic takes care of it automatically for you!

Resizing Regions

Splitting isn't the only way you can alter a region in the Arrange; you can also resize it. Logic offers a few simple ways to resize regions. The most straightforward way to resize a region is simply to move the pointer to the lower half of the edge of a region; the Pointer tool will become the Resize tool, and you can now drag to the right or left to expand or shorten the region. The info tag beneath the cursor will display your action and position. Figure 6.59 shows a region being resized in this manner.

Figure 6.59   When you move the pointer to the lower half of the right or left edge of a region, the pointer turns into the Resize tool, and you can drag right or left to lengthen or shorten selected regions. The info tag displays what you are doing.

You can also resize multiple regions this way: Simply select a group of regions and click on the lower-right corner of one of the selected regions, and then Logic will lengthen or shorten all the regions by the amount you adjusted the region that you clicked. If you want to adjust multiple regions to the same absolute length (meaning the same number of bars), even if they were originally of varying length, hold down the Option+Shift keys while resizing.

There are some limitations to your ability to resize regions, however. You cannot shorten a region out of existence—Logic will always retain at least a sliver of the region. Also, if you are expanding an audio region, you cannot lengthen it past the end of the audio file itself, since there is no audio after that point. However, you can expand a MIDI region past existing MIDI data. You cannot shorten a MIDI region to cover up its original starting point. This means that you will usually find that you're limited to extending a region outward to the left.

If you shorten a boundary of a region that includes data, Logic will no longer consider that data part of that region. The data will not be deleted or modified in any way, however, and if you later lengthen the region, the original data will still be there, exactly as it was before you shortened the region.

Sometimes, however, when you adjust the length of a region, you may want to compress or expand the data inside to fit the new region boundary. If you have selected a region, you can do this by holding down the Option key while dragging the right region boundary.

You can also use two different procedures to resize an audio region and compress or stretch its contents to fit with the Adjust Region Length to Locators and Adjust Region Length to Nearest Bar commands from the Audio local menu. These commands invoke the chosen Time Stretching Algorithm to adjust the length of your audio region. Compressing or stretching audio using any of these approaches is different than using Flex Time on an audio region. Flex Time editing will be covered in detail in the "Using Flex Time" section later in this chapter.

Other local menu functions, such as Set Optimal Region Sizes, Remove Overlaps, and Tie Regions, are also useful for resizing regions. Review "The Region Menu" subsection to learn about these commands. There are also unassigned key commands that will allow you to nudge the length of regions shorter or longer by varying degrees. If you find any of them useful, remember to assign key commands to them.

Splitting and Resizing Regions Using the Marquee Tool

The Marquee tool is a special tool, perhaps one of the most powerful editing tools available in Logic Pro, and thus it gets its own subsection here. As described in the "Making Selections with the Marquee Tool" subsection earlier, you can use the Marquee tool to select portions of regions, not just entire regions. Once you have made a selection with the Marquee tool, you can perform most Arrange edit options, such as the following:

- Erase. (Press Delete or click with the Eraser tool.)

- Move (drag the selection) or copy (hold down Option while dragging the selection) using the Pointer tool. (See the upcoming "Moving and Copying Regions" section.)

- Cut and copy. (Press Command+X for cut and press Command+C to copy.)

- Paste at the playhead. (Press Command+V.)

- Cut at the selection border. (Click inside the selection with the Scissors tool.)

- Mute (via either a key command or the Mute tool; this results in a cut at the selection borders with the regions inside the selection borders muted).

- Solo (via either a key command or the Solo tool; this results in a cut at the selection borders with the regions inside the selection being soloed).

Moving and Copying Regions

Now that you've split and resized some regions in the Arrange, you probably want to, well, *arrange* them! Moving regions around is certainly one of the central functions of the Arrange window, and it couldn't be simpler. Just select a region or regions, hold down the mouse button, drag your selection anywhere you want, and then drop the region or regions in the new location. Done!

Of course, Logic gives you many more options for moving regions. If you want to restrict the movement to either the horizontal or vertical axis (depending upon whether you initially move the region horizontally or vertically), there is a check box preference labeled Limit Dragging to One Direction in Arrange in the Editing tab of the General Preferences, accessible through Logic Pro > Preferences > General. You can also toggle this feature on and off by pressing the Shift key while dragging. (In other words, if you've checked the Preference, pressing Shift will allow normal movement, and if the Preference is unchecked, you can press Shift to limit region movement to one axis.)

If you hold Control while dragging a region, you can move the region in one-division increments. If you press Control+Shift while dragging a region, you can move the region in increments of one tick or one sample, depending on your zoom setting. There are also unassigned key commands that you can use to nudge a region forward or backward by varying amounts. Search for "nudge" in the Key Commands window to find them. If you find any of them useful, be sure to assign keys to them.

Sometimes you may want to duplicate the data in a given region or regions in another location. Logic allows you to copy regions very easily. To move a copy of your selected region(s) instead of the original region(s), hold the Option key while moving the region, leaving the original regions in their original positions. If you want the copied regions to be aliases (see following Method Tip) that point to the original regions instead of actual copies, press Option+Shift when moving the regions. You can also make multiple duplicates that will follow your selected region or regions by using the Repeat Regions command either via key command or by choosing Region > Repeat Regions. This command presents you with a dialog box in which you may select the number of copies you want and specify whether you want them to be aliases or copies.

Moving and copying operations snap automatically to the Snap menu setting, which we'll discuss in "The Snap and Drag Menus" section later in this chapter.

Method Tip: Aliases versus Copies   Copying a region creates a completely new region with its own MIDI notes or audio data. It is a duplicate of the original region, but you can edit the original region without affecting the copy, and vice versa. An *alias*, however, looks like a copy of the original region, but it doesn't contain any data of its own; instead, it is just a reference to the original region. This means that any editing you do to the original will be reflected in the alias.

Aliases are perfect for when you want to ensure that each instance of your copied region exactly reflects the original region, since any edits and changes to the original affect all the aliases as well. If you want to edit an alias without affecting the original, you can always turn your alias into a real copy.

Editing Multiple Regions

There will probably be times when you will want to perform the same edits on multiple tracks. For example, you may want to remove a couple of bars from a multitracked drum performance and a guitar part and then drag the resulting regions one bar closer to each other. This kind of editing could take a bit of time, particularly if the tracks aren't all in order in the Track List. Fortunately, Logic allows you to group channel strips for just this kind of work.

To assign channel strips to a group, you need to click the Group slot on a channel strip you wish to assign to a group. The Group slot is the empty dark-gray box above each channel strip fader. Select an available group from the pull-down menu that appears, which is shown in Figure 6.60.

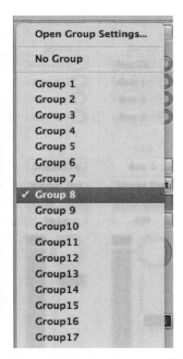

Figure 6.60   The Groups pull-down menu. You can assign channel strips to groups in this list.

When you select a group for the first time, the Group Settings window shown in Figure 6.61 will open.

Select the Editing (Selection) option and close the Group Settings window. You can now assign other channel strips to that same group. When you perform an edit on any single track assigned to a channel strip in the group, the same edit is performed on all tracks in the group. If you select an area of any region on a group track with the Marquee tool, the same area will be selected on all group tracks. If you select a whole region on a group track, all regions on group tracks that

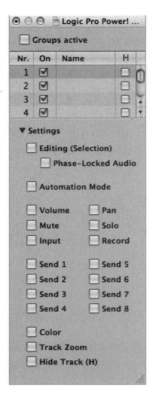

Figure 6.61 The Group Settings window.

overlap the selected region anywhere along its length will be selected. You can then move or delete these regions collectively.

Groups can be used for many other functions, as you can see in Figure 6.61. Groups and the Group Settings window will be covered in greater detail in Chapter 11.

Comping in Logic

Comping, or compiling pieces of different performances of the same material into one cohesive performance, used to involve a lot of work—keeping track of different performances on different tracks, selecting which parts to keep and editing sections into new regions, keeping the new edited bits organized, and so forth. Logic Pro gives you an incredibly powerful set of features that not only simplify the management of different Takes, as we explored in Chapter 5, but that also make creating audio Comps from those Takes a breeze thanks to Quick Swipe Comping.

Creating and Editing Comps

To begin, open an audio Take folder by clicking its disclosure triangle at the upper-left corner. Next, enable Quick Swipe Comping by clicking the Quick Swipe Comping button at the upper-right corner of your audio region, by selecting Quick Swipe Comping in the Take Folder menu, or by using the key command Option+Q. Now you can use the Pointer to select sections from different Takes. As you select a Comp area from one Take, that same area in every other Take is deselected. Also, when you select different pieces of your Takes to create your Comp, the waveform in the topmost track in the audio Take folder is updated to reflect those selections. Figure 6.62 shows an open audio Take folder that has Takes that have been comped.

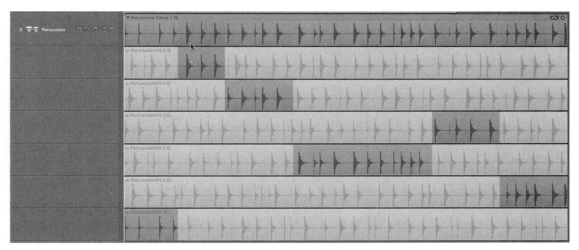

Figure 6.62   An open audio Take folder containing Takes that have been comped. Selecting an area of one Take deselects that same area on all other Takes, and the waveform in the topmost track updates to reflect the selection.

You can also create a Comp using the Region > Folder > Pack Take Folder command (key command Control+Command+F). When you use this command on selected regions on different tracks, they are packed into a Take folder using the channel strip of the topmost track. You can then create Comps in your new Take folder, but if you use this command on regions that are on the same track lane, then a Comp is automatically created.

You can change the length of a Comp section by click-dragging on its border. If there are any Comp sections that share that border with the section you are editing, they will automatically be resized. If you hold Shift while shortening a Comp section, adjacent Comp sections will not be lengthened. You can also move a Comp section. If you click-drag a Comp section, you can move the entire section left or right. Any adjacent Comp sections will be automatically resized.

When you create a Comp, the various sections that make up the Comp are automatically cross-faded per the settings in the Crossfades for Merge and Take Comping section of the General tab of the Audio Preferences window. You can access the Crossfades for Merge and Take Comping Preferences by selecting Logic Pro > Preferences > Audio or by selecting Audio from the

Preferences menu in the Toolbar and then clicking the General tab in the Audio Preferences window, or by pressing Option+=. Figure 6.63 shows the Crossfades for Merge and Take Comping section of the General tab of the Audio Preferences window.

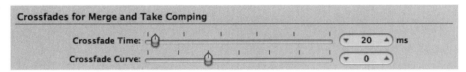

Figure 6.63   The Crossfades for Merge and Take Comping section of the General tab of the Audio Preferences window. You can determine how Logic cross-fades the sections of any Comps you create with the parameters in this section.

The Crossfade Time parameter determines how long in milliseconds each crossfade will take. The Crossfade Curve parameter allows you to control the kind of curve Logic will use to crossfade your Comps. A setting of zero will give you linear crossfades, while positive or negative values will give you symmetrical, exponential fades.

After you have selected the various sections of your different Takes that will make up your Comp, you can quickly replace an individual section of your Comp with the same section of a different Take by clicking in the desired area of the desired Take. If the Take folder is closed, you can do this by Control-clicking (or right-clicking) on the section in the Take folder. A menu like the one shown in Figure 6.64 will appear, in which you can select the alternate Take for use in that section.

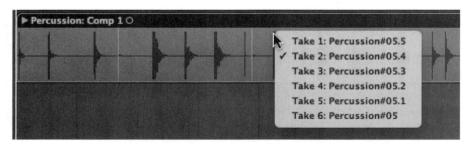

Figure 6.64   If you want to replace the Take used for a particular section of your Comp in a closed Take folder with the audio from another Take, simply Control-click (or right-click) on that section in the Take folder. You can select a different Take from the menu that appears.

If you wish to remove a Comp section, simply Shift-click on that section on its parent Take. If you Shift-click on a Take's header, it will remove all Comp sections from that Take.

Treating Takes as Regions.   Let's say you have found the exact Comp you want from a set of Takes, but there's one Comp section that's just a little late. You can easily slice a Take into sections via either of two commands found in a Control+click contextual menu specific to audio

Takes folders—Slice at Comp Selection Borders and Trim to Active Comp Sections. Both of these commands fundamentally create new regions from the selected Take that reside in the Takes folder. The Slice at Comp Selection Borders command slices the Take into separate regions defined by the borders of any Comp selections for the particular Take. Trim to Active Comp Sections slices the Take into separate regions too, but it removes any regions that are not used as Comps. You can see the effect of both of these commands in Figure 6.65.

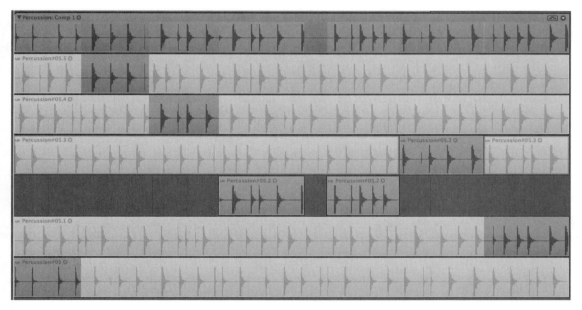

Figure 6.65   The third Take in this Takes folder after using the Slice at Comp Selection Borders command has been divided into three regions—one that is derived from the Comp section from the Take, and two from the remaining sections of the Take. The fourth Take has been divided into two separate regions derived from the Comp sections from the Take using the Trim to Active Comp Sections command.

You can now move these regions freely using the mouse or any nudge commands. Note that you must turn off Quick Swipe Comping mode to move any of these Take regions.

Saving Comps

You can store multiple Comps created with the same Take folder. Once you are satisfied with your Comp, click on the triangle in the upper-right corner of the Take folder to open the Take Folder menu and select New Comp. A new, freely editable Comp will be created, and your previous Comp will be saved. If you wish to rename a saved Comp, open the Take Folder menu and select the desired Comp. Then open the Take Folder menu again and select the Rename Comp command. This opens the Rename Comp dialog, discussed with the Rename Take dialog in Chapter 5.

Flattening and Merging Comps

Once you have comped your Takes and you have decided that you have a Comp you want to use, you have the option to either flatten or flatten and merge your Comp. Both of these commands are found in the Take Folder menu and are assignable to key commands. The Flatten command replaces your Take folder with individual regions that encompass each Take selection. Figure 6.66 shows regions that have been created by the Flatten command. Note that the crossfades created by Crossfades for Merge and Take Comping Preference are visible.

Figure 6.66   Regions created by the Flatten command in the Take Folder menu. The crossfades created by the Crossfades for Merge and Take Comping Preference are visible on the newly created regions.

The Flatten and Merge command takes the Flatten command one step further by taking the individual Take selections, merging them into one region, and creating a new audio file for that region. Figure 6.67 shows the effect of the Flatten and Merge command on the same Comp used in Figure 6.66.

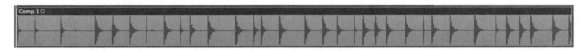

Figure 6.67   This region, created with the Flatten and Merge command, is from the same Comp used in Figure 6.66.

What makes these commands so powerful is that the new regions created by these commands are fully editable and movable, just like any other region.

Exporting and Unpacking Takes and Comps

There are a few more commands for manipulating Takes and Comps that you may find useful: Export to New Track, Unpack, and Unpack to New Tracks. All three commands can be found in the Take Folder menu, and the two Unpack commands can also be found in the Region > Folder submenu.

The Unpack commands both take the contents of the Take folder and place them on individual tracks, getting rid of the parent Take folder in the process. Takes are unpacked to individual tracks as whole regions, and Comps are unpacked to individual tracks as regions representing each Take selection. The Unpack command (Control+Command+U) places all Takes and Comps on their own track lanes, and they all share the same channel strip with the same configuration as the parent Take folder's configuration. The Take or Comp that was active when the folder was unpacked remains active, and all other Takes and Comps are muted. The Unpack to

New Tracks command (Shift+Control+Command+U) functions like the Unpack command, except each new track is given its own channel strip with the configuration of the original Take folder's channel strip. Figure 6.68 shows an unpacked Take folder.

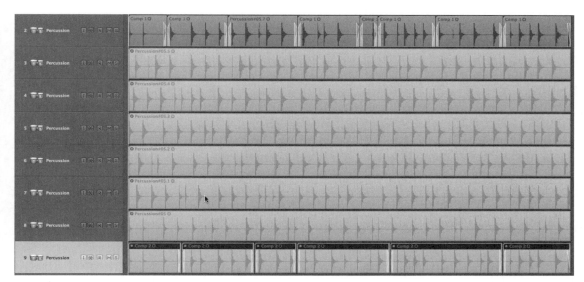

Figure 6.68   Unpacking a Take folder sends all Takes and Comps to individual tracks.

The Export to New Tracks command allows you to export an individual Take or Comp from the Take folder to a new track using the same channel strip as the parent track, while maintaining the existence of the parent Take folder. You just need to select a Take or Comp and then select the Export to New Tracks command (or assign a key command), and the selected Take or Comp will be exported to a new track directly below the parent Take folder in the Track List. If you export a Comp, the Take selections will be exported as individual regions.

The Snap and Drag Menus

To the left of the Arrange Tool menu are two very important menus: the Snap menu and the Drag menu. Figure 6.69 shows these two menus.

Figure 6.69   The Snap and Drag menus of the Arrange window.

Both of these menus affect the way you can move regions around the Arrange in Logic Pro. The following subsections explain each menu in more detail.

The Snap Menu

The Snap menu affects precisely where a region you move will "snap," or be affixed to, in the Arrange. You have a number of options for snap resolutions in this pull-down menu, designed to give you the ultimate say on where you want Logic to place your region. Your Snap options are as follows:

- **Smart.** Smart snap determines the snap resolution based on the zoom level of the Arrange. For example, if you are zoomed out to see all 200 bars of your project, if you move a region, Smart snap will snap to even bars. However, if you are zoomed in so you can accurately see 32nd notes, Smart snap will snap to 32nd notes. The limit is the sample level.

- **Bar.** This option will always snap every region you move in one-bar increments relative to the region's start position, regardless of zoom level. If your region's position is 1 1 2 67, dragging your region one bar to the right will result in a position of 2 1 2 67.

- **Beat.** This option will snap to the denominator of your time signature (which determines the beat) relative to the region's start position, regardless of the zoom level. For example, if your project is in 4/4 time, Beat snap will snap your regions to quarter-note increments; if your project is in 6/8 time, Beat snap will snap to eighth-note increments. If you have time changes in your Signature track, Beat snap will follow those signature changes and snap to the correct beat increment. As with the Bar snap setting, the Beat setting moves your regions by beats relative to the region's starting position.

- **Division.** This option snaps to the note value increments displayed in the Division display of the Transport window (sixteenth notes, eighth notes, and so on) relative to the region's start position, regardless of the zoom level.

- **Ticks.** This option will always snap to ticks, regardless of the zoom level.

- **Frames.** Frames snap to SMPTE frames regardless of the zoom level. The exact snap will depend on which frame rate you have set in your synchronization options. (See Chapter 15, "Synchronizing Hardware with Logic Pro.")

- **QF.** This option will always snap to quarter frames (one quarter the length of a full SMPTE frame) regardless of the zoom level.

- **Samples.** This option snaps at the sample level for extremely precise editing. You must be at extremely high zoom levels to use this snap resolution.

- **Snap to Absolute Value.** Selecting this option snaps any move to the nearest absolute position described by the Snap value. In other words, if your region begins at 1 1 2 67, and your Snap value is set to Bar, any drag will move the region to an even bar. Moving the region to the immediate right would result in a position of 2 1 1 1.

- **Snap Automation.** With this option enabled, all automation, track-based or region-based, will snap to the absolute Snap value, regardless of the Snap to Absolute Value setting.

- **Automation Snap Offset.** Selecting this option enables Automation Snap Offset, which allows you to offset any automation to compensate for any latency you may incur because of hardware, plug-in processing needs, or any other source of latency. Automation Snap Offset is covered in more detail in Chapter 10.

The Drag Menu

The majority of the Drag menu options determine how regions will react when two regions are moved into the same space, called *overlapping* (as the regions will then overlap each other). The exceptions are the Shuffle modes, which determine how regions respond when dragged or cut. The Drag menu options are as follows:

- **Overlap.** In this mode, two regions can overlap, as shown in Figure 6.70. Be careful not to lose one region behind another in this mode! You can always move regions to expose a region hidden due to overlapping.

Figure 6.70   Two regions that overlap in Overlap mode. The black vertical line represents where the Bass riff region ends underneath the Logic Power region.

- **No Overlap.** In this mode, two regions are not allowed to overlap. If you move a region into a position in which it would overlap another, the region that would be overlapped is simply cut and the hidden portion discarded, as shown in Figure 6.71.

Figure 6.71   In No Overlap mode, you can see that the portion of the Bass Riff region that would have been hidden underneath the Logic Power region was simply removed.

- **X-Fade (Crossfade).** This mode acts like Overlap mode for MIDI regions. However, if you overlap two audio regions, Logic Pro will automatically generate a crossfade between the two regions, as shown in Figure 6.72. See Chapter 7 for more information on audio crossfades. You can see the crossfade graphically represented over the overlapping regions.

Figure 6.72   Logic will automatically create crossfades for overlapping audio regions with the Drag mode set to X-Fade.

- **Shuffle R.** With Shuffle R mode enabled, if you move a region any distance to the right, it will automatically snap to the region to its immediate right, as shown in Figure 6.73. Obviously, if there is no other region to the right of the region you are moving, this will not happen.

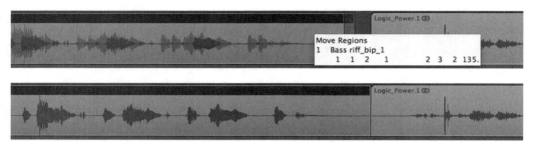

Figure 6.73   As you can see from the two figures, in Shuffle R mode, if you (a) move a region even a slight distance to the right, it will snap to the nearest region to its right. (b) Shuffle L mode is identical, but for regions you move left.

- **Shuffle L.** Shuffle L mode operates identically to Shuffle R mode, with the difference that if you move any region to the left, it will snap to the region to its immediate left. Shuffle L operates the same as the Pro Tools Shuffle mode. (Pro Tools does not have two shuffle modes—only one, which operates like Logic Pro's Shuffle L.)

Using Flex Time

When you work with MIDI, moving around individual notes or groups of notes to improve their timing or place them exactly where you want is easy, and there are many different tools you can use to accomplish this—Logic's many robust MIDI editors give you complete control over every detail of a MIDI performance, and quantization lets you easily align notes to a grid. Speeding up or slowing down a MIDI performance alters nothing about the pitch or timing of the performance.

Audio, traditionally, has been much more difficult to deal with in these regards. Sampled sound is completely time reliant, which means making it "elastic" while maintaining an audio file's sound quality is challenging at best. Logic used to handle this solely through use of the Time and Pitch Machine, which is covered in Chapter 7. Basically, you needed to work very deliberately with your audio to get the desired effect without drastically altering the character of your recording. Then you had the issue of lining up parts of audio performances—in other words, quantizing the audio. To handle this kind of work previously, a lot of precision cutting and arranging of audio regions was necessary. For a single timing issue, this is no big deal, and this is still an easy and effective way to correct such a simple issue, but when you're dealing with entire sections that have "gotten off the grid," you're talking about a significant amount of tedious work.

Flex Time editing helps make manipulating the timing of your audio files much easier and even gives you the ability to actually quantize your audio to the same grid your MIDI performances utilize. It offers a number of different modes, which allow you to tailor its effect to each individual track you wish to Flex, and it does this all nondestructively.

Enabling Flex View

In order to work with Flex Time, you need to enable Flex view. Flex view is an Arrange window state that adds a Flex Time menu to each audio track header, and therefore hides any automation lanes that may have been visible, along with the automation controls in the track header. To enable Flex view, select View > Flex View, click the Flex button in the Toolbar, or use the key command Command+F. Figure 6.74 shows a track header with Flex view enabled.

Figure 6.74   Enabling Flex view gives you access to the Flex menu in each audio track header.

The default Flex state for each audio track is Off. Clicking on the Flex menu reveals the different Flex modes available, which are assignable on a per-track basis. When you select a Flex mode on a track for the first time, Logic will analyze the audio and create transient markers—makers that generally denote meaningful points in your audio, such as higher amplitude transients, from which you can stretch or compress your audio. Transient markers will be discussed in greater detail in Chapter 7, but for now the important thing to remember is that initially, Flex will use these transient markers as the "pivot points" around which it will stretch or compress your audio.

Figure 6.75 shows the Flex menu.

Figure 6.75   The Flex menu lets you choose the Flex mode you will use for the selected track.

Each Flex mode is optimized for working on different types of material. Knowing which Flex mode to use with a particular kind of source will greatly improve the results you can achieve with

Flex Time. While we'll cover all the different Flex modes in more detail in the following sections, here are brief descriptions of the different Flex modes:

- **Off.** When Off is selected, Flex Time for the selected track is turned off.

- **Slicing.** Slicing mode allows you to flex your audio without applying any time compression or stretching; it works best with percussive sounds.

- **Rhythmic.** Rhythmic mode is great for flexing chordal rhythm parts.

- **Monophonic.** Monophonic mode is great for flexing single vocal parts and other single-note passages.

- **Polyphonic.** Polyphonic mode is best used on chordal material, particularly less rhythmic material you want to flex.

- **Tempophone.** Tempophone mode provides an effect similar to a tape-based time-stretching device called the Tempophone.

- **Speed.** Speed mode simply affets the playback speed of the source material. Your audio's pitch will be affected in Speed mode.

You can also set the Flex mode in the Track Parameter box of the selected track. There are added Flex parameters available in the Track Parameter box for most Flex modes. Let's deal with the basics of Flex Time, such as creating and moving Flex markers, which are generally derived from transient markers. Then we'll look at each Flex mode's parameters in more detail.

Flex Time Editing Basics

The basics of Flex Time stretching or compressing are incredibly simple. You can stretch or compress an entire region if you wish, or you can just alter the timing of a small section of a region. Figure 6.76 shows a region with Flex view engaged. Note the white vertical lines—these are the Flex markers.

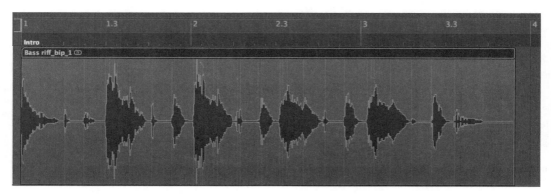

Figure 6.76 When Flex view is on, regions on tracks that have Flex Time enabled show vertical Flex markers. Flex markers are points in your audio from which you can stretch or compress your audio.

To stretch or compress an audio region on a Flex-enabled track, simply move your cursor to the beginning or end of the region and click-drag the region. Figure 6.77 shows the region in Figure 6.76 stretched to the next barline.

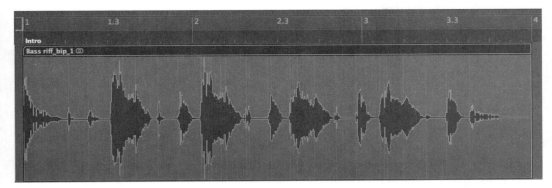

Figure 6.77   To stretch or compress an entire audio region, simply click-drag either end of the region.

Stretching or compressing a section of your audio within a region is just as simple. First, drag the cursor into the top half of your Flex Time–enabled audio region. You'll notice the cursor changes to a vertical line. We'll discuss the function of that cursor mode in the next section. What we need to do now is drag the cursor near a transient marker. This changes the cursor from a simple vertical line to a line with a triangle at the top. When you see this cursor tool mode, shown in Figure 6.78a, click your mouse, and a Flex marker will be created at the location of the selected transient marker, as shown in Figure 6.78b.

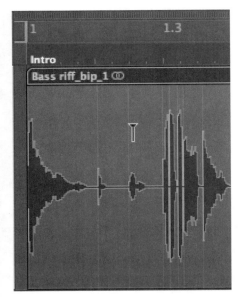

Figure 6.78a   Moving the cursor near a transient marker in a Flex Time–enabled audio region changes the cursor to a Flex marker tool.

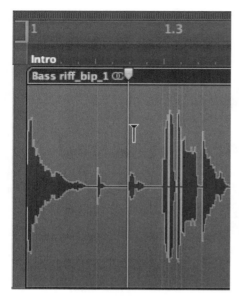

Figure 6.78b   The Flex marker tool lets you change a transient marker to a Flex marker with a simple click of the mouse.

Now you can drag the selected Flex marker left or right. Again, when you move the cursor over the Flex marker, the cursor mode changes to a tool that adds what look like minature audio waveforms emanating from either side of the Flex marker tool, as shown in Figure 6.79. When the cursor changes to this mode, you can click-drag the selected Flex marker.

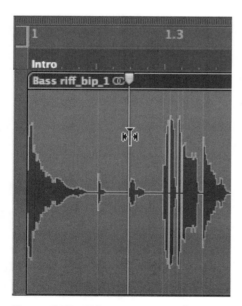

Figure 6.79   When you move the cursor over a Flex marker, the cursor gives you the ability to move the Flex marker by simply click-dragging it.

If you move your newly created Flex marker, you'll notice something that you could find problematic—the entire region is affected, not just the audio in the immediate area of the Flex marker. If this is all you could accomplish with Flex Time editing, it would make Flex Time editing less than "flexible." In order to affect the timing of a particular section of your audio region, you need to create Flex markers to either side of the Flex marker you wish to move. Obviously, this means that if you are moving the beginning or end of a region, you only need to create one Flex marker to the right or the left, respectively.

In the middle of a region, you would need to create three Flex markers to flex a particular bit of audio—the Flex marker you wish to move and markers to create boundaries to either side. You can, of course, create these individually, and there may be times when that would be advantageous—for example, when flexing an area that encompasses multiple transient markers—but you can also utilize another cursor tool mode to accomplish this. Move the cursor to the bottom half of your Flex Time–enabled audio region. The Flex marker tool now has three vertical lines, as you can see in Figure 6.80.

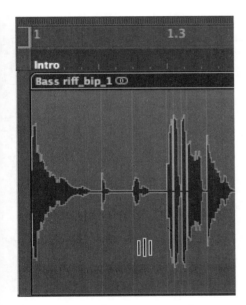

Figure 6.80   When you move the cursor to the lower half of a Flex Time–enabled region, the Flex marker tool has three vertical lines.

As with the Flex marker tool in the upper half of an audio region, moving the tool next to a transient marker adds triangles to the top of each vertical line. Clicking your mouse will then create Flex markers for the selected transient marker and the transient markers immediately to the right and left of the selected transient marker, as shown in Figure 6.81.

You can now move the middle Flex marker, which will only affect the audio between the outer Flex markers, which you can see in Figure 6.82.

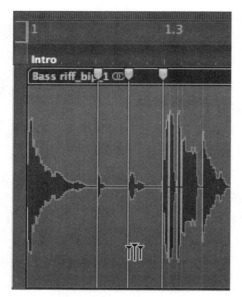

Figure 6.81 Clicking on the selected transient marker changes it and the transient markers to its immediate right and left into Flex markers.

Figure 6.82 With three Flex markers now created, you can freely move the middle Flex marker and only affect the audio within the outer Flex markers.

Flex Markers versus Transient Markers   If you think that Flex and transient markers are the same things, and you're confused about the difference, don't be alarmed—they *are* similar, and this can be quite confusing! Thankfully, once explained, it becomes obvious, you'll never forget again, and it will make all of Logic's Flex Time features make more sense.

As we wrote above, *transients* refer to the characteristics of the audio file—generally moments of peak amplitidude that are rhythmically and musically important. Therefore, *transient markers* are part of the audio file, as they relate to the recorded material itself. These markers inform the time stretching algorithms how to work their magic.

Flex markers, however, relate to the Arrange time stretching and compression feature of Logic. So it is the Flex markers (and the Flex markers *alone*) that you use for stretching and compressing your audio on the Arrange. In other words, with few exceptions, if you are working with Flex mode in the Arrange, you'll be working with Flex markers, and if you're working with audio transient markers, you'll be working in the Sample Editor. (More on transient markers in Chapter 7.)

You'll see in a moment that there are a few exceptions, such as creating Flex markers from another audio file's transient markers or using Flex with regions that don't have tempo information, but the above is true in all other cases. If you're "flexing" audio on the Arrange, just worry about Flex markers.

Flexing your audio is just that simple, but there's a lot more depth in Flex Time editing than these simple elements. What if the transient markers don't line up with the points in your audio you want to flex? Let's find out.

Creating New Flex Markers

Creating your own Flex markers, independent of the transient markers Logic has created, is every bit as easy as it was to convert a transient marker into a Flex marker. Remember that we mentioned that when the Flex marker tool is in the upper half of a Flex Time–enabled audio region and is not near a transient marker, it is a single, vertical line? To create a single Flex marker at a location you determine, simply move the Flex marker tool to the point in your audio where you would like to create a Flex marker and click your mouse. Figure 6.83 shows the same section of audio that we have been using since Figure 6.78a, but notice the Flex marker created in a location where there was no transient marker.

Similarly, when you click the mouse in the lower half of your audio region away from a transient marker, a Flex marker will be created at that point and at the transient markers to the immediate right and left of that point, which you can see in Figure 6.84.

Creating Flex Markers with the Marquee Tool

You can also use the Marquee tool to create Flex markers. Select an area of your Flex-enabled audio region with the Marquee tool. Switch the cursor back to the Pencil tool. When you drag the cursor over the upper half of the audio region in the marquee area, it becomes a Hand tool. Click

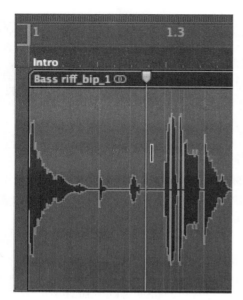

Figure 6.83   To create a new Flex marker, click your mouse in the upper half of your Flex Time–enabled region at the point you want to flex.

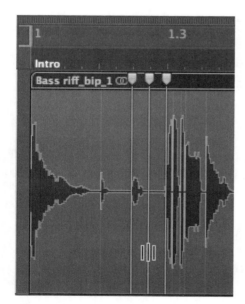

Figure 6.84   Clicking in the lower half of a Flex-enabled audio region away from a transient marker creates Flex markers at the point you click and at the transient markers to the immediate right and left.

on the marquee area with the Hand tool, and Flex markers will be created at the edges of the marquee area and at the transient markers to the immediate right and left, as shown in Figure 6.85.

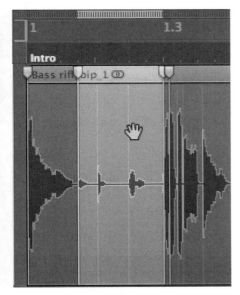

Figure 6.85   When you click with the Hand tool on the upper half of a marquee selection in your Flex-enabled audio region, Flex markers are created at the edges of the marquee area and at the transient markers to the immediate right and left of the marquee region.

When you click in the lower half of your marquee selection, Flex markers are created at the edges of the marquee area and at the point you clicked.

Creating Flex Markers from Another Audio Region's Transients

There may come a time when you're working on a project and you want to line up a Flex marker in one audio region with a transient marker in another audio region. First, make sure the regions are on adjoining tracks. Next, click on the region in which you would like to create the new Flex marker, and while holding the mouse button, drag the cursor to the adjacent track, find the transient maker from which you'd like to create your new Flex marker, and release the mouse button. When you drag the cursor over the second region, a Flex marker line will extend through both regions, allowing you to see what you're doing clearly, and the line will snap to the transient markers of the second region as you move the cursor. You can see this process in action in Figures 6.86a, 6.86b, and 6.86c. Figure 6.86a shows two Flex-enabled regions. The lower region has few transient markers in the selected area, and we'd like to create a new Flex marker from a transient in the upper region. Therefore Figure 6.86a shows the two regions before we do anything. Figure 6.86b shows the two regions as we drag the cursor from the lower region into the upper region. Figure 6.86c shows the resulting Flex marker.

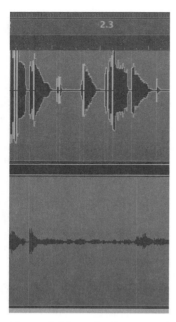

Figure 6.86a   The lower region has few transtient markers, and we'd like to create a Flex marker at the exact location of a transient marker in the upper region.

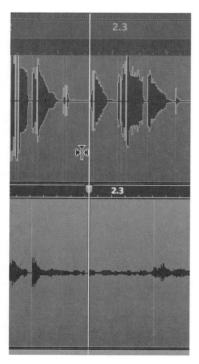

Figure 6.86b   Clicking on the lower region and dragging the cursor to the upper region lets you snap the Flex marker tool to the transients in the upper region.

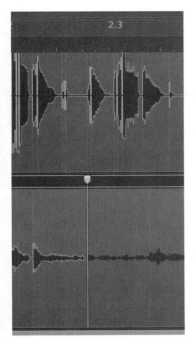

Figure 6.86c   The Flex marker in the lower region is at the exact location of its parent transient marker in the region above.

If you click on the lower half of the destination region and drag to the second region, three Flex markers will be created—two at the transient markers to the right and left of where you clicked, and one in line with the parent transient marker in the second region. Note that regardless of where you click in the destination region, moving the cursor left or right as you select a parent transient will affect the audio in the destination region, so you want to begin by clicking in an area very close to the location of the parent transient to avoid any unnecessary impact on your audio.

Flexing Audio with an Unknown or Inconsistent Tempo   Flexing audio when Logic doesn't know the tempo of the audio material, either because the file has no tempo information or because it wasn't played to a click or it otherwise changes tempo, can lead to some pretty awful results. Luckily, with the Detect Tempo command and Beat Mapping track, we can make Flex work wonders even in these difficult situations.

In Chapter 5, we talked about the Beat Mapping track, which lets you create a tempo map for an audio file that doesn't keep a consistent tempo. You can use this to generate tempo information and then embed that tempo information to the audio file.

First, refer to Chapter 5 on how to create a Beat Mapping global track and use that to create a tempo map of your audio file. If your audio file is consistant in tempo, the Options > Audio > Detect Tempo command might be enough.

Once Logic has generated tempo information for the audio file, use the command Options > Tempo > Export Tempo Information to Audio File. Once you export the tempo information to the audio file, that tempo information will then be used to create transient markers when Logic subsequently detects transients in Flex mode. Now you should be able to flex your audio with good results!

Moving and Deleting Flex Markers

There will probably be times when you create a Flex marker, but you're not entirely happy with the exact location of the marker. You could always Undo and create another Flex marker, or you could just move the one you have. To move a Flex marker, Option-click on the marker and drag it to the desired location, as in Figure 6.87. You can see the parent transient marker to the right of the moved Flex marker.

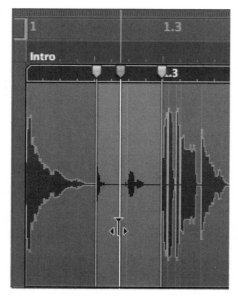

Figure 6.87   To move an existing Flex marker to a new location, Option-click and drag the marker.

To delete a Flex marker, you can double-click it or click it with the Eraser tool. You can delete multiple Flex markers by click-dragging the Eraser tool across them.

Flex Mode Parameters

Each Flex mode, with the exception of Speed, has at least one paramater available in the Track Parameter box. In addition, you can change the Flex mode of selected track in the Track Parameter box. Figure 6.88 shows the Track Parameter box of a track in Slicing mode.

Figure 6.88   The Track Parameter box for a track in Slicing mode.

Let's look at the parameters of the different Flex modes.

Slicing Mode

Slicing mode basically slices the audio and flexes it without stretching or compressing the audio.

When a track is in Slicing mode, its Track Parameter box offers the following parameters:

- **Fill Gaps.** Selecting Fill Gaps lets you ensure that any gaps between slices are filled per the Decay parameter setting.

- **Decay.** The Decay parameter lets you set a decay time for the Fill Gaps parameter.

- **Slice Length.** This parameter lets you control the length of each slice as a percentage. When you set this parameter below 100%, you are effectively shortening each slice, so the Fill Gaps and Decay parameters are not available.

Rhythmic Mode

Rhythmic mode is good for rhythmic chordal parts, and as such, flexing the audio can create some unwanted artifacts that the Rhythmic mode parameters help to mitigate. The Rhythmic mode parameters are:

- **Loop Length.** The Loop Length parameter lets you define the length as a percentage of the end of a time-stretched section of your audio that will be looped. This is similar to the looping that one might perform in the decay phase of a sampled instrument to help ensure a more natural decay phase.

■   **Decay.** The Decay parameter lets you define the decay time of any looping that will occur.

■   **Loop Offset.** The Loop Offset parameter lets you move the start point of the looped section up to 100 ms earlier.

Monophonic Mode

Monophonic mode works best on monophonic sources. There is only one parameter for Monophonic mode, and that is the Percussive check box. Select the Percussive check box if your source audio is more percussive, or staccato. Otherwise, leave this option unselected.

Polyphonic Mode

Polyphonic mode works best on more legato polyphonic material and is a very processor-hungry Flex mode. As with Monophonic mode, Polyphonic mode offers only a single paramater, Complex. Selecting Complex allows for more internal transients in your audio.

Tempophone Mode

Tempophone mode is not the mode you would want to use for natural-sounding flexing, as it produces a more grainy effect. Tempophone mode offers two parameters:

■   **Grain Size.** The Grain Size parameter defines the size of each grain of audio in milliseconds, from 0.10 ms to 500 ms.

■   **Crossfade.** The Crossfade parameter controls the amount of crossfade from one grain to the next. The lower the setting, the less crossfading you will hear.

Using the Flex Tool

The Flex tool is useful for quick Flex edits of audio when you are not in Flex Editing mode. It can use the transients detected in your audio as guides, much like you would see when creating three Flex markers with the Flex Marker tool and moving the middle Flex marker. Figure 6.89 shows the Flex Tool being used to flex a bit of audio.

When the Flex tool nears a transient, its appearance changes, and you can then flex your audio at that transient. Figure 6.90 shows the Flex tool near a transient.

You can also use the Marquee tool in conjunction with the Flex tool. Select an area of your audio region with the Marquee tool, switch to the Flex tool, and you can flex the selected area as you would when you click the upper half of a marquee selection in Flex Editing mode.

In addition, you can move Flex markers with the Flex tool in the same way you can when in Flex Editing mode. Drag the Flex tool to a transient, as in Figure 6.90, and Option-drag the marker to the desired location.

Figure 6.89   The Flex tool lets you flex your audio when you're not in Flex Editing mode.

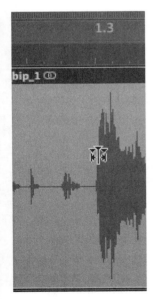

Figure 6.90   You can flex your audio at transients with the Flex tool, too.

Adding Files to the Arrange Window

As noted previously, recording audio and MIDI is not the only way to create regions. You can also add preexisting files into the Arrange window in Logic. There are a number of ways to add files:

- As already explained, if you Shift-click the Pencil tool in an Audio track, Logic will present you with the Add File dialog box to select an audio file to add at the clicked position.

- By choosing File > Import, you can import audio or MIDI files into Logic. If you use the Open dialog box to navigate to an audio or MIDI file, this command imports the file into Logic. If you selected a MIDI file, this command creates one or more regions on the Arrange; if you selected an audio file, this command imports it to the Audio Bin, from which you can drag the audio file into a track in the Arrange or use the Add to Arrange command to create a region for it.

- You can drag audio or MIDI files from your computer's desktop (or any file directory) onto your Arrange. This method drops the dragged audio or MIDI file directly onto a track on the Arrange. If it is an audio file, this method also adds the file to the Audio Bin.

- You can drag audio or MIDI files from the Library to the Arrange. The Library is explained in detail in Chapter 12.

- If you are working with an audio file, you can add it to the Audio Bin using the Add Audio File command and then drag that file from the Audio Bin into the Arrange or use the Add to Arrange command. These methods are explained in more detail in the next chapter.

Expert Tip: Using Folders When Importing Standard MIDI Files   Sasso has another great tip for how Folder tracks can assist when importing Standard MIDI Files into Logic:

"If a Standard MIDI File (SMF) has multiple tracks, dragging it to the Arrange window will create a separate region for each track. To keep them together and well organized, first create an empty folder, then open it and drag the SMF into the Arrange window displaying the folder's contents. If some of the resulting regions contain multiple channels, use 'Demix by MIDI Channel' to further separate them."

Bouncing in Place

Bouncing tracks and regions in place, like Freeze tracks, is another great way to conserve system resources. A track or region that is bounced in place is given some of the same options that you see when you bounce your project, with added control over things such as volume and pan automation and whether new tracks are created for the bounced files. It allows you to bounce tracks directly into your project that you are "finished" with, without the extra burden of deleting regions on your selected track or adding tracks to your project and dragging the bounced file into the new track and lining it up properly. It also allows you the flexibility to use external gear via the External Intstrument or I/O plug-in.

Bouncing Tracks in Place

The Bounce Track in Place command lets you bounce an entire track and have the resulting bounce file automatically added back into the Arrange. To use the Bounce Track in Place command, select the track you wish to bounce in place and then select Track > Bounce Track in Place, or use the key command Command+Control+B. The Bounce Track in Place dialog, shown in Figure 6.91, will open, giving you some options for how Logic will handle the bounce in place.

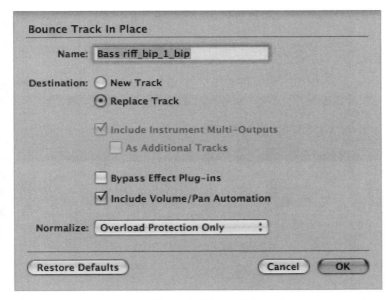

Figure 6.91 The Bounce Track in Place dialog gives you a number of different options for controlling how Logic performs the bounce in place.

The options in the Bounce Track in Place dialog are:

■ **Name.** The Name field is automatically named based on the track name, but you can rename the bounced file if you wish.

■ **New Track.** If you select New Track as the destination for your bounced file, Logic will create a new track below the selected track, and the bounced file will be added to the new track.

■ **Replace Track.** If you select Replace Track as the destination for your bounced file, Logic will bounce the selected track and place it on a new track that replaces the original track.

- **Include Instrument Multi-Outputs.** If you are bouncing a multi-output software instrument in place, selecting this command will also bounce the output of any dependent aux channels into your bounce file.

- **As Additional Tracks.** This sub-option of the Include Instrument Multi-Outputs option lets you create a separate bounce file for each multi-instrument aux output.

- **Bypass Effect Plug-Ins.** When you select this option, any effects plug-ins on the track will be bypassed for the bounce.

- **Include Volume/Pan Automation.** When you select this option, any volume or pan automation on the selected track will be performed during the bounce in place process.

- **Normalize.** The Normalize menu gives you options for normalizing the signal in the bounce, or finding the peak transient and increasing it to 0 dBFS, and increasing the level of the rest of the file by the same amount. For more on the Normalize menu and its functions, see the section "Bouncing Your Mix" in Chapter 11.

Click OK, and the track will be bounced, with the resulting file(s) added back to the Arrange window per your instructions. Figure 6.92 shows a track before and after a bounce in place.

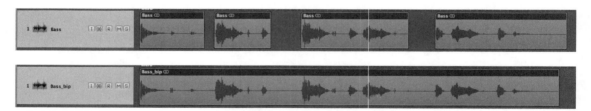

Figure 6.92   A track before and after using the Bounce Track in Place command.

Bouncing Regions in Place

Bouncing regions in place is very similar to bouncing a track in place. This command allows you to selectively bounce the regions on a track either alone or in combination with other regions. To use the Bounce Regions in Place command, select the regions you wish to bounce in place and then select Region > Bounce Regions in Place or use the key command Control+B. The Bounce Regions in Place dialog, shown in Figure 6.93, will open, giving you some options for how Logic will handle the bounce in place.

As you can see, some of the options in the Bounce Regions in Place dialog are identical to those in the Bounce Track in Place dialog shown in Figure 6.91. There are a few differences though. The options in the Bounce Regions in Place dialog are:

- **Name.** The Name field is automatically named based on the track name, but you can rename the bounced file if you wish.

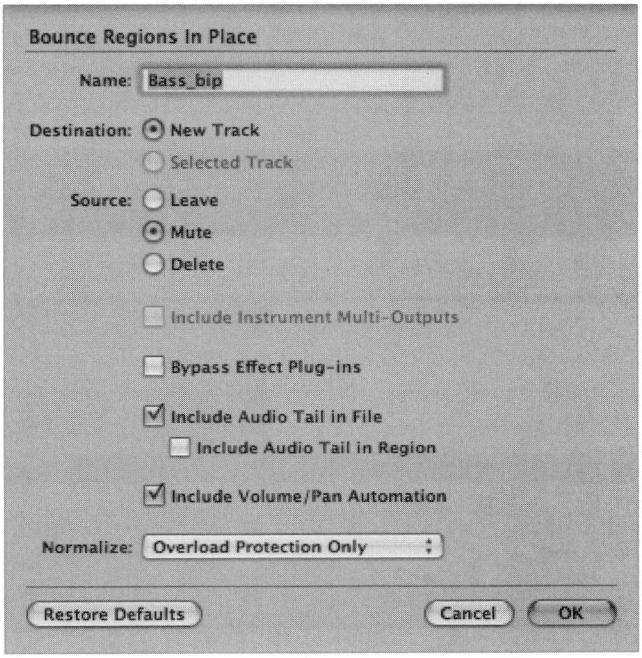

Figure 6.93   The Bounce Regions in Place dialog.

- **New Track.** If you select New Track as the destination for your bounced file, Logic will create a new track below the selected track, and the bounced file will be added to the new track.

- **Selected Track.** If you select Selected Track as the destination for your bounced file, Logic will bounce the selected regions and place them on the selected track.

- **Leave.** Selecting Leave keeps the parent regions intact and active after the bounce.

- **Mute.** Selecting Mute mutes the parent regions after the bounce.

- **Delete.** Selecting Delete deletes the parent regions from the Arrange after the bounce.

- **Include Instrument Multi-Outputs.** If you are bouncing a multi-output software instrument in place, selecting this command will also bounce the output of any dependent aux channels into your bounce file.

- **Bypass Effect Plug-Ins.** When you select this option, any effects plug-ins on the track are bypassed for the bounce.

- **Include Audio Tail in File.** Selecting this option ensures that the bounce will continue until the very end of the region's audio tail.

- **Include Audio Tail in Region.** This option ensures that the full extent of the audio tail will be included in the resulting bounce file.

- **Include Volume/Pan Automation.** When you select this option, any volume or pan automation on the selected track will be performed during the bounce in place process.

- **Normalize.** The Normalize menu gives you options for normalizing the signal in the bounce, or finding the peak transient and increasing it to 0 dBFS, and increasing the level of the rest of the file by the same amount. For more on the Normalize menu and its functions, see the section "Bouncing Your Mix" in Chapter 11.

Click OK, and the selected regions will be bounced and added back to the Arrange per your instructions in the Bounce Regions in Place dialog. Figure 6.94 shows two regions selected on one track and the bounce file that is produced when those regions are bounced in place.

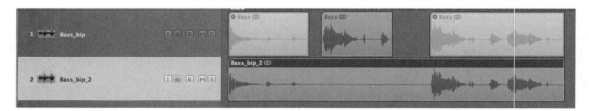

Figure 6.94   Two regions on the top track are selected and bounced in place, resulting in the new lower track and the new region on it.

Bouncing All Tracks in Place

In addition to these track and region bounce in place functions, you can also bounce your entire project in place. Select Track > Bounce-Replace All Tracks. First you will be greeted with a warning dialog inviting you to save your project. Since you're a smart Logic user, you'll select Yes because even though you save your projects regularly, it never hurts to save it one more time before performing a huge operation. Once you select your save option, the Bounce Replace All Tracks dialog, shown in Figure 6.95, will appear.

There are two options and one menu in the Bounce Replace All Tracks dialog, which are identical in function to the same commands in the Bounce Track in Place dialog. Click OK, and your entire project will be bounced in place!

Other Transient-Related Functions in the Arrange

The use of transient markers in Logic Pro is extensive, and the more you get used to working with them and their related processes, the more mileage you'll get out of Logic. There are a few more processes in the Arrange that utilize transient markers to perform their functions, and we'll explore those processes now.

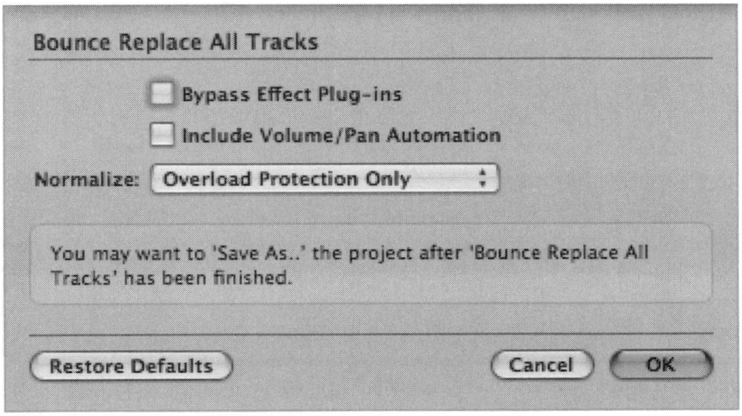

Bounce Replace All Tracks

☐ Bypass Effect Plug-ins

☐ Include Volume/Pan Automation

Normalize: [Overload Protection Only ‡]

You may want to 'Save As..' the project after 'Bounce Replace All Tracks' has been finished.

(Restore Defaults)　　　　　(Cancel)　(OK)

Figure 6.95　The Bounce Replace All Tracks dialog.

Replacing and Doubling Drum Tracks

One very handy function in the Arrange that makes use of transient markers is the Drum Replacement/Doubling command found in the Track menu or accessed via the key command Control+D. When you run this command on a track, the regions on the track are analyzed for transients, a software instrument track with EXS24 loaded and trigger notes in place is created immediately below the selected track, as shown in Figure 6.96, and the Drum Replacement/Doubling dialog, shown in Figure 6.97, opens. The Library tab is also opened, allowing you to select a different replacement drum sound.

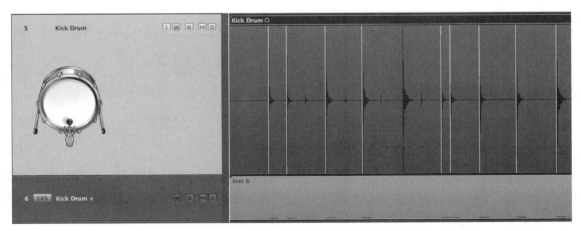

Figure 6.96　When you run the Drum Replacement/Doubling command, the regions on the selected track are analyzed for transients. A Software Instrument track is added directly below the selected track. A region with trigger notes in line with the transients derived from the Audio track is created, and an EXS24 instance with the appropriate triggered drum sound is instantiated.

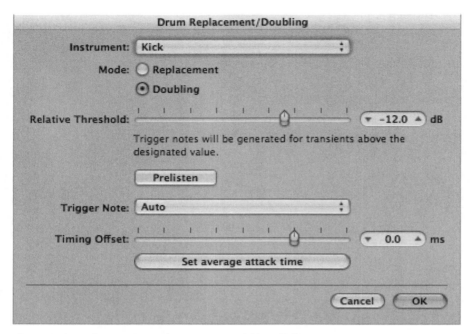

Figure 6.97 The Drum Replacement/Doubling dialog.

The Drum Replacement/Doubling dialog gives you a variety of options for defining how your drums are doubled or replaced:

- **Instrument.** The Instrument menu lets you define what kind of drum will be processed. The type of drum you define here will be loaded in the EXS24 instance on the related Software Instrument track. The Instrument menu options are Kick, Snare, Tom, and Other. You could therefore, for example, analyze a kick drum pattern but replace it with a snare drum if you wanted.

- **Replacement.** If you select Replacement, the original track will be muted, and the new Software Instrument track sound will replace the original sound.

- **Doubling.** If you select Doubling, the new Software Instrument sound will double the original Audio track.

- **Relative Threshold.** The Relative Threshold control lets you define the threshold below which transients will be ignored. The lower the setting, the more transients will be doubled or replaced; the higher the setting, the fewer will be doubled or replaced.

- **Prelisten.** Clicking Prelisten lets you hear the results you will achieve with the current Drum Replacement/Doubling dialog settings.

- **Trigger Note.** The Trigger Note menu lets you define what note will be triggered. This is particularly handy if you are going to use a custom drum kit for replacement or doubling or a drum at a non-standard note in Ultrabeat, for example. Auto sets the note based on the Instrument setting to the appropriate General MIDI note.

■ **Timing Offset.** The Timing Offset setting lets you alter the placement of the replaced or doubled drums forward or backward in milliseconds.

■ **Set Average Attack Time.** This command sets an offset for the slicing position for all regions on the parent Audio track.

When you're finished tweaking the settings to achieve the desired result, click OK, and you're done!

Converting Regions to Sampler Tracks

You can also turn regions into EXS24 sampler instrument settings by executing the Convert Regions to New Sampler Track command in the Audio menu, also accessible via the key command Control+E. When you select an audio region or regions and execute the Convert Regions to New Sampler Track command, the Convert Regions to New Sampler Track dialog, shown in Figure 6.98, will open.

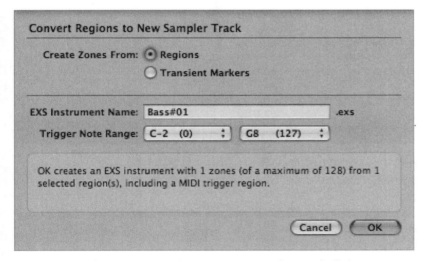

Figure 6.98   The Convert Regions to New Sampler Track dialog.

The options in the Convert Regions to New Sampler Track dialog are:

■ **Regions.** When you select the Convert Zones From Regions radio button, a new EXS24 zone will be created for each selected region.

■ **Transient Markers.** When you select the Convert Zones from Transient Markers radio button, the zones in the new EXS24 instrument will be created using the transient markers in the selected audio regions. The result is similar to what you would find in a ReCycle file, where the audio is sliced into "playable" bits.

■ **EXS Instrument Name.** You can name your new EXS24 instrument here.

■ **Trigger Note Range.** The Trigger note range menus let you define the upper and lower extent the newly created zones will be mapped to in EXS24, from C-2 to G8.

When you click OK, the audio will be processed per your instructions, a new Software Instrument track will be created directly below the parent track with an instance of EXS24 loaded with your new sampler instrument, and a region will be created on the new track with trigger notes created to play back your new instrument exactly like the parent audio region(s). You can see this in Figure 6.99.

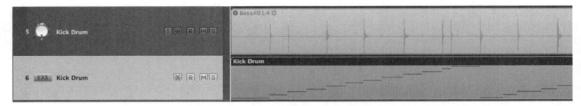

Figure 6.99   After executing the Convert Regions to New Sampler Track command, a new Software Instrument track is created under the parent track, with your new sampler instrument loaded into EXS24. A region featuring the appropriate trigger notes for playing back your sampler instrument exactly like the parent audio region is also created.

Using Logic Pro Synthesizers   There isn't nearly enough room in this book to explore the EXS24 mkII and all the other professional, world-class software instruments that come with Logic Pro. However, if you are interested in more information on Logic Pro's instruments, *Using Logic Pro Synthesizers* by Kevin Anker (Course Technology PTR, 2010) is the perfect companion to *Logic Pro 9 Power!*

Slicing Audio Regions at Transient Markers

There is one more command you can use in the Arrange that utilizes transient markers. When in Flex Editing mode, you can Control-click on a region and select the Slice at Transient Markers command. The selected region will be split into new regions at its transient markers, as shown in Figure 6.100.

There are many powerful things you can accomplish with transient markers. Now that you've seen some of these things, you're probably thinking that all this is great, but what's the point if you can't customize your transient markers? No worries—Logic has this covered too in the Sample Editor, as you'll learn in the next chapter.

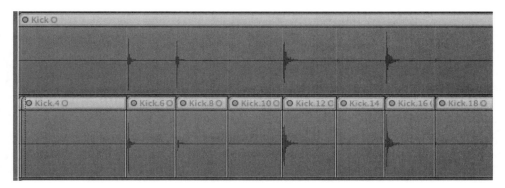

Figure 6.100   An audio region before and after executing the Slice at Transient Markers command. You can see that the new regions all line up with the transient markers.

Automation

Automation is one of Logic's more extensive features, and Chapter 10 will examine automation in depth. However, since most automation functions are in the Arrange window, a brief explanation of automation follows.

Track-Based Automation

Track-based automation (TBA) is the most powerful, accurate, and modern automation in Logic. With TBA, your automation is not connected to the regions on a particular track lane, but to the actual track lane itself. This is how automation would function with an actual hardware mixer, in which you automate a mixer channel, not the material that is playing through the channel. It is possible, however, to tie TBA to the regions on a track, which is explained in Chapter 10.

When you turn on track-based automation by choosing View > Track Automation or by pressing A, the track lane expands, and you will see the various automation options. Figure 6.101 shows a track with track-based automation visible.

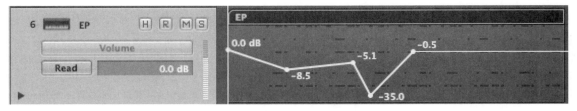

Figure 6.101   This track has track-based automation turned on, and you can see volume automation data in the track lane.

Because the automation lane takes up the majority of the track lane, when you want to edit, move, and resize regions, you'll need to be careful to click only in the top label portion of the region above the automation data—otherwise, Logic assumes that you are trying to edit your automation data, not the region.

Region-Based Automation (Hyper Draw)

Before Logic introduced TBA, the only method of automation was called Hyper Draw. Hyper Draw uses standard MIDI messages to automate MIDI data. These MIDI messages are directly tied to the region for which they were created; hence, Hyper Draw is also known as region-based automation (RBA). Figure 6.102 shows a track with RBA information visible.

Figure 6.102   This track has volume Hyper Draw (region-based automation) data displayed. The Track List does not show as much information for the RBA data as for the TBA data in Figure 6.101. Notice also that the RBA information is included as an actual part of the region itself, unlike TBA information, which is connected to the track.

One of the main advantages to RBA is that as you move regions around, RBA automatically moves with them. In general, however, RBA does not have the high resolution or show you as much information on the Track List as TBA does. You can turn RBA data into TBA data, as you will explore in Chapter 10.

Caps Lock Keyboard

Finally, although this isn't technically a part of the Arrange window, since you may want to use it to record software instrument performances, we'll mention the Caps Lock Keyboard here. If you have Enable Caps Lock Keys checked in the Caps Lock Keys tab of the Global Preferences window, pressing the CAPS LOCK key will bring up the onscreen keyboard shown in Figure 6.103.

The Caps Lock Keyboard is a real-time MIDI keyboard with a maximum of six notes of polyphony. You can use it to audition software instruments without having to reach for your MIDI controller, or you can even use the Caps Lock Keyboard to record a MIDI performance in real time! The numeric keys can select from among the 10-octave range of the Caps Lock Keyboard, you can use the spacebar as a sustain pedal (also set in the aforementioned Preferences window), and you can assign its velocity in the Z-row of your computer keyboard! Obviously, you toggle the Caps Lock Keyboard by pressing the CAPS LOCK key.

The Caps Lock Keyboard clearly doesn't replace a full MIDI keyboard controller, but if you are on a plane, train, or automobile with no access to a real keyboard, Logic's Caps Lock Keyboard is

Figure 6.103   The Caps Lock Keyboard.

very convenient. If you want to record a MIDI performance using it, just select your Software Instrument track in the Arrange, press the CAPS LOCK key, start recording, and play!

The Arrange window is perhaps the most complex window in Logic. There's a lot of information to digest here, but when you're comfortable with the Arrange, you'll be far along the path to being comfortable with Logic as a whole. The next chapter specifically explores using audio and Apple Loops in Logic.

7 Working with Audio and Apple Loops

Now that you've explored manipulating and editing regions, it's time to address manipulating and editing the data within those regions. Logic's handling of audio has always been one of its most lauded features. In this chapter, we'll examine how Logic Pro 9 handles audio and Apple Loops, as well as some useful and creative tips and tutorials for using these features.

Let's start by going into greater detail about the various audio channel strips types available in Logic Pro 9.

Types of Channel Strips

Logic offers many different audio channel strip types. Software instrument and audio channel strips are automatically assigned their own Arrange tracks, but you can assign any of the other audio channel strips to an Arrange track. They will then appear as channel strips in the Arrange Inspector, in the Mixer, and in the Mixer layer of the Environment.

A brief description of the different channel strip types follows:

- **Audio channel strips.** The audio channel strip is analogous to the standard Audio track on a hardware mixer. You record and play back audio files on Audio tracks. You will normally record or place audio onto an Audio track in the Arrange and then use the Audio track as a playback track. Audio tracks can be mono, stereo, or surround. They can use a hardware input or a bus as an input. A Logic project can include up to 255 stereo, mono, or surround Audio tracks.

- **Software instrument channel strips.** Like External MIDI tracks, Software Instrument tracks utilize MIDI regions instead of audio regions. Unlike External MIDI channel strips, software instrument channel strips actually pass the audio from software instruments through the effects and routing defined in each software instrument channel strip. Software instrument channel strips allow you to access the built-in or third-party plug-in software synthesizers that can be integrated into Logic. When you play back the MIDI regions of a software instrument, those MIDI regions will trigger the DSP algorithms of the software instrument to generate sound. Software instruments can be mono, stereo, surround, or multi-output.

Multi-output software instruments use aux objects for their additional outputs. (See Chapter 9, "Working with Software Instruments.") A Logic project can include up to 255 software instruments.

- **Aux channel strips.** Aux (auxiliary) channel strips in Logic do not record or play back audio regions. Instead, aux channel strips are routing destinations that can accept their input from a number of sources. They can accept the input of a bus, becoming a send destination for any send-capable channel strip. (See the upcoming "Channel Strip Components" section.) This also means that you can assign the output of a channel strip to a bus and assign the input of an aux channel strip to that bus. If you assign the outputs of multiple channel strips to the same bus, you can then assign an aux channel strip's input to that bus and use the aux channel strip as a master fader for those channels. Aux channel strips can accept their input from a multi-output software instrument, so each aux channel strip becomes the destination of a different output from the software instrument. If you are using Logic as a ReWire master, you use aux channel strips to bring the ReWire slave's audio into Logic. Finally, aux channel strips can take their inputs from your audio interface, allowing for complex routing of live audio. Aux channel strips can be bussed to other aux channel strips via either their sends or their output assignment. Aux channel strips can be mono, stereo, or surround. Logic supports up to 255 aux channel strips.

- **Input channel strips.** Input channel strips are used as a "live audio play-through" track in Logic. Unlike Audio tracks, on which you record audio and then play back audio regions, Arrange tracks with input channel strips are used for tracks that are always live—for example, a hardware synthesizer that you want to mix with the rest of your tracks in the Logic Mixer but you do not want to record onto an Audio track. Input channel strips can be mono or stereo and can output in mono, stereo, or surround. The number of hardware inputs on your audio interface determines how many input channel strips are available in Logic.

- **Output channel strips.** Output channel strips are used to send audio to your external hardware. They are usually the output destination of your other channel strips. You can use output objects to "bounce" audio—which means to create an audio file that contains the summation of all the channel strips routing their output to that particular output channel strip. Output channel strips can be mono, stereo, or surround. The number of hardware outputs on your audio interfaces determines how many output channel strips are available in Logic.

- **Master channel strip.** Logic offers a master channel strip. This channel strip does exactly what it says—it serves as a "master volume" for your song. The master channel strip does not stream any audio or MIDI data itself; it simply is used to adjust volume. If you are doing a surround mix or you are sending each track to a hardware mixer and using many output channel strips, having a master channel strip offers a convenient way to adjust the overall level.

- **External MIDI channel strip.** This isn't an audio channel strip at all, but we're including it here for completeness, since it appears in the Mixer along with your audio channels if you create External MIDI tracks. Like software instrument channel strips, these channel strips utilize MIDI data. If you are using a ReWire application with Logic and sending that application MIDI from Logic, you will use an External MIDI track assigned to your ReWire application. (Chapter 9 goes into using ReWire applications in more detail.) If you are using hardware synthesizers or other instruments and not using the External Instrument plug-in (again, see Chapter 9), the MIDI on this track will be directed to them.

The aforementioned channel strips are the only channel strips you'll ever need to use in Logic 9. However, there are two additional channel strip types that existed in Logic 7 and are still included in Logic 9 for compatibility purposes. We're including their descriptions here in case you are working on a project that began in Logic 7, but otherwise you will not need to use these channel strips—in fact, we strongly advise against using these, because they have been superseded by Aux tracks, which you should use instead.

- **Bus channel strips.** The bus channel strip does not play or record audio files at all—it is more of a "patch bay" track. Traditionally, busses on mixers were often push buttons that sent the audio on an audio channel to an auxiliary track or auxiliary output. Busses in Logic Pro 8 serve a similar purpose of being a patch bay between destinations for your audio, although in Logic you can also use an actual bus channel strip as a destination itself. Still, it's best to think of a bus as an internal routing between other channel strips in Logic, because the more flexible aux channel strip has supplanted the bus channel strip. The reasons for this change will be covered in Chapter 11, "Mixing in Logic." In the meantime, we'll briefly mention some of the things you can do with busses. You can have a bus route audio from other channel strips to hardware outputs. Aux channel strips may use busses as their input source. In addition, other channel strips can use their sends to route signal through or to a bus. Busses do not have sends on their own channel strips, because busses are the destination of sends from other channel strips, but you can put effects directly in the channel strip of a bus if you want. Bus channel strips can be mono, stereo, or surround. Logic offers up to 64 busses.

- **ReWire channel strips.** In previous versions of Logic, if you used ReWire applications with Logic, you would create unique ReWire channel strips that used the output of the ReWire application as their input. Now this task is handled completely by aux channels, and you cannot create ReWire channel strips. However, if you are working on an older project, you may see these channel strips.

Channel Strip Components

You've seen the channel strip in previous chapters. Now that we've described the different channel strip types, we'll go over the components of the channel strip and the subtle differences in the strips for various channel strip types. The channel strip is mostly utilized during mixing, which is covered in Chapter 11. However, editing audio requires some knowledge of the channel strip. You can use the channel strip in Figure 7.1 as your reference.

Figure 7.1   An audio channel strip.

Each of the components of this channel strip can be toggled on or off in the View menu in the Mixer or in the Inspector in the Mixer layer of the Environment or by Control-clicking in the Mixer and selecting items from the menu that appears. Both of these Mixers are covered in detail in Chapter 11. The following descriptions of the various components of the channel strip explain any differences that exist for a specific type of channel strip:

- **Channel strip Setting menu.** Clicking on a channel strip's Setting menu opens a menu that allows you to browse for and select, as well as manage, channel strip settings.

- **EQ.** If you double-click inside this rectangle, you will enable a thumbnail of the Channel EQ effect graph (using Logic's EQs is discussed in Chapter 11) inside the rectangle, and the Channel EQ effect is instantiated in the first insert slot. (Inserts are described next.) If there is already a plug-in inserted in the first insert slot, you can hold the Option key down while double-clicking inside the rectangle, and the Channel EQ will be instantiated in the first insert. If you have instantiated the Linear Phase EQ, then the EQ graph from this effect will be shown in the EQ rectangle. If the thumbnail image of the Channel or Linear Phase EQ is already showing in the channel strip, double-clicking on the thumbnail opens the respective EQ's Editor window. All audio channel strips contain the EQ section.

- **Inserts.** These rectangles represent slots into which you can "insert" effects into the channel strip. Logic Pro comes with 80 built-in effects, and you can also use various third-party plug-in effects. (This is discussed further in Chapter 11.) You add effects to inserts by clicking and holding the button until a pull-down menu of effects appears. When you select an effect, it appears in that insert slot, and the insert glows blue, indicating the effect is functioning. You can have up to 15 inserts in Logic. If you see fewer than the maximum number of insert slots on your channel strip, don't worry; when you fill the last insert slot on the screen, another slot will appear beneath it, and this will continue until you reach your version's maximum number of inserts. All channel strips can have inserts, although the nature of your project defines whether your output channel strips or the master channel strip has inserts. Your master channel strip will not have inserts unless you are working in surround, and then your outputs will not have inserts.

- **Sends.** Send knobs are used to route (send) a variable amount of the audio signal from channel strips through busses. When empty, sends appear to be empty rectangles (slots). When you click and hold on a send rectangle and add a send destination, not only does the destination appear in the slot, but a small dial appears to the right of the send for you to adjust the send level. If you see fewer than the maximum number of send rectangles on your channel strip, don't worry; when you fill the last send slot on the screen, another rectangle will appear beneath it, and this will continue until you reach the maximum of eight sends. Because busses are the destinations of sends, bus channel strips do not have sends themselves. When you assign an unused bus to a send, a new aux channel strip is automatically created as the destination for the bus.

- **I/O.** There are two rectangles under I/O; the upper rectangle is for selecting the input of the channel strip, and the lower rectangle is for selecting the output.

- **Input.** Each channel strip type features a different method of handling its input slot:

  - **Audio channel strips.** You may select any of your audio interface's physical inputs, as the input for this slot. You may also select any bus. You can also configure an Audio channel strip as a surround channel strip if your audio interface has enough inputs. If you choose surround, the input configuration is dictated in the Input tab of the I/O Assignments pane of the Audio Preferences window, which was covered in Chapter 3.

  - **Software instrument channel strips.** You may select any available software synthesizer as the input for this slot.

  - **Aux channel strips.** You may select your hardware inputs, busses, ReWire channels, or multi-output instrument outputs as the input for this slot. You can also choose to utilize your hardware inputs in surround if your audio interface has enough inputs.

- **Input channel strips.** Input channel strips have their input determined by the selected hardware input in the input channel strip's Channel parameter in the Inspector of the Mixer layer of the Environment, so the Input slot does not appear in the input channel strip. Currently, you can only configure input channel strips in mono or stereo.

- **Output channel strips.** These channel strips do not have rectangles for input, because they can only be used as destinations for other channel strips.

- **Output.** The output for all channel strips, except actual output channel strips, can be any available bus or output channel strip. If you are using a channel strip in surround, the master channel strip will automatically function as its output. The hardware output is selected in an output channel strip's Channel Parameter box in the Inspector of the Mixer layer of the Environment, so output channel strips do not have an output rectangle.

- **Group menu.** This window shows the group number of the selected channel strip. If the channel strip is not assigned to a group, this window is a darker gray than the rest of the channel strip. Groups are explained in Chapter 11. All types of channel strips, including MIDI channel strips, may belong to groups.

- **Automation Mode menu.** This window shows whether the channel strip is currently using Logic's track-based automation. If the channel strip is utilizing automation, the window displays whether the track is currently reading automation data, or which mode it is using to write automation data. Automation is explained in Chapter 10, "Using Automation in Logic." All channel strips, including MIDI channel strips, have automation slots.

- **Pan knob.** The large rotary knob below the Automation Mode menu is the Pan knob. This knob allows you to adjust the panorama—or stereo position—of the channel strip's audio in the stereo field. If you are in surround mode, you may adjust the channel strip's panorama on more than two axes. All channel strips except the master channel strip (but including MIDI channel strips) have Pan knobs.

- **Volume slider.** This long slider below the Pan knob, directly to the right of the channel strip audio meter, allows you to adjust the volume of the channel strip. All channel strips, including MIDI channel strips, have Volume sliders.

- **Channel strip meter.** This meter displays a bar line that represents the volume of the audio passing through the channel strip. It changes with each variation in volume of the channel strip's audio. The small box above the channel strip meter displays the highest volume peak that the channel strip's audio has hit up to that point in the project in the Clip Detector, directly above the channel strip meter. The channel strip meter has a range from –60 dB to +0 dBFS. There are two display scale options for the channel strip meters: Sectional dB-linear and Exponential. The Exponential scale gives you a higher metering resolution the closer the signal gets to +0 dBFS. The Sectional dB-linear scale provides a very high level of resolution along the entire metering range. You can change the display mode of the channel strip meters in the Mixer tab of the Display Preferences window or by Control-clicking on the dB scale at the left side of the Mixer. All audio channel strips have audio meters.

- **M.** This is the Channel Mute button. Clicking on this button mutes the channel strip (and all the tracks in the Arrange window assigned to the muted channel strip are silenced). All channel strips have the Channel Mute button.

- **S.** This is the Channel Solo button for a channel strip. Pressing this button silences all other currently unsoloed channel strips (and only those Arrange tracks assigned to the soloed track will be heard). All audio channel strips have Solo buttons.

- **Format button.** The single or double circle icon underneath the channel strip meter is the Format button. If the button is a single circle, the channel strip format is mono. If the button is a double circle, the channel strip format is stereo. Clicking the button toggles between mono and stereo. If you click and hold on an audio, aux, or bus channel strip's Format button, you can assign the channel strip to mono, stereo, left, right, or surround. If you select left or right, the Format button displays two separate circles, and the circle on the side you have chosen will be darkened. If you choose surround, the Format button will display five small circles. Software instrument channel strips do not have this button because the type of software synthesizer you selected will determine whether the software instrument channel strip is mono, stereo, or surround.

- **I.** This is the Input Monitoring button. Turning on this button allows you to monitor the signal through an audio channel strip without record-enabling the track.

- **R.** This is the Record-Enable button. If you click this button, the audio channel strip is ready to record audio through your audio interface. Only audio channel strips have R buttons, because they are the only channel strips that can record audio.

- **Bounce.** The Bounce button is only found on output channel strips or, in the case of surround projects, the master channel strip. Clicking this button brings up a dialog box enabling you to create a mono or stereo audio file from all the channel strips routed to that output channel strip or a surround bounce through the master channel strip. Bouncing is discussed further in Chapter 11.

- **D.** This is the Dim button, found only on the master channel strip. Switching on the Dim button drops the level of your audio to the predetermined level set in the General tab of the Audio Preferences window. This button is directly linked to the Dim button in the Transport.

The Audio Bin

The Audio Bin is, in a sense, a repository for recorded and imported audio files. You do not have to use every audio file listed in the Audio Bin in your project, but every audio file used in your project will be listed in the Audio Bin. The Audio Bin is far more than a simple list of files, however. First of all, the Audio Bin also keeps track of every audio region into which an audio file has been split. You can drag audio regions from the Audio Bin directly onto an audio track on the Arrange. The Audio Bin itself offers many ways to manage, group, and manipulate audio files and audio regions as well. The Audio Bin is available in the Media area of the Arrange window and as its own window. The Audio Bin window is unlike many other integrated browsers and their separate windows in that the Audio Bin window is slightly different in look and is a little more powerful in functionality than its integrated twin. If we mention that an operation can be performed in the Audio Bin, then that operation can performed in either the integrated Audio Bin or the Audio Bin window, but if we specifically mention that something can be done in the Audio Bin window, then that operation *cannot* be performed in the integrated Audio Bin. Figure 7.2 shows an integrated Audio Bin filled with audio files and audio regions. Figure 7.3 shows an Audio Bin window filled with the same audio files and regions.

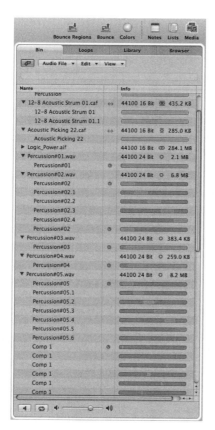

Figure 7.2   The Audio Bin.

The Audio Bin consists of local menus, buttons, and a Volume slider around its perimeter, an audio list in which the names of all your audio files and audio regions are listed, and then the Audio Bin Graphic Overview window. In this section, which is the majority of the Audio Bin, not

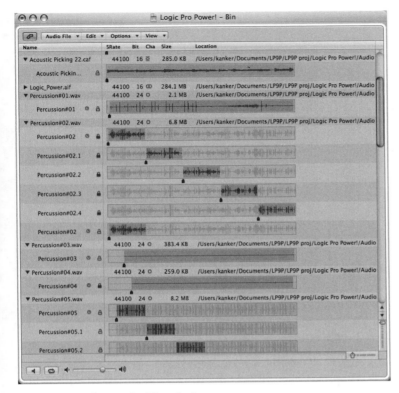

Figure 7.3 The Audio Bin window.

only do you see your audio regions represented in relation to the entire audio file that they are part of, but you can see sample rate, bit depth, size, and location information for all your audio files. In the Audio Bin window, you also see the actual waveforms of your audio files, their anchor points, and zoom controls that allow you to resize the view of your audio files.

We'll start our exploration of the Audio Bin with the local menus.

The Audio Bin Local Menus

Like all windows and editors in Logic, the Audio Bin features its own local menu containing commands that specifically affect audio and audio files. Keep in mind that for those commands that do not have key commands assigned by default, you can assign keys to them in the Key Commands window.

The Audio File Menu

The Audio File menu contains commands that operate on the audio files themselves. Figure 7.4 shows the Audio File menu of the Audio Bin.

An explanation of the Audio File menu commands follows.

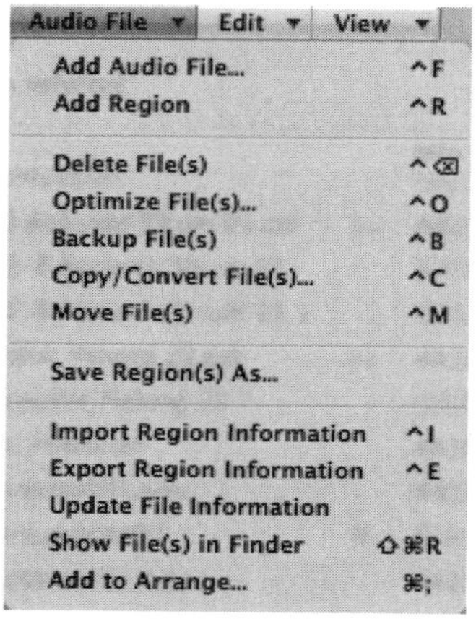

Figure 7.4   The Audio File menu of the Audio Bin.

- **Add Audio File.** This command brings up an Open File dialog box, which allows you to import audio files from your hard drive into the Audio Bin of your Logic project. You can then drag your file into the Arrange window or process it further in the Audio window. Logic is capable of importing files in WAV, Broadcast WAV, AIFF, CAF, SDII (Sound Designer II), MP3, or AAC format. The key command for this is Control+F.

- **Add Region.** If you select an audio file in the audio list, this command creates a new audio region for that audio file. The new audio region will initially be the full length of the audio file, but you can adjust this length. The key command for this is Control+R.

- **Delete File(s).** This command deletes all selected files. The key command for this is Control+Delete.

- **Optimize File(s).** This command deletes sections of audio files that are not used in your song. You can use this command to save hard drive space by eliminating unnecessary data, but beware that you don't accidentally erase a piece of audio that might prove useful. Because of this, you should use this command only when you are reasonably sure that you are completely finished with a given song. The key command for this is Control+O.

- **Backup File(s).** This command creates a duplicate of all selected audio files. These files are given the extension .dup. Generally, since any edits to regions are nondestructive (that is, they don't touch the file), this command is mostly useful if you are using time and pitch processing or editing samples, which each affect the actual audio file itself. The key command for this is Control+B.

- **Copy/Convert File(s).** This command brings up a dialog box in which you can duplicate or convert your selected audio file or files to AIFF, WAV, SDII, CAF, Apple Lossless, AAC, or MP3; for example, you could convert an AIFF file into a WAV file, or an SDII file into an AIFF file. You can, of course, choose the original format and simply make duplicate files.

This function is particularly useful when you want to export one or more files to a different format. You can also perform stereo conversion from a split format to an interleaved one or from an interleaved format to a split one, you can dither your audio file if you are changing bit rates, and you can choose to have the results of the process added to the Audio Bin. Figure 7.5 shows the Copy/Convert File As dialog.

These copy and conversion options are basically identical to the options you are given when you perform a bounce in Logic, which is covered in detail in Chapter 11. The key command for this is Control+C.

- **Move File(s).** When you choose this command, a dialog box appears, prompting you for a new location on your hard drive to move one or more selected audio files in the Audio Bin. If you move audio files without using this command, Logic will not know the new location of your audio file and will prompt you to find it. If you use this command, Logic will be able to keep track of where you moved your audio files. The key command for this is Control+M.

- **Save Region(s) As.** This command allows you to save one or more specific audio regions as separate audio files. This is very useful if you want to export only those selected regions to another application.

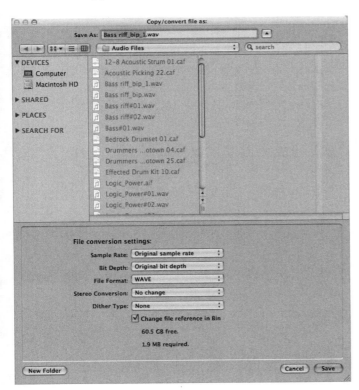

Figure 7.5   In the Copy/Convert File As dialog, you can duplicate files and convert them from one format to another.

- **Import Region Information.** This command allows you to import information from AIFF, CAF, WAV, and SDII audio regions you have added to your project. This allows you to add the information embedded in your audio file, such as tempo or position data, to the Audio Bin. The key command for this is Control+I.

- **Export Region Information.** This command allows you to export the information for the current audio file into the selected audio file. The key command for this is Control+E.

- **Update File Information.** If you find one or more of your audio regions is grayed out, that means Logic couldn't find the original audio file used by that audio region. When you select those grayed-out audio regions and choose this command, Logic presents a dialog box prompting you to navigate to the missing audio files. After using this command (and saving your song), Logic will remember the new file information.

- **Show File(s) in Finder.** If you select one or more audio regions, this command will then open Finder windows showing you the actual audio files on your hard drive that these regions point to. The key command for this is Shift+Command+R.

- **Add to Arrange.** You can select one or more audio regions and use this command to place them in the Arrange window. See the section "Adding Audio to the Arrange Window" later in this chapter for more details. The key command for this is Command+;.

The Edit Menu

This menu consists of some standard application editing functions and some functions specific to Logic. Figure 7.6 shows the Edit menu of the Audio Bin.

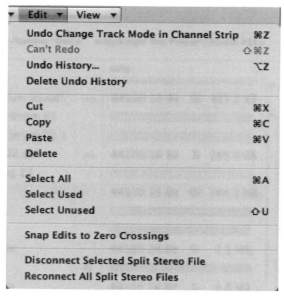

Figure 7.6   The Edit menu of the Audio Bin.

The first four commands in this menu—Undo, Redo, Undo History, and Delete Undo History—are the same commands as from the Arrange window's local Edit menu. See the previous chapter for detailed information. Definitions of the rest of the commands follow:

- **Undo.** This command reverts Logic to the state before the previous action. The key command for this is Command+Z.

- **Redo.** This command allows you to bring back an action you have undone. The key command for this is Shift+Command+Z.

- **Undo History.** This command opens the Undo History window, which was covered in Chapter 6. The key command for this is Option+Z.

- **Delete Undo History.** This command empties all previous actions from the Undo History window.

- **Cut.** This command removes the selected audio files and audio regions from their locations on the audio list and places them on the Clipboard. The key command for this is Command+X.

- **Copy.** The Copy command places a copy of the selected audio files and audio regions on the Clipboard. The key command for this is Command+C.

- **Paste.** This command pastes the contents of the Clipboard beneath the currently selected audio region or audio file in the audio list. The key command for this is Command+V.

- **Delete.** The Delete command removes any selected audio regions or audio files from the Audio Bin.

- **Select All.** You can select every audio file and audio region in the Audio Bin with this command. The key command for this is Command+A.

- **Select Used.** This command selects all the audio regions that are currently used in your song.

- **Select Unused.** This selects all the audio regions that are not currently used in your song. The key command for this is Shift+U.

- **Snap Edits to Zero Crossings.** A *zero crossing* occurs when the amplitude of the audio wave is at the zero line. If you turn on this option, all adjustments to audio regions fall at the nearest zero point. The advantage to this option is that you are far more likely to have seamless playback between two adjacent audio regions, since the amplitude of both audio regions will be at the zero crossing when they meet. The disadvantage is that this will sometimes interfere with where you want to make an edit if there doesn't happen to be a zero crossing at that point. Keep in mind that if you turn this option on, it also holds true for audio region resizing and splitting in the Arrange window.

- **Disconnect Selected Split Stereo File.** This command converts a split stereo file into two un-linked mono audio files. This is useful if you want to process or edit each side of the split stereo file separately.

- **Reconnect All Split Stereo File(s).** This command reconnects all unlinked mono files that used to be part of a split stereo file. This is especially useful when you import Audio tracks that were originally split stereo files, but their link was broken in the process of exporting them from their original application.

The View Menu

The View menu offers options for viewing and sorting audio regions and audio files in the Audio Bin. Figure 7.7 shows the View menu of the Audio Bin.

Figure 7.7   The View menu of the Audio Bin.

The various options in the View menu are as follows:

- **Files Sorted By.** This entry opens a hierarchical menu, which allows you to check one of six options for sorting audio files in the audio list: None, Name, Size, Drive, Bit Depth, and File Type. When you re-sort your audio files, all the audio regions that originate from that file always move with the file. The default category is None, meaning your audio files are sorted by the order in which you added them. If you find it useful to have all your files in alphabetical order or in order of their file size, hard drive, or audio file bit depth, select the appropriate option.

- **Show File Info.** If this is checked, Logic displays the file information for all audio files in the audio list to the right of their names. The information displayed in the integrated Audio Bin is, from left to right, the sample rate of the audio file, the bit rate, the file format, and the file size. The Audio Bin window also displays the file path. (File path information is displayed for the selected audio file in the integrated Audio Bin directly above the audio list, regardless of the Show File Info setting.) The file format (Cha in the Audio Bin window) tells you whether the file is mono (single circle), stereo (overlapping circles), surround (five small circles), or an audio Apple Loop (an oval between two horizontal lines).

- **Show All Regions.** This command expands the disclosure triangle of all audio files so that all audio regions are displayed in the Audio Bin. The key command for this is Option+Down Arrow.

- **Hide All Regions.** This command contracts the disclosure triangle of each audio file so that none of the audio regions appears in the Audio Bin. The key command for this is Option+Up Arrow.

- **Sort Regions By.** This entry opens a hierarchical menu, which allows you to check one of three options for sorting audio regions used by a given audio file: Start Point, Length, or Name. This sorts only the audio regions attached to each audio file; the files themselves do not change positions in the audio list.

- **Show Length As.** If you want to display the length of each audio region above the graphic representation of the region in the Audio Bin window (this command is not available in the integrated Audio Bin), you can choose one of the Show Length As options that you are offered in the hierarchical menu that opens when you select this command. These are your options:

  - **None.** This is the default. The audio region length is not displayed above the region.

  - **Min:Sec:Ms.** This displays the length of the region in the format minutes: seconds: milliseconds.

  - **Samples.** This command displays the number of samples in the region.

  - **SMPTE Time.** This displays the length of the region in SMPTE time code.

  - **Bar/Beat.** This command displays how long the region is in bars and beats.

- **Create Group.** This command allows you to create a new grouping of audio files in the Audio Bin. Audio groups are discussed further in this chapter in the upcoming "Audio Bin Groups" section. The key command for this is Control+G.

- **Group Files By.** You can automatically create Audio Bin groups by grouping files by location, file attributes, or selection in the Arrange. Audio groups are discussed later in the chapter.

- **Delete Selected Groups.** This command will delete any selected Audio Bin group(s).

- **Show Region Use Count.** If this option is checked, there will be a number representing how many times that region appears in the Arrange window beside the overview of each audio region in the integrated Audio Bin and beneath the name of every audio region in the Audio Bin window.

■ **Colors.** This command brings up the Color palette so you can color your audio regions. The key command for this is Option+C.

The Options Menu

The final local menu is only available in the standalone Audio Bin window. The Options menu contains one command, Strip Silence. The key command for this is Control+X. Strip Silence was briefly mentioned in the previous chapter's subsection on the Arrange window's local Audio menu; it is also available here. Strip Silence allows you to remove the silence in audio regions, creating many new audio regions that include only those areas that have content. Strip Silence is a very valuable function and is explained in detail in the section "Using Strip Silence" later in this chapter.

The Audio Bin Buttons

The left-hand corners of the Audio Bin house three buttons that affect how the Audio Bin operates. Figure 7.8 shows those buttons.

Figure 7.8　The Audio Bin's buttons.

From the top corner to the bottom corner, the buttons do the following:

■ **Link button.** As in other windows, the chain link icon is the Link button. If this is glowing purple, the Audio Bin is linked to the Arrange window, meaning that the most recently selected audio region will be selected in the Audio Bin. If this button is not glowing, the Audio Bin does not reflect the Arrange at all.

- **Playback button.** When the speaker icon is glowing green, the selected audio region plays back. If you have an audio file selected, the first audio region of that audio file plays back. If you have nothing selected at all, you cannot activate the button. If you click and hold the mouse button over any audio region, the cursor itself will become a speaker icon, your audio region will play back as long as you hold the button down, and the Playback button will remain lit during playback.

- **Loop button.** With this button glowing green, the selected audio region loops continuously. This is especially useful when you are adjusting loop points in the Audio Bin. (See the section "Using Looping in the Audio Bin" later in this chapter.)

Cursor Modes in the Audio Bin Window

Although neither the integrated Audio Bin nor the Audio Bin window has a Tool menu, the cursor does serve a variety of functions in the Audio Bin window. Obviously, you can perform standard pointer functions in the Audio Bin window, such as dragging and dropping files, but where you place the cursor over an audio region in the Audio Bin window changes the function of the cursor.

If you drag the cursor over the lower half of either edge of an audio region, the cursor will change into a resize cursor, which you can then use to change the start or end point of the region. If you keep the cursor in the lower half of the region and move it in from a start point or an end point, the cursor will become a two-headed arrow cursor. You can use this cursor mode to move the entire selected area that comprises the audio region over the parent audio file. If you move the cursor over the anchor point indicator, which is the black indicator under a region overview in the Audio Bin window, the cursor will change into a finger, which allows you to drag the anchor to a new position in the selected audio region. Anchor points will be covered in detail later in this chapter.

Finally, if you drag the cursor over the top half of an audio region, the cursor will change into a speaker icon. If you click and hold on a region when the cursor is in speaker mode, the selected region will play from the point in the region that you clicked until either you release the mouse button or you reach the end of the region. If Loop mode is engaged, then playback will begin at the point in the region where the cursor is, but the entire region will then loop until the mouse button is released.

Protecting Regions in the Audio Bin Window

Because there are so many different ways you could inadvertently edit your audio regions in the Audio Bin window, Logic offers you the choice of protecting audio regions by locking them. A region that is locked in the Audio Bin window cannot have its start or end point altered, and the anchor point is protected, too. To lock or unlock an audio region, simply click on the padlock icon next to the audio region's name in the Audio Bin window. Figure 7.9 shows one locked audio region and one unlocked audio region in the Audio Bin window.

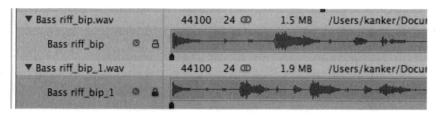

Figure 7.9   Locking audio regions protects them from inadvertent edits while you are working in the Audio Bin window. Here you see one region that has been locked and another that is unlocked.

You can still perform Strip Silence on a locked audio region, you can still edit a locked audio region in the Arrange, and you can still delete a locked audio region from the Audio Bin. When an audio region is locked, the only cursor mode that is available for use with that region is the speaker cursor. Although you cannot lock or unlock audio regions in the integrated Audio Bin, locked regions do have a closed padlock icon displayed in the middle column in the audio list.

The Prelisten Channel Strip

When you are working in the Audio Bin, any audio region you play back will by default play back through the Prelisten channel strip, which is an audio channel strip that you can find in the Mixer next to the last audio channel strip when the Mixer is in the All view mode. The Mixer and Mixer view modes are covered in detail in Chapter 11. The Prelisten channel strip is directly tied to the slider shown in Figure 7.8. The Prelisten channel strip also services the Sample Editor, the Loop Browser, and the Browser. Therefore, if you change the volume of the Prelisten channel strip using the slider in the Audio Bin, for example, the slider in the Loop Browser will reflect that change. The Sample Editor and the Loop Browser will be covered later in this chapter, and the Browser will be covered in Chapter 12, "Working with Files and Networks."

At first, the need for a Prelisten channel strip might seem counterintuitive—why doesn't the Audio Bin simply play back each region using the audio channel to which that region is already assigned? Remember, the Audio Bin is a repository for all the audio files and regions that you have imported or recorded for your project, regardless of whether you use them. This means that a good number of your audio regions are likely not assigned to any audio channel. By offering an assignment of a single track for playback of everything in the Audio Bin, Logic ensures that each region, regardless of whether it is currently used in the project, will be able to play back. It also ensures that Logic is far more resource-efficient than if it had to constantly use resources to enable it to switch to any audio channel, turn on new effects processing, and so on for the various windows that utilize the Prelisten channel. It also allows you to easily hear any changes you make to an audio file in the Audio Bin without any effects that may be instantiated on the audio file's parent channel strip.

Looking at it another way, the Prelisten channel strip is not a limitation, but a feature. Many other DAWs don't include a Prelisten channel strip at all. Instead, when you play audio from any editor or window except the main editor and Mixer, the audio is simply routed directly to the master outputs. You have no opportunity to adjust the volume, add effects, or otherwise process the "audition" channel. Logic gives you the ability to do that, thanks to the Prelisten channel strip.

Still, if you want to monitor the audio files in the Audio Bin that have been assigned to an Arrange track through their parent channel strips, you can Control+click on the Playback button in the lower-left corner of the Audio Bin. This opens the contextual menu shown in Figure 7.10.

Figure 7.10   Control-clicking on the Playback button in the Audio Bin opens a contextual menu in which you can assign the playback routing of audio files in the Audio Bin.

Selecting the Auto-Select Channel Strip option ensures that audio files that have been assigned to an Arrange track will play through their parent channel strip. Note that this playback setting applies to both the Audio Bin and the Sample Editor—if you change the playback setting in the Audio Bin, you also change the playback setting for the Sample Editor, and vice versa.

Zooming in the Audio Bin Window

The Audio Bin window includes two horizontal zoom sliders. These are identical to the zoom sliders in the Arrange window (and, indeed, all other windows with zoom sliders). You can also use the zoom-related key commands if you want to zoom in or out.

Adding Audio Files to the Audio Bin

Every time you record using Logic, the resulting audio file is automatically placed in the Audio Bin. Sometimes, however, you'll want to use audio in your song that you didn't record. If you want the audio to be in the Arrange of your song, you can, of course, open an audio file from the Arrange, drag audio from the Finder to the Arrange window, or drag audio files from the Browser. Sometimes, however, you'll want to have a number of prerecorded audio files available for your song but not placed in the Arrange yet; in these circumstances, you'll need to add them to the Audio Bin yourself. Luckily, this is very easy to do.

The easiest way to add audio to your song is simply to drag the audio files from your desktop or a Finder window into your Audio Bin. At that point, Logic creates an overview for the file, and it appears in your audio list like all the rest of your audio. You can select as many audio files as you want on your desktop or in the Finder, and when you drag them into the Audio Bin, all of them will be added.

You can also use the Add Audio File command described previously. This command opens an Open File dialog box with one Logic-specific addition: a Play button. This button auditions the selected audio file on the Prelisten channel. You can select one or more files to add, and when you click the Add button at the bottom-right corner of the dialog (or press Return), Logic will add any selected files to the audio list in the Audio Bin.

Exporting Audio from the Audio Bin

Sometimes, you may want to use an audio file you have recorded in Logic in another application. In these cases, you'll want to export your audio. The usual way to export audio is to do a bounce, which is discussed in Chapter 11, or to export one or more tracks, which is discussed in Chapter 12. However, this section discusses a couple of options for exporting audio directly from the Audio Bin.

You can use the Copy/Convert File(s) command to save your file in the same or a different format. When you select one of these commands, the resulting dialog box prompts you for a name and a destination for your file and then exports the audio file in the format you have selected.

Using Strip Silence

Early in this chapter, we mentioned Strip Silence; now it's time to give this essential function a closer look. When you record an audio performance of an instrument that does not play constantly throughout the entire performance—for example, a vocal that weaves through the music or instruments that come and go for the duration of a song—your audio file will play back with moments of silence. At best, these moments take up unnecessary CPU cycles as Logic plays and processes segments of an audio file that are empty. At worst, the portions where your instrument or vocal aren't performing aren't truly silent at all, but filled with background noise, guitar amplifier hiss, and the like. The Strip Silence command is designed to search your audio file for these segments of low to no audio and remove them from your song.

Strip Silence does not actually remove anything from the audio file on your hard drive. Because Logic plays audio regions in the Arrange or Audio Bin, Strip Silence divides the selected audio region into several audio regions, leaving out those portions in which it did not detect any audio. The command allows you to set the threshold or minimum level for audio to be considered "not silence," so you have a certain amount of control over how many new audio regions the command will create. Figure 7.11 shows the Strip Silence window for a selected audio region.

The Strip Silence window gives you a number of settings:

- **Threshold.** This is the amplitude above which Strip Silence detects the audio as audio and not as silence. Logic's default value is 4 percent, which is good for removing the silence in quiet tracks. If you have a noisier performance, such as a vocal that recorded a fair amount of background noise when there was no singing or a guitar amplifier with a loud hum or hiss when it wasn't playing, you will get better results if you set the threshold higher.

- **Minimum Time to Accept as Silence.** You wouldn't want Strip Silence to detect any moment below a threshold as silence, or else Logic will split up those nanoseconds between notes into

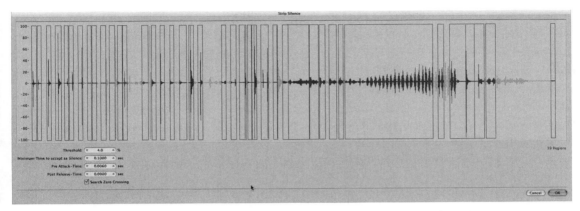

Figure 7.11   In the Strip Silence window, you can fine-tune the Strip Silence function.

their own audio regions! This parameter allows you to set how much time must pass before Logic detects silence. The default is 0.1 seconds, which is generally a very good setting. You might want to raise the setting if you find that Strip Silence is chopping off the decay of very quiet notes.

■ **Pre Attack-Time.** This parameter ensures that Strip Silence will not cut off the attack of notes with slower amplitudes (or *rise times*). If you find that Strip Silence is cutting off your notes, increase this value.

■ **Post Release-Time.** Similar to the preceding parameter, this setting is used to ensure that the decay of notes isn't removed. If you find that Strip Silence is cutting off your notes, increase this value.

■ **Search Zero Crossing.** This command ensures that Logic always begins and ends audio regions at the point that the amplitude crosses the zero line. This way, no glitches or clicks will be audible at the beginning or end of newly created regions. You'll pretty much always want this option to be checked.

The actual operation of the command is quite simple:

1.   Select an audio region.

2.   Choose the Strip Silence command.

3.   Use the graphic display of your waveform to adjust the settings. Your goal is for Logic to create exactly as many regions as you need, with no extra regions and without excess silence being included within the regions.

4.   Click OK. The Strip Silence dialog will disappear, and your new regions will appear in the Arrange and/or Audio Bin.

As you can see, Strip Silence is a powerful tool for quickly splitting the musically relevant portions of a performance or audio file into separate audio regions. If you want the silenced audio to also be removed from your hard drive after using Strip Silence, you can use the Edit > Select Unused command followed by the Audio Files > Optimize Files command in the Audio Bin. You can also use this function as a creative tool. For example, you can set the Pre Attack-Time and Post Release-Time parameters specifically to cut off audio for a unique gated audio effect or split different beats from a drum loop apart and then rearrange them to create an entirely new rhythm. Don't be afraid to experiment with Strip Silence—creativity is the name of the game, and remember, you can always undo it later!

Method Tip: Using Strip Silence and Folder Tracks to Loop Audio   We've placed this tip in the "Working with Audio and Apple Loops" chapter instead of the chapter on the Arrange to follow the section on the Strip Silence function, but this really should be done completely in the Arrange page. Remember that the Strip Silence function appears in the Arrange window in Audio > Strip Silence as well as in the Audio Bin.

Sometimes you might want to use Strip Silence to remove the irrelevant segments of an audio region but still retain the ability to manipulate the result as a single region. For example, suppose you have a four-bar drum performance you want to loop throughout the choruses of a song. You want to use Strip Silence to eliminate the noise between the beats, but trying to loop eight tiny audio regions representing a part of a whole would interfere with your looping. Folder tracks to the rescue! After using Strip Silence, you can place all resulting audio regions in a new Audio track in the Arrange with no other audio regions and then use the Region > Folder > Pack Folder command in the Arrange to pack that track into a folder. You can now manipulate the folder track as you would any other Arrange track.

Also, as you get more familiar with Logic, you can expand on this trick. For example, you could put each of the audio regions on a separate track, being careful not to alter their spacing from one another. In fact, you'll find there's even an assignable key command, New Tracks for Selected Regions, that is really handy for this. You would select the right-most new region, use the key command to assign that region to a new track, then move to the previous region, select it, then use the key command to assign it to its own track, and so on. This way, you would end up with each audio region on its own track. Since each audio region in the folder gets its own channel strip, you could have different effects on every audio region, as well as submix the audio regions in the folder track. (More on mixing in Chapter 11.)

Using Looping in the Audio Bin

As mentioned previously, you can turn on looping by clicking the Loop button on the Audio Bin, selecting an audio region, then clicking on the Playback button (the one represented by the speaker icon). That audio region will then repeat until you disengage the Playback button. This may not seem particularly useful at first, but let's look at how you can use this functionality in the Audio Bin window in tandem with the Arrange window.

If you have an audio region in the Arrange that just doesn't seem to begin and/or end where you'd like it to, and your attempts to resize it in the Arrange window are not giving you the desired results, the Audio Bin window is your answer. If you've turned on the Link button of the Audio Bin window, it should already have the region you're working on selected. With the Loop button engaged, click the Playback button, and your region will repeat. If you move the cursor over the bottom half of the start or end point of the region, it will become a resize cursor, and you can use that to adjust the start and end points of your audio region. You can even use the zoom sliders (or key commands) to make the regions larger in the Audio Bin window for more accurate dragging of start and/or end points. The Arrange window immediately reflects any changes you make, so you need not drag or move anything between windows.

Using this method to adjust regions can be a timesaver, and if you have painstakingly set the locators, cycle, and/or autodrop points in the Arrange, this method gives you a way to loop the audio region you need to adjust without affecting any other aspect of your Arrange window setup. Give it a try—you'll find using looping in the Audio window is a great way to resize individual audio regions.

Audio Bin Groups

Logic gives you the ability to organize audio files into groups inside the Audio Bin. You'll find this to be a great organizational help if you have lots of different types of audio material. For example, you could create one group called Guitars, one called Drums, one called Synths, and so on, and use these to keep your audio files organized within the Audio Bin.

Creating groups in the Audio Bin couldn't be easier. Simply select those audio files (not regions representing segments of a larger file, but regions representing a complete file) in the Audio Bin that you wish to group together and then select the Create Groups command. A text box will appear for you to name the new group, and the selected audio files will be placed inside the group. You can also use the Create Groups command without any audio files selected in the Audio Bin and then simply drag audio files into the group later. Finally, Logic can automatically group your audio files together by their location on your hard drive or their file attributes, or it can group those files selected in the Arrange with the Group Files By command. (If you already have groups created, you will be prompted about whether you want them to be deleted.)

The names of audio file groups will be in a bolder and slightly smaller font than the names of your audio files, and the audio list will identify the group as an audio file group. (If you double-click this text, however, you can add your own comment.) Figure 7.12 shows an Audio Bin with two audio file groups created.

You can open and close audio file groups by clicking on their disclosure triangles. You can also Option-click on a group triangle to open or close all groups.

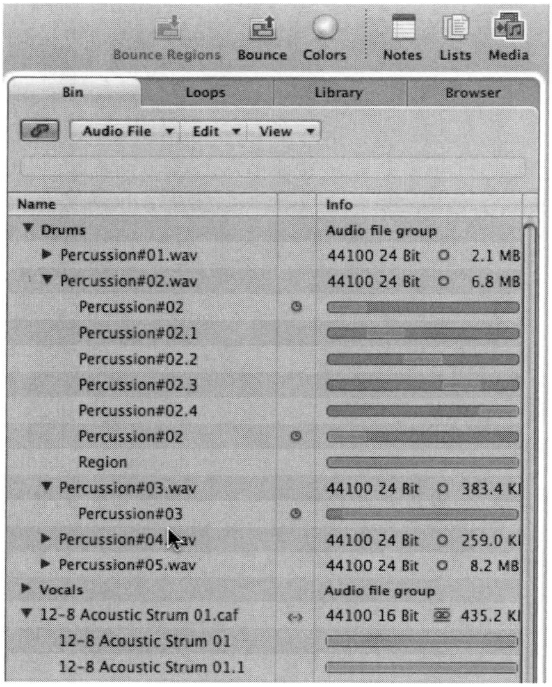

Figure 7.12   This Audio Bin has two audio file groups: Drums and Vocals. You can see the audio regions in the expanded Drums group with some of the region data hidden; the Vocals group has been collapsed, so its audio files are not displayed.

Keep in mind that audio file groups are strictly organizational groups. Grouping audio files does not affect their location on your hard drive, their use or their track placement in the Arrange window, and so on.

Adding Audio to the Arrange Window

The Audio Bin is a great organizational and processing tool for audio, but to actually use your audio in a project, you'll need to add it to the Arrange window. You can do this either by selecting one or more audio regions and dragging them to the Arrange window or by using the Add to Arrange command.

If you use the Add to Arrange command or drag multiple audio files/regions from the Audio Bin (or the Finder) to the Arrange, you will be prompted with the dialog box shown in Figure 7.13 so that you can instruct Logic how to handle the audio region(s).

Depending on your radio button and/or check mark selections, Logic Pro will:

■   Create a new Audio track in the Arrange for each audio region you wish to add.

■   Use the existing Audio tracks in the Arrange and add one audio region to each.

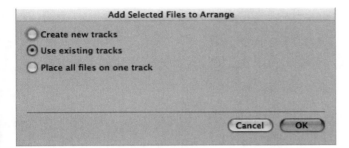

Figure 7.13   The Add Selected Files to Arrange dialog.

- Place all the audio regions you are adding to the Arrange on the selected Audio track.
- Copy the names of the audio files to the track names.

As you can see, Logic makes adding audio from the Audio Bin to the Arrange window simple and intuitive and gives you plenty of options to make sure it handles the audio the way you want it to.

The Sample Editor

Sometimes, resizing or editing audio regions won't be enough; you'll want to alter the audio data itself permanently. This is where the Sample Editor comes in. The Sample Editor operates on the actual data in the audio file. This means that the Sample Editor's edits are *destructive,* because they forever alter the contents of the actual audio file, unlike edits to audio regions, which are *nondestructive,* meaning that the audio data itself is never touched. Figure 7.14 shows the Sample Editor window.

Double-clicking an audio region in the Arrange opens that region in the Arrange window's integrated Sample Editor. Selecting an audio region in the Audio Bin opens that region in the Sample Editor. In either case, the region will be displayed inside the waveform overview and detailed waveform display. You can also launch the Sample Editor by choosing Window > Sample Editor or open the integrated Sample Editor in the Arrange window by clicking the Sample Editor button at the bottom of the Arrange window or by pressing W.

As with the other windows, we'll start with a discussion of the Sample Editor's local menus.

Local Menus

The local menus provide file, editing, and processing commands specific to the Sample Editor. A description of the local menus follows.

The Audio File Menu

This menu contains the file operations that are possible from the Sample Editor. Figure 7.15 shows the Audio File local menu of the Sample Editor.

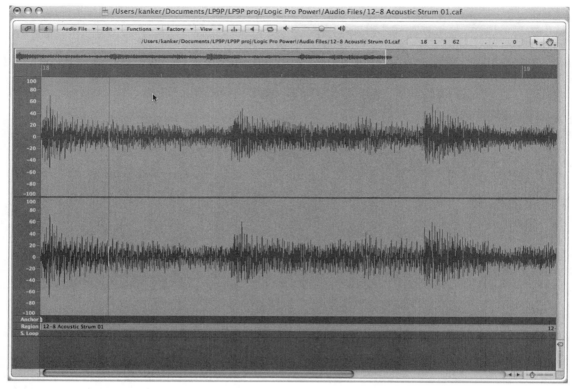

Figure 7.14   The Sample Editor window.

Figure 7.15   The Audio File menu of the Sample Editor.

An explanation of the commands follows:

■   **Create Backup.** Because the actions that you make in the Sample Editor are destructive, you may want to make a backup of your file, so that if you do something you don't like, you still have your original audio. The key command for this is Control+B.

- **Revert to Backup.** If you've previously made a backup of your audio file, this command replaces your current processed and edited audio file with the backup. You can use this command if you've made a backup and are not happy with the changes you've made to your audio file. The key command for this is Control+Option+Command+B.

- **Save a Copy As.** You can create a copy of an audio file using this command.

- **Save Selection As.** Using this command, you can save only the portion of your file that you have selected with your mouse. The key command for this is Option+Command+S.

- **Detect Transients.** This command detects transients in your audio file and marks them with transient markers, which can aid you in general editing but also gives you a very powerful tool for customizing the transients for Flexing, deriving a Groove Template from your audio, and for use with the Convert Regions to New Sampler Instrument command. We'll look into this in a little more detail in the "Editing Transient Markers" section later in this chapter.

- **Update File Information.** This updates the information that Logic has stored for the file you are editing. Saving your project performs this updating, but you can use this command to update the file information without saving the project.

- **Refresh Overview(s).** This command refreshes the waveform overview of the audio region you are editing in the Sample Editor.

The Edit Menu

The Edit menu contains functions that involve the selection and manipulation of audio and audio regions. Figure 7.16 shows the local Edit menu of the Sample Editor.

Following are details about the commands in this menu:

- **Undo.** This command undoes the last action made to your audio in the Sample Editor. You can have as many levels of undo as you set in the Preferences > Audio > Sample Editor tab. The key command for this is Command+Z.

- **Redo.** This command will redo the last undone action in the Sample Editor. Note that the Sample Editor Undo and Redo functions are unique to the Sample Editor (meaning you can't undo an Arrange action in the Sample Editor, whereas in a MIDI editor, for example, Undo will include windows outside the MIDI editor). The key command for this is Shift+Command+Z.

- **Cut.** This command removes a selected area of audio and places it on the Clipboard. The cut selection can only be pasted in the Sample Editor. The key command for this is Command+X.

- **Copy.** This command copies a selected area of audio and places it on the Clipboard. The copied section can only be pasted in the Sample Editor. The key command for this is Command+C.

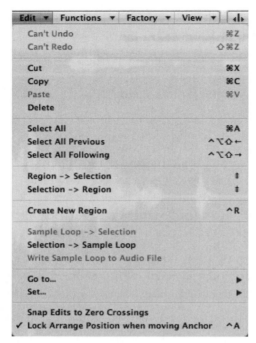

Figure 7.16   The Edit menu of the Sample Editor.

■ **Paste.** This command pastes audio from the Clipboard at the current locator position. Only audio that has been cut or copied from the Sample Editor may be pasted in the Sample Editor with the Paste command. The key command for this is Command+V.

■ **Delete.** This command removes the selected audio from your audio file.

■ **Select All.** This command selects your entire audio file. The key command for this is Command+A.

■ **Select All Previous.** This command adds the area from the beginning of the audio file to the currently selected area. The key command for this is Control+Option+Left Arrow.

■ **Select All Following.** This command adds the area from the end of the audio file to the currently selected area. The key command for this is Control+Option+Right Arrow.

■ **Region -> Selection.** This command selects the entire audio region that you are currently editing. The key command for this is Page Up.

■ **Selection -> Region.** This command replaces the original audio region that you are editing with the selected audio. The key command for this is Shift+Command+R.

■ **Create New Region.** This creates a new audio region from your current selection. The original audio region you are editing remains unchanged. The key command for this is Control+R.

- **Sample Loop -> Selection.** This function turns a loop you have loaded into the Sample Editor from Emagic's EXS24 Sampler into a normal audio selection that you can edit.

- **Selection -> Sample Loop.** This turns a selection of audio into a loop for use with Logic's EXS24 Sampler.

- **Write Sample Loop to Audio File.** This command saves an audio file from the contents of an EXS24 loop.

- **Go To.** The Go To submenu is covered in the following subsection.

- **Set.** The Set submenu will be covered in its own subsection following "The Go To Submenu" subsection.

- **Snap Edits to Zero Crossings.** You learned about zero crossings earlier in this chapter. If you select this command, Logic always looks for the point at which the amplitude crosses the zero mark while you are editing. This is to ensure glitch- and click-free playback, but it might restrict you from making edits at the exact location you want.

- **Lock Arrange Position When Moving Anchor.** With this command engaged, the left boundary of an audio region will stay fixed in the Arrange window regardless of any changes you make to an audio region in the Sample Editor. If this is not engaged, anchor points will remain fixed in the audio regions in the Arrange. The key command for this is Control+A.

The Go To Submenu.   The Go To submenu gives you a variety of commands for quickly navigating to specific points in your audio file. Figure 7.17 shows the Go To submenu.

Figure 7.17   The Go To submenu.

The functions in the Go To submenu are:

- **Selection Start.** This command moves the waveform display and the highlighted area in the waveform overview to the beginning of the selected area of the audio region. The key command for this is Control+Shift+Left Arrow.

- **Selection End.** This command moves the waveform display and the highlighted area in the waveform overview to the end of the selected area of the audio region. The key command for this is Control+Shift+Right Arrow.

■ **Region Start.** This command moves the waveform display and the highlighted area in the waveform overview to the beginning of the audio region. The key command for this is Control+Left Arrow.

■ **Region End.** This command moves the waveform display and the highlighted area in the waveform overview to the end of the audio region. The key command for this is Control+Right Arrow.

■ **Region Anchor.** This command moves the waveform display and the highlighted area in the waveform overview to the anchor point of the audio region. The key command for this is Control+Down Arrow.

■ **Previous Transient.** This command moves the waveform display and the highlighted area in the waveform overview to the closest transient before the current selection. The key command for this is Command+Left Arrow.

■ **Next Transient.** This command moves the waveform display and the highlighted area in the waveform overview to the closest transient after the current selection. The key command for this is Command+Right Arrow.

The Set Submenu.   The Set submenu gives you a variety of commands for assigning start, end, and anchor points for your audio file. Figure 7.18 shows the Set submenu.

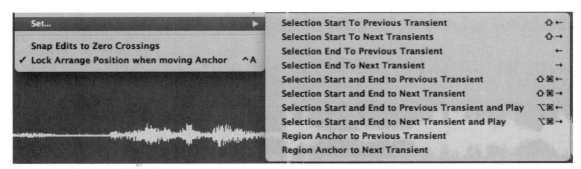

Figure 7.18   The Set submenu.

The functions in the Set submenu are:

■ **Selection Start to Previous Transient.** This command moves the start of the selected area to the first transient immediately before the selected area. The key command for this is Shift+Left Arrow.

■ **Selection Start to Next Transients.** This command moves the start of the selected area to the first transient immediately after the current start point of the selected area. The key command for this is Shift+Right Arrow.

- **Selection End to Previous Transient.** This command moves the end of the selected area to the first transient immediately before the current end of the selected area. The key command for this is Left Arrow.

- **Selection End to Next Transient.** This command moves the end of the selected area to the first transient immediately after the selected area. The key command for this is Right Arrow.

- **Selection Start and End to Previous Transient.** This command moves the start and end points of the selected area to the first transients immediately before the current start and end points, respectively. The key command for this is Shift+Command+Left Arrow.

- **Selection Start and End to Next Transient.** This command moves the start and end points of the selected area to the first transients immediately after the current start and end points, respectively. The key command for this is Shift+Command+Right Arrow.

- **Selection Start and End to Previous Transient and Play.** This command moves the start and end points of the selected area to the first transients immediately before the current start and end points, respectively, and then the selection is played. The key command for this is Option+Command+Left Arrow.

- **Selection Start and End to Next Transient and Play.** This command moves the start and end points of the selected area to the first transients after the immediately current start and end points, respectively, and then the selection is played. The key command for this is Option+Command+Right Arrow.

- **Region Anchor to Previous Transient.** This command moves the region anchor to the transient immediately before its current position.

- **Region Anchor to Next Transient.** This command moves the region anchor to the transient immediately after its current position.

The Functions Menu

The Functions menu consists of Sample Editor functions that process your audio in one way or another. These functions only operate on the area of your audio region that is selected. If you want to process your entire file, be sure to choose Edit > Select All or use the key command Command+A first. You can generally cancel any process in progress by pressing Command+. (period). Figure 7.19 shows the Functions menu of the Sample Editor.

These functions are as follows:

- **Normalize.** To *normalize* audio means to increase its level as much as possible without changing the dynamics or distorting the audio file. Logic does this by finding the loudest point in the currently selected audio, determining its distance from the maximum attainable level for the audio passage, and then increasing the audio for the entire selection by that amount. This way, the dynamics are preserved, the audio is not maximized to the point that it

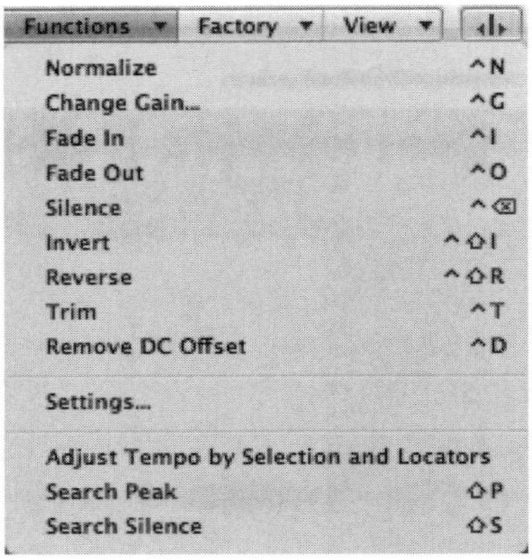

Figure 7.19   The Functions menu of the Sample Editor.

distorts, and the entire selection is louder by a specified amount. You can set the desired maximum level in the Settings dialog box. The key command for this is Control+N.

Sample Editor Normalize versus Bounce Dialog Normalize   The Sample Editor Normalize feature is not the same as the Normalize feature in the Bounce dialog. The Sample Editor Normalize operates directly on your audio file. This means that it is destructive—meaning it permanently changes the audio file—and it is limited to the bit depth (16- or 24-bit) of your audio file. The Normalize in the Bounce feature is really a nondestructive, 32-bit (when running Logic in 32-bit mode) or 64-bit (when running Logic in 64-bit mode) floating-point precision bit-mapping function. Don't mix up the two! See Chapter 11 for more information on the Normalize feature of the Bounce dialog.

- **Change Gain.** This command raises or lowers the level of the selected audio by a specified amount. You can determine this amount in the dialog box that appears when you select this command. You can choose to change the gain by either inputting a percentage of the current level or entering absolute decibels. If you click Search Peak, Logic finds the highest peak in the selection and calculates how much it can safely raise the gain (much as it does with the Normalize function). You can also view the Results in Absolute, which shows you an absolute value rather than a percentage. Keep in mind that if you raise the gain more than 100 percent, you will clip your file, producing a very nonmusical digital clipping. The key command for this is Control+G.

- **Fade In.** This allows you to create a destructive fade-in at the front of your selection. This is in contrast to creating a fade-in on the Arrange, which only affects how the audio region is played back and is nondestructive. You can adjust the curves of the fade-in in the Settings dialog box. The key command for this is Control+I.

- **Fade Out.** With this command, you can create a destructive fade-out at the end of your selection. This contrasts with creating a fade-out on the Arrange, which only affects how the audio region is played back and is nondestructive. You can adjust the curve of the fade-out in the Settings dialog box. The key command for this is Control+O.

- **Silence.** Silence removes all audio data inside your selection. The key command for this is Control+Delete.

- **Invert.** This inverts the phase of the audio selection. In other words, what originally was the peak of the amplitude of the waveform becomes the bottom, and so on. This command doesn't affect the sound, but it can help fix phase cancellation problems with your audio file that become apparent during mixing. The key command for this is Control+Shift+I.

- **Reverse.** This command reverses the audio in your selection. (In other words, the audio plays backward.) The key command for this is Control+Shift+R.

- **Trim.** Trim erases any part of the current region outside of the area you have selected. Make sure you don't delete any areas that you'll need for your song! If you try to trim away portions of a region you are using in the Arrange window, a warning screen will appear, asking you to confirm that you want to do so. The key command for this is Control+T.

- **Remove DC Offset.** When you are using lower-quality audio hardware, it is common for stray direct current (DC) to be layered over your audio signal, which causes the waveform to look like it's not centered around the zero line, but shifted vertically up or down. This can cause crackling and artifacts at the beginning and end of audio regions. This command removes the effect of DC and centers the audio around the zero bar. The key command for this is Control+D.

- **Settings.** Settings isn't a function itself, but rather a dialog box of parameters for other functions. Figure 7.20 shows the Function Settings dialog box.

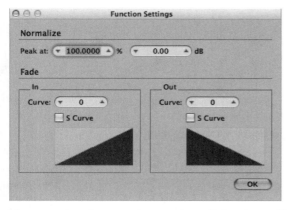

Figure 7.20   The Function Settings dialog box offers settings for the Normalize, Fade In, and Fade Out functions.

Here you can set the maximum value to which you want the Normalize function to increase the selection's level, either as a percentage of the maximum amplitude or in decibels. The dialog box also presents options to adjust the curves for the Fade In and Fade Out functions. If you check their boxes and adjust the curve value from −100 to +100, the graphic display will change to illustrate the current shape of the curve.

- **Adjust Tempo by Selection and Locators.** This command adjusts the tempo of your audio by stretching or compressing it to fit the length of the current locator positions while maintaining the integrity of its pitch. This is very similar to the Arrange option to Adjust Tempo Using Region Length Locators.

- **Search Peak.** If you select this option, Logic will search the currently selected audio for the sample with the greatest amplitude value and will center the cursor in the waveform display around this point. The key command for this is Shift+P.

- **Search Silence.** With this option, Logic searches the currently selected audio for silence and places the cursor at the start of the first section of silence detected. The key command for this is Shift+S.

The Factory Menu

Most of the options on the Factory menu allow you to choose one of the available functions in the Digital Factory, Logic's built-in audio processing tool. The remaining options in the Factory menu are functions from the Quantize Engine. All of these operations are destructive. Figure 7.21 shows the Factory menu.

Figure 7.21   The Factory menu of the Sample Editor.

The Digital Factory Machines and Functions are both given individual subsections later in this chapter. However, the contents of the Factory menu are described briefly here:

- **Time and Pitch Machine.** The Time and Pitch Machine enables you to independently adjust the tempo and pitch of your selected audio. The key command for this is Control+P.

- **Groove Machine.** This allows you to "regroove," or alter the rhythm and feel of your audio.

- **Audio Energizer.** The Audio Energizer raises the perceived loudness of audio.

- **Silencer.** The Silencer, which is the last component of the Digital Factory Machines on this local menu, allows you to reduce the level of noise and/or volume spikes (such as pops or clicks) in your audio.

- **Audio to MIDI Groove Template.** This powerful feature allows you to extract the rhythm and feel of an audio selection for use as a Groove Template that you can apply to MIDI notes. You can help customize the Groove Template by editing your audio file's transients.

- **Audio to Score.** Audio to Score works best using a mono audio file with monophonic content—audio content that includes only one note at a time, such as a vocal, horn, kazoo, and so on. Audio to Score converts that audio data into MIDI data. You can use this MIDI data in the Score Editor or as another MIDI region in the Arrange assigned to a MIDI instrument or an audio instrument. The key command for this is Control+S.

- **Quantize Engine.** This locks points you specify in your audio file to a quantize grid, just as MIDI quantize locks MIDI notes to a grid.

The View Menu

The View menu offers you a number of options for changing the units of measurement on the waveform display and the way the audio wave itself is displayed. Figure 7.22 shows you the View menu of the Sample Editor.

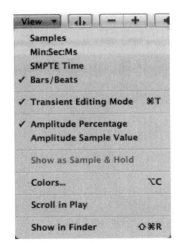

Figure 7.22   The View menu of the Sample Editor.

The Samples, Min:Sec:Ms, SMPTE Time, and Bars/Beats options determine the units that the Bar ruler displays. The Samples option displays the actual number of the sample or the samples you are currently viewing. Min:Sec:Ms shows the elapsed time on the Bar ruler. SMPTE Time displays the SMPTE position, and Bars/Beats shows the musical location of the audio. By choosing View > Amplitude Percentage or View > Amplitude Sample Value, you can specify whether the vertical axis of the waveform display measures the amplitude of the audio wave as a percentage of the maximum amplitude or as a number of samples.

You can enable Transient Editing Mode, allowing you to modify your audio file's transients. A few more options determine how a waveform will be displayed. Show as Sample & Hold displays the actual data structure of the waveform (that is, the wave appears blocky, not rounded). This is very useful if you are using the Pencil tool to remove pops and clicks. (See the section "The Sample Editor Tool Menu" later in this chapter.) Colors brings up the now-familiar Color palette, where you can assign a color to your waveform's parent region and to the region bar beneath the waveform. Scroll in Play moves the audio file past a stationary playhead, instead of moving the playhead across your audio file. Finally, Show in Finder opens a Finder window displaying the location on your hard drive of the audio file being edited.

The Audiosuite Menu

This local menu is only of interest if you are using Avid hardware and the DAE audio engine. It allows Audiosuite plug-ins to be applied destructively in the Sample Editor. If you have any Audiosuite plug-ins, they will appear here. If you don't (as most users will not), then simply ignore this menu. Refer to your plug-in's manual for how to apply any specific Audiosuite process. Remember that Pro Tools|HD 8.0.3 and later no longer support the DAE audio engine.

The Sample Editor Tool Menu

The Sample Editor Tool menu contains the five tools available to you in the Sample Editor. Figure 7.23 shows the Sample Editor Tool menu.

Figure 7.23   The Sample Editor Tool menu.

A description of how each tool functions in the Sample Editor follows:

■ **Pointer Tool.** Drag the Pointer tool across the audio in the waveform display to select audio.

■ **Eraser Tool.** The Eraser tool is used for removing transients from your audio file.

■ **Hand Tool.** The Hand tool allows you to reposition a selection box (made previously with the pointer) to the right or left.

- **Zoom Tool.** Drag the selection "rubber band" over a portion of audio to increase the magnification of the selected audio down to the single-sample level. Double-click anywhere to return the selection to its original zoom resolution. If you have already used the zoom rectangles or key commands to zoom in on your audio, this tool has no further effect.

- **Solo Tool.** This tool will scrub (play back slowly) a selection of audio.

- **Pencil Tool.** This tool will allow you to redraw the audio waveform at high zoom levels. If you are not at a high zoom level, the Pencil tool can be used as a Zoom tool to increase the zoom setting by rubber-banding an area of the waveform. The main use for this tool is to smooth out sudden sharp peaks in your audio, as these sudden sharp peaks are usually pops or clicks. This tool works well in tandem with Show as Sample & Hold, which enables you to see exactly which samples are peaking. Be very careful when redrawing waveforms, however—if you don't know what you are doing, you are likely to redraw a waveform incorrectly and compromise the sound of your audio.

The Sample Editor Region Locators Display

To the left of the Tool menu is a position display that shows you the start point and length of the audio region in the Sample Editor using the unit display you selected in the local View menu. You obviously cannot place audio regions graphically using the Sample Editor, only numerically. When you open the Sample Editor from the Arrange, the Bar ruler reflects the region's location in the Arrange window; when you open the Sample Editor from the Audio Bin, the Bar ruler instead measures from the start of the audio region.

The Sample Editor Mode Buttons

On either side of the local menus are the Sample Editor's five mode buttons and two more buttons to accompany Transient Editing mode. Figure 7.24 shows the Sample Editor buttons.

Figure 7.24   The Sample Editor buttons.

The functions of the Sample Editor buttons are as follows:

- **Link Mode.** This button enables Link mode. This means that the audio region selected in the Arrange window also appears in the Sample Editor.

- **Catch Mode.** The "walking man" button enables Catch mode. If this button is lit, the Sample Editor is linked to the current song position. If there is no audio, the playhead simply stops at the end of the audio region.

- **Transient Editing Mode.** The Transient Editing mode button enables Transient Editing mode, which gives you the ability to increase and decrease the number of transients Logic uses when Flexing audio and stretching Apple Loops by using the + and − buttons to the right of the Transient Editing mode buttons, and to move transient markers.

- **Play Mode.** The speaker icon represents Play mode. If the Loop button is also enabled, Logic will continuously play back your selection from start to finish. If the Loop button is not also enabled, it will play through your selected audio one time. If the Play button is not enabled, your selection will not play back.

- **Loop Mode.** If you enable Loop mode, playback of the selected portion of audio repeats continuously if the Play button is also enabled.

The Waveform Display

The main feature of the Sample Editor is the waveform display. This is the main window you use to edit your audio and transients in the Sample Editor. You can use the zoom controls in the bottom-right of the Sample Editor (as well as key commands) to zoom in and out on your audio and display and edit your audio region down to single-sample accuracy.

Beneath your audio on the waveform display is the anchor point, represented by an orange indicator. The anchor point represents the first musically relevant point on which you want the audio region to pivot. It is the anchor point that gets placed at a specific time position when you drag regions around the Arrange window. For example, if your audio region begins with a fade-in, you might want to place the anchor point at the end of the fade-in, so that the audio past the fade-in falls exactly on the bar as you move the region in the Arrange window.

Beneath the anchor point is the region area, which displays a bar similar to the one you would see in the integrated Audio Bin that runs the entire length of the selected region. You can change the start and end points of the region by clicking and dragging the ends of the region area bar with the resize cursor, which automatically appears when you move the cursor over either end of the bar. Under the region area is the Sample Loop (S. Loop) display. If you use the Edit > Selection > Sample Loop command, then a sample loop bar similar to the region area bar will appear. You can change the length of the sample loop by dragging the ends of the sample loop bar in the same manner as the region area bar. When you select Edit > Write Sample Loop to Audio File, the sample loop information is added to the looped audio file's file header. This information can be used by other applications capable of reading loop data in the file header and by EXS24. Figure 7.25 shows a waveform with the anchor, the region area bar, and the sample loop bar clearly visible.

As you use the Digital Factory or otherwise process or edit your audio, the waveform display reflects your changes. Use the Bar ruler to ensure that the audio region is still positioned where you want it to be as you process and edit your audio.

Editing Transient Markers

Among the many editing functions that can be performed in the Sample Editor, transient marker editing gives you some of the most varied possibilities. Any action that involves using transient

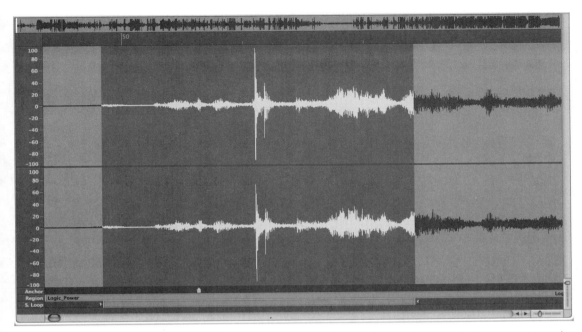

Figure 7.25   The waveform display of the Sample Editor. Notice the anchor point, the region area bar, and the sample loop bar of the audio region under the waveform.

markers can be impacted by judicious use of transient marker editing. From altering Apple Loops, to defining a Groove Template, to improving the reliability of your transient markers for Flexing, to creating musically, technically, or creatively meaningful selections in the Sample Editor, Transient Editing mode can open multiple paths for the manipulation of a single audio file. Before you begin working with a file's transient markers, run the Detect Transients command in the Audio File menu. This will analyze your audio file for transients (which can take a while with longer audio files) and enable Transient Editing mode automatically. Figure 7.26 shows an audio file in the Sample Editor after running the Detect Transients command.

Note that if you Detect Transients on an audio file that Logic has already analyzed, a dialog will appear asking whether you really want to overwrite the existing transient markers.

Just looking at an audio file, or looking at it while it's playing back, can give you a good indication of whether you need to increase or decrease the number of transient makers in your audio file. You can quickly increase or decrease the number of transients for your audio file by clicking the + or − button, respectively. Figure 7.27 shows the same audio file with a greater number of transients detected.

You create new transient markers with the Pencil tool while in Transient Editing mode. You can delete transient markers by double-clicking them, by clicking them with the Eraser tool, or by selecting the area containing the transient markers you wish to remove and pressing Delete.

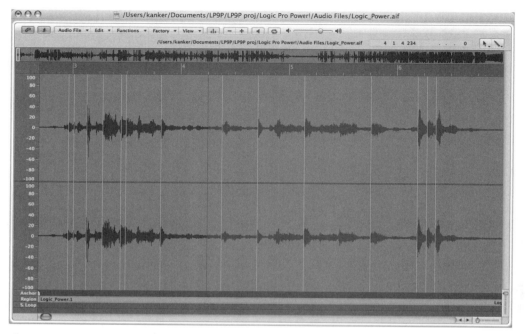

Figure 7.26   An audio file in the Sample Editor with transients displayed after running the Detect Transients command.

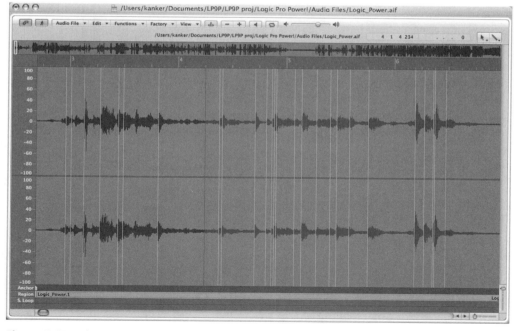

Figure 7.27   The same audio file as seen in Figure 7.26, but with more transients diplayed.

When you move the pointer near a transient marker, it changes to a Transient Editing tool, which allows you to grab and drag a transient to a new position. Figure 7.28 shows the Transient Editing tool moving a transient marker.

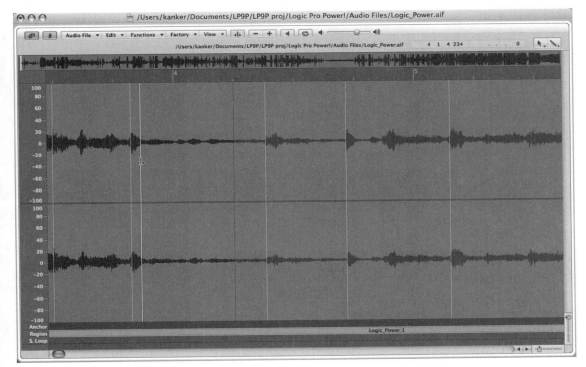

Figure 7.28   Use the Transient Editing tool to move transient markers.

You can toggle Transient Editing mode by clicking the Transient Editing mode button or by using the key command Command+T.

The Digital Factory Machines

The Digital Factory is a repository of destructive offline processes that Logic offers to process audio. As the local Factory menu illustrated, four different processes comprise the Digital Factory Machines: the Time and Pitch Machine, the Groove Machine, the Audio Energizer, and the Silencer. Each of these components is detailed in this section.

Time and Pitch Machine

The Time and Pitch Machine can change the tempo of audio by stretching or compressing that audio. In fact, when you stretch and compress audio in the Arrange window without using any Flex tools, you are technically invoking the tempo-adjusting function of the Time and Pitch Machine. When you access the Time and Pitch Machine in the Sample Editor, either by selecting the local Factory > Time and Pitch Machine option or by pressing Option+P, you can also transpose audio up or down in pitch. You can link these functions together, or they can be independent. Figure 7.29 shows the Time and Pitch Machine dialog box.

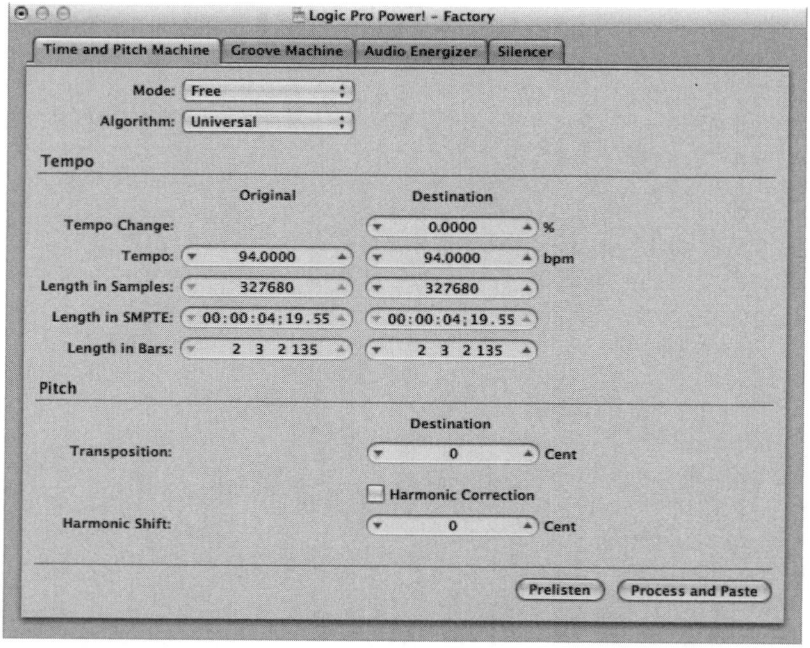

Figure 7.29   You can access the Time and Pitch Machine via the Sample Editor.

Most parameters include a text field for the original (current) value of the audio and a text field to input the desired new value. If you know the specific numeric values you want to use for your parameters, you can enter those numbers in the text fields to the right. The parameters are as follows:

■ **Mode.** The Mode pull-down menu in the Time and Pitch Machine contains two options: Free and Classic. *Free* mode indicates that tempo and pitch adjustments are independent. *Classic* mode means that pitch and tempo are adjusted together, like on an old tape machine, which gets higher in pitch when the tape speeds up and lower in pitch as the tape slows down.

■ **Algorithm.** This selects which algorithm the Time and Pitch Machine uses to adjust the tempo of the audio. These options are already detailed in "The Time Stretching Algorithm Submenu" section in Chapter 6. Remember that if you are in 64-bit mode, any additional Time and Pitch compatible plug-ins you have installed will need to be 64-bit in order to integrate into Logic. If a 64-bit version of your preferred plug-in is not available, you can always save your project, quit Logic, and reopen Logic in 32-bit mode, process your audio file, and then reopen Logic in 64-bit mode.

- **Tempo Change.** This parameter tells you how drastic your tempo change will be by giving you the percentage of change from the original tempo. For example, if the tempo of your original audio track was 120 BPM and you change the tempo to 240 BPM, the parameter will indicate a 100-percent tempo change. You cannot increase the Tempo Change parameter to more than 300 percent or reduce it by more than −75 percent.

- **Tempo.** The Original box lists the current tempo of your audio. You can input a new tempo in the Destination box. You can increase the tempo as much as 300 percent or decrease it as much as 75 percent depending on the algorithm used.

- **Length in Samples.** This is the exact length of the audio in samples. If you know exactly how many samples you want your processed audio to be, you can enter that value in the Destination box. You cannot adjust the number of samples so drastically that the result would be beyond the boundaries of the tempo restrictions mentioned for the Tempo setting.

- **Length in SMPTE.** The length of your audio in SMPTE frames is listed here. If you know exactly how many SMPTE frames you want your processed audio to be, you can enter that value in the Destination box. You cannot adjust the SMPTE frames beyond the boundaries of the Tempo setting's restrictions.

- **Length in Bars.** This is perhaps the most musically useful setting and the closest to the way the Time Machine is used in the Arrange window. Here you see how long your audio is in bars. You can enter the number of bars you want your audio to be in the Destination box. Again, you cannot adjust the bar length beyond the Tempo setting's restrictions.

- **Transposition.** Now you are getting into the transposition settings that affect *pitch,* not tempo. The text-entry box allows you to enter the number of cents, or hundredths of a semitone, by which you want to adjust your audio. Positive numbers raise the pitch, whereas negative numbers reduce the pitch.

- **Harmonic Correction.** As you adjust the pitch of audio, its formants (timbre) are also changed. This means that not only the pitch of the audio changes, but the sonic character of the sound as well. If you turn on Harmonic Correction, Logic attempts to adjust the harmonics of the pitched audio so that the formants remain the same as the original audio. If Harmonic Correction is off, Logic makes no such correction, and the formants change along with the pitch.

- **Harmonic Shift.** If you activate Harmonic Correction, you can use Harmonic Shift to adjust the formants of the audio independently. A Harmonic Shift setting of 0 means that Logic will attempt to keep your formants in the pitched audio identical to the original audio. If you input any other number, Logic shifts the formants by that number, regardless of the Transposition (Cent) setting. In fact, you can choose to only alter the formants of audio by not transposing the audio at all, but turning on Harmonic Correction and inputting a value for Harmonic Shift. This value is also adjusted in cents (hundredths of a semitone).

Because using the Time and Pitch Machine is a destructive process, Logic offers a Prelisten button to the left of the Process and Paste button. Prelisten gives you a sample of what your new audio will sound like before you commit to processing your audio and pasting the newly processed audio into your song.

The Groove Machine

The Groove Machine allows you to "regroove" or change the feel of your audio by adjusting the level and placement of the up and down beats. Figure 7.30 shows the Groove Machine window.

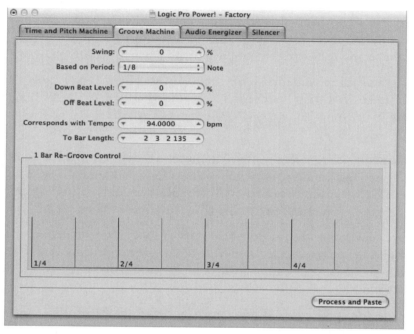

Figure 7.30   The Groove Machine, one of the Digital Factory Machines of the Sample Editor.

The lower half of the Groove Machine window offers you a graphic representation of how the changes are affecting your audio. The parameters of the Groove Machine are as follows:

- **Swing.** This allows you to adjust how far from the beat the change in level occurs. A value of 50 percent means the level change occurs directly on the beat, and you can adjust the value to +70 percent from that value. In general, subtler settings are most useful.

- **Based on Period.** You can choose whether the regroove will be based on eighth notes or sixteenth notes. Select the period most relevant to your audio material.

- **Down Beat Level.** This allows you to raise or lower the level of the down beat (the beat on the bar) from −100 percent to +100 percent.

- **Off Beat Level.** This setting allows you to raise or lower the level of the off beat (the beat between the bar) from −100 percent to +100 percent.

- **Corresponds with Tempo.** This setting reflects the project tempo at the current playhead position.

- **To Bar Length.** This setting reflects the length in bars, beats, divisions, and ticks of the selected audio.

The Audio Energizer

The Audio Energizer attempts to raise the perceived loudness of audio by reducing the distance between the peaks and valleys in the audio wave, resulting in audio with less dynamic range but more consistent loudness. This is the same idea as that of the Maximizer and Loudness Maximizer plug-ins that work in real time in Logic's Mixer. Figure 7.31 shows the Audio Energizer dialog box.

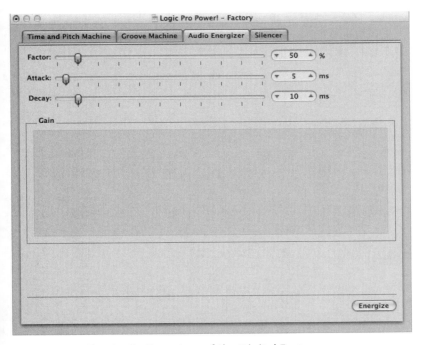

Figure 7.31   The Audio Energizer of the Digital Factory.

The Audio Energizer has only three parameters, and the display below them shows you graphically what adjustments are being done to the audio waveform. The parameters are as follows:

- **Factor.** Factor is the main parameter. This is the average level boost. High values flatten out your audio at the maximum possible amplitude for the waveform. Lower values have little effect.

- **Attack.** This affects the steepness of the effect's onset. Low values mean a very quick, steep onset of the Energizer. High values result in a more gradual ramp up.

- **Decay.** This affects the steepness of the effect's release. Low values stop the Energizer's effect very abruptly after making an adjustment. High values result in a gradual decline of the effect.

Because real-time limiters and maximizers that you can insert in the channel strips of your audio offer more control and are nondestructive, you will most likely not find yourself using the Audio Energizer often, if at all. It's also important to note that the Audio Energizer is different than the Normalize function, as Normalize raises the greatest audio peak to 0 dBFS and brings the rest of the file's amplitude up by the same amount, keeping the difference from peak to valley proportionate.

The Silencer

You can use the Silencer to reduce noise and audio spikes destructively. It offers selector buttons for adjusting the strength of each function and another parameter for configuring how gentle or aggressive the spike reduction will be. Figure 7.32 shows the Silencer.

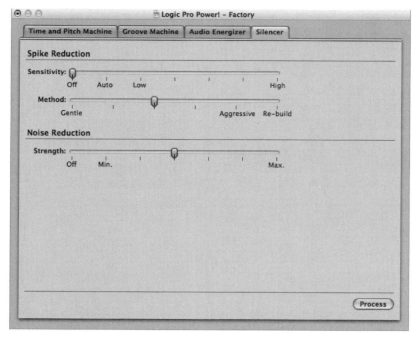

Figure 7.32 The Silencer, the final Digital Factory Machine.

Simply click the button representing the level of noise or spike reduction you want and choose how gently or aggressively the spike reduction algorithm should be in detecting noise. If you choose values too low, the Silencer might not have a noticeable effect. If you choose values too high, you risk adversely affecting your audio.

Logic's Silencer is convenient and of acceptable quality, but there are many plug-ins and stand-alone applications devoted to high-quality noise and spike reduction. If you find yourself doing a significant amount of noise reduction, you would be best served by using one of those applications, such as iZotope's AudioRestore or TC Electronic's Restoration Suite for the TC PowerCore.

The Digital Factory Functions

The Digital Factory Functions relate to the interaction and interchanging of audio and MIDI and the quantization of audio (locking the timing to a grid). There are three options: Audio to MIDI Groove Template, Audio to Score, and the Quantize Engine. Each of these is described in its own subsection.

The Audio to MIDI Groove Template

This function takes the rhythm and feel of an Audio track and creates a Groove Template to superimpose that feel onto MIDI data. To use this feature, you'll need a one-bar drum part displayed in the Sample Editor. (You can either have recorded one bar of drums or have used Add Audio File in the Audio Bin to add a one-bar drum file.) Then select Factory > Audio to MIDI Groove Template or press Control+M. When you select this command, the dialog box shown in Figure 7.33 will appear.

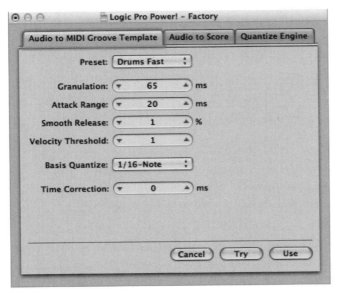

Figure 7.33   The Audio to MIDI Groove Template dialog box. Adjust these parameters to capture more accurately the rhythm of your audio selection.

The Preset menu contains a number of different algorithms designed make it easy to create Groove Templates for different types of source material, such as a fast drum part or a picked guitar part. You use the first four parameters under the Preset menu to fine-tune the analysis algorithm:

■ **Granulation.** To make a Groove Template, Logic must analyze segments of your audio. This parameter determines the length in milliseconds of the slices that Logic will use to derive "velocity points" in the Groove Template. How long you want to set this depends on the tempo of your audio and how distinct each beat and rhythmic element in your audio is. More distinct and loud elements do not require as much time to analyze, but softer or less distinct elements do. Generally, you'll want to keep this parameter between 50 and 200 milliseconds.

■ **Attack Range.** Use this setting to specify the length of the attack times (in milliseconds) of the audio's rhythmic elements. Generally, drums and percussion have very short attack times (1 ms to 10 ms), and other instruments have longer attack times (10 ms to 40 ms).

■ **Smooth Release.** This smoothes out the analyzed release times of instruments with long fades, which generally don't make as good of Groove Templates as instruments with short decay times.

■ **Velocity Threshold.** Logic ignores any sound whose value falls below that which you set in the Velocity Threshold parameter. While the default setting of 1 works well, you can, of course, experiment with this setting to find out what works best for your material.

You use the remaining parameters to fine-tune the MIDI Groove Template created by the analysis algorithm that the preceding settings generated:

■ **Basis Quantize.** This is a pull-down menu that contains all of Logic's usual MIDI quantization options. You can select one of these to ensure that your Groove Template has a standard groove as a basis, in addition to any audio hits that are saved to the Groove Template.

■ **Time Correction.** You can use this setting to compensate for any noticeable delay when playing MIDI tracks or multichannel software instruments. Compensating for delay is addressed in more detail in Chapter 11.

As you adjust the parameters of the Audio to MIDI Groove Template window (or any of the Digital Factory Functions), you will notice your settings being reflected in a Quantize ruler that appears below the waveform display in the Sample Editor, as shown in Figure 7.34.

If you click Try, Logic will apply your MIDI Groove Template to any selected MIDI regions so you can audition your new template. If you like the template, you can click Use to save your Groove Template and install it in the current song. You can now access your Groove Template from the Arrange in the Quantize pull-down menu in the Parameter box of MIDI regions and MIDI objects.

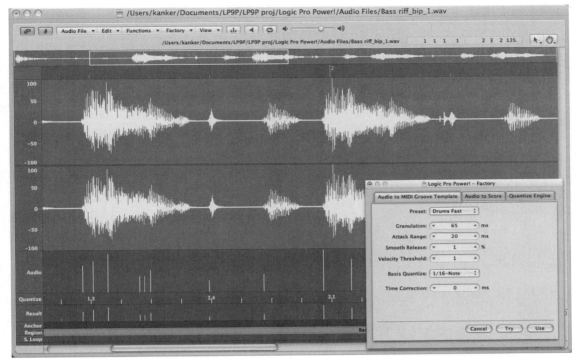

Figure 7.34   The Audio Quantize ruler appears below your audio waveform when you select the Audio to MIDI Groove Template function of the Digital Factory.

Remember, you can also use transients to derive a Groove Template from an audio file by selecting an audio file in the Arrange, going to the Quantize menu in the Region Parameter box, and selecting Make Groove Template.

Audio to Score

Usually, audio data and MIDI data never have anything to do with one another. MIDI data will not make sound, and audio data doesn't send messages to MIDI devices. Logic has a unique and powerful function, however, that tries to convert audio data to MIDI data using the same underlying Quantize Engine as the Audio to MIDI Template function.

This is a very difficult procedure—Logic tries to estimate MIDI notes from the shape of an audio waveform—and the function is limited. You should use this function only with monophonic material—that is, material in which only one note sounds at a time.

When you select Audio to Score or press Control+S, the dialog box shown in Figure 7.35 appears.

As you can see in Figure 7.35, almost all of these parameters are the same as those in the Audio to MIDI Groove Template dialog box. The Audio to Score function brings up the same Audio

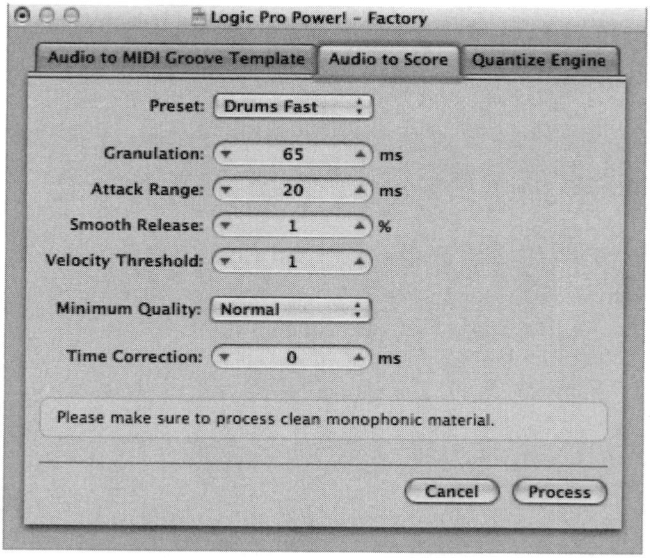

Figure 7.35   The Audio to Score dialog box.

Quantize ruler in the Sample Editor waveform display as shown in Figure 7.34. Logic uses the same analysis parameters and the same analysis engine for both functions. Refer to the section "The Audio to MIDI Groove Template" earlier for descriptions of these parameters. The only different parameter is Minimum Quality, which gives you two options, Normal and High. The Normal setting is more tolerant of notes slightly off pitch but may capture wrong notes. The High setting is far more exacting, but it only converts those notes that it can discern accurately, so it may miss notes. Experiment with both settings to see what works better for any given audio selection.

When you are ready, click Process. Logic then converts your audio into MIDI data and opens up the Score Editor with the newly created MIDI region. Logic uses the Score Editor because this function was initially conceived as a method of writing sheet music from audio. This is why the function is called Audio to Score instead of Audio to MIDI. Don't worry; you can copy and paste the data into any editor or a new MIDI region however you see fit.

The Quantize Engine

Quantizing audio in the Sample Editor isn't as easy a process as it is using Flex Time editing—but depending on the source material, you can still achieve good, and sometimes more interesting, results. If you choose Quantize Engine, the dialog box shown in Figure 7.36 will appear.

Once again, most of the parameters are the same as in the other Digital Factory Functions, and the Audio Quantize ruler shown in Figure 7.34 appears. The only new parameters are Quantize By, which opens the standard Quantize pull-down menu from the MIDI Region Parameter box, and Maximum Range, in which you set the maximum number of milliseconds that a peak in the

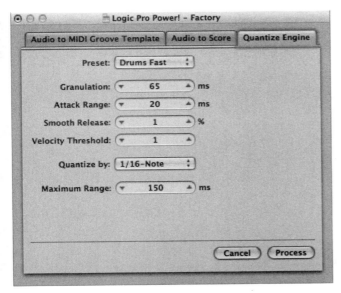

Figure 7.36   The Quantize Engine dialog box.

audio material is allowed to diverge from the quantization grid. To get a tighter quantization, set this value as small as possible; for a looser quantization, use a larger value.

While the Audio to MIDI Groove Template and Quantize Engine functions have been largely supplanted by Flex Time and its related processes, you can still achieve very interesting results with these "old" processes. Experiment a little with these functions—you might just find that they lend themselves to your creativity better than Flex from time to time.

Setting Up Sample Editor Undo Preferences

As you now see, Sample Editor is a very powerful destructive audio editor. Because of this, you might be wondering what happens if you perform a process whose results are less than satisfactory, but you forgot to make a backup of your original audio file. Never fear, not only does the Sample Editor have its own set of preferences that specifically deal with the facility and extent of the Undo command in the Sample Editor, but it also has its own Undo History that is separate from Logic's global Undo History! Unfortunately, given the destructive nature of the Sample Editor's processing, there is no way to open the Sample Editor's Undo History. You can access the Sample Editor's Undo Preferences by opening the Sample Editor tab of the Audio Preferences window, shown in Figure 7.37.

The functions of the Sample Editor's Undo Preferences are as follows:

- **Warning before Processing Function by Key Command.** Selecting this option ensures that when you use a key command to process audio in the Sample Editor, a warning dialog will open, asking you whether you are sure you want to process the selected audio.

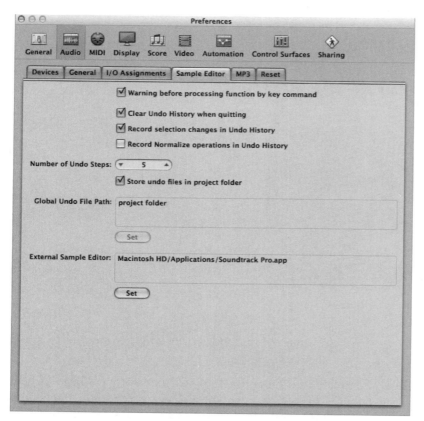

Figure 7.37   The Sample Editor tab of the Audio Preferences window.

- **Clear Undo History When Quitting.** With this option selected, the Sample Editor's Undo History is automatically cleared when you quit Logic.

- **Record Selection Changes in Undo History.** This option enables or disables the Sample Editor's Undo capability. It is best to leave this option selected.

- **Record Normalize Operations in Undo History.** This option allows you to record normalize operations in the Undo History. Since normalization is typically the last process performed on an audio file, when you leave this selection unchecked, the Undo History is automatically deleted when you normalize an audio file. Just to be on the safe side, if this option is not selected, Logic will open up a dialog, asking you whether you want to add the normalize process to the Undo History when you invoke the Normalize command.

- **Number of Undo Steps.** You can set the number of Undo steps that are stored for the Sample Editor in this field by clicking on the up and down arrows, by clicking on the number and scrolling with your mouse, or by double-clicking in the field and entering a number on your keyboard.

- **Store Undo Files in Project Folder.** With this option selected, Logic will store Undo files in a subfolder of your project's main folder.

- **Global Undo File Path.** If you would rather store all your Sample Editor Undo files in one location, you can deselect the Store Undo Files in Project Folder option and use the Global Undo File Path's Set button to open a typical file browser dialog where you can select or create a Global Undo folder for all your Logic projects.

Configuring Logic to Use an External Sample Editor

Although the Sample Editor in Logic is a great place to edit and process your audio files, you might be more comfortable performing those processes in another application. Logic makes this a piece of cake. To tell Logic which application to use as an external sample editor, you simply open the Sample Editor tab of the Audio Preferences window and click the Set button beneath the External Sample Editor heading, shown in Figure 7.37. A file dialog will open, allowing you to browse for your sample editor of choice.

"But I don't have an external sample editor," you say. Apple's Soundtrack Pro 3 was included in the Logic Studio package, so you can set Soundtrack Pro 3 as your external sample editor! Soundtrack Pro 3 has a far more modern editor, a really excellent sound design and processing feature called "actions" for application of plug-ins to an audio region, and other great features. It's beyond the scope of this book to explain all of Soundtrack Pro 3's qualities, but suffice it to say it's a great program worth checking out in its own right. Be sure to check out its user manual for more information.

Once you have selected an external sample editor, you can open audio regions from Logic in your external sample editor either by selecting Options > Audio > Open in [*insert name of your selected sample editor here*] or by pressing Shift+W. Your external sample editor will automatically launch and open with the selected audio region.

Audio Fades and Crossfades

There are three types of audio fades: a fade-in, in which audio ramps up in volume; a fade-out, in which audio ramps down in volume; and a crossfade, in which two audio regions fade into each other. Many times, fading is used as a creative effect, such as fading out a song over a 20-second coda, building in an effect, or cross-fading between two songs. However, sometimes you will want to use fades as tools to cover up clicks at the beginning or end of audio regions or clicks caused by overlapping two audio regions. These fades, rather than being seconds long, are usually measured in milliseconds. For these micro-fades, Logic allows each audio region to have one fade-in and one fade-out or crossfade associated with it. When a fade is associated with an audio region, the length of the fade will appear in the Region Parameter box, and the fade will appear as a light shading on the region itself, as shown in Figure 7.38.

Figure 7.38 The audio region here has a fade-out 300 ms long, as you can see on the region and in the Region Parameter box.

Creating Audio Fades

There are three ways to create fades in the Arrange:

- Typing fade settings into the Region Parameter box

- Using the Crossfade tool in the Arrange Toolbox

- Setting the Arrange Drag mode to X-Fade and overlapping two audio regions

Fade Files

Whenever you set up a fade, Logic creates a fade file. This is a very short temporary audio file that contains just the faded segment. This file is stored in a Fade Files folder in your Project folder. These files cannot be edited. Whenever you adjust a fade in the Arrange, the fade file will be re-created.

Adjusting Audio Fades

If you want your fade to have a curve (in other words, instead of a linear increase or decrease in volume, a logarithmic increase or decrease) you can adjust the curve parameter from −99 to 99 to create various symmetrical curves in the Region Parameter box. This number determines the strength and direction of the curve. You can also select whether the right region fade will be a fade-out, a linear crossfade (X), an equal power crossfade (EqP) for crossfading between two regions that are not phase coherent (for example, two completely different instruments), or an S-shaped crossfade (X S) for material that is hard to crossfade with a standard-shaped crossfade. Generally, just sticking to a straight crossfade (X) will work in most common situations, and you should only try the other curves if you find yourself getting audio dropouts with a linear cross-fade. The Time and Curve parameters for the X-Fade drag mode's crossfades can be set in the General tab of the Audio Preferences dialog.

You can also use the Crossfade tool to adjust the curve of a fade. To do this, simply press Control+Shift while using the Crossfade tool and click and drag the fade to change its curve.

To delete a fade, just change the value of the Fade In or Fade Out parameter to zero or Shift+Option-click on the fade with the Fade tool.

Apple Loops

If you are a new Logic user but are familiar with the Apple audio applications GarageBand or Soundtrack Pro, you will already be familiar with Apple Loops. Users familiar with ACID-ized WAV files will already have an idea of what Apple Loops can do, although Apple Loops go much further than ACID-ized WAVs.

To put it simply, Apple Loops are special audio or MIDI regions that contain embedded pitch, tempo, channel strip, and even sample information.

Audio Apple Loops

Audio Apple Loops are AIFF or CAF audio files with specially embedded tempo and pitch information. Audio Apple Loops:

■   Automatically play at the current song tempo, regardless of the tempo at which the audio was originally recorded

■   Automatically adjust to the key of the current song, regardless of the key of the original performance

Audio Apple Loops behave just like normal audio regions—you can loop them, resize them, cut them, and so on. They even appear in the Audio window like other audio regions. However, you *cannot* edit an Apple Loop in the Sample Editor, because this would compromise the embedded information in the Apple Loop. If you want to edit an Apple Loop, make a copy of it that is a normal audio file and edit that. You can then convert the edited audio file into Apple Loop format. Creating Apple Loops is covered in the section "Creating Your Own Apple Loops," later in this chapter.

To add an audio Apple Loop to your Logic song, simply drag it into an Audio track in the Arrange as you would any other audio file. That's it! You don't need to set up anything—Logic automatically will handle it as an Apple Loop. You can even drag the audio Apple Loop to a blank area of the Arrange, and a new track will be created.

Software Instrument Apple Loops

Software Instrument Apple Loops are MIDI files with specially embedded information. In addition to their MIDI notes, Software Instrument Apple Loops include:

■   **Channel strip settings.** This means that the software instruments and effects that the loop uses will be instantly recalled as soon as you add the loop to a Software Instrument track. You can also drag a Software Instrument Apple Loop to a blank area of the Arrange, and a new track will be created with the correct channel strip setting!

■ **Sample information.** If the Software Instrument Apple Loop uses a sample-based instrument, all the samples it uses will automatically load and be ready for use.

■ **Audio information.** If you drag a Software Instrument Apple Loop to an Audio track, it will behave exactly as an audio Apple Loop!

To use a Software Instrument Apple Loop, just drag it into a MIDI, Software Instrument, or Audio track. Remember that unlike audio Apple Loops that only work on Audio tracks, Software Instrument Apple Loops also contain an embedded audio version of the Apple Loop as well and can be used on either MIDI or Audio tracks. If you drag a Software Instrument Apple Loop to a blank area of the Arrange, it will create a Software Instrument track with the Apple Loop.

Software Instrument Apple Loops: Audio versus Instrument Track?   As mentioned in the text, Software Instrument Apple Loops also include audio information and can be used on either Audio or MIDI tracks. So when would you want to use a Software Instrument Apple Loop in an Audio or MIDI track? There are advantages and disadvantages to both uses.

Software Instrument Apple Loops allow you far more ability to adjust the software instrument, effects, and MIDI data in the loop itself. However, loading software instruments and effects can take up significant CPU power, depending on the individual plug-ins that are part of the loop.

Audio Apple Loops don't let you fine-tune the notes inside the loops themselves or the recorded tone of the loop, since it's a prerecorded audio performance that is looped. However, audio Apple Loops take up very little CPU, but they do take up RAM; the longer the loop, the more RAM they require.

So if you don't need to adjust the loop itself, and you want to conserve CPU, you might want to place your Software Instrument Apple Loop on an Audio track. However, if you want to adjust the instrument used in the loop itself, or you want to conserve RAM, you want to load your Software Instrument Apple Loop onto a Software Instrument track.

The Loop Browser

Because Apple Loops are a special kind of file, there is a special kind of window to organize them. Those of you who are used to Soundtrack or GarageBand are already familiar with the concept of the Loop Browser. Basically, the Loop Browser allows you to search and audition your loops by various criteria. The Loop Browser can index more than just Apple Loops; if you have many ACID loops, for example, you can use the Loop Browser to index them as well. The Loop Browser is available in the Media area of the Arrange and also can be accessed by using the key command O. Figure 7.39 shows the Loop Browser.

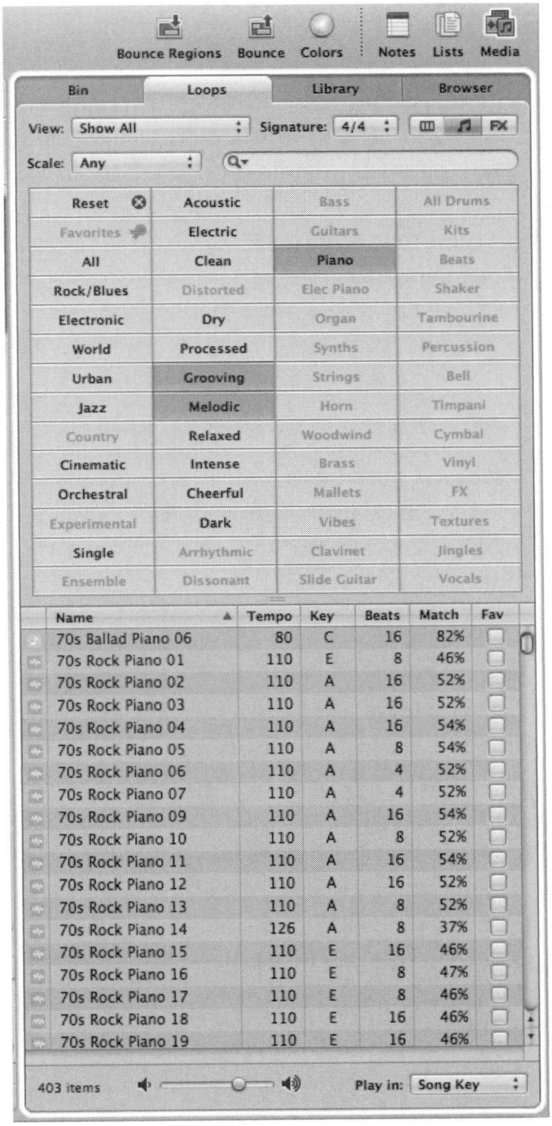

Figure 7.39   The Loop Browser allows you to search for your Apple Loops via category, text search, and more.

Browsing Loops

Searching for loops couldn't be simpler. You can either type in search words in the search field or press the category buttons to limit your search to various instrument and sound effects categories and genres, or both. If you prefer lists of categories instead of buttons, the buttons at the top-left of the Loop Browser will switch you between button view and column view, as shown in Figure 7.40.

You can also select a scale and time signature of Apple Loop to look for and limit your search to specific Jam Packs in the View menu.

The left-hand column in the results window will display either a blue audio wave or a green MIDI note to indicate whether the loop is an audio Apple Loop or a Software Instrument Apple Loop. To the right of the loop name is the Tempo column, displaying the original tempo of the loop. The Key column tells you the original key of the loop, if any. The Beat column tells you how many beats are in the Apple Loop. The Match column lets you know how close the loop is to your search criteria. Finally, if you want to store a loop in your Favorites category in the Loop Browser, just check the box in the Fav column.

Auditioning Loops

To audition a loop, simply click the name of the loop (or anywhere on the same line). The loop will play back using the Prelisten channel strip (as discussed previously), with the volume determined by the Volume slider and the key determined by the Play In pull-down menu. The Play In menu gives you the option to play the loop in the song key, the loop's original key, or any other key you define. To stop the loop from playing, click the loop again.

Adding Loops to the Loop Browser

You add new loops to the Loop Browser by dragging them from the Finder to the results window of the Loop Browser. Your Apple Loops will then be added to ~/Library/Audio/Apple Loops/User Loops/SingleFiles if you are adding a single Apple Loop, and if you add a folder with multiple Apple Loops, an alias of the folder will be added to ~/Library/Audio/Apple Loops/User Loops. If the Apple Loops are on a different drive, you will be asked whether you want to copy the loop to Loop Browser's default loop location or if you'd rather that the Loop Browser just index your loop in its current location. After you make your selection, your loop will be entered into the Loop Browser's database and will be ready for use in Logic. If you are adding ACID loops, be sure to drag the entire folder (or CD) containing the ACID loops onto the Loop Browser, because with Apple Loops, the folder name is used as the category name.

Adding Loops from the Loop Browser to Your Logic Song

If you find a loop you want to use in your song, simply drag it to an appropriate track on the Arrange window—an Audio track for an audio Apple Loop (or another kind of loop, such as an ACID loop) or a Software Instrument Apple Loop, or a MIDI or audio Instrument track for a Software Instrument Apple Loop. The loop will now be part of your song, and if it's an audio loop, it will be added to the Audio window as well.

If, for example, you want a number of audio loops in your song, but not necessarily placed on the Arrange yet, you can also add audio loops directly to your Audio Bin. Just drag the audio loops to the Audio window like you would any other audio file.

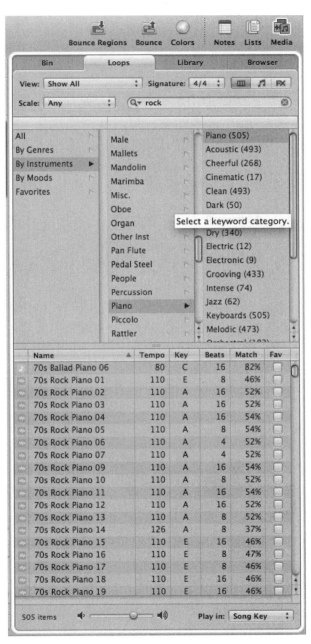

Figure 7.40   The Loop Browser in column view. Notice that there is also text in the text search field, further restricting the results.

Creating Your Own Apple Loops

At this point, you may be very excited by the potential of Apple Loops. It won't be long until you'll want to make your own Apple Loops. In Logic Pro 9, you can create audio and Software Instrument Apple Loops quickly and easily.

Creating Apple Loops in Logic

In the Arrange window, select the audio or software instrument region that you want to convert into an Apple Loop. Next, select Region > Add to Apple Loops Library. You can also drag an Audio or Software Instrument region to the Loop Browser and drop it. Either action opens the dialog shown in Figure 7.41.

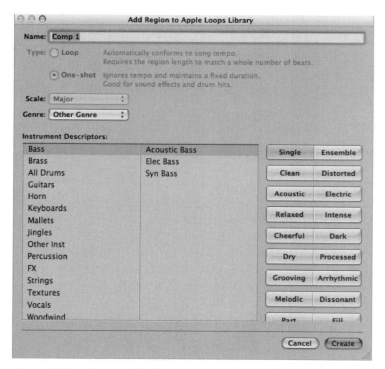

Figure 7.41   The Add Region to Apple Loops Library dialog. You can use the options in this window to name, tag, and otherwise define properties of your Apple Loop.

The Add Region to Apple Loops Library box allows you to tag your Apple Loop with the following information:

- **Name.** You can name your Apple Loop in this field.

- **Type.** The Type parameter defines whether the Apple Loop will follow the tempo or key of any project it is used in (Loop), or whether it will play for its normal duration and pitch, regardless of tempo or transposition (One-Shot). If you are trying to convert an audio region that is not an exact number of bars in length, then One-Shot will automatically be selected. If you want to use the audio region as a Loop-type Apple Loop, then you need to process it in the Apple Loops Utility.

- **Scale.** This menu allows you to define the tonality of your Apple Loop.

- **Genre.** This menu allows you to define a genre for your Apple Loop.

- **Instrument Descriptors.** The Instrument Descriptors area consists of a list area, which allows you to define an instrument type for your Apple Loop, and a button area that allows you to add other descriptive tags to your Apple Loop. In the Instrument Descriptors list area, the list to the left allows you to define a general instrument family for your Apple Loop. Most of the general instrument families have a secondary list that appears in the column to the right when you select a general instrument family. This secondary list allows you to define a more specific instrument type. For example, in Figure 7.41, you see that Bass is selected in the general instrument list, and there are three more specific options you can select from: Acoustic Bass, Elec Bass, and Syn Bass. In the Instrument Descriptors button area, you can add up to nine of the descriptors to your Apple Loop. You can only select one descriptor from each horizontal pair of buttons, so if you chose Single from the first row, clicking on Ensemble would automatically deselect Single.

When you are finished tagging your Apple Loop, click the Create button. Your new Apple Loop will automatically be added to the Loop Browser.

Adjusting the Transients of Your Custom Audio Apple Loops   When you make your own custom Apple Loop using the Add to Apple Loops Library command, it uses the currently detected and edited transients from the Sample Editor to determine where to stretch your loop. So if you want to adjust the "stretch points" of your Apple Loop, you can use Transient Edit mode as described earlier to set and adjust the transients. If you create an Apple Loop without adjusting the transients, Logic simply creates its own grid based on the project's beat divisions.

Creating Apple Loops in the Apple Loops Utility

Thanks to Logic Pro 9's new Transient Edit mode in the Sample Editor, you don't have to use the Apple Loops Utility every time you want to adjust the "stretch points" of an audio Apple Loop. Nevertheless, you still have that option if you want to create an Apple Loop that is not an exact number of bars, or if the audio doesn't match the project's tempo. To do this, select the audio region you want to turn into an Apple Loop in the Arrange and then select the command Open in Apple Loops Utility from the Arrange local Audio menu. You will be asked to select how many bars or beats long your audio region is, as shown in Figure 7.42.

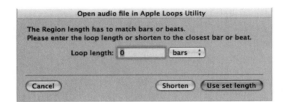

Figure 7.42   Selecting the Open in Apple Loops Utility command in the Arrange window's Audio menu opens the Open Audio File in Apple Loops Utility dialog, where you define the length of your audio file in bars or beats. After selecting Use Set Length, the Apple Loops Utility will open.

Set the number of bars or beats in the box and select Use Set Length.

For this to work properly, your audio region must be its own unique audio file. If the region you wish to make into an Apple Loop is part of a longer audio file, use the Regions to New Audio Files command from the Audio menu of the Arrange to make the desired region into a unique audio file first, and then use the Open in Apple Loops Utility command.

The Apple Loops Utility is a separate application, much like Propellerhead's ReCycle application, if you are familiar with that program. Your selected audio region will be loaded into the Apple Loops Utility's waveform display, and you will be able to reselect how long you want your loop to be and manually set transient points. Figure 7.43 shows you the Apple Loops Utility.

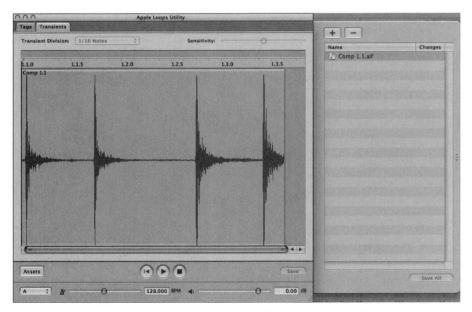

Figure 7.43   You can use the Apple Loops Utility to turn an audio region into an audio Apple Loop.

It is beyond the scope of this book to delve into the art of transient setting and making the perfect Apple Loop using the Apple Loops Utility, but the basic process is that you adjust the tempo and transient points in the Transients tab of the Utility, and then in the Tags tab, you select genre and other information, as shown in Figure 7.44.

Figure 7.44   In the Tags tab of the Apple Loops Utility, you can set the beats, tempo, categories, and other information for your audio Apple Loop before you save it.

After you save your Apple Loop, it should be in the Audio Files folder in your Project folder. You'll need to manually add it to your Loop Browser or drag it back into the Arrange, and then you will have access to your selected audio region as a brand-new Apple Loop.

Adding ACID Loops to the Loop Browser

ACID loops are audio loops that are designed to work in Sony Creative Software's ACID programs. ACID Loops are similar to Apple Loops in that they are designed to automatically adjust to the tempo and key of a project in an ACID program. They are in WAV format, unlike Apple Loops.

Suppose you have a bunch of ACID loops, but you want to find some way to easily integrate them into Logic. You can add ACID loops to the Loop Browser, allowing you to manage all your loop libraries in one location. Because ACID loops aren't embedded with tags like Apple Loops are, you can't import ACID loops without the context of their folder structure. So, if you want to add ACID loops to the Loop Browser, simply drag the highest-level folder in your ACID loops' folder structure into the Loop Browser. You can now access your ACID loops in the Loop Browser.

Using ReCycle Files in Logic

The ReCycle format is a file format originally designed to work in Propellerhead Software's Reason program. A file that is in ReCycle format contains an audio file that has been sliced into smaller pieces to allow the file to be played back at different tempos with little degradation in sound quality.

As of this writing, ReCycle files are not supported in 64-bit mode, so if you plan on working with ReCycle files in a project, be sure to run Logic in 32-bit mode.

Importing ReCycle Files into Logic

If you have some ReCycle files you'd like to incorporate into your project, Logic offers you a variety of options regarding how the ReCycle file is handled. First, you need to import a ReCycle file by selecting File > Import Audio File, by pressing Shift+Command+I, by Control-clicking on an Audio track in the Arrange window, or by dragging a ReCycle file into the Arrange from the Finder. Logic Pro can import ReCycle files with an .ryc, .rex, or .rx2 suffix. When you import a ReCycle file, the ReCycle File Import dialog shown in Figure 7.45 will open.

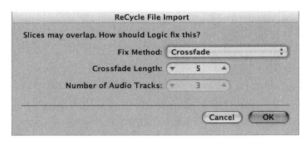

Figure 7.45   The ReCycle File Import dialog.

Because the ReCycle file probably will not match your project tempo, there is a possibility that the slices could overlap each other. Logic allows you to define how it handles your ReCycle file in the ReCycle File Import dialog. The options in the Fix Method menu determine how Logic handles the imported ReCycle file. The different options and their functions are:

- **Don't Fix.** This option imports the files as they are, without performing any extra processing. If you import your ReCycle file using this option, the slices may overlap.

- **Crossfade.** If you select this option, Logic adds all the slices to the same Audio track and automatically crossfades the slices per the Crossfade Length setting. The Crossfade Length setting is in milliseconds.

- **Add Tracks.** If you select the Add Tracks option, Logic will distribute the slices onto the original Audio track, plus any additional tracks as defined in the Number of Audio Tracks field.

- **Render into Single File.** This option renders the ReCycle file into a single audio file per the current project tempo.

- **Render into Apple Loop.** Selecting this option imports the ReCycle file as an Apple Loop.

If you import the ReCycle file using the Don't Fix, Crossfade, or Add Tracks option, then Logic will create a ReCycle folder in the Arrange on the selected track. You can then open the folder and manipulate the individual slices as audio regions.

Converting ReCycle Files into Apple Loops

As you now know, you can import ReCycle files into Logic and have them converted into Apple Loops in the process. You can also use the Browser to convert ReCycle files into Apple Loops. What's really handy about this Browser function is that you can also use it to batch convert your ReCycle files into Apple Loops, meaning you can convert an entire folder full of ReCycle files at one time.

To convert ReCycle files into Apple Loops in the Browser, you need to navigate to the folder containing your ReCycle files in the Browser. Next, select Convert ReCycle Files/Folders to Apple Loops from the Action menu at the bottom of the Browser, as shown in Figure 7.46.

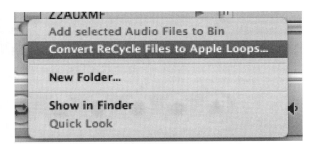

Figure 7.46   The Action menu in the Browser. Selecting Convert ReCycle Files/Folders to Apple Loops allows you to convert ReCycle files to Apple Loops in the Browser.

Once you select this command, a file browser dialog will appear, asking you to choose which folder to put your new Apple Loop(s) in.

Now that you've explored how to work with Apple Loops and audio data inside audio regions, the next chapter will look at working with the MIDI data inside MIDI regions.

8 Working with MIDI

Because MIDI messages are simply numerical messages instead of actual sound, like an audio file, you can move, alter, program, and view those MIDI messages in many different ways. Thanks to these properties and Logic's origins as a MIDI-only application, there are far more editors and windows relating to MIDI information than to audio. Each MIDI editor offers its own unique view of MIDI data and allows you to work with your MIDI information in whichever way is most comfortable for you. Logic offers perhaps the most comprehensive and powerful MIDI editing and re-imagining functions of any sequencer, and these obviously take some time to master. If you're already pretty familiar with the MIDI editors in Logic, you should be aware of the addition of the Chord Grid Library to the Score Editor; it's a comprehensive tool for the creation and management of guitar tablature. Be sure to check out "The Chord Grid Library" section later in this chapter.

This chapter is not going to explore every possible detail and use of every possible option in all the editors, but it will go over the functionality, operation, and potential of each one specifically enough for you to explore deeper on your own.

MIDI Editors and MIDI Regions

We've previously discussed MIDI regions. Just as double-clicking an audio region brings you to the Sample Editor in which you edit your audio, double-clicking a MIDI region opens the MIDI editor of your choice in the Arrange window. You can choose which MIDI editor will open automatically when you double-click a MIDI region by clicking Logic Pro > Preferences > General and selecting the Editing tab. If you click on the pull-down menu beside the Double-Clicking a MIDI Region Opens option, Logic presents you with a menu of the four MIDI editors in Logic, as shown in Figure 8.1.

Logic defaults to opening up the Piano Roll Editor when you double-click a MIDI region, because graphically editing MIDI is the most popular form of MIDI editing and programming. Others may like to use the Event List or another editor. When you get used to the various editors and how you like to use Logic, you can change the default to reflect your personal working method.

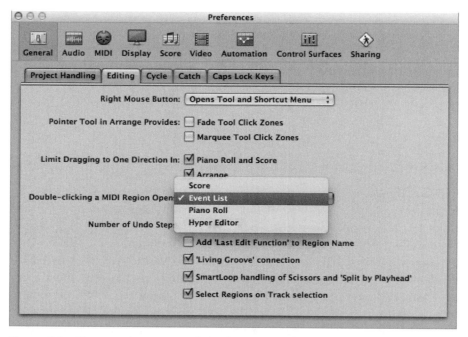

Figure 8.1   You can choose any of the four MIDI editors as the default editor in the Global Preferences.

MIDI regions can be viewed in the MIDI editors in ways besides simply double-clicking the region in the Arrange window. Each editor can be viewed not only in the Arrange window, but in its own dedicated window. All the MIDI editors have Link buttons, which allow you to keep one or more of the MIDI editors in your screenset, and those editors automatically contain the data from any MIDI region selected in the Arrange window. The Event List, Piano Roll, and Score Editors even allow you to view multiple regions at one time. There are also key commands you can use when selecting regions to open specific editors.

In addition, you can always open the various MIDI editors by using menu and key commands, regardless of what is selected on the Arrange window.

The Piano Roll Editor

The Piano Roll Editor offers a graphical piano roll–like view of MIDI data. It displays MIDI notes as colored bars in different positions, with different lengths, colors, and velocities. You can even use the Piano Roll Editor to visually edit MIDI controller data (called *Hyper Draw data*), as you'll see later in this section. Figure 8.2 shows the Piano Roll Editor.

The Piano Roll Editor contains now-familiar elements of buttons, a position display, and a Tool menu, but its most striking feature is the large window that displays the MIDI notes. The playhead moves across all the notes of the MIDI region as you play the song, much like a piano roll

Figure 8.2   The Piano Roll Editor allows you to edit your MIDI notes graphically.

spins as the song plays. You can use the Piano Roll Editor not only to edit notes, but also to create MIDI parts. The Piano Roll Editor also has a Bar ruler display, complete with global tracks to help you navigate and edit.

This section explores the various elements of the Piano Roll Editor and how you can use them.

Local Menus
The Piano Roll Editor contains three local menus: the Edit, Functions, and View menus. Figure 8.3 shows the local menus of the Piano Roll Editor.

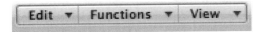

Figure 8.3   The local menus of the Piano Roll Editor.

The following subsections contain descriptions of each local menu.

The Edit Menu
The Edit menu contains options for moving and selecting data. Figure 8.4 shows the Edit menu of the Piano Roll Editor.

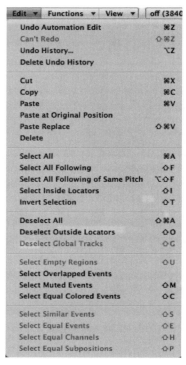

Figure 8.4   The Edit menu of the Piano Roll Editor.

The commands in this menu are as follows:

■ **Undo.** This undoes your last action in the Piano Roll Editor. The key command for this is Command+Z.

■ **Redo.** This command redoes your last action in the Piano Roll Editor. The key command for this is Command+Shift+Z.

■ **Undo History.** This command opens the Undo History window. See the Arrange local menu for details. The key command for this is Option+Z.

■ **Delete Undo History.** Choose this command to delete the Undo History. See the Arrange local menu for details.

■ **Cut.** This removes all selected notes from the grid and places them in the Clipboard. The key command for this is Command+X.

■ **Copy.** This command copies any MIDI notes into the Clipboard. The key command for this is Command+C.

■ **Paste.** Paste places any MIDI notes in the Clipboard on the grid at the current playhead position. The key command for this is Command+V.

- **Paste at Original Position.** This command places MIDI notes from the Clipboard back into the notes' original location. This is useful if you cut notes and decide you still want them where they were, or if you copy notes, subsequently delete them from their original positions, and decide you want them back.

- **Paste Replace.** This command replaces notes you select in the Piano Roll Editor with those from the Clipboard. It pastes notes at the current playhead and replaces all notes within the time range of the pasted notes. The key command for this is Shift+Command+V.

- **Delete.** Delete removes the selected MIDI information from the Piano Roll Editor.

- **Select All.** This selects all the notes in the Piano Roll Editor. The key command for this is Command+A.

- **Select All Following.** Use this command to select all the notes after the currently selected note. The key command for this is Shift+F.

- **Select All Following of Same Pitch.** Use this command to select all the notes of the same pitch after the currently selected note. The key command for this is Option+Shift+F.

- **Select Inside Locators.** This command selects all the notes inside the two locators. The key command for this is Shift+I.

- **Invert Selection.** This command inverts the selection status of all the notes in the Piano Roll Editor. In other words, if you have a single note selected, this command toggles between that single note and every note except that selected note. If you had previously used the Select Inside Locators command, Invert Selection alternates between all notes inside the selected locators and those outside those locators. The key command for this is Shift+T.

- **Deselect All.** This command deselects any selected events. The key command for this is Shift+Command+A.

- **Deselect Outside Locators.** This command deselects any selected events outside the right and left locators. The key command for this is Shift+O.

- **Deselect Global Tracks.** This command deselects any selected global tracks. The key command for this is Shift+G.

- **Select Empty Regions.** This is one of the selection commands common to a number of edit windows, but since Piano Roll Editor notes are never empty, this command has no real effect. The key command for this is Shift+U.

- **Select Overlapped Events.** You can use this command to select all notes that overlap each other in time, such as chords.

- **Select Muted Events.** This command selects all notes that you have muted. The key command for this is Shift+M.

- **Select Equal Colored Events.** This command selects all notes with the same color based on the Colors mode enabled in the local View menu. The key command for this is Shift+C.

- **Select Similar Events.** This selects all notes that are the same (for example, all D#4 notes). The key command for this is Shift+S.

- **Select Equal Events.** This usually selects the same notes you would select by using Select Similar Events, making this command fundamentally redundant. The key command for this is Shift+E.

- **Select Equal Channels.** This selects all notes on the same MIDI channel. This is useful when viewing more than one MIDI track in the same Piano Roll Editor. (See the "Editing Multiple Regions in the Piano Roll Editor" section for details on viewing options in the Piano Roll Editor.) The key command for this is Shift+H.

- **Select Equal Subpositions.** Select Equal Subpositions is a powerful selection option—it selects all MIDI notes that have the same relative position in the Bar ruler. This means if you select a note directly on the bar line, you select all notes that fall on a bar line as well; if you select a note in between the third and fourth bar, you also select all notes that fall on that relative position between the third and fourth bar; and so on. The key command for this is Shift+P.

The Functions Menu

The Functions local menu contains commands that operate on MIDI notes or require MIDI notes to operate. Figure 8.5 shows the Functions local menu.

Figure 8.5   The Functions menu of the Piano Roll Editor.

The functions included in this menu are as follows:

- **Include Non-Note MIDI Events.** If you check this option, editing and moving notes also edits and moves any controller data acting on those notes.

- **Set Locators by Events.** This sets the left locator by the leftmost selected note and the right locator by the rightmost selected note. The key command for this is Control+=.

- **Quantize Selected Events.** This command applies the current quantization setting to the selected events. The key command for this is Q.

- **Undo Quantization.** This removes any quantization that may have been applied and returns the selected notes to their original location. The key command for this is Control+Shift+Q.

- **Delete MIDI Events submenu.** The Delete MIDI Events submenu offers the options shown in Figure 8.6.

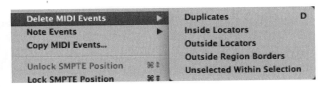

Figure 8.6 The Delete MIDI Events submenu of the Functions menu.

These commands offer different options for erasing groups of MIDI events in the Piano Roll Editor. Here is a brief description of each:

- **Duplicates.** This erases the second instance of all MIDI events that are duplicated by other MIDI events (in other words, same pitch, time, controller number, and so on). The key command for this is D.

- **Inside Locators.** This command erases all MIDI events between the locators.

- **Outside Locators.** This erases all MIDI events not between the locators.

- **Outside Region Borders.** If you are editing more than one MIDI region in the Piano Roll Editor, this command erases MIDI events inside the selected region but outside the current region boundaries. This is useful when a region has been resized. The other regions will not be affected.

- **Unselected Within Selection.** If one or more notes/events are unselected between the first and last selected notes, this command erases those MIDI events.

- **Note Events submenu.** The Note Events submenu offers the options shown in Figure 8.7.

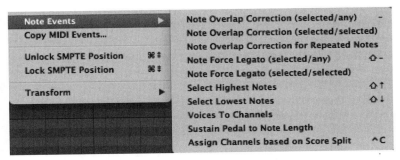

Figure 8.7 The Note Events submenu of the Functions menu.

These commands give you different ways to affect the position and length of notes. A description of each follows:

■ **Note Overlap Correction (Selected/Any).** This shortens any selected overlapping notes so they do not overlap. It does not matter whether one or both of the overlapping notes is selected. The key command for this is -.

■ **Note Overlap Correction (Selected/Selected).** This shortens any selected overlapping notes so they do not overlap. You must select both of the overlapping notes to correct a given pair of overlapping notes.

■ **Note Overlap Correction for Repeated Notes.** This shortens any selected repeated overlapping notes of the same pitch so they do not overlap. The first note in the overlap must be selected in order for this command to work.

■ **Note Force Legato (Selected/Any).** This lengthens any note to extend to the beginning of any following notes. (This sort of smooth transition from one note to another without space in between is called *legato*.) The initial notes to be extended must be selected. The key command for this is Shift+-.

■ **Note Force Legato (Selected/Selected).** This lengthens any note to extend to the beginning of any following notes. You must select both the initial notes to extend and the notes to which they will extend.

■ **Select Highest Notes.** This command selects all the topmost notes across the length of your MIDI region. If your region contains a monophonic performance, such as a melody line, all the notes will be selected. The key command for this is Shift+Up Arrow.

■ **Select Lowest Notes.** This command selects all the bottommost notes across the length of your MIDI region. If your region contains a monophonic performance, such as a melody line, all the notes will be selected. The key command for this is Shift+Down Arrow.

■ **Voices to Channels.** For selected notes that start at approximately the same time or are overlapping, this places each voice (note of different pitch) on a separate MIDI channel.

■ **Sustain Pedal to Note Length.** If you use this command, Logic uses any sustain pedal MIDI controller data to adjust the lengths of the MIDI notes that the messages were sustaining.

■ **Assign Channels Based on Score Split.** This splits selected notes to different MIDI channels, based on the Auto Split Pitch setting in the Score Preferences—notes above get one channel, and notes below get another. The key command for this is Control+C.

■ **Copy MIDI Events.** You can copy all MIDI events with this command. You will be presented with a dialog asking you the range of notes to copy and how you want them to be copied.

■ **Unlock SMPTE Position.** This releases the MIDI events from being tied to their current SMPTE positions. The key command for this is Command+Page Up.

- **Lock SMPTE Position.** This command locks the MIDI events to their current SMPTE positions. The key command for this is Command+Page Down.

- **Transform submenu.** One of Logic's most powerful MIDI tools is its Transform feature, which lets you literally "transform" data in nearly unlimited ways. The Transform submenu offers a selection of Transform presets, as shown in Figure 8.8.

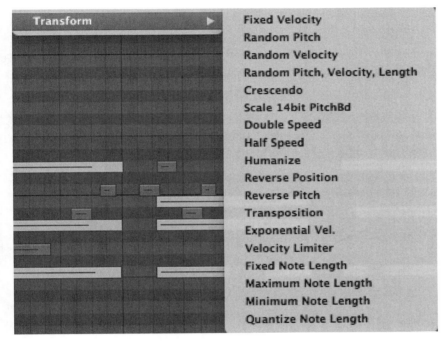

Figure 8.8   The Transform submenu of the Functions menu.

If you select one of these presets, you launch the Transform window, which is configured to run the task you have chosen. The Transform window is one of the more complex aspects of Logic and is examined further in "The Transform Window" section later in this chapter.

The View Menu

The View menu allows you to alter the appearance of the Piano Roll Editor and gives you access to the Hyper Draw functions. Figure 8.9 shows the View menu of the Piano Roll Editor.

The View menu options are as follows:

- **Scroll in Play.** If you select Scroll in Play, instead of the playhead scrolling across the Piano Roll Editor window, the playhead remains stationary in the center of the window, and the MIDI data scrolls horizontally past it, from right to left.

Figure 8.9   The View menu of the Piano Roll Editor.

- **Auto Zoom.** If you select Auto Zoom, when you open a region in the Piano Roll Editor, the horizontal zoom level is automatically set to a point at which the entire length of the region can be displayed.

- **Velocity Colors.** When Velocity Colors is selected, the velocity of each note in the Piano Roll Editor is displayed in color, ranging from purple at the lowest velocities through the colors of the rainbow to red at the loudest velocities. Editing velocity in the Piano Roll Editor is easy in the Piano Roll Editor using the Velocity tool, which is covered in the next section. Velocity Colors is the default view in the Piano Roll Editor.

- **Region Colors.** This command displays the notes of each MIDI region with the same color from the Arrange window. This is most useful when more than one region is in the Piano Roll Editor at the same time. (See the section "Editing Multiple Regions in the Piano Roll Editor" later in this chapter.)

- **MIDI Channel Colors.** This command allows you to display notes of the same MIDI channel with the same color. For example, if you decide to use the Voices to Channels command on a region, and you want to see what notes are on which MIDI channels, selecting MIDI Channel Colors makes the changes readily apparent.

- **Scroll to Selection.** You can have the Piano Roll Editor scroll only until a specific selection in the Arrange window with this option. The key command for this is Shift+'.

- **Global Tracks.** You can toggle the global tracks on or off with this command. Global tracks were discussed in depth in Chapter 4. The key command for this is G.

- **Configure Global Tracks.** This command opens a menu that lets you toggle on or off individual global tracks you wish to view. The key command for this is Option+G.

- **Track Protect Buttons.** If this is checked, Track Protect buttons will appear on the global tracks.

■ **Event Float.** This launches a small, one-event-tall Event List that floats above the Piano Roll Editor. The list displays and allows you to numerically edit text information for the specific note selected in the Piano Roll. The key command for this is Option+E.

■ **Piano Roll Colors.** If you choose this command, the Piano Roll tab of the Display Preferences window opens, presenting different color choices for the Piano Roll Editor background elements and grid lines. If you spend a lot of time working in the Piano Roll Editor and want to create a custom look or perhaps create a workspace that is not fatiguing to your eyes, you can use this Preference pane to accomplish that.

■ **Hyper Draw.** As mentioned briefly in Chapter 6, Hyper Draw enables you to enter and edit MIDI controller data to automate a MIDI region. (Hyper Draw is also called *RBA, region-based automation.*) Since the MIDI controller data is part of the region itself, when you are editing a region in the Piano Roll Editor, you can edit the controller data as well. This command displays a hierarchal menu that offers a selection of possible MIDI controllers you may want to view alongside your note data, as shown in Figure 8.10.

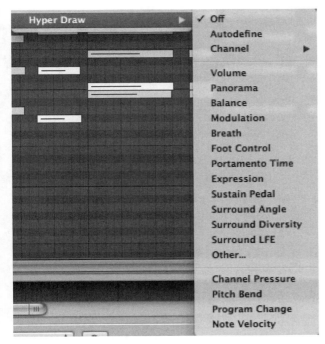

Figure 8.10   The Hyper Draw submenu of the View menu.

If you select one of these options, a controller data lane opens in the bottom half of the Piano Roll Editor. This area is filled with any existing controller messages that you already have in the region, as shown in Figure 8.11.

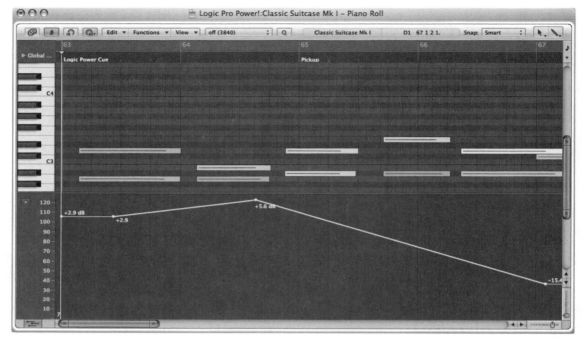

Figure 8.11 A Piano Roll Editor showing the Hyper Draw window. Currently, the volume MIDI controller data is showing.

You can adjust the height of the Hyper Draw area by dragging the bar between the Hyper Draw and Piano Roll areas up or down. You'll learn more about Hyper Draw in Chapter 10, "Using Automation in Logic."

The Piano Roll Editor Tool Menu

Because the Piano Roll Editor is designed for graphic editing, it makes sense that the Piano Roll Editor would have a rather extensive Tool menu of graphic editing tools. Figure 8.12 shows the Piano Roll Editor Tool menu.

Here is a description of the tools, in order from top to bottom.

- **Pointer Tool.** This tool is the standard pointer for selecting and making "rubber band" selections of multiple notes.

- **Pencil Tool.** The Pencil tool allows you to draw new notes into the Piano Roll Editor. You'll learn how to use the Pencil tool later in this chapter, in the section "Inserting and Deleting Notes in the Piano Roll Editor."

- **Eraser Tool.** This tool removes notes from the Piano Roll Editor.

- **Finger Tool.** This tool allows you to resize notes.

Figure 8.12   The Tool menu in the Piano Roll Editor.

- **Scissors Tool.** The Scissors tool splits notes into multiple notes.

- **Glue Tool.** This tool merges adjacent notes, forming one note from multiple notes.

- **Mute Tool.** The Mute tool mutes or unmutes notes in the Piano Roll Editor.

- **Quantize Tool.** The Quantize tool allows you to quantize only selected notes, leaving the rest of the region unquantized. This is very useful if you have a great performance with only one portion in which the timing is slightly off. You can use this tool to quantize just those few notes and not alter the rest of the performance.

- **Velocity Tool.** The bar inside each note indicates the velocity of that note relative to the length of the note itself. In Velocity Colors mode, the bar for each note also displays its velocity using colors from purple through the rainbow to red. With the Velocity tool, you can raise or lower the velocity of one or more notes graphically, by selecting the note and then scrolling up or down with the mouse to shorten or lengthen the velocity bar inside the note or notes. When you adjust the velocity of all selected notes at once by clicking on any selected note and moving the mouse, every note retains its relative value compared to the other notes (so if you raise the velocity of a loud note and a soft note, both will get louder, but the numeric difference between their velocities will remain the same). You can hold down Option+Shift while clicking to adjust all selected notes to the same velocity.

- **Zoom Tool.** For zooming in on a particular group of notes, use the Zoom tool to "rubber band" them and zoom in to the maximum level. Click anywhere that has no notes to return to the original zoom level.

- **Automation Select Tool.** The Automation Select tool resembles a bent arrow pointing upward and left, with a solid arrowhead. The Automation Select tool can select automation data in the Piano Roll Editor Hyper Draw automation lane. Chapter 10 discusses automation and the Automation Select tool in depth.

- **Automation Curve Tool.** The Automation Curve tool resembles a bent arrow pointing upward and left, with an open arrowhead. The Automation Curve tool can create curves between two automation Nodes in the Piano Roll Editor Hyper Draw automation lane. Chapter 10 discusses automation and the Automation Curve tool in depth.

Piano Roll Editor Buttons

At the upper-left corner of the Piano Roll Editor are the four Piano Roll Editor buttons. Figure 8.13 shows those buttons.

Figure 8.13   The Piano Roll Editor buttons.

The functions of each of these buttons are as follows:

- **Link.** Engaging the Link button ensures that the editor always displays the same content as the topmost window. The Link button in the Piano Roll Editor functions in an on or off manner—when the Link button is on, the Piano Roll Editor displays the contents of the currently selected region(s).

- **Catch.** The now-familiar walking man icon is the Catch button of the Piano Roll Editor. With this button engaged, the visible window in the Piano Roll Editor always follows the playhead. You will almost always want this button engaged.

- **MIDI IN.** When the MIDI IN button is engaged, you can use your MIDI controller to directly input MIDI into the Piano Roll Editor. This is very useful for Step Input, which is explained later in this chapter, in the section entitled "MIDI Step Input."

- **MIDI OUT.** With this engaged, you hear each note as you select and edit it. This is useful if you want to monitor what you are doing as you work in the editor.

Inserting and Deleting Notes in the Piano Roll Editor

You may already have a region filled with MIDI information from recording a keyboard performance. If, however, you want to enter MIDI data without recording and performing a keyboard part in its entirety, and if working with your music graphically appeals to you, the Piano Roll Editor is *the* place to create MIDI performances in Logic. There are two ways to insert notes in the Piano Roll Editor: You can use a MIDI controller or onscreen keyboard to "Step Input" MIDI, or you can use the Pencil tool to draw your MIDI performance onscreen.

To use either method of inserting notes, first you must have an open MIDI region in the Piano Roll Editor. This can be an empty region that you created in the Arrange window just so you could fill the region in the Piano Roll Editor, or it could be a region that already contains MIDI data. In the following subsections, you'll learn how to use each method of inserting notes.

MIDI Step Input

The Piano Roll, Score, and Event List Editors allow you to use your hardware MIDI controller to input MIDI in what is known as *Step Input* or *Step Recording* mode. In this mode, you enter your MIDI performance one step at a time. This is useful if you want to create a MIDI performance that is beyond your technical ability to play in real time or if you know precisely which notes you want to input and you want to insert them quickly, but not in real time. Step Input in Logic is fast and intuitive once you understand the basics, and it is a powerful tool when you know how to use it.

First, make sure you have the MIDI IN button engaged so that the Piano Roll Editor can receive external MIDI. Next, set the Division value in the Transport for the length of notes you'll be playing. Drag the mouse up or down to raise or lower the value. The Division display is shown in Figure 8.14.

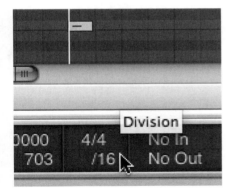

Figure 8.14   The Division display in the Transport. Drag the mouse up or down to raise or lower the Division value for Step Input in the Piano Roll.

At this point, start playing your controller. Logic considers any notes you hold down at the same time to have been input at the same point, so you can play either single notes or chords. As soon as you release the key(s), the playhead advances by one division, and you will see the notes you performed (complete with the velocity with which you pressed the keys) onscreen. It's as simple as that!

As you'd expect, Logic offers more control over Step Input than the basic procedure we have just described. You can adjust the Division setting using the Division display or key commands throughout the Step Input process. So you could, for example, Step Input a few eighth notes, then a passage of sixteenth notes, then two quarter notes, then back to eighth notes. You can lengthen notes you have just input by using the sustain pedal or the Sustain Inserted Notes key command. You can also insert a rest by depressing the sustain pedal without inputting notes or by using the Rest key command. You can also step forward and backward via key commands, or you can press the Delete key to erase what you have just input and thus move the playhead backward.

We've made references to some of the key command options for Step Input; in fact, you can use Step Input entirely by means of key commands. In the Key Commands window, look for the Step Input Keyboard section. You will find key commands for everything, from all the notes and divisions to different velocity settings.

If you would rather use Step Input completely with the mouse, you can use Logic's Caps Lock Keyboard (described in Chapter 6) or the Step Input Keyboard. You can launch the Step Input Keyboard either by selecting Options > Step Input Keyboard or via key commands. The Step Input Keyboard is shown in Figure 8.15.

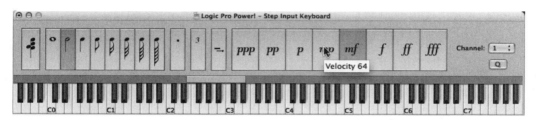

Figure 8.15   Use the Step Input Keyboard window to Step Input MIDI notes onscreen with the mouse.

This window includes buttons representing the various quantization settings, velocity ranges, advance playhead, and so on. As with MIDI hardware or keyboard input, you can adjust these features at any point while inputting, so you can create complex MIDI performances using the Step Input Keyboard.

Step Input versus Caps Lock Keyboard for Step Input Recording   As mentioned in the text, you can use the Caps Lock Keyboard or the Step Input Keyboard to Step Input MIDI notes. Because the Step Input Keyboard has so many more options relating to MIDI Step Input, we highly recommend you use it for Step Recording instead of the Caps Lock Keyboard. The Caps Lock Keyboard is more designed for onscreen input of live performances from the Arrange window.

All of these Step Input methods and key commands offer you rich and creative tools to create and develop MIDI performances. Feel free to experiment with them, and be sure to check out the available key commands. Don't think that Step Input is only for those who are not piano virtuosos—even the best performers may just need to add a few notes to a MIDI region, and there's nothing faster than using Step Input key commands!

Entering MIDI Notes with the Pencil Tool
You can also "draw" your MIDI performance using the Pencil tool. If you know exactly what you want, this is a great way to create MIDI parts quickly. When you click the Pencil tool in the Piano Roll Editor, it creates a note at that pitch and the nearest division. The created note will be the same length and velocity as the previously created note, so if you created an eighth note, then used the Finger tool to lengthen it to a whole note, the next note you created would be a whole note. If you select a note with the Pointer tool and then use the Pencil tool to create notes, all subsequent notes will have the length and velocity of the previously chosen note. If you click and drag with the Pencil tool, you can shorten or lengthen the note you are creating.

Entering Notes Using the Piano Roll Shortcut Menu
The Piano Roll Editor shortcut menu, which can be opened by Control-clicking (or right-clicking if you have selected Right-Click Preferences to open shortcut menus) in the Piano Roll Editor, offers a Create Note command, which places a note at the playhead at the same pitch and with the same length as the last note you selected or edited.

Deleting Notes in the Piano Roll Editor
You can delete notes in the Piano Roll Editor by pressing the Delete key to delete any selected notes or by using the Eraser tool. If you want to restore notes you have deleted, you can undo the action.

Resizing and Moving Notes in the Piano Roll Editor
After creating notes, resizing and moving notes are two of the things you will use the Piano Roll Editor for most often. Because the Piano Roll Editor is designed for graphic editing, it's no surprise that it includes tools to make these tasks as easy as possible. This section explores some of the methods for moving and resizing notes in the Piano Roll Editor.

Resizing Notes
You can resize notes using a number of tools. To resize notes from the front, leaving the end point the same, you can grab a note from the lower-left corner (the cursor should change into a Resize pointer), hold down the mouse button, and drag right or left to move the beginning of the note forward or backward in the region. If you select multiple notes, when you click on the lower left of one note, you adjust the beginning point of all the selected notes.

The Finger tool is designed to allow you to adjust the length of one or more notes quickly. You can click on a single note to resize, or you can select a group of notes and resize them all. As you hold down the mouse and drag right and left, the note becomes longer or shorter. You can resize a note to be as long as the entire MIDI region in the Piano Roll Editor or as tiny as the smallest possible note division. Keep in mind that the smallest division to which you can graphically reduce a note depends on the zoom resolution of the Piano Roll Editor. You can change the zoom level using the Zoom tool or the zoom sliders in the bottom right of the Piano Roll Editor, or via key commands.

If you hold down the Shift key while using the Finger tool to resize multiple notes, every selected note will then end at the same point as the note you are resizing. If you hold down Shift+Option, every selected note will be made the exact same length as the note you are resizing.

Moving Notes

You can move notes around the Piano Roll Editor by selecting them with the Pointer tool and dragging them to a new location. When you hold the mouse button down with one or more notes selected, the Pointer turns into a hand to give you a visual cue that you can now move your notes around the Piano Roll Editor. You can move at the highest resolution possible for the current zoom level by holding down the Control key as you move your notes. To move at the single-tick level (the finest resolution possible in Logic) regardless of zoom level, you can hold down the Control+Shift keys.

To make and move a copy of one or more notes, you can hold down the Option key while dragging your notes.

Expert Tip: Adjusting Pitch and Velocity Using a MIDI Keyboard   If you select a note in a MIDI editor, you aren't limited to using the computer to change the note's pitch or alter its velocity. If you double-click the MIDI IN button, every time you select a note in a MIDI editor in Logic, you can edit the pitch and change its velocity by pressing a note on the keyboard. The note in the editor will change pitch and velocity based on which MIDI note you trigger and its velocity, and the note will retain the timing and length it already had.

Editing Multiple Regions in the Piano Roll Editor

The most common use of the Piano Roll Editor is to open a single MIDI region for editing. However, sometimes you might want to view and/or edit more than one region in the Piano Roll Editor simultaneously. You can accomplish this very easily.

To view multiple regions in the Piano Roll Editor, simply select the regions you want to view in the Arrange window, and the contents of all your selected MIDI regions will appear in the Piano Roll Editor. Lines delineating the start and end points of MIDI regions in the Arrange window will appear as thick vertical lines in the editing window, reflecting the colors of their parent region. If you have Region Colors engaged, the notes of the various regions will have the same colors in the Piano Roll Editor as their regions do in the Arrange window.

When showing multiple regions, you can make selections, resize, and move notes from more than one region as if they were all in the same region. To return to showing only a single MIDI region at a time, simply double-click on a MIDI note; the Piano Roll Editor then displays the region to which the double-clicked note belongs, and the rest disappear.

The Event List

The Event List is the oldest method of recording, storing, and entering MIDI data, both in general and in Supertrack, Logic's earliest predecessor. Given this long heritage, the Event List is extremely robust and feature-laden while admittedly looking a bit anachronistic. Put simply, the Event List features a scrolling text window containing MIDI information. You view, edit, and modify this information by changing the text in the list. Figure 8.16 shows the Event List in the Lists area of the Arrange window.

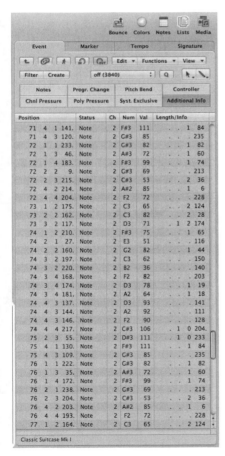

Figure 8.16 In the Event List, you can view and edit your MIDI data as text.

The Event List displays the position of events, the specific type of event it is (which the editor labels as Status), the MIDI channel of the event (Ch), any numerical values associated with that event, and the length or other relevant information about that MIDI event.

At first glance, it might seem as if editing music as text would be more tedious than creative. When you get used to the Event List, however, you'll find this is far from the reality. Many times, you'll want to have a linked Event List even when using another editor or the Arrange window, simply to view the detailed information available in the Event List. In some cases, some MIDI information, such as note release velocity, can be viewed and edited only in the Event List. And you might just find that when you know what you are doing, being able to quickly find and replace MIDI data as text is the most efficient method of editing available.

Let's start looking at this vital and powerful tool by going through its local menus.

Event List Local Menus

Like the Piano Roll Editor, the Event List has three local menus: Edit, Functions, and View. Figure 8.17 shows the local menus of the Event List.

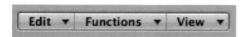

Figure 8.17   The local menus of the Event List.

The similarities between the Piano Roll Editor's and the Event List's local menus don't end there. Because all the MIDI editors are essentially working with the same data, many of the commands are also shared, as you will see in the following subsections.

The Edit Menu

Figure 8.18 shows the Edit menu of the Event List.

As you can see, this menu is exactly the same as the Edit menu in the Piano Roll Editor. Refer to the descriptions of the commands in that subsection.

The Functions Menu

Once again, take a look at the Functions menu of the Event List in Figure 8.19 and compare it to the Functions menu in the Piano Roll Editor.

Refer to the description of the commands in subsection "The Functions Menu" in "The Piano Roll Editor" section.

The View Menu

Unlike the other two local menus in the Event List, the View menu offers selections unique to this editor. Figure 8.20 shows the View menu of the Event List.

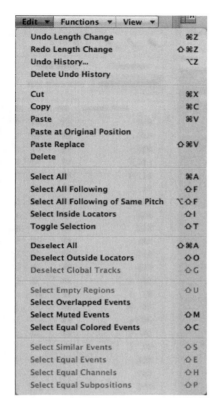

Figure 8.18   The Event List's Edit menu is identical to the Piano Roll Editor's Edit local menu. (The Undo option displayed may be different, but that changes with each action.)

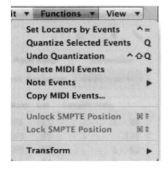

Figure 8.19   Like the Event List's Edit menu, the Functions local menu in the Event List shares the same options as the Piano Roll Editor's Functions menu.

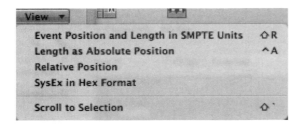

Figure 8.20   The View menu in the Event List.

This menu offers a selection of commands that allow you to customize the display of events in the Event List:

- **Event Position and Length in SMPTE Units.** With this engaged, the Position and Length columns in the Event List display SMPTE units instead of bar units. The key command for this is Shift+R.

- **Length as Absolute Position.** If this is engaged, the Length display shows the absolute song position of the note-off message, as opposed to the note length (which is the usual way of displaying length). The key command for this is Control+A.

- **Relative Position.** With this engaged, the position of notes does not reflect their position in the song, but their relative position inside the MIDI region you are editing.

- **SysEx in Hex Format.** If your Event List is displaying any System Exclusive (SysEx) information for a hardware MIDI device, engaging this option displays the data in hexadecimal format. Consult your MIDI hardware unit's instruction manual for details of its SysEx implementation.

- **Scroll to Selection.** With this engaged, the Event List scrolls to the region selected in the Arrange window. The key command for this is Shift+'.

The Event Editor Tool Menu

Because the Event List is designed for text, not graphic, editing, its Tool menu contains fewer tools than in the other MIDI editors. Figure 8.21 shows the Event List Tool menu.

The Event List Tool menu offers the following tools.

- **Pointer Tool.** The Pointer tool is the standard tool for selecting single or multiple MIDI events. To make multiple selections with the Pointer tool, hold down the mouse button over an area in the Event List outside the Position column and drag over a group of notes to make a "rubber band" selection, or hold down the Shift key while clicking on individual messages.

- **Pencil Tool.** You can click in the Event List to create a new MIDI event. This is described in more detail in the upcoming section, "Inserting and Deleting MIDI Messages in the Event List."

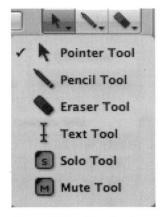

Figure 8.21   The Tool menu of the Event List.

- **Eraser Tool.** The Eraser tool removes one or more MIDI messages from the Event List. This has the same effect as selecting MIDI messages and pressing the Delete key.

- **Text Tool.** If your Event List is not showing MIDI notes, but is instead showing the names of regions and folders from the Arrange window, you can use this tool to rename them.

- **Solo Tool.** The Solo tool allows you to audition events in the Event List. By clicking on an event with the Solo tool, Logic begins a soloed playback of all events in the selected region, beginning from the selected note.

- **Mute Tool.** You can click on one or more MIDI notes in the Event List to mute them. Click again to unmute the muted notes.

Event List Buttons

The Event List holds many more buttons than any window you have explored so far. Figure 8.22 shows the Event List buttons.

Figure 8.22   The Event List buttons allow you to select which data to show and which to filter out.

Some of these buttons are familiar from other windows, but others are unique to the Event List and allow you to display only those specific types of MIDI messages with which you want to work. The familiar buttons located to the left of local menus include, from left to right:

- **Hierarchy button.** Clicking this button when it is active will move you up a level in the Event List from a list of the events in a region to a list of the regions in the project.

- **Link button.** Engaging the Link button ensures that the editor always displays the same content as the topmost window. If you do not have a MIDI region selected, and the topmost window is an Arrange window, a list appears of the folders and regions in the Arrange window rather than the MIDI messages inside the regions. Double-clicking or Option-clicking the Link button while the Catch button is also engaged activates Contents Catch mode, which means that the Event List always shows the contents of the currently playing region as the song plays.

- **Catch button.** With this button engaged, the visible window in the Event List always follows the playhead position. You will almost always want this button engaged.

- **MIDI IN button.** When the MIDI IN button is engaged, you can use your MIDI controller to input MIDI directly into the Event List. This is described in the earlier subsection, "MIDI Step Input."

- **MIDI OUT button.** With this engaged, you hear the currently selected MIDI note that you are editing.

In addition to these buttons, there are two other sets of buttons available in the Event List. The first set contains the Filter and Create buttons, seen under the Hierarchy, Link, and Catch buttons in Figure 8.22. These buttons control what actions are performed by the other set of eight buttons at the bottom of Figure 8.22, the Event Type buttons. The functions of these buttons are as follows:

- **Notes button.** With the Filter button engaged, selecting the Notes button hides the MIDI notes in the MIDI region that you are editing. With the Create button engaged, clicking the Notes button creates a new note event at the current playhead position.

- **Progr. Change button.** With the Filter button engaged, selecting this button hides any program change messages in the MIDI region you are editing. With the Create button engaged, clicking the Progr. Change button creates a new program change event at the current playhead position.

- **Pitch Bend button.** With the Filter button engaged, selecting this button hides any pitch bend messages in the MIDI region you are editing. Keep in mind that if your region has pitch bend information, you may find literally *hundreds* of pitch bend messages representing every instant the pitch bend wheel was touched, so this button comes in very handy! With the

Create button engaged, clicking the Pitch Bend button creates a new pitch bend event at the current playhead position.

- **Controller button.** With the Filter button engaged, selecting this button hides any control change messages in the MIDI region you are editing. With the Create button engaged, clicking the Controller button creates a new controller event at the current playhead position.

- **Chnl Pressure button.** With the Filter button engaged, selecting this button hides any aftertouch messages in the MIDI region you are editing. With the Create button engaged, clicking the Chnl Pressure button creates a new aftertouch event at the current playhead position.

- **Poly Pressure button.** With the Filter button engaged, selecting this button hides any polyphonic key pressure messages in the MIDI region you are editing. With the Create button engaged, clicking the Poly Pressure button creates a new polyphonic key pressure event at the current playhead position.

- **Syst. Exclusive button.** With the Filter button engaged, selecting this button hides any System Exclusive messages in the MIDI region you are editing. With the Create button engaged, clicking the SysEx button creates a new System Exclusive event at the current playhead position.

- **Additional Info button.** If the Filter button is engaged, selecting this button will hide extra information (the "full message") about the displayed MIDI messages. If the Create button is engaged, this button changes to the Meta Events button.

- **Meta Events button.** If the Create button is engaged, clicking the Meta Events button will create a new meta event at the current playhead position.

Inserting and Deleting MIDI Messages in the Event List

As with the other MIDI editors, you can insert and delete MIDI information. Because the Event List is a text editor, you do not have the visual cues that you do in the Piano Roll Editor or the musical notation cues you have in the Score Editor. Still, some people may find it convenient to add notes directly while using the Event List, and you can employ a number of methods.

First of all, you can use the same process described in the earlier "MIDI Step Input" subsection to input MIDI information into a MIDI performance one note at a time. The major difference is that you will not see a graphic representation of the note you have performed, but a line of text information instead.

You can also insert an event using the Pencil tool. Simply click the Pencil tool in the Status column, and it adds a new event, identical to the currently selected event, at the current song position. A text input box appears, in which you can type in the position where you want to place the duplicate event. Type in the desired position and press Return. If you press Return without specifying a new position, the duplicate appears in the same position as the original event (although because this is a text list, it appears right under the original event but with the same position value).

If you click on an event with the Pencil tool in the Position column, it copies the event to the Clipboard. When you paste the event, a text entry box also appears, in which you can enter position values; follow the same procedure of entering their position, and the editor will paste them in the new location.

You can delete MIDI events by clicking on them with the Eraser tool or by selecting them and then pressing the Delete key. If you are not happy with any insertions or deletions you have made, you can always use the Undo command, or open the Undo History window if you have made a number of edits you dislike.

Moving and Adjusting the Values of MIDI Messages in the Event List

Even though you do not have the graphic bar to move, lengthen, or shorten for each note as you do in the Piano Roll Editor, you can easily accomplish these things in the Event List, and with even more precision. The important thing to remember is that you are accomplishing everything through text entry, so you need to know the precise values of how much you want to resize a MIDI note or the exact position to which you want to move a MIDI event.

First of all, to move a single event, simply double-click its position data with the Pointer. A text entry box appears, in which you type the new value. When you press Return, the event moves to the new location. If you select multiple MIDI messages, they all move relative to the event whose position you changed. So if you selected three MIDI notes that occurred on Bar 1, Bar 2, and Bar 3, and you double-clicked on the note at Bar 2 and changed its position to Bar 3, the note at Bar 1 would move to Bar 2, and the note at Bar 3 would move to Bar 4.

The procedure for adjusting any other value, such as a MIDI event's length or velocity, is basically the same: You simply double-click the desired data with the Pointer tool, enter a new value in the text box, and press Return. If you select more than one MIDI event, they all maintain their values relative to each other, just as previously described; all selected events maintain their relative length.

You can also adjust values and move events without entering text, but by selecting one or more events and then using the mouse as a vertical slider to adjust values up or down.

When adjusting values for a group of MIDI events with the mouse, when any selected event reaches its maximum or minimum value (remember, MIDI values are between 0 and 127), no further adjustments in that direction will be possible for any event in that group, so that each event may maintain its relative value. If you want to continue to change the events from the selected group that have not reached their maximum or minimum more than this, you can do so by holding the Option key down while dragging one of those events. If you want to set the same value for all selected events, hold down Shift+Option while dragging one of the events.

The Hyper Editor

The Hyper Editor is another MIDI editor with a heritage that goes back to the early versions of Notator. It offers a unique way to build drum parts and to edit MIDI controller data graphically. It looks a bit like a cross between an Arrange window and a Piano Roll Editor, with lanes for different notes or controller messages like tracks in the Arrange window and vertical bars representing MIDI events. You can also view global tracks in the Hyper Editor. Figure 8.23 shows a Hyper Editor window.

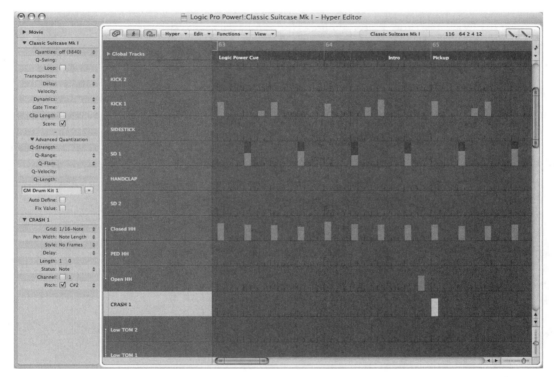

Figure 8.23   You can use the Hyper Editor as a MIDI drum or controller editor; here it is being used as a drum editor.

The Hyper Editor not only offers a step-entry graphic editor for drums and controller messages, but it also allows you to save combinations of event definitions and drum note names as hyper sets, which you'll explore in the "Hyper Sets" section later in this chapter. Due to the uniqueness of the Hyper Editor, it is often overlooked. After reading this section, I hope you will feel comfortable enough to integrate it into your working method.

Note: Hyper Editor and Hyper Draw   It's tempting to confuse the Hyper Editor with Hyper Draw. Although both share the word "hyper" in their names and both can operate on

MIDI control messages, they do not refer to the same thing. *Hyper Draw* is the name for the automation-like protocol in which you can enter MIDI control data in the Arrange window or the Piano Roll Editor for specific MIDI regions. The *Hyper Editor* is a grid-based editor that does allow for the input and editing of MIDI control data, but its grid-based editing does not allow for the smoothness of changes that are possible with Hyper Draw. Hyper Draw is not suited for one-off and non-continuous MIDI control—Hyper Draw wants to connect control messages together. On the other hand, you'll find the Hyper Editor is far too tedious if you are trying to create automation-like effects—you'd be far better served using Hyper Draw or track-based automation. Finally, there's no way to use Hyper Draw as a drum editor, whereas the Hyper Editor's grid-based Edit window is uniquely suited for drum programming.

Hyper Editor Local Menus

Like the Event List, the Hyper Editor shares some local menus that the other MIDI editors offer. The unique menus and commands are as follows in the next few subsections.

The Hyper Menu

As you might have guessed, the local Hyper menu includes commands unique to the Hyper Editor. Figure 8.24 shows the Hyper menu.

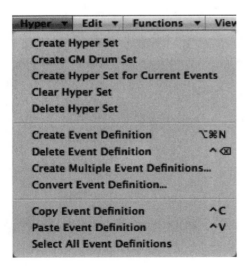

Figure 8.24 The Hyper menu of the Hyper Editor.

This local menu contains most of the commands related to using hyper sets. The "Hyper Sets" subsection later in this chapter explains in detail how to use hyper sets. Following are descriptions of these commands:

- **Create Hyper Set.** This creates a new hyper set.

- **Create GM Drum Set.** This command creates a new General MIDI drum set.

- **Create Hyper Set for Current Events.** This creates a hyper set using the events currently selected in one of the MIDI editors. This is very useful if you have used Hyper Draw in other windows to add controller messages to MIDI regions, and you want to create a hyper set with just those previously defined messages (events) represented.

- **Clear Hyper Set.** This command empties the current hyper set.

- **Delete Hyper Set.** This command deletes the current hyper set.

- **Create Event Definition.** This command creates a new event definition on the selected lane of the Hyper Editor. Event definitions determine which MIDI event a given lane of the Hyper Editor will edit. The key command for this is Option+Command+N.

- **Delete Event Definition.** This erases the event definition of the selected lane(s) in the Hyper Editor. The key command for this is Control+Delete.

- **Create Multiple Event Definitions.** You can automatically create event definitions for either all MIDI events or all selected events. When you choose this command, a dialog box appears asking whether you want to create a new set with definitions only for those events you have selected or for all events. Select the option you desire and press Return, and all those event definitions will appear to the right of the lanes in the Hyper Editor.

- **Convert Event Definition.** This redefines the selected event definition, as well as all the events in its lane. The events retain their values after conversion.

- **Copy Event Definition.** This command copies an event definition into the Clipboard. The key command for this is Control+C.

- **Paste Event Definition.** This pastes an event definition from the Clipboard. The key command for this is Control+V.

- **Select All Event Definitions.** This command selects all the event definitions in the current hyper set.

The Edit Menu

Figure 8.25 shows the Edit menu of the Hyper Editor.

As you can see, the Hyper Editor also shares its Edit menu with the Piano Roll Editor. Refer to the previous subsection covering the Edit menu of the Piano Roll Editor for descriptions of these commands.

The Functions Menu

Figure 8.26 shows the Functions menu of the Hyper Editor.

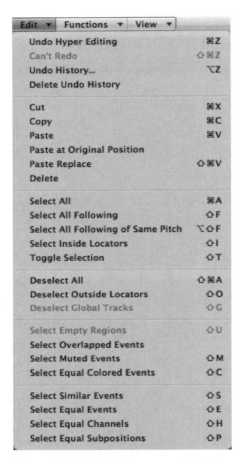

Figure 8.25   The Edit menu of the Hyper Editor is the same as the Edit menus of the Piano Roll Editor and Event List.

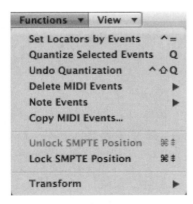

Figure 8.26   The Functions menu of the Hyper Editor is also the same as that of the Piano Roll Editor and the Event List.

Once again, this menu is also the same Functions menu as that of the Piano Roll Editor and the Event List. Refer to the previous subsection covering the Piano Roll Editor's Functions menu for descriptions of these commands.

The View Menu

The View menu for the Hyper Editor offers unique options. Figure 8.27 shows the View menu of the Hyper Editor.

Figure 8.27 The View menu of the Hyper Editor.

The various view options are as follows:

- **Scroll in Play.** If this is engaged, instead of the playhead scrolling through the Hyper Editor, the Hyper Editor tracks scroll past the stationary playhead.

- **Global Tracks.** You can toggle the global tracks on or off with this check box. The key command for this is G.

- **Configure Global Tracks.** This command opens a drop-down menu that lets you toggle on or off individual global tracks you wish to view. The key command for this is Option+G.

- **Track Protect Buttons.** If this is checked, Track Protect buttons will appear on the global tracks.

- **Inspector.** This command shows or hides the Inspector at the left side of the Hyper Editor window. The key command for this is I.

- **Scroll to Selection.** The Hyper Editor scrolls to a selected MIDI region in the Arrange window when this control is engaged. The key command for this is Shift+'.

- **Event Float.** This command launches a small, one-event-tall Event List that floats above the Hyper Editor and displays text information regarding the specific note you are editing. The key command for this is Option+E.

The Hyper Editor Tool Menu

Figure 8.28 shows the Hyper Editor Tool menu.

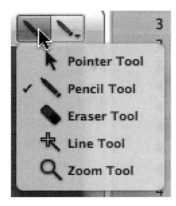

Figure 8.28   The Tool menu of the Hyper Editor.

The Line tool is unique to the Hyper Editor, but the other four tools are standard. Descriptions of the five tools follow:

- **Pointer Tool.** This is the standard Pointer for selecting and making "rubber band" selections of multiple notes.

- **Pencil Tool.** The Pencil tool allows you to draw in new drum notes if you are using the Hyper Editor as a drum editor or new controller information if you are using the editor to edit controller data. You learn how to use the Pencil tool later in this chapter in the subsections that cover editing.

- **Eraser Tool.** This tool removes notes and controller data from the Hyper Editor.

- **Line Tool.** This tool is valuable if you want to make linear changes in your data. To use this tool, click the mouse on the note or controller message that you want to begin your line, drag the vertical line until you reach your end point, then click the mouse again. The velocity or controller data in any event between the line's end points will snap to the value at which the line bisected the event. In other words, if you wanted to fade up the velocity of drum hits slowly, you could click the crosshair on the first drum hit at the very bottom of the hit; then, at the end of the measure, click the mouse again, drawing a diagonal line up through your drum hits. The velocities of your drum hits now have the upward ramp formed by the Line tool, giving you an even, linear fade-in.

- **Zoom Tool.** To zoom in on a particular area, use the Zoom tool to "rubber band" it. You then zoom in to the maximum zoom level. Click in any empty space in the Edit window to return to the original zoom level.

The Hyper Editor Buttons

Because the Hyper Editor is unique in its functions, it relies less on the standard Logic window components. As you can see in Figure 8.29, the Hyper Editor has three basic function buttons common to the other MIDI editors.

Figure 8.29   The buttons of the Hyper Editor.

The Hyper Editor buttons control these familiar functions:

■ **Link button.** Engaging the Link button ensures that the editor always displays the content of the currently selected region in the Arrange window. The Link button functions in an on or off manner.

■ **Catch button.** With this button engaged, the visible window in the Hyper Editor always follows the playhead position. You will almost always want this on.

■ **MIDI OUT button.** With this engaged, you will hear the currently selected MIDI note or event change (if you are working with pitch bend data, for example) while you are working.

The Hyper Editor Event Parameter Box

Unlike the Piano Roll Editor or the Event List, the Hyper Editor has an Inspector. The Hyper Editor's Inspector contains parameters to define the currently selected lane in the Hyper Editor. Every event definition has its own Parameter box. Figure 8.30 shows a parameter box for the Volume lane.

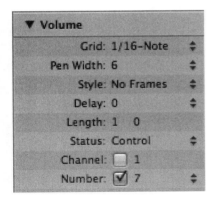

Figure 8.30   The Parameter box for the volume events in the Hyper Editor.

The functions of these parameters are as follows:

■ **Grid.** This determines the grid, meaning how many events will fit in one bar in the Edit window. The size of the grid determines the resolution of the events.

■ **Pen Width.** With this parameter, you can adjust the width of the bars that appear in the Edit window. You can adjust this parameter between 1 and 16. In general, you'll want to find the value that almost completely fills the grid space, but that still leaves a few pixels so you can differentiate the different bars. You need to determine the correct value based on your chosen grid resolution.

- **Style.** This parameter gives you two options for how data is displayed in the Hyper Editor. No Frames displays the event as a vertical line. Framed Values displays the event as a vertical line with a hollow frame that fills the remainder of the Hyper lane, allowing you to see the event as a proportion of its full range. You can see the Framed Values displayed in the lane named SD 1 in Figure 8.23.

- **Delay.** With this parameter, you can offset all the events in a lane by a number of ticks. Simply double-click the left side of the parameter box next to the word Delay and enter a value in the text box. Positive values delay events; negative numbers advance events. If you click the right side of the Delay area by the up and down arrows, a pull-down menu appears in which you can select your note divisions.

- **Length.** The Length parameter determines how long added notes will be. The first number is the current division, and the second is ticks. You will not normally need to set this unless you have some particularly long or short drum samples.

- **Status.** Here you can change the event definition from one type of message (note, volume, pitch bend, and so on) to another.

- **Channel.** Normally, the Hyper Editor displays all matching MIDI events in the region being edited. If you set the MIDI Channel parameter and check the box, the Hyper Editor shows only those events on the selected channel. If the box is unchecked, the parameter is ignored.

- **Number or Pitch (First Byte).** With this box checked, this parameter determines what the initial byte (note pitch for notes, controller type for MIDI control messages) must be for the lane to display data. In other words, if the First Byte parameter is set for C#2, the editor displays only those notes that fall on C#2. Generally, for drum editing and specific MIDI control message events, you'll want this box checked. For more generic columns (such as the All Velocities option), you'll want to leave this box unchecked.

Where Did My Inspector Go? Let's say you've become very comfortable working with Logic's editors in the Arrange window. You've looked at the picture of the Hyper Editor in Figure 8.23 and you've looked at the integrated Hyper Editor in the Arrange window, and you don't see the Hyper Editor window's Inspector in the integrated Hyper Editor. Instead of wasting what space you *do* have in the Arrange window's Hyper Editor, Logic uses the Arrange window's own Inspector for controlling the currently selected Hyper lane!

Hyper Sets

Hyper sets are unique to the Hyper Editor. They are basically stored lists of MIDI note or MIDI control message definitions, complete with parameters for each lane. Hyper sets allow you to configure the editor for your specific needs, then save that configuration with all of your parameter settings, note names, and so on, and recall that configuration at will. If you like to use a few specific MIDI control events, you can create a hyper set of only those event definitions. You can also have a hyper set for your specific MIDI drum kit, and whenever you want to program drums, the exact setup that you need will be ready for you right in the Hyper Editor.

Hyper sets not only are powerful tools, but they are also very easy to use. You can access your available hyper sets from a pull-down menu in the Inspector. Simply click the arrow to open the pull-down menu and select the hyper set you want to use. This menu also includes the commands for creating and clearing hyper sets found in the Hyper menu. Figure 8.31 shows the Hyper Set selection field.

Figure 8.31   All the hyper sets you create are available in the Hyper Set selection field.

Logic offers hyper sets for MIDI controls and GM (General MIDI) drums, which you can use as they are, or you can use them as templates for your own hyper sets. Simply adjust each lane using the Hyper local menu and key commands, set the Parameter box for the event definitions in the Inspector to taste, use the Select All command, then choose Create Hyper Set for Current Events to create a hyper set of your current configuration. (The "Setting Up the Hyper Editor as a Drum Editor" subsection describes this in more detail.) If you'd prefer to start from a blank slate, you can always start the process by using the Create Hyper Set command. You can name your hyper set by double-clicking in the Hyper Set selection field, which presents you with a text box in which to enter a new name for the hyper set. You need not worry about saving anything—Logic automatically saves each new hyper set in Logic's Preferences, so it's available in any of your songs.

Editing MIDI Control Messages Using the Hyper Editor

The Hyper Editor is ideal for editing situations in which you want to see your controller data in a grid or in vertical bars. You can also view many different MIDI messages in one hyper set and get an overall view of how your various MIDI messages are interacting with each other (such as how volume and pan messages are interacting).

You can use the Pencil tool to place MIDI events directly on the grid where you want them. If you want to create many messages at once, simply hold the mouse button down and move across the grid. As you move the mouse up or down, you draw in higher or lower values for your data. The bar for each note is solidly colored to represent how high the value of the event is. A totally solid event means the event has a value of 127, the highest MIDI value. If the solid portion of the bar is only a third of the way up the bar, the value may be only 42. After creating your data with the Pencil, you can use the Line tool to make smooth, linear value adjustments across an entire lane.

If you are used to viewing messages as continuous data, viewing them in the shape of static bars instead might seem tricky at first, but what you might think is continuous is actually nothing but a series of individual messages, each assigning a given controller a value at a particular position. After using the Hyper Editor to edit those individual messages and values, you might just fall in love with having that level of control over your data!

Editing MIDI Notes (Drums) Using the Hyper Editor

A MIDI note is actually just a type of MIDI control message that tells a sound module to play a sound at a given pitch. This means that the Hyper Editor can be configured to edit MIDI note messages just as easily as any other MIDI control message. Because the Hyper Editor allows you to place notes directly on a grid, using the Hyper Editor as a drum editor is a natural fit. If you enjoy programming drums in the computer, rather than via a performance on a MIDI keyboard, drum controller, or MIDI percussion set, the Hyper Editor offers you the ability to draw notes on a grid quickly, exactly where you want them. Thanks to hyper sets, you can even name each lane with the name of the drum instrument the lane triggers. See the subsection "Setting Up the Hyper Editor as a Drum Editor" a bit later in this chapter for specific details on using the Hyper Editor with drums.

The procedure for using the Hyper Editor to program drums is exactly the same as described previously for MIDI control messages: You draw in the event you want, in the lane you want, at the velocity you want. You'll see a bar line representing your drum hit and the velocity you selected. You can hold the Pencil down and roll over many positions to create multiple notes, and you can use the Line tool to create fade-ins, fade-outs, steady velocity at a particular value, and so on. If you like programming drum parts directly into Logic, you'll find the Hyper Editor especially suited to your needs.

Expert Tip: Hyper Editor Isn't Limited to Drum Programming Clearly, the Hyper Editor assumes if you want to program notes in its grid, they will be for drum parts—as its inclusion of a GM Drum hyper set and commands to create them illustrates. That doesn't mean you *must* use the Hyper Editor for drum tracks. However, if you are programming heavily quantized MIDI parts and looking for that old-school "analog" Step Sequencer style of grid in which to place your arpeggiated synth pulses and techno hits, you just might find that the Hyper Editor suits your needs as well.

Simply create a GM Drum hyper set, which will give you a hyper set with all notes, then erase the drum name in the Parameter box and give each event its standard note name.

You'll end up with a hyper set of notes without drum names. Rename the hyper set, and you now have a MIDI Step Sequencer hyper set, ready for you to program synths right to the grid!

Setting Up the Hyper Editor as a Drum Editor

If you happen to be using an external General MIDI drum module (or a synthesizer with GM drum sounds), then the Hyper Editor is already set up for you—just select the GM Drums hyper set, and you're done! Everything is already configured for you. But it's far more likely that you are using a software instrument or a more advanced drum module. In this case, you should start with the GM Drum Kit set, but you'll want to customize it to your specific instrument.

If your software instrument or drum module matches some or all of the GM drum notes, customizing your hyper set will be a breeze. Simply select those event definitions that you don't need and select Hyper > Delete Event Definition (or use the key command, which is Control+Delete by default); see Figure 8.32. You can delete more than one definition at a time by Shift-clicking multiple lanes.

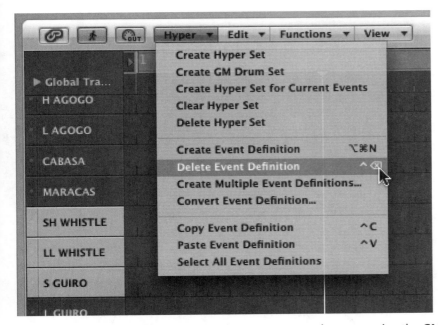

Figure 8.32   Use the Delete Event Definition command to customize the GM Drum Kit to your specific drum instrument.

Very often, your drum instrument may match its main drums with the names in the GM Drum Kit, but not all of them. For example, the kick, snares, and most cymbals may match up between your instrument and the GM Drum Kit hyper set, but your instrument's crash sound may be in the GM Drum Kit lane for RIDE 2. Thankfully, the Hyper Editor lets you easily change the names of event definitions. To do this, in the Inspector simply double-click on the event name and type in the new name. Figure 8.33 shows the name of the High TOM 2 event definition being changed.

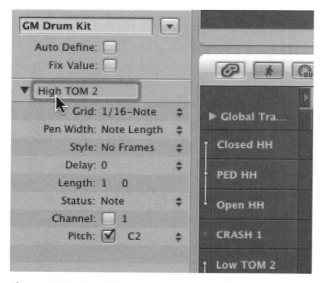

Figure 8.33 Double-click the event definition name in the Inspector to quickly change its name.

If you find that your instrument doesn't match any of the GM Drum Kit names, you can create a brand-new hyper set specifically using the notes of your instrument. To do this, select a MIDI region of notes, open that region in the Hyper Editor, and select Create Hyper Set for Current Events from the Hyper menu. As Figure 8.34 shows, this will leave you with a new hyper set containing one lane for each MIDI note in your MIDI region. The event definitions will be named for their MIDI note by default. The hyper set will have the same name as your MIDI region. You can rename both the hyper set and event definition names in the Inspector.

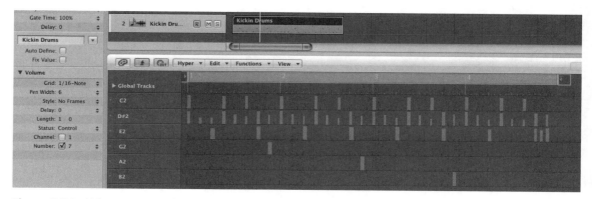

Figure 8.34 When you use the Create Hyper Set for Current Events command, a new hyper set named after your MIDI region is created with one lane for each MIDI note.

Expert Tip: A Lane for Every Drum   Suppose you're creating your own hyper set from the Create Hyper Set for Current Events command, and you want to ensure that you have a lane for every single drum hit. In this case, create a MIDI region that contains one note for each drum hit. You can even play each drum hit in the order from first to last that you want the lanes to appear in your new hyper set. Then select that MIDI region, open it in the Hyper Editor, and when you select Create Hyper Set for Current Events, it will have a lane for every single hit, with the first note appearing in the top lane and the last note appearing in the bottom lane.

Expert Tip: Using the Hyper Editor Even When Your Instrument Has Its Own Sequencer   Even if you are using a software instrument such as Ultrabeat that already has a built-in Step Sequencer, you might want to use the Hyper Editor. Most software instruments with Step Sequencers only allow a single-step division setting to be used at once; in other words, you can't have a quarter-note grid for your kick drum, a sixteenth-note grid for your snare, a thirty-second-note grid for your hi-hats, and so on. The Hyper Editor gives you that level of flexibility. Give it a try!

The Score Editor

As cutting edge as Logic is, musicians who like working with notation are not left out in the cold. One of the most powerful editors in Logic is the Score Editor, which offers traditional music notation recording, editing, and score printing. Even if you don't feel at home using computers to manipulate MIDI performances, you will find the Score Editor to be the "digital music notation paper" you always wanted, where you can perform, move, erase, redraw, and print out sheet music with the ease that only a computer can bring. Figure 8.35 shows the Score Editor.

If you do not read and write music notation, you might find this editor superfluous to your working method. However, if you do use—and sometimes even think in—music notation, you'll find the Score Editor to be one of Logic's most important features, with advantages over other sequencers that do not offer the power and flexibility of Logic's notation facilities.

The Scope of this Section   This section is not intended to teach music theory or the reading and writing of music notation. Instead, the purpose is to introduce those already familiar with these concepts to the way that Logic allows users to write and edit music in notation form—and I do mean *introduce*. The Score Editor is perhaps the deepest editor in Logic, because music notation itself is truly an advanced symbolic language, with all the inherent complexity and flexibility that implies. If this chapter inspires you to explore music notation on your own, *great!* Music theory will always help your music productions, regardless of genre.

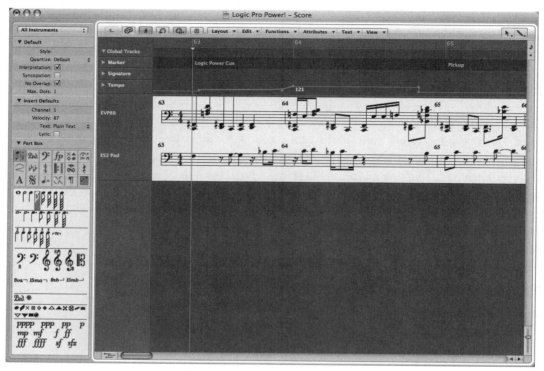

Figure 8.35   The Score Editor.

Score Editor Local Menus

Because of the comprehensive nature of music notation, the Score Editor has a lot of commands relating to how to format, lay out, and enter musical information. To accommodate this, the Score Editor has more local menus than the other MIDI editors. A couple of the local menus are shared with the other MIDI editors, but most are unique to the Score Editor. The subsections that follow describe the various options available in the local menus.

Layout Menu

The Layout local menu contains options for how to format your score. Figure 8.36 shows the Layout menu.

The various options are as follows:

■   **Staff Styles.** This command opens the Staff Styles window, which allows you to access Logic's predesigned staff styles as well as create your own. The Staff Styles window is described in

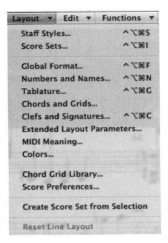

Figure 8.36 The Layout menu of the Score Editor.

the subsection "Staff Styles" later in this chapter. The key command for this is Control+ Option+Command+S.

- **Score Sets.** This command brings up a window that allows you to select which MIDI instruments from the Arrange tracks you want to appear in your score. The key command for this is Control+Option+Command+I.

- **Global Format.** This command opens the Score Project Settings window to the Global Format tab, which allows you to configure the page setup for printing, the spacing of your score, the chord symbols, and so on. You can also access this Preference pane by choosing File > Project Settings > Score. Figure 8.37 shows this window. The key command for this is Control+Option+Command+F.

- **Numbers and Names.** This command opens the Score Project Settings window to the Numbers & Names tab, in which you can configure page numbers, bar numbers, and instrument names for printing and so on. You can also access this Preference pane by choosing File > Project Settings > Score. Figure 8.38 shows this window. The key command for this is Control+Option+Command+N.

- **Tablature.** This command opens the Score Project Settings window to the Tablature tab, which allows you to configure how Logic will format guitar tablature and similar features. You can also access this Preference pane by choosing File > Project Settings > Score. Figure 8.39 shows this window. The key command for this is Control+Option+Command+G.

- **Chords and Grids.** This command opens the Score Project Settings window to the Chords & Grids tab, which allows you to configure the way Logic displays chord symbols and to define settings for the way tablatures are displayed. You can also access this Preference pane by choosing File > Project Settings > Score. Figure 8.40 shows this window.

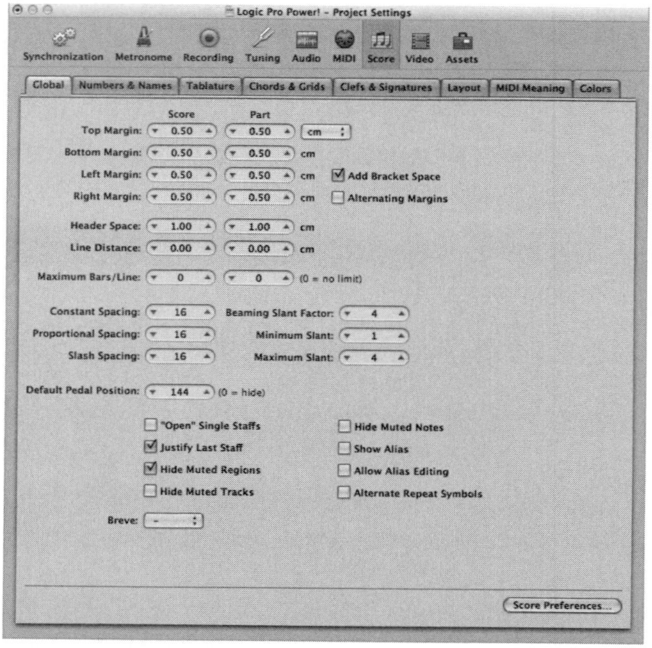

Figure 8.37   The Score Project Settings window open to the Global Format tab.

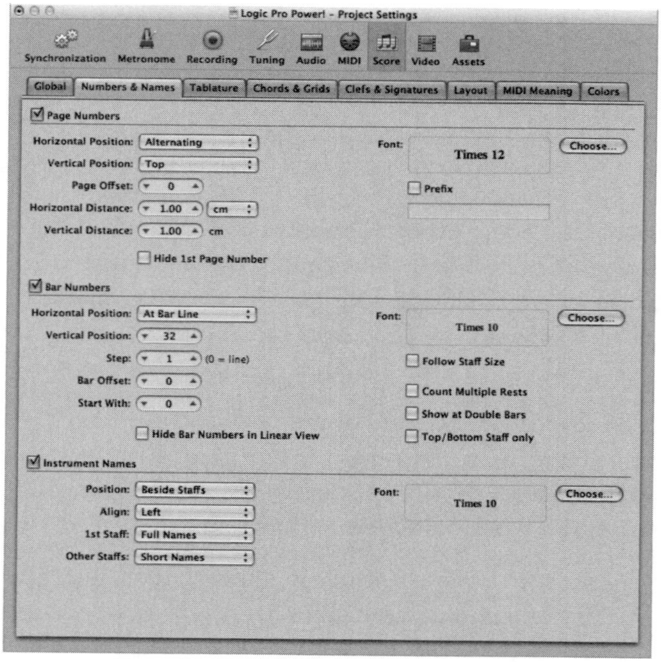

Figure 8.38   The Score Project Settings window open to the Numbers & Names tab.

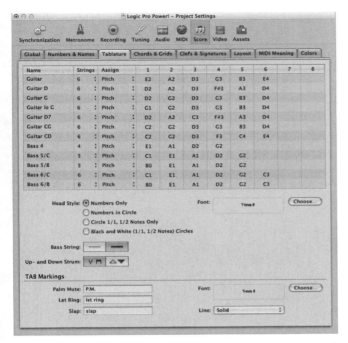

Figure 8.39 The Score Project Settings window open to the Tablature tab.

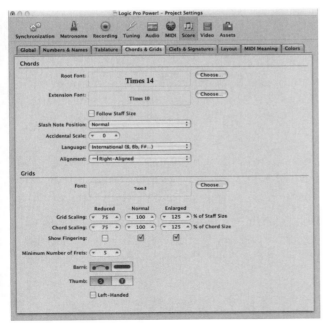

Figure 8.40 The Score Project Settings window open to the Chords & Grids tab.

■ **Clefs and Signatures.** This command opens the Score Project Settings window to the Clefs & Signatures tab. This window offers parameters for how Logic displays clefs, key signatures, time signatures, and octave symbols. You can also access this dialog box by choosing File > Project Settings > Score. Figure 8.41 shows this window. The key command for this is Control+Option+Command+C.

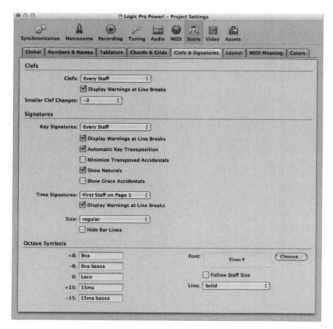

Figure 8.41   The Score Project Settings window open to the Clefs & Signatures tab.

■ **Extended Layout Parameters.** This command opens the Score Project Settings window to the Layout tab. This window offers extra parameters for more esoteric and aesthetic display options. You can also access this dialog box by choosing File > Project Settings > Score. Figure 8.42 shows this window.

■ **MIDI Meaning.** This command opens the Score Project Settings window to the MIDI Meaning tab. This window lets you assign MIDI values to score symbols. You can also access this dialog box by choosing File > Project Settings > Score. Figure 8.43 shows this window.

■ **Colors.** This command opens the Score Project Settings window to the Colors tab. This window lets you assign colors to pitch and velocity, as well as construct your own user palettes. You can also access this dialog box by choosing File > Project Settings > Score. Figure 8.44 shows this window.

■ **Chord Grid Library.** Selecting Chord Grid Library opens the Chord Grid Library, a repository of thousands of guitar tablatures. The Chord Grid Library will be covered in detail in "The Chord Grid Library" section later in this chapter.

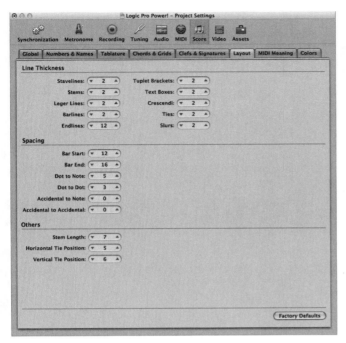

Figure 8.42   The Score Project Settings window open to the Layout tab.

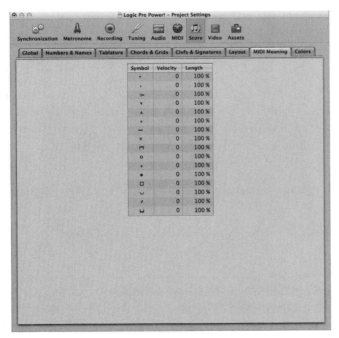

Figure 8.43   The Score Project Settings window open to the MIDI Meaning tab.

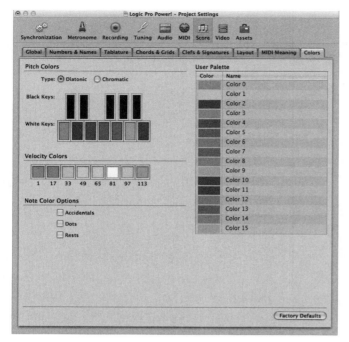

Figure 8.44   The Score Project Settings window open to the Colors tab.

- **Score Preferences.** This command launches the global Score Preferences dialog box. You can also open this dialog box by choosing Logic Pro > Preferences > Score or by clicking on the Preferences menu in the Toolbar and selecting Score. Figure 8.45 shows the Score Preferences dialog box.

  The Score Preferences dialog box includes Preferences for how you want the Score Editor to operate. The specific settings that you want will depend completely on how you use the Score Editor—for example, do you use it more for editing or just for printing? Many Score Preferences options are self-evident if you are familiar with music notation.

- **Create Score Set from Selection.** This creates a new score set from all the instruments assigned to the MIDI regions you have selected.

- **Reset Line Layout.** You can reset the layout of the notation lines with this command.

Printing a Score that Includes Both a Transposed and a Non-Transposed Instrument   Noted film and television composer Jay Asher, author of *Going Pro with Logic Pro 9* (Course Technology PTR, 2010), is a longtime Logic user who, as he puts it "lives in the Score

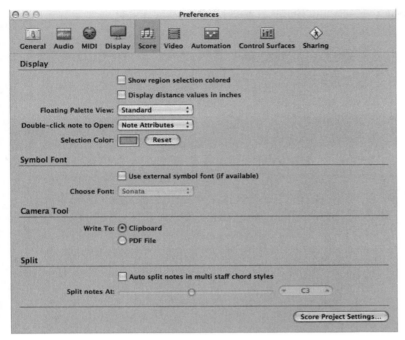

Figure 8.45   The Score Preferences dialog allows you to define how the Score Editor will behave in all of your projects.

Editor." Asher shares with us a very helpful tip he learned for printing scores that begin on a non-transposing instrument and switch to a transposing instrument:

"Let us say you need to print out a part that begins on a non-transposing (C) instrument—for example, the oboe—and then switches to a transposing instrument—for example, the English horn, which transposes up a 5th (+7). You could highlight all the notes in one of the editors and manually transpose them, but the result would be that the notes would sound different when played back. Here's how you can do it without changing the sound:

1. Make sure that your Score Editor is showing the default instrument set All Instruments.

2. If your oboe and English horn parts are already different MIDI regions on the same Arrange track, you can skip to Step 4.

3. Cut the MIDI region into two MIDI regions and put them on the same Arrange track.

4. Make sure that both have the proper transposition—in our example, none for the oboe sequence, and +7 for the English horn.

5.   Open the Score Editor. Make sure that you are in Full Score mode in Page Edit view and select both MIDI regions by holding the Shift key while selecting.

6.   In the Layout local menu, choose Create Score Set from Selection. This will create a new score set (which you can rename if you would like).

7.   Then double-click anywhere in the white area around the MIDI regions.

8.   Switch to Print view.

The result is [a single] score part with both MIDI regions properly transposed for a [professional musician] to read, and your MIDI parts will sound [as they did originally]. Remember, of course, to insert text to [inform] the player…when he is playing one instrument (oboe, in our example) and when he switches (to English horn, in our example)."

The Edit Menu

As Figure 8.46 illustrates, the Edit menu in the Score Editor is fundamentally the same as in the other MIDI editors.

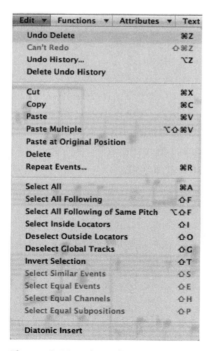

Figure 8.46   The Edit menu in the Score Editor is similar to the Edit menu in all the other MIDI editors in Logic.

Although you can refer to the subsection covering the Piano Roll Editor's Edit menu to learn about the various functions of the Edit menu, there is one in particular that is unique to the Score Editor that we need to cover.

At the bottom of the Score Edit menu is the Diatonic Insert command. When you are using the Pencil tool, engaging Diatonic Insert limits you to inserting only notes that are diatonically correct for the current key. You can alter the notes chromatically once they have been inserted, however. Also, this function does not work for MIDI input notes, only drawn notes.

The Functions Menu

The options of the Functions menu, shown in Figure 8.47, are also similar to the other MIDI editors with a few notable exceptions.

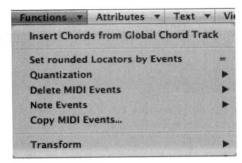

Figure 8.47   The Functions menu in the Score Editor.

- **Insert Chords from Global Chord Track.** This command adds the chord names from the Chord track to your score at the correct location.

- **Set Rounded Locators by Events.** This command rounds the locators to the bar lines nearest the selected events.

- **Quantization.** Figure 8.48 shows the Quantization submenu.

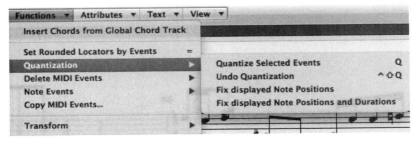

Figure 8.48   The Quantization submenu of the Functions menu in the Score Editor.

The Quantization submenu gives you options to control the quantization of events in the Score Editor.

- **Quantize Selected Events.** This command applies the current Quantization setting to the selected events. The key command for this is Q.

- **Undo Quantization.** This removes any quantization that may have been applied and returns the selected notes to their original location. The key command for this is Control+Shift+Q.

- **Fix Displayed Note Positions.** This command fixes the display quantization of the notes in your project, allowing you to export it to another notation program, maintaining the display quantization settings.

- **Fix Displayed Note Positions and Durations.** This command fixes the display quantization of the notes and their duration.

Refer to the subsection "The Functions Menu" in the section "The Piano Roll Editor" for descriptions of the other commands in the Functions menu.

The Attributes Menu

The Attributes menu is filled with note and score symbol display parameters that you can set individually per note, regardless of your settings in other menus. For example, you can change the direction of the stem of a note, shift a sharp note to its enharmonic flat note, or change the display color of a note with commands from this menu. Figure 8.49 shows the Attributes menu.

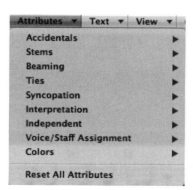

Figure 8.49   The Attributes menu of the Score Editor. This local menu contains different options to change the attributes of a selected note or symbol.

The Attributes menu contains nine hierarchal menus with more than 40 options for altering the attributes of the selected note or notes. To apply any of these options, select one or more notes and/or symbols in the editor display, then choose the desired option from this menu.

It's beyond the scope of this book to cover all the possible note and symbol attribute alterations in this menu. If you write music notation and need to alter note attributes, you should find it easy to locate the desired attributes in this menu.

The Text Menu

The Text menu should look familiar to anyone used to word processing and desktop publishing applications. Figure 8.50 shows the Text menu.

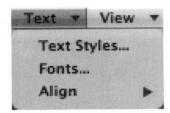

Figure 8.50   The Text menu of the Score Editor offers you the use of your currently installed fonts and basic style options for score text.

The Text menu offers a standard selection of text formatting menus from which to choose any of your installed fonts, size, style, left/right alignment, and so on, allowing you to select which one of your installed fonts you would like to use for lyrics, notes on your score, and more.

The View Menu

The View menu contains options for configuring your view of the Score Editor. Figure 8.51 shows the View menu.

The various options available in the View menu are as follows:

- **Colors.** This View menu option allows you to colorize notes by pitch, velocity, or voice assignment. You can also force a note to be black and white instead of colorized. The different choices are available in the hierarchal menu that opens when you select this menu option.

- **Page View.** This switches to Page view, where you can edit your printable score page. The key command for this is Control+P.

- **Page Display Options.** This submenu offers more page layout display options when Page view is selected, such as Print view, which allows you to see your score as it will print.

- **Go to Page.** When you are in Page view, selecting this option opens the Go to Page dialog, where you can directly enter a page number and click OK or press Return, and the selected page will be displayed. The key command for this is Control+/.

- **Duration Bars.** Duration bars are similar to the bars for notes in the Piano Roll Editor—they provide a visual, editable representation of the length of each note. The Duration Bars submenu, shown in Figure 8.52, gives you a few options for the display of duration bars.

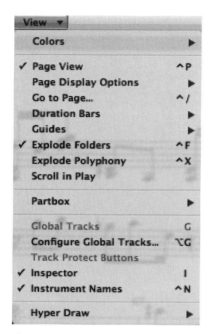

Figure 8.51   The View menu of the Score Editor.

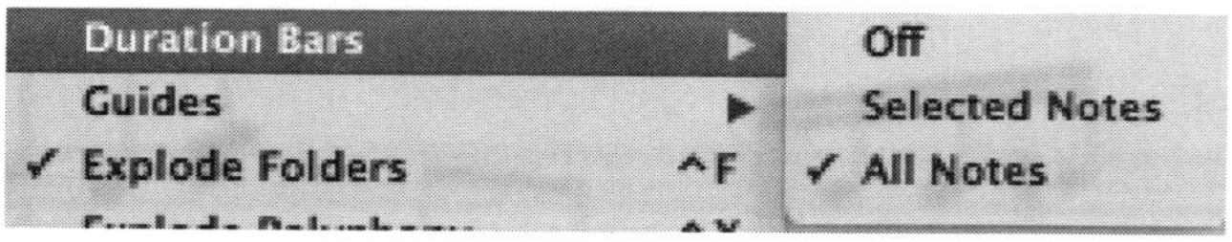

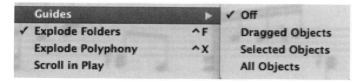

Figure 8.52   The Duration Bars submenu gives you options for the display of duration bars.

You can chose to switch the display of duration bars off, only for notes you have selected, or for all notes.

■   **Guides.** The Guides submenu gives you a variety of options for displaying vertical dotted-line guides, which can help you align objects in the score as you work on its layout. Figure 8.53 shows the Guides submenu.

Figure 8.53   The Guides submenu gives you options for the display of guide lines to aid in tweaking a score's layout.

You can turn guides off or display them for dragged objects, selected objects, or all objects. If you want to clean up your score to look as professional as possible, guides are an invaluable aid.

- **Explode Folders.** This separates folder tracks into their component tracks. The key command for this is Control+F.

- **Explode Polyphony.** This command separates into separate staves the various separate voices playing together. The key command for this is Control+X.

- **Scroll in Play.** If this is engaged, instead of the playhead scrolling through the Score Editor, the score scrolls past the stationary playhead.

- **Partbox.** In this hierarchal submenu are two options: one is Show All Groups in the Part Box (the box of notes, staffs, and other symbols on the left of the Score Editor), and the other option is Lock Group Positions. The Part box is described in its own subsection, "The Part Box," later in this chapter.

- **Global Tracks.** You can toggle the global tracks on or off with this check box when Page view is off. The key command for this is G.

- **Configure Global Tracks.** This command opens a drop-down menu that lets you toggle on or off individual global tracks you wish to view. The key command for this is Option+G.

- **Track Protect Buttons.** If this is checked, Track Protect buttons will appear on the global tracks.

- **Inspector.** Engaging this option displays the Score window's Inspector to the left of the Edit window. You should keep this option engaged until you are so familiar with the Score Editor that you can use it completely via key commands. The key command for the Inspector is I.

- **Instrument Names.** This determines whether the name of the instrument to which your MIDI region is assigned is displayed. The key command for this is Control+N.

- **Hyper Draw.** Just like the Piano Roll Editor View menu option, this command creates a track lane beneath the Score Editor where you can view, edit, and create Hyper Draw or MIDI control message information. Figure 8.54 shows a Score Editor displaying the Hyper Edit lane.

The Score Editor Tool Menu

Because the Score Editor is geared toward both graphic editing and printing, its Tool menu is the largest of all the MIDI editors, housing 17 tools. Figure 8.55 shows the Score Editor Tool menu.

Many of these tools are familiar, but a few are unique to the Score Editor. Following are descriptions of these tools from top to bottom.

- **Pointer Tool.** The standard Pointer tool is for selecting and making "rubber band" selections of multiple notes.

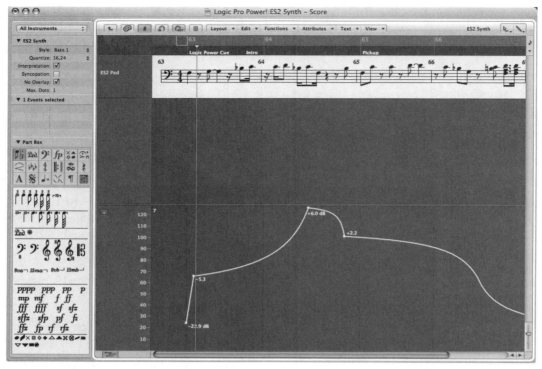

Figure 8.54 The Hyper Draw View option selected in the Score Editor, displaying volume automation.

- **Pencil Tool.** The Pencil tool allows you to insert new notes into the Score Editor.

- **Eraser Tool.** This tool removes notes from the Score Editor.

- **Text Tool.** With this tool, you can enter text into your score.

- **Layout Tool.** Use this tool to move objects around in your score without actually affecting the timing of the parent MIDI event.

- **Zoom Tool.** If you want to zoom in on a particular group of notes, use the Zoom tool to "rubber band" them. You then zoom in to the maximum zoom level. Click anywhere there are no notes to return to the original zoom level.

- **Voice Separation Tool.** This tool allows you to separate polyphonic voices into different staves by drawing a dividing line. For this tool to be effective, you must be using a polyphonic staff style.

- **Solo Tool.** This tool solos or unsolos notes in the Score Editor.

- **Mute Tool.** The Mute tool mutes or unmutes notes in the Score Editor.

- **Resize Tool.** This tool can adjust the size of objects in the Score Editor.

Figure 8.55   The Score Editor Tool menu.

- **Quantize Tool.** The Quantize tool allows you to quantize only selected notes, leaving the rest of the region unquantized. This is very useful if you have a great performance with only one portion in which the timing is slightly off. You can use this tool to quantize just those few notes to improve the readability of the score and leave the rest of the performance alone.

- **Velocity Tool.** With the Velocity tool, you can raise or lower the velocity of one or more notes graphically, by selecting the note and then scrolling up or down with the mouse to increase or decrease the velocity of the selected note. When you adjust the velocity of all selected notes at once by clicking on a single note and moving the mouse, every note retains its value relative to the other notes (so, if you raise the velocity of a loud note and a soft note, both become louder, but the soft note becomes the same amount softer). You can hold down Option+Shift to adjust all selected notes to the same velocity.

- **Camera Tool.** Use the Camera tool to select sections of your score and export them into graphics files.

- **Scissors Tool.** The Scissors tool can be used to cut a score piece into multiple regions, and in the Signature track for cutting bars into smaller divisions, creating time signature changes in the process.

- **Glue Tool.** This tool works in the Signature track to merge measures, affecting the time signature of those measures in the process.

- **Automation Select Tool.** The Automation Select tool resembles a bent arrow pointing upward and left, with a solid arrowhead. The Automation Select tool can select automation data in the Score Editor Hyper Draw automation lane. Chapter 10 discusses automation and the Automation Select tool in depth.

- **Automation Curve Tool.** The Automation Curve tool resembles a bent arrow pointing upward and left, with an open arrowhead. The Automation Curve tool can create curves between two automation Nodes in the Score Editor Hyper Draw automation lane. Chapter 10 discusses automation and the Automation Curve tool in depth.

The Score Editor Buttons

The Score Editor offers six buttons, five of which are common to the other windows in Logic. Figure 8.56 shows the Score Editor buttons.

Figure 8.56   The Score Editor buttons.

Following are descriptions of the buttons, moving from left to right:

- **Hierarchy button.** This button takes you from a view of the selected region(s) to a master Score view of all the project's regions.

- **Link button.** Engaging the Link button ensures that the editor always displays the same content as the topmost window. Double-clicking or Option-clicking the Link button while the Catch button is also engaged activates Contents Catch mode, in which the Score Editor always shows the contents of the currently playing MIDI region as the song plays.

- **Catch button.** With this button engaged, the Edit window in the Score Editor will always follow the playhead position. You will almost always want this on.

- **MIDI IN button.** The MIDI IN button engages Step Input mode, described earlier in the section "The Piano Roll Editor."

- **MIDI OUT button.** With this engaged, you hear the currently selected MIDI note or event change (if you are working with pitch bend data, for example) while you are working.

- **Page View button.** This button toggles between the Edit view—the normal Score Editing mode seen in Figure 8.35—and Page Layout view, a full-page overview of how your score will print out. Page Layout view was not really designed for real-time input or editing operations, but for final finishing touches before printing.

The Score Editor Inspector

As you can see in Figure 8.35, the Score Editor's Inspector is loaded with boxes. Two of them are Parameter boxes for the region being edited in the Score Editor. The following subsections describe these Parameter boxes.

The Display Parameter Box

The Display Parameter box, located directly underneath the Score Set selection box, contains parameters that configure the rhythmic display of the selected MIDI region. Figure 8.57 shows the Display Parameter box.

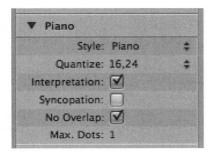

Figure 8.57   The Display Parameter box.

Descriptions of the parameters follow:

- **Style.** This parameter indicates the staff style used for the score display of the selected MIDI region. Clicking to the right of the parameter name opens a pull-down menu of all available staff styles from which you can choose.

- **Quantize.** The Display Quantize parameter determines the shortest note value that the currently selected region can display. The value can be either a single number, called a *binary quantization*, or two numbers (a binary and a ternary value), called a *hybrid quantization*. As with the Style parameter, you choose your desired value from the pull-down menu that appears when you click to the right of the parameter name.

- **Interpretation.** With Interpretation on, the Score Editor displays notes with length values that fall on the beat, to make the score easier to read. The display is far less precise than when Interpretation is off and the Score Editor shows notes at their true length. At the same time, when Interpretation is off, your Score can be *too* accurate, showing every possible miniscule division of the beat that was played. You can also turn this feature on or off on a per-note basis by choosing the appropriate option in the Attributes menu or via a key command. Generally, you probably want to leave Interpretation on.

- **Syncopation.** If Syncopation is turned on, instead of displaying syncopated notes as several tied notes, the Score Editor displays syncopated notes as a single note. As with the Interpretation option, you can turn this feature on or off per note by choosing the appropriate option in the local Attributes menu or via the key command.

- **No Overlap.** This prevents the overlapping of notes in the display. Except when you want to display visually repeated and overlapping notes, you will want to keep this option on.

- **Max. Dots.** The Max. Dots option determines how many dots Logic allows a single note to display. You can change unwanted dotted notes by inserting user rests.

Event Parameter Box

Each event in the Score Editor gets its own parameter set. The Event Parameter box displays those parameters for each individual event (note, rest, time signature, and so on) in your score. Figure 8.58 shows the Event Parameter box.

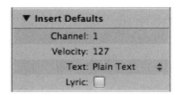

Figure 8.58   The Event Parameter box.

Depending on whether you have selected a note or a non-note event, the Event Parameter box displays different options. Following are all the possible parameters that can appear in this box:

- **Channel.** The selected event is on the MIDI channel set in this parameter. In general, your entire MIDI region should send all of its notes on the same channel, but you might want to send a few notes to other devices. An exception is if you are working on a drum score, and you are sending different drum instruments on different MIDI channels.

- **Pitch.** This sets the pitch of the selected note. This parameter appears only when notes are selected.

- **Velocity.** This parameter is for setting the MIDI velocity (volume of the event). If the event is a rest, even though the parameter contains a value, it is still sending silence.

- **Length.** This parameter sets the length of the note. This parameter appears only when notes are selected.

- **Text.** Use this parameter to select a text style from the pop-up menu of text styles that appears when you click on this parameter. You'll learn about text styles in the "Text Styles" section later in this chapter. This parameter does not appear for note events.

- **Lyric.** You should check this box if you are writing lyrics above this event or leave it set to off if you are not. This parameter does not appear for note events.

The Part Box

The Inspector view of the Score Editor contains a unique notation toolset underneath the Event Parameter box called the Part box—so named because it contains various parts you might like to use in a score. Figure 8.59 shows a Score Editor Part box.

Figure 8.59 The Score Editor Part box.

The Part box is so expansive that the entire box fits into the Score Editor only at the highest resolutions of very large displays. Figure 8.59 only shows a portion of the Part box. This isn't a problem, however, because the top portion of the Part box consists of 18 Group buttons. As you press different buttons, different sections of the Part box move to the top of the box under the Group buttons, so the specific section of the Part box you need is never more than one click away.

Inserting parts from the Part box couldn't be easier: Simply select the Group you need, click on a part you want to add to your score, and then drag it to the location in your score where you want to place the part, or use the Pencil tool to insert a part. You can also click and hold one of the Group buttons, and all the parts in that group will appear in a pop-up menu below the Group button. If you want a group to appear as a floating menu, you can double-click the Group button. And of course, you can use key commands to switch between parts in the Part box.

Staff Styles

You can think of staff styles as similar to style sheets in word processor or desktop publishing applications: They each contain a set of formatting and layout preferences for you to apply when needed. You can access staff styles from the Layout local menu or via the key command Control+Option+Shift+S. Figure 8.60 shows the Staff Style window.

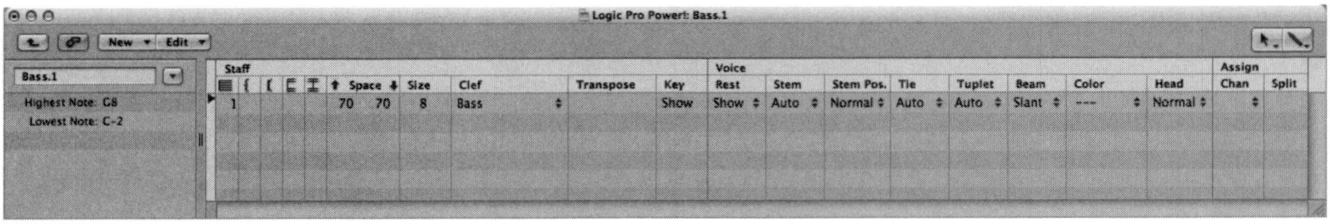

Figure 8.60   The Staff Style window.

The Staff Style window allows you to select one of the default staff styles or to create your own. These staff styles are then accessible through the Display Parameter box in the Score Editor or the Instrument Parameter box in every MIDI instrument.

You can create your own staff styles by selecting Duplicate from the Style selector panel at the left of the window or by choosing one of the varieties of new staff styles from the New local menu. After designing your style by typing new values in and/or using the basic tools (Pointer, Pencil, and Eraser), you can double-click the name of the style you have been creating to type in your own name. That staff style then appears in every pull-down menu of staff styles.

Text Styles

Just as there is a Staff Style window to create format and layout templates for your score, there is also a Text Styles window for creating text formatting templates. Figure 8.61 shows the Text Styles window, accessible in the Text menu.

Clicking on a text style under the Example heading opens a Fonts window, shown in Figure 8.62, which lets you select a font, size, and formatting style. You can also access the Fonts window from the Text local menu in the Score Editor window.

You can edit the selected text style in the Fonts window or create your own by choosing New > New Text Style in the Text Styles window and defining the new style's attributes in the Fonts window. Your new text style will appear at the bottom of the Text Styles window and at the bottom of the Text Style pull-down menu.

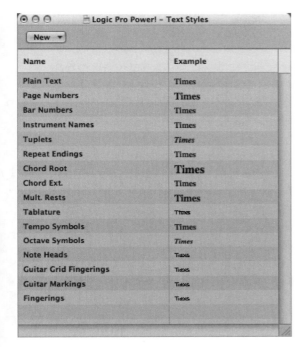

Figure 8.61   The Text Styles window.

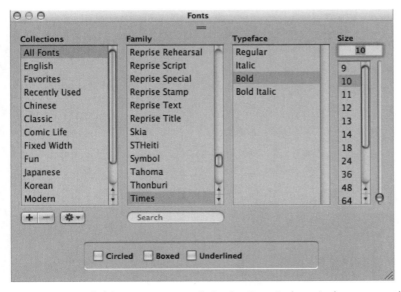

Figure 8.62   Clicking on a text style in the Text Styles window opens the Fonts window.

A Brief Primer on Working in the Score Editor   After reading through all the information on the various menus and tools in the Score Editor, it would be unfair of us to leave you without even the slightest knowledge of how to use any of those tools to create your own scores. Although it is well outside of the scope of this book to go into much more depth on this very powerful editor, we can at least give you a couple of basic building blocks.

The Chord Grid Library

The Chord Grid Library contains thousands of preconfigured chords in tablature. It's an easily searchable database, but it also offers you a great deal of latitude to create and edit chord grids of your own using tunings of your own creation. The Chord Grid Library has three different tabs—the Instrument Editor, the Chord Grid Selector, and the Chord Grid Editor. You can open the Chord Grid Library by selecting Chord Grid Library in the Layout menu. We'll start by looking at the Instrument Editor.

The Instrument Editor

The Instrument Editor lets you create, delete, import, and export different instruments for which you can create chord grids. Although it only has a standard six-string guitar instrument configuration in standard tuning to begin with, you can create an instrument with up to 16 strings tuned almost any way you can imagine. Figure 8.63 shows the Instrument Editor.

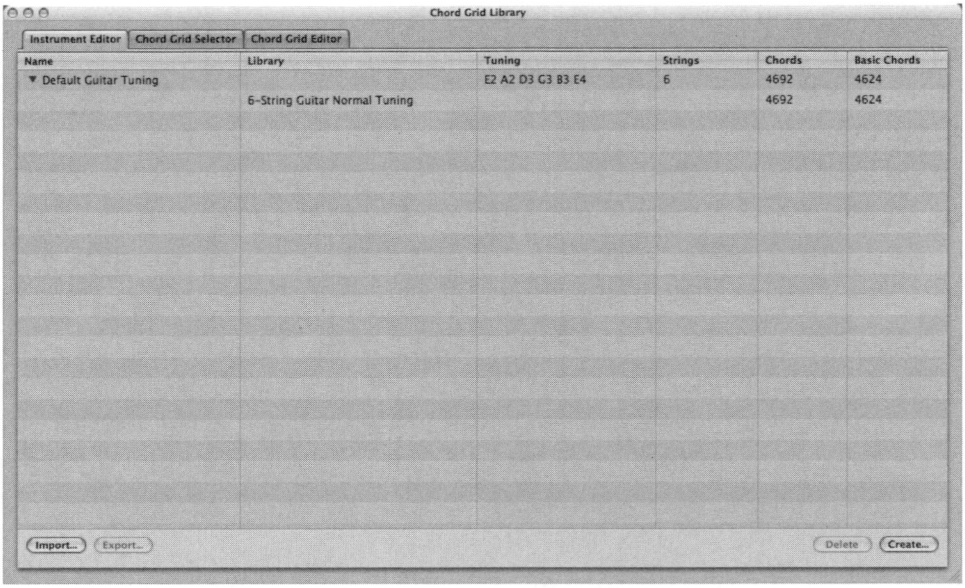

Figure 8.63   The Instrument Editor tab of the Chord Grid Library. You can create new instruments with up to 16 strings in any number of tunings in the Instrument Editor.

To create a new instrument, click the Create button in the lower-right corner of the window. This opens the Create Library dialog, shown in Figure 8.64.

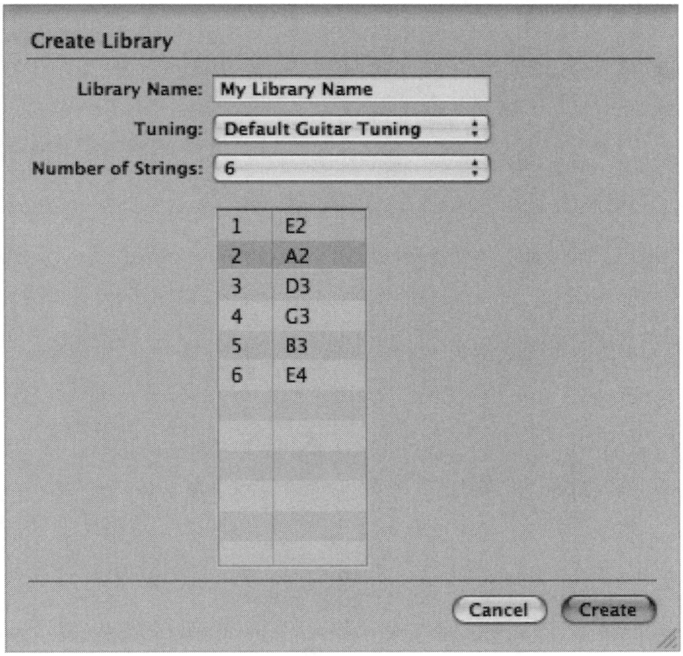

Figure 8.64   The Create Library dialog.

The Create Library dialog offers the following options:

- **Library Name.** To name your library, select the text in the text box and enter your new library name.

- **Tuning.** The Tuning menu allows you to select a tuning to use as a starting point. To begin with, there is only the Default Guitar Tuning option, but as you add your own libraries, they will appear in this list. This menu may become unavailable depending on the settings in the Number of Strings menu.

- **Number of Strings.** Use this menu to define the number of strings for your new instrument, from 1 to 16.

- **Tuning Area.** The Tuning area lets you define the tuning for each string of your new instrument. Simply double-click the pitch name for string you wish to alter and enter the new pitch name manually. Be sure to enter the right octave number for the string, too!

Once you have finished defining the properties of your new instrument, click the Create button, and your new instrument will be added to the Instrument Editor. You can rename an instrument or Library in the Instrument Editor by double-clicking the name you want to edit, entering the new name, and pressing Return.

You can delete an instrument in the Instrument Editor by selecting it and clicking the Delete button in the lower-right corner. Clicking Import or Export opens a typical file browser dialog in which you can search for an instrument file to import or choose a directory into which you will export, respectively.

The Chord Grid Selector

The Chord Grid Selector lets you browse for, view, and even hear any chord in the Chord Grid Library. Figure 8.65 shows the Chord Grid Selector.

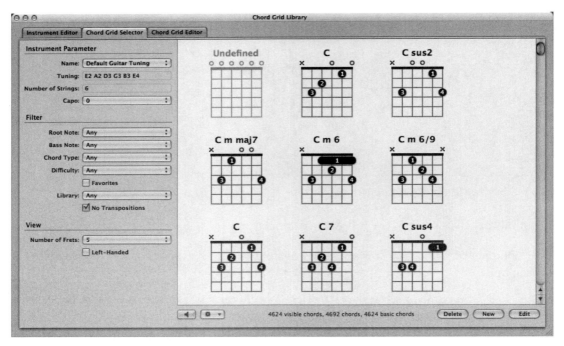

Figure 8.65   The Chord Grid Selector.

The Chord Grid Selector has a bunch of different menus, enabling you to browse for a very general set of chord grids or extremely specific ones quickly and easily. The Chord Grid Selector's options are:

■ **Name.** Select the instrument whose chord grids you wish to view in this menu.

■ **Tuning.** This field displays the tuning for the selected instrument.

■ **Number of Strings.** This field displays the number of strings for the selected instrument.

- **Capo.** If you desire, you can assign a capo setting for the selected instrument in this menu, anywhere from the first fret to the twelfth.

- **Root Note.** The Root Note menu allows you to assign a root note for the chord grids you are looking for, filtering out all chord grids with different root notes. You can also select Any, which displays all chord grids, or Undefined, which displays any undefined chord grids.

- **Bass Note.** The Bass Note menu allows you to assign a bass note for the chord grids you are looking for, filtering out all chord grids with different bass notes. You can also select Any, which displays all chord grids, or Undefined, which displays any undefined chord grids.

- **Chord Type.** The Chord Type menu allows you to assign a chord quality—such as major, minor, or any other of a wide variety of chord types—for the chord grids you are looking for, filtering out all chord grids of different chord types. You can also select Any, which displays all chord grids, or Undefined, which displays any undefined chord grids.

- **Difficulty.** The Difficulty menu allows you to filter the chord grids based on their difficulty— Easy, Medium, or Advanced. You can also select Any, which displays all chord grids, or Undefined, which displays any undefined chord grids.

- **Favorites.** Selecting the Favorites check box allows you to display only those chord grids tagged as favorites.

- **Library.** The Library menu allows you to select whether to display the chord grids from any library for your selected instrument or from a specific library.

- **No Transpositions.** This check box allows you to exclude chord grids that have been transposed.

- **Number of Frets.** This menu lets you define the number of frets shown for each chord grid—4, 5, or 6.

- **Left-Handed.** Selecting Left-Handed reverses the chord grids so they appear as they would on a left-handed guitar.

You can select any chord grid simply by clicking on it. If you want to hear what that particular chord grid looks like, click the Playback button at the bottom of the Chord Grid Selector pane. You can even decide how chord grids will be played when you press the Playback button by using the self-explanatory options in the Action menu immediately to the right of the Playback button. The Playback Action menu is shown in Figure 8.66.

To delete a chord grid, select the chord grid and click the Delete button. You can edit a chord grid by selecting it and clicking the Edit button, and you can create a new chord grid by clicking the New button. Either one of these actions opens the Chord Grid Editor.

Figure 8.66   The Playback Action menu lets you define how chord grids will be played when you click the Playback button.

The Chord Grid Editor

The Chord Grid Editor allows you to create new chord grids, edit existing ones, and save them to the desired library. Figure 8.67 shows the Chord Grid Editor.

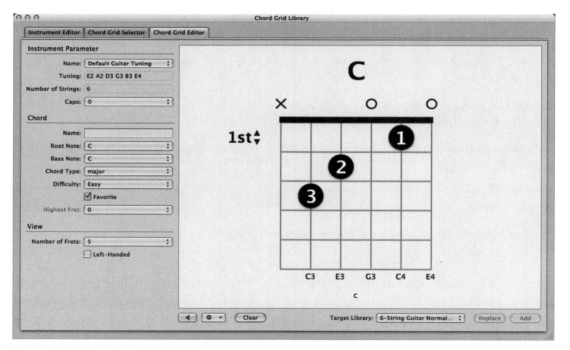

Figure 8.67   The Chord Grid Editor.

As you can see, the parameters to the left of the window are almost identical to those in the Chord Grid Selector, but instead of using them to filter chord grids, you use them to classify the chord grid you are editing.

To add a note to a chord grid, simply click on the desired string and fret with your mouse. A dot will appear. You can move the dot by clicking and dragging it. You can assign the new note a fingering by Control-clicking on the dot and selecting a finger number from the menu that opens. To create a barre, click and hold on one of the desired outer strings and drag the mouse across the chord grid to the desired end of the barre. If you click and drag vertically, a selection box will be drawn, allowing you to select multiple notes to edit. Above the chord grid in Figure 8.67, you'll notice an X (meaning don't play that string) and a couple O's (meaning let the open string ring). You can change from an X to an O by clicking on the X, and vice versa. Finally, you can assign the lowest fret for the chord grid by clicking on the number to the left of the chord grid—1st in Figure 8.67—which opens a menu in which you can select any fret number from 1 to 15.

The Clear button at the bottom of the window lets you clear the entire chord grid. If you have performed any edits, it becomes a Reset button, letting you return the chord grid to its original state. The Target Library menu lets you determine which library the chord grid will be added to when you've finished creating or editing it. The Replace button immediately replaces the original chord grid with your edited chord grid. The Add button immediately adds it to the selected chord grid library.

Inserting and Deleting Events in the Score Editor

Although the Score Editor deals with MIDI information as traditional notation instead of as text or piano roll–like graphics, you can still use some of the same familiar event entry methods that are available in the other MIDI editors.

As with the Piano Roll Editor and the Event List, you can use the process described in the "MIDI Step Input" subsection to input MIDI information into the Score Editor. Before you do, make sure that you have turned Interpretation off in the Display Parameter box and that you have set the Quantize setting to the smallest note value you'll be using. You can set the playhead either by clicking the position you want in the Bar ruler or by holding Option while clicking in the staff. As you hold down the mouse button while Option-clicking, a help tag appears that shows you the current position of the cursor.

To enter notes in the Score Editor with a mouse, make sure you have the Notes button selected in the Part box, as in Figure 8.59. You can then drag a note of the desired value directly onto the staff and place it at the appropriate location. As you drag the note across the staff, a help tag appears, showing you the MIDI channel, pitch, velocity, and position of the note. You can also use the Pencil tool to add events to the Score Editor by selecting the note value you wish to use in the Part box and clicking in the staff at the position and pitch you want the event to be. Be aware that the Quantize setting determines the smallest note value you can enter with the mouse, too.

What if you need to add a tempo marking or a slur to your score? You can also add any of the other notation symbols to your score directly from the Part box. Just drag the symbol to the location where you want it, and it's added to the score just like a note.

If you insert a chord grid from the Part box, a two-tab version of the Chord Grid Library will open, offering the Chord Grid Selector and Chord Grid Editor tabs. You can drag the desired chord grid from the Chord Grid Selector directly to the inserted chord.

Deleting events from the Score Editor is just as easy as it is in the other editors. Simply select the notes you want to delete and either press Delete or click on the note with the Eraser tool.

Moving and Adjusting Events in the Score Editor

You've finished your score and you notice a few things you want to adjust. Perhaps there is a wrong note, or a note isn't lining up where you'd like it. Maybe a note you entered via Step Input isn't long enough. Making these adjustments in the Score Editor is quick and easy.

Changing the Length of Events in the Score Editor

Entering events into the Score Editor via Step Input creates notes that are the same length as the Quantize setting you selected earlier. To alter the length of a note you have entered, you simply select the note and change it to the desired length using the Length setting in the Event Parameter box or via key commands. You can also enable duration bars in the View menu and edit the length of notes using the Resize cursor as you would in the Piano Roll Editor. Figure 8.68 shows some notes in the Score Editor with duration bars enabled. Notice the Resize cursor next to one of the very light gray duration bars.

Figure 8.68   You can edit the length of notes in the score using duration bars.

Changing the Pitch of Events in the Score Editor

Adjusting the pitch of a note in the Score Editor couldn't be easier. Simply select the note(s) you want to change and drag them vertically to the correct pitch. As you hold down the mouse button, a help tag will appear, telling you what pitch the note is currently on and how far you have transposed it. You can also use the Pitch parameter in the Event Parameter box to alter a note's pitch or do so via key commands.

Adjusting the Layout of Events in the Score Editor

Once you have all of your events at the correct time and pitch in the Score Editor, the score itself might have a few places that aren't as easily readable in Page view as you would like. Perhaps a couple of notes are a little too close together, or a bar is smaller than you would like it to be. This is where the Layout tool, seen in the Tool menu in Figure 8.55, comes in handy.

The Layout tool allows you to adjust the position of events in the Score Editor graphically while maintaining their timing. Select the Layout tool from the Tool menu, grab the event(s) you want to adjust, and then drag them horizontally to their correct location. A help tag will open up, telling you how far you have moved the event. The entire bar that the event is in will adjust some as a result of the move. A little bit of experimentation with the Layout tool will make anticipating the effects of these adjustments much more intuitive. Also, don't forget to enable Guides to help you align elements of your score. Figure 8.69 shows an element of a score with Guides enabled.

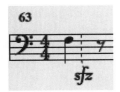

Figure 8.69   Notice the dotted vertical line above the sforzando marking. Enabling Guides makes it easy to line up elements of your score with the note to which you intend them to relate.

For Further Score Editor Information   The Score Editor is the deepest MIDI editor in Logic, and there is far more to delve into than space in this book allows. As you see, just the preceding explanation of the surface functionality of the Score Editor has already taken more figures and pages of this book than any other MIDI editor has! Going into minute detail could easily fill half this book. Instead, let me point you to two resources for further information on the Score Editor. The first, of course, is the Logic Pro manual itself, which includes more than 140 pages on the Score Editor. For a really excellent guide on how to use the Score Editor, we recommend Johannes Prischl's *Logic Notation Guide,* which has more than 200 pages of explanation, tutorials, valuable Logic Environments, and more to help you get the most out of the Score Editor. The book is only available through the author's website: http://prischl.net/LNG/. Prischl wrote this guide for an earlier version of Logic, so you'll clearly notice that the look of the Score Editor is different. However, the fundamental workflow and functionality of the Score Editor hasn't changed much over the years—his examples will look different, but the methodology and procedures are fundamentally the same, and his Environments still work. We cannot recommend his book highly enough for those who want a complete Score Editor reference.

The Transform Window

The Transform window is not exactly a MIDI *editor,* but it offers you the ability to alter (or "transform") large amounts of MIDI data at once. You can consider it a MIDI event batch processor window if you want. If that sounds a bit complicated, that's because its functionality can be incredibly far-reaching. You can use it for processes as straightforward as changing every instance of one note in a selected MIDI region into another note, or you could set up a very complex map, which would filter out only specific notes of a specific velocity and map them to selected new notes. Logic comes with a number of transform sets that are preconfigured for many popular transformations, including a few new ones for Logic 9, and you can create your own transform sets. The Transform window is one of those features in Logic that you won't use constantly, but when you can use it, knowing how to will allow you to automate the transformation of your MIDI data in ways that would take forever manually.

Users often overlook the Transform window. First of all, it's not an editor, so it's not a window absolutely necessary to the basic recording and editing of music, but another reason that users frequently overlook the Transform window is that it initially appears to be very mathematical in nature and not very intuitive. Figure 8.70 shows a Transform window.

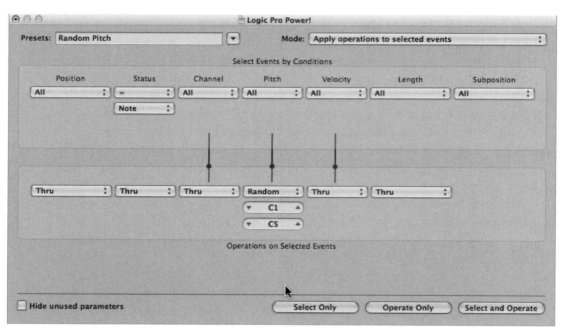

Figure 8.70   You can use the Transform window to make batch transformations of MIDI data.

Unless you already have a mathematical understanding of MIDI data and values, the Transform window doesn't seem very inviting, does it? Despite its initial complexity, however, it is a very powerful tool to have in your arsenal. Our goal for this section is to demystify the Transform window for you!

How the Transform Window Works

The Transform window becomes easier to grasp once you have a general idea of how it works. Remember that at its root, MIDI represents musical ideas mathematically, and the Transform window uses the form and flow of a mathematical formula to operate on your data.

You'll start by setting the Operation mode from the pull-down menu at the upper-right of the window. The mode you choose determines how the transformation will affect the selected events. The different modes are described in the "Setting the Transform Mode" section that follows this one.

Next, you set up the conditions for the transformation. Here you define which events to transform. You set up these conditions in the area labeled Select Events by Conditions. You'll learn how to do this in the section titled "Setting Up Transform Conditions" later in this chapter. Once you have set up your conditions, you define the operation that you want to execute. You can select the various parameters of your operation in the area labeled Operations on Selected Events. You'll learn how to set these parameters later in this chapter, in the section entitled "Setting Up Transform Operations."

Finally, you perform your transformation by clicking on one of the Action buttons at the bottom of the window. The different buttons are described in the "Action Buttons of the Transform Window" section later in this chapter.

Setting the Transform Mode

At the upper-right side of the Transform window is the Mode pull-down menu. Apply Operations to Selected Events is the mode showing in Figure 8.71.

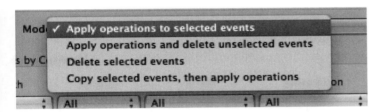

Figure 8.71 In the Mode pull-down menu, you shape how the transformation will affect your selected events.

The modes available from this menu are as follows:

- **Apply Operations to Selected Events.** In this mode, the operation that you set up in the Mode menu is applied to the events you select via the conditions you set. This is the default mode.

- **Apply Operations and Delete Unselected Events.** When the only events you want to remain after the transformation are those events that are operated on, choose this option. It operates on the selected events and deletes any other events in the region.

- **Delete Selected Events.** In this mode, you can use the Transform window as a programmable delete function. You set up which events to select in the Select Events by Conditions box, and when you apply the transformation, those events are deleted.

■ **Copy Selected Events, Then Apply Operations.** If you don't want to modify your original events but you want to add transformed events to your region, you can do so in this mode. This mode copies your selected events and then operates on those events, so you retain the original events and add the transformed copies of those events.

Setting Up Transform Conditions

The Select Events by Conditions box in the Transform window gives you seven parameters with which to define those events you want to select. Figure 8.72 shows you the Select Events by Conditions box.

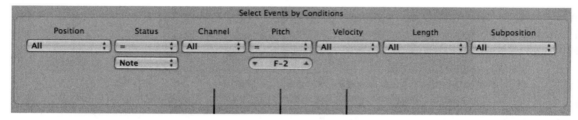

Figure 8.72   The Select Events by Conditions box in the Transform window allows you to focus precisely on the exact events you want to transform.

Notice that all the parameters offer pull-down menus filled with options for that parameter. Sometimes, a given option then gives you another pull-down menu in which you can enter a further value. This allows you to precisely configure the condition you want for the selected events. The various parameters and your options for setting them are as follows:

■ **Position.** This option is for setting the time position in the song of your selection relative to the conditions you set. In other words, should Logic select only those notes that happen at an earlier or equal time to your conditions, or should it also select those that are unequal to the time position you are setting? Or should it select those events that are equal or those events inside a specific time range (map) of values? Figure 8.73 shows the pull-down menu of all your options.

Remember that your MIDI data is mathematical at its base, so it's easy to create mathematical relationships between the conditions you set up and to specify how you want those conditions to determine which notes to select.

■ **Status.** First, the pull-down menu allows you to choose whether you want your conditions to be equal to a specific kind of MIDI event or to apply to all MIDI events. If you choose to limit your conditions to one type of MIDI event, another pull-down menu appears—this one with a black background and blue text—from which you can choose your event type. Figure 8.74 shows the pull-down list of event types.

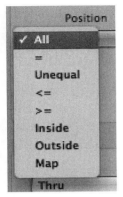

Figure 8.73   The pull-down menu of Position options. Use this menu to determine where to place the selected notes relative to the value determined by your conditions.

Figure 8.74   In this pull-down menu, you can choose the event type to which you want to limit your conditions.

Note events are the most commonly chosen, but you can also choose fader (automation) events, meta events, MIDI program changes, or other common MIDI performance events.

- **Channel.** Here you can specify whether you want the conditions to apply to events on all MIDI channels, only channels equal to or less than the recorded MIDI channel of the event, and more. The pull-down menu has the exact same options as the Position pull-down menu.

- **Pitch.** The white pull-down menu under the title is the same menu as displayed for the Position and Channel parameters; this menu allows you to specify the range of pitches, controller number, and so on of the selected notes or controller numbers relative to the conditions you are setting. Underneath this menu is a text entry box. If the event you selected in the Status menu is a note, then in this box you type in the note you want. If you selected a control message type in the Status menu, you input the controller number here.

- **Velocity.** The white pull-down menu under the title is the same menu as displayed for the Position, Channel, and Pitch parameters; this menu allows you to specify the range of the velocity or controller value relative to the conditions you are setting. Underneath this menu is a text entry box. If the event you selected in the Status menu is a note, then in this box you type in the velocity you want for the note. If you selected a control message type in the Status menu, you input the controller value here.

■ **Length.** Here you can determine what the relative length of the events selected by your conditions should be, whether the events all need to be equal or unequal in length, and more. This option presents the same pull-down menu as displayed for the Position, Channel, Pitch, and Velocity parameters. This field is irrelevant except for with regard to note events.

■ **Subposition.** This parameter determines whether events must have the same subposition inside a bar as other selected notes. Once again, this parameter features the same pull-down menu as the Position, Channel, Pitch, Velocity, and Length parameters.

Setting Up Transform Operations

In the Operations on Selected Events box, shown in Figure 8.75, you can specify any changes that you want executed on those MIDI events that match all the conditions you set in the Select Events by Conditions box.

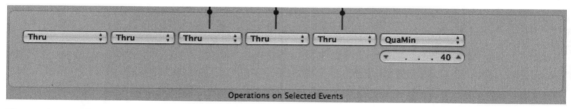

Figure 8.75   The Operations on Selected Events box is where you specify which transformations you want to perform on the events selected by the conditions you set.

Notice the pull-down menus in the Operations box directly beneath each parameter in the Conditions box. Each pull-down menu in the Operations box directly affects the parameter above it. (You can refer back to Figure 8.70 for a view of the whole Transform window.) In other words, if you want your transformation to operate on the pitch of a note, you would use the pull-down menu under the Pitch condition. The default for each of the pull-down menus is Thru, which specifies that no operation is performed. Figure 8.76 shows the Operations pull-down menu and all of the possibilities for transformations it offers. This Operations pull-down menu is the same menu for every column in the Operations box except Status.

Figure 8.76 shows all the ways in which you can operate on your data. As soon as you select an option, a text box appears below for you to type in the value that you want for the operation. A brief explanation of the options follows:

■ **Fix.** The parameter is fixed (changed) to the value you choose.

■ **Add.** This option adds the value you choose to the event.

Figure 8.76   The Operations pull-down menu. Every column but Status uses this same menu.

- **Sub.** This subtracts the value you choose from the event.

- **Min.** If any events that met your conditions have values in this column less than the number you set for this parameter, Logic changes the event values to the number you set here.

- **Max.** If any events that met your conditions have values in this column that exceed the value you set, this value replaces those event values.

- **Flip.** You can flip, or reverse, data around a set point. If the value of the event in this column is above the flip value, Logic reduces the value below the flip point by the same amount it was originally over it. If the value in the selected event is below the flip point, Logic raises it above the flip point by as much as it originally had under it.

- **Mul.** The event is multiplied by the value you choose.

- **Div.** The event is divided by the value you choose.

- **Scale.** In this complex action, two text entry boxes appear underneath the Operations box, one above the other. Logic first multiplies the value of events that match your conditions by the top number and then adds the bottom number to the result.

- **Range.** This limits the range of values to the lower and upper values entered in the text boxes.

- **Random.** This generates random values for the events that match the conditions, within limits that you set.

- **+−Rand.** This adds to the event a random number between zero and a value you set. You can use either a positive or a negative number as a value.

- **Reverse.** This option reverses the value of the event within its parameter range (so a velocity of 13 becomes 115, for example).

- **Quantize.** This quantizes the event to a multiple of the value you chose.

- **QuaMin.** This is a combination of the Qua and Min operations. The operation quantizes the event, but if the quantized value falls below the value you choose, Logic replaces the value with the minimum value you chose.

- **Expon.** This scales the parameter value according to an exponential function. The value you choose shapes the curve of the exponential function. A positive value scales exponentially; a negative value scales logarithmically.

- **Cresc.** If you have selected "inside" as your value for your condition above, this operation creates a smooth alteration between the set boundaries.

- **Rel. Cres.** This has a similar effect as Cresc. does, except it takes the original values of your selected event into account to create a more natural crescendo and preserve the original feel of the MIDI event.

- **Use Map.** When you select this option, the map at the bottom of the Transform window becomes interactive, and you can select, deselect, and map different values as you see fit. Figure 8.77 shows the Universal Map under a Velocity operation.

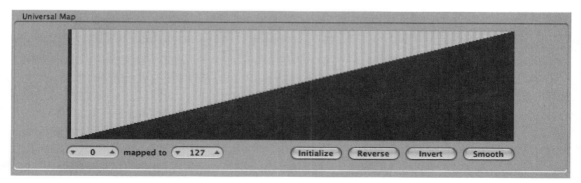

Figure 8.77 The Transform Universal Map can be used to map one parameter value to another, only operate on specific values within the map, and more.

You use this map by typing a value in each text box in the lower-left (such as 81 in the first box and 67 in the second box), by scrolling the numbers in the text boxes, or by clicking in the map itself. The vertical columns represent every permissible value, and the black lines represent the location to which that value is currently mapped.

Action Buttons of the Transform Window

The bottom of the Transform window contains a couple of general controls, the parameter to hide any menus you aren't using in the Conditions and Operations boxes, and the Action buttons. These three Action buttons give you a number of different ways to use the Transform window. Figure 8.78 shows the three Action buttons of the Transform window.

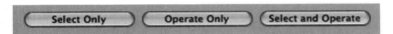

Figure 8.78   The Action buttons of the Transform window.

Once you have your conditions and operations defined, you must click one of these buttons to begin the transformation. These buttons are as follows:

- **Select Only.** This selects all the events that fulfill your conditions, but it will not operate on them. This is useful if you want to use the Transform as a programmable selection tool or if you want to verify that your conditions select the right events.

- **Operate Only.** This button processes any selected events according to the Operations settings, regardless of the Conditions settings. This is useful if you have already manually selected all the events you want to be operated on.

- **Select and Operate.** This button selects events according to your Conditions settings and processes those events according to the Transform mode and your Operations settings.

Transform Sets

As mentioned previously, in the top-left corner of the Transform window is the Transform Sets pull-down menu. These transform sets are already configured for many popular transformations to save you the trouble of having to set up each transformation from scratch. You can simply select the transform set and modify any specific parameters to suit your needs, and you're ready to process your data. Figure 8.79 shows you the pull-down menu of available transform sets.

You may also find that there are specific transformations that you like to do regularly. Logic allows you to save your own transformations as transform sets. Notice the last item on the Transform Sets menu is named **Create Initialized User Set!** If you select this option, a dialog

Figure 8.79   The pull-down menu of available transform sets. At the bottom of the menu is the option to create your own transform set.

opens, asking whether you would like to create a new transform parameter set or rename the current set. If you choose to create a new set, you can now configure your transformation any way you want, and Logic will automatically save your settings in this new transform set. You can rename it by double-clicking the name and changing it to anything you want.

9 Working with Software Instruments

One of the most exciting developments in the world of computer music, without a doubt, is the software synthesizer. Knowing a bit about the development of software synthesis will help you understand the philosophy, uses, and limitations of software instruments, so the next few paragraphs will explain how software instruments came to be and what they are.

From the late 1960s through the 1980s, synthesizers were electronic devices that used physical oscillators and filters to make sound. These devices sounded spectacular (at least to synthesizer enthusiasts!) but were incredibly bulky and expensive. Starting at the end of the 1970s and into the 1980s, the first steps in digital synthesizers were being made—in effect, a dedicated computer chip that had specially written software to control sound production, including the development of "virtual" oscillators and filters. Digital synthesizers took over in the 1980s and 1990s, and even though these synthesizers were housed in rackmount boxes or in keyboards, it was in fact the software that was doing the synthesis.

With the rise of home computers in the 1980s and 1990s, programmers began to experiment with writing programs that used the built-in sound potential of the computer for making music. Although fun and innovative, these initial forays into desktop software synthesis were limited by the primitive sound delivery components, CPU power, and memory. As the 1990s progressed, however, computers became more powerful and more sophisticated. With DSP (*digital signal processing*), programmers began to try to bring their understanding of programming hardware digital synthesizers to bear in the desktop computer world. Some of the stand-alone software synthesizers developed in these days, while rudimentary, were orders of magnitude better than anything previously available. In the late 1990s, Steinberg blew the computer music world off its collective feet when the second version of its audio plug-in format, Virtual Studio Technology (VST), allowed for not only audio processing plug-ins, but also synthesizer plug-ins. These were small pieces of code that could be "plugged in" to the host audio sequencer, accepted MIDI data, and translated that MIDI data into sound—just like any hardware synthesizer, but completely inside the computer, with no cabling required, sample-accurate timing, and total integration into your software mixing environment. The computer music world has never been the same.

As time passes, software synthesizers keep getting better and better, both reaching the quality of hardware synthesizers and in many cases surpassing it in terms of ease of use and integration into computer recording environments. There is a downside to all of this, however; the more processing we ask our computers to do, the sooner they run out of power. For example, imagine that simply playing back, editing, and mixing your 32-track audio and MIDI project requires 30 percent of your available CPU power. Now suppose that you want to add your favorite software synthesizer plug-in, which requires 25 percent of your available CPU by itself. As you can see, your computer could only comfortably handle two such processor-intensive software synthesizers with your project.

Logic is very efficient with CPU resources and offers the Freeze and Bounce in Place functions described in Chapter 6, "The Arrange Window," along with Node functionality discussed in Chapter 11, "Mixing in Logic," to help manage CPU resources even further. This enables you to get even more power out of your computer(s) than ever before, but as you can see, although software synthesizers are a spectacular new development in the computer music world, they require some compromises and, occasionally, careful resource management.

Logic and Software Instruments

Emagic embraced the idea of software synthesizers (softsynths) very early. In fact, Emagic's release of its ES1 synthesizer and EXS24 24-bit software sampler represented two of the very first integrated synthesizers available for any sequencer. Unlike VST plug-ins, Logic's own softsynths are not additional programs that can be integrated into Logic; Logic's software instruments are actual extensions of the main Logic application and are already 100-percent integrated into the application. In addition to offering Logic's own software instruments, Logic can also accept third-party softsynths compatible with Apple's Audio Units format. These plug-ins will be called *components* on your hard drive, because Audio Units are technically a "component" of the audio architecture of the Macintosh OS X operating system.

Although incorporating softsynths is typical in the modern DAW, the software instrument channel strip object (the Environment's extension of the software instrument) sets Logic apart. Not only does it allow for a single Arrange track that allows you to insert a software instrument and enter MIDI data onto the track, producing audio from the software instrument, but it also allows you to apply any of the large array of MIDI tools in the Environment to your softsynths and to insert effects in the channel strip to enhance or affect the softsynth's audio output.

Using Logic Pro Synthesizers   For a complete guide and "master class" tutorial on how to use Logic Pro's many excellent built-in synthesizers, be sure to pick up *Using Logic Pro's Synthesizers* by Kevin Anker (Course Technology PTR, 2010).

Accessing Logic Software Instruments

Logic's own software instruments don't need any special installation—they are part of the Logic code itself. This means there's no procedure necessary to install them; your installation of Logic included all of them.

To instantiate any of Logic's softsynths into a software instrument channel, simply click and hold the mouse on the Instrument slot of the channel strip under the I/O label. A menu appears, allowing you to select the Logic instrument you want from its submenu. Each submenu lists the available channel format options for the instrument, such as mono, stereo, multi-output, and 5.1 (surround). Simply select the Logic instrument in the format you want to use, and it will be loaded into the software instrument channel strip. The channel strip will automatically be configured to the correct format. Figure 9.1 shows Logic's EVD6 being instantiated into a software instrument channel strip in the Arrange window.

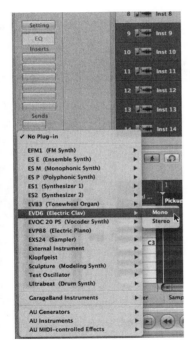

Figure 9.1   This Arrange channel strip for a Software Instrument track shows Logic's EVD6 softsynth being selected from the Instrument hierarchal menus.

The selected software instrument automatically opens its Graphic Editor window when you instantiate it. If you close the editor and want to access it again, double-click on the Instrument slot displaying the name of the software instrument. The softsynth's Graphic Editor launches, giving you full access to all the parameters and functions of the instrument. Figure 9.2 shows the Graphic Editor window of Logic's EVP88 software instrument and its parent channel strip.

Figure 9.2 A software instrument channel strip with Logic's built-in EVP88 softsynth instantiated. If you double-click on the Instrument slot displaying the name of the instrument, you launch the Graphic Editor for that instrument.

Installing and Accessing Non-Logic Software Instruments

You need to install any third-party software instruments into either the local (system-wide) or user (yours specifically) Components folder of your Macintosh. The exact method of installation depends on whether the developer included an installer application that automatically places files where they need to go or whether you need to move the plug-in application to where it belongs manually.

If you have to install the plug-ins manually, the local Components folder resides at /Library/Audio/Plug-ins/Components, and the user Components folder is at ~/Library/Audio/Plug-ins/Components. It shouldn't make a difference which location you choose or whether your components are split among both Components folders. Logic sees all Audio Unit plug-ins in both folders.

If you are running Logic in 32-bit mode, you will need to have 32-bit versions of any third party Audio Units plug-ins you plan to use installed. If you are running Logic in 64-bit mode, you can access either 64-bit AUs natively or 32-bit AUs via the 32-Bit Audio Unit Bridge, which will launch automatically when you instantiate a 32-bit AU in 64-bit mode. The 32-Bit Audio Unit Bridge actually works as a host for your 32-bit AUs.

You instantiate third-party softsynths into software instrument channel strips using the same procedure as with Logic's softsynths, except that you navigate the AU Instruments portion of the hierarchal menu. The AU Instruments menu contains additional hierarchal menus that divide software instruments into groups based on the manufacturer of the instrument. If you are running Logic in 64-bit mode, and you have 32-bit AUs installed, you will also see a hierarchal AU Instruments (32-bit) menu, which will contain all your 32-bit AU instruments. Figure 9.3 shows the FM8 software synthesizer by Native Instruments being selected. In this figure, Logic is in 64-bit mode, and FM8 is accessed through the AU Instruments (32-bit) menu hierarchy.

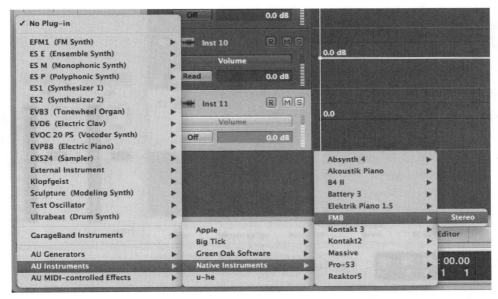

Figure 9.3   A third-party synthesizer—in this case, FM8 by Native Instruments—is being instantiated on this software instrument channel strip.

Just as with the Logic softsynths, double-clicking the Instrument slot displaying the name of the software instrument launches the instrument's Graphic Editor. Because 32-bit third-party plug-ins are not hosted by Logic when in 64-bit mode, but are instead accessed via the 32-Bit Audio Unit Bridge, Logic cannot actually display the 32-bit AU's Graphic Editor. Logic instead launches a window that you can click in to launch the AU's Graphic Editor in the 32-Bit Audio Unit Bridge. Figure 9.4a shows FM8's Graphic Editor launched next to the channel strip in which the instrument is instantiated, with Logic in 32-bit mode. Figure 9.4b shows the FM8 Graphic Editor launched in the 32-Bit Audio Unit Bridge after clicking the Click to Open Plug-In Interface window, also shown, with Logic in 64-bit mode.

Method Tip: Using the External Instrument to Connect MIDI Synthesizers   Considering how many software instruments and effects Logic comes with, it is impossible for this

Figure 9.4a   Just as with Logic's own software instruments, you can double-click the Instrument slot of a software instrument channel strip with a third-party instrument to launch its Graphic Editor.

Figure 9.4b   When you instantiate a 32-bit AU in Logic when Logic is in 64-bit mode, the plug-in's Graphic Editor can only be accessed by clicking in a "dummy" window, which launches the plug-in Graphic Editor in the 32-Bit Audio Unit Bridge.

book to go into them all. However, one of Logic's software instruments is so special that it warrants going over. And it's not even a true software instrument in that it makes no sound itself.

Many times, you might want to send MIDI performances to an external MIDI device, such as a MIDI sound module or MIDI synthesizer, and then send the stereo audio from your MIDI hardware back into the Logic Mixer to be processed and summed with all your other tracks. This used to take a fair amount of preparation. You needed to create an instrument or multi-instrument object for your MIDI hardware device in the Environment. This object would then need to have a track created for it in the Arrange window in order for Logic to record MIDI from and send MIDI to the device. Then you needed to configure audio channels for the audio outputs of your MIDI device.

The External Instrument plug-in is designed expressly for this situation. You still need to have created an instrument, multi-instrument, or mapped-instrument object for your MIDI device. Select either a mono or a stereo external instrument in a software instrument channel strip's Instrument slot. The plug-in editor gives you only a few options. First, set its MIDI destination to your instrument, multi-instrument, or mapped-instrument object. Then set its input to the input(s) on your audio interface into which you plugged your MIDI hardware device.

That's it! You now have a single track that both sends and receives information from your hardware MIDI device. Keep in mind that you can only use one (mono) or two (stereo) outputs of your MIDI hardware with this instrument—there is not a multichannel option.

Plug-In Window Controls

Software instruments and audio effects (which are discussed in Chapter 11) use the same basic form of plug-in window. Each plug-in window features Link, Bypass, Compare, Copy, and Paste buttons, two arrow buttons, and either four or five pull-down menus, as shown in Figure 9.5.

Figure 9.5   The two varieties of controls you'll find on software instrument plug-in windows. They are identical except for the number of pull-down menus: (a) Software instrument windows typically have four pull-down menus; (b) some software instruments have side chains, which gives them five pull-down menus, with the Side Chain menu offset from the others.

The elements of the plug-in window in which your software instrument will open are described in the following sections.

Plug-In Window Buttons

There are seven buttons at the top of the plug-in window:

- **Link.** By default, the Link button is disengaged, so multiple plug-in windows can be on the screen simultaneously. If the Link button is engaged, only a single plug-in window at a time is allowed onscreen. This is useful if you have a limited amount of screen space. You can also open a number of windows with the Link button disengaged and then engage the Link button on one of the open plug-in windows so that all subsequent plug-ins will appear in this window.

- **Bypass.** The Bypass button turns the plug-in on and off. This has the same effect as Option-clicking in the plug-in's box in the channel strip in which the plug-in is instantiated.

- **Compare.** The Compare button allows you compare any changes you have made to a plug-in's settings to the last saved setting.

- **Next Setting and Previous Setting.** These are the two arrow buttons, which allow you to select the next or previous preset.

- **Copy.** Use this button to copy a plug-in's setting.

- **Paste.** Use this button to paste a copied plug-in setting.

Plug-In Window Menus

The plug-in window contains either four or five pull-down menus in its top bar, depending on the capabilities of the plug-in.

- **View menu.** This menu contains two options: Editor, which offers the standard Graphic Editor view of plug-ins, and the Control view, which simply lists the parameters of the synth and offers a slider for each. Most plug-ins have too many parameters to offer useful graphic feedback in Control view, so you'll almost always want to use the Editor view.

- **Show Channel Strip menu.** This menu lists the current channel strip in which you are viewing a plug-in, as well as all the other channel strips used in the current Logic song. To switch to a different channel strip, just select it.

- **Show Insert menu.** The Show Insert pull-down menu contains all the plug-ins used by the current dependent plug-in's channel strip. To change the current plug-in window to that of another plug-in being used by the same channel strip, you can use this menu to select the new plug-in.

- **Side Chain menu.** Some softsynths are capable of processing the audio from an audio channel. To do this, you will need to use the Side Chain menu to select which audio channel to process. Side chains are discussed in detail in Chapter 11.

■ **Settings field.** The Settings field is the pull-down menu to the right of the Next Setting and Previous Setting buttons. This menu has commands for loading and saving Logic plug-in setting files. These files store the current parameter conditions of your plug-in, which you can then reload later and even reuse in other songs. This is useful for creating your own unique collection of commonly used settings for your various plug-ins. As you save your settings, they appear in this pull-down menu for easy access. The presets for Logic's own instruments and effects are listed at the bottom of this menu as well. Plug-in settings are stored in the Plug-In Settings folder inside the Logic Application Support folder. You can also manually add settings collected from other users by copying them to this folder. This field also displays the name of the currently selected preset. Note that many third-party plug-ins have their own methods for loading and saving presets and do not rely on the host application for preset handling. You can still use the commands in this menu if you want to create and manage settings for a plug-in within Logic's preset hierarchy rather than the plug-in's.

Extended Parameters

Not all of Logic's plug-ins have every parameter available in their Editor view. In such cases, a disclosure triangle at the bottom-left corner of the plug-in allows you to open an Extended Parameters area, as shown in Figure 9.6, giving you access to any remaining controls the plug-in offers.

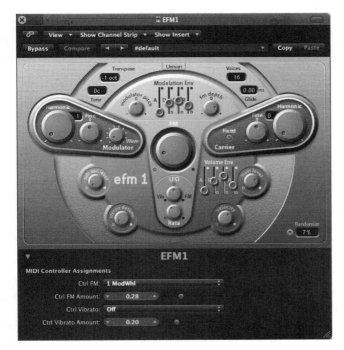

Figure 9.6   The Extended Parameters area of the EFM1 plug-in. Some Logic plug-ins have parameters that are not found in the plug-in's Editor view but are available by clicking on the window's disclosure triangle in the lower-left corner.

Software Instruments and the Environment

As we've already discussed, a software instrument channel strip is both a channel strip object and a MIDI object. As such, you can route software instrument objects to other MIDI objects to create unique MIDI effects and routings, just like you can any other MIDI device. You'll learn about the Environment routing and macro construction possible in Logic in Chapter 13, "The Environment," but for now, keep in mind that you can use software instrument objects just like MIDI instrument objects for any sort of Environment work.

Using Multi-Output Software Instruments

The vast majority of the software instruments you use will be either mono or stereo instruments. Moreover, you'll probably only need stereo outputs from softsynths that allow for more than two outputs. However, sometimes you might want to have an independent output for each sample from a sampler, each voice of a synthesizer, or each drum from a drum instrument to allow for more precise mixing, processing, or automation control. For these situations, you can instantiate a multi-output instrument in a software instrument channel strip.

Logic is far more efficient than other DAWs in the management of resources when using software instruments. The price for this efficiency, unfortunately, is that accessing the additional outputs of softsynths takes a few more steps than in other applications. Most other applications automatically create every allowable output channel for multiple-output instruments as soon as you instantiate the plug-in. This is very convenient because there are no steps required to access the additional outputs. There are two drawbacks to this, however. The first is that if your instrument is set up to allow 32 outputs, your Mixer will be cluttered with 32 additional output channels, making it huge and unwieldy—especially if you only wanted to use four outputs! The other drawback is that all of those unused outputs may drain your computer's CPU power and RAM. Logic allows you to activate only those additional outputs that you will actually use, conserving both screen real estate and computer resources, but giving you this flexibility means that activating the additional outputs requires some configuration.

The first step is to make sure that you have instantiated a multi-output softsynth in a software instrument channel strip. Then, you may need to change the output assignments in the softsynth's graphical interface. For details, consult the documentation for your specific software instrument.

Next, open the Mixer and use the + button on the multi-output instrument's channel strip to add as many aux channels as you need for routing your multi-output instrument. Figure 9.7 shows the + button on a multi-output channel strip in the Mixer. After you have used the + button to add aux channel strips to the Mixer, a − button appears next to it, allowing you to delete that multi-output instrument's dependent aux channels one by one.

Now you need to assign your aux channels to the outputs of the multi-output instrument. In addition to submenus for hardware inputs and available busses in each aux channel strip's Input

Figure 9.7   Use the + button to add more aux channel strips to the Mixer for the outputs of a multi-output instrument.

pull-down menu, you will find a hierarchal menu of all the outputs available for your multi-output instrument. If the aux channel's Format button shows a single circle, mono outputs are displayed, and if the Format button is pressed so it shows two overlapping circles, stereo outputs are displayed. Choose the output (or outputs if you are using stereo) that you want this aux channel to use as its input(s). Figure 9.8 shows an aux channel's input being assigned to a multi-output instrument's output.

Figure 9.8   To access the additional outputs of multi-output instruments, create an aux channel and select the desired output from its input menu. Here, Output 3 is being chosen as the input for this aux channel.

If your Mixer's display mode is set to Arrange, the new aux channel strips will be shown directly to the right of their parent multi-output channel strip. Different Mixer display modes will be covered in detail in Chapter 11, but for the moment you can find the display mode buttons at the top center of the Mixer window's local menu bar. You can see some of these buttons at the top of Figure 9.8. Figure 9.9 shows an Ultrabeat multi-output instrument channel strip in an Arrange view procedure. Note that in addition to the main software instrument channel strip that serves as the main stereo output pair, this multi-output instrument has been configured with two additional mono aux channel strips and then a stereo aux channel strip. This is the power of Logic—only 6 of Ultrabeat's 16 outputs were needed, and the configuration matches exactly the user's desired combination of mono and stereo outputs.

The Arrange track for this multi-output instrument is the track in which you will record, program, and edit the MIDI data that will operate the software instrument. The multi-output instrument's own outputs will be the "master outputs." This means that depending on how the specific softsynth you are using operates, it may serve as your master stereo output, or it may be a

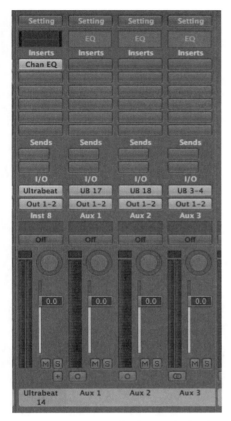

Figure 9.9   The multichannel Ultrabeat has now been configured to include the main outputs, two additional mono outputs, and an additional stereo output. If you needed more outputs, you could easily continue creating aux objects and choose more Ultrabeat outputs, to the limit of the instrument's capacity.

summation output of all the other outputs for the entire instrument. You'll need to consult your instrument's documentation for specifics on how it utilizes its master outputs.

For multi-output instruments, you won't need to have any of the additional outputs in the Arrange window if you don't want them there. However, you might want to put some or all of them in the Arrange window in order to automate those outputs. Automation will be discussed in the next chapter, "Using Automation in Logic." You can add your aux channels to the Arrange window in a couple of different ways. In the Mixer, you can Control-click on an aux channel strip and choose Create/Select Arrange Track from the resulting menu, as shown in Figure 9.10.

In the Arrange window, you can also change a freshly created track or a currently unused one to an aux channel by Control-clicking on the track header. Under the Mixer submenu of the Reassign Track Object menu, go to the Aux submenu and select the aux channel you want, as shown in Figure 9.11.

Figure 9.10 To create an Arrange window track for an aux in the Mixer, simply Control-click on an aux channel strip and choose Create/Select Arrange Track from the menu.

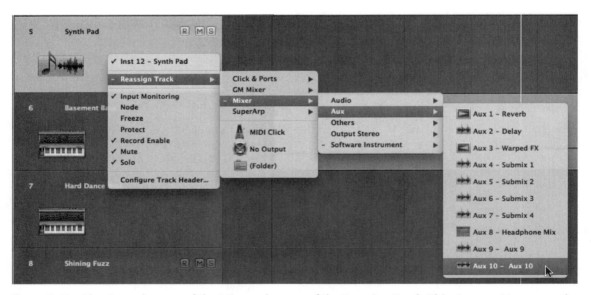

Figure 9.11 The Aux submenu of the Mixer submenu of the Reassign Track Object menu. You can assign an Arrange track to the aux channel output of a multi-output instrument in this menu.

Another way to add your multi-output instrument's dependent aux channels to the Arrange window is to create a new channel of any type in the Arrange window for each aux you want to add. Next, open the Environment Mixer and select the aux channels you want to add to the Arrange window and then drag them to the Arrange area over the new tracks. You will see boxes highlighting the track headers of the channels that the aux channels will be affecting. Once you have selected the correct tracks, release the mouse button. The selected tracks will automatically be changed to aux channels. Be careful, though—if you release the aux over any channel, even one with regions on it, it will be converted into an aux channel. If this does happen, you can simply undo the action. You can also assign any aux to an automation mode, and it will automatically be added in the Arrange.

This is a perfect example of the "Logic way." It might take a little extra initial configuration, but when you understand how it works and how to do it, not only is it simple, but you can really take advantage of the power and flexibility it offers over other applications!

Using Multitimbral Software Instruments

Some software instruments allow for multitimbral operation, meaning they'll allow you to load completely different plug-in settings, presets, and so on for each different MIDI channel the instrument can receive. Not all instruments allow for this—in fact, Apple doesn't currently make any software instruments that are multitimbral—but if you *do* have some Audio Unit instruments that allow this function, here's how you would access them from within Logic. One method is to simply have the MIDI regions on your Software Instrument track send different MIDI events to different MIDI channels. For example, you could create a single MIDI region with a bass line sending to MIDI Channel 1 and a high lead part sending to MIDI Channel 2. Your software instrument will take care of routing the different notes to the proper MIDI channels. This technique comes in handy for scoring, when you might want several voices in a single MIDI region going to different channels. However, if you want separate tracks for each MIDI part being routed to different channels, you can easily create them in the Arrange window.

Open the New Tracks dialog to create a new software instrument, either by clicking the + or by using the key command Option+Command+N. There you can define the number of new tracks you wish to create, and by checking the Multi-Timbral box next to the Number field, shown in Figure 9.12, the channel strip and region parameters will be identical for all of the new tracks. That's because the exact same software instrument channel strip is being used on all the newly created Software Instrument tracks.

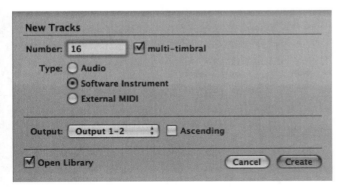

Figure 9.12   The New Tracks dialog. Checking the Multi-Timbral box creates the defined number of multitimbral tracks in the Arrange window.

Now you can create new MIDI regions on these tracks and send those MIDI regions to different MIDI channels of your multichannel software instrument. This way, you have the MIDI parts for each channel separated on different tracks.

Unfortunately, it is currently not possible to use the standard volume and pan automation on individual tracks that belong to a single-parent multitimbral software instrument, as the automation will affect the multitimbral software instrument as a whole, and not on a per-track basis.

Using ReWire 2 Instruments

We briefly described how to create ReWire Instruments in Chapter 3, but now we'll go into more detail. As mentioned previously, ReWire 2 is a protocol, developed by Propellerhead Software, through which one program can access and control another music software program, with both applications running on the same computer. ReWire 2 slaves function as software instruments because all their processing is being done inside the host computer, but they are different from software instruments in the sense that they are not part of the Logic application like Logic's own softsynths, nor are they literally "plugged in" to the Logic application like third-party plug-ins. So while all the connections that Logic needs to make are "virtual connections" that do not require hardware interfaces and cables, Logic must still create these connections *out* of Logic *into* another application. The Environment's ReWire object, therefore, is the "virtual MIDI cable" between Logic and the ReWire 2 application and is also the "virtual audio cable" between Logic and the ReWire 2 application. This section explains how to configure these objects in order to use a ReWire 2 application with Logic.

Working with ReWire 2 Applications

ReWire 2 has two modes: Master mode and Slave mode. Generally, the application that is launched first is the default ReWire Master, and the ReWire 2 application launched subsequently is the ReWire Slave. The Master application is the one that controls the synchronization between the two applications, and the sound from the ReWire Slave application plays through the ReWire Master application. Logic is only capable of being a ReWire Master, so be sure that the ReWire 2–capable application you want to use can be operated in ReWire 2 Slave mode.

No special configuration is required to initialize ReWire operation. Be sure to launch Logic first, then launch your ReWire 2 Slave application. The application should automatically load in ReWire Slave mode. Remember that as of this writing, ReWire is not available when Logic is in 64-bit mode. If using ReWire is vital to your workflow, you must keep Logic in 32-bit mode.

Creating ReWire Instruments for MIDI Transmission

Before you can use Logic with your ReWire slave, you need to create and configure the necessary tracks in the Arrange window.

First, create as many new External Instrument tracks as you will need for your ReWire slave, as discussed in Chapter 3. Open the Library tab of the Media area, as shown in Figure 9.13. From here, you can launch your ReWire slave by double-clicking its name.

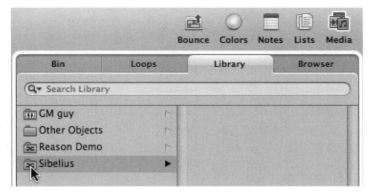

Figure 9.13   The Library tab of the Media area in the Arrange window. Clicking on the ReWire Slave name—in this case, Sibelius—will launch it as a ReWire Slave.

Once the ReWire Slave has launched, you will see a list of the available ReWire instruments in the Library, as shown in Figure 9.14. You can assign a ReWire Slave instrument to an External Instrument track by simply clicking on the name of the desired instrument.

If at any time you decide to change a ReWire track's settings, you can change the settings in the Inspector. Following are descriptions of each parameter:

- **Device.** This refers to the specific ReWire 2 application to which the ReWire instrument is connecting. For example, if you were using three different ReWire 2 applications, all three applications would appear in this pull-down menu, and you could select which of the three applications to connect this ReWire instrument to.

- **Bus.** This parameter allows you to choose which ReWire bus to use from your available ReWire busses. For Reason, the Propellerhead application, the Bus parameter allows different functions depending on the value. Bus 1 addresses only the instrument chosen as the Live instrument in Reason. Busses 2–5 address Busses A–D of Reason's MIDI In device. And Busses 6 and above address the individual instruments inside the Reason Rack. (These devices appear by name in Busses 6 and above.)

- **Channel.** The Channel parameter specifies the MIDI channel on which you want your ReWire instrument to send and receive MIDI data.

In the Devices tab of the Audio Preferences dialog box, accessible from Logic Pro > Preferences > Audio, you will find a pull-down menu for ReWire mode with two options: Playback and Live mode. For normal use, you will leave this setting in Playback mode. If you are going to use your ReWire Slave for live performance of its instruments over the ReWire connection, you will want to set the ReWire mode to Live mode. This setting diverts extra CPU resources to ensure the best possible synchronization between Logic and your ReWire application during live performance. If you use ReWire applications extensively, even if not strictly for live use, you will want to keep this option on.

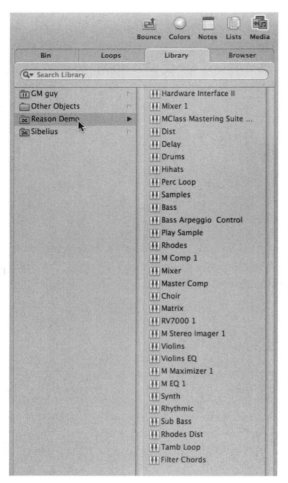

Figure 9.14 You can select the desired ReWire instrument directly in the Library tab of the Media area in the Arrange window.

Setting Up ReWire Objects for Audio Transmission

Now that you have set up your ReWire instrument's MIDI connection between Logic and your ReWire 2 application, you need to create and configure aux channels to receive audio from the ReWire Slave. To create a new aux, simply open the Mixer, and in the Mixer's local Options menu, select Options > Create New Auxiliary Channel Strips or press Option+Command+N. A New Auxiliary Channel Strips window, shown in Figure 9.15, will open, allowing you to define the number of aux channel strips, the input, and the output of the new channel strips.

Enter the number of aux channel strips you wish to create. You can then define the ReWire bus of your first aux channel strip using the Input menu, shown in Figure 9.16.

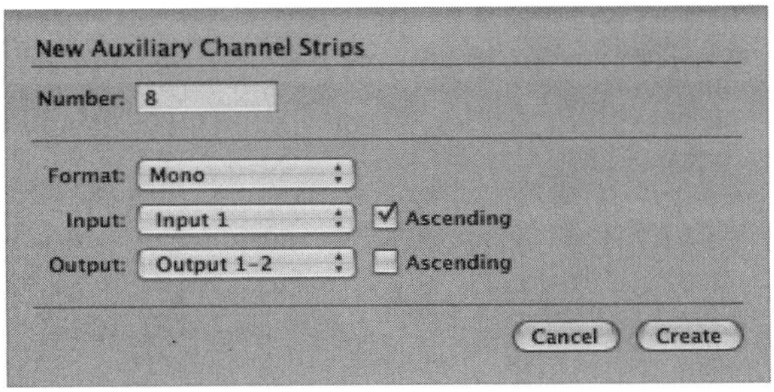

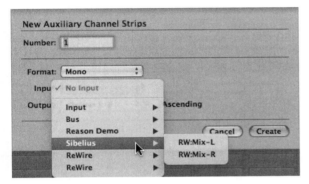

Figure 9.15   The Create New Auxiliary Channel Strips command opens a window allowing you to define the number of channel strips and their parameters.

Figure 9.16   Use the Input menu in the New Auxiliary Channel Strips dialog to define the ReWire bus of your new aux channel strip.

If you are creating more than one aux channel strip, you can easily assign a ReWire bus to each channel strip's input by checking the Ascending box next to the Input drop-down menu. This will assign the channel strips' ReWire busses sequentially. The output of your channel strips can be assigned by using the Output drop-down menu, and selecting the Ascending option allows you to assign outputs sequentially.

Using QuickTime Instruments

QuickTime (Apple's multimedia technology) comes with its own Roland-licensed soundset, which you can also access within Logic. Since the QuickTime Synth is a software instrument that is inside your computer but outside of Logic, just like a ReWire application, the QuickTime object looks almost identical. You create a QuickTime instrument by choosing it from the New local menu in the Environment window via the path New > Internal > QuickTime. Figure 9.17 shows a QuickTime instrument.

Notice the QuickTime instrument has the same parameters as the ReWire instrument. Refer to the section "Using ReWire 2 Instruments" for a description of the parameters. You'll likely never

Figure 9.17   The QuickTime instrument. This is an internal instrument that makes virtual MIDI connections like the ReWire instrument.

need to adjust them, with the exception of the Channel parameter if you are using more than one QuickTime instrument.

The QuickTime Music Synthesizer offers you a complete collection of Roland GS General MIDI sounds. You can double-click on the QuickTime instrument to bring up the QuickTime instrument interface shown in Figure 9.18. You can use the various pull-down menus to select the specific sound you want to use for your QuickTime instrument.

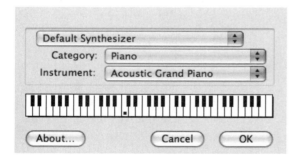

Figure 9.18   You can use the pull-down menus in the QuickTime instrument interface to access the various installed sounds of the QuickTime Synth.

You will probably not want to use the QuickTime Synth much at all. Its sounds are very basic, and in most cases you will be better off using one of Logic's included software instruments. Its main use would be to get a feel for what a MIDI file may sound like on a webpage or some other instance where a General MIDI sound set will be used.

10 Using Automation in Logic

I n the early days of recording, if you wanted to capture the sound of moving one of the controls—for example, to create a wild stereo panning effect with an instrument, to have sound fade out gradually, or simply to level out the volume of a track that fluctuated wildly in level—you would need to move the control carefully by hand while the mixdown was happening. Any error in movement meant starting the whole thing over from scratch, and there was no way to exactly repeat anything. If you wanted to repeat the move for a new mixdown, the only option was to do it again manually and hope that the result was close to that of the original mixdown. In the 1970s, large mixing consoles began to offer *automation*—a way to write, rewrite, and save these moves in memory so that as you mixed your material, it would automatically make your move for you. This was not only more convenient, but it meant that you could audition, change, and repeat any move an infinite number of times, and it would be the same each time. This opened the door not only for more accurate mixing, but also for much more creative mixing by experimental artists who wanted to use the studio itself as an instrument.

With the advent of computer sequencers, automation has become an even more powerful tool, available to all. You can use automation to turn static effects into living, dynamic parts of a track's sound; you can tailor the volume of a track exactly to the source material; you can perfect mixes to previously unimaginable accuracy; and you can use your DAW not only as a tool, but as an instrument in its own right. Logic's automation system is fairly intuitive, but it still takes a while to get used to its "Logic!"

Types of Automation

As we introduced in Chapter 6, there are two ways to automate your song data in Logic. Both types are useful and very similar in many ways, but each has distinct advantages and disadvantages.

The first method is called *track-based automation (TBA)*, so named because the automation data is stored with the Arrange track lane. This paradigm of storing the automation data with the track harkens back to the days of hardware mixing consoles, where you automated a specific channel of the mixer. TBA allows for incredibly high (sample-accurate) resolution, which gives

437

you precise control over automation points and lines. Since TBA is the more recent and powerful automation system, you will probably use TBA for most of your automation in Logic.

Unlike using a hardware mixing console, in which the console doesn't know what type of audio you are sending through a channel, a computer *does* know what sort of data you have in your song. This means that unlike a hardware console, a computer sequencer doesn't need to automate a channel, but it can instead include automation information as part of the audio or MIDI region itself. This type of automation in Logic is called *Hyper Draw,* or *region-based automation (RBA).* Emagic developed Hyper Draw long before TBA, back when all automation of MIDI hardware and Audio tracks was based on MIDI (hence the term *Hyper Draw,* as it is basically a "hyper set" of the MIDI control messages). This means that RBA is limited to controlling parameters that have MIDI control message values, and that RBA's values are limited to the standard MIDI range of 0–127 (as opposed to TBA's 32-bit resolution). While RBA is definitely limited compared to TBA, it still has its uses.

Both forms of automation can be used together, so you can have a region in which you've automated some plug-in parameters using Hyper Draw as well as done some track-based automation. When you have Track Automation view enabled, there will be a disclosure triangle in the bottom-left corner of the track; if you click on the triangle, you can get as many additional lanes for Hyper Draw and track automation as you need. Figure 10.1 shows a track that has track-based automation turned on, while the MIDI region itself has some RBA on it as well, and two automation lanes visible to view them both. You can even turn RBA into TBA and vice versa, as you'll explore later in this chapter. But be careful not to use TBA and RBA for the same parameter—the results will be random and unusable.

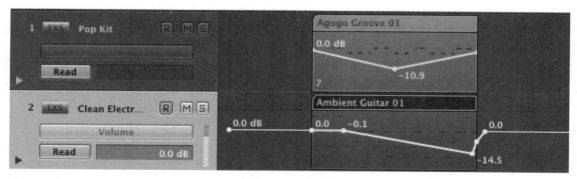

Figure 10.1   This screenshot shows both Hyper Draw (region-based automation) and track-based automation. You can see the Agogo Groove region with volume RBA above the Ambient Guitar region with TBA automating its volume. You can use both of them interchangeably, depending on your needs. Because TBA is the newer and more robust automation system, you will most likely use TBA more often.

Using Track-Based Automation

Using TBA couldn't be simpler. If you've already turned on track-based automation in the local View menu of the Arrange, the automation display is visible for all your tracks. If you haven't done that, select View > Track Automation or press A, and your tracks will all enlarge to fit the automation display data (unless you have already zoomed the tracks). Figure 10.2 shows a few tracks in an Arrange Track List.While they all have Automation view enabled, only one of the tracks actually has any automation.

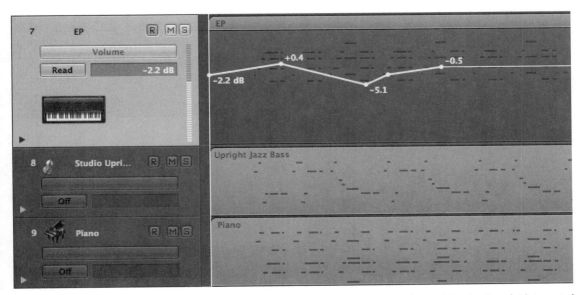

Figure 10.2   By choosing View > Track Automation, you ensure that each track in the Track List contains the pull-down menus for track-based automation. Note that only the first of the three visible tracks actually has automation data visible in the track lane, but all three tracks are ready to be automated.

The first pull-down menu is the Parameter Display. Here you can select from all the available parameters for all the automatable elements of the track itself (volume, pan, solo, mute, send, insert bypass, and so on), as well as each automatable plug-in and software instrument parameter. Choose from this menu the parameter you want to automate. Figure 10.3 shows the pull-down menus in the Parameter Display.

As you automate more parameters, they appear in the automation lane behind the currently live parameter. Volume appears as a yellow line, pan as a green line, and other parameters appear in a range of other colors. How easy the dark colors are to see depends on the Automation Transparency value you set by choosing the Arrange tab in Logic Pro > Preferences > Display.

Then you need to choose the automation mode. There are five automation modes:

- **Off.** To disable automation, set the mode to Off. This doesn't erase any existing automation data, but any existing data will not play back, and you cannot write any new data. If you already have automation data on the track and you edit that data while in Off mode, the mode switches to Read, so that the next time you play your song, Logic will play back the

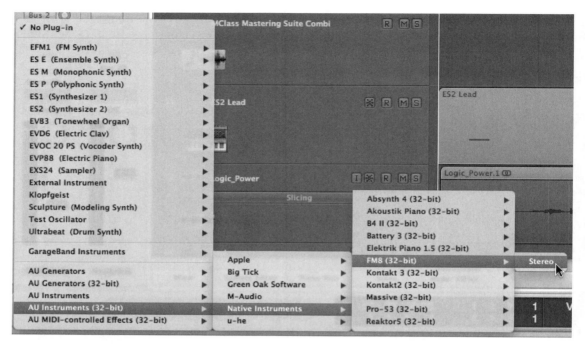

Figure 10.3   You can see from the Parameter Display box of this track that in addition to the shortcuts to Display Off, Volume, and Pan, there are hierarchal menus to choose to display parameters from the main track, software instrument, or effects.

automation data you just edited. You can set all tracks to Off using the key command Shift+Control+Command+O.

- **Read.** This mode tells Logic to "read" the automation data on the track. When you play your song, Logic automates your track. You cannot write automation data in real time in this mode, but you can create and edit automation data in the track lane itself (as explained later in the "Manipulating Automation Data" section). You can set all tracks to Read using the key command Shift+Control+Command+R.

- **Touch.** In Touch mode, if you "touch" an element of the channel strip with your mouse or a software control surface, such as the Euphonix MC Artist or Mackie controller, Logic starts writing automation data for that element. This is real-time, live automating, so any move you make is recorded live into Logic's track automation, although you can of course edit the data later. As soon as you release the mouse or the control surface or stop "touching" the onscreen element, Logic stops writing automation data and returns the chosen parameter to its original value at the playhead position where you quit "touching" the parameter. For example, if you are in Touch mode and during playback you click the mouse on the Pan knob and move it from its current value—let's say –25—you will write pan automation data in real time. When you release the mouse button, you will stop writing pan automation data, and the pan value will return to –25 at the current playhead position. Keep in mind that if you already had pan data written in that specific place in which you wrote new data, the new data recorded in Touch mode will overwrite the previous data. Touch mode is the standard mode for real-time onscreen or software controller automation. You can set all tracks to Touch using the key command Shift+Control+Command+T.

- **Latch.** Latch mode is like Touch mode except that once you click your mouse or move your control surface to start writing automation, Logic continues to write new data for that parameter even after you release the control. Only when playback stops will Logic stop writing automation for that parameter. Latch mode is desirable when you know that after a certain point in your song, you want to overwrite all the remaining data for a particular parameter. You can set all tracks to Latch using the key command Shift+Control+Command+L.

- **Write.** Write mode deletes all existing track automation as the playhead passes it. If you write new data, the new data is recorded. If you do not write new data, Write mode acts as a "real-time eraser" of previous automation data, which it replaces with nothing. Write mode is useful only if you want to start your mix over without using any of the delete commands described later in this chapter. You will find this mode to be less useful than the other automation modes.

After setting the parameter you want to display and the automation mode, all that's left to do is to actually write the automation data! There are basically two ways to do this: in real time or in the track lane (non–real time).

You can automate in real time by clicking the mouse on the various elements of the channel strip (Volume fader, Pan knob, Solo button, Mute button, insert and send slots) or the graphic interface of a plug-in or software instrument, then adjusting those elements by dragging them with the mouse (or just clicking on them, if the option is a button) as your song plays. As you change the values of various elements, you will create *automation Nodes,* which are points in which the value of an automatable parameter has changed. When you do real-time automation, as you might imagine, you may create hundreds of these Nodes at a time in a mix with lots of complex motion.

You can also use a control surface, such as the Euphonix MC Artist controllers, Mackie Control, or any other MIDI hardware controller that you have set up, using the Controller Assignment function described in Chapter 3. In this case, you would use the hardware controls on your controller to manipulate the onscreen channel strip and plug-in elements. If you are used to hardware mixers, automating by using a controller will seem more natural to you. Also, unlike a mouse, using hardware controllers gives you the ability to manipulate more than one parameter at the same time. Finally, some hardware controllers offer 10-bit or greater resolution in their faders and knobs, which means that you'll be able to make finer resolution moves with the controller than you could with a mouse.

If you don't want to automate in real time, you can also directly add automation Nodes (points) and drag them up and down with your mouse in the track lane itself. This offers more precise placement of automation data than real-time mixing but also less feedback, because you can't hear what you're doing as you make the move.

You can also quickly create Nodes on the borders of a selected region or regions by using two commands found in the Track > Track Automation menu in the Arrange window: Create 2 Nodes at Region Border and Create 4 Nodes at Region Border. The benefit of these commands is that they create new Nodes at the precise region borders, allowing you to easily control any automatable parameters on a per-region basis. With two Nodes, you can create single-region fades, panorama movement, or filter sweeps without having to worry about creating precisely placed Nodes on a region border. With four Nodes you can add quick volume, compressor threshold, or individual EQ band gain changes that affect only the selected region. In essence, these two commands bring region-based automation–like benefits to the more flexible track-based automation.

Parameter Display versus Parameter Write   Although you need to select a parameter for the automation lane in order to display automation data, in fact you can write automation data for any parameter that is automatable, even if it is not currently being displayed. For example, let's say you select Volume to be the parameter displayed in the automation lane. Then, while in Touch mode, you write some volume automation data, but you also make some panning moves. Logic will write both the volume and the pan moves, even though the automation lane will reflect only the volume moves while you are recording automation data.

Keep in mind that you are not limited to any one method of writing automation data—you can use the mouse to automate volume in a track in real time, then add a few more points and adjust them in the track lane, and use one of the Create Nodes commands on a few of the track's regions. We will discuss this further in the upcoming "Expert Automation Editing" section.

Method Tip: Viewing Multiple Automation Lanes   A track's automation lane only lets you choose one live parameter to display; however, you can automate more than one parameter at a time with a software controller. What if you want to view more than one parameter that you are automating? As mentioned earlier, you can view multiple parameters on separate displays by clicking the small disclosure triangle at the bottom-left of a track displaying automation to open a new track lane to display another automation parameter. The new automation display lane will also contain a disclosure triangle. You can use this technique to open as many new automation display lanes as you need for each track you are automating. You can also Option-click on the triangle to open up one new automation display lane for each parameter currently automated and then Option-click the triangle again to close all those automation lanes. Figure 10.4 shows a track that is displaying more than one automation lane this way.

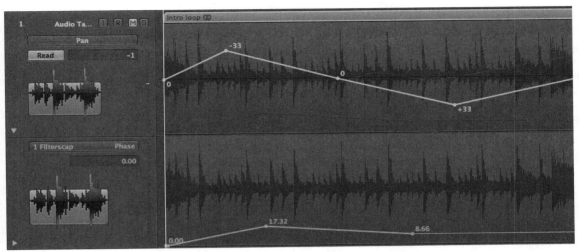

Figure 10.4   This track displays pan automation on its track lane, but then by clicking the triangle in the lower-left corner, the user created an additional automation display lane for LFO Phase automation.

A Tale of Two View Modes   Both Automation and Flex Time offer view modes that add information to every track on the Arrange. This means that Automation view and Flex view are mutually exclusive—in other words, you can't have the Automation view displaying on one track and the Flex view displaying on another track simultaneously. If you have both Flex and Automation enabled, you can toggle between both views with Toolbar buttons and key commands.

Manipulating Automation Data

Because you can write automation either by using the mouse or a hardware controller in real time or by simply adding it to an Arrange track while not in playback, you can use the methods in this section to alter existing data or to create new data. All you need to do is turn on track-based automation and select a parameter in the Parameter Display.

Using the Pointer Tool

To move a Node, simply grab it with the Pointer tool and then move the Node in any direction you want. Notice that the position line representing the continuous parameter value simply shifts positions and values depending on wherever you move the Node. If you click on a point in the automation lane in which there isn't currently a Node, Logic creates a Node in that location, which you can manipulate as described previously.

The Pointer tool can manipulate automation data in additional ways:

- Short-clicking on a Node deletes it.

- Long-clicking on a line between two Nodes enables you to move the line.

- If you click and hold a Node and then hold the Shift key, you restrict the movement of the Node to one plane, horizontal or vertical, whichever direction you move first.

- If you click and hold a Node and press the Control key, you gain fine control of the Node in the vertical plane, moving 0.1 units at a time.

- Long-clicking while holding down the Shift key enables you to select a length of automation data (from one tick away to the entire project).

- Option-clicking selects the area from the Node to the right of the Pointer to the last Node on the track lane.

- Option-double-clicking selects all automation data in the current track lane.

- If you Command-click on either the automation value fader or numerical display in the track header, you select all automation of the displayed type in the current track lane.

- Command-dragging either the automation value fader or the numerical display in the track header scales all automation data of the displayed type in the current track lane.

- You can move a selected area by clicking and dragging anywhere in the selected area.

- If you Option-drag the selection, it will copy selected automation data to the new location.

- Finally, Shift+Control-clicking in an automation lane changes the pointer into the Automation Curve tool, discussed in the next section.

To change the value of a group of Nodes, simply alter the value of one of the selected Nodes inside the selected area. All the selected Nodes then change by the same amount. If you click outside of a line or Node but inside a selected area, or you alter the value of either of the two Nodes at the edges of the selected area, you alter the values proportionally to where you clicked, but the values do not change by the same absolute amount.

Using the Automation Tools

You can also use the Automation tools described in the section "The Arrange Tool Menu" in Chapter 6. There are two Automation tools: Curve and Select. Figure 10.5 shows the Automation tools in the Tool menu.

In Curve mode, you can use the Automation tool to grab the line between any two Nodes and bend it into a curve. Logic offers a number of preset curve types: convex, concave, and S-curves.

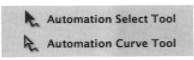

Figure 10.5   The Automation Select tool is the solid arrow with the jagged stem. The Automation Curve tool is the open arrow with the jagged stem.

Which variety of curve you create depends on where on the line you start your bend and in which direction you bend the line.

In Select mode, the Automation tool can make "rubber band" selections in the automation lane. If you click outside the automation lane into a region title bar, you select all the automation that falls within that region. You can make noncontiguous selections of automation with this tool by holding down the Shift key while selecting additional automation data on the track. You can also extend a selection by Shift-clicking on a Node in front of or behind an existing selection; everything from the selected area to the Node you clicked is then selected. Finally, if you Option-click the Automation tool on a region in the area above the automation lane, Logic will place one Node at the beginning and one Node at the end of the selected region.

Expert Automation Editing

As you would expect, Logic offers myriad key commands to control various automation functions. Figure 10.6 shows all the automation key commands.

Feel free to assign keys to any of the options you want—you'll find using Logic's automation even faster and more natural when you master the key commands. The Automation Event List key command, Control+Command+E, opens the Event List window to show all automation data for the selected track. These views of automation data are normally invisible. We call the Automation Event List an "expert option" because unless you know what you are doing, you will probably find this window too confusing to be of much use. If you want to explore it, however, the following subsection describes it briefly.

Automation Event List

You can view automation data in the Event List, just like other command data, such as MIDI control messages. Because automation data is technically a special proprietary type of data known as *fader messages,* you'll notice that the Automation Event List consists exclusively of fader and control data, depending on what the entry is automating. Figure 10.7 shows an Automation Event List.

As you can see, the Automation Event List is a specialized view in the Event List Editor, so you can use all the options and techniques described in Chapter 8 regarding the Event List Editor to edit your MIDI automation. You may find the Automation Event List useful if you know exactly what you want to edit or if you are more comfortable editing data numerically than graphically.

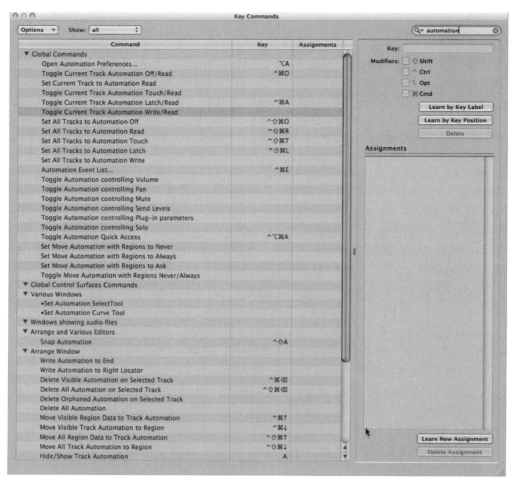

Figure 10.6 The Key Commands window showing the automation-related commands.

Moving Automation Data from One Parameter to Another

If you have automation data written for one parameter, but you'd like to move it to another parameter—say you automated a filter cutoff for a software instrument, and now you want that data to control the envelope level—you can do this easily. With the parameter you want to move displayed in the automation lane, hold the Command key while opening the Parameter Display pop-up menu. (Be sure to hold the Command key after you release the mouse button.) Now when you choose a destination parameter, a dialog box appears, asking whether you want to convert (move) the current automation to the new parameter or copy and convert it, which leaves the data you have recorded in the current parameter but also adds it to the new parameter. Select the option you prefer, and that's it!

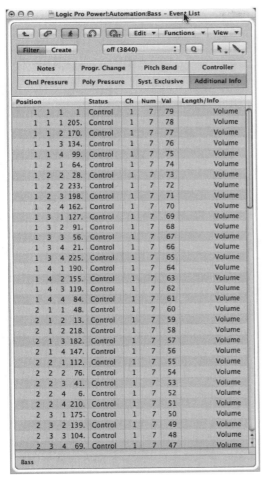

Figure 10.7   An Automation Event List. Because this is displayed in the Event List Editor, you have all the options previously described in Chapter 8 to edit your automation data.

Moving Automation with Regions

As with so many other things, Logic gives you options for controlling its behavior when you move regions on tracks that contain automation. To define how Logic handles automation data when you move a region, open Logic Pro > Preferences > Automation by selecting Automation in the Preferences menu in the Toolbar or by pressing Option+A. Figure 10.8 shows the Automation Preferences window.

The Move Automation with Regions menu gives you three options: Never, Always, and Ask. If you select Never, Logic will not move any associated automation data when you move a region. If you select Always, Logic will always move all associated automation data when you move a region. If you select Ask, then Logic will open a dialog asking whether you would like to move the

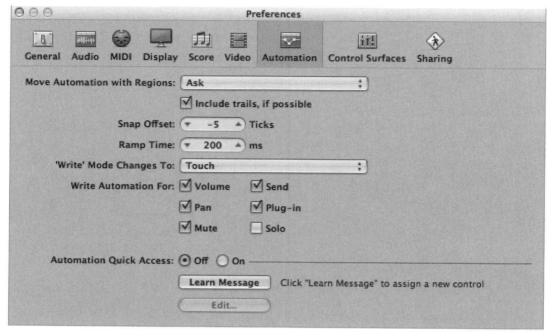

Figure 10.8 The Automation Preferences window.

automation data with the region. It is generally best to select Ask, because this gives you the power to choose what happens to automation data on a per-case basis.

Snapping Automation

If you want to snap automation Nodes to a grid, you can select Snap Automation from the Snap pull-down menu in the Arrange, shown in Figure 10.9, or use the key command Option+Shift+A.

Figure 10.9 To snap automation Nodes to the grid, select Snap Automation from the Snap menu in the Arrange window.

You can offset the placement of Nodes created with Snap Automation enabled by changing the Snap Offset value in the Automation Preferences window, as shown in Figure 10.8. Changing the Snap Offset value will automatically offset the snap position of newly created Nodes by the defined number of ticks.

Deleting and Converting Automation Data

Eventually, you may find yourself wanting to completely rid a track of all the automation for a given parameter you have recorded and start over. Perhaps you want to attach your track-based automation to a track's regions, or maybe you want to convert MIDI control information into TBA. Luckily, Logic allows you to delete automation and convert between RBA and TBA easily. You can find the basic commands to convert automation data by choosing Track > Track Automation. Figure 10.10 shows the submenu that appears.

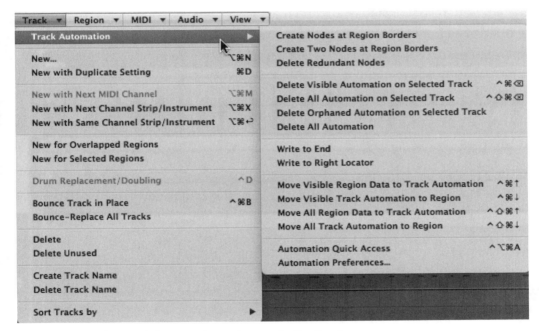

Figure 10.10 The Track Automation submenu in the Track menu.

Here is a brief description of these commands:

- **Create Nodes at Region Borders.** If you select this option, a Node will be created at each end of the selected region.

- **Create Two Nodes at Region Borders.** If you select this option, two Nodes will be created at each end of the selected region.

- **Delete Redundant Nodes.** Selecting this command removes any redundant Nodes. For example, suppose you are automating the volume of a track and you have created a few Nodes in a row that share the same value. Using the Delete Redundant Nodes command will remove all but the first and last of these Nodes.

- **Delete Visible Automation on Selected Track.** This command erases all the automation data on the selected track for the parameter in the Parameter Display. The key command is Control+Command+Delete.

- **Delete All Automation on Selected Track.** This command erases all automation data on the selected track. The key command is Control+Shift+Command+Delete.

- **Delete Orphaned Automation on Selected Track.** This command erases all orphaned automation data from the selected track.

- **Delete All Automation Data.** This command erases all automation data on all tracks.

- **Write to End.** With this command, you can zero (erase) all automation data on the selected track from the current playhead location to the end of the song.

- **Write to Right Locator.** Like the preceding command, this command zeroes all automation data on the selected track, but only as far as the right locator.

- **Move Visible Region Data to Track Automation.** This command converts the Hyper Draw information currently displayed into TBA data. When you use this command, TBA data in the automation lane replaces the Hyper Draw display inside your region. The key command is Control+Command+Up Arrow.

- **Move Visible Track Automation to Region.** You can convert your currently displayed TBA data to Hyper Draw with this command. When you use this command, your TBA data turns into Hyper Draw information that is part of the region. The key command is Control+Command+Down Arrow.

- **Move All Region Data to Track Automation.** This command converts all of a region's Hyper Draw information into TBA data. When using this command, TBA data in the automation lane replaces the Hyper Draw display inside your region. The key command is Control+Shift+Command+Up Arrow.

- **Move All Track Automation to Region.** You can convert all your current TBA data to Hyper Draw with this command. When you use this command, your TBA data turns into Hyper Draw information that is part of the region. Since Hyper Draw is MIDI data, keep in mind you'll need a MIDI region under the TBA for this to work. (For Audio tracks, you can always create a MIDI region on an External MIDI or Software Instrument track, then move it under the TBA with your mouse.) The key command is Control+Shift+Command+Down Arrow.

- **Automation Quick Access.** This turns on Automation Quick Access, which is explained later in this chapter. The key command is Control+Option+Command+A.

- **Automation Preferences.** Selecting Automation Preferences opens the Automation Preferences window. The Automation Preferences window is covered in the next section.

Automation Quick Access

Sometimes, you may want to record a single parameter live to track automation as part of a MIDI performance—for example, let's say you want to perform a synthesizer track, but you want to record your pitch shifting as TBA instead of as Hyper Draw information. You can, of course, record the information as normal MIDI and then convert it to TBA using one of the commands discussed previously, but Logic offers you an even more elegant shortcut: Automation Quick Access. This feature allows you to use any single hardware controller able to send MIDI data to write track-based automation data. Automation Quick Access is very easy to set up, thanks to Logic's very intuitive Learn function.

To configure and engage Automation Quick Access, open the Automation Preferences dialog box that contains the Automation Quick Access controls shown in Figure 10.11 by choosing Track > Track Automation > Automation Quick Access or by pressing Control+Option+Command+A. You can, of course, also access this window via the Automation Preferences window.

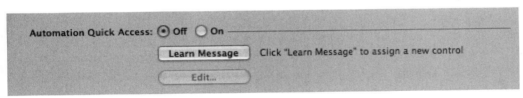

Figure 10.11   The Automation Preferences window contains the options to configure Automation Quick Access.

You'll immediately notice that the bottom of the Automation Preferences window consists of settings for Automation Quick Access. All you need to do is click the large Learn Message button at the bottom of the window. As soon as you engage this button, Logic is ready to "learn" the specifications of the controller you want to use as your Automation Quick Access control. The text to the left of the button now reads, "Slowly move/turn the control up and down you want to assign." In other words, simply take hold of the control you want to assign, slowly adjust the control to its maximum value, and then adjust the control to its minimum value.

That's it! Click Done, and you're ready to use your control to input TBA data. You can now engage or disengage Automation Quick Access by selecting Track > Track Automation > Automation Quick Access or by pressing Control+Option+Command+A.

11 Mixing in Logic

Whenever you have more than one track in your DAW, you will have to mix together the different tracks so you can hear all the various tracks out of the same set of speakers or headphones. The simplest form of mixing is when you simply sum (in other words, add the different audio streams of) all of your audio to the same outputs so all your different tracks play from the same speakers. For example, you could take a song with material on 16 different audio channels and combine them into a single stereo output so you can listen to all 16 channels through your stereo monitors. After doing this, your audio has been mixed together. However, mixing music is far more of an art than simply that. You can adjust the volume and position of your audio in a stereo or surround panorama for each track. You can process your tracks through effects individually or in groups. You can process the song as a whole through effects. And, of course, you can *bounce*—or print—the mix to a single audio file.

Logic offers some of the most comprehensive and intuitive options and features for mixing that are available in the digital realm. Logic can build a mixer for you from the tracks you have in your Arrange window, or you can build your own mixer in the Environment. You can route your audio directly to your outputs or use myriad creative methods to allow you to group tracks for mixing and processing. You can insert effects directly into a given audio track, send your audio to other channels for processing, or change the output of your tracks to group them with others for processing. You can bounce your audio down to a file in real time so you can hear exactly what is going into the file, or you can bounce the audio offline when you know exactly what you have and you don't need to hear it again. Logic does all this using channel strips that offer you a complete view of each track's settings at a glance.

This chapter will not teach you how to create a professional radio-ready mix of your music. It will, however, explain how you can use Logic to achieve the best mix you can and offer some techniques for using Logic to mix in creative and exciting ways.

Mixer or Mixer Layer?

As discussed previously, channel strip objects in Logic show a complete channel strip reminiscent of a hardware mixer channel strip. Logic gives you two options for how you can arrange these channel strips. The first method is to allow Logic to put together your mixer for you.

As mentioned in Chapter 3, Logic creates a mixer, called—wait for it . . . —the *Mixer*, based on the tracks you have in the Arrange window. The other way you can create a mixer is to do so manually, by adding your own channel strip objects to the Mixer layer of the Environment window and organizing them yourself. Each method has its advantages and disadvantages, and they are not mutually exclusive; because any channel strips in the Mixer represent channel strip objects in the Environment, both mixers coexist in the same project. You may prefer to access either or both, depending on your workflow and the specific project on which you are working. The specific features of each mixer are described in this section.

The Mixer

The Mixer is a very powerful tool in Logic. Not only does it reflect all of the MIDI and Audio tracks you have in your Arrange window, but it automatically reflects all channel strip objects in your project that you have created in the Environment. You can access the Mixer from the Window global menu by selecting Window > Mixer or by pressing the key command Command+2. You can also open it inside the Arrange window by clicking on the Mixer button or by pressing X. Figure 11.1 shows the Mixer window.

Figure 11.1   The Mixer reflects all the tracks you have in your project.

One of the best features of the Mixer is that Logic automatically configures it for you—there is no setup at all to do. As you add tracks to the Arrange window, the Mixer automatically reconfigures, too. Also, the Mixer is the only mixer that shows MIDI channel strips, so if you use a fair number of MIDI tracks, the Mixer allows you to see channel strips for your MIDI tracks alongside your audio channel strips.

You can use the channel strip Filter buttons at the top of the Mixer to filter the types of channel strips in the Mixer (omit the Audio tracks, instruments, outputs, MIDI tracks, and so on). You can also use the Single, Arrange, and All View buttons to affect your view in the Mixer.

The Mixer's biggest weakness is that it is limited to only a single horizontal row of channel strips. You could, however, open multiple Mixers, each set to a different channel strip type, and arrange them as you see fit. In fact, you can use the "magnetic windows" feature of Logic Pro 9's windows here to excellent effect, building two Mixers, one above or next to the other, and using the single bar to resize them both (see Figure 11.2). You can even "stick" more than two windows together—for example, stacking two windows on top of one other window—and then you can resize the windows both vertically and horizontally.

Figure 11.2   When arranging Mixer windows, you can take advantage of magnetic windows, allowing you to resize adjacent windows in tandem.

Finally, if you want to rearrange the order of tracks in the Mixer, you'll need to reorganize the tracks in the Arrange window.

The Mixer Layer of the Environment

Because you can create channel strip objects in the Environment, by simply adding multiple channel strip objects in the Environment window, you can create your own custom-configured Environment Mixer layer. The Layer menu includes a command to open the Mixer layer; this command opens an Environment window to the Mixer layer of the Environment. Normally, this is where Logic keeps all of your channel strip objects, but if you create your own mixer on a new layer, the Mixer layer command will not open your custom mixer. The Mixer layer in the Environment can have any shape you want and can include as many or as few channel strip objects in any given layer as you want (with the caveat, of course, that all the tracks in your song will have objects created for them on some Environment layer). Figure 11.3 shows the Mixer layer of the Environment for the same project as in Figure 11.1.

Figure 11.3   The Mixer layer of the Environment offers great flexibility but doesn't automatically adapt to the tracks in your Arrange window like the Mixer does.

The main advantage of building Mixers in the Environment is that you can create and organize them however you like, allowing your Mixer to reflect exactly how you want to work. The Mixer layer does not reflect your Arrange window at all, however. This can create extra navigation headaches; for example, if your Mixer layer contains 64 Audio track channel strips and then three software instrument channel strips, but your song uses only 16 Audio tracks and two software instruments, you'll have to scroll from Audio track 16 through 48 empty Audio tracks to your two software instruments—or continually create Mixer layers reflecting what your song looks like. By contrast, the Mixer can be filtered to only contain your 16 Audio tracks, so you'll have no extra tracks to navigate. On the other hand, in the Mixer layer, you can instantly rearrange any of the objects, so you can simply move your Mixer around or open new layers for different channel strip objects. Of course, since the Mixer layer only contains channel strip objects, it does not show you any of the External MIDI tracks in your Arrange.

Adding Input Channel Strips

Although most Audio tracks can be added to your Logic project in the Arrange window, input channel strips still need to be added in the Environment. In the Mixer layer of the Environment, go to the Channel Strip submenu of the New local menu and select Input. A new input channel strip object will be created in the Mixer layer.

You can add as many mono input channel strips as your audio interface has inputs. If you change an input channel strip's format to stereo, then it will use two of your audio interface's hardware inputs. Therefore, if your audio interface has eight inputs, you could have eight mono input channel strips in Logic, four stereo input channel strips, or any other combination of stereo and mono input channel strips that does not exceed your audio interface's eight total hardware inputs.

What's in a Name?   Although Logic Pro is full of many great features that have simplified previously tedious and confusing tasks, possible new sources of confusion are the names *Mixer* and *Mixer layer*.

In earlier versions of Logic, the Mixer was known as the *Track Mixer,* and it only reflected what was in the Arrange window. The Mixer layer of the Environment was known as the *Audio Mixer,* and it was where you needed to create and configure your audio objects (now known as channel strip objects), which you could then transform into the kind of customized workspace for which Logic is famous. The problem back then was that you needed to add all of your audio objects to the Arrange window in order to have access to them in the Track Mixer, and you didn't have access to MIDI tracks in the Audio Mixer.

Now, in addition to the ability to quickly and easily create any type of track in the Arrange window and have that reflected in the Mixer, the Mixer also automatically reflects anything you add to the Mixer layer of the Environment. The Mixer layer, on the other hand is still crippled by its inability to incorporate External MIDI tracks.

This means that the Mixer will be your preferred mixer in Logic, with the Environment's Mixer layer being reserved for special customization and incorporation of Environment widgets.

The problem is keeping track of which Mixer is which. Unless we state that something is to be done in "the Mixer layer of the Environment" or in some way refer specifically to "the Mixer layer," then "the Mixer" refers to the Mixer that opens in its own window or inside the Arrange window, with its own local menus.

The Mixer Local Menus

Like all windows in Logic, the Mixer includes its own local menus with commands specific to itself. The following subsections describe the Mixer local menus and their options.

The Edit Menu

The Mixer Edit menu contains the typical Edit menu commands, but it does add a few Mixer-specific commands, which you can see in Figure 11.4.

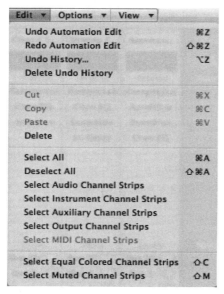

Figure 11.4   The Mixer Edit menu.

Select Equal Colored Channel Strips selects all channel strips of the same color as the currently selected channel strip. The key command for this is Shift+C. You can assign colors to your channel strips by opening the Colors window (View > Colors or press Option+C), selecting a channel strip, and clicking on a color. This also updates the associated track color in the Arrange. Select Muted Channel Strips selects all muted channel strips. The key command for this is Shift+M.

The Options Menu

The Options menu consists of a few miscellaneous functions you may want to use. Figure 11.5 shows the Options menu of the Mixer.

Here are brief descriptions of these functions:

- **Create New Auxiliary Channel Strips.** This command opens the New Auxiliary Channel Strips dialog, which was covered in Chapter 9. The key command for this is Option+Command+N.

Figure 11.5   The Options menu of the Mixer.

- **Create Arrange Tracks for Selected Channel Strips.** This command adds any selected Mixer channel strips to the Arrange window. For example, you can use this command to add Aux tracks to the Arrange from aux channel strips in the Mixer. The key command for this is Control+T.

- **Send All MIDI Mixer Data.** This command sends all the Mixer-related information that is on MIDI tracks to your MIDI devices.

- **Group Clutch.** This command allows you to temporarily disable groups. Groups will be covered in detail in the "Mixer Groups" section of this chapter. The key command for this is Command+G.

- **Change Track in Record Mode.** If you select this option, changing a setting on any channel strip while recording automatically selects that track. If you keep this option deselected, you can change the settings on any channel strip during recording without changing the track that is selected.

- **Change Track in Play Mode.** If you select this option, changing a setting on any channel strip during playback automatically selects that track. If you keep this option deselected, you can change the settings on any channel strip during playback without changing the track that is selected.

- **I/O Labels.** This command opens the I/O Labels window, shown in Figure 11.6.

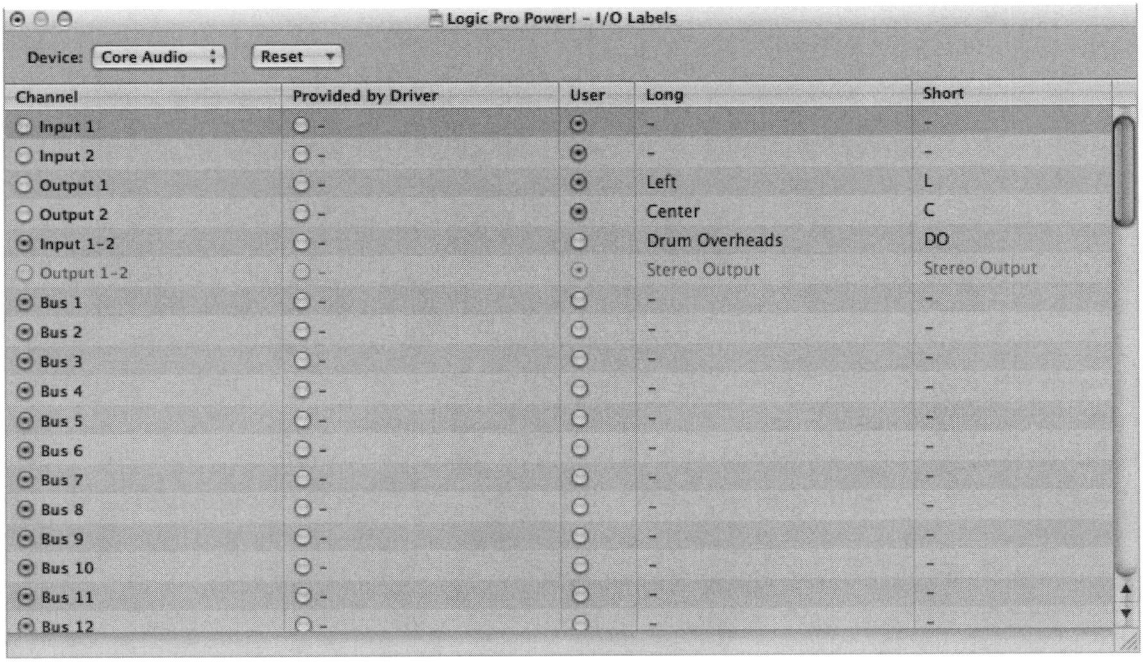

Figure 11.6   The I/O Labels window.

In this window, you can assign names to your inputs, outputs, and busses, which can be provided by Logic (channel), your driver, or you. Double-clicking in the Long and Short columns allows you to assign long and short user I/O labels. The Device menu allows you to select the driver you want to use, and the Reset menu gives you options to reset all the labels or by specific channel type: Input, Output, or Bus. Note that these labels are a global setting and will apply across all projects.

- **Copy Audio Configuration.** This command allows you to copy your entire Mixer plug-in configuration to transfer it into another project. The key command for this is Control+Option+Command+C.

- **Paste Audio Configuration.** This command allows you to paste a Mixer that you have copied to the Clipboard. In order for this command to have a useful effect, you must be pasting to a Mixer containing the same basic channel strip configuration as the Mixer from which you copied. This is particularly useful if you are copying and pasting among Mixers built off the same template project. The key command for this is Control+ Option+Command+V. Logic's extensive Track Import options have largely supplanted this command.

The View Menu

The View menu offers a number of options that relate to MIDI tracks and the overall look of the Mixer. Figure 11.7 shows you the View menu.

The various options in the View menu are as follows:

- **Link Control Surfaces.** If you have a hardware control surface connected to Logic, selecting this option ensures that the track selected in the Mixer always reflects the channel you have selected on your control surface.

- **Scroll To.** This hierarchal submenu includes options that allow you to jump to various track types in your Mixer. The submenu includes the same group of track types as the channel strip filter buttons. These navigation options can be very useful if you have a large Mixer and you keep your track types organized together. If your Mixer is small or you mix up your track varieties, you most likely will not use these options. You can also assign key commands for these options, of course, with which you can navigate among the track varieties even faster.

- **Add Signal Flow Channel Strips.** Selecting this option allows you to see the entire signal flow of channel strips, of a selected channel strip in Single view, or of all Arrange channel strips in Arrange view.

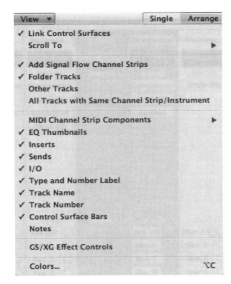

Figure 11.7   The View menu of the Mixer.

- **Folder Tracks.** Check this view option if you want folder tracks to get channel strips in the Mixer. Uncheck this view option if you do not.

- **Other Tracks.** Check this view option if you want other types of tracks that do not have any mixing options, such as a No Output track, to get channel strips in the Mixer.

- **All Tracks with Same Channel Strip/Instrument.** If checked, this option gives you a separate channel strip in your Mixer for each track that accesses the same object. With this option unchecked, if more than one track is assigned to the same object, you will only see a single channel strip for that instrument in the Mixer.

- **MIDI Channel Strip Components.** This submenu allows you to check or uncheck individual components within the MIDI track. You can toggle the Instrument Name, Program, Bank, and Assign 1–5 controls for MIDI track strips by checking or unchecking the relevant components.

- **EQ Thumbnails.** If checked, this option displays the channel EQ thumbnail of each audio/software instrument channel strip in the Mixer.

- **Inserts.** If checked, this option displays the inserts of each audio channel strip in the Mixer.

- **Sends.** If checked, this option displays the sends of each audio channel strip in the Mixer.

- **I/O.** If checked, this option displays the I/O slots of each audio channel strip in the Mixer.

- **Type and Number Label.** If checked, this option displays the channel strip type and number below the I/O slots.

- **Track Name.** If checked, this option displays the track name of each channel strip in the Mixer.

- **Track Number.** If checked, this option displays the track number of each channel strip in the Mixer.

- **Control Surface Bars.** If checked, this options displays which channel strips are being controlled by your control surface.

- **Notes.** If checked, this option displays a Track Notes field under each channel strip. You can double click on a Notes field to create or edit a note, and those changes will be reflected in the parent track's Notes.

- **GS/XG Effect Controls.** This command adds rotary knobs to MIDI tracks. These knobs can control the built-in effects that use the Roland (GS) or Yamaha (XG) General MIDI parameters.

- **Colors.** This opens the Color window so you can assign colors to the various tracks in the Mixer. Any colors you assign to a channel strip in the Mixer will also apply to any tracks and regions in the Arrange window assigned to that channel strip.

The Tool menu

The Mixer's Tool menu consists of two tools, as shown in Figure 11.8.

Figure 11.8   The Tool menu of the Mixer.

The Pointer tool is used for selecting things in the Mixer, for manipulating faders, and so on. The Hand tool is used for moving effects from one slot on a channel strip to another, or even from one channel strip to another. If you Command+Option-click on an effect slot, you can copy it to another slot, as shown in Figure 11.9.

Figure 11.9   You can copy effect settings from one channel strip to another by Command+Option-clicking them.

Mixer Buttons

The Mixer has a number of buttons alongside the local menus. Figure 11.10 shows the Mixer buttons.

Figure 11.10   The Mixer buttons.

The Mixer Link and Hierarchy Buttons

The functions of these two Mixer buttons are as follows:

■   **Hierarchy button.** This button moves you up a level in your project's hierarchy when working with folder tracks.

- **Link button.** If this button is lit, the Mixer follows your Arrange window track selections. The Mixer will also follow your selections in and out of folder tracks on the Arrange.

The Mixer View Buttons

The Mixer View buttons allow you three different Mixer display options. You can also use the Cycle through Mixer Views key command, Shift+X.

- **Single button.** This button displays the selected Arrange track's channel strip.

- **Arrange button.** This button displays the channel strips of all Arrange window tracks. If you have the Add Signal Flow Channel Strips command selected, then all the other channel strips that the Arrange window tracks utilized will also be displayed.

- **All button.** This button displays all the channel strips in your project.

The Mixer Filter Buttons

The Mixer Filter buttons allow you to toggle the display of specific channel strip types. Although only two of these filters have default key commands, the remaining ones can be assigned their own key commands.

- **Audio button.** This button toggles the display of audio channel strips in the Mixer.

- **Inst button.** This button toggles the display of software instrument channel strips in the Mixer.

- **Aux button.** This button toggles the display of auxiliary channel strips in the Mixer.

- **Bus button.** This button toggles the display of bus channel strips in the Mixer.

- **Input button.** This button toggles the display of input channel strips in the Mixer.

- **Output button.** This button toggles the display of output channel strips in the Mixer.

- **Master button.** This button toggles the display of the master channel strip in the Mixer.

- **MIDI button.** This button toggles the display of MIDI channel strips in the Mixer.

Recording Audio from the Mixer

Throughout the rest of this chapter, everything discussed applies to either the Mixer or the Mixer layer. First, you likely need to set up your audio recordings directly from your Mixer. This process consists of two steps.

The first step is to select the physical input you want to use from the Input box of your channel strip. When you click and hold the box, a pull-down menu of all available inputs will appear, as Figure 11.11 illustrates. From this menu, select the input you want to use.

Next, click the R button at the bottom of the channel strip. The R button flashes red, as you can hopefully somewhat discern from Figure 11.12. This indicates that when you press Record on the Transport, the track will record audio.

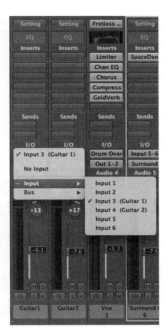

Figure 11.11   From the Input pull-down menu, choose the hardware input you want to use for this track.

Figure 11.12   When you click the R button at the bottom of an Audio track channel strip, it flashes red to indicate that the channel is now armed for recording.

If this is the very first track of audio that you are recording for your song, and you didn't set a record path when you created the project, then Logic will ask you to set the record path for the recording you are about to make. This record path is also where all subsequent audio for this project will be recorded. You'll know that there is no record path set if a dialog box such as the one in Figure 11.13 appears.

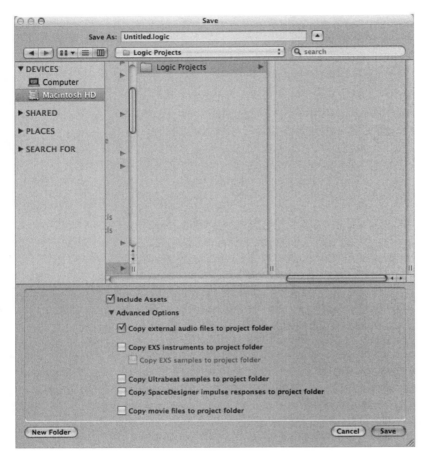

Figure 11.13   If you haven't already set a record path, when you record-enable a channel, a file dialog box will appear, in which you can select the record path for the song.

Repeat the preceding two steps for each track on which you want to record audio, remembering that only one track per input can be armed at any given time. After that, just press the Record button on the Transport (via mouse, hardware controller, or key command) and record away!

Basic Mixing: Summing Volume and Panorama

The most basic mixing that you'll want to do is simply to adjust the volume of one track in comparison to another and to place tracks at different points in the stereo field, or panorama. If this is all you'll ever want to use Logic's Mixers for, then this section will tell you all you'll ever need to do to mix in Logic.

Volume Summing

Because each individual track is usually recorded with an ear toward getting the best recording of that specific source material, you almost never will initially record your tracks at the perfect level in relation to each other. This is why, since the beginning of recorded music, engineers have brought the level of one track up in a mix, while perhaps bringing another track down. The result is creating the perfect balance among all the various sounds in the mix.

You adjust the volume of a channel by moving the onscreen Volume fader on its channel strip. If you are using a mouse, you'll generally be able to adjust only one fader at a time, but if you have a hardware control surface, you may be able to adjust many faders at once. The numbers inside the fader represent either how many decibels you have added or subtracted from the initial volume of the track or the current MIDI volume, from 0 to 127. Figure 11.14 shows a Mixer in which the Volume faders have been adjusted to different levels to create a pleasing overall volume balance.

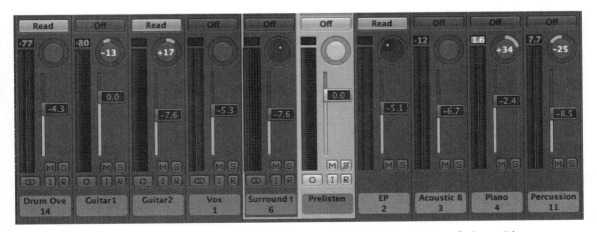

Figure 11.14 Mixing the volume of your tracks is as easy as sliding the Volume faders with your mouse or controller. You can also adjust the volume numerically.

Option-clicking a Volume fader sets it to its *null value,* or the center point at which no adjustment is made. This is 0 dB for decibel faders and 100 for MIDI data faders. Double-clicking the number field in a fader allows you to enter a volume value numerically.

Remember, if you have customized your Transport to include the Pre-Fader button, and you have Pre-Fader metering engaged, you'll only see the input values of your track in the meter, and not the impact of the Volume fader on the track's level.

Panning

The other basic mixing technique you'll find yourself wanting to do is placing tracks at different spots in the stereo panorama. This is known as *panning*. Panning can make tracks more distinct by placing them in a stereo location in which there is no other sound "competing" for the space. The technique can make mixes come alive by making the material sound as if it is coming from all over the stereo spectrum, instead of all sounds originating from the exact middle of the listening field. The Pan rotary knob is above the Volume fader, and you can adjust the pan value for any track by moving the knob to the right or left with either your mouse or a hardware control surface. Pan values range from –64 (full left) to +64 (full right), with 0 being the exact middle. Figure 11.15 shows a pair of tracks that have been panned differently to enhance the mix.

Figure 11.15   To adjust the pan of a track, rotate its Pan knob to the desired setting. You can also directly enter a pan value numerically.

You can double-click the Pan knob to enter a pan value numerically, and Option-clicking on the Pan knob returns the pan value to the center. Shift+Option-dragging lets you move the Pan knob with greater precision. Keep in mind that you can automate these parameters as explained in the previous chapter so that your mix can be dynamic, with automatic changes happening exactly on cue.

The Direction Mixer Plug-In

If you adjust the Pan knob on a stereo track, you aren't really panning the signal between left and right, because the stereo signal already exists in both channels. Instead, you are adjusting the balance between the two channels. Sometimes this can work like panning, but sometimes it won't. If you want more control over the track's stereo panorama, check out Logic Pro's built-in Direction Mixer effect, found in the Imaging submenu of an Insert slot. You can see the Direction Mixer interface in Figure 11.16.

The Direction Mixer will allow you to not only adjust the balance of the signal, but also adjust the width of the stereo image and its location between the two channels. To apply this effect to a stereo signal, select LR as the input. You can then change the perceived width of the stereo signal with the Spread control and the perceived location of the signal with the Direction rotary knob. You can also double-click in either parameter's numerical display to enter a value directly.

This effect is also designed to decode mid-side audio recordings. To decode mid-side recordings with the Direction Mixer, select MS as your input. If you're wondering what mid-side recording is, you probably shouldn't select MS as your input, but the short answer is that mid-side

Figure 11.16   The Direction Mixer effect.

configuration refers to a method for setting up two microphones, one with a figure-eight pattern and another with a cardioid pattern, to accurately record space and depth—but the resulting tracks need to be decoded in order to be used effectively. You can find a discussion of this and other multiple microphone techniques in *Getting Great Sounds: The Microphone Book* by Tom Lubin (Course Technology PTR, 2008).

The Binaural Panner

The Binaural Panner is a very powerful, very flexible stereo imaging tool. It adds spatial directional clues to your audio, giving your source a depth or presence in a mix that a typical pan control can't achieve. To add a Binaural Panner to a mono or stereo channel strip, click on the channel strip's Output box and select Binaural. The Pan rotary knob will be replaced with the Binaural Pan control shown in Figure 11.17.

Figure 11.17   Selecting the Binaural option in a channel strip's Output box replaces the typical Pan rotary knob with the Binaural Pan control.

Figure 11.18   The Binaural Panner window. Double-clicking the Binaural Pan control opens this plug-in-style window.

Double-clicking on the Binaural Pan control opens the Binaural Panner window, shown in Figure 11.18.

You can drag the L or R dots to change the width of the stereo image. The middle circle determines the perceived direction and distance from which the sound will come. If you hold the Command key while dragging the blue dot, you can change the position of your audio while maintaining the same distance. Holding Option+Command while dragging the L or R dot locks the angle so you can tweak the distance.

The Binaural Panner has two modes: Planar and Spherical. Selecting Planar limits the motion of the controls to a plane. The Extended Parameters area of the Binaural Panner interface gives you three Planar mode controls: Vertical Offset, Tilt Amount, and Tilt Direction. These parameters give you control over orientation of the circular plane relative to the listener. Spherical mode, which you can see in Figure 11.18, allows you to simulate the positioning of sound in space.

The Size parameter defines the maximum size of the plane or sphere that the Binaural Panner will allow. The Doppler parameter simulates the pitch shifting that a listener experiences as his distance relationship to a source changes, known as the *Doppler effect*. The Diffuse Field parameter in the Extended Parameters region delivers a more neutral sound to the listener.

The Binaural Panner's effect is most obvious when listening through headphones. That said, the power of the effect is such that you might be tempted to try it on a number of tracks through your studio monitors. To get the most out of the Binaural Panner, send all the channels strips you have set to Binaural through the same aux or output channel strip. In an insert of the destination channel strip, instantiate the Binaural Post-Processing plug-in, found in the Imaging submenu and shown in Figure 11.19.

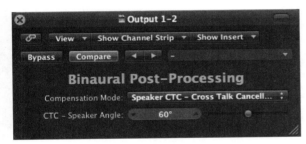

Figure 11.19   The Binaural Post-Processing plug-in.

Set the Compensation mode to Speaker CTC – Cross Talk Cancellation . Then, set the CTC – Speaker Angle parameter to match the angle at which you have your studio monitors.

When using the Binaural Post-Processing plug-in, turn off the Diffuse Field parameter in all of your Binaural Panners, as the Binaural Post-Processing plug-in will handle this operation for all of your Binaural Panner channels, freeing up CPU power.

Bussing Tracks in Logic

When you play back your audio material in Logic, the most direct signal path your audio can follow in order for you to hear it is for the source audio channel strip to output its audio directly to the output channel strip connected to your hardware. Logic offers you more signal path options than this, however. As we discussed when introducing bussing and auxiliary channel strips in Chapter 7, these are basically "parallel mixers" that allow you to send a portion of your signal to another channel strip or that allow you to output a track into another Mixer channel strip for further grouping and processing instead of having to output that track directly to your hardware.

Using Aux Channel Strips

Aux channel strips are perhaps the most powerful and flexible channel strips in the Mixer. When you click the Input box of an aux channel strip, you'll access the Input pull-down menu for the aux channel strip, as shown in Figure 11.20. Notice that the aux channel strip can accept a hardware input, a bus, a ReWire output, or a multichannel output from a software instrument.

Figure 11.20   When you click on the Input box of an aux channel strip, you access its Input pull-down menu.

Using an aux channel strip for multi-output software instruments and ReWire outputs was already discussed in Chapter 9, so the next two sections address using aux channel strips with live inputs and bus inputs.

Using Aux Channel Strips with Live Inputs

Sometimes you may want to record some audio without effects but hear your source audio with some effects on it while recording. One way to do this is by setting up an aux channel strip with a live input as its input source. This allows you to use an aux channel strip as a true "auxiliary mixer," in which one set of audio goes to your hard disk and another goes to the speakers or headphones.

To use an aux channel strip this way, simply select one of your live inputs as the input for the aux channel strip. As soon as the source starts to play, you will hear the audio through the aux channel strip, as well as any Audio track or input channel strip through which the audio is routed. Figure 11.21 shows an example of a setup with both an Audio track and an aux channel strip using the same input for a source.

Such a setup is particularly useful when you have software monitoring turned off so that Logic is not monitoring the actual track doing the recording, and only the aux channel strip is playing back the source material during recording. This is also very useful if your vocalist likes to hear some effects—for example, a bit of reverb or chorus—while recording that are separate from whatever effects you're actually tweaking on the vocal track's audio channel strip; by setting up an Aux track with effects, the vocalist will hear the performance through the Aux with effects, but Logic will record the performance on the Audio track without effects.

Figure 11.21   Here an Audio track will record using audio hardware interface Input 1, while an aux channel is also getting its input from Input 1. The aux channel is being used to add chorus and reverb effects.

Using Aux Channel Strips with Busses

Often you might want to assign a group of channels to a bus so you can use an aux channel strip to process all the tracks together and serve as a master fader for the group. In other words, say your song has 12 tracks of drums (a full drum kit, miked using 12 microphones). In addition to having individual controls for each track, you may want a master fader, or to apply effects to all the drums at once (such as putting them all through the same compressor). Logic allows you to set up an aux channel strip to serve this purpose by using its busses as a virtual patch bay between your source channels and the aux channel strip.

To do this, first you need to set the output setting of your source channels to a bus. Then, set the input of your aux channel strip to the same bus to which you have set the output of the source channels. Figure 11.22 shows a simple setup in which two tracks are using an Aux track as their bus destination.

Figure 11.22   Here the two channel strips on the left are guitar tracks with their outputs set to Bus 10. The channel strip (on the right) is an aux channel strip with its input set to Bus 10. The aux channel strip can now be used as a master fader for the two source tracks, and effects can be added to both tracks via the aux.

If you end up using aux channel strips as master group faders, as in Figure 11.22, we highly recommend you use aux channel strips as described here—having the option to use sends on your master group fader is definitely worth it!

It's also important to note that multiple aux channel strips can use the same bus as an input and that any aux can bussed to another aux, so you can create some complex and creative routings if you desire.

Using a Send to Feed an Aux Channel Strip

If you want to use a send to feed audio to an aux channel strip, simply click and hold a Send box, and a pull-down menu of all your available busses will appear. Select the bus you want and turn the Send knob to send to the bus the amount of audio you want. You then assign the destination aux channel strip's input to the desired bus. Figure 11.23 shows the pull-down menu of a Send box with all the busses available for you to choose.

Figure 11.23   To send audio to an aux channel strip using a send, simply select the bus you want from the Send box pull-down menu and then adjust the Send knob to send the desired amount of signal to the bus. Assign the input of an aux channel strip to the send's bus.

The Send pull-down menu includes options for Post, Pre, and Post Pan. If you select Post, Logic feeds your audio through the send *after* the Volume fader has adjusted its level. If you select Pre, Logic feeds the audio through the send *before* the fader adjusts the volume of the channel. If you select Post Pan, Logic feeds your audio through the send *after* both the Volume fader and the

Panorama knob have adjusted. To turn off a send, you can click on it with the Option key held down. Your Send box will stop glowing, indicating that it is turned off. It still retains the bus you chose for it, so Option-clicking on the send again will reengage it.

Bussing audio to sends is especially useful when you want to use time- and modulation-based effects, such as delay, chorus, and reverb, to process your audio. Because you rarely want to process all your audio using these effects, you can insert the effect into the Insert box of an aux channel strip and send a variable amount of your audio to that aux channel strip, adjusting the Send knob until you get just the right balance for your music. Figure 11.24 shows a software instrument that is using a send to add a reverb that is inserted in an aux channel strip. Inserting effects is discussed in more detail later in this chapter.

Figure 11.24   The channel strip on the left is for a software instrument. The software instrument is using a send to feed the second channel strip, which is an aux channel strip in which Logic's built-in Space Designer impulse response reverb is instantiated. By adjusting the Send knob on the software instrument channel strip, you can control how much reverb is added to the software instrument.

What about Bus Channel Strips?   If you've been using Logic for a long time, you may wonder what happened to bus channel strips—especially if you have projects that use them. Don't worry; bus channel strips are included in Logic Pro 9, but *solely* for compatibility with older projects. Put another way, unless you are working on a Logic project that originated in Logic 7 or earlier, there is no reason why you should ever need to use bus channel strips—auxes do everything bus channel strips did and more. If you're just starting with Logic Pro 9 and have never seen a bus channel strip, aux channel strips do everything you need, and that's all you need to know.

''But why?'' we can hear (well, anticipate) some of you asking. As you can see from the bus channel strip in Figure 11.25, bus channel strips do not have Send or Input boxes, which auxes do.

Figure 11.25   A bus channel strip.

In other words, there's nothing more that you can do with a bus channel strip than you can do with an aux channel strip, and the aux channel strips are much more flexible because of their inputs and sends. For these reasons, whenever you need to bus audio in the Mixer, you should use always an aux channel strip as the bus destination.

Output Channel Strips

Output channel strips are the final destination for your audio; output channel strips connect directly to your hardware audio interface. You can have as many output channel strips as you have physical outputs on your audio hardware. Output channel strips have insert slots for effects, but no sends, since output channel strips portion out audio to hardware, not to additional processing channels within Logic. Output channel strips also don't have Input boxes, as they are destinations for any audio that they receive. These objects include the Bnce button, which allows you to sum all the audio going to that output channel strip into a file on your hard disk.

Usually, a song has only a single output channel strip, which represents the hardware output that leads to your speaker system. Figure 11.26 shows an output channel strip for the main outputs to the audio hardware.

Figure 11.26 This output channel strip is hardwired to Outputs 1–2, the main stereo outputs for the hardware interface used with this project.

Sometimes you might want to use more than the main output channel strip. If you are mixing surround audio, for example, you may need 6–12 outputs, each sending to a discrete input on a hardware surround encoder. Perhaps you are not doing all your mixing in Logic, but sending tracks from Logic into a large studio mixing console. Or maybe you are sending out various tracks to various hardware processors and mixing your song on a tape deck. Whatever your use, you will use output channel strips to interface Logic with your audio hardware.

Using Effects

Mixing is not simply a matter of bringing together multiple source signals. Sometimes, you'll want to process them as well. You can process audio in all sorts of ways—you can compress and distort audio; add EQ, delays, modulation, and reverb; link a track to external hardware for additional processing; and more. In traditional hardware studios, you need to cable an audio channel to a hardware effects processor in order to process a channel with effects. Just as software sequencers feature software mixers, they also feature software effects.

Effects in Logic generally have their own graphic editor that displays the parameters of the effect and often gives you some visual representation of the current effect settings. This is called the *Editor view*. Figure 11.27 shows the Editor view of a Logic effect.

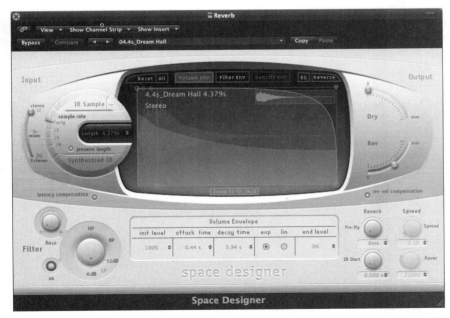

Figure 11.27   This is the graphic control window of Logic's built-in reverb effect, Space Designer. Notice that not only are the parameters given graphic controls, but the impulse response audio file and volume envelope are represented graphically.

Notice that the plug-in window for effects has the same controls already discussed in Chapter 9 regarding software instruments. The menus and functions are identical in their operation, and the windows are fully resizable. You will most often want to use Editor mode to work with your effects because this is where you get the most pleasing user experience, as well as graphical feedback. Sometimes, however, if you know exactly what you want and you just want to adjust a parameter numerically, or if you are working with older effects without graphics, you might want to use Controls mode. As Figure 11.28 shows, when an effect is in Controls mode, no graphics other than a slider for each parameter are displayed. You still have full control over your effect, but you do not get the aesthetic experience or graphical feedback that the Editor mode offers.

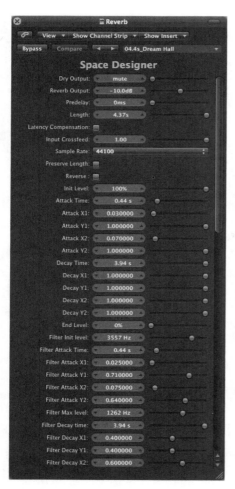

Figure 11.28   This is the Controls window of the Space Designer from Figure 11.27. It displays only a slider for each parameter.

This section explores using audio effects within Logic's Mixer and also offers some tips and suggestions for using effects in a mix.

Logic Effects

Apple ships Logic with a collection of professional-quality effects, which you can access from within Logic's Mixer. You will often hear Logic's effects referred to as *plug-ins,* since almost all other software effects are separate applications that are "plugged in" to a host digital audio sequencer, such as Logic. Logic's effects, while accessed the same way as third-party plug-ins, are in fact built into the code of the application itself, just like Logic's own softsynths. This is why you cannot access Logic's effects in other applications that allow effects plug-ins.

To access a Logic effect, click and hold on an Insert slot in a channel strip. A hierarchal menu opens, listing the effects by type, such as Modulation, Dynamics, and Reverb. Once you select an effect type, another menu will open, displaying the individual effects of the selected type. If the channel is mono, the hierarchal menu that appears will offer you either a mono effect or a mono -> stereo effect, or it may offer you both. If your channel is stereo, your only option is a stereo effect. To instantiate a Logic effect, simply choose a Logic effect from the menus offered. After selecting the effect you want and releasing the mouse button, the effect appears in the Effect slot in the channel strip, and the effect Editor window opens, ready to be configured. Figure 11.29 shows a Logic effect being selected.

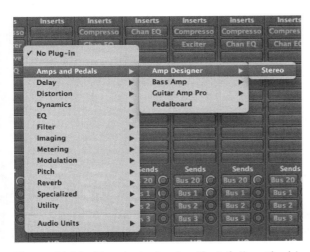

Figure 11.29   To select a Logic effect, follow the hierarchal menus and select the Logic effect you desire—in this case, Amp Designer.

Logic gives you a complete selection of all the effects you will need in modern music production, including all the standard dynamics-based effects (compression, limiting), time-based effects (delay, reverb), modulation effects (chorus, flange), and many completely unique offerings (Spectral Gate, Delay Designer).

Using the Channel and Linear EQ

There is not enough space in this book to go over how to use each effect included with Logic Pro 9. However, there are two plug-ins that interact with the channel strip differently than the others: the Channel EQ and the Linear Phase EQ. Therefore, this unique interaction is explained in this subsection.

As stated, Logic Pro 9 includes two professional-quality equalizer plug-ins: the Channel EQ and the Linear Phase EQ. Both are filters that can adjust the frequency response of your audio; the two EQs look and operate identically. The main difference is that the Linear Phase EQ maintains the exact phase relationship of the frequencies of your audio material, which at extremes non-linear phase EQ algorithms can alter. In other words, it does a better job of maintaining the integrity of your material the more intensely you apply equalization.

The price of this advanced linear phase algorithm is both increased CPU overhead and increased processing delay. We will discuss processing delay later in this chapter, in the "Plug-In Delay and Logic's Plug-In Delay Compensation" section. The point is, you'll want to be judicious in your use of Linear Phase EQs. The Channel EQ is actually just another effect, like any other of Logic's effects. The Channel EQ offers a few special features beyond other plug-ins that are worth noting.

If you have the EQ Thumbnails parameter turned on in the Mixer or in an audio channel strip's Parameter box in the Mixer layer, the top of the channel strip has a rectangular box that displays a thumbnail representation of the current EQ curve, as in Figure 11.30. This EQ thumbnail box offers you both easy access to the Channel and Linear Phase EQ plug-ins and a visual reference of the current EQ curve.

Figure 11.30   A channel strip's EQ thumbnail box above the Inserts parameter. This box is where you can access your Channel EQ and see the current EQ curve.

If the EQ thumbnail box is empty, the box simply displays the letters "EQ." Figure 11.31 shows a channel strip with an empty EQ thumbnail box.

To activate the Channel EQ, you can simply double-click inside the thumbnail box. Logic opens a new window with the Channel EQ plug-in, places a thumbnail of the grid display of the new Channel EQ in the EQ thumbnail box, and instantiates the Channel EQ plug-in into the topmost

Figure 11.31   An EQ thumbnail box for a channel strip that does not have a Channel EQ instantiated.

available Insert slot. You cannot click into the box to instantiate the Linear Phase EQ, but if you add a Linear Phase EQ effect on your own, it also will show its grid in the EQ thumbnail box. As you adjust the parameters in the Channel or Linear Phase EQ, this thumbnail box reflects the EQ curve that is created in the plug-in window. This offers you a quick visual reference as to how you have EQ'd that channel. If you need to make an adjustment, you can double-click the EQ thumbnail box to open the Channel or Linear Phase EQ (depending which you have instantiated).

If you have multiple Linear Phase or Channel EQ effects in one track, only the topmost EQ will have its grid showing in the EQ thumbnail box.

Effects Side Chains

Some effects, such as Logic's Compressor, Expander, and AutoFilter, as well as some third-party plug-ins, have what is called a *side chain* input. A side chain is an input to an effect or plug-in that allows another Audio track to trigger that effect or plug-in. You can use side chains to configure an effect to activate only when another signal is present. One example of this would be to have a compressor on a bass track triggered by a kick drum on another track, so that the bass is compressed only when the kick drum sounds, in order to create a tighter feel for the rhythm. Side chains are also very useful for "ducking" (making a signal softer when another signal is present), for vocoder effects and instruments (where an audio channel is sent into the side chain of a vocoder software instrument to "play" the vocoder), and so on. The side chain input looks like an additional pull-down menu on the plug-in window control bar, as shown in Figure 11.32.

To select a track to use as the side chain input, simply select an available audio source from the pull-down menu, as in Figure 11.33. The track that you choose triggers the operation of the effect.

Not all plug-ins or effects have side chain inputs, but for those that do, it opens a whole new creative way to use effects.

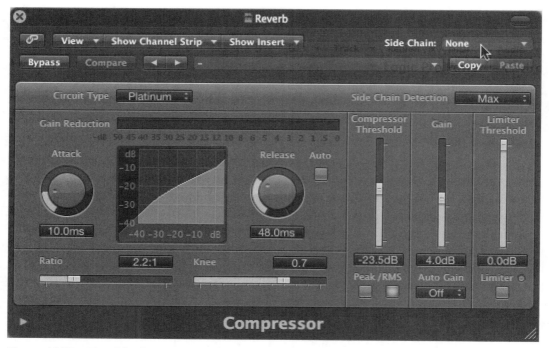

Figure 11.32   The side chain input can be seen on the Compressor effect in Logic as a new pull-down menu on the far right of the control bar.

Figure 11.33   To use one of these available tracks as the side chain trigger, select it from the pull-down menu.

Expert Tip: Using the Side Chain Input to Rescue Lackluster Kick Drums   Producer, co-author of *Logic 7 Ignite!,* and Logic guru Don Gunn offers his expert method for how you can use the side chain input feature to add "guts" to a kick drum performance that isn't punchy enough:

"If you find yourself mixing a song and the kick drum just isn't providing the bottom end you'd like, there's an easy way to create low-frequency content. This tip utilizes Logic's software instruments as well as the side chain feature on the Noise Gate plug-in.

"With your kick drum track in the Arrange window, assign an unused bus to one of the sends; as you can see in Figure 11.34, I've used Bus 23.

"Next, create a Software Instrument track and assign the track a software instrument of your choice for generating low tones. In Figure 11.35, I've used the ES2, but any of the built-in Logic synthesizers (ESM, ESE, ESP) will work as well. You can see that to create the tone, I'm using one oscillator set to generate a sine wave, as well as the secondary sine sub-oscillator for additional fatness.

"Now insert a Noise Gate plug-in on the Software Instrument track and assign the side chain input to the bus that was assigned to the send on the kick drum track, as shown in Figure 11.36.

"If you play this track as it is currently set up, you will still only hear the original kick drum; for the instrument to produce sound, it needs a note that is affected by the incoming signal via the Noise Gate side chain. You can see in Figure 11.37 that I

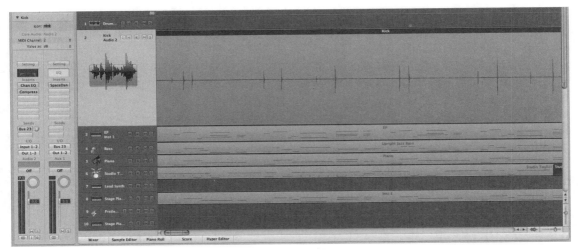

Figure 11.34   To begin the process of adding low-frequency content to a lacking kick drum, assign an unused bus to a send; here, Bus 23 is assigned.

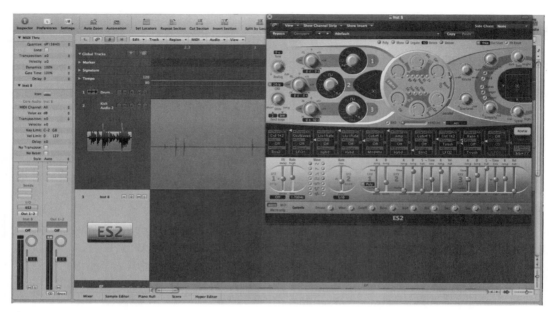

Figure 11.35 Next, Emagic's ES2 synthesizer is instantiated in a Software Instrument track. This instrument actually generates the new low-frequency content.

have inserted the note A1 and made its length be the duration of the kick drum region that needs reinforcement. One benefit to this technique is that you can have the kick drum trigger a note that is in key with your song, helping to reinforce the notes being played by the bass part.

"At this point, when the song is played back, the kick drum will trigger the side chain on the Noise Gate to open, allowing the tone of the synthesizer to go to the output. Using the envelope controls in the Noise Gate (Attack, Hold, Release), you can make the tone of the synthesizer longer or shorter; give the note a short, clipped attack; or have the low-frequency material swell in behind the original kick drum. You can also adjust the sensitivity of the Noise Gate with the Threshold and Reduction parameters. Experimentation is the key, and while the Drum Replacement/Doubling function gives you one great tool for beefing up a kick drum, this side-chain method can produce results that the other method just can't achieve!"

Audio Units Effects

You may want to use an effect not included with Logic, or you may prefer to use a different version of an effect than the one Logic includes. Toward this end, all versions of Logic allow you to use third-party effects plug-ins within the Mixer as well. As discussed previously, these third-party applications literally "plug in" to Logic's Mixer and offer extended processing functionality from within Logic. There are a number of different plug-in formats with which

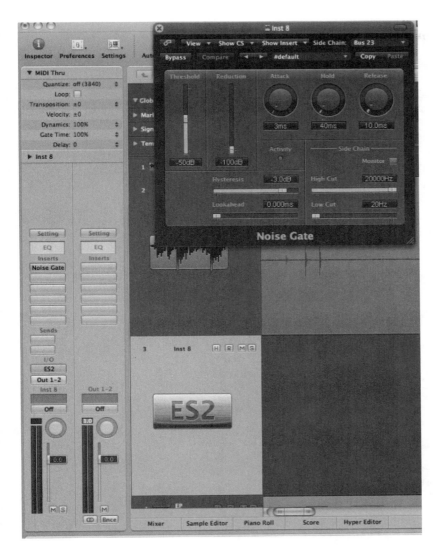

Figure 11.36   A Noise Gate plug-in is inserted onto the Software Instrument track with its side chain input set to the same bus used in Figure 11.35.

different sequencers are compatible, and Logic Pro 9 is compatible with Apple's native Audio Units (AU) format.

To access third-party effects, you follow the same basic procedure as you use with Logic effects. The difference is that instead of selecting Logic effects, you select Audio Units and then choose your effect from the list of manufacturers. Remember that if you're running Logic in 64-bit mode, 32-bit effects will be found in a separate menu and will launch via the 32-Bit Audio Unit Bridge. You will have to click in the effect's plug-in window to open the plug-in's GUI in the 32-Bit Audio Unit Bridge. Figure 11.38 shows a third-party 32-bit Audio Units effect being selected.

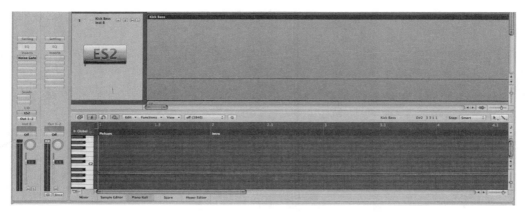

Figure 11.37 In the Piano Roll Editor, a single note that is the duration of the entire audio region is used to trigger the software instrument controlled by the Noise Gate side chain.

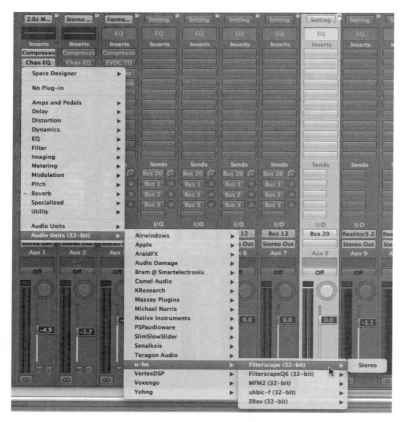

Figure 11.38 To select a third-party Audio Units effect, you follow the same general procedure as when selecting a Logic effect, except that you follow the hierarchal menu of Audio Units plug-ins. 32-bit Audio Units effects will be run in the 32-Bit Audio Unit Bridge, and you will have to click in the plug-in window in Logic to access the plug-in GUI in the Bridge.

Expert Tip: Plug-In Format Converters   What if a third-party effect that you really want to use within Logic is not available in the format that Logic supports? Well, in most cases, you are simply out of luck. However, if the plug-in you wish to use is available for the Mac OS X VST format, you can use the VST–AU Adapter from FXpansion to convert Mac OS X–compatible VST effects to Audio Units. Unlike "wrapper" plug-ins that basically require you to run two plug-ins (the original third-party plug-in and the wrapper plug-in) so that you can use an additional format, the FXpansion VST–AU converter actually creates a working Audio Units plug-in from those third-party plug-ins with which the adapter is compatible. Be sure to check out www.fxpansion.com for the latest third-party plug-in compatibility charts and pricing if you are interested in this. As with so many other things, as of this writing, there is no 64-bit VST–AU Adapter, and FXpansion's website does not officially state compatibility with Logic 9 or Mac OS X 10.5 or 10.6. Therefore, you should proceed with caution if you're going to give VST-AU wrapping a go.

The Audio Units Manager

As you can imagine, there are hundreds of third-party Audio Units effects available, some of which come in bundles that are quite inexpensive. You may find that in no time flat your lists of available AUs will become huge! Thankfully, Logic Pro 9 includes a much-requested feature: an integrated way to manage your Audio Units plug-ins. This is called the *Audio Units Manager*. You launch the Audio Units Manager by selecting Logic Pro > Preferences > Audio Units Manager, which you see in Figure 11.39.

The Audio Units Manager displays each of your Audio Units plug-ins in a row, one after the other. The Audio Units Manager contains seven columns.

- **Logic.** Check this box if you want a plug-in to appear in the plug-in menus within Logic. Uncheck this box if you do not.

- **Nodes.** Check this box if you want a plug-in to be available for use on a Logic Node. Note that not all plug-ins can be run on a Node. Nodes will be explored in more detail in the section "Logic Nodes—Distributed Audio Processing" later in this chapter.

- **Name.** This is the name of the Audio Units plug-in.

- **Manufacturer.** This is the name of the developer of the Audio Units plug-in.

- **Type.** This column tells what kind of plug-in each Audio Units plug-in is, such as effect, instrument, or MIDI-controlled effect.

- **Version.** The version number of the Audio Units plug-in.

- **Compatibility.** This column tells you whether the plug-in passed, failed, or crashed Apple Computer's Audio Units Validation scan. Audio Units Validation is covered in the next section.

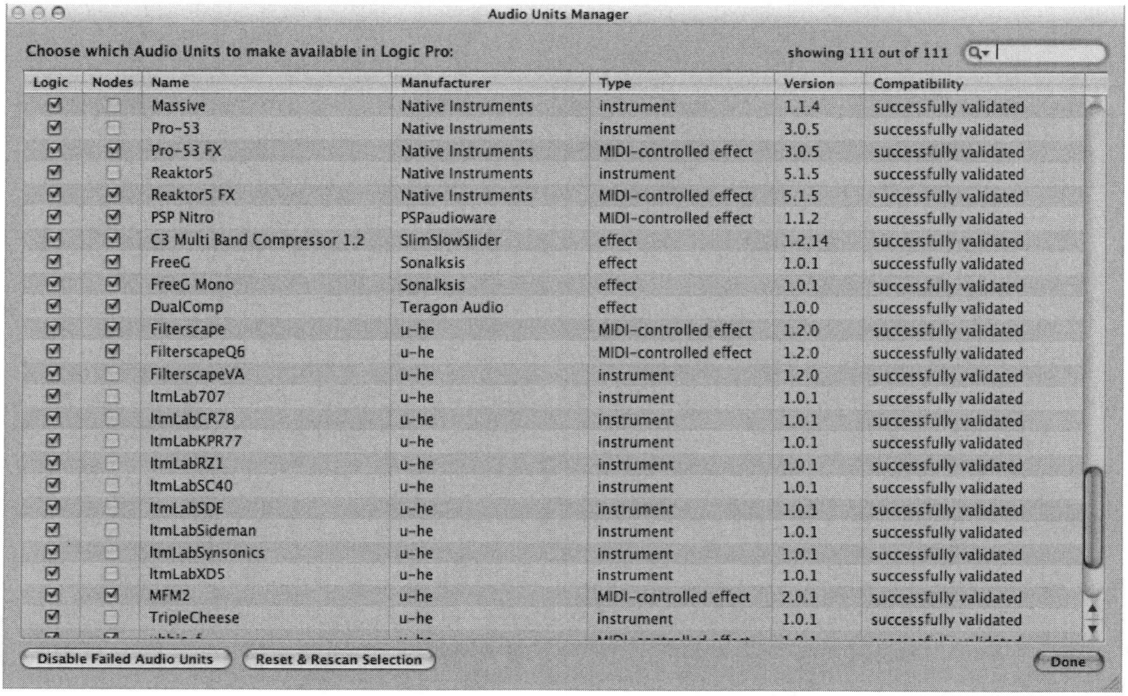

Figure 11.39   The Audio Units Manager. You can check and uncheck the Logic boxes to select which AUs will be available in the plug-in menus in Logic Pro 9.

Using the Logic AU Manager couldn't be easier. If you don't need an AU to appear in the plug-in menus within Logic, uncheck the box in the Logic column. If you want to reactivate a plug-in that you deactivated, recheck its box. When you're finished, simply click the Done button at the bottom-right of the Audio Units Manager.

The Audio Units Manager includes one additional, vital function besides Audio Units management. It also scans your Audio Units for compatibility with the Audio Units format and deactivates them for you if they fail or crash validation. This is explained in more detail next.

Initial AU Scan.   Apple wants Logic Pro 9 to be the most stable audio application possible. To ensure this, they take pains to test the application rigorously before release. Unfortunately, third-party plug-ins, such as Audio Units, are not within Apple's power to test and debug. In the past, this has meant that plug-ins that didn't "play nice" with Logic could crash Logic, or in some cases, bring down your entire computer! To help mitigate this, Apple created a free test diagnostic application for developers—the AU Validation Tool. This tool basically runs a number of diagnostic tests on an Audio Units plug-in in an attempt to ensure that it properly complies with the Audio Units format specifications and will not destabilize the host application.

When you first run Logic Pro 9 and every time you install a new Audio Units plug-in, Logic will scan the plug-in with AU Validation to test it for compatibility and stability. Normally, all you will see is a progress bar indicating scanning is taking place, and that's it. When Logic Pro opens, your new plug-ins will be available in the appropriate menus.

Sometimes, however, you may find that a plug-in you installed does not appear in the menu. This most likely means that the plug-in failed validation. At this point, if you open the Audio Units Manager, you will find that your plug-in is not checked, along with the message that it failed or crashed validation. Figure 11.40 shows an AU plug-in that has failed the Logic AU Validation scan.

☐	☐	MonalisaAudioUnit	Monalisa-au.org	effect	1.0.0	failed validation
☑	☐	Absynth 4	Native Instruments	instrument	4.0.4	successfully validated

Figure 11.40   Here you see one Audio Unit plug-in that passed the Validation scan and is checked for use in Logic Pro and another unchecked plug-in that did not pass the Validation scan.

If you believe that the scan results were somehow incorrect, you have the option to hit the Rescan button. The Audio Units Manager will then rescan just the selected AU and present you with the results, as shown in Figure 11.41.

If the plug-in still fails validation, we highly recommend that you contact the developer with the information that their plug-in fails AU Validation. If you want to be extra helpful, you can even copy and paste the rescan results into an email and send it directly to the developer, saving them from having to run it themselves. It is up to the developer to release an update that will comply properly with the Audio Units specifications. When they do, Logic will scan the updated plug-in, it will pass the scan, and your plug-in will work properly!

Activating Incompatible AU Plug-Ins.   What if you absolutely, desperately need an incompatible Audio Units plug-in within Logic in order to finish a previous project or the like? For these emergency situations, you *can,* if you want to, activate an incompatible plug-in within Logic. To do this, simply click its Logic box, just like a compatible plug-in, as shown in Figure 11.42.

Audio Units that you activate this way are filtered into their own special hierarchal menu for incompatible plug-ins, as shown in Figure 11.43.

We *highly* recommend against activating incompatible Audio Units unless for some compelling reason you have no choice. The whole purpose of scanning Audio Units is to try to ensure that Logic Pro will not be destabilized by an errant plug-in. If you activate a plug-in that crashes or fails validation, you defeat the whole purpose of the scan! This is truly a feature of last resort. Waiting for an update that successfully passes AU validation is always the best policy.

Using Insert Effects

Insert effects are really simple to use, as we have already discussed—simply select an insert effect for a slot, and you're ready to use it! Bypassing an insert effect is just as easy. To bypass an

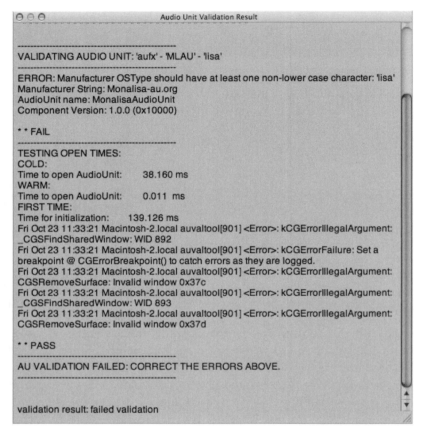

Figure 11.41   Here is the same plug-in after being individually scanned by Apple's AU Validation Tool in the Audio Units Manager.

| ☑ | ☑ | Spectral Tracing | Michael Norris | effect | 1.0.0 | successfully validated |
| ☑ | ☑ | MonalisaAudioUnit | Monalisa-au.org | effect | 1.0.0 | **failed validation** |

Figure 11.42   Even if a plug-in fails its AU Validation scan, you can still activate it at your own risk, as shown here.

insert effect, Option-click on that insert. The insert will stop glowing, indicating the effect is bypassed.

Saving or Loading Channel Strip Settings

In addition to being able to save and load individual effects settings, Logic gives you the option to save and recall entire configurations of channel strip inserts—including software instruments. If you click and hold the Setting box on a channel strip, a pull-down menu like the one in Figure 11.44 will appear, offering you options to save, load, and navigate channel strip settings.

Figure 11.43   Any incompatible Audio Units that you activate
will be available to you in the [Incompatible] submenu.

Figure 11.44   Clicking the Setting box on a channel strip opens the
Setting menu, where you can manage and navigate channel strip settings.

The functions of the commands in the Setting menu are as follows:

- **Next Channel Strip Setting.** This command changes the configuration of the channel strip to the next channel strip setting. The key command is Shift+].

- **Previous Channel Strip Setting.** This command changes the configuration of the channel strip to the previous channel strip setting. The key command is Shift+[.

- **Copy Channel Strip Setting.** This command allows you to copy an entire channel strip configuration to the Clipboard so you can paste it into another channel strip. The key command is Option+Command+C.

- **Paste Channel Strip Setting.** This command allows you to paste an entire channel strip setting from the Clipboard into a channel strip. The key command is Option+Command+V.

- **Reset Channel Strip.** The Reset Channel Strip command allows you to quickly remove all plug-ins from a channel strip.

- **Save Channel Strip Setting As.** This command allows you to save your own channel strip settings. When you save a channel strip setting, a Save dialog like the one in Figure 11.45 opens.

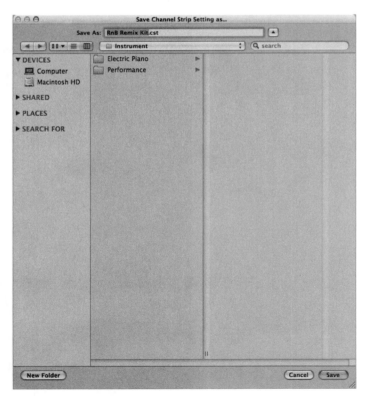

Figure 11.45 The Save Channel Strip Setting As dialog.

It is helpful to create a new folder structure inside the default folder to organize your channel strip settings. Otherwise, all of your channel strip settings will show up as a list in the Setting menu. Figure 11.46 shows a Setting menu with two instances of the same software instrument channel strip setting—one saved in the default Instrument folder, and another saved in a folder created inside the Instrument folder.

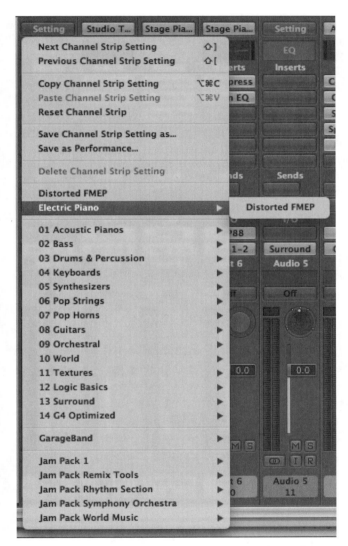

Figure 11.46   This Setting menu shows one channel strip setting directly in the menu and another that has been nested in a submenu. Creating subfolders in the Save Channel Strip Setting As dialog allows you to create submenus in the Setting menu, which will help you keep your channel strip settings organized.

- **Save as Performance.** This command allows you to save your channel strip setting as a performance, which will allow you to recall the channel strip setting via a MIDI program change message. Selecting the Save as Performance command opens the Save Channel Strip Setting as Performance dialog shown in Figure 11.47.

Figure 11.47   The Save Channel Strip Setting as Performance dialog. Saving your channel strip setting as a performance gives you the ability to recall your channel strip setting via a MIDI program change message.

Simply name your performance, enter the program change number you wish to use in the Program Number box, and select OK. You can now use a program change message with the number you selected to recall your channel strip setting. Be aware that the program change message will transmit on MIDI channel 1.

- **Delete Channel Strip Setting.** This command allows you to delete the current channel strip setting.

Beneath the Setting menu commands you'll find submenus full of channel strip settings. Channel strip setting files include all the insert effects instantiated on the channel strip (complete with their effects settings as they were saved), and if you are on a software instrument channel strip, it will include the software instrument as well. The beauty of channel strip settings is that you can save configurations of channel strip inserts that you use regularly—for example, if you have a particular set of plug-ins you like to use to process vocals. You can save them as a channel strip setting and have quick access to your favorite configuration at all times. Logic Pro comes with a very wide variety of factory preset channel settings for you to explore as well—give them a listen!

Using Send Effects

Using a send to add effects to a track is a bit more complicated than using inserts, because sends don't directly connect to effects; instead, they connect through busses to aux channel strips. To use a send to add effects, you assign a bus to a send, then add the effect you desire in an insert of the aux channel whose input is assigned to that bus. You control how much of your audio signal is bussed to the aux via the Send rotary knob.

Plug-In Delay and Logic's Plug-In Delay Compensation

Most effects do their processing nearly instantly. Some, however, do not. They may involve highly mathematically complex processes, like convolution reverbs such as Logic's Space Designer. They might have a "look ahead" feature, by which the effect increases its accuracy by scanning the recorded audio—literally "looking ahead" before it processes it, which requires that the effect hangs on to the audio signal for a while instead of instantly processing it. Some Audio Units plug-ins run on FireWire or PCI Express or ExpressCard DSP devices, such as the UAD-2 cards or the TC PowerCore; it takes time to get the audio out to these devices. The point is that some devices and plug-ins will introduce a delay into your signal path if you use them. This can be a real problem. For example, if you have two tracks that are both in sync with each other and set to play at Bar 1.0.0.0, but one track has plug-ins that introduce 2,000 samples of delay, that track will play late and out of sync. If you are not careful, plug-in delay can really ruin your song.

Luckily, Logic tries to make things a bit easier for us. There is a Compensation menu in the General tab of the Audio Preferences window for plug-in delay compensation, as shown in Figure 11.48.

Figure 11.48 The Compensation menu in the General tab of the Audio Preferences window. You can determine how plug-in delay compensation will work in your project from this menu.

There are three options in the Compensation menu: Off, Audio and Software Instrument Tracks, and All. Off means there will be no plug-in delay compensation. If you're not using any plug-ins that need compensation, then this is the preferred setting. Selecting Audio and Software Instrument Tracks will automatically adjust any of your Audio and Software Instrument tracks to be in sync with any other Audio and Software Instrument tracks that have delay-causing effects on them. Selecting All allows you to compensate for delay-inducing plug-ins across your entire project, including outputs and auxes. All is the default plug-in delay compensation mode of Logic Pro 9.

Keep in mind that plug-in delay compensation only works during playback, not during recording. If you have no choice but to record with plug-ins that cause some processing delay, be sure to use Low Latency mode, as explained in Chapter 5.

Final Notes on Using Effects

Using effects is arguably one of the most dramatic ways to alter an audio mix. Sometimes, the effects become instruments themselves, and their processing is an integral part of the music, but like all things, it's very easy to get carried away both musically and computationally if you are not careful.

Keep in mind that your computer has only a finite amount of CPU power. If you try to process every track to death in a large project, you'll most likely overtax your computer to the point that your project no longer plays back. And if you *really* overdo it, you might so overextend your resources that your project won't play unless you engage Freeze for every track! Of course, this is exactly the situation for which you will want to use Logic Nodes, which are described in the following section. Also, don't forget to utilize Bounce in Place whenever possible—once a track is finished, there's no point in having it steal more CPU cycles than are absolutely necessary.

If you are using a fair amount of software instruments and effects in a given song, keep a close watch on your system performance to make sure your computer is up to your demands. You can get a gauge of Logic's audio CPU and hard disk usage from the load meters in the Transport, which you can open in their own window by double-clicking on them. This is another advantage to using some effects on aux channel strips and having tracks access them via sends—you can have more than one track access the same aux, thereby saving you from having to instantiate that same effect on more than one track.

Beware of the pitfall of EQing and effecting one track until it is perfect when played by itself, but then it muddies everything up when placed in the context of the mix. That infinite delay line that you love so much might just start getting jumbled when you bring in 24 more tracks and it's been repeating for 90 seconds! Even as you work on perfecting individual tracks, always try to keep a holistic view of what you want the completed project to sound like. Logic Pro's signal analysis effects—Correlation Meter, Multimeter, and Levelmeter—can help you get a better picture of your material, where there is too much "signal energy," and where you might want to adjust your mix to sound more open or less overloaded. The saying "less is more" definitely applies to mixing!

Lastly, remember that there are no hard-and-fast rules as to how to add effects to a mix. Listen to effects on a lot of your favorite CDs, read magazines and books that discuss effects placement and usage in detail (Course Technology PTR sells a fair number of books on mixing; go to courseptr. cengage.com to check them out), and, of course, don't forget to experiment for yourself!

Logic Nodes—Distributed Audio Processing

As explained earlier, if you use a lot of effects and software instruments, it's very easy to run out of processing power. Even with a top-of-the-line 8-core Mac Pro, if you run dozens of software instruments along with scores of effects, you're going to bring your computer to its knees. Bounce in Place is a great solution for when you are finished with some tracks, and Freeze is great for when you want to load a song onto a computer that isn't beefy enough to run it normally—for example, if you want to open a song that you composed on your Mac Pro on your MacBook, you can freeze all the tracks on your Mac Pro, then copy the entire project to your MacBook. Still, freezing your whole song isn't very conducive to spontaneous composing or mixing, and depending on how you performed a Bounce in Place you may or may not have included effects and possibly even deleted the original region. Enter one of the aces up Logic Pro's sleeve: Logic Nodes, also known as *distributed audio processing.*

The idea of using many computers to process audio is not new. People have been hooking up multiple computers for a long time. First, simply using audio and MIDI connections, users could configure an auxiliary computer as if it were simply another external sound module, just like a synthesizer. Steinberg raised the bar from there by developing VST System Link. This was a protocol that used an available digital audio channel to send both audio and MIDI between VST plug-in hosts. It was a real breakthrough—the first time that users could legitimately harness the power of additional computers to run software plug-ins. But VST System Link was very clunky and inelegant, requiring multiple cables to get a two-way connection between computers. It required that users keep track of two project files, one on each computer, and that users manually load all the VST plug-ins on the client computer that would be available on the host. Because it relied on the digital clock inside multiple audio interfaces for synchronization, it was very prone to sync errors.

Apple may not have been the first to the table when it presented the Logic Node method of distributed audio processing, but they certainly developed the most elegant and intuitive implementation to date.

Using only a single Gigabit Ethernet connection between computers, you can use any connected computer as a Node to process Logic's effects and synthesizers. You can use a MacBook as your main Logic Pro computer and then attach it to a network of Logic Node Mac Pros if you want. You could use an old MacBook as your main Logic Pro computer and have an entire rack of Xserves for a truly monstrously powerful studio. As you will see in the next section, the configuration is absolutely minimal. Simply install the Logic Node application on the Macintosh you wish to be the Node, and then the rest is handled from within the Logic Pro application. Simple. Neat. Efficient. The way it should be!

Using Nodes

As explained previously, the first step is to have installed the Logic Node application onto the computer you wish to be a Node. The Node computer should have its firewall turned off. At this point, you're ready to turn on Nodes in Logic Pro. Open the Nodes tab via Logic Pro > Preferences > Audio, and you will see a simple check box to turn on Node processing and a list of all available Nodes on your network, as shown in Figure 11.49.

To enable Logic Nodes, simply check the box enabling Logic Nodes and any individual check boxes for attached Macintosh computers running the Logic Node application.

After that, any time you want a Node to handle the processing of the built-in effects and synthesizers on an Audio or Software Instrument track, simply click its Node button, as shown in Figure 11.50. The button graphic will change from three dots to a right and left arrow, indicating the track is distributing its processing to the Node.

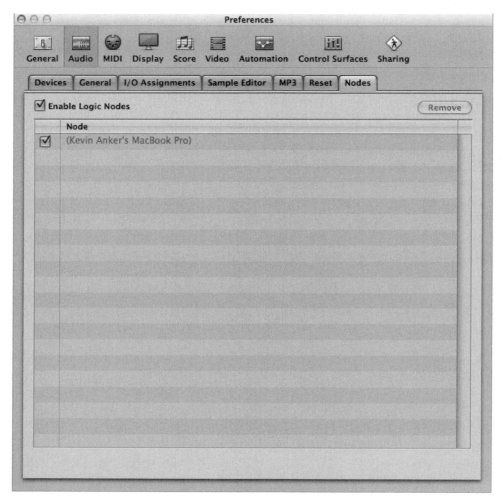

Figure 11.49   The Nodes tab of the Audio Preferences window. Here you can enable Logic Nodes and any Macintosh computers attached as Nodes.

Figure 11.50   By clicking the Node buttons on the two bottom tracks, all of the Logic effects and plug-ins on these tracks will be processed on the active Logic Node.

That's all there is to it! You send or stop sending each Audio and Software Instrument track to a Logic Node by clicking the Node button. You can tell how heavy the load is on your various Logic Nodes by looking at the Load Meters window. You'll notice that when Nodes are turned on, the Load Meters window will expand to include a Nodes meter.

Current Limitations of Logic Node Technology

Logic Nodes make mixing huge songs more possible than ever—especially when you consider that you can have up to 128 Nodes attached to one main Logic Pro system! But you should also be aware of the limitations of using Logic Nodes in Logic Pro 9.

First of all, you can't use the EXS24mkII Sampler; any multi-output instrument, such as Ultrabeat; or any Audio Units software instruments. Many Audio Units effects, however, can be used on Nodes as long as you are running the same version of the plug-in on your host and your Node.

Also, sending the audio across an Ethernet cable and back again takes time. Luckily, Logic Pro 9's automatic delay compensation handles this seamlessly.

As of this writing, Logic Node processing is not available in 64-bit mode, so if you plan on using Logic Nodes, you'll need to run Logic in 32-bit mode.

Finally, Apple Computer lists Intel Macs as the minimum system requirement for Logic Studio, including the Nodes, and all Intel Macs have featured Gigabit Ethernet, which was a previous recommended feature of a Logic Node. Does this mean that you can't hook up a Macintosh without Gigabit Ethernet, such as the iMac G5? Or that you can't use a G4 as a Node? As the Logic Node is still a Universal Binary, meaning it has code for both Intel and PPC architectures, slower Ethernet and Macintosh computers can possibly work as Nodes; there is no technical reason that it wouldn't work, but the extra horsepower available from a G4 will be minimal. And not having Gigabit Ethernet reduces the throughput of your Logic Node. So while you can certainly try to hook up your old G4s and other computers to get a little more power for your system, you may find that the payoff is small. Also, since Apple does not actually list support for PPC processors with Logic Studio, you won't be able to get any support from Apple if you have problems with your G4 or G5 Logic Nodes.

Muting Channels

From Chapter 6, you're already familiar with the Mute button on each track of the Arrange. That button mutes or unmutes either a single track or all tracks routed to a single channel strip, depending on the Track Mute/Solo setting in the General tab of the Audio Preferences window. Each channel strip also has a Mute button at its bottom, as shown in Figure 11.51. Clicking this button mutes or unmutes the channel in question.

Muting a channel strip mutes the Mixer output of all dependent tracks of the muted channel strip, regardless of the Preference setting. If you have the Track Mute/Solo Preference set to Fast

Figure 11.51   The button with the M is the Mute button for this channel strip. If mute is engaged, the button on the channel strip glows light blue.

(Remote Channel Strips), then muting a channel strip in the Mixer engages the Mute button of all the channel strip's dependent tracks in the Arrange window. If you have the Track Mute/Solo Preference set to CPU-Saving (Slow Response), you can still activate a channel strip's dependent Arrange window track's Mute buttons remotely by Option-clicking. This can be useful for temporarily lightening a track's CPU load while mixing.

Soloing Channels

Each channel strip, except for output channel strips, has a Solo button like the one in Figure 11.52. When the Solo button is engaged, all other channel strips, other than dependent aux channel strips and output channel strips, are silenced unless they have their Solo buttons engaged. When one or more tracks are soloed, the M's in the Mute buttons of the non-soloed tracks flash.

Figure 11.52   When the Solo button of a channel strip is activated, all non-soloed channel strips are silenced, except for output and aux channel strips. The Solo button will glow yellow when activated.

Keep in mind that Solo does not silence output channel strips, because output channel strips are necessary for the soloed tracks to be heard. Also, soloing channels is strictly an audio function; MIDI tracks are not muted unless their audio is routed into Logic. Additionally, soloing a channel strip that is bussed to an aux channel strip does not mute the dependent aux, as you can see in Figure 11.53.

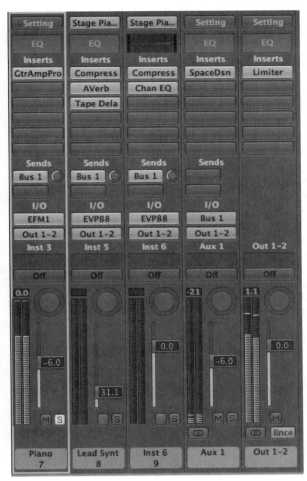

Figure 11.53   Soloing a channel strip that is bussed to an aux channel strip does not mute the dependent aux. Here you can see signal in the level meters of the soloed channel strip, its dependent aux channel strip, and the output channel strip.

If you are using an aux as the destination of a send and do not wish to hear the processing you are applying on the aux while soloing a parent channel strip, you can mute the aux.

Soloing an aux channel strip passes all audio routed to that aux through to its output. If the parent channel strips are assigned to an output channel strip, then their output signal is muted. In Figure 11.54, Aux 1 is using Bus 1 as an input. The three software instrument channel strips to the left of Aux 1 are sending signal to Aux 1 through Bus 1. Notice that while there is no signal registering in any of the software instrument's level meters, Aux 1 is sending signal to the output channel strip.

Figure 11.54 When you solo an aux channel strip that is the destination of a send, the dry signal of its parent channel strips is muted. The aux still receives signal from its parent channel strips through its input bus and sends its soloed signal to the output channel strip.

This can be very handy for dialing in the settings on insert effects with precision.

It's important to note that the Solo button in the Mixer interacts with the Solo buttons in the Arrange window in a similar way to the Mute buttons depending on the Track Mute/Solo Preference. Also, Option-clicking a currently unsoloed channel strip will solo that particular channel strip and turn solo off on any currently soloed channel. Option-clicking a soloed channel strip turns solo off on any currently soloed channel strip, including the selected track.

Because of the many different ways that soloed channels can interact, you may want to solo safe certain channels in your project. What is Solo Safe mode, you ask? Good question . . .

Solo Safe Mode

If you want to make sure that no matter which tracks are soloed, you never silence certain tracks, effects, busses, and so on, you can make them solo safe to exempt them from being silenced. Control-clicking the Solo button turns on Solo Safe mode for a given channel strip. You can tell whether a track is in Solo Safe mode because its Solo button will have a line through it, as in Figure 11.55. Control-clicking the Solo button a second time disengages Solo Safe mode.

Figure 11.55   A red line through an unactivated Solo button on a channel strip indicates the channel strip is in Solo Safe mode.

Mixer Groups

Sometimes you may want to link some properties of different channel strips—for example, you might want the volume, solo, and mute functions of all your drum tracks to change together as a group, or you might want to link the Pan control of a group of tracks that are all panned to the same location. The Group function allows you to do this and more. You can use the Group function not only to group Mixer operations, but also to link Arrange window functionality for group editing.

The Group slot is the dark-gray display window directly below the channel label in each channel strip, as illustrated in Figure 11.56. This is where you can select and create groups. You can create as many as 32 groups, and channels can belong to multiple groups.

Figure 11.56   Directly under the channel label and above the Automation Mode menu is the Group slot. In this figure, the channel strip is assigned to Group 1.

Assigning Channels to Groups

To assign a channel to a group, click in the Group slot on the channel strip. A pull-down menu will appear with the numbers (and names, if assigned) of all 32 possible Mixer groups, as well as the option to open the Group Settings window. Select the group number you want and then release the mouse. The number of the group you have selected appears in the Group display of your channel strip. Figure 11.57 shows the Group pull-down menu.

You can assign a channel to more than one group by holding down Shift while selecting groups in the pull-down menu. If you Option-click in the Group slot, the last Group selection is applied to the current channel strip. This is especially handy for quickly assigning a large number of channel strips to the same group.

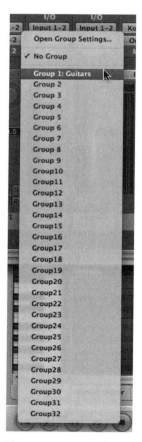

Figure 11.57   In the Group pull-down menu, you can choose the number of the group to which you want to assign your channel, or you can open the Group Settings window.

Group Settings

You can access the Group Settings window in two ways. If you assign a group to a channel, but you have not yet defined that group, the Group Settings window will automatically open. You can also select the Open Group Settings option in the Group pull-down menu if you want to define or change the settings of a group. Figure 11.58 shows the Group Settings window.

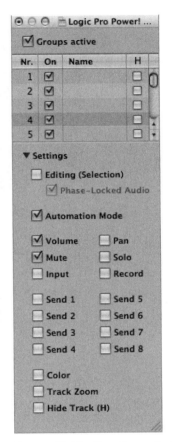

Figure 11.58   The Group Settings window.

The window contains a list of options, each with a check box (except for the Name option). If you check the box next to an option, that option will be set to the group. So, if you adjust the control or do any editing or automation in one channel in the group, that action affects all channels in the group. The following list describes the various options.

■ **Groups Active.** This check box allows you to turn all groups on or off globally.

■ **Groups List.** This list lets you control the following group options.

- **Nr.** This column dispays each group's number.

- **On.** To turn a particular group on, select its check box.

- **Name.** In this text box, you can type a name for your group. The name of the group will appear in the Group display in the channel strip, at least the first 7 or 8 letters, along with the group number.

- **H.** Selecting a group's H check box hides that group. If one or more tracks in the group are already hidden, the check box will display a dash in it, but you still have the ability to hide all the group's tracks by clicking on the check box. This is different from using an individual track's Hide function, as you have to access this menu to toggle a group's Hide status.

- **Group Settings area.** The group Settings area lets you configure what functions affect your group as a whole. The group settings are:
  - **Editing (Selection).** With this option selected, if you select a region on one track in the group on the Arrange, every track in the group will have any regions at the same relative time in the song selected.

  - **Phase-Locked Audio.** With this option selected, a group that has Editing (Selection) enabled will remain phase-locked if you quantize its audio.

  - **Automation Mode.** Changing the Automation mode of one member of the group changes all of them.

  - **Volume.** Changing the Volume fader of one channel strip in the group changes all of them. Note that these are relative changes, so if two channels in the group are at different volumes, Logic raises or lowers both volumes by the amount of the change to the group, but they retain their relative difference in volume.

  - **Mute.** If one channel in the group is muted/unmuted, every channel in the group is muted/unmuted.

  - **Input.** With Input selected, all tracks in the group will utilize the same Input setting.

  - **Pan.** Logic adjusts the panorama of every channel in the group if you adjust one channel's pan. As with the Volume option, all channels retain their relative differences from each other.

  - **Solo.** If one channel in the group is soloed/unsoloed, every channel in the group is soloed/unsoloed.

  - **Record.** Record-enabling/disabling one channel in the group record-enables/disables all of the channels in the group.

  - **Send 1–8.** As with the Volume and Pan options, if you check any of these sends, Logic links them.

- **Color.** If you assign a color to one member of the group, all of them are assigned that color.

- **Track Zoom.** Adjusting the zoom of one track in the group zooms all the tracks in the group.

- **Hide Track (H).** If you hide one track in the group using a track's H button, all members of the group are hidden.

When you link the automation of a group, any track can be the "master" that you use to control the mode, and if you draw or write automation for any linked parameter, Logic writes the automation for each individual track in the group. Therefore, if you later ungroup your tracks, they will still have the automation you wrote. There is also a "clutch" to disable group links temporarily, if you want to adjust one single track without affecting the rest of the group. You can access the Toggle Group Clutch command by pressing Command+G. The numbers in the Group slot change color from yellow to gray as a visual cue that the group clutch is engaged.

Temporary Groups by Selecting Multiple Channel Strips

There is also a very down-and-dirty way to make a change to more than one fader without going through the process of creating a group. If you just want to adjust the Volume faders of four channel strips, for example, you can select them all, either by Shift-clicking on them or via a "rubber band" selection with the Pointer tool (if they are contiguous) in the Mixer. Logic Pro indicates which channels are selected by their color; they will all be light gray instead of dark gray. Once selected, you can adjust an attribute on one of them, and all of the selected tracks will also adjust. You can click anywhere outside the selected channel strips to deselect the channel strips.

Bouncing Your Mix

At any point in the mixing process, you might want to "bounce" your mix down to a stereo (or surround) master mix. This is different than the Logic's Bounce in Place function, where you are bouncing individual tracks and automatically adding them back to the project—the goal of bouncing here is to provide a usable, listenable audio file for use outside of Logic. The term *bounce* originated from the days in which this process required you to play your audio from a multitrack tape machine and then re-record your mixed audio onto a stereo tape deck—hence "bouncing" the audio from one tape deck onto another. With computer recording, however, bouncing to a file requires far less setup and effort, so you no longer need to wait until your mix is complete to bounce tracks—you can bounce mixes regularly during the mixing process to listen to them on different stereos, to share your mixes with others, and so on.

Because bouncing consists of outputting your mix, Logic puts the Bounce button on the bottom-right of output channel strips, as well as the master channel strip when you are working in surround. It is the button labeled Bnce, as shown in Figure 11.59.

Figure 11.59   Press the Bnce button of an output channel strip to display the Bounce dialog box and create an audio file of your mix.

There are two other ways to bounce your mix. You can select the global Bounce command from File > Bounce. This will only bounce Outputs 1–2. If you have one or more output channel strips in the Arrange window, you can click the Bnce button on an output channel strip to bounce its dependent Audio tracks.

The Bounce Dialog Box

When you select the command to bounce audio by any of the aforementioned means, the Bounce dialog box appears, as shown in Figure 11.60. This window contains all your options to bounce your mix down to a file.

The top of this window consists of a standard Save As dialog box where you can type in a file name and navigate to the directory to which you want to save your bounced audio. Underneath the navigation bar on the left are your four file type selections in the Destination table.

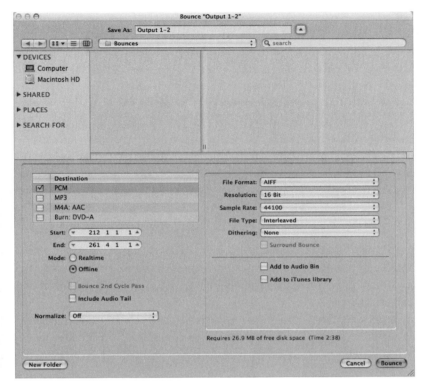

Figure 11.60   In the Bounce dialog box, you can set the parameters for how to bounce your mix.

- **PCM.** This option bounces a standard, uncompressed audio file into AIFF, Broadcast WAV, or Sound Designer II format.

- **MP3.** This bounces to the MP3 compression format.

- **M4A.** This bounces to either the AAC or the Apple Lossless compression format. The selected sub-format will be listed after M4A, such as M4A: AAC.

- **Burn.** This song burns your Logic project onto a recordable CD or DVD. The selected sub-format will be listed after Burn, such as Burn: CDDA.

Below the Destination table, Logic lets you enter the start and end positions of your bounce by click-dragging in the Start or End field, by clicking on the arrows for the desired field, or by double-clicking in the desired field and entering a value manually. If you have Cycle mode engaged, the start and end positions will reflect the cycle region. If you have Cycle mode disengaged and have a region selected in the Arrange, the start and end postitions will reflect the boundaries of the selected region. Otherwise, the start and end positions will reflect the length of the entire project.

Bounce Mode Options

Once you have your start and end potitions set, you can choose between Realtime or Offline Bounce mode. In Realtime mode, Logic plays the selection you want to bounce and prints the file as it is playing. The advantage of this mode is that you get to hear exactly how the bounced file will sound, and you can include the signals from input channel strips. However, it can be slow if the file is long. In Offline mode, Logic bounces your mix internally. If your Logic song is not taxing your CPU, offline bouncing can be much faster than real-time bouncing. If your song squeezes every last bit of your CPU to do complex processing, offline bouncing will not be faster than real-time bouncing—in fact, since offline bouncing is limited to running on a single CPU core, if you are using a multi-core Mac, offline bouncing may be many times slower than a real-time bounce. If your song is too complex to play in real time at all, you can still do an offline bounce—but it will take longer than if you played your song in real time.

Below the Realtime/Offline radio buttons are two check boxes that let you dictate a couple of very specific aspects of your bounce. The first option, Bounce 2nd Cycle Pass, works when you are bouncing a cycle region. Logic will play through one cycle of the region and then bounce the second cycle. The tails from effects such as reverbs and delays from the first pass will end up bounced at the front of the second cycle. The other option, Include Audio Tail, automatically lengthens the bounce to include all effect tails. For final mixes in particular, this option should be checked to avoid clipping your track's end prematurely.

Nomalize Options

Below the Bounce mode options is the Normalize drop-down menu shown in Figure 11.61.

Figure 11.61   The Normalize menu.

The Normalize menu gives you three options for normalizing your bounce: Off, Overload Protection Only, and On. Normalizing means a file is scanned to find its highest peak, and the level of that peak is increased to the highest possible level (technically, 0 dBFS) without clipping, and the level of the rest of the audio is raised by the same amount. If you select Off, your bounce will not be normalized. If you select On, your bounce will be normalized in the manner described. If you select Overload Protection Only, Logic will perform a very specialized normalization. The file will be scanned for any overloads, and those peaks will be decreased to 0 dBFS, leaving the rest of your bounce unaltered. The Normalize feature in the Bounce dialog is really a special feature—be sure to read the note on it for the full skinny.

When to Use Logic's Floating-Point Bounce   The Normalize functions in the Bounce dialog are actually quite special: They use floating-point math instead of fixed-point math. This means that they normalize the floating-point audio information and then map each bit to its optimal level in the final fixed-point audio file. The result is that the full dynamic range of Logic's 32-bit or 64-bit floating-point audio engine (depending on whether you are in 32-bit or 64-bit mode, respectively) is preserved much more accurately than the traditional fixed-point Normalization feature, such as the one found in Logic's own Sample Editor. Traditional fixed-point normalization methods may result in distortion or audio degradation, but the floating-point Normalize features of the Bounce dialog will never compress, limit, or distort your audio.

So does this mean that you should always use Normalize your bounces? It depends. Here are some guidelines:

- If your peak levels are already at 0 dBFS, the floating-normalize feature will do absolutely nothing, so there is no point.

- If you're delivering your final bounce to a mastering engineer, he generally won't want your peak levels to be at 0 dBFS, so in this case, don't normalize your bounce.

- If the levels of your audio are above 0 dBFS (in other words, if it sounds like your track is digitally clipping), be sure to normalize using the Overload Protection Only option. It will re-map your audio to 0 dBFS, your audio will not be clipped anymore, and your overall bounce will maintain its accuracy.

- If you are bouncing a single track to be reused in your Logic project, and you want to make sure you bounce at the optimal level, use the On setting.

- If you're bouncing particularly dynamic material to a compressed file format, such as MP3 (unavailable in 64-bit mode) or AAC, using the Normalize feature will help you get optimal dynamic range into the compressed file.

As you can see, while normalization is not a cure-all or something you always want to use when you bounce, Logic's exceptional floating-point Normalize features are extremely useful in the right circumstances.

Near the bottom of the Bounce dialog, Logic informs you how much disk space you'll need for your bounce and how long your file will be. You also have options to create a new folder for your bounces, to cancel the operation, and to commence the bounce.

You can bounce to multiple file formats by checking the Destination boxes of more than one file type. The Bounce parameters to the right of the Destination table will change depending on which destination is highlighted. The parameters for each bounce destination will be explained in the following subsections.

Bounce to PCM

This bounce destination includes bouncing to uncompressed Sound Designer II, AIFF, Broadcast Wave, or CAF files. Figure 11.62 shows the PCM destination parameters.

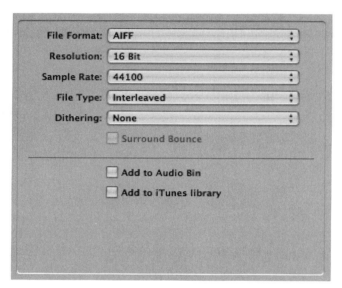

Figure 11.62   The PCM bounce destination parameters.

The parameters for this bounce are:

- **File Format.** This is where you select Sound Designer II (SDII), AIFF, Broadcast Wave (Wave), or Core Audio Format (CAF) for your PCM bounce. There is no sonic difference among the different formats. What format you bounce to ultimately can be guided by compatibility—if you are bouncing audio that will be imported into another DAW or across platforms, you'll want to bounce in the most compatible format for the destination application. For example, WAV is the native audio format on PCs. If you are sending audio files to someone who is working on a PC, it will probably make the most sense to bounce your audio to WAV. In general, if you are only working with the audio on your Macintosh, AIFF and CAF are the native formats, although AIFF is ubiquitous.

- **Resolution.** Here you can choose the file bit depth for your bounce. Your choices are 8-, 16-, or 24-bit. You will almost never want to print an 8-bit bounce. If you are going straight to CD, you might want to print a 16-bit file with dither (see the description of the Dithering option later in this list). Normally, you'll want to archive your mix at 24 bits, which is the highest bit rate that Logic currently allows.

- **Sample Rate.** You can select the sample rate for your bounced file here. Logic will default to the same sample rate as your Logic song, but you can change it to any of 12 different sample rate options between 11 kHz and 192 kHz. If you select a different sampling rate than the sample rate of your song, Logic will sample rate convert your bounced file using its very high quality sample rate conversion algorithms.

- **File Type.** This option is available only if you are bouncing a stereo file. If your destination file is an SDII file, some applications cannot import interleaved SDII files and require split stereo files (meaning you bounce one file for the left track and another for the right). Unless you know you need split stereo files, leave this set to Interleaved. If you are bouncing a mono file, this will be grayed out.

- **Dithering.** If you are bouncing your 24-bit audio to a 16-bit file for CD or compressed format uses (for example, MP3, Internet), you'll want to turn on dithering. Normally, when you save 24-bit audio into a 16-bit file, the 8 bits that don't make it to the 16-bit file are simply those that happen to be filling the lowest bits of the audio stream. Unfortunately, sometimes you have desired audio in those bits, and this truncation can end up sounding harsh. Dithering adds imperceptible amounts and frequencies of noise to your file, so that the noise "pushes" all the desired audio into the 16 bits that are saved, and only the noise is eliminated. As you can imagine, not all dither is created equal. Logic includes the industry-standard POW-r dithering algorithms. There are three algorithms—the first is plain, and the second and third have various amounts of noise shaping to attempt to tailor the dither even more to your audio material. Logic also includes the Apogee UV22HR dithering algorithm. Use the algorithm that sounds best with your material. If you are bouncing 24-bit files, leave dithering off.

- **Surround Bounce.** If you are bouncing for a surround mix, Logic will bounce to any of the six surround formats it supports. If you turn on Surround Bounce, this grays out the Add to iTunes Library option. Logic doesn't do any actual surround encoding or decoding, so if you plan to do a surround bounce, you need additional hardware or software (such as Compressor, which is included in the Logic Studio bundle) to play and encode the bounced files in the proper format. Unless you need to bounce surround files, you should leave this set to Off.

- **Add to Audio Bin.** This check box allows you to add the bounced file to the Audio Bin for reuse in your Logic song. This is very useful if you are only bouncing a small portion of audio to capture some effects processing or you are doing a real-time bounce to record audio from inputs and you want the result to be available for later use.

- **Add to iTunes Library.** This check box will add the bounced file to iTunes for you. This is a great timesaver if you like to audition your mixes in iTunes or you want your song to be ready to add to your iPod, and so on. This option is grayed out if you are bouncing a surround file.

Bounce to MP3

MP3 (or MPEG-1 audio layer 3) currently reigns as the ubiquitous compression format for sharing music across platforms. Figure 11.63 shows you the MP3 destination parameters. Bounce to MP3 is unavailable in 64-bit mode as of this writing.

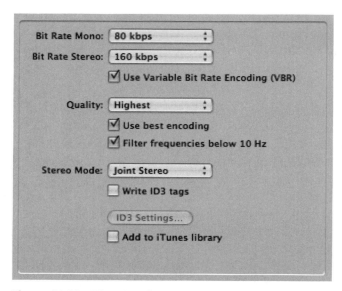

Figure 11.63   The MP3 destination parameters.

The parameters for this bounce are:

- **Bit Rate (Mono/Stereo).** You can select bit rates between 32 kbps and 320 kbps. Typically, bit rates of 160 kbps or 192 kbps offer the best balance between quality and file size for MP3 compression. The quality improvement for bit rates above 192 kbps is minimal.

- **Use Variable Bit Rate Encoding (VBR).** Check this box if you want to use variable bit rate encoding instead of constant bit rate encoding. Variable bit rate encoding compresses simpler passages more heavily than more harmonically rich passages, which in theory encodes better-quality MP3s at a smaller file size.

- **Quality.** If you use VBR encoding, this pull-down menu allows you to select the quality of your variable bit rate. Generally, you should keep this set to Highest. Reducing the quality speeds up the conversion process, but at the expense of audio quality.

- **Use Best Encoding.** If you uncheck this option, you gain encoding speed at the price of audio quality. Again, you should always keep this setting checked.

- **Filter Frequencies below 10 Hz.** Frequencies below 10 Hz are usually not reproduced by speakers and are not audible to human ears anyway. Such frequencies can, however, create a muddier MP3. If you check this box, Logic removes those frequencies, leaving slightly more data bandwidth for the frequencies that people can hear and resulting in an improvement in perceived quality.

- **Stereo Mode.** You can choose between Joint Stereo and Normal Stereo modes. The differences are very subtle, if any, so go ahead and experiment to see which sounds better on your source material. Don't be surprised if both sound the same. This option is not available for mono bounces.

- **Write ID3 Tags.** MP3 files can have ID information, such as song title, artist, and so on encoded with the audio. If you want to enter this information for your bounce, check this box.

- **ID3 Settings.** If you check the Write ID3 tags box, this button will be available; click it to open a window in which you can enter song title, artist, album, genre, and other information. ID3 tags are useful if you plan to share your MP3 or you want the information to display in iTunes. Otherwise, there's no need to bother.

- **Add to iTunes Library.** This check box will add the bounced file to iTunes for you. This is a great timesaver if you like to audition your mixes in iTunes or you want your song to be ready to add to your iPod, and so on.

Bounce to M4A

AAC, or Advanced Audio Coding, and Apple Lossless are the "next generation" of audio encoding, based on the MP4 (MPEG-4) format, the successor to MP3. Figure 11.64 shows you the M4A destination parameters.

Figure 11.64   The M4A destination parameters.

AAC gets better audio quality at the same bit rate compared to MP3. Apple Lossless is a format that compresses the audio to a smaller file size than an uncompressed format, with absolutely no loss of data or quality. AAC and Apple Lossless files can be decoded by iTunes and QuickTime on both Mac OS X and Windows. AAC is also compatible with some other media players and is used by the iTunes Music Store for its commercially available songs.

When you select M4A in the Destination window, there are only four visible options.

- **Encoding.** You can choose to encode your audio in AAC or Apple Lossless format.

- **Bit Rate.** You can choose the bit rate of your AAC file from between 16 kbps and 320 kbps. Typically, bit rates of 160 kbps or 192 kbps offer the best balance between quality and file size for AAC compression. The quality improvement for bit rates above 192 kbps is minimal. If you are bouncing in Apple Lossless format, this option is grayed out.

- **Encode with Variable Bit Rate (VBR).** Check this box if you want to use variable bit rate encoding instead of constant bit rate encoding. Variable bit rate encoding compresses simpler passages more heavily than more harmonically rich passages, which in theory encodes better-quality AACs at a smaller file size. If you are bouncing in Apple Lossless format, this option is grayed out.

- **Add to iTunes Library.** This check box will add the bounced file to iTunes for you.

Bounce to CDDA/DVD-A (Burn)

This option lets you bounce your Logic project directly to a CD or DVD. This option does not allow you the complete facilities for properly mastering a commercial CD—for that, you'll want to use WaveBurner, which came bundled in Logic Studio. If you want to quickly bounce your Logic project to a CD-R/CD-RW or DVD-A to audition it in various stereo or surround systems, to share with friends, and so on, this option will do the trick. Figure 11.65 shows the Burn destination parameters.

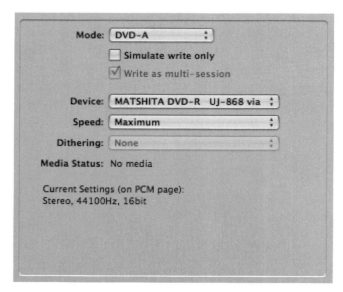

Figure 11.65 The Burn destination parameters.

The parameters for this bounce are:

- **Mode.** This pull-down menu allows you to choose between CDDA (*Compact Disc Digital Audio*) and DVD-A (*Digital Versatile Disc Audio*).

- **Simulate Write Only.** If you want to try a test run to make sure that everything is set up and working properly to do either a CDDA or a DVD-A burn, check this box.

- **Write as Multi-Session.** If you write your session as multi-session, you will be able to write other files to the CD-R after you burn your Logic project. If this box is unchecked, Logic will "close" the CD-R when it is finished. If you want to use your CD-R for more material, check this box. Otherwise, leave it unchecked. If you are bouncing to DVD-A, this option is grayed out.

- **Device.** This drop-down menu allows you to select any connected CD or DVD burner.

- **Speed.** This allows you to select the maximum speed your CD or DVD burner can write to disc or any lower speed your drive is capable of. How many options appear here will depend on your model of drive.

- **Dithering.** Refer to the dithering definition in the "Bounce to PCM" section earlier in this chapter.

- **Media Status.** This tells you what kind of disc is in the selected drive.

Method Tip: Including MIDI Tracks in Your Bounce   Clearly, bouncing your Audio tracks from an output channel strip includes only audio. What if you want to include the output of your MIDI hardware modules in your bounce file?

There are basically two ways to go about this. The first method requires that before you do your final bouncing, you record the output of all your MIDI hardware into Audio tracks in Logic. This takes extra time, but it allows you to move and edit your newly recorded MIDI as you would any other audio performance, which you may enjoy. Once your MIDI has been committed to Audio tracks, Logic bounces them with all your other Audio tracks. This is especially easy if you use the External Instrument effect as described in Chapter 9. Simply send the output of your Software Instrument track to a bus, then create an Audio track and set its input to the same bus to record it into your song. You can do this simultaneously for all your MIDI hardware.

If you want to keep your MIDI hardware in the MIDI realm as long as possible and never record it as audio, one way to do this is simply to delay doing the above until right before you print your final bounce. However, if you know that you'll never want to record your MIDI in advance, you can instead create input channel strips for all of your MIDI hardware modules. Because input channel strips are audio channel strips, you can mix, process, and bounce them to a file just like the audio on any other audio channel strip. Using input channel strips requires that you have as many physical hardware inputs as you have MIDI module outputs you want to use. Creating input channel strips is a bit more complicated because you can't create them on the Arrange; you can only create them on the Mixer layer of the Environment. But using the Mixer layer of the Environment, you can create an entire "input mixer" if you want, for just this sort of thing.

Also, to compensate for your audio hardware latency, you may need to adjust the setting Delay All MIDI Output that you can access by choosing File > Project Settings > Synchronization and going to the MIDI tab. If you don't know exactly how much latency your audio hardware has, and its documentation lists no approximations in milliseconds, then you can use trial and error to determine the point at which your audio sounds in sync with your MIDI.

Surround Mixing

In addition to allowing for the usual stereo mixing, Logic Pro 9 includes complete, comprehensive, and arguably best-in-class support for surround mixing, including surround effects, panning, and bouncing functions. Logic supports the most common surround formats (such as quad, Pro Logic, 5.1, and 7.1) and even some additional, more esoteric surround formats. To access Logic's surround functions, you must have audio hardware with more than two physical outputs. Logic also offers surround upmixing and downmixing in software.

Changing an audio channel strip from a mono or a stereo channel to a surround channel is very simple. Click and hold the Format button, which opens a pull-down menu, and then select Surround, as shown in Figure 11.66.

Figure 11.66 If you want an audio channel strip to be a surround object, select Surround from the Format pull-down menu.

When an audio channel strip is placed into Surround mode, its Panorama dial is replaced by special Surround control, as shown in Figure 11.67. Your surround speakers are represented by colored dots and the pan position by a white dot. You can grab the white dot and rotate it anywhere around the Surround control.

You can mix stereo and surround objects in the same Logic song with no restrictions.

Figure 11.67   After placing an audio channel strip into Surround mode, its Pan dial changes into a special Surround panorama control like the channel above.

The Surround Panner Window

If you double-click the Surround control on a surround channel, you will open a Surround Panner window like the one shown in Figure 11.68. This gives you a more detailed view of the surround panorama, as well as access to the surround format, LFE Level, and Center Level.

Figure 11.68   In the Surround Panner window, you can access the surround format, LFE Level, and Center Level, and also see a more detailed image of the surround panorama.

The Surround Panner window offers you more options than just grabbing and moving your signal in the surround panorama. To lock the diversity, you can hold Command down while dragging the blue dot. You can also hold down Command+Option to lock the angle while dragging, and you can hold down the Option key to reset the angle and radius to the exact center.

The slider at the bottom of the window is the Low-Frequency Enhancement, or LFE, control. Generally, the LFE channel is a subwoofer, but it doesn't have to be. This slider controls how much of the signal from this channel is directed toward the LFE channel. The Center Level determines signal level at the dead center of the surround panorama.

The Extended Parameters area offers three controls: Separation XF, Separation XR, and Separation Y. Separation XF changes the separation of the front left and right channels. Separation XR changes the separation of the rear left and right channels. Finally, Separation Y changes the separation of the front and rear speakers.

Assigning Surround Channels to Audio Outputs

You determine which physical output will correspond to which surround channel in the Output tab of the Surround tab of the Audio Preferences window. You can access this dialog box from the global menus, by choosing Logic Pro > Preferences > Audio. Selecting the I/O Assignments tab will open the dialog box shown in Figure 11.69.

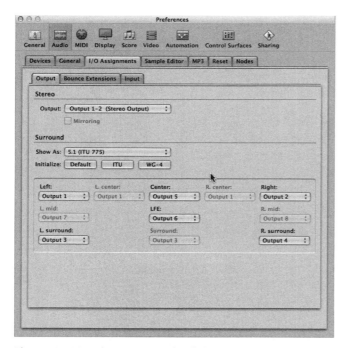

Figure 11.69 The Output tab of the I/O Assignments tab of the Audio Preferences window.

In the Show As pull-down menu, you can select which surround format Logic will output. At this point, the appropriate pull-down menus are accessible for assigning your hardware outputs to the surround channels dictated by your chosen surround format. You might want to place a low-pass filter effect into the Insert box of the output object that is your LFE, since that is the standard LFE cutoff for surround subwoofer channels. The three buttons under the Show As menu allow you to select the Default, ITU, or WG-4 configuration of hardware outputs automatically, without having to set each pull-down menu manually.

Applying Surround Effects

Logic supports the use of surround effects, and some of Logic's own effects have native 5.1 support. You can insert Stereo > 5.1 effects on stereo channel strips and 5.1 effects on surround channel strips, such as surround software instrument channel strips and master channel strips.

Applying Surround Effects to a Surround Channel Strip

Inserting a surround effect on a surround channel strip is just as easy as inserting a stereo effect in a stereo channel strip. Simply select an Insert box and navigate to the effect you would like to insert and then select whichever format the plug-in offers for your project's surround format, such as 5.1 or Multi Mono, as shown in Figure 11.70.

When you instantiate a Multi Mono effect, you'll notice that the effect's Editor window offers new tabs that are unavailable on stereo or mono effects, which you can see in Figure 11.71.

The Configuration tab allows you to alter the content and number of the remaining tabs. Clicking the Configuration tab reveals a new set of controls in the plug-in window, as shown in Figure 11.72.

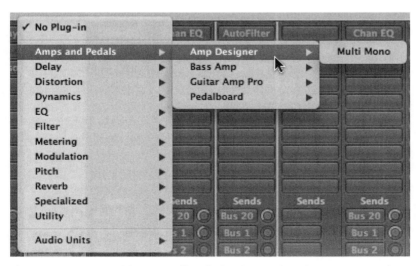

Figure 11.70   A Multi Mono effect being instantiated on a surround aux channel strip.

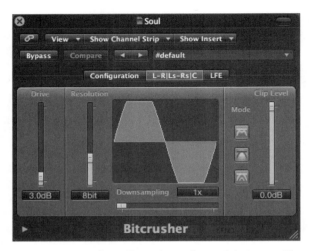

Figure 11.71   The Editor view of a Multi Mono effect.
Notice the Configuration, L-R|Ls-Rs|C, and LFE tabs.

The Link menus under each surround channel in the Configuration tab allow you to assign each channel to a linked group: A, B, C, or –. Each Link group has its own tab, which appears as channels are added to that group. Each tab basically allows the effect to act as a dedicated effects unit for the channels assigned to that tab. The – option assigns the selected channel to its own individual tab. You can see in Figure 11.73 that the L, C, and R channels have all linked in the same tab, and that the Ls and Rs channels are each assigned to discrete tabs, and that the LFE

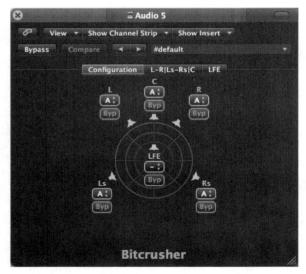

Figure 11.72   Clicking the Configuration tab reveals
a new set of controls in the plug-in window.

Figure 11.73   The L, C, and R channels coming through this effect have been linked to Group A, allowing them to be processed together. The Ls and Rs tabs are being processed individually, while the LFE channel is not being processed.

channel is bypassed. This means that the L, C, and R channels are being processed with the same plug-in setting, while the Ls and Rs channels can each be processed separately within the same plug-in instance, and the LFE channel undergoes no processing. You can save these configuration and effects settings as presets for recall at a later time.

Note that when you use the side chain on a side chain–capable plug-in, the source audio is routed to all surround channels and the side-chain detection is linked, so that the plug-in can maintain the integrity of the surround image.

It is also possible to insert effects that do not match the channel strip's format. Option-clicking on an Insert slot will display every format the plug-in offers. Logic will perform any necessary format down- or upmixes automatically. In other words, if you were to insert a stereo effect after a surround effect, Logic would automatically downmix the audio to stereo.

Applying Surround Effects to a Mono or Stereo Channel Strip

If your audio interface supports six or more outputs, inserting a Mono > Surround or Stereo > Surround plug-in on a stereo channel whose output has been assigned to Surround automatically changes the level meters of the channel to surround metering, as shown in Figure 11.74. The Mono > Stereo or Stereo > Surround option should reflect your project's surround format, meaning that if your project is in 5.1, then a surround plug-in inserted on a stereo channel will be instantiated as a Stereo > 5.1 format plug-in.

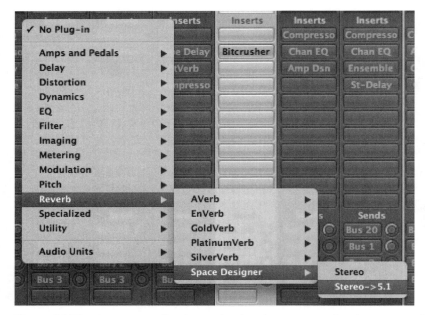

Figure 11.74   A stereo audio channel strip whose output has been set to Surround. When you instantiate a Stereo > Surround effect in an insert, like the Space Designer in this instance, the level meters switch to surround metering. Note that the Format button of the channel strip still displays the stereo symbol.

Effects that are inserted before the Mono > Surround or Stereo > Surround effect maintain the channel strip's original format. Effects inserted after the Mono > Surround or Stereo > Surround effect can be either Multi Mono or Surround, depending on what format(s) the plug-in supports.

Using the Down Mixer Plug-In
The Down Mixer plug-in, found in the Utility submenu of the master channel strip's inserts, allows you to change the format of the master channel strip from Surround to Stereo, Quad, or LCRS (Pro Logic). This gives you the ability to quickly check how your surround mix sounds in another format. Figure 11.75 shows a 5.1 To Stereo Down Mixer instance.

The level controls allow you to change the levels of different channel groupings, along with the overall signal level.

The Surround Compressor
There is one other Logic effect worth mentioning—the Surround Compressor. Although it is outside the scope of this book to go into any detail about the Surround Compressor, it bears mentioning because this effect is only available on surround channel strips. It functions like any typical compressor, but it is specifically designed for surround application, with the Link menus of a Multi Mono plug-in available directly in its Editor view.

Figure 11.75   The Down Mixer plug-in. This master channel strip plug-in allows you to quickly check the compatibility of your surround mix in different formats.

Bouncing in Surround

As mentioned in the preceding section describing the Bounce dialog box, you can choose to bounce in surround by selecting Surround Bounce in the Bounce dialog. Logic gives the files the extensions shown in the Bounce Extensions tab in the I/O Assignments Preferences window, shown in Figure 11.76.

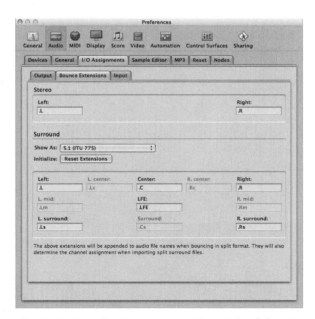

Figure 11.76   The Bounce Extensions tab of the I/O Assignments tab of the Audio Preferences window.

Mixing Using Control Surfaces

How to set up a control surface with Logic was already discussed in Chapter 3. But considering that most control surfaces are geared toward mixing, we wanted to briefly bring them up again here.

Depending on how you like to work, these devices can be a godsend. They let you manipulate more than one fader, Pan knob, and so on at a time. Control surfaces usually let you adjust plug-in parameters as well, and as with faders, you can control multiple parameters simultaneously. You can use a control surface to record automation for one or more tracks at a higher resolution than you can using a mouse. They usually include Transport controls to start and stop the song. The more advanced controllers also include shortcut buttons for advanced automation, editing, and other useful functions. As you can see, control surfaces can help you mix both faster and more accurately.

Control surfaces range in price from incredibly inexpensive small plastic devices with a few knobs and sliders that cost less than most Audio Units plug-ins, to completely professional full-size mixers that cost hundreds of thousands of dollars. This book can't possibly cover all the different types of control surfaces and ways in which control surfaces can be connected and used with Logic Pro. However, we did want to mention two controllers.

The Euphonix MC Artist series of controllers for audio applications (see Figure 11.77) consists of the MC Control, the MC Mix, and the MC Transport. These controllers look like Mac products

Figure 11.77   The Euphonix MC Artist series was designed to work hand in hand with your Mac and Logic Pro for a level of integration not possible with any other control surface.

for good reason: Apple was involved in their development, and they were created with Logic in mind. Euphonix has a long and well-earned reputation for making high-end, professional audio products, and if you can afford these controllers, you won't be disappointed.

The MC Control was designed to be a complete editing and mixing "brain" that gives you one-button touch-screen access to as many editing, arranging, and mixing features as you like. You can add MC Mix units for a system offering as many high-quality, touch-sensitive motorized faders as you need. Euphonix also invented their own high-end, two-way communication protocol between control surface and software program, called EuCon, that is supported by most media applications, such as Logic, although it is currently not supported by Logic in 64-bit mode. You can learn more about the MC Arist series at www.euphonix.com/artist.

Many years ago, the controller that initially blew open the controller market was the Logic Control, designed by Mackie. Today's Mackie Control Universal Pro series of controllers is the direct evolution of that original Logic-only control surface. And this controller truly is universal: Most software and controller devices support Mackie Control emulation (including the Euphonix MC Artist series). The Mackie Controllers (or the Mackie Control protocol) are not as robust as the Euphonix MC Artist series, but they are extremely capable. You can read more about them at www.mackie.com/products/mcupro.

12 Working with Files and Networks

At this point, you should have a pretty solid foundation in how to set up, compose, and mix a project in Logic. You're now ready to start learning about file management within Logic. Some general aspects of file management, such as creating new documents and opening and saving files, should already be familiar to you. Other more specialized operations, such as exporting your project to a variety of standard formats, require a little more explanation. This chapter should hit on everything you need to know to manage your project's files properly in Logic.

Creating New Projects

As explained in Chapter 3, Logic can be configured to launch to your default template. You can also have Logic launch with an empty project or to the Templates dialog, among other options. Normally, new songs are based on one of these starting points. Your template is your "virtual studio," representing an ideal configuration for the way you like to work, but what if you have a number of ideal configurations based on the specific project? Luckily, Logic lets you create and save multiple templates for access at any time.

Templates

We discussed templates in some detail in Chapter 3. Because the template is a powerful way to have a preferred Logic configuration ready to go whenever you need it, having multiple templates allows you to have a number of different Logic configurations at your disposal. For example, you might want one virtual studio set up for compositions with lots of software instruments, one for recording lots of instruments simultaneously, one for different video setups if you do sound-to-picture, and so on. You may have more than one Macintosh and want different templates based on the different monitor sizes and CPU power of each machine, or perhaps you use a laptop and require one template for when you're on the go and another for when you have a second monitor connected.

Logic Pro 9 comes with a number of templates that are installed in the directory /Library/ Application Support/Logic/Project Templates. You will notice that there are different base configurations optimized for composing, recording, working in surround, and so on. You can also save any project you create as a template by selecting File > Save As Template. After you name the project in the dialog box, your project will be saved in the directory ~/Library/Application Support/Logic/Project Templates. You can create a subfolder structure in the Project Templates folder to organize multiple templates if you wish. Every time you create a new project template, the template you created will appear in the list of available templates in the New window either on startup or when using the New command.

Using the New Command to Create New Songs

Obviously, the easiest way to create a new project is to simply start working in your default template and then save it as a new project later. However, if you set the Startup Action Preference (discussed in the "Configuring Logic's Startup Action" section later in this chapter) in the Project Handling tab of Logic Pro > Preferences > General to Automatically Open Most Recent Project, for example, you will not get your default template or an empty project on startup. Also, you may want to start a new song from one of your other templates or one of the templates included with Logic. In these situations, you'll want to use the New command from the global File menu.

When you select the New command, you will get the New dialog box shown in Figure 12.1.

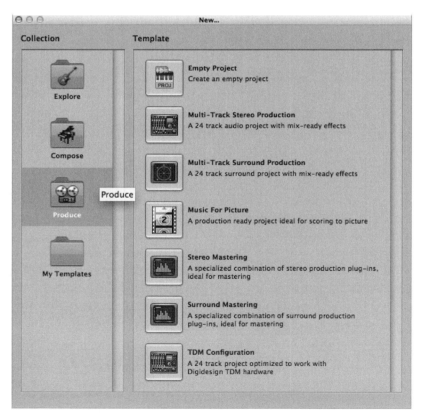

Figure 12.1   The New dialog box.

From here, you can select the project template you want to use from the various menus of project templates.

Saving Logic Projects
In pre-Logic 8 versions of Logic, songs were saved independently of their various dependent files, or assets. In order to save a song with its assets, you had to specifically tell Logic to save the song as a project. Logic would then create a folder hierarchy containing all the assets you wanted saved in the project. In Logic Pro 9, the project is the default format.

The Save Dialog
To save your project in Logic, choose File > Save or press Command+S. The first time you save your Logic project, the Save dialog, shown in Figure 12.2, will open.

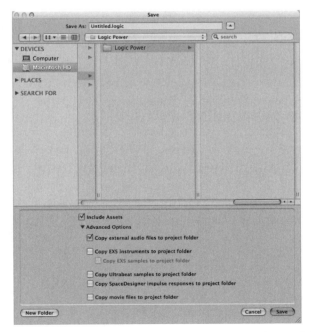

Figure 12.2   The Save dialog. In addition to determining the file path of your Logic project, you can choose which of its assets to save in the Project folder.

The Save dialog looks very similar to a typical Save dialog you might see in any application, until you look at the area directly above the Save button. The first thing you may notice there is the check box labeled Include Assets. Selecting this option will include the project's assets in the Project folder. Below that is a disclosure triangle giving you access to the Include Assets Advanced

Options. If this disclosure triangle has not been opened, clicking it reveals the options shown in Figure 12.2. The Advanced Options are as follows:

- **Copy External Audio Files to Project Folder.** When you select this option, Logic will save all the audio files used in your project in the Audio Files subfolder of the Project folder.

- **Copy EXS Instruments to Project Folder.** This option allows you to save any EXS instrument files (.exs) used in your song to the Sampler Instruments subfolder of the Project folder. When you select this option, the Copy EXS Samples to Project Folder option below it becomes available.

- **Copy EXS Samples to Project Folder.** If you want to keep all the actual EXS samples used in your project in the Project folder, select this option. All EXS samples are stored in the Samples subfolder of the Project folder.

- **Copy Ultrabeat Samples to Project Folder.** You can also save any Ultrabeat samples used in your project to the Project folder by selecting this option. Ultrabeat samples are then added to the Ultrabeat Samples subfolder of the Project folder.

- **Copy SpaceDesigner Impulse Responses to Project Folder.** This option moves any SpaceDesigner impulse responses you use in the song into the Project folder.

- **Copy Movie Files to Project Folder.** This option moves any QuickTime movies used by the song into the Project folder. If you select this option, Logic will open a dialog asking whether you really want to store a copy of your movie in the Project folder.

You may not want—or even need—to use all of these options all the time. What these options do is allow you to create an easily portable version of your project encompassing all the files associated with it. This is perfect for backing up important projects, transferring projects between computers, and even transferring projects to other Logic users. You can therefore ensure that all necessary assets are not only included with your project but also are located in the directory structure in which Logic expects to find them.

Changing Your Project's Included Assets

Let's say you've already saved your project for the first time, and since then you decided you needed to use an instance of Ultrabeat in your project. You'd like to save the Ultrabeat samples in the Project folder, but you didn't allow for that the first time you saved your project. If you have already saved your project, and you decide you need to reconfigure the assets that Logic is saving, simply open File > Project Settings > Assets or select Assets from the Settings menu in the Toolbar. This opens the Assets tab of the Project Settings window, shown in Figure 12.3.

The asset options in the Assets tab of the Project Settings window are identical to those in the Save dialog with the exception of one option—Convert Audio File Sample Rate When Importing. This option is a good one to leave enabled. If you import audio into your project that is of a different sample rate than your project, it will not play correctly. Imagine that your project sample rate is

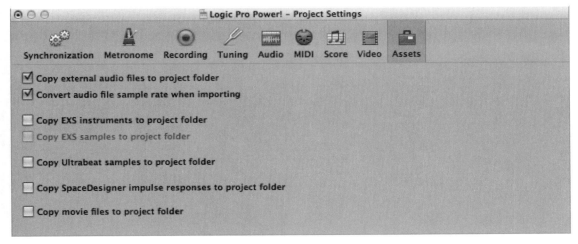

Figure 12.3   The Assets tab of the Project Settings window.

44.1 kHz, and you import a one-second audio file whose sample rate is 48 kHz. If you do not have Convert Audio File Sample Rate When Importing selected, Logic will read 41,000 samples of the 48,000 samples the imported audio contains in one second, reading the remaining 7,000 samples in the first 7/48ths of the next second. Your audio will play back too slow—and flat to boot. Unless you're looking for that sort of effect (to each their own), having Logic handle the sample rate conversion automatically will save you a lot of headaches.

Saving Backups of Your Project

Logic automatically creates a backup of your project file each time you save your project. Each backup song for your project is numbered and automatically placed in your current project's Project File Backups folder.

To save your Logic project with a new name or in a new directory, choose File > Save As or press Shift+Command+S. You can also save a copy of your file by selecting File > Save a Copy As. A file dialog box will appear, in which you can type a new name for your file and select a directory in which to save your project. This is similar to other software applications. While Logic does automatically create backups of your projects, it is still wise to manually back up projects (and even templates) as a normal part of your work routine.

Configuring Logic's Startup Action

Logic offers you a number of options as to what occurs when you launch Logic. Opening the Project Handling tab of the General Preferences window allows you to access the Startup Action menu, shown in Figure 12.4.

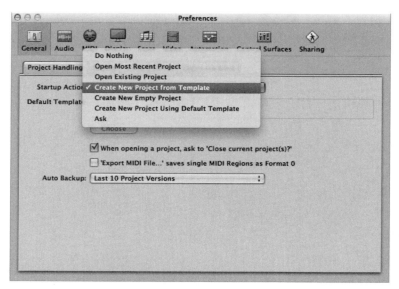

Figure 12.4   The Startup Action menu in the Project Handling tab of the General Preferences window.

The options in the Startup Action menu are as follows:

- **Do Nothing.** Selecting this option allows you to choose what you do each time you launch Logic. You can decide to create a new project, open a recent project, open a template from the Templates dialog, and so on.

- **Open Most Recent Project.** If you select this option, each time you launch Logic it will open the project on which you last worked.

- **Open Existing Project.** If you select this option, Logic will display the Open dialog to the most recent save location when launched.

- **Create New Project from Template.** If you select this option, Logic will display the Templates dialog when launched.

- **Create New Empty Project.** If you select this option, Logic will launch an empty project.

- **Create New Project Using Default Template.** If you select this option and have assigned a default template, Logic will open your default template upon startup.

- **Ask.** If you select Ask, every time you open Logic, a dialog containing the options above will appear. Select the option you prefer and click OK. If you select Cancel, Logic will remain open, and you can select a project using any method you prefer—Open command, New command, Open Recent menu, and so on.

Obviously, the best startup action for your workflow is a matter of personal preference, but oftentimes a well-thought-out default template is the perfect starting point.

The Project Menu

You have a number of project-related options beyond simply saving Logic projects and their assets to Project folders and then opening the projects within them. Figure 12.5 shows the Project submenu of the File menu.

Figure 12.5   The Project submenu of the File menu.

These options give you the ability to do a little housecleaning to your project if the need arises.

Clean Up Project

You can clean up Project folders by deleting unused files with the Clean Up command. If you select File > Project > Clean Up, you will open a window listing any files in the Project folder that are currently unused in your song, as shown in Figure 12.6.

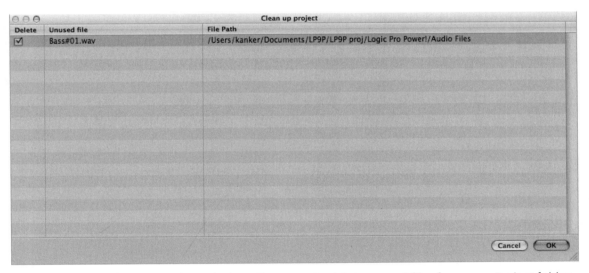

Figure 12.6   The Clean Up Project window allows you to delete unused files from your Project folder.

You can select which files to delete and which unused files you wish to keep and then click OK, and Logic will clean up your Project folder for you.

Consolidate Project

If you have been working with a project that has managed to link to files all over your hard drive or otherwise get unorganized, you can select File > Project > Consolidate to bring your Logic song and associated files together. After selecting this command, you will be presented with the Consolidate Project: Options dialog, which looks almost exactly like the Save As Project dialog, as shown in Figure 12.7.

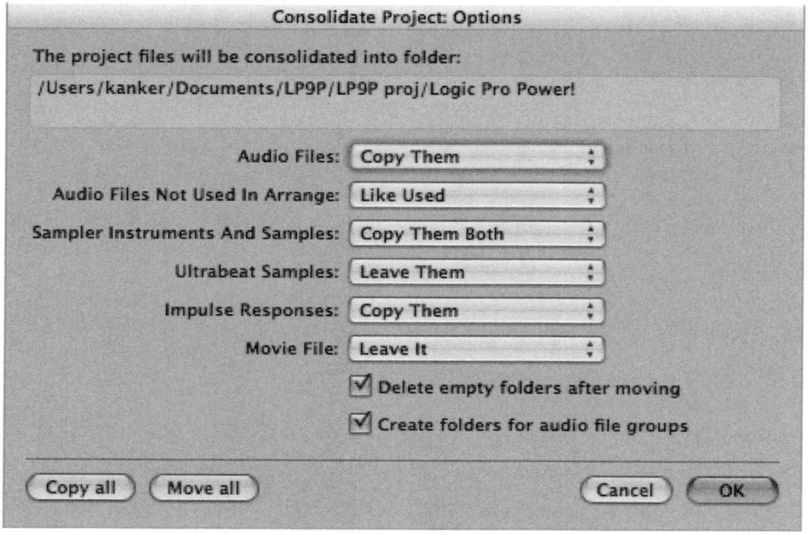

Figure 12.7   The Consolidate Projects: Options dialog.

After your project is consolidated, you can use all the other project-related functions (such as cleaning up and opening its settings) to further operate on the consolidated folder.

Rename Project

If you want to rename a Project folder that already has songs and files in it, the File > Project > Rename command will allow you to rename your file and its included songs. Figure 12.8 shows the Rename Project dialog.

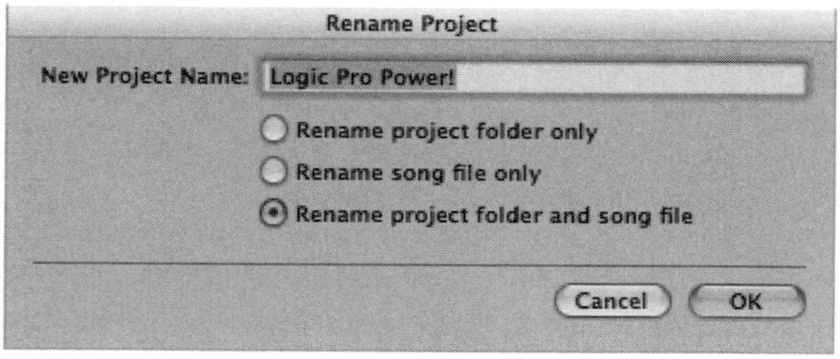

Figure 12.8   The Rename Project dialog.

You can choose to rename the Project folder only, the song only, or both the Project folder and the song file. This command is very useful if you save a project before you name your song, and then you want to rename it all in one go.

The Project Settings Menu

The Project Settings menu can be found in the File menu or in the Toolbar of your Logic project. Most of the Project Settings are covered in depth in other chapters. These settings affect the current project only. You can configure these settings as you desire and save them to your template project to ensure that each time you start a new project, you are using your preferred settings. The Import Project Settings command will be explored later in this chapter.

Opening or Importing Projects and Files

In Logic Pro, the Open dialog not only opens Logic and GarageBand Projects, but also lets you import all the formats that Logic can import. When you select File > Open or press Command+O, Logic displays the Open dialog box. In this dialog, you select which file formats Logic will look for and navigate to the file you wish to open. In Figure 12.9, you can see the Open dialog with the File Type pull-down menu extended to show the various additional file types Logic can open.

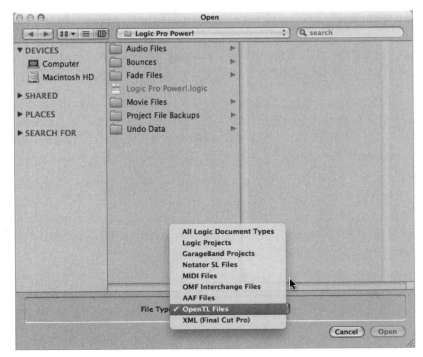

Figure 12.9 The Open dialog, showing the menu of all supported file types.

The options in the File Type menu are as follows:

- **All Logic Document Types.** This option allows you to open a file in any of the formats Logic supports.

- **Logic Projects.** This option opens Logic projects only.

- **GarageBand Projects.** This option opens GarageBand projects only.

- **Notator SL Files.** This option opens Notator SL files only.

- **MIDI Files.** This option opens Standard MIDI Files (SMF) only.

- **OMF Interchange Files.** This option opens Open Media Framework (OMF) Interchange files only. OMF Interchange format was developed by Avid, parent company of Digidesign, and this format is currently supported by most major sequencers. As of this writing, OMF import and export are unavailable when Logic is in 64-bit mode.

- **AAF Files.** This option opens Advanced Authoring Format (AAF) files only. This interchange format is currently supported by high-end professional audio applications, such as Pro Tools HD. As of this writing, AAF import and export are unavailable when Logic is in 64-bit mode.

- **OpenTL Files.** This option opens OpenTL format files only. The OpenTL format was developed by Tascam and is supported by applications such as Nuendo.

- **XML (Final Cut Pro).** This option opens Extensible Markup Language (XML) files only. XML allows you to integrate Logic Pro with Apple's video editing application, Final Cut Pro.

If you are opening a song from an earlier version of Logic, a dialog box tells you that Logic is converting the file to the newer song format. Note that Logic Pro 9 can only open Logic songs created in any version of Logic 5, 6, 7, 8, or 9. If you need to open a song created in Logic 4 or earlier, the song must be opened and saved in a version of Logic 5, 6, or 7 first. Be aware that pre-Logic 5 projects do not open in Logic 8 either.

You can open Logic 9 projects in Logic 8, but you will get a message that the project was created by a newer version of Logic and might not operate properly. This is because Logic 9 features such as Flex Time don't exist in Logic 8, so if you use Flex, your audio may play back incorrectly. Logic 9 projects will not open in any version of Logic earlier than Logic 8.

If you click File > Open Recent, Logic will display the submenu shown in Figure 12.10. This Open Recent submenu lists all Logic songs that you have opened, and you can simply select your song from this submenu.

If your Open Recent submenu gets too long and unwieldy, you can choose the Clear Menu option at the bottom of the Open Recent submenu to reset the list.

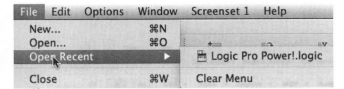

Figure 12.10   The Open Recent submenu in the global File menu.

Importing Files into Logic

As stated earlier, the Open dialog both opens and imports files. However, Logic also contains an Import command, which you can access by choosing File > Import. The main difference is that when you use Open, Logic Pro opens a new project, whereas with the Import command, Logic attempts to import the file into the currently open project. (This only works for non-Logic songs.) If it cannot add the imported material to the current song, it will open a new project, just like the Open command.

You can also import SMF files by dragging them onto the Arrange window in Logic. When you open an SMF file this way, Logic will place it on your Arrange page; one track for each MIDI channel is created, and any data on that track appears in the track lane as a single MIDI region.

Logic also includes a specialized window called the *Browser,* which we will explore now.

Using the Browser

The Browser is available in the Media area of the Arrange. The key command to open the Browser is F. The Browser is akin to having a Finder window incorporated into Logic—and in fact, the Browser is kept automatically in sync with your drives via Spotlight, the Finder's built-in search technology. Figure 12.11 shows the Browser. You can use the Browser to search for and add any file supported by Logic.

The Browser has a very simple interface. Its main function allows you to quickly search for and add files to your Logic project. The Browser has two view modes: List view and Column view. These two views are similar to List view and Column view in the Finder. You switch between these two views using the two buttons at the upper-right corner of the Browser. Figure 12.11 shows the Browser in Column view.

To the left of the View buttons are the Bookmark buttons. The buttons are, from left to right, the Computer button, the Home button, and the Project button. Selecting one of these buttons moves the Browser to that particular level of your computer's file hierarchy.

The pull-down menu in the Browser is the Path menu. Opening the Path menu allows you to view and navigate through the file path of your project. When you select a different level in the file hierarchy, the Browser shows the files and folders contained in that level, similar to a Path menu in a Save dialog.

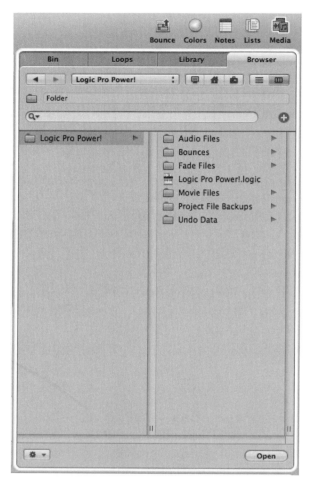

Figure 12.11   The Browser in the Media area of the Arrange window.
The Browser functions similarly to a Finder window.

In the upper-right corner are two buttons with arrows in them, the Back and Forward buttons. These buttons allow you to move backward and forward through your navigation history in the Browser, independent of file path.

The Browser also includes a Search field. To the right of the Search field is a + symbol in a circle. Clicking the + symbol opens a set of advanced search parameters, as shown in Figure 12.12.

You can use these parameters to narrow and fine-tune your search to specify things such as the file type, sample rate, bit depth, format, and so on. You can add more search parameters by clicking the + symbol next to the advanced search parameters, or you can remove search parameters by clicking the – symbol.

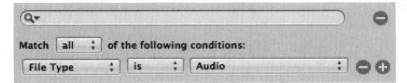

Figure 12.12   Clicking the + symbol next to the Search field opens a set of advanced search parameters.

When you find the file(s) you are looking for, you can click the Add button to add the selected file(s) to the Arrange. Audio files are also added to the Audio Bin. Selecting a movie opens the Drop Movie dialog, covered in Chapter 16, "Working with Video."

The bottom of the Browser also includes a few familiar features, such as the Speaker button, which allows you to preview audio files in the Browser, and the Prelisten slider. There is also an Action menu at the bottom of the Browser, which was mentioned briefly in Chapter 7. Figure 12.13 shows the Action menu of the Browser.

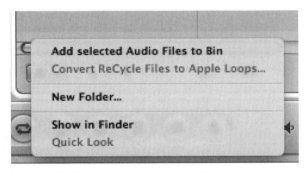

Figure 12.13   The Action menu of the Browser.

The Action menu contains the following options:

- **Add Selected Audio Files to Bin.** Using this command will add the files selected in the Browser to the Audio Bin.

- **Convert ReCycle Files/Folders to Apple Loops.** This command allows you to convert the selected audio files or folders into Apple Loops. This command was covered in detail in Chapter 7.

- **New Folder.** Selecting New Folder opens a dialog in which you can name your new folder. After you name the new folder, it is added to the currently displayed folder in the Browser.

- **Show in Finder.** This command will open a Finder window with the selected file displayed.

- **Quick Look.** If you have selected a Logic project document, this option allows you to see a Quick Look of the project in its most recent saved state, just as you would see with Quick Look in the Finder.

Importing Track Settings from Other Projects

One of the really handy features in Logic is the ability to import different settings directly from other Logic projects. After selecting a Logic project in the Browser, clicking the Import button at the bottom of the Browser invokes the Track Import view, shown in Figure 12.14.

Figure 12.14   The Track Import view in the Browser, where you can import settings from individual tracks in other Logic projects directly into your current Logic project.

The Track Import view shows all the tracks in the selected project, including the Marker, Signature, and Tempo global tracks. You can select what type of settings will be imported from each individual track by selecting the appropriate check boxes. You can also filter the types of tracks that are displayed using the Global, Audio, Inst, Aux, I/O, and MIDI filter buttons that appear at the top of the list of tracks, similar to the way you can filter tracks in the Mixer. The columns and options of the Track Import view are:

- **Num.** The Num column displays track numbers in the selected project where applicable.

- **Name.** This column displays the name of each track in the selected project.

- **Content.** If you select Content and click the Add button, the region data or global track data for the selected track(s) will be imported, and a new track will be created for each imported track. The channel strip settings for any track imported via the Content option will not be imported.

- **Plug-Ins.** If you select Plug-Ins and click Add, the region data (if applicable) and channel strip settings will be imported for each selected track to new tracks.

- **Sends.** If you select Sends and click Add, tracks that share the send structure of the selected track will be imported, creating tracks with no regions in the Arrange and no loaded channel strip settings.

- **I/O.** If you select I/O and click Add, tracks that share an I/O configuration will be imported, creating new tracks in the Arrange with empty channel strips.

- **Auto.** If you select Auto and click Add, the automation data for the selected track(s) will be imported into new tracks in the Arrange with empty channel strips.

You can select multiple options per track, and all the selected options for a track will be imported to a single track. You can click on one option for a track and press the right arrow key to select all options for the selected track. Pressing the left arrow key deselects all options on the selected track.

If you have only chosen to import data from one track, you can click the Replace button at the bottom of the Track Import view to transfer that data to the currently selected track in the Arrange, replacing all data of the selected types on the selected Arrange track. Otherwise, click the Add button to import everything you have selected into the current project.

The Import Project Settings Window

There may be times when you want to import different settings from other projects, such as screensets, staff styles, or hyper sets. Selecting File > Project Settings > Import Settings, pressing Option+Command+I, or clicking the Import Project Settings button at the bottom of the Track Import view opens the Import Project Settings window, shown in Figure 12.15.

The settings from which you can choose are Screensets, Transform Sets, Hyper Sets, Score Sets, Staff Styles, Text Styles, Score Settings, Sync Settings, Metronome Settings, Record Settings, Tuning Settings, Audio Settings, MIDI Settings, Video Settings, and Asset Settings. Simply select the settings you wish to import, select the file from which you wish to import the settings, and click Import. The chosen settings will be imported into the current project.

Exporting Files from Logic

If you want to export your Logic project in a different format for use in a different application (or an earlier version of Logic), Logic offers an Export submenu in the global File menu. Figure 12.16 shows this submenu.

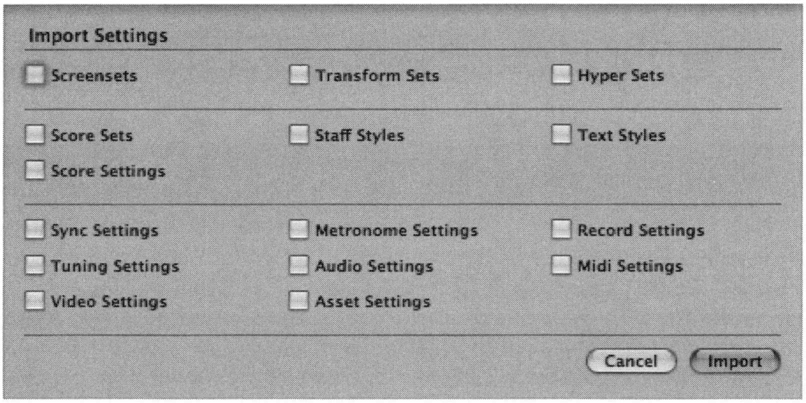

Figure 12.15   The Import Project Settings window.

Figure 12.16   The Export submenu from the global File menu features your options for exporting files from Logic into different formats.

These export options are explained in the following subsections.

Export Selection as MIDI File

To export MIDI data from Logic, first select one or more MIDI regions (across as many tracks as you'd like) and then choose this option or press Option+Command+E. A file dialog box will prompt you to choose a name and a directory for your exported file, and then your MIDI selection will be exported with a .mid extension to denote that it is a Standard MIDI File (SMF). By default, Logic exports SMFs in Format 1, where the file can contain one or more MIDI tracks. In the Project Handling tab of the Global Preferences window, shown in Figure 12.4, there is an option to export single MIDI as Format 0. Format 0 SMFs consist of one multichannel track. To export a Format 0 SMF, you would first need to merge all your MIDI regions into one region on one track. First, select all your MIDI regions and then, in the Arrange window, select Region > Merge > Regions or press =. You can now export your MIDI file as a Format 0 SMF.

Export Region as Audio File

This command allows you to export the selected audio or software instrument region as an audio file. When selected, this command opens the Region as Audio File dialog shown in Figure 12.17.

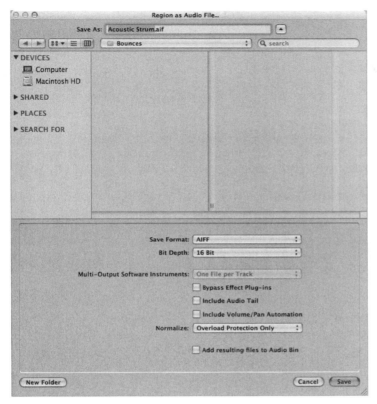

Figure 12.17   The Region as Audio File dialog.

In addition to the normal Save As dialog features, this window gives you a number of different options regarding how Logic will bounce your regions. These options are:

- **Save Format.** Use this menu to select the save format for your exported audio file: AIFF, CAF, or Broadcast Wave.

- **Bit Depth.** Select the bit depth (8-, 16-, or 24-bit, or 32-bit float) of your exported audio file in this menu.

- **Multi-Output Software Instruments.** This menu offers two options: One File per Track, and One File per Channel Strip. The One File per Track option creates one bounce file for every multi-output Software Instrument track in the Arrange. The One File per Channel Strip option creates one file for every channel strip a multi-output software instrument utilizes, including aux channel strips.

- **Bypass Effect Plug-Ins.** Selecting this option lets you bypass effect plug-ins for the exported audio file.

- **Include Audio Tail.** When you select this option, the exported audio file is automatically lengthened to include any effects tails, similar to the Include Audio Tail command in the Bounce dialog.

- **Include Volume/Pan Automation.** With this option selected, all volume and pan automation that occurs over the selected region will be performed during the export.

- **Normalize.** The Normalize menu offers the same options for export as the Normalize menu in the Bounce dialog: On, Off, and Overload Protection Only. With On selected, the exported file will be normalized. With Off selected, the exported file will not be normalized. With Overload Protection Only selected, the file will be scanned for peaks over 0 dBFS, and those peaks will be reduced to 0 dBFS, and the rest of the file will not be altered.

- **Add Resulting Files to Audio Bin.** Select Add Resulting Files to Audio Bin to have the exported audio added to the Audio Bin.

When you click Save, Logic will perform an offline bounce of the selected region.

Export Track as Audio File

This command allows you to export the selected Arrange audio or Software Instrument track as an audio file. Selecting this command brings up a dialog identical to Figure 12.17. Logic Pro will do an offline bounce of the selected track that begins at the project's beginning and ends at the project's end. The key command for this is Command+E.

Export All Tracks as Audio Files

This command allows you to export all of your Audio and Software Instrument tracks as separate audio files. Selecting this command or pressing Shift+Command+E brings up a dialog identical to Figure 12.17. The export options you specify will be applied to every track you export. For example, you can't choose different formats and/or bit depths for different tracks—they will all have the same format and bit depth. Logic Pro will do an offline bounce of each track that begins at the project's beginning and ends at the project's end.

Export Project as OMF File

To export a song in Avid's popular inter-application OMF (*Open Media Framework*) Interchange file format, select this option. The OMF Export dialog box will then appear, as shown in Figure 12.18.

The OMF Export options are described as follows:

- **OMF File Version.** You can select Version 1 or Version 2. Version 1 is an older version of OMF that was not as robust; you will nearly always use the default setting of Version 2 here.

- **Include Audio.** If you check this box, all of your audio regions will be integrated into the OMF file itself, resulting in a potentially very large file that will take longer to export. On the

Figure 12.18   The OMF Export dialog. Here you can set the parameters for your OMF file.

other hand, it is also the most compatible with other applications. If you uncheck this box, only the references to the used audio files are included, which some applications have a problem reading. As long as you have the disk space, you should include the audio in your OMF file.

- **Convert Interleaved to Split Stereo.** This option lets you create split stereo files for compatibility with any other DAW that may not be capable of importing interleaved stereo files.

  If you intend to import your OMF file into an application that cannot use interleaved stereo files, you'll want to check this box. If you are not sure, it's always safer to leave it checked.

- **Convert 24 Bit Files to 16 Bit.** If you know that the application you want to import your tracks cannot import 24-bit files, you may want to convert all your 24-bit audio files to 16-bit with this option.

- **Dither Type.** If you are converting your files down to 16-bit, you may want to use dither. This is the same Dither pull-down menu as from the Bounce dialog box described in Chapter 11.

When you have configured your OMF export the way you want, clicking OK brings up a file dialog box in which you can choose the name and directory for your OMF file. After you select a location and name for your file, Logic begins the OMF export. A progress bar indicates the status of the process, as it will tie up Logic until the operation is complete. When you are finished, the result is a portable song file in OMF format (with a file extension of .omf) that contains all the audio regions in your Logic song. As of this writing, OMF export and import are unavailable when Logic is in 64-bit mode.

Export Project as OpenTL File

When you choose to export your song in Tascam's proprietary OpenTL file format, first a file dialog box will appear in which to name your OpenTL file and choose a directory. Once that is accomplished, a dialog box will appear, asking whether you want to create a new folder to contain your OpenTL file and all relevant audio files. After you click either Create or Don't Create, a new dialog box will appear, asking whether you want to add the project's SMPTE start time to the event start positions. This allows you to stamp the files with your Logic project's SMPTE start position. After selecting Add or Don't Add, another dialog box will appear, asking whether you'd like to make a copy of all audio files used in the song. Once you click Yes or No in response, the OpenTL exporting will take place, resulting in an OpenTL file (with a file extension of .tl) that you can import into any application that can import OpenTL files.

Export Project as AAF File

When you choose to export your song as a new, professional Advanced Authoring Format (AAF) file, you are presented with a specialized Save AAF File As window, shown in Figure 12.19.

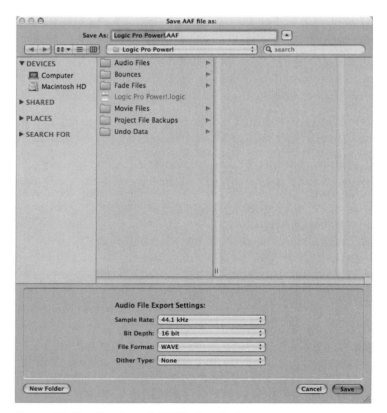

Figure 12.19   The Save AAF File As window.

In addition to the normal Save As window options, this window offers four Audio File Export Settings:

- **Sample Rate.** You can select a sample rate from 44.1 kHz to 96 kHz.

- **Bit Depth.** You can select a bit depth of either 16- or 24-bit.

- **File Format.** You can select either WAVE or AIFF format for your audio files.

- **Dither Type.** If you have selected 16-bit audio files from 24-bit originals, you should select one of Logic's dither algorithms to dither your files.

When you are finished setting up the AAF Audio File Export Settings, click Save, and Logic will export your Logic song as an AAF. As of this writing, AAF export and import are unavailable when Logic is in 64-bit mode.

OMF or AAF? Since both AAF and OMF are music interchange formats, the same applications can normally import both formats. So the question often arises, which format is better? Unfortunately, there is no hard-and-fast rule. In general, OMF is an Avid-owned format, and Avid controls the libraries to it. This means that if an application has a problem supporting OMF, the developers may have to wait for Avid to help them come up with a solution—which may or may not happen. AAF is an open standard format created by the Advanced Media Workflow Association (AMWA), and it *tends* to be more robustly supported. So you might want to use AAF first. However, if you then experience issues between Logic's AAF file and your destination software's AAF import capability, don't hesitate to try OMF as well.

Export Project to Final Cut Pro/XML

This option will save your Logic song in Extensible Markup Language (XML) for use in Final Cut Pro. When you select this option, it will present you with a standard Save As dialog. Simply name your file, choose where to save your XML file, and press Return. Logic will save your song as an XML file that you can then import into Final Cut Pro.

Sharing and Backing Up Logic Settings

Networks are a common part of daily computing life, be they local networks among the computers around the home or in an office or larger networks, such as the Internet. Networks offer the convenience of easy access to files, information, and in the case of Logic Nodes, more processing power. You can easily transfer files between machines by logging into another computer remotely and retrieving files from the remote machine. You can manually perform a lot of backup routines with connected or networked hard drives, or if you are using Mac OS X 10.5 or higher, you can use Time Machine to back up your entire hard drive.

With Logic Pro 9, you can use Bonjour and MobileMe to share and back up channel strip settings, plug-in settings, and key commands. Bonjour is an Apple technology for networking computers over a local network. Bonjour devices automatically look for and offer their network services to other Bonjour devices. MobileMe is the successor to .Mac. With MobileMe, you can back up and sync devices over the Internet, allowing you remote access to important data. These technologies make it possible for you to easily transfer your settings and key commands into Logic projects on other machines either on your local network or over the Internet!

Let's look at how you can configure Logic to work with these technologies.

Accessing Sharing Preferences

Before you can use Bonjour or MobileMe with Logic, you need to set up Logic's Sharing preferences. To do this, select Logic Pro > Preferences > Sharing, select Sharing from the Preferences menu in the Arrange window Toolbar, or select Sharing Preferences from the Action menu at the bottom of the Library tab of the Media area or in the contextual menu that opens when you Control-click in the Media area. Figure 12.20 shows the Action menu.

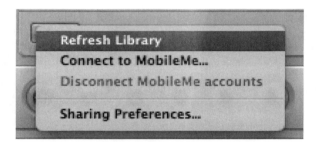

Figure 12.20   The Action menu in the Library tab. Selecting Sharing Preferences opens the Sharing Preferences window.

The Sharing Preferences window, shown in Figure 12.21, allows you to determine what types of data are accessible via Bonjour, what types of data are shared from your MobileMe account, whether or not to look for shared data on your local network, and whether to back up your settings to or restore them from MobileMe.

Sharing Logic Data via Bonjour

To allow Logic to actively look for settings and key commands on other machines on your local network via Bonjour, select the Look for Shared Data on the Local Network check box in the Sharing Preferences window shown in Figure 12.21. Logic will then search the ~/Library/Application Support/Logic folder of the computers on your local network for any shared settings. To actively share settings or key commands on your current machine over your local network, select the check boxes of the desired data types in the Bonjour column in the Data Sharing pane of the Sharing Preferences window.

Settings that are being shared via Bonjour have a red dot to the left of their folder or setting file icon, as shown in Figure 12.22.

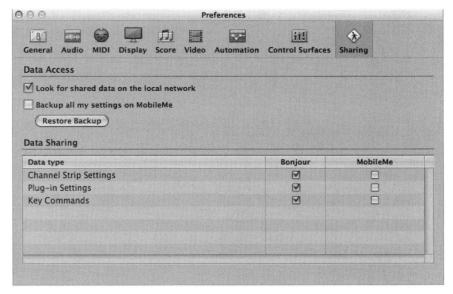

Figure 12.21   The Sharing Preferences window.

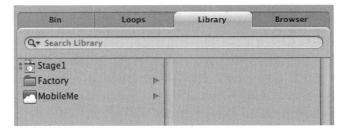

Figure 12.22   Settings that are shared via Bonjour have a red dot next to the left icon in the Library.

If there are any specific setting files you wish to exclude from sharing, you can Control-click on them and uncheck Share via Bonjour in the menu that opens. Settings shared from other computers can be found in the Bonjour folder in the Library.

You can access shared key commands in the Key Commands window. Simply open the Options menu in the Key Commands window and look in the Presets submenu.

Sharing and Backing Up Logic Data via MobileMe

Sharing settings via MobileMe is just as easy as it is with Bonjour. Select the settings you would like to share in the MobileMe column of the Data Sharing pane of the Sharing Preferences window. Those settings will then be available in the /Public/MusicAudioData directory of your iDisk. Again, you can exclude specific settings by Control-clicking on the settings you wish to exclude and unchecking Share via MobileMe, and you can access shared key commands in the Presets submenu of the Options menu in the Key Commands window. Channel strip settings and plug-in settings and folders that are shared via MobileMe have a blue dot to the left of their icons in the Library.

You can access either your or another user's MobileMe account by opening the Action menu in the Library, shown in Figure 12.20, and selecting Connect to MobileMe. This command will open the Connect to MobileMe dialog shown in Figure 12.23.

Figure 12.23   The Connect to MobileMe dialog. You can log into either your MobileMe account or another user's to access channel strip and plug-in settings.

To log into your MobileMe account, select My MobileMe account and click OK. To log into another user's MobileMe public folder or to log into your own public folder, select Another Account and input the MobileMe account name. You will then see a MobileMe folder in the Library, in which you can access shared channel strip and plug-in settings. To disconnect, simply select Disconnect MobileMe Accounts in the Action menu in the Library.

To back up your settings to MobileMe, select Back Up All My Settings on MobileMe. This copies all your settings to your iDisk in a format you can restore from at any time. Note that the computer from which you initially back up becomes the master machine. If you try to back up your settings from another machine, a warning dialog will ask whether you want to make the new machine the backup master. If you deselect Back Up All My Settings on MobileMe on the master machine, then there is no longer a master machine. To restore your settings, just click the Restore Backup button in the Sharing Preferences window.

Now that you understand more about working with files in Logic and sharing your settings and key commands, it's time to take a look into one of the deepest and most misunderstood parts of Logic, the Environment.

13 | The Environment

D o you wish you had a complete virtual model of your hardware synthesizer's controls inside Logic for easy programming while sequencing? Do you have some great ideas for running the notes you perform through a couple of arpeggiators and delay lines to create amazing and unique rhythms that follow your playing dynamics? Have you thought about having single keys play unique chords and then be delayed and play additional chords? Would you like to create structures in which the type of processing done to any data is conditional upon the notes you are playing or the velocity of your notes, and so on? Would you like to be able to use Logic itself as a live performance tool? Then welcome to the Environment.

We have touched on the Environment in other chapters, but now it's time to dive into it in more detail. The Environment is perhaps the most unique and daunting aspect of Logic. If the Environment seems like something you aren't ready to explore, don't worry—you can successfully use Logic without ever using the routing and transforming power of the Environment. Logic is highly competitive with the other sequencers simply by virtue of its audio and MIDI editing, recording, mixing, and arranging. On the other hand, if you want to use the power of the Environment, no other sequencer can possibly compete with Logic. The Environment puts Logic into a league all its own.

Understanding the Environment

The Environment, as you know, is a virtual representation of your studio. Channel strip objects represent available audio channels inside Logic as well as your available audio hardware. MIDI objects represent available MIDI hardware and MIDI processors. There are internal objects that represent connections to software synthesizers that are running on your computer but outside the Logic application, such as the Apple QuickTime object and the ReWire object.

Let's take the "virtual studio" paradigm further. In a hardware studio, you can cable different processors to different channels, you can have splitters that split up signals, you can monitor signals, and you can access entire racks of effects. By cabling objects, using transformer and splitter objects, and creating macros, you can do that in the Environment as well. This chapter will touch on the more complex types of routings and structures you can make with the Environment. No single chapter can cover everything you could possibly create with Logic's

Environment, but hopefully you'll learn enough about what is possible to facilitate your own creativity and invention!

Keep in Mind: Can Does Not Mean Must!   Unfortunately, the Environment plays a large part in why Logic has traditionally been considered difficult. Sometimes users who cannot find anything they are familiar with in the Environment feel that Logic must require a degree in programming in order to do the simplest things. Hopefully, you will realize how false that idea is. To reiterate, just because the Environment will allow you to build complex constructions and macros that can do amazing MIDI processing, that doesn't mean you *have* to do this! You don't need to use the Environment at all. If you don't feel comfortable or interested in delving into the Environment yet, just put this chapter off for now.

Environment Local Menus

Like all windows in Logic, the Environment has its own local menus of functions. Unlike many local menus, since the Environment is designed to be a graphical object workspace, not too many of them are accessible via key commands. Learning the options and functions available in the local menus is the first step toward understanding the potential of the Environment. The following subsections will detail the Environment local menus.

New Menu

The New menu contains all the various types of objects you can create in the Environment. When you want to add an object, you will find it in this local menu. Figure 13.1 shows the New menu.

You'll notice that a number of these objects have already been discussed in previous chapters. Rather than describe each object in a short list, the next section will go into each object in detail.

Edit Menu

As with the Edit local menus in other windows, the Edit menu in the Environment window includes commands for selecting and editing selections. Figure 13.2 shows the Edit menu of the Environment window.

A brief description of the available commands follows.

- **Undo.** This will undo the most recent action. The key command for this is Command+Z.

- **Redo.** This will redo the most recent action. The key command for this is Shift+Command+Z.

- **Undo History.** You can use this command to open the Undo History window. The key command for this is Option+Z.

Figure 13.1   The New local menu of the Environment window.

■   **Delete Undo History.** This command will empty your Undo History window.

■   **Cut.** You can use this command to remove the selected object from the Environment window and place it on the Clipboard. The key command for this is Command+X.

■   **Copy.** This command will place a copy of the selected object onto the Clipboard. The key command for this is Command+C.

■   **Paste.** You can paste the contents of the Clipboard into the Environment window at the current cursor position with this command. The key command for this is Command+V.

■   **Delete.** This will delete the selected objects from the Environment window.

■   **Clear Cables only.** This will clear all the cables running to or from the selected objects but will not delete the objects themselves. The key command for this is Control+Forward Delete.

■   **Select All.** This command selects everything in the current Environment layer. See the "Environment Layers" section later in this chapter for more information on layers. The key command for this is Command+A.

■   **Invert Selection.** This command will toggle between the selection you have made and everything in the current Environment layer except your selection. The key command for this is Shift+T.

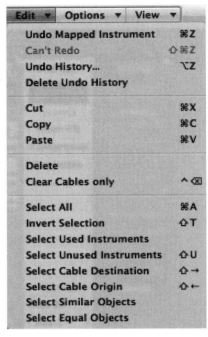

Figure 13.2   The Environment's local Edit menu.

- **Select Used Instruments.** This command selects all instruments that are currently used in your song.

- **Select Unused Instruments.** This command selects all instruments that currently are not used in your song. The key command for this is Shift+U.

- **Select Cable Destination.** If you have an object selected, this command will select the object(s) to which the selected object is cabled. The key command for this is Shift+Right Arrow.

- **Select Cable Origin.** If you select an object that is the destination of another object's cable, this command will select the later object. The key command for this is Shift+Left Arrow.

- **Select Similar Objects.** This will select fader objects similar (such as the same type of object) to the currently selected fader object(s).

- **Select Equal Objects.** This will select additional objects that are identical (such as the same type of object with the same settings) to the currently selected object(s). All objects of the same type are "equal" except faders. All faders are "similar," but only faders with the same style are "equal."

Options Menu

The Options menu is a catchall local menu for additional Environment functions. Figure 13.3 shows the Options menu.

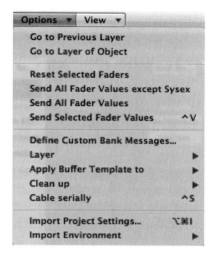

Figure 13.3   The local Options menu of the Environment window.

The various commands and submenus contained in the Options menu are detailed here, with each submenu seen in Figure 13.3 detailed in separate subsections:

- **Go to Previous Layer.** This will switch the current Environment layer to the previous Environment layer.

- **Go to Layer of Object.** If you have an object selected in the All Objects layer, this command will switch the Environment to the layer that the selected object is on.

- **Reset Selected Faders.** This command will cause all selected faders to return to their original values.

- **Send All Fader Values except SysEx.** This will send all fader values to their recipient objects except those faders sending SysEx data.

- **Send All Fader Values.** This will send all fader values to their recipient objects, including those faders sending SysEx data.

- **Send Selected Fader Values.** This will send the fader values of selected faders to their recipient objects. The key command for this is Control+V.

- **Define Custom Bank Messages.** If you have a multi-instrument object selected, you can choose this option to launch a special Edit window in which you can define custom bank messages for each channel of your multi instrument. Figure 13.4 shows the special Edit window.

  When you are finished, simply close the Edit window, and your multi instrument will have its custom bank messages defined.

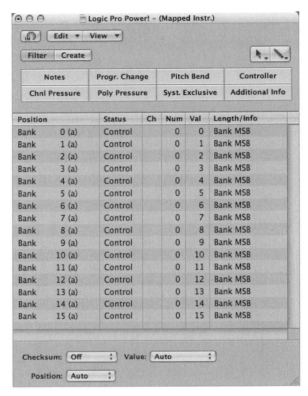

Figure 13.4 When you select a multi-instrument object, you can use the Define Custom Bank Messages command in the Environment's local Options menu to launch this special Edit window to enter custom bank messages for your multi instrument.

- **Cable Serially.** This will cable all selected objects. The key command for this is Control+S.

- **Import Project Settings.** This will open an open file dialog box with additional options at the bottom of the window for you to select which elements of a Logic project you wish to import into the current Logic project. Figure 13.5 shows this dialog. The key command for this is Option+Command+I.

Layer Submenu

The Layer submenu of the Options local menu includes two options, as shown in Figure 13.6: Delete and Create. Create will open a new, empty Environment layer that you can name anything you want by double-clicking on its name in the parameter bar. Delete will erase the current Environment layer.

Apply Buffer Template To Submenu

When you build a virtual mixing desk or a synthesizer controller in the Environment, you might find yourself using a significant number of objects of the same type (such as a row of fader objects

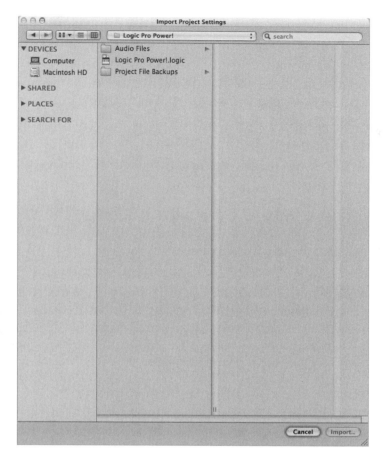

Figure 13.5   The Import Project Settings dialog box is essentially an open file dialog with additional options for which song elements to import to the current Logic song.

Figure 13.6   The Layer submenu of the local Options menu of the Environment window.

or channel splitters, all with the same spacing and settings). To save time defining and aligning all of these similar objects, you may copy one or more objects into the Clipboard using either the Copy or the Define Template command and use that object (or group of objects) as a template for the rest of your objects in your construction. The Apply Buffer Template To submenu, shown in Figure 13.7, consists of options to apply specific characteristics of your template objects to the selected objects.

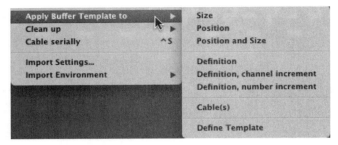

Figure 13.7   The Apply Buffer Template To submenu of the local Options menu of the Environment.

To align a group of objects, choose two or more objects in rows or columns whose horizontal or vertical alignment you want transferred to the rest of your objects and copy them onto the Clipboard. You can then select the rest of your objects and use the Size, Position, or Position and Size command to transfer the positioning and size of your template objects.

If you want to transfer the parameters of your template objects, select the objects and use the Definition command. You also can use the Definition, Channel Increment command to have the channel number of each object increase from the top-left object onward or the Definition, Number Increment command to increment the first data byte of whatever is being defined (such as a MIDI controller number). Definition; Definition, Channel Increment; and Definition, Number Increment apply only to faders. Finally, you can use your template to transfer the cabling of your template with the Cable(s) command.

Clean Up Submenu

The Clean Up submenu of the Options menu, as shown in Figure 13.8, contains three options for organizing your Environment window: Align Objects, Positions by Grid, and Size by Default.

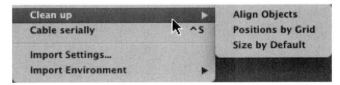

Figure 13.8   The Clean Up submenu of the local Options menu of the Environment.

The three options have the following effects on the currently selected objects:

- **Align Objects.** This command will put all selected objects into a row or column, depending on the orientation of the top or leftmost two objects.

- **Positions by Grid.** This command will position all selected objects in a grid pattern in case View > Snap Positions is not checked.

- **Size by Default.** This command will size all selected objects to their default size.

Import Environment Submenu

The Import Environment submenu of the local Options menu, shown in Figure 13.9, contains seven options for importing Environments from other Logic songs. These options enable you to import parts of an Environment or even an entire Environment from another song.

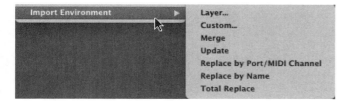

Figure 13.9   The Import Environment submenu of the local Options menu of the Environment.

The options in this submenu are explained below:

- **Layer.** If you have two Logic songs open, this option will present you with a dialog showing a pull-down menu of the other song's Environment layers. If you do not have two songs open, this option will first present you with a dialog box to select another Logic song from which you want to import an Environment. When you choose the Environment layer you want to import, it will be added to the Environment of your current song.

- **Custom.** This opens a special version of the All Objects layer of the song from which you want to import and lets you pick which individual objects you want to import. You will notice that this option creates the same Import local menu that the Import Options command in the local View menu opens. This menu enables you to mark each individual object as one you want to keep, delete, reassign in some way as you import the Environment, and so on. Figure 13.10 shows the Environment window opened by the Custom command.

  When you are finished assigning each object in the Environment you want to import, choose Import Environment Using Current Assignment, and your custom import will be complete.

- **Merge.** This will merge the Environment you want to import into the Environment of the current song.

- **Update.** This is useful if you have a song with a very similar or identical Environment that you want to import. This will update your current song's Environment with more recent changes made in the Environment you want to import.

- **Replace by Port/MIDI Channel.** This will import objects from another Environment by replacing only those objects that are set to similar ports and MIDI channels as objects in the current song.

- **Replace by Name.** This will only replace Environment layers in the current song with Environment layers of the same name.

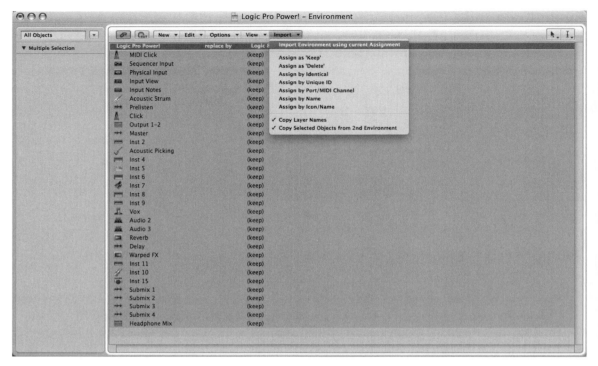

Figure 13.10 The specially colored All Objects Environment layer of the Environment to be imported. Use the Import local menu, also shown, to assign each object, and then select Import Environment Using Current Assignment.

- **Total Replace.** This command completely replaces the Environment of the current song with the Environment you are importing.

View Menu

The View menu includes options for what will be displayed in the Environment window. Figure 13.11 shows the View menu of the Environment window.

A description of each View option appears below:

- **Protect Cabling/Positions.** With this checked, you will not be able to move objects or remove any existing cabling between objects. The key command for this is Control+P.

- **Snap Positions.** With this checked, Logic will snap newly created objects to an internal grid to keep them more organized into rows and columns. Objects moved by dragging are also snapped to the grid.

- **Cables.** With this option engaged, you will be able to see the cabling between objects; if it is unchecked, all cables will be hidden. The key command for this is Control+C.

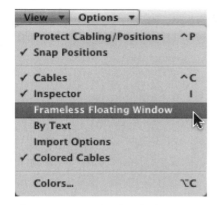

Figure 13.11   The local View menu of the Environment window.

- **Inspector.** This option, when checked, shows the Inspector box of the selected object on the left side of the Environment window. The key command for this is I.

- **Frameless Floating Window.** When you select this option, the current Environment window changes into a frameless floating window, which you can then resize and position anywhere. This is helpful for bringing some of your custom Environment tools into your screensets.

- **By Text.** With this checked, Environment objects will be displayed as text instead of as graphic objects.

- **Import Options.** This option adds an entire new local menu to the Environment window, the Import menu. This is useful when you are importing Environments from other Logic songs. This is discussed in detail in the "Environment Layers" section later in this chapter.

- **Colored Cables.** With this option, cables will be the same color as the Environment object.

- **Colors.** This launches the Color Palette window so you can color your Environment objects. The key command for this is Option+C.

Environment Tool Menu

The Environment Tool menu is found at the upper-right corner of the Environment window, as shown in Figure 13.12.

The tools in the Environment's Tool menu are described below, from top to bottom:

- **Pointer Tool.** This is the standard pointer for selecting, dragging, and rubber-banding objects.

- **Pencil Tool.** The Pencil tool will add an instrument object to the Environment.

- **Eraser Tool.** With this tool, you can delete any object you click.

Figure 13.12   The Environment Tool menu.

- **Text Tool.** You can enter text in text boxes that you click on with this tool. Simply click the text at the bottom of an object to type a new name for it.

- **MIDI Thru Tool.** When you click on a MIDI instrument with this tool, the selected Arrange track will immediately change its assignment to the object you clicked on.

Environment Window Buttons

The Environment window has two buttons next to its local menu bar, as shown in Figure 13.13: a Link button to link the Environment to the front-most window in the screenset and a MIDI OUT button to enable MIDI to be sent from the Environment. You will generally want to leave both of these buttons engaged.

Figure 13.13   The Environment window buttons.

Environment Objects

Objects are the building blocks of the Environment. Objects represent the devices and processes you will use to construct your virtual studio. The following subsections offer some details about each object not already discussed in previous chapters. As always, remember that these descriptions are designed to get you started, not to cover every single possible setting and option for each object.

You create objects by choosing them from the New local menu in the Environment. Refer back to Figure 13.1 for all of the objects available in this menu.

Instrument Object

The instrument object represents a simple MIDI device that plays on only one MIDI channel. You create this object by selecting New > Instrument, and you'll see the icon for an instrument in your current Environment layer. Figure 13.14 shows a newly created instrument object and its Parameter box.

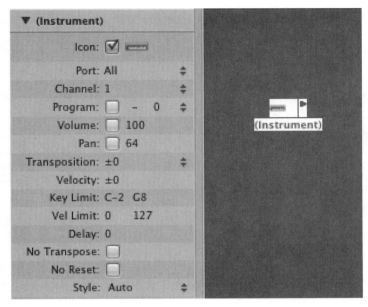

Figure 13.14 An instrument object with its Parameter box.

The instrument object's parameters are the same as the parameters for individual channels of the multi-instrument object discussed in Chapter 3.

Multi-Instrument Object
The multi-instrument object was covered in detail in Chapter 3.

Mapped Instruments Object
Mapped instruments are a different sort of object than either instrument or multi-instrument objects. Mapped instruments allow settings to be specifically defined, or *mapped*, for every note in the instrument. This means that with a mapped instrument, you can:

- Name the notes.

- Map notes to sounds in MIDI sound sources. (You can even map multiple sound sources to the same note or different notes to the same sound source.)

- Assign each note its own MIDI channel.

- Send each note to its own output cable.

- Give each note its own musical notation parameters, such as note head shape, relative vertical position in the staff, and drum group assignment.

As you've probably guessed, mapped instrument objects are most often used with drum kits, where each MIDI note represents a different drum sound, and you might even play a complete kit across different MIDI devices (if you are constructing a single drum kit from drum sounds scattered among several synthesizers, for example). You can create a mapped instrument by selecting New > Mapped Instrument in the Environment window. Logic then displays the icon and Parameter box shown in Figure 13.15. Logic also automatically opens the Mapped Instrument window.

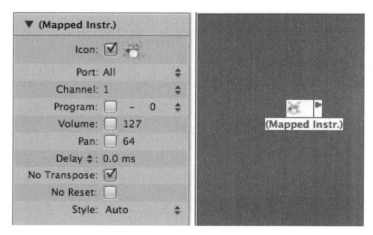

Figure 13.15   A mapped instrument object and its Parameter box.

Notice that a mapped instrument has the exact same parameters as a subchannel of a multi-instrument object, except for those parameters relating to the notes themselves: Transposition, Velocity, Key Limit, and Vel Limit. That's because these missing parameters are set for each note of the mapped instrument, and not the object as a whole. When you are ready to continue with your setup, click into the Mapped Instrument window shown in Figure 13.16. This is where you do the main work of defining the mapped instrument object.

The first thing you'll notice is the graphic keyboard at the left of the Mapped Instrument window. The notes on these keys represent the input notes, meaning the notes that you play from a controller that are received by the mapped instrument. You can play this keyboard by clicking on a note, or you can select a range of notes by dragging the mouse across the desired notes. To add notes to an existing range, hold the Shift key down while clicking on the desired notes. Directly above the keyboard, you'll notice that the Mapped Instrument window has its own local menu, the Initialize menu, as shown in Figure 13.17.

The explanations of the various columns in the Mapped Instrument window also detail the functions of the various menu items in the Initialize local menu:

■ **Input Name.** This is where you can name your note. For example, you could name the note G8 Piccolo Snare to represent the drum sound that G8 triggers, and so on. You can also reset

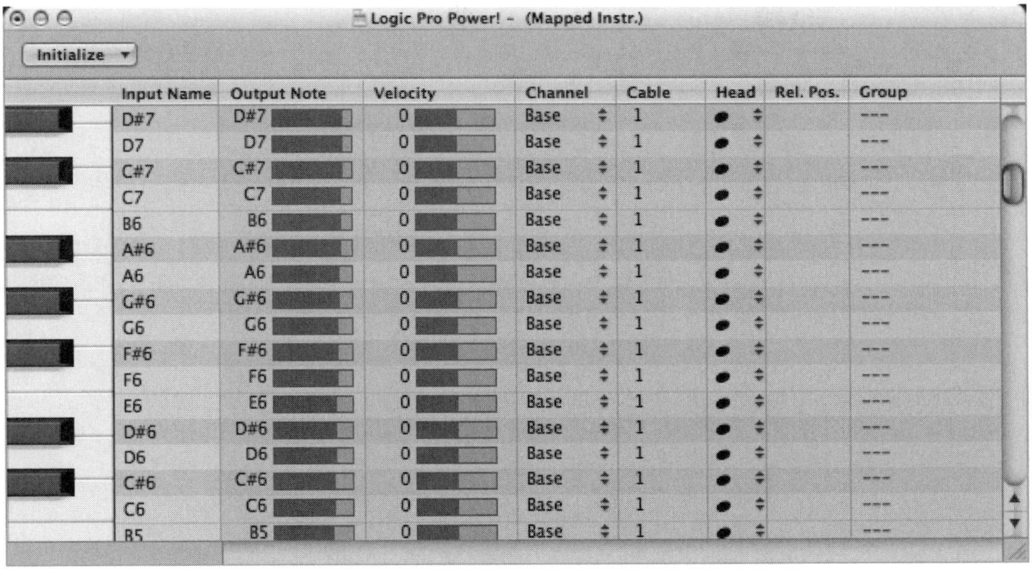

Figure 13.16   The Mapped Instrument window presents the majority of settings for mapped instrument objects.

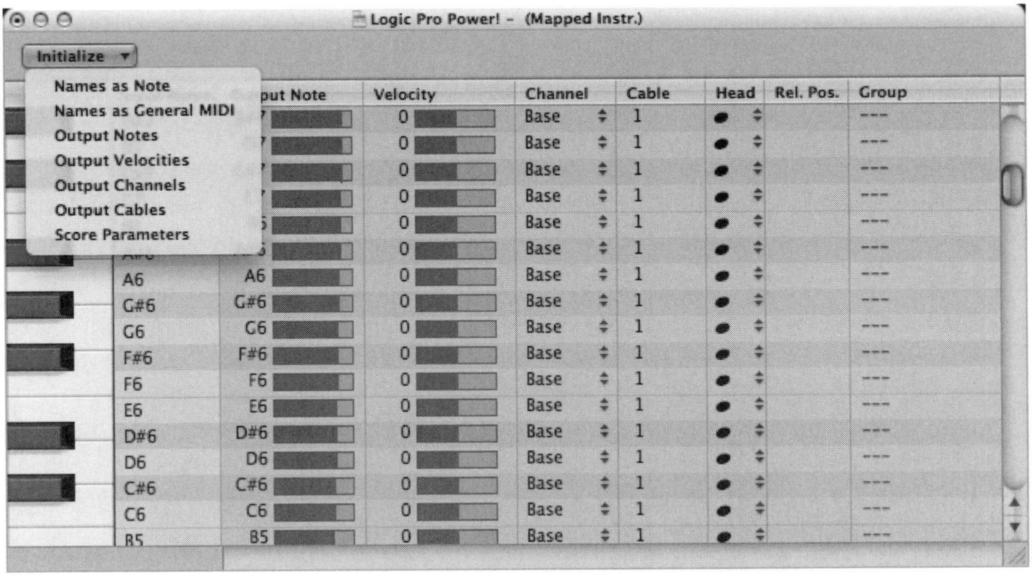

Figure 13.17   The Initialize local menu of the Mapped Instrument window.

all the names back to the default note pitch by selecting Initialize > Names as Note. If you want to assign the General MIDI drum names to notes, you can select Initialize > Names as General MIDI.

■ **Output Note.** Here you can set the output note independently, so it can actually be different from the input note. For example, if you are playing a drum controller that sends out a C#3 when you hit a particular pad, but you want that pad to trigger the drum sound located in your sound module at G#5, you could set the output note of C#3 in your mapped instrument to G#5. You can quickly return all the output note assignments to the same as the input notes by selecting Initialize > Output Notes.

■ **Velocity.** This is the same as the velocity adjustment for instrument objects. You can grab the beam with the mouse by clicking on it and dragging it, add or subtract from the offset value by dragging, or simply click inside the beam at the desired point. You can quickly reset all offsets to zero by selecting Initialize > Output Velocities.

■ **Channel.** In this column, you can set the MIDI channel for each note. This allows you to trigger drum sounds from different modules on different MIDI channels. The default setting for the parameter is Base, which specifies that each note uses the MIDI channel that has been set globally for the mapped instrument in its Parameter box. You can change any note's MIDI channel to any of the available 16 MIDI channels, or to All if you wish to send a note on all available channels. If you want to reset all selected notes to the Base value, you can select Initialize > Output Channels.

■ **Cable.** This parameter allows you to have up to 16 different cables, so you can send individual notes from the mapped instrument to unique objects to trigger sounds or to be further processed. If you ever wanted to reset all the cables of the multi instrument to cable #1 (the default cable), you can select Initialize > Output Cables.

■ **Head, Rel. Pos, Group.** These parameters specifically relate to the score notation and don't really affect MIDI performance at all. You can use these parameters to adjust how each note will appear on the staff. To reset them, you can select Initialize > Score Parameters.

Touch Tracks Object

The touch tracks object, shown in Figure 13.18, enables you to use Logic as an interactive live sequencer, not simply as a recording tool. With touch tracks, you can play an entire MIDI region (or even a Folder track full of MIDI regions) live from a MIDI controller (a keyboard, guitar synthesizer, and so on). This is really useful for groups and artists with sequenced tracks in their music who want to be able to trigger entire sequences during a live performance.

Setting up a touch tracks object couldn't be easier. After you create and double-click your touch tracks object, simply drag your MIDI regions (or your folder with MIDI regions inside) to the key that you want to trigger that region. You also can drag a MIDI region into the Environment, and

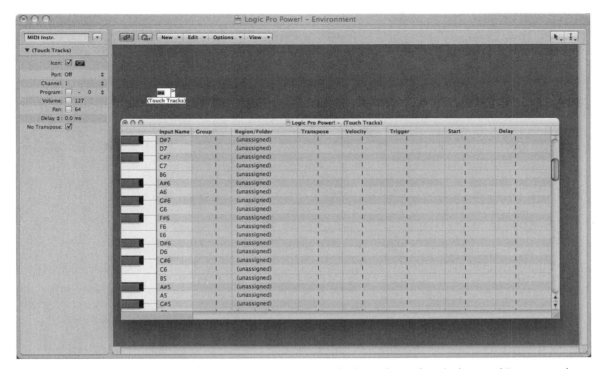

Figure 13.18   The touch tracks object, including its expanded Touch Tracks window and Parameter box.

Logic will create a touch tracks object automatically configured for every key on the keyboard to trigger your MIDI region.

Notice that the Parameter box of the touch tracks object includes the same basic MIDI parameters that are defined for instrument objects. Keep in mind that even though the touch tracks object has an output triangle to cable it to other objects, you cannot actually cable touch tracks to anything else.

When you use touch tracks live, you might want to mute those regions and folders in the Arrange assigned to the touch tracks object to ensure that those regions only play when you trigger them, and not as part of your preprogrammed sequence. Of course, if you *want* your MIDI regions to play exactly as programmed in addition to being available for you to perform live via touch tracks, do not mute those regions in the Arrange.

You can see in Figure 13.18 that the expanded Touch Tracks window shows the name of the MIDI region or folder assigned to a given note. There are a number of parameters across the top bar of the window that are defined here:

- **Input Name.** This is the name of the note. If you select a number of notes by dragging on them and then drag a MIDI region or folder into the Touch Tracks Region/Folder column, the MIDI region or folder will be assigned to the selected notes.

- **Group.** As in the Hyper Editor, if you assign a number of MIDI regions to the same group, when you trigger one of them, all the other regions in the same group will stop playing.

- **Region/Folder.** This is where the name of the MIDI region or folder will appear. If the notes below a given region are assigned to that region, you will see a vertical line instead of a name.

- **Transpose.** This column lets you know how many steps your part is transposed at that note. If your region is played across the entire keyboard, the transposition at the extreme ends will be pretty severe. If your region is not transposed at all, this column will be blank.

- **Velocity.** This determines how much the velocity at which you trigger a region will affect the velocities already in the region you are playing. A value of 100% means your trigger velocity will affect the velocity at which the region plays back significantly. A value of 50% means there will be some effect, and Off means there will be no effect on the region's velocities.

- **Trigger.** This column determines how playback will be handled. There are a number of different Trigger modes:

  - **Multi.** Playing the trigger note starts playing the MIDI region; playing the note again starts a second playback of the region without stopping the original region's playback.

  - **Single.** Playing the trigger note starts the MIDI region playing; playing the note again restarts playback of the MIDI region.

  - **Gate.** The MIDI region plays until the note is released or the end of the MIDI region is reached.

  - **Gate Loop.** The MIDI region loops until the trigger note is released.

  - **Toggle.** Playing the trigger note starts playback; playing it again stops playback.

  - **Toggle Loop.** The MIDI region loops until the note is played again.

- **Start.** You can quantize how playback will begin and end with this parameter. Free means there is no quantization. Next 1/16, 1/4, or 1/1 will start the next region you trigger playing at the next 1/16, 1/4, or bar interval, depending on your selection.

- **Delay.** This enables you to set a delay for when playback will begin. The left side of the column sets the delay in note values; the right side sets the delay in ticks.

Expert Tip: Using Touch Tracks to Trigger Audio   Touch tracks work only with MIDI regions, not audio regions, but you can still use touch tracks to trigger audio parts if you have a sampler, such as the EXSmkII sampler that comes with Logic Pro 9. Record the audio parts you want to be triggered as samples, and then trigger those samples from a MIDI region in Logic. The EXS24mkII (or other software sampler) will then stream samples directly from your hard drive. You might need to adjust the Delay parameter if you notice some latency. This way, the touch tracks object will allow you to trigger a sampler that will in turn trigger your audio! Between this method and the ability to convert regions to new sampler tracks, Logic gives you a couple of different methods to enable you to sequence your audio tracks as creatively as your MIDI tracks.

Fader Object

Fader objects enable you to send MIDI events to different objects. There are many different fader varieties, as Figure 13.19 shows.

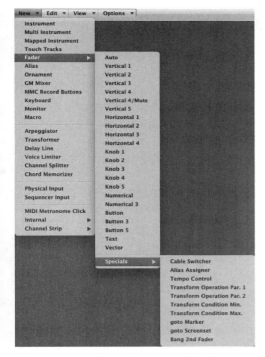

Figure 13.19 The submenus of fader types in the New local menu of the Environment. Despite how many varieties of faders there are, they all do basically the same thing—send MIDI events to objects.

All faders have the same parameters, as shown in Figure 13.20. All of them can be set to accept various MIDI message types as inputs or outputs, can be set to different values, and can be adjusted by the user.

The Parameter box for fader objects includes the following parameters, from top to bottom:

■ **Object Name.** You can name your fader by clicking in this text box.

■ **Icon.** You can select an icon for your text box. This is of limited use because you'll rarely want a fader to show up in the Arrange window.

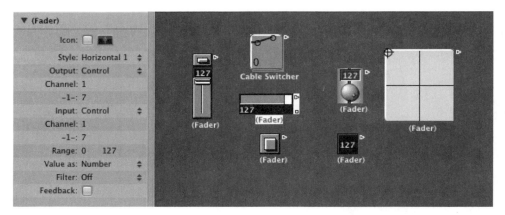

Figure 13.20   Despite the varieties of faders, all have the same Parameter box.

- **Style.** You can use this to change the style of your fader; for example, you can turn your knob fader into a horizontal fader or change your cable switcher to look like a knob.

- **Output.** This enables you to select the sort of event that will be output from the fader. Your choices are various MIDI events and the following Logic-only options: Switch (for a cable switcher), Fader (to send automation data to Logic), or Meta (for sending Logic's internal meta messages to other Environment objects or to Logic's sequencer).

- **Channel.** This determines the MIDI channel on which the fader will output.

- **-1-.** This determines the control message the fader will output. It is the note number if the fader definition is Note or P-Pres, the MSB if the fader definition is Pitchbend, and it has no meaning for C-Pres and SysEx.

- **Input.** This determines the type of input message that the fader will accept. The In definition and its components determine which MIDI messages will control the fader remotely. The special thing about the cable switcher in this context is that the message corresponding to the In definition will switch the switch rather than passing through it.

- **Channel.** This determines the MIDI channel on which the fader looks for input.

- **-1-.** This determines the MIDI message number the fader looks for on input.

- **Range.** This is the minimum and maximum MIDI values for the fader. Full range is 0 to 127, but you can narrow the range for your fader if you wish.

- **Value As.** You can choose your fader to display its value as a number, a dB value, a Hz value, a pan value, and so forth, depending on the type of data the fader is handling.

- **Filter.** Usually, this is used to filter the type of incoming messages to which the fader responds, in order to prevent MIDI doubling or feedback for MIDI hardware devices that do not have a Local Off or MIDI Thru Off function. When used properly, the Filter parameter can be one of the fader's most useful features, but because it deals with advanced MIDI metadata and hardware MIDI functioning, it is far beyond the scope of this book. It is better to ignore this parameter, which is why the default is Off.

■ **Feedback.** The Feedback check box enables you to create cabling feedback loops (which Logic otherwise prevents). Leave it unchecked unless you know what you're doing.

There is one notable exception to this list. The Vector fader substitutes the Input and Output parameters with Vertical and Horizontal parameters, which define the type of MIDI data that is transmitted as you move the crosshair along each axis of the fader. As you start creating your own macros and Environment construction in Logic, you can cable fader objects to other objects so that you can send data and change parameters with the mouse. As your Environment creations become more advanced, you will find fader objects to be very important in your arsenal.

Alias Object

If you select an object and then choose New > Alias from the local New menu of the Environment, you will create an alias—or duplicate—of your original object. Figure 13.21 shows an alias of a MIDI instrument object next to its parent object.

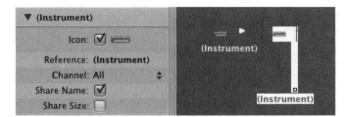

Figure 13.21   An alias object next to its parent object.

The alias object is effectively identical to the original, but it does have a Parameter box that allows you to rename it, choose a new icon, set which object it is referring to, and choose whether you want it to share its name and size with its parent object. The main use for alias objects is when you need many identical faders. You can configure a single fader object and then create as many alias objects as you need. Each will be set to the proper style, channel, MIDI event, and so on automatically, and each fader can be adjusted independently.

Ornament Object

This object is simply an empty box. Seriously. The Color parameter has no effect on the ornament object. Its sole purpose is to be background behind an Environment construction. You can perhaps use the ornament object as an organizational aid by putting a boundary around your Environment construction. If you are a little doubtful as to the value of this object, join the club!

GM Mixer Object

The GM mixer object is designed to control the 16 MIDI channels of a MIDI hardware device that conforms to the GM, XG, or GS standard. The object appears as a self-contained mixer consisting of MIDI channel strips from the Mixer, as Figure 13.22 shows.

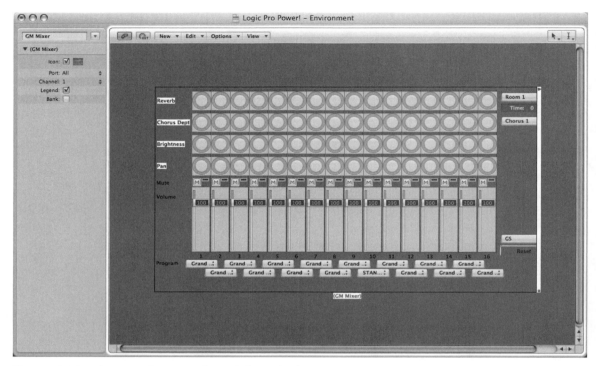

Figure 13.22   The GM mixer. You'll need this only if you are using Logic to control 16 MIDI channels of a General MIDI device.

This mixer should be pretty straightforward to operate, since we discussed channel strips in detail previously. You will most likely never use this object unless you use an external General MIDI sound source, and even then I'd highly recommend you use the simpler, more intuitive, and more powerful Mixer for mixing your MIDI tracks.

MMC Record Switches Object

The MIDI Machine Control (MMC) record switches object gives you 21 memory buttons (or switches) that you can use to trigger various setups on your MIDI hardware. Not many hardware boxes use MMC, and for those that do, usually the most important functions are the Transport functions, which do not require this object.

Keyboard Object

The keyboard object, as shown in Figure 13.23, creates a virtual MIDI keyboard in the Environment.

Figure 13.23   The keyboard object. You can cable this to other objects in order to send them MIDI notes.

This keyboard can be cabled to Environment objects, and when you click on a key in the virtual keyboard, that MIDI note will be sent. The main purpose for the keyboard object is that you can use it to monitor and test your Environment constructions to ensure that they react properly when receiving MIDI notes. This saves you from needing an external keyboard hooked up if you just want to test something quickly.

Monitor Object

The monitor object is a window that displays all events passing through it. It is a very useful testing tool, and it also can be used to branch cables because it accepts input from one source but can output to many sources. Figure 13.24 shows a keyboard object feeding a monitor object.

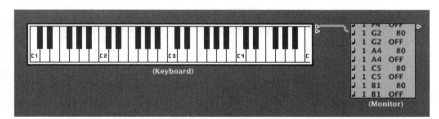

Figure 13.24   A monitor object displaying all the notes being sent by the keyboard object.

Macro

Macros are not actually objects, but collections of Environment objects and their cabling. You create a macro by selecting all the objects that you have in your construction and then choosing New > Macro from the New local menu of the Environment. Figure 13.25 shows an Environment construction that has been packed into a macro. If you wish to create a macro that cannot be unpacked, select New > Macro with the Control key pressed.

You can cable macros to other objects just like any other object, you can check their Icon parameter to have them available in the Arrange window's track hierarchical menus, and so on. You can even nest macros within macros! Be aware that there is a limit to the number of objects you can have in a macro, based on how much processing they are doing. (Generally 100 to 200 objects is the maximum.)

The advantage of macros is that they are more portable to other Logic songs, and because they are single structures, you can access them in the Arrange Track List.

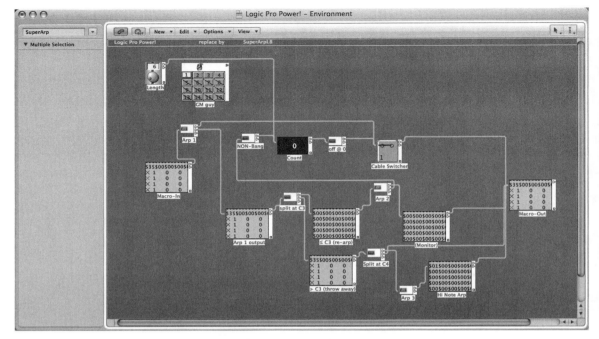

Figure 13.25 In this figure, you can see a complex construction of signal splitters, monitors, and arpeggiators that has been packed into a macro, shown at the upper-left corner of the Environment window, called SuperArp.

Arpeggiator Object

The arpeggiator object will "arpeggiate" chords by cycling through all held notes in a user-selectable pattern. To be used, the arpeggiator object must be cabled to a MIDI device, and Logic's Transport must be running. You can use the arpeggiator to arpeggiate MIDI data in real time, or you can record its output by cabling it to the sequencer input object. (Be sure to record to a No Output track so you don't hear everything doubled!) Figure 13.26 shows the arpeggiator object and its Parameter box.

The arpeggiator object offers the following parameters:

- **Direction.** You have seven options for the direction of your arpeggio:

  - **Up.** Lowest note to highest note.

  - **Down.** Highest note to lowest note.

  - **Up/Down.** Up and down; low to high, then high to low. The highest and lowest notes repeat after each cycle.

  - **Auto.** Up or down, depending on whether the second note in the chord is played before or after the first note.

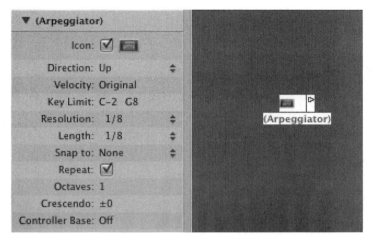

Figure 13.26   The arpeggiator object and its Parameter box.

- **Up/Down2.** Similar to Up/Down above, but the highest and lowest notes do not repeat.

- **Random.** Notes play in random order.

- **All.** All notes play at the same time.

- **Velocity.** This lets you choose the velocity of the arpeggiated notes. Original will retain the original velocities of the notes, and Random will randomize the velocities between 1 and the original value, or you can select a fixed velocity between 1 and 127.

- **Key Limit.** You can define the pitch limits of the arpeggiator here, down to a pitch of C–2 and up to a pitch of G8.

- **Resolution.** This lets you set the note resolution of the arpeggios. All note divisions are represented in the pull-down menu. A value of None means the arpeggiator is switched off.

- **Length.** This lets you set the length of each arpeggiated note. This parameter offers a pull-down menu with all the note divisions represented. Original will keep the same length as the performed notes for the arpeggiated notes, and Random will randomize the note lengths.

- **Snap To.** If you want the arpeggiator to start and end arpeggiations only on a specific note division, you can set that here. This can be helpful in trying to sync the arpeggiator to other MIDI data.

- **Repeat.** If this is set to On, the arpeggiator will continue as long as you hold the chord down. If this is set to Off, the chord will stop as soon as all notes in the arpeggio have been played one time.

- **Octaves.** You can set the arpeggiator to repeat over up to 10 octaves.

- ■ **Crescendo.** This will add or subtract the given velocity value each time the arpeggio is repeated.

- ■ **Controller Base.** This will enable the parameters of the arpeggiator to be controlled remotely by controller events if the parameter is set to On. The setting for this parameter is a number representing the lowest MIDI CC# used to control arpeggiator settings. That CC# controls the top parameter (Direction), and consecutive CC#s control the remaining parameters, counting down from the top.

You can use more than a single arpeggiator object in a single Environment construction, so even if you don't feel Logic's arpeggiator offers the most cutting-edge options, you can build your own cutting-edge arpeggiator macro or structure. That's the power of the Environment!

Transformer Object

The transformer object enables you to cable a real-time Transform window into your Environment creations. As you can see in Figure 13.27, when double-clicked, the transformer opens up to a smaller Transform window that is functionally similar to the Transform window discussed in Chapter 8, with the exception that there are no time-based parameters because the transformer object works in real time.

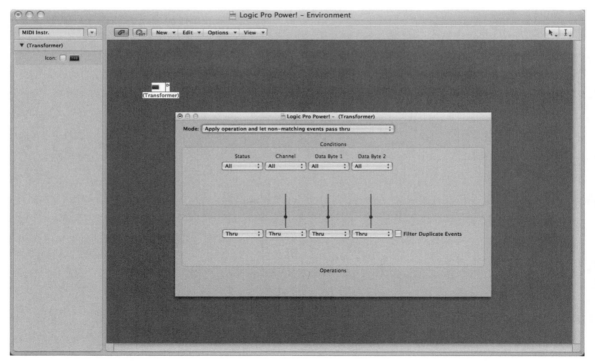

Figure 13.27 The transformer object is an Environment object version of the MIDI Transform window. Use this to make complex transformations of your MIDI data in your Environment constructions.

As your Environment creations become more complex, you can use the transformer to select and transform MIDI data running through your Environment as you would use the Transform window to modify your region data. Please refer to the Transform window section in Chapter 8 for more on the full power of this object.

Delay Line Object

This object creates a MIDI echo effect by adding multiple repeats of MIDI data. Figure 13.28 shows the delay line object and its Parameter box.

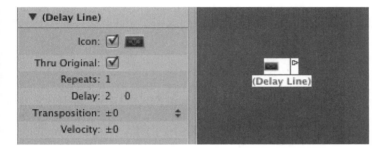

Figure 13.28   The delay line object and its Parameter box.

The delay line object offers the following parameters:

■   **Thru Original.** If this box is checked, the original signal also will pass through the delay line along with the repeats. If this box is unchecked, the original MIDI data will not pass through.

■   **Repeats.** This is the number of repeats, from 0 to 99. (No repeats means the delay line is off.)

■   **Delay.** The delay time between repeats. The left value is divisions; the right value is ticks.

■   **Transposition.** You can choose to transpose the repeats with this parameter, either up or down 96 semitones.

■   **Velocity.** You can change the velocity values of the notes by adding or subtracting a MIDI value of up to 99 per repeat.

If you feel like experimenting, you can cable together the arpeggiator and the delay line to create some very wild and interesting MIDI repeats! However, if you use multiple outputs of the delay line, individual repeats will cycle through them. Also keep in mind that the delay line repeats all messages, not just notes.

Voice Limiter Object

The voice limiter object restricts the number of voices that are sent to a MIDI object by turning off any MIDI notes over a selected limit. You can restrict a MIDI instrument to between 1 and 32 notes. There are only two parameters: Voices, where you define how many voices the voice limiter will limit the instrument to, and Priority, where you decide which notes will be turned off first—the highest (Bottom, giving low notes priority), lowest (Top, giving high notes priority), or first performed (Last, giving most recently performed notes priority).

If you are making a MIDI Environment that sends out more notes than your MIDI devices can handle, this can be useful. If you have older synthesizers that do not have the high voice counts (64 or more) of modern instruments, you might find this object useful.

Channel Splitter Object

The channel splitter object, shown in Figure 13.29, routes MIDI events according to their MIDI channel. It offers one output for each of the 16 MIDI channels and an additional SUM output that combines all channels not specifically routed to other objects.

Figure 13.29   The channel splitter object enables you to route individual MIDI channels to different locations.

This object is great for constructions in which you want to route specific MIDI channels to specific destinations. You can process each MIDI channel separately this way, or you can separate only a few channels, and the rest will appear at the SUM output.

Chord Memorizer Object

The chord memorizer object has a number of functions. It can map single notes into chords. The chords can contain 12 notes or fewer. The chord memorizer also can be used as a "scale filter" by mapping out-of-scale notes to nothing. The Chord Memorizer window consists of two keyboards: one for inputting the note to map to a chord, and a second for inputting the chord. Figure 13.30 shows the chord memorizer object, its Parameter box, and its window.

The Parameter box of the chord memorizer contains the following parameters:

■ **Channel.** The chord memorizer will output all notes to this MIDI channel.

■ **Key Limit.** The notes within this range will be mapped to chords. Notes outside this range pass through the chord memorizer unchanged.

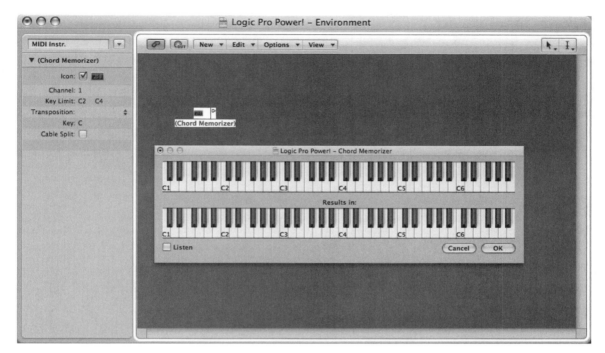

Figure 13.30   The chord memorizer object, its Parameter box, and the Chord Memorizer window.

- **Transposition.** You can transpose the chords that are output up or down 96 semitones with this parameter.

- **Key.** The entire chord map will be transposed to the key you set here.

- **Cable Split.** If On, this parameter will split each note of the chord down a different cable, if you have enough cables.

The easiest way to configure the chord memorizer is to click on an input note in the top keyboard and then click on the notes on the bottom keyboard until the entire chord you want has been played. If you click a key by mistake and turn on a note you do not want in your chord, a second click will turn that note off. When you are finished with the chord, click the OK button or another input note to configure another note in the same chord memorizer.

You can have a single chord memorizer memorize only one chord for each input note—so if you input a C and then selected a chord, then input a D and selected a chord, and then input C again and input a final chord, the only chords that would be stored in the chord memorizer would be the chord for the D note and the second chord for the C note. Of course, you can create as many chord memorizer objects as you'd like.

All octaves within the chord memorizer range use the same chords, and the relations between the input note's octave and the output chord notes' octaves are preserved.

Physical Input Object

This object has an input for up to 64 physical MIDI interface channels. In general, the only physical input object you will need is the one created with your initial song. It is the virtual interface between your hardware MIDI interface's MIDI IN(s) and Logic, and normally is connected to the sequencer input object, allowing your MIDI hardware to be recorded by the sequencer.

You can have only one physical input. If you create a new one, the old one is deleted along with all its cabling. If you have no physical input, all MIDI input is automatically routed to Logic's sequencer.

Sequencer Input Object

This object represents the input to Logic's sequencer (in other words, the Arrange tracks). You will generally have a single sequencer input object in a song, and that will be enough. Logic automatically creates one with each song.

You can have only one sequencer input. If you create a new one, the old one is deleted along with all its cabling.

The only reason to have the physical input/sequencer input combination is to insert other processes between them. Otherwise, you can do without either.

MIDI Click Object

The MIDI click object was discussed in Chapter 5. It enables you to use an external MIDI device to act as the Metronome by generating a click in time with Logic's tempo. Figure 13.31 shows the MIDI click object and its Parameter box.

The MIDI click object is pretty complete. As you can see in Figure 13.31, it enables you to send different notes for up to three beats and lets you set the note, channel, and velocity for each. However, MIDI timing can never be as accurate as the KlopfGeist software click, which is sample accurate. Therefore, I recommend that you do not use this object.

Another use for the MIDI click object (made more convenient by the addition of the KlopfGeist) is as a timer for other Environment processes. For example, you can use it to drive a MIDI LFO made from arpeggiators or delay lines.

Internal Objects

These objects were discussed in Chapter 9.

Channel Strip Objects

Channel strip objects should be very familiar by now. They were covered in particular depth in Chapter 7.

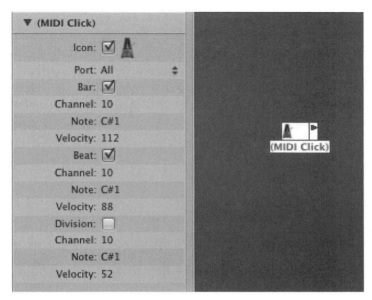

Figure 13.31   The MIDI click object and its Parameter box. You can set up which MIDI note the object will send to your MIDI device for different beats.

Cabling Environment Objects

Now that you have an overview of the objects you can use to create your own unique Environment constructions, let's talk about cabling. The basics of cabling are extremely simple: As you grab the small triangular outlet found at the top right of every object and drag the mouse, the mouse pointer will turn into a patch cord plug. You simply drag that patch cable to the object to which you want to cable your initial object, and when you release the mouse, a gray line will connect the two objects, indicating they are cabled together. Figure 13.32 illustrates a very simple cabling.

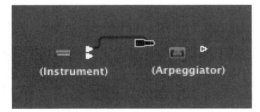

Figure 13.32   Here you see an instrument object being cabled to the arpeggiator object. After clicking on the triangle at the top right of the instrument object, the pointer turns into the patch plug, and when the mouse is released on the arpeggiator object, the two objects will be cabled together. At that point, the arpeggiator can be selected on an Arrange track, and when you hit Play in Logic and perform with your MIDI instrument, the result will be arpeggiated.

As Figure 13.32 shows, creating a basic Environment structure is very simple. As you've no doubt already surmised, you can cable far more than two objects together. In fact, you can cable an unlimited number of cables into an object. All incoming MIDI data is simply mixed at the input of the object. You'll also notice from Figure 13.32 that as soon as one output cable was used, another output triangle appeared directly beneath the first triangle. Again, this is so you can output as many cables from an object as you wish. Keep in mind the limit mentioned earlier of about 100 to 200 objects in a macro. To delete cabling, simply click on a cable with the Eraser tool or press Delete.

You can cable objects serially by selecting Options > Cable Serially. You might want to do this to cable all the faders in a synthesizer mixer you are constructing, for example. You can use the Apply Buffer Template To > Cable(s) function if you want to cable many objects to the same destination. And if you want each cable to be the same color as the object from which it originated, choose View > Colored Cables. You can even cable objects between more than one Environment layer; layers are discussed in the next section.

Special Cable Outputs

Certain objects—channel splitter; cable switcher; delay line; chord memorizer in Cable Split mode; transformer object in Condition Splitter, Alternating Split, and TA Splitter modes; and physical input—have functionally different outputs, as opposed to normal objects where each additional output sends the same data. When using one of these special objects, if you want to route a signal from a single output to more than one destination, you'll need to use a monitor object. The monitor object itself doesn't do anything to the data (other than give you a window to view it), but like other objects, it can have as many outputs as you need.

Environment Layers

Layers are different display windows of the Environment. They enable you to organize your Environment so that you are not flooded with too much information at a time, and you can create layers to house only those constructions you want to use at a given time. You can easily switch from one Environment layer to another by choosing the Options > Go to Previous Layer command or by using the Layer pull-down menu directly under the Toolbox in the parameter bar of the Environment. Figure 13.33 shows you the Layer pull-down menu in the parameter bar.

Figure 13.33 The Layer box, inside the parameter bar of the Environment. Here you see the Mixer layer. If you click on the box, the pull-down menu of all available layers will appear.

To create a new layer, you have two options. You can choose Options > Layer > Create to insert a new layer above the current layer. You can also select the last option in the Layer box pull-down menu, Create Layer. This will create a new layer at the end of the Layer list. You can then name the layer by double-clicking the Layer box to open a text window for you to type into. All newly created layers are devoid of objects, waiting for you to fill them with your constructions.

Specialized Layers

You can do anything you want with all the layers in your Environment—even the layers automatically created for you by Logic—except for two protected layers: the All Objects layer and the Global Objects layer.

The first layer in the Environment is always the All Objects layer, with one exception (noted in a moment). This layer lists every object in the Environment. You can use this layer to quickly get an overview of all the objects you are using or to navigate to a specific object. You can also select an object and choose Options > Go to Layer of Object in order to switch from the All Objects layer to the layer on which your selected object resides.

The other protected layer is the second one, the Global Objects layer. In this layer you can place objects that you wish to appear in every layer in your Environment. This is useful if you want particular output ports on every layer, for example. Be very sparing in the objects you place here, however, because they can clutter up your Environment layers pretty quickly.

Objects and Layers

Layers are purely an organizational and aesthetic partition; they do not actually separate the objects from each other in any way. You can move an object from one layer to another by selecting an object and then choosing a different layer from the Layer box while pressing the Option key. You also can use the Clipboard to cut, copy, and paste objects from one layer to another. Because you can open more than one instance of any window in Logic, you can also open multiple Environment windows and simply drag an object from a layer in one Environment window to a different layer in the second Environment window.

Not only can you easily move objects between layers, but you can cable objects between layers as well. As noted earlier, you can simply open two Environment windows and drag a cable from an object in one Environment window to an object in the other Environment window, regardless of the layer each window has visible. You can also hold down the Option key while clicking and dragging on the output triangle of an object to bring up a pop-up menu of available instruments to which you may cable your object simply by selecting it. A cable connection between layers looks like a cable that goes through a hole in the ceiling, as shown in Figure 13.34.

Building Your Own Environments

Everyone ends up with a completely customized workspace in Logic, thanks to the power and flexibility of the Environment. Hopefully, the details provided in this chapter are enough to get you started cabling your own Environment constructions together. Go ahead and experiment—that's the best way to learn!

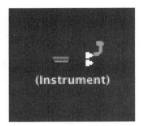

Figure 13.34 An object cabled to an object on a different layer of the Environment.

Space requirements mean that since this chapter is already around the 40-page mark, there aren't as many tips, tricks, and tutorials as you might have liked. Luckily, the author of *Emagic Logic Tips and Tricks* (Course Technology PTR, 2003) wrote an entire book in the form of PDF tutorials and prebuilt Environments called *The Environment Toolkit*—and it's free! You can obtain it directly from his website: www.swiftkick.com. This website is perhaps the best Environment support site on the Internet, with hundreds of free Environments and multi-instrument objects created by Logic users and freely offered to the Logic community. In fact, the Super Arpeggiator that Orren Merton designed (see Figure 13.25) is available for free download on that site, as well as myriad others. Have yourself a look around the site, get the Environment Toolkit, and enjoy creating your virtual studio!

Swiftkick.com Environments and Logic 9   Some of those contributed Environments on swiftkick.com (such as Orren's SuperArp) were initially created and uploaded using Logic 4 or earlier. This means that you'll need to open the file first in Logic 5, 6, or 7 and re-save it, since Logic 9 can only open Logic songs from Logic 5 and up, and Logic 8 is also incapable of opening pre-Logic 5 files. If you don't have an earlier version of Logic, ask for help on the Logic User Group at www.logic-users-group.com—someone will undoubtedly be able to help.

14 Advanced Tempo Operations

Tempo, meaning speed and timing, is one of the most important elements in music. Tempo management can be as simple as agreeing on the tempo of a song and asking all the musicians to play in time. It can be as complicated as keeping track of multiple tempo changes throughout a musical movement—or even continuous tempo changes. With digital audio sequencers being the nerve center for both electronic and acoustic, programmed and performed tracks, it becomes vital that the sequencer keeps everything synchronized and gives the user the tools to fully implement whatever tempo requirements he has.

Luckily, Logic is up to the task. Logic offers many different tempo functions and, in typical Logic fashion, many ways to use them, depending on your own personal style. It can sync with external hardware through a number of common protocols, and it keeps perfect internal sync.

We have already discussed the most innovative and intuitive controls Logic gives you over tempo—the Tempo and Beat Mapping tracks, discussed in detail in Chapter 4. By contrast, in this chapter, you'll explore Logic Pro's other tools to work with tempo and synchronization.

Tempo Operations versus Flex Time   If you're not familiar with the musical concept of tempo, we forgive you for thinking that "tempo operations" are part of Logic Pro's Flex Time functions. After all, Flex is supposed to adjust audio to the tempo, right? But in fact, it is the reverse: Flex Time relies on Logic's facility with tempo. Here's a quick explanation.

As explained above, Logic includes lots of functions to manage the tempo—that is, the speed and timing—of your *project*. Flex Time is a subset of features that lets you manage the tempo of your *audio regions*. So for example, let's say that you use Flex Time's quantize features to adjust your audio to the song tempo. Flex is relying on Logic's tempo operations to define and manage the project tempo, which then determines how Flex will quantize the "flexed" audio region.

So as you can see, while Flex relies on Logic's tempo management to work its magic, Logic's tempo operations are far more than simply an aspect of Flex Time.

The Tempo Display

The first step in tempo management is to know what the tempo is. As we discussed previously in Chapter 5, the tempo is displayed in the Tempo display in the Transport, along with the Project End. Figure 14.1 shows this.

Figure 14.1   As you recall from Chapter 5, the Tempo/Project End display on the Transport shows the current song tempo. Chapter 5 also explained how to change the Display Preferences for the Tempo display if you want.

The Tempo display will show the current song tempo even if an external device to which Logic is synched is determining the tempo. If your Logic project has only a single tempo, and Logic is the master of any external devices (or if you have no external devices, and Logic is the only tempo master), the easiest way to set the tempo is simply to double-click the tempo in the Tempo display and manually enter the correct number. For more involved tempo manipulations, Logic offers a number of methods to edit tempo.

Recording and Editing Tempo

Whether you want to add only a few subtle tempo changes or a complex set of evolving tempos for different movements, Logic gives you a number of methods to record and edit tempo changes. This section will discuss the variety of ways you can either perform or program tempo changes.

Programming Tempo Changes on the Tempo Track

The Tempo track discussed in Chapter 4 not only displays any tempo changes in your song, but gives you an intuitive track on which to enter your tempo changes as well. Please refer to "The Tempo Track" section of Chapter 4 for the complete details.

Recording Tempo Changes

To record tempo changes while you are performing (for example, by adjusting a Tempo slider on external hardware), make sure the Allow Tempo Change Recording box is checked in the Project Settings > Recording window. You can access this window from File > Project Settings > Recording or by pressing Option+*. Figure 14.2 shows this preference turned on.

After you check this box, any tempo changes you make will be saved into the Tempo track, which is the internal list of tempo changes that Logic maintains to manage a song's tempo. The next subsections discuss the two ways to access, add to, and edit that Tempo track.

The Tempo Interpreter

If you want to record your tempo live, perhaps the best way to do it is to tap your tempo into Logic as you are performing. To accomplish this, Logic includes a Tap Tempo key command and

Figure 14.2   Check the Allow Tempo Change Recording preference in the Recording tab of the Project Settings window if you want to record tempo changes in real time.

a Tempo Interpreter window. You can access the Tempo Interpreter by selecting Options > Tempo > Tempo Interpreter or by clicking and holding the Sync button on the Transport to reveal its pull-down menu and selecting Open Tempo Interpreter. Figure 14.3 shows the Tempo Interpreter.

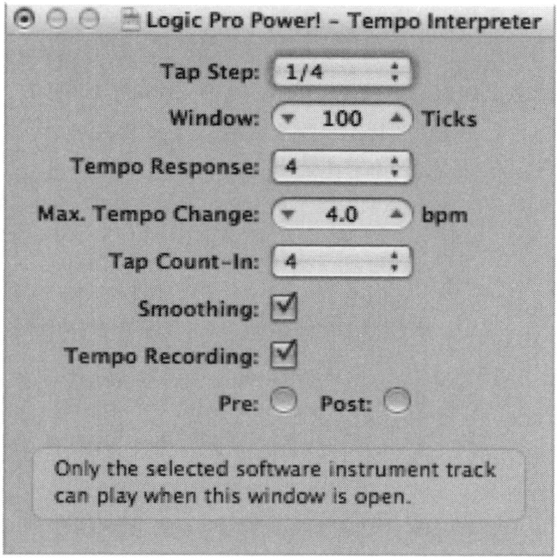

Figure 14.3   The Tempo Interpreter.

This window enables you to configure how Logic will interpret those tempos that you tap in with the Tap Tempo key command. A description of the parameters follows.

- **Tap Step.** This sets the note value that Logic will assign to each of your taps. Generally, the best possible selection is 1/4 notes. Smaller figures will give you too much variation, and larger divisions will not accurately capture the tempo.

- **Window [Ticks].** This adjusts how much of a window in time there is in which taps will be interpreted as tempo taps. In other words, if you set a huge window, only taps that are a very large number of ticks apart will be counted as taps for determining tempo. If you set a tiny window, nearly every tick will be counted. In general, you'll want this value to be large enough that double-clicks or ghost-clicks won't be counted but anything else will.

- **Tempo Response.** This sets Logic's internal sensitivity for tempo changes. The higher the value, the more responsive Logic will be—meaning, the more often Logic will change the tempo of the song. If you are hoping for a constant tempo, a value of 2 should work. If you are expecting some tempo changes, a value of 4 is recommended.

- **Max. Tempo Change.** You probably don't want wild changes in your song. You should set as small a value as possible here so that any inconsistencies in your tapping don't result in outlandishly large tempo variations.

- **Tap Count-In.** This enables you to tap a count into your song. Type in the number of taps you want as a count (if any).

- **Smoothing.** If you check this box, any jumps in tempo will be smoothed out. If you want your taps to be followed exactly, do not check this box.

- **Tempo Recording.** This will create a real-time Tempo List if you are creating tap tempo events in Record mode. Normally, you will not need this, so you'll want to leave it off.

- **Pre and Post.** This has to do with how your taps are displayed onscreen. If you check Pre, every tap that is input will be displayed. If you check Post, only those taps that are in the accepted timeframe defined in the Window parameter above will be displayed. Accepted taps flash yellow; unaccepted taps flash red. If you do not check either box, of course, no taps will flash at all.

You will need to set the Sync mode to Manual and ensure that the Auto Enable External Sync box is checked in the General tab of the Synchronization window, shown in Figure 14.4. You can access this window by selecting File > Project Settings > Synchronization or by pressing Option+Y. You can also change the Sync mode by clicking and holding the Sync button in the Transport bar and selecting the desired Sync setting.

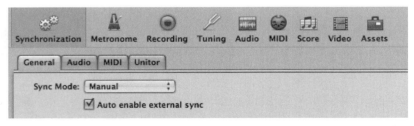

Figure 14.4 The Synchronization pane of the Project Settings window. Under the General tab, set Sync mode to Manual and check Auto Enable External Sync for Logic to recognize tap tempo.

Finally, use the Tap Tempo key command Shift+T to record tempo this way.

Real-Time Tempo Fader

One of the special Environment fader objects is a Tempo fader. To create this object, in the Environment local menus select New > Fader > Specials > Tempo Control. This fader can create real-time tempo changes in Logic by using the mouse to adjust the fader value. The range of this fader is 50 BPM–177 BPM.

If you only want to adjust the tempo during playback, you do not need to cable the fader to any-thing—you can simply click and drag the fader, and the playback tempo will change. However, if you want to record your tempo changes or control the fader from something like a hardware MIDI device's pitch bend wheel (you can set this to another controller if you like, but using the pitch bend wheel generally works best during a MIDI performance), you'll need to connect the fader between the physical input and sequencer input objects. Fortunately, when you create the Tempo fader, a window opens, reminding you how to cable the tempo fader!

If you'd like to configure a MIDI controller for your Tempo fader, select Control in the Tempo fader's Object Parameter box and set the Channel to the correct MIDI channel and the -1- parameter to the desired MIDI controller number.

Tempo List Editor

The Tempo List Editor is available in the Lists area of the Arrange window <T> and as a floating window. You can create and edit tempo events in a text-based format using this window. If you click and hold the Transport's Sync button (see Chapter 5), you can select Open Tempo List from the pull-down menu. You also can access the Tempo List Editor from the global Options menu via Options > Tempo > Open Tempo List or via key command. Figure 14.5 shows the Tempo List Editor.

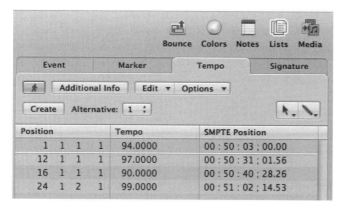

Figure 14.5   The Tempo List Editor.

You will notice that this looks basically like a standard Event List. You can manipulate the events in the Tempo Event List similarly to how you would in a normal Event List, as described in

Chapter 8. You can add tempo events at the current playhead position by clicking in the Tempo List with the Pencil tool or by clicking the Create button. A new tempo event will appear, which you can edit by double-clicking on any parameter (Position, Tempo, or SMPTE Position). Press Return to enter the data. Also, you can click on any of the parameters and scroll up or down with your mouse to change the value. Finally, you can delete tempo events by pressing the Delete key or using the Eraser tool.

Expert Tip: Keeping Track of Multiple Tempo Lists   Sometimes, you may want more than a single Tempo List in order to experiment with different tempos, changes in different places, and so on. To facilitate this, Logic allows you to store up to nine alternative Tempo Lists. In the global Tempo track or the Options local menu of the Tempo List Editor, select Tempo Alternatives, and in the hierarchical menu, you will be able to view any of your nine available alternatives. Remember that since the Tempo List Editor and the global Tempo track are showing the same information different ways, any changes you make to tempo events in one editor will show up in the other editor.

Tempo Operations

You can access the Tempo Operations window in a number of ways. In the global Options menu, you can select Options > Tempo > Tempo Operations. From the Tempo List Editor, you can access the Tempo Operations window from the local Options menu. From the global Options menu, you can choose Options > Tempo > Tempo Operations. You can open the Tempo Operations window from the pull-down menu accessible from the Sync button, again as with the Tempo Editors, and you can use the Open Tempo Operations key command Option+Shift+T. Figure 14.6 shows the Tempo Operations window.

As with the Tempo track or Tempo List Editor already discussed, the Tempo Operations window is another option for creating and editing tempo changes. To use the Tempo Operations window, you'll need to make a selection in another Tempo Editor; your tempo will be shown in the window. You might have to re-open the Tempo Operations window to reflect any recent tempo changes.

The Operation pull-down menu, shown in Figure 14.7, contains the six functions possible in the Tempo Operations window.

The following subsections describe each of the Tempo Operations window functions. You will find that most of these processes can be accomplished more quickly and intuitively in the Tempo track.

Create Tempo Curve

This function enables you to create a tempo curve. To generate a curve, first choose one of the three curves available from the Curve Type pull-down menu, shown in Figure 14.8.

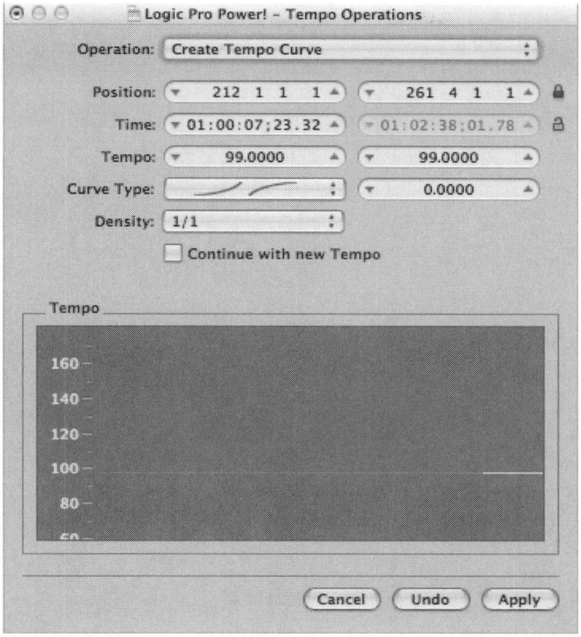

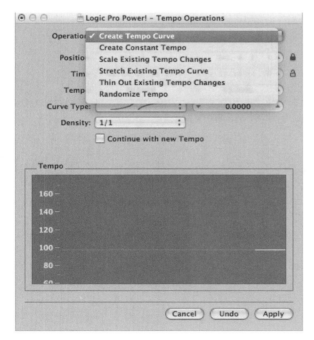

Figure 14.6   The Tempo Operations window.

Figure 14.7   The Operation pull-down menu lists the six functions possible in the Tempo Operations window.

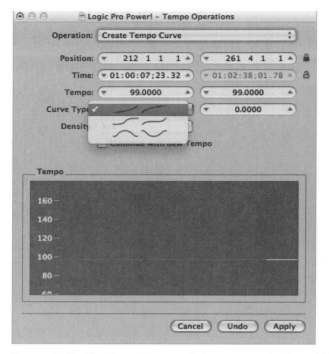

Figure 14.8 The Curve Type pull-down menu in the middle left of the Tempo Operations window contains the three curve shapes that you can choose for your tempo curve.

After you've chosen a curve, adjust the Position and Time settings to set the song position and length of your tempo change curve. Below those parameters, enter the starting and ending tempos you want in the Tempo track. Finally, set the Curvature parameter in the field to the right of the Curve Type menu, which determines the curve on which your tempo will speed up or slow down, depending on whether you enter a positive or a negative number. Values between 1 and –1 are allowed. After that, clicking the Apply button will create your tempo curve.

If you need more tempo events for a smoother curve, you can enter a smaller note denomination in the Density parameter. Figure 14.9 shows a descending tempo curve created using eighth notes.

You can check the Continue with New Tempo button if you want your song to maintain the tempo at which your curve ends. If you want to revert to the original song tempo after your curve, leave this option unchecked.

As you can see, creating tempo curves on the Tempo track is *far* simpler than using the Tempo Operations window!

Create Constant Tempo

If you want to eliminate all tempo events for a given area and simply set one tempo for a given length of time, this operation will do it.

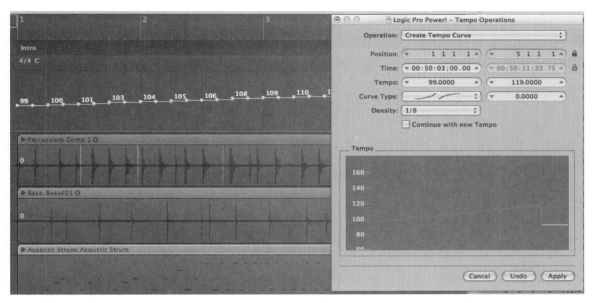

Figure 14.9   This curve was created by the Create Tempo Curve operation generating one tempo event every eighth note over the area specified by the chosen parameters.

As you can see in Figure 14.10, the only options with this function are the Position and Time settings for where and how long your constant tempo should be set and the Tempo box to enter what the tempo should be.

You can use the Continue with New Tempo button to either maintain this tempo for the rest of the song or revert to the original tempo after your section of constant tempo. Again, this process has been superseded by the Tempo track.

Scale Existing Tempo Changes

This lets you adjust currently existing tempo functions proportionally. You can set the Position and Time settings to determine where and how long you want your scaling to occur. You then enter the percentage of scaling you want to apply to the current tempo events and the average tempo. Figure 14.11 shows the Scale Existing Tempo Changes function.

Stretch Existing Tempo Curve

This enables you to shrink or elongate an existing tempo curve. You can set New End Position, New End Time, and the percentage of stretching you want as you adjust the length of the existing tempo curve. Figure 14.12 shows the Stretch Existing Tempo Curve screen.

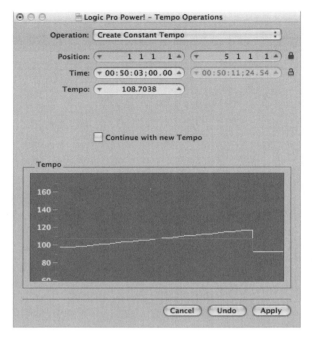

Figure 14.10   The Create Constant Tempo function display of the Tempo Operations window.

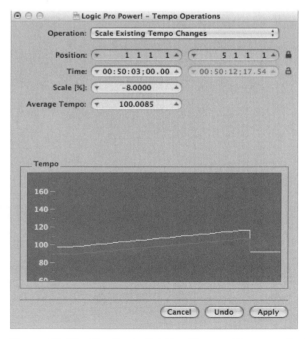

Figure 14.11   The Scale Existing Tempo Changes display.

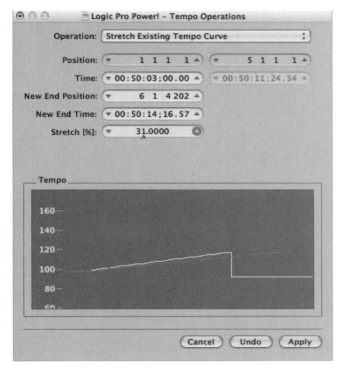

Figure 14.12 The Stretch Existing Tempo Curve display.

Thin Out Existing Tempo Changes

This lets you remove tempo events from a given length of time. You can set the Position or Time at which you want the thinning to occur and the Density of events you want to remain after processing. Figure 14.13 shows the Thin Out Existing Tempo Changes screen.

This is something that the Tempo Operations window might come in handy for, because the Tempo track doesn't offer a simpler way to thin out specific tempo changes, and manually deleting tempo events from the Tempo List could be time consuming.

Randomize Tempo

Finally, you can randomize your tempo—create a random deviation in beats per minute (BPM) from your current tempo. The Position and Time parameters determine where and how long the section of random tempo deviation should be, and Density defines how many program changes will appear per bar. Figure 14.14 shows the Randomize Tempo screen.

This is another thing that you might want to use the Tempo Operations window for, because the Tempo track doesn't lend itself to randomizing tempo changes.

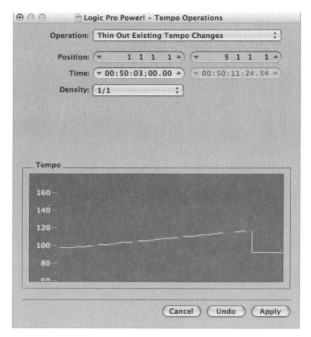

Figure 14.13   The Thin Out Existing Tempo Changes display.

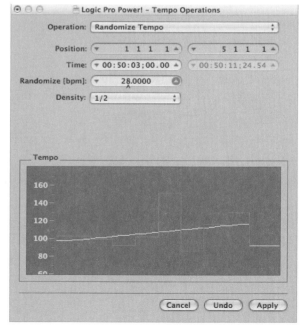

Figure 14.14   The Randomize Tempo display.

Matching the Project Tempo to an Audio Region

There might be times when you want to build a song, or even just a section of a song, around an audio clip. For example, you have a two-bar bass pattern, but you don't know its tempo. Now you have a problem—how to figure out how to set the project's tempo to a value that matches the tempo of your audio. Logic allows you to set your project's tempo to match your audio region with ease.

First, you need to select the audio region you will use to define the tempo. Next, set the locators either in the Bar ruler or in the Transport to start at the beginning of your audio region and end at a musically meaningful location, typically the end of a bar. Using the two-bar bass pattern as an example, you would set the cycle length to two bars, as shown in Figure 14.15.

Figure 14.15   To match the project tempo to an audio region, first set the locators to match the length you want your audio region to define.

Next, select Options > Tempo > Adjust Tempo Using Region Length and Locators or press Command+T. This opens the dialog shown in Figure 14.16, which asks whether you want to change the project's global tempo or simply change the tempo inside the locators.

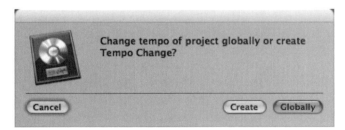

Figure 14.16   The Change Tempo of Project Globally or Create Tempo Change dialog.

Selecting Globally changes the entire project tempo to match that of your audio region. Selecting Create allows you to only change the tempo of the area inside the locators. Figure 14.17 shows the end result of this process—the selected audio region now fits the locators, and the project's tempo has changed to reflect the length of the audio region.

Figure 14.17   After matching the tempo to an audio region, the audio region fits the locators, and the project's tempo has changed.

Using Beat Detection to Adjust the Project Tempo

Logic Pro 9 gives you a new method of setting the project tempo. Using beat detection as a guide, you can have Logic analyze a region and offer a number of suggestions for possible tempos derived from the selected region. First, you need to select one or more regions. Use the Transients buttons in the Beat Mapping global track header to adjust the beat detection sensitivity. The more sensitive the beat detection, the more tempo options Logic will present you with when you invoke the Adjust Tempo Using Beat Detection command. You can access this command by selecting Options > Tempo > Adjust Tempo Using Beat Detection or by using the key command Option+Command+T. The Adjust Tempo Using Beat Detection command opens the Adjust Tempo Using Beat Detection dialog, shown in Figure 14.18. The Advanced Options area has been opened by clicking its disclosure triangle.

The parameters in the Adjust Tempo Using Beat Detection dialog are:

■ **Resulting Tempo.** The Resulting Tempo field displays the tempo that will result from using the settings assigned throughout the rest of the Adjust Tempo Using Beat Detection dialog.

■ **Detection Results.** The Detection Results area lists the potential results from which you can choose. The more transients you have detected, the more results you will see. The Tempo column lists the tempo of each result, and the Reliability column shows bars to demonstrate graphically the extent to which Logic believes a particular tempo to be correct. Logic automatically selects the first result. To select a different result, simply click on the desired result. The Resulting Tempo field will update to reflect the tempo of the selected result.

■ **Adjust Value By.** The Adjust Value By fields allow you to set a ratio that will affect the Resulting Tempo. A ratio of 3:1 will triple the tempo. A ratio of 1:3 will cut the tempo to one

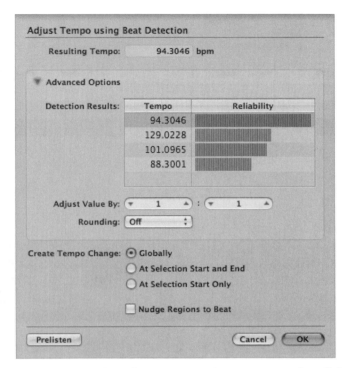

Figure 14.18   The Adjust Tempo Using Beat Detection dialog.

third of its original setting. Each Adjust Value By field can be set from 1 to 16 by clicking and dragging in the desired field, by clicking the up or down arrows in the desired field, or by double-clicking in the desired field and entering a value manually.

■ **Rounding.** The Rounding menu lets you define the type of rounding Logic will apply to the tempo value the Adjust Tempo Using Beat Detection command creates. Figure 14.19 shows the Rounding menu.

   If you select Off, the tempo will not be rounded. Selecting 1 Decimal, 2 Decimals, or 3 Decimals will round the tempo to tenths, hundredths, or thousandths place, respectively. Selecting Integer rounds the tempo to a whole number.

■ **Create Tempo Change.** Create Tempo Change gives you three options to define the extent to which the Adjust Tempo Using Beat Detection command affects the project tempo. If you select the Globally option, the tempo of the entire project will be altered to reflect the result of the Adjust Tempo Using Beat Detection command. If you select At Selection Start and End, the tempo of the area defined by the selected region(s) will be altered to reflect the result of the Adjust Tempo Using Beat Detection command, and the previous tempo will begin again at the end of the selected region(s). If you select At Selection Start Only, the tempo of the project

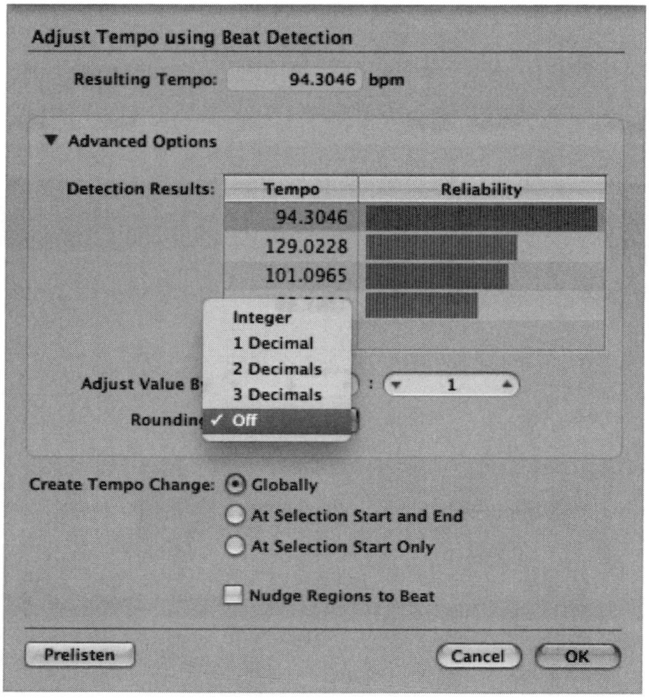

Figure 14.19 The Rounding menu lets you define what type of rounding, if any, will be applied to the tempo value resulting from the Adjust Tempo Using Beat Detection command.

will be altered at the beginning of the first selected region to reflect the result of the Adjust Tempo Using Beat Detection command. That tempo will remain in effect through the end of the project, unless there is another tempo change event later in the project.

- **Nudge Regions to Beat.** With this option checked, all selected regions will be nudged by the same amount as it takes to move the first transient in the first selected region to the closest beat.

- **Prelisten.** Click the Prelisten button to hear the resulting tempo change the Adjust Tempo Using Beat Detection command will create before actually finalizing the command.

Once you have set the parameters in the Adjust Tempo Using Beat Detection dialog to your liking, click the OK button, and the project tempo will change!

Working with Tempo Data in Audio Files

Logic Pro 9 automatically saves tempo data into audio files bounced or exported from Logic. The Options > Tempo menu gives you three options for handling this data, as seen in Figure 14.20.

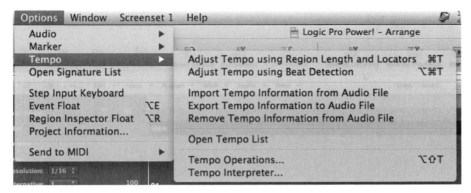

Figure 14.20   The Options > Tempo menu offers three options for dealing with tempo information in audio files.

First, you can select Import Tempo Information from Audio File. Simply select an audio region in the Arrange, select this command, and the tempo data from the region will automatically be added to the global Tempo track. You can also export data from the Tempo track into an audio region by selecting the Export Tempo Information to Audio File command. Finally, the Remove Tempo Information from Audio File command removes all tempo data from the selected region.

15 Synchronizing Hardware with Logic Pro

S ome composers and producers do not want to produce an entire composition inside the computer. Other producers want to, but do not have access to a computer powerful enough for the most demanding projects. At the time of this writing, Logic Pro features performance optimizations for the 8-core Mac Pro, which offers the highest level of performance from any personal computer. As previously mentioned, you can also create an entire distributed audio processing network, with additional Macintosh computers being used as Logic Nodes for nearly unprecedented processing capability. However, those who want to use external hardware recorders and other devices or who have older computers still need a way to synchronize external recording hardware with Logic. Luckily, Logic Pro can sync with hardware using a number of different formats. This chapter will explain how.

The Synchronization Window

The main synchronization settings are located in the Synchronization window, which can be accessed from the Project Settings submenu via File > Project Settings > Synchronization, from the Settings menu in the Toolbar, by clicking and holding Sync button in the Transport, or via the key command Option+Y. Any of these options will launch the Synchronization window, shown in Figure 15.1.

There are four different tabs across the top of the Synchronization window: General, Audio, MIDI, and Unitor (which is a truly excellent, and unfortunately out of production, MIDI interface that Emagic made, although Apple recently released a new driver for it, so they are apparently continuing to support it). The following sections deal with these tabs.

General Tab

As Figure 15.1 shows, the Synchronization window defaults to the General tab. These are the synchronization options you will most often need to configure—assuming you need to configure any of the default options. The following list offers an explanation of each option in the General tab of the Synchronization window, from top to bottom.

- **Sync Mode.** The Sync Mode pull-down menu lets you choose from three synchronization modes, as shown in Figure 15.2.

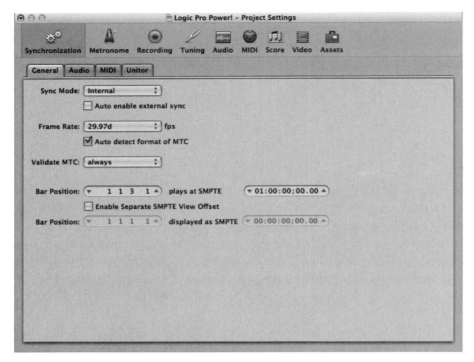

Figure 15.1   The Synchronization window.

Figure 15.2   The Sync Mode pull-down menu.

Each synchronization mode is described below:

- **Internal.** Logic will sync to its own internal clock—in other words, it will be the "master." Any external hardware connected to Logic can synchronize to Logic as a slave by using either MTC (MIDI Time Code) or MIDI Clock.

- **MTC.** Logic will synchronize to incoming MIDI Time Code (MTC) from an external device. The MTC can be generated directly by an external device, or the external device can generate a different time-code format (such as SMPTE time code), which some MIDI interfaces, such as the Unitor, can translate into MTC for Logic.

- **Manual.** In this mode, Logic will synchronize to the Tempo Interpreter (described in the previous chapter). In this case, the Tempo Interpreter can base its tempo on external pulses as well as on the computer keyboard.

- **Auto Enable External Sync.** With this option selected, Logic will synchronize to its own internal clock until it receives a synchronization signal from an external device in either MTC or Tempo Interpreter format. Logic will automatically sync to the first synchronization signal it receives. This is very important—make sure Logic doesn't receive multiple synchronization signals simultaneously! That will cause Logic to synchronize to the wrong source (or throw up an error message if it is truly confused).

- **Frame Rate [fps].** Frame rate refers to how many frames per second are set. A *frame* is the basic unit because most often these formats were used to synchronize audio to picture, and pictures raced by at a certain number of frames per second, depending on the format. Figure 15.3 shows the pull-down menu for the Frame Rate option.

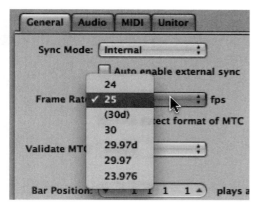

Figure 15.3   The Frame Rate pull-down menu.

The Frame Rate options include the following:

- **24.** The frame rate for motion pictures.

- **25.** This frame rate is common in Europe for PAL video and audio.

- **(30d).** This format stands for *30 fps drop* frame. This means that a certain number of frames are dropped from the normal 30 per second. This format is unusable in Logic because it cannot handle it in real time. This is why the option is in parentheses.

- **30.** This frame rate is no longer common in the United States for NTSC video and audio.

- **29.97d.** This is a more usable, real-time version of the 30d format. It is common in the United States for NTSC video and audio.

- **29.97.** As above, but without frame drop. This format is rarely used because the 29.97d format is far more accurate for synchronizing audio and video.

- **23.976.** This is 24 fps at 99.9 percent of full speed, generally used for transferring 24-fps film to NTSC video.

- **Auto Detect Format of MTC.** This option should almost always be engaged because it usually chooses the correct frame rate. Why the qualifiers "almost" and "usually?" Unfortunately, the MTC standard does not provide a way for a host to make the distinction between the 29.97 and 30 frame rates. Logic generally will interpret both those rates as either 29.97d or 30, depending on whether you are using a drop frame. If you know that you need either 30 or 29.97 as your frame rate, uncheck this option and set the frame rate manually.

- **Validate MTC.** This option enables you to select how often Logic will verify that it is getting the proper synchronization signal at the proper frame rate. Figure 15.4 shows the Validate MTC pull-down menu.

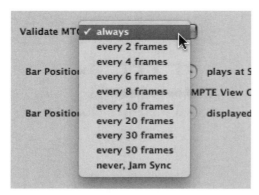

Figure 15.4   The Validate MTC pull-down menu.

In general, you want to leave this option set to Always so that Logic will verify sync after every message. On the other hand, if you know that the sync will be erratic but you want to use sync anyway, you might not want Logic to check the synchronization signal and simply accept whatever is thrown at it (which is known as *Jam Sync*).

- **Bar Position/Plays at SMPTE.** These boxes enable you to enter a bar position or SMPTE time for Logic to start at instead of starting at the very beginning of the song. This is known as *SMPTE offset* because it enables you to start running anywhere in your song that you want as soon as sync is received.

- **Enable Separate SMPTE View Offset.** With this option engaged, the second set of text fields for entering bars and SMTPE values becomes available. Unlike the option above, in which you can set which bar position *plays* at which SMPTE location, in this field you can set which bar position will be *displayed* at the specified SMPTE location.

Audio Tab

The Audio tab of the Synchronization window reveals a number of displays that offer a more detailed view of the synchronization code being transmitted to Logic. Figure 15.5 shows the Audio tab of the Synchronization window.

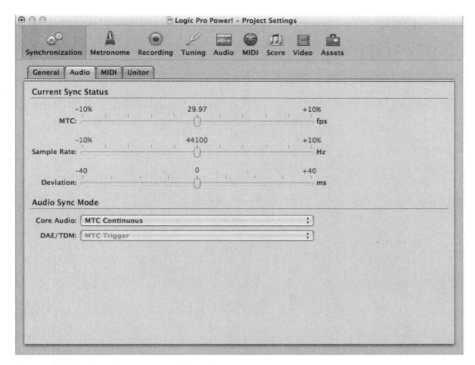

Figure 15.5   The Audio tab of the Synchronization window.

The following sections explain what the different displays mean and how to interpret them.

Current Sync Status

These items display the current status of your synchronization with your external hardware.

- **MTC [fps].** This display shows the percentage of deviation—if any—between the incoming MIDI Time Code and its nominal frame rate. Your goal, of course, is for the yellow line to be in the exact middle (meaning no deviation at all). If there is some deviation, adjust the speed of the master machine until the yellow line shows no deviation. If your deviation is too extreme, you might have chosen an incorrect frame rate in the General tab; try different settings to see whether that eliminates the deviation.

- **Sample Rate [Hz].** This display shows any deviation of the sample rate from its nominal value. In general, if your synchronization signal is accurate, your sample rate will be. If there is a problem with your time-code deviation, you may see your sample rate deviate as well. This can be particularly troublesome because some audio interfaces simply cannot handle any variation in sample rate.

- **Deviation [ms].** This will show you any deviation between Word Clock and time code—in other words, any deviation between audio and MIDI. Tiny deviations are inevitable, but if you believe you have a major problem syncing your audio and MIDI, this display will enable you to determine the actual deviation in milliseconds.

Audio Sync Mode

These two submenus are linked to the specific audio driver you are using in Logic Pro.

- **Core Audio.** This pull-down menu enables you to determine how each piece of audio hardware should synchronize to an external time-code master that the Core Audio engine can understand. Figure 15.6 shows the Core Audio pop-up menu.

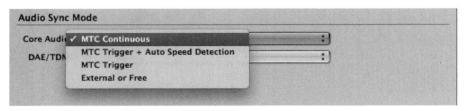

Figure 15.6 The Core Audio pop-up menu in the Audio tab of the Synchronization Settings window.

Not all hardware can work in every synchronization mode; see your hardware manual for details. A description of each mode follows.

- **MTC Continuous.** In this mode, audio regions start in sync, and the sample rate is regulated continuously according to the time-code master to ensure constant sync of even very long audio regions.

- **MTC Trigger + Auto Speed Detection.** In this mode, audio regions start in sync but are then played at a constant sample rate regardless of any variations in the time-code master. When Logic stops and restarts, it starts playback at the current sample rate of the time-code master. This is useful when you must keep your audio playing at the same rate to maintain the absolute pitch of a recording.

- **MTC Trigger.** As above, Logic starts the audio regions in sync, but they are then played at a constant sample rate regardless of any variations in the time-code master. When Logic stops and restarts, however, the time-code master is not queried again for the current sample rate. The initial sample rate in which Logic started playback will continue.

- **External or Free.** In this mode, Logic completely relinquishes all influence over the sample rate to the external hardware. If you have a very high-quality external SMPTE/Word Clock synchronizer, this can be a valuable option. Otherwise, this can be a disaster.

- **DAE/TDM.** This pull-down menu enables you to determine how each piece of audio hardware should synchronize to an external time-code master that the Digidesign Audio Engine (DAE) can understand. It is identical to the Core Audio submenu except for the addition of two settings (Digital and SSD/VSD Type) that are unique to TDM systems. Remember that as of Pro Tools|HD version 8.0.3, Avid has discontinued DAE support.

MIDI Tab

The MIDI tab includes valuable options when synchronizing external MIDI hardware to Logic. Figure 15.7 shows the MIDI tab of the Synchronization window.

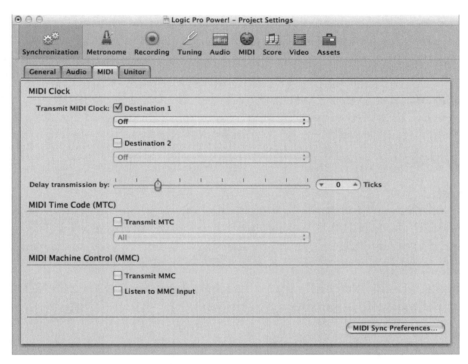

Figure 15.7   The MIDI tab of the Synchronization window.

The options in this window are explained in the following list:

■ **Transmit MIDI Clock.** With either of these check boxes engaged (for Destination 1 or Destination 2), you will send MIDI Clock to all external MIDI devices. The pull-down menus next to the check boxes include all the MIDI ports available. There are two check boxes with two pull-down menus, in case you have two MIDI interfaces and you want to send MIDI Clock via a port on each. If you do not have two MIDI interfaces connected, Destination 2 will have its pull-down menu grayed out. You will generally get the best timing by sending MIDI Clock to all ports instead of individual ports.

■ **Delay Transmission By.** This command will delay the transmission of MIDI Clock. Setting a negative delay will start Logic transmitting MIDI Clock before the song begins playback. This will enable you to compensate for any reaction delays in your external hardware.

- **Transmit MTC.** This check box enables the transmission of MIDI Time Code (MTC) to one of your available MIDI ports from the pull-down menu next to the box. Unlike MIDI Clock, MTC is very data intensive and should not be sent to the All ports option. You will get the best performance if you transmit MTC on a port that is being used for nothing else.

- **Transmit MMC.** With this option enabled, Logic will be able to transmit MIDI Machine Control (MMC). MMC enables Logic to control the Transport of an external device using MIDI commands. These commands will be transmitted whenever you operate Logic's Transport. Normally, MMC will be used if you are slaving Logic to an external MTC master, such as an ADAT machine, but you want to use Logic to control the Transport of the MTC master. Enabling this check box will let Logic control the Transport of the MTC master device, even as Logic itself is slaved to that device.

- **Listen to MMC Input.** When you select this check box, Logic not only transmits MIDI Machine Control, but can itself be controlled by MMC commands. This is useful if you want to use your external hardware to control Logic's Transport, the record-arming of Audio tracks in the Arrange, and so on.

MIDI Sync Preferences

On the bottom right of the Synchronization settings MIDI tab is a button to open the MIDI Preferences window to the Sync tab. This can also be accessed by choosing Logic Pro > Preferences > MIDI and clicking into the Sync tab or by selecting MIDI in the Preferences menu in the Toolbar. Figure 15.8 shows the MIDI Preferences window open to the Sync tab.

The MIDI Sync Preferences includes additional options that control synchronization with MIDI hardware, as described in the following sections.

All MIDI Output

- **Delay [ms].** In order for your MIDI hardware to play in sync with Logic, you'll probably need to delay the MIDI output by a certain amount. This is because your audio hardware will have a certain latency that depends on the audio buffer, as explained earlier in this book. By delaying the MIDI output the same amount as your interface's buffer delays your audio, everything will play in sync. You will want to set a positive delay value in milliseconds, which in effect gives your audio a pre-roll so that everything will start together. Negative values can be used to sync your MIDI devices' audio if you are monitoring the audio through Logic.

MIDI Clock

- **Allow to Send Song Position Pointer While Playing.** Logic will also send Song Position Pointer (SPP) commands to your MIDI devices. However, many MIDI devices cannot process this message. If you know your device can process this message, go ahead and engage this option. If you aren't sure or if you know your device cannot process SPP messages, do not engage this option.

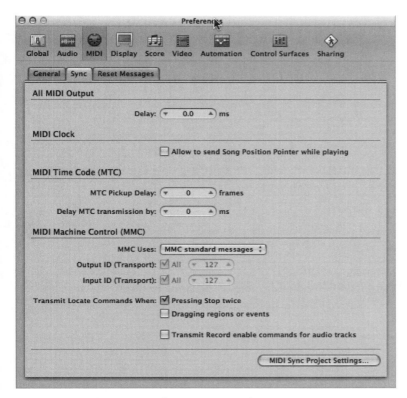

Figure 15.8   The MIDI Preferences Sync tab.

MIDI Time Code (MTC)

- **MTC Pickup Delay.** You will normally keep this parameter set to zero to ensure the quickest pickup time while Logic is in MTC Sync mode. Some devices, unfortunately, take a while to get in sync and, as such, transmit imprecise MTC commands at first. This inaccuracy can result in an offset every time you attempt to sync Logic Pro to the device. In these cases, use this parameter to set a delay for MTC pickup. When you do, Logic will ignore the initial MTC commands for as long as the delay in frames that you set. Generally, 25 to 30 frames correspond to a delay of about a second, depending on the selected frame rate.

- **Delay MTC Transmission By.** This parameter enables you to delay the transmission of MTC. As with MIDI Output Delay, negative values will start the transmission of MTC earlier, which can compensate for reaction delays in MTC slave devices.

MIDI Machine Control (MMC)

- **MMC Uses.** You can select in this pull-down menu whether MMC will use MMC standard messages or the old Fostex format. Only select the old Fostex format if you know that is the only format your device can accept.

- **Output ID (Transport).** This enables you to set a specific MMC Output ID in the text box if you need to. You can select any ID number from 1 to 127. Consult the manual for your external hardware to determine whether you need to input a specific MMC Output ID.

- **Input ID (Transport).** This enables you to set a specific MMC Input ID in the text box if you need to. You can select any ID number from 1 to 127. Consult the manual for your external hardware to determine whether you need to input a specific MMC Input ID.

- **Transmit Locate Commands When:**

  - **Pressing Stop Twice.** With this option engaged, pressing Stop on Logic's Transport two times will transmit the MMC Locate command.

  - **Dragging Regions or Events.** With this option enabled, dragging regions in the Arrange when Logic is stopped will send MMC Locate commands to your external device with the new position of the dragged region.

- **Transmit Record Enable Commands for Audio Tracks.** When this option is engaged, record-enabling tracks in Logic will send MMC Record-Enable commands to your external device. This works both ways, so MMC Record-Enable commands sent to Logic will arm the audio tracks in the Arrange.

Unitor Tab

The Unitor tab is useful only if you own Emagic's Unitor8 MIDI interface. If you do, you can click on this tab in the Synchronization window in order to access the Unitor8's synchronization functions. If you have a different MIDI interface that has synchronization features, it most likely came with its own software to enable you to configure the interface.

Unfortunately, the Unitor8 is out of production. However, it is still supported. Having its synchronization functions integrated into Logic does not give it any special features compared to any other quality MIDI interface, however. It simply means that you will not need to access a separate application to configure it. Because this book is not going into how to configure specific hardware devices, please read the Unitor8 manual for more information about how to configure your Unitor8 MIDI interface using this tab.

The Sync Button Menu

Clicking and holding the Sync button in the Transport opens the Sync button menu, shown in Figure 15.9, which offers some familiar commands listed earlier.

You can select your Sync mode, auto sync, and MMC settings in this menu. You can also open the Synchronization Settings window from here and access some tempo-related windows, covered in Chapter 14.

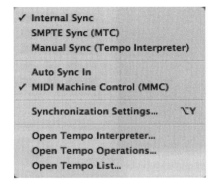

✓ Internal Sync
SMPTE Sync (MTC)
Manual Sync (Tempo Interpreter)

Auto Sync In
✓ MIDI Machine Control (MMC)

Synchronization Settings...   ⌥Y

Open Tempo Interpreter...
Open Tempo Operations...
Open Tempo List...

Figure 15.9 Clicking and holding the Sync button in the Transport opens the Sync button menu.

Switching On External Synchronization

If you want Logic to synchronize with external hardware, simply engage the Sync button on the Transport, shown in Figure 15.10.

Figure 15.10 To engage external sync in Logic, switch on the Sync button on the Transport; the button will light up when engaged, and the Bar ruler will turn blue.

Not only does the button glow blue when you engage sync, but so does the Bar ruler. When you disengage sync by clicking the Sync button again, the button and Bar ruler will stop glowing. You can use the Sync button to engage and disengage sync at any time, which is useful if you need to disengage sync for a moment while doing some editing in Logic, then reengage sync.

When Logic is actively receiving sync, a dot will flash in the Sync button on the Transport. This indicates that everything is running smoothly. If you see the dot stop flashing, that indicates there is a sync error. Although Logic has a fairly robust handling of MTC, if you notice the dot stick, you should check your configuration of your external master device to make sure that the MTC or SMPTE signal is sending a high-quality, uncompromised signal. In the case of SMPTE time code that is being translated to MTC by another hardware device (such as your MIDI interface), be sure to check both hardware devices to make sure they are sending proper sync.

Bar Ruler to Time Ruler

In every graphical window in Logic, you have the option to turn the Bar ruler into a SMPTE time ruler (or simply a Time ruler), or you can also display both the Bar ruler and the Time ruler. To do this, click the arrow icon at the end of the Bar ruler on the right side. This opens the menu shown in Figure 15.11.

Figure 15.11   Clicking the arrow icon at the right end of the Bar ruler opens a menu, allowing you to change the Bar ruler display mode.

There are four Bar ruler display modes:

- **Bar.** This mode shows the typical Bar ruler.

- **Bar and Time.** This mode adds a SMPTE time ruler over the Bar ruler.

- **Time.** This mode changes the display to just a SMPTE time ruler.

- **Time and Bar.** This mode adds a Bar ruler over the SMPTE time ruler.

Figure 15.12 shows the Bar ruler display mode set to Bar and Time.

Figure 15.12   You can change the Bar ruler in the graphical windows in Logic to display either a SMPTE time ruler or both the Bar ruler and the Time ruler.

You can also change the Bar ruler display mode via key command. The Event Position and Length in SMPTE Units key command (Shift+R) toggles between either the Bar ruler mode and the Time ruler mode or the Bar and Time ruler mode and the Time and Bar ruler mode, depending on the initial mode setting. The Secondary Ruler key command (Shift+Option+R) toggles between single ruler mode (Bar or Time) and double ruler mode (Bar and Time or Time and Bar).

The Event Lists are exceptions, of course, because they are not graphical windows. You still can choose to switch the positions and lengths to show SMPTE values instead of bar positions by selecting View > Event Position & Length in SMPTE from their local View menu or by using the key command. Your Event List will change to show all positions in SMPTE time code, as shown in Figure 15.13.

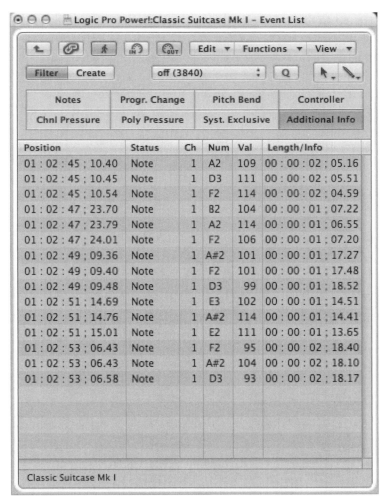

Figure 15.13 You can change the position and length displays in Event Lists to show SMPTE time code instead of bar positions.

This is particularly valuable when you're syncing audio to picture because you may want to lock specific regions to specific frames. Holding down the Control key while performing an editing operation in the Arrange window will change your rate of movement to frames, and holding down Control+Shift will switch you to sub-frame movement. You can then use Arrange window commands such as Regions > Lock SMPTE Position to lock your region to its SMPTE position, and so on.

Expert Tip: Positioning a Bar at a Specific SMPTE Frame   If you want a particular bar of your project to fall at a specific SMPTE frame, you'll need to create a tempo event, as discussed in the previous chapter, so that your song's tempo will change at the exact SMPTE position where you want the bar to fall. When you create the tempo event at the bar you want, open the Tempo List and then set its SMPTE position to the exact frame you want. Logic will ensure that your bar with the tempo change will fall at the SMPTE position you selected. At this point, Logic has adjusted the Bar ruler itself to match the SMPTE position you chose, so you can go ahead and delete the tempo event, and the bar will still fall where you want it!

---

16 Working with Video

For those involved in scoring commercials, industrial videos, motion pictures, games, or any other visual medium that integrates music and/or sound, Logic provides features to enable you to synchronize your music production with the video. Logic does not enable you to edit your video; for that you need a video production application, such as Apple's world-class Final Cut Pro—and as you saw in Chapter 12, you can export your Logic Pro project to Final Cut Pro/XML via the Export command. Logic Pro will, however, enable you to open your video, view your video alongside your Logic project, and lock your music to particular frames of video.

Logic supports Apple's QuickTime format for digital video. QuickTime is not only the Macintosh standard, but the professional standard of choice. If you want to use video with Logic, make sure it is in the QuickTime format. You should also be aware that as of this writing, there are a few video options that are unavailable when Logic is in 64-bit mode. FireWire video streaming, Digital Cinema Desktop, and the Export Audio to Movie command are only available in 32-bit mode.

Opening Movies

There are number of ways to open a QuickTime video in Logic. The first is by choosing File > Open Movie from the global File menu (or typing Option+Command+O). You can also select Open Movie in the Video track or click anywhere in the Video track with the Pencil tool. Control-clicking in the Video track opens a shortcut menu in which you can select the Open Movie option. If you use any of these methods, you will be presented with the Open File dialog to choose your video. When you open your video, it will appear in its own window along with your Logic song. Figure 16.1 shows a video opened as part of a Logic song.

You can also use the Browser to navigate to and open your movie. If you use this option to open a movie, by highlighting it and pressing Open or by double-clicking on it, Logic will present you with the Drop Movie dialog, shown in Figure 16.2.

The Drop Movie dialog gives you more flexibility regarding the way Logic handles your movie than any of the other Open options—you can choose whether you want to open your movie,

Figure 16.1   After selecting File > Open Movie from the global File menu, you will be able to view a QuickTime movie along with your Logic project.

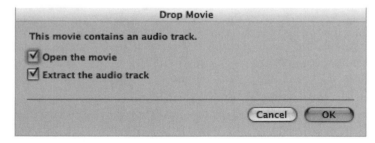

Figure 16.2   The Drop Movie dialog.

extract its audio track, or both. If you open your movie using one of the other methods, you can still extract the audio from it using the Import Audio from Movie command covered later in this chapter

You can adjust the image size via the Movie Options menu, which is discussed in the following section.

Movie Options

If you Control-click anywhere on your QuickTime Movie window, you will be presented with the Movie Options menu, as shown in Figure 16.3.

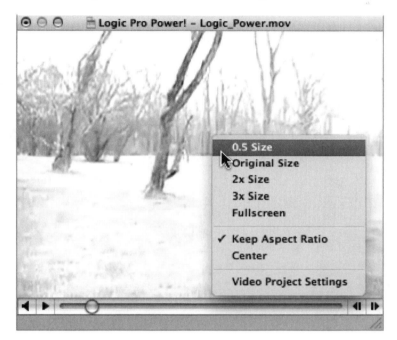

Figure 16.3 You can access the Movie Options menu by Control-clicking the mouse button anywhere on your QuickTime Movie window.

This menu gives you a number of resizing and synchronization options:

- **0.5 Size.** Display your movie at half its original size.

- **Original Size.** Display your movie at its original size.

- **2x Size.** Display your movie at double its original size.

- **3x Size.** Display your movie at triple its original size.

- **Fullscreen.** Display your movie in a full-screen window.

- **Keep Aspect Ratio.** If you resize your Movie window, the aspect ratio of the video will be maintained.

- **Center.** This will place your Movie window in the middle of your screen. (If you have multiple monitors, your video will be placed in the middle of the monitor it is currently on.)

- **Video Project Settings.** This opens the Video Project Settings window. This window is described in the "Video Project Settings" section, later in this chapter.

Movie Scene Markers

Movie scene markers are special markers locked to a specific SMPTE time. They were discussed in Chapter 4 in the section on the Video track. You can also create them via the Create Movie Scene Markers submenu found in Options > Marker > Create Movie Scene Markers, shown in Figure 16.4.

Figure 16.4   The Create Movie Scene Markers submenu gives you a variety of options for creating markers from your QuickTime movie.

The Create Movie Scene Markers submenu commands function more or less the same as the Detect Cuts button on the Video track, one of the global tracks discussed in Chapter 4. They search for scene cuts in your QuickTime movie and create movie markers in the Marker track. Unlike the Video track Detect Cuts button, the Create Movie Scene Markers submenu commands can restrict Logic to looking for cuts within a cycle range, a Marquee tool selection, or a region selection.

Movie markers can be deleted via a dialog that opens if you remove the movie from your project. You can also remove them via the commands in the Options > Marker > Remove Movie Scene Markers submenu. The Remove Movie Scene Markers submenu offers the same options for marker removal as the Create Movie Scene Markers submenu does.

Don't Forget about Global Tracks!   Remember that in Chapter 4 we discussed the Video track, which is the global track that lets you view video thumbnails of your QuickTime movies along with your song. Also, your movie markers will show up on the Marker track, another important global track. Remember to use these features in tandem with the Video window.

Power User Tip   As experienced film/TV composers know, a "hit point" that is exactly on a cut to the frame will actually seem to sound a little early, so they will frequently wish to delay it by one to six frames. Although a movie scene marker's SMPTE position cannot be edited, it can be converted to a standard marker and then adjusted as desired.

Video Project Settings

Among the various Project Settings is the Video Project Settings window. You can access this via File > Project Settings > Video, by selecting Video in the Settings menu in the Toolbar, by right-clicking on the Movie window and selecting Video Project Settings, or by pressing Option+V. Figure 16.5 shows the Video Project Settings dialog.

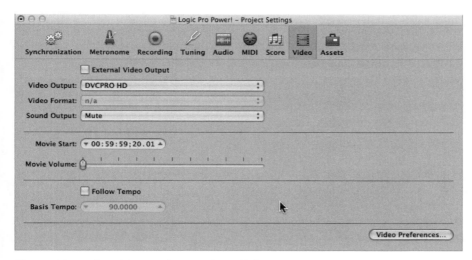

Figure 16.5   The Video Project Settings dialog.

The options of this dialog are:

- **External Video Output.** Selecting this option enables external video output.

- **Video Output.** In this pop-up menu, you can select a device to which Logic can output video. The Video Output menu options are:

  - **DVCPRO HD.** Selecting this option allows you to output your video to a connected DVCPRO HD device.

  - **Digital Cinema Desktop.** Selecting this option allows you to output your video to any display connected to an AGP graphics card using the Video Format parameter discussed in a moment. This function is currently only available when Logic is in 32-bit mode.

- **FireWire.** Selecting this option outputs QuickTime movies to your FireWire video device as defined by the Video Format parameter discussed in a moment.

For specific details on how your external Video Output device can use the video being output by Logic, please see the documentation that came with your hardware.

- **Video Format.** The Video Format pop-up menu provides different options if your Video Output option is set to Digital Cinema Desktop or FireWire. If you have chosen DVCPRO HD for your Video Output setting, the Video Format menu is not available. If you have selected Digital Cinema Display as your Video Output setting, the Video Format menu offers three options: Preview, Full Screen, and Raw. If you have selected FireWire as your Video Output setting, you can choose from a variety of NTSC or PAL formats. This enables you to select one of your FireWire digital video device's video modes.

- **Sound Output.** This determines whether a soundtrack that is already attached to a Quick-Time movie you import will be played back through the Macintosh's sound system or through an external device or will be muted.

- **Movie Start.** The Movie Start setting allows you to offset the start of your video file in SMPTE units to match a particular bar position.

- **Movie Volume.** You can use this slider to adjust the level of your video's audio.

- **Follow Tempo.** Selecting the Follow Tempo check box allows your QuickTime movie to follow tempo change events using the Basis Tempo parameter as its baseline.

- **Basis Tempo.** The Basis Tempo parameter defines the base tempo for any tempo changes the video may undergo when the Follow Tempo option is active.

Video Preferences

As you can see in Figure 16.5, there is a button on the bottom right of the Video Settings window to open the Video Preferences window. You can also access the Video Preferences window via the global menu by selecting Logic Pro > Preferences > Video or by selecting Video in the Preferences menu in the Toolbar. Figure 16.6 shows the Video Preferences window.

The Video Preferences window includes the following options:

- **Video to Project.** This is a global setting to fine-tune exactly which quarter frame your movie will start on. You can either adjust the slider or type in a number. The range is –48 to 48 quarter frames.

- **External Video to Project.** This is the same as above, except it fine-tunes the start point for external FireWire video devices in quarter frames. Basically, this lets you compensate for any video hardware latency. The range is the same as above (–48 to 48 quarter frames).

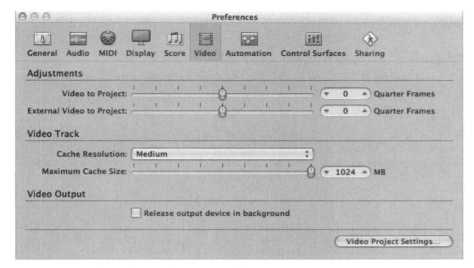

Figure 16.6   The Video Preferences window.

- **Cache Resolution.** This determines the resolution of video thumbnails stored in the temporary internal memory cache. Your options are Low, Medium, High, and Best. Obviously, the higher the quality, the more detail in your video thumbnails, but the more memory they take up.

- **Maximum Cache Size.** This determines how large your cache for video thumbnails can be. The memory is only filled when movie data is displayed.

- **Release Output Device in Background.** Selecting this option allows you to release the output device defined in the Video Project Settings window from Logic's control when Logic is not using it.

Importing Audio from a QuickTime Movie

If you want to use the soundtrack from a QuickTime movie in your Logic project, you can use the Import Audio from Movie command to bring the QuickTime audio into your song. Once you select the Import Audio from Movie command, Logic will automatically bounce the audio from the movie, perform any necessary sample rate and format conversions, and add the new audio file to your Audio Bin using the name of the movie as the name of the new audio file. A new Audio track will be created at the top of the Arrange area, and the audio from the movie will be placed on this track.

Exporting Audio to a QuickTime Movie

As of this writing, the Export Audio to Movie function is only available when Logic is in 32-bit mode. If you wish to add the bounced audio from your 32-bit project into a QuickTime movie soundtrack using the Export Audio to Movie command, first you will be presented with the QuickTime Sound Settings dialog box to choose your export options, as shown in Figure 16.7.

You are then presented with a Save dialog to save your new movie that includes the exported audio, as shown in Figure 16.8.

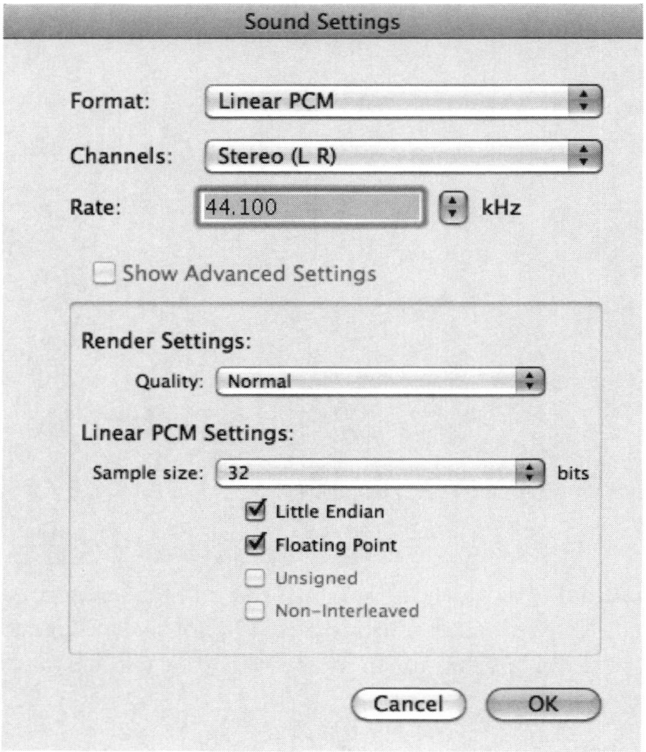

Figure 16.7   The QuickTime Sound Settings dialog is where you set your export preferences.

After you have chosen a location and a name to save your new QuickTime movie, you are prompted to specify which, if any, soundtracks from the original QuickTime movie should be included in the new QuickTime movie file. Figure 16.9 shows this window.

Finally, Logic will bounce your Logic song (just as if you'd pressed the Bnce button on an output channel strip or selected File > Bounce) and then save that bounced audio to your new QuickTime movie.

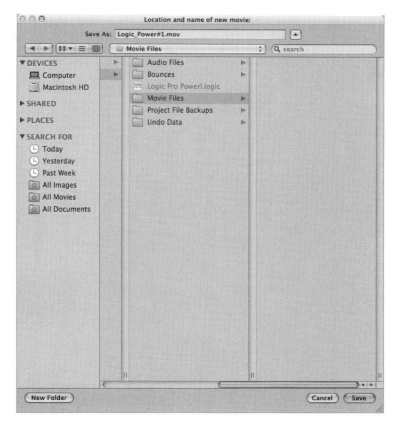

Figure 16.8   You are prompted to save the new movie that includes your exported audio.

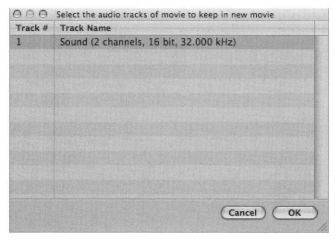

Figure 16.9   You can select which original tracks from the original QuickTime movie to include in the new QuickTime movie.

Appendix: Logic Studio Utilities

To make Logic a complete professional music production solution, Apple has bundled a lot of great tools not only into Logic Pro 9, but into the entire Logic Studio package. Logic has always been one of the leading applications in the world of computer-based music production, and Logic Studio expands on that legacy with a number of powerful, complementary applications bundled into the Logic Studio suite: Apple Loops Utility, Compressor, Impulse Response Utility, MainStage 2, Soundtrack Pro 3, and WaveBurner. Although it would be impossible for us to detail the functions of these applications in any depth—to do that would take at least an entire separate book—we can at least briefly introduce you to each application and describe its general purpose. If you are a Logic Express user, this can serve as an introduction to some of the other features that separate Logic Express and Logic Studio.

Apple Loops Utility

Apple Loops are a powerful tool for manipulating audio in an "elastic" manner—Logic automatically changes the tempo and pitch of Apple Loops to fit your project. Logic Studio ships with a massive collection of Apple Loops, but you may want to make Apple Loops from your own audio files to enjoy the time-stretching and pitch-shifting capabilities that Apple Loops can impart to your audio across different projects. The Apple Loops Utility, shown in Figure A.1, provides this functionality.

Apple Loops and the Apple Loops Utility were covered in more detail in Chapter 7.

Compressor

Compressor is a file compression and conversion utility for video and audio files. You can use it to batch convert video files into multiple delivery formats; tweak your files for specific purposes, such as web delivery; and perform a wide variety of other functions. The primary reason it is included in the Logic Studio package is as a surround encoder. While Logic can record, mix, process, and bounce your audio to a variety of surround formats, you need to use Compressor to actually deliver your mix in a usable format. Figure A.2 shows the Compressor interface.

Figure A.1   You can use the Apple Loops Utility to convert your audio files into Apple Loops.

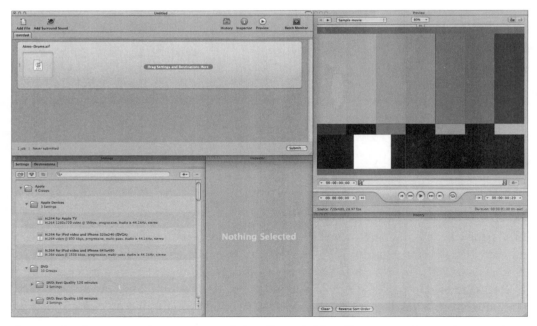

Figure A.2   Compressor is a very powerful audio and video file compression and conversion utility. You can use Compressor to encode your surround mixes to the correct surround format.

Impulse Response Utility

One of the great advances in modern audio processing is the use of convolution-based processing to provide very high levels of detail and realism to effects such as Logic's own convolution reverb, Space Designer. Convolution effects use special audio files called *impulse responses* to process your audio files. An impulse response is a recording of a sound in a space—either a transient, such as a balloon popping or starter pistol firing, or a deconvolved broadband sine wave sweep—that includes all the reflections from the surfaces in the space. A transient provides the quickest and easiest method of creating an impulse response. A full-spectrum sine wave sweep provides a more detailed impulse response, but the recording must be deconvolved, or time aligned, into a usable impulse response. If creating impulse responses for Space Designer sounds like something you'd be interested in trying, the Impulse Response Utility is the tool for the job. Figure A.3 shows the Impulse Response Utility.

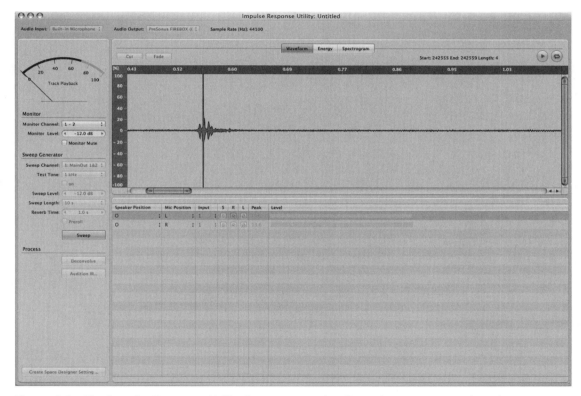

Figure A.3   The Impulse Response Utility lets you record, edit, and save your own impulse responses for use in Space Designer.

The Impulse Response Utility allows you to record, edit, deconvolve, and save your impulse responses. You can record mono, stereo, or surround impulse responses, allowing you to create reverberant spaces for use in your everyday work or highly specialized reverbs for individual projects.

MainStage 2

While Logic Pro is an unparalleled recording platform containing a truly unique set of audio and MIDI editors and processors, it also has a comprehensive and industry-leading set of software synthesizers and effects that are perfect for use in live performance. MainStage 2, a streamlined extension of Logic Pro containing all of Logic's softsynths and effects, is optimized for use as a live performance host. Many elements of MainStage's interface will be very familiar because they are derived from Logic. Figure A.4 shows MainStage 2 in Edit mode.

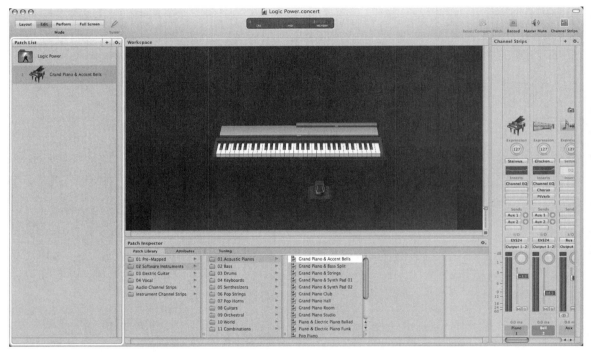

Figure A.4   In MainStage, you can set up complex layers, splits, and patches complete with effects for use in live performance.

MainStage lets you create patches with very complex layers, splits, effects routings, and controller setups, using Logic's plug-ins in addition to third-party plug-ins. MainStage 2 gives you an ideal platform for taking Logic to the stage!

Soundtrack Pro 3

Although the audio editing capabilities of Logic expand and become more powerful with each new version, Logic Studio includes Soundtrack Pro 3 to provide an alternative audio editor for Logic users. Soundtrack Pro 3 is a full-featured audio editor, giving you the ability to edit and process your audio files outside of Logic. You can even configure Logic to use Soundtrack Pro 3 as your default audio editor, which was discussed in Chapter 7. Figure A.5 shows an audio file opened in Soundtrack Pro 3.

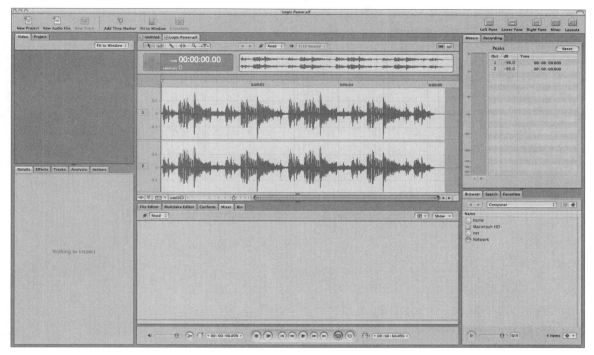

Figure A.5 Soundtrack Pro 3 is a full-featured audio editor, allowing you to edit and process your audio files outside of Logic.

Soundtrack Pro 3 lets you view and edit individual audio files or entire multitrack projects, and it includes all of Logic Pro's audio effects, making it a versatile tool to have in your arsenal.

WaveBurner

Once you have mixed your projects, the only things left to do are master and sequence your tracks and then burn them to a Red Book CD for duplication. Since Logic Studio is a complete audio production solution, it's only natural that a professional CD-master authoring tool is included in the package. When you have reached the final stages of production, WaveBurner is the application for the job. Figure A.6 shows WaveBurner in action.

WaveBurner gives you access to all of Logic Pro's effects for use in your mastering tasks and offers a range of other tools to ensure the highest possible quality final product for your Red Book CD authoring needs.

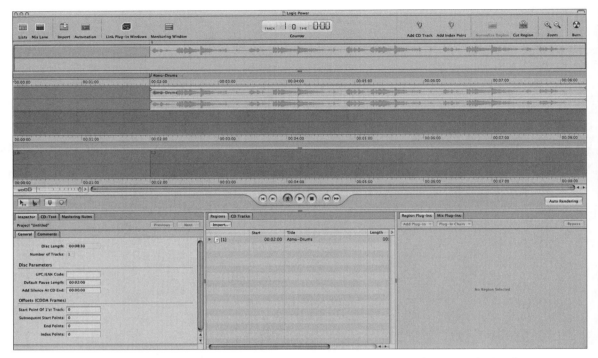

Figure A.6   WaveBurner is a complete mastering, sequencing, and CD authoring solution for your Logic projects.

Index

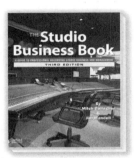